Program Authors

Peter Afflerbach
Camille Blachowicz
Candy Dawson Boyd
Elena Izquierdo
Connie Juel
Edward Kame'enui
Donald Leu
Jeanne R. Paratore
P. David Pearson
Sam Sebesta
Deborah Simmons
Alfred Tatum
Sharon Vaughn
Susan Watts Taffe
Karen Kring Wixson

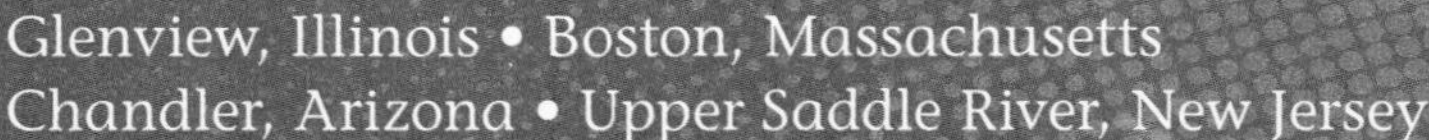
Glenview, Illinois • Boston, Massachusetts
Chandler, Arizona • Upper Saddle River, New Jersey

We dedicate Reading Street to
Peter Jovanovich.

His wisdom, courage,
and passion for education
are an inspiration to us all.

ISBN-13: 978-0-328-47000-6
ISBN-10: 0-328-47000-7
2 3 4 5 6 7 8 9 10 V064 14 13 12 11 10
CC1

Any Path, Any Pace

Reading Street

Calle de la Lectura

PEARSON

Who said so?

The Leading Researchers,

Program Authors

Peter Afflerbach, Ph.D.
Professor
Department of Curriculum and Instruction
University of Maryland at College Park

Camille L. Z. Blachowicz, Ph.D.
Professor of Education
National-Louis University

Candy Dawson Boyd, Ph.D.
Professor
School of Education
Saint Mary's College of California

Elena Izquierdo, Ph.D.
Associate Professor
University of Texas at El Paso

Connie Juel, Ph.D.
Professor of Education
School of Education
Stanford University

Edward J. Kame'enui, Ph.D.
Dean-Knight Professor of Education and Director
Institute for the Development of Educational Achievement and the Center on Teaching and Learning
College of Education
University of Oregon

Donald J. Leu, Ph.D.
John and Maria Neag Endowed Chair in Literacy and Technology
Director, The New Literacies Research Lab
University of Connecticut

Jeanne R. Paratore, Ed.D.
Associate Professor of Education
Department of Literacy and Language Development
Boston University

P. David Pearson, Ph.D.
Professor and Dean
Graduate School of Education
University of California, Berkeley

Sam L. Sebesta, Ed.D.
Professor Emeritus
College of Education
University of Washington, Seattle

Deborah Simmons, Ph.D.
Professor
College of Education and Human Development
Texas A&M University

Alfred W. Tatum, Ph.D.
Associate Professor and Director of the UIC Reading Clinic
University of Illinois at Chicago

Sharon Vaughn, Ph.D.
H. E. Hartfelder/Southland Corporation Regents Professor
Director, Meadows Center for Preventing Educational Risk
University of Texas

Susan Watts Taffe, Ph.D.
Associate Professor in Literacy
Division of Teacher Education
University of Cincinnati

Karen Kring Wixson, Ph.D.
Professor of Education
University of Michigan

Consulting Authors

Jeff Anderson, M.Ed.
Author and Consultant
San Antonio, TX

Jim Cummins, Ph.D.
Professor
Department of Curriculum, Teaching and Learning
University of Toronto

Lily Wong Fillmore, Ph.D.
Professor Emerita
Graduate School of Education
University of California, Berkeley

Georgia Earnest García, Ph.D.
Professor
Language and Literacy Division
Department of Curriculum and Instruction
University of Illinois at Urbana-Champaign

George A. González, Ph.D.
Professor (Retired)
School of Education
University of Texas-Pan American, Edinburg

Valerie Ooka Pang, Ph.D.
Professor
School of Teacher Education
San Diego State University

Sally M. Reis, Ph.D.
Board of Trustees Distinguished Professor
Department of Educational Psychology
University of Connecticut

Jon Scieszka, M.F.A.
Children's Book Author
Founder of GUYS READ
Named First National Ambassador for Young People's Literature 2008

Grant Wiggins, Ed.D.
Educational Consultant
Authentic Education
Concept Development

Lee Wright, M.Ed.
Pearland, TX

Practitioners, and Authors.

Consultant

Sharroky Hollie, Ph.D.
Assistant Professor
California State University
Dominguez Hills, CA

Teacher Reviewers

Dr. Bettyann Brugger
Educational Support Coordinator—Reading Office
Milwaukee Public Schools
Milwaukee, WI

Kathleen Burke
K–12 Reading Coordinator
Peoria Public Schools, Peoria, IL

Darci Burns, M.S.Ed.
University of Oregon

Bridget Cantrell
District Intervention Specialist
Blackburn Elementary School
Independence, MO

Tahira DuPree Chase, M.A., M.S.Ed.
Administrator of Elementary English Language Arts
Mount Vernon City School District
Mount Vernon, NY

Michele Conner
Director, Elementary Education
Aiken County School District
Aiken, SC

Georgia Coulombe
K–6 Regional Trainer/ Literacy Specialist
Regional Center for Training and Learning (RCTL), Reno, NV

Kelly Dalmas
Third Grade Teacher
Avery's Creek Elementary, Arden, NC

Seely Dillard
First Grade Teacher
Laurel Hill Primary School
Mt. Pleasant, SC

Jodi Dodds-Kinner
Director of Elementary Reading
Chicago Public Schools, Chicago, IL

Dr. Ann Wild Evenson
District Instructional Coach
Osseo Area Schools, Maple Grove, MN

Stephanie Fascitelli
Principal
Apache Elementary, Albuquerque Public Schools, Albuquerque, NM

Alice Franklin
Elementary Coordinator, Language Arts & Reading
Spokane Public Schools, Spokane, WA

Laureen Fromberg
Assistant Principal
PS 100 Queens, NY

Kimberly Gibson
First Grade Teacher
Edgar B. Davis Community School
Brockton, MA

Kristen Gray
Lead Teacher
A.T. Allen Elementary School
Concord, NC

Mary Ellen Hazen
State Pre-K Teacher
Rockford Public Schools #205
Rockford, IL

Patrick M. Johnson
Elementary Instructional Director
Seattle Public Schools, Seattle, WA

Theresa Jaramillo Jones
Principal
Highland Elementary School
Las Cruces, NM

Sophie Kowzun
Program Supervisor, Reading/ Language Arts, PreK-5
Montgomery County Public Schools
Rockville, MD

David W. Matthews
Sixth Grade Teacher
Easton Area Middle School
Easton, PA

Ana Nuncio
Editor and Independent Publisher
Salem, MA

Joseph Peila
Principal
Chappell Elementary School
Chicago, IL

Ivana Reimer
Literacy Coordinator
PS 100 Queens, NY

Sally Riley
Curriculum Coordinator
Rochester Public Schools
Rochester, NH

Dyan M. Smiley
Independent Educational Consultant

Michael J. Swiatowiec
Lead Literacy Teacher
Graham Elementary School
Chicago, IL

Dr. Helen Taylor
Director of English Education
Portsmouth City Public Schools
Portsmouth, VA

Carol Thompson
Teaching and Learning Coach
Independence School District
Independence, MO

Erinn Zeitlin
Kindergarten Teacher
Carderock Springs Elementary School
Bethesda, MD

Changes

Key
- SI Strategic Intervention
- OL On-Level
- A Advanced
- ELL ELL

In this Teacher's Edition Unit 3, Volume 2

In the First Stop on Reading Street

GO Digital!

See It!

- Big Question Video
- Concept Talk Video
- Interactive Sound-Spelling Cards
- Envision It! Animations
- Sing with Me Animations

Hear It!

- Sing with Me Animations
- eSelections
- Grammar Jammer
- eReaders
- Leveled Reader Database

Do It!

- Vocabulary Activities
- Story Sort
- 21st Century Skills Activities
- Online Assessment
- Letter Tile Drag and Drop

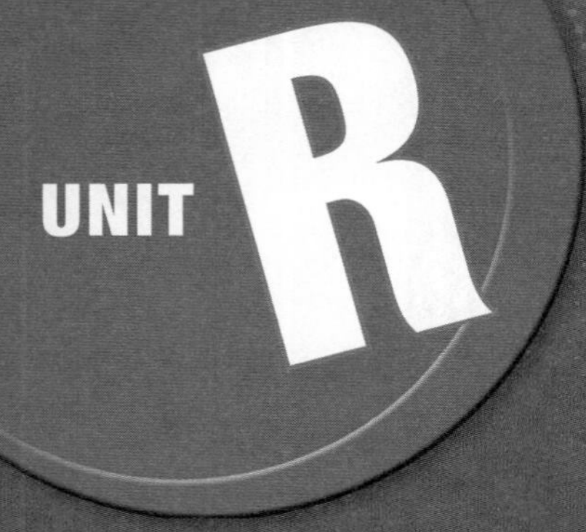

My World

Key
- SI Strategic Intervention
- OL On-Level
- A Advanced
- ELL ELL

Animals, Tame and Wild

Key
- SI Strategic Intervention
- OL On-Level
- A Advanced
- ELL ELL

Communities

Key
- SI Strategic Intervention
- OL On-Level
- A Advanced
- ELL ELL

Changes

Key
SI Strategic Intervention
OL On-Level
A Advanced
ELL ELL

Treasures

Key
SI Strategic Intervention
OL On-Level
A Advanced
ELL ELL

Great Ideas

Key
- SI Strategic Intervention
- OL On-Level
- A Advanced
- ELL ELL

UNIT 3

Skills Overview

Key
T Tested Skill
◎ Target Skill

	WEEK 1	WEEK 2
	 **A Place to Play** Realistic Fiction pp. 20–33 **My Neighborhood, Then and Now** Autobiography pp. 38–41	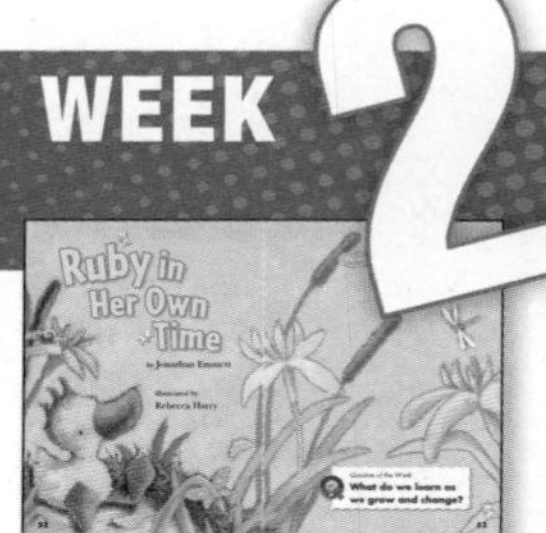 **Ruby in Her Own Time** Animal Fantasy pp. 52–73 **The Ugly Duckling** Fairy Tale pp. 78–81
Get Ready to Read		
Question of the Week	How do places change?	What do we learn as we grow and change?
Amazing Words	*growth, population, public, teeter, shuffle, crooked, makeshift, spindly*	*attempt, event, time line, famous, flatter, correct, awkward, common*
Phonemic Awareness	Segment and Blend Phonemes, Add Initial Phonemes	Segment and Blend Phonemes, Add Initial and Final Phonemes
Phonics	T ◎ Vowel Sounds of *y* T ◎ Syllable Pattern CV Review Long *e: e, ee;* Syllables VC/CV	T ◎ Consonant Patterns *ng, nk* T ◎ Compound Words Review Vowel Sounds of *y*, Syllable Pattern CV
Spelling	Vowel Sounds of *y*	Words with *ng, nk*
Read and Comprehend		
Comprehension	T ◎ **Skill** Sequence ◎ **Strategy** Summarize Review **Skill** Author's Purpose	T ◎ **Skill** Compare and Contrast ◎ **Strategy** Inferring Review **Skill** Sequence
High-Frequency Words	T *things, always, day, become, nothing, stays, everything*	T *ever, sure, were, enough, every, any, own*
Vocabulary	Antonyms	Synonyms
Fluency	Accuracy and Rate	Appropriate Phrasing
Language Arts		
Writing	Realistic Story Trait: Organization	Comments About a Story Trait: Voice
Conventions	T Action Verbs	T Verbs that Add *-s*
Speaking/Listening	Relate an Experience in Sequence	Respect
Research Skills	Interview	Glossary

The Big Question

What is changing in our world?

WEEK 3	WEEK 4	WEEK 5	WEEK 6
The Class Pet Expository Text pp. 92–105 **Belling the Cat** Fable pp. 110–115	**Frog and Toad Together** Animal Fantasy pp. 126–141 **Growing Plants** How-to Article pp. 146–147	**I'm a Caterpillar** Literary Nonfiction pp. 158–173 **My Computer** 21st Century Skills pp. 178–179	**Where Are My Animal Friends?** Drama pp. 190–207 **Poetry Collection** Poetry pp. 212–215
What can we learn about animals as they grow and change?	What changes happen in a garden?	What changes can be seen in nature?	What do animals do when the seasons change?
mature, natural, features, tumble, swoop, crumple, nudges, nibble, wriggle	*gardener, sprout, nature, dim, shade, sprinkling, destroy, humongous*	*insect, develop, cycle, rearrange, flurries, emerge, fragile, vessel*	*hibernate, migrate, temperature, autumn, freeze, bitterly, weary*
Segment and Blend Phonemes, Add Initial and Final Phonemes	Isolate Phonemes, Add Phonemes	Isolate Phonemes, Add Phonemes	Segment and Blend, Change Initial Phonemes
T Ending *-es,* Plural *-es* T Vowels: *r*-Controlled *or, ore* Review Consonant Patterns *ng, nk;* Compound Words	T Inflected Endings T Vowel: *r*-Controlled *ar* Review Ending *-es,* Plural *-es; r*-Controlled *or, ore*	T Vowels: *r*-Controlled *er, ir, ur* T Contractions *'s, 've, 're* Review Inflected Endings *-ed, -ing; r*-Controlled *ar*	T Comparative Endings T Consonant Pattern *-dge* Review *r*-Controlled *er, ir, ur;* Contractions
Words with *-es*	Words with *-ed*	Words with *er, ir, ur*	Words with *-er, -est*
T **Skill** Fact and Opinion **Strategy** Monitor and Clarify Review **Skill** Compare and Contrast	**Skill** Author's Purpose **Strategy** Visualize Review **Skill** Plot	T **Skill** Fact and Opinion **Strategy** Text Structure Review **Skill** Sequence	T **Skill** Draw Conclusions **Strategy** Background Knowledge Review **Skill** Compare and Contrast
T *very, car, away, our, house, school, friends*	T *few, afraid, read, soon, how, again*	T *know, push, done, wait, visit*	T *does, good-bye, before, won't, oh, right*
Descriptive Words	Dictionary/Glossary	Dictionary/Glossary	Context Clues
Appropriate Phrasing	Expression and Intonation	Expression and Intonation	Expression and Intonation
Writing for Tests Summary	Lists Trait: Sentences	Captions and Pictures Trait: Focus/Ideas	Play Scene Trait: Sentences
T Verbs That Do Not Add *-s*	T Verbs for Past and Future	T Verbs *Am, Is, Are, Was, Were*	T Contractions with *Not*
Give Descriptions	Poetry Presentation	Share Information and Ideas	Give Announcements
Classifying and Categorizing	Diagram	Technology: My Computer	Picture Graph

Monitor Progress

Make Data-Driven Decisions

Data Management
- Assess
- Diagnose
- Prescribe
- Disaggregate

Classroom Management
- Monitor Progress
- Group
- Differentiate Instruction
- Inform Parents

Don't Wait Until Friday

SUCCESS PREDICTORS	WEEK 1	WEEK 2	WEEK 3	WEEK 4
Word Reading — **Phonics**	T Vowel Sounds of *y* T Syllable Pattern CV	T Consonant Patterns *ng, nk* T Compound Words	T Ending *-es,* Plural *-es* T Vowels: *r*-Controlled *or, ore*	T Inflected Endings T Vowel: *r*-Controlled *ar*
WCPM — **Fluency**	Read with Accuracy and Rate 20–30 WCPM	Read with Appropriate Phrasing 20–30 WCPM	Read with Appropriate Phrasing 20–30 WCPM	Read with Expression and Intonation 25–35 WCPM
Vocabulary — **High-Frequency Words**	T things T always T day T become T nothing T stays T everything	T ever T sure T were T enough T every T any T own	T very T car T away T our T house T school T friends	T few T afraid T read T soon T how T again
Vocabulary — **Oral Vocabulary/ Concept Development** (assessed informally)	growth population public teeter shuffle crooked makeshift spindly	attempt event time line famous flatter correct awkward common	mature wriggle natural features tumble swoop crumple nudges nibble	gardener sprout nature dim shade sprinkling destroy humongous
Retelling — **Text Comprehension**	T **Skill** Sequence **Strategy** Summarize	T **Skill** Compare and Contrast **Strategy** Inferring	T **Skill** Fact and Opinion **Strategy** Monitor and Clarify	T **Skill** Author's Purpose **Strategy** Visualize

Key

T Tested Skill

◎ Target Skill

WEEK 5	WEEK 6
T ◎ Vowels: *r*-Controlled *er, ir, ur* T ◎ Contractions	T ◎ Comparative Endings T ◎ Consonant Pattern *-dge*
Read with Expression and Intonation 25–35 WCPM	Read with Expression and Intonation 25–35 WCPM
T know T push T done T wait T visit	T does T good-bye T before T won't T oh T right
insect develop cycle rearrange flurries emerge fragile vessel	hibernate migrate temperature autumn freeze bitterly weary
T ◎ **Skill** Fact and Opinion ◎ **Strategy** Text Structure	T ◎ **Skill** Draw Conclusions ◎ **Strategy** Background Knowledge

ReadingStreet.com

Online Classroom

Manage Data

- Assign the Unit 3 Benchmark Test for students to take online.
- Online Assessment records results and generates reports by school, grade, classroom, or student.
- Use reports to disaggregate and aggregate Unit 3 skills and standards data to monitor progress.
- Based on class lists created to support the categories important for AYP (gender, ethnicity, migrant education, English proficiency, disabilities, economic status), reports let you track adequate yearly progress every six weeks.

Group

- Use results from Unit 3 Benchmark Tests taken online through Online Assessment to measure whether students have mastered the English-Language Arts Content Standards taught in this unit.
- Reports in Online Assessment suggest whether students need Extra Support or Intervention.

Individualized Instruction

- Tests are correlated to Unit 3 tested skills and standards so that prescriptions for individual teaching and learning plans can be created.
- Individualized prescriptions target instruction and accelerate student progress toward learning outcome goals.
- Prescriptions include remediation activities and resources to reteach Unit 3 skills and standards.

Assessment and Grouping

for Data-Driven Instruction

4-Step Plan for Assessment
1 Diagnose and Differentiate
2 Monitor Progress
3 Assess and Regroup
4 Summative Assessment

STEP 1 Diagnose and Differentiate

Baseline Group Tests

Diagnose

To make initial grouping decisions, use the Baseline Group Test, the Texas Primary Reading Inventory (TPRI), or another initial placement test. Depending on children's ability levels, you may have more than one of each group.

Differentiate

If... student performance is SI **then...** use the regular instruction and the daily **Strategic Intervention** small group lessons.

If... student performance is OL **then...** use the regular instruction and the daily **On-Level** small group lessons.

If... student performance is A **then...** use the regular instruction and the daily **Advanced** learners small group lessons.

Small Group Time

SI Strategic Intervention

- Daily small group lessons provide more intensive instruction, more scaffolding, more practice, and more opportunities to respond.
- Reteach lessons in the *First Stop on Reading Street* provide additional instructional opportunities with target skills.
- Leveled readers build background and provide practice for target skills and vocabulary.

OL On-Level

- Explicit instructional routines teach core skills and strategies.
- Daily On-Level lessons provide more practice and more opportunities to respond.
- Independent activities provide practice for core skills and extension and enrichment options.
- Leveled reader provides additional reading and practice for core skills and vocabulary.

A Advanced

- Daily Advanced lessons provide instruction for accelerated learning.
- Leveled reader provides additional reading tied to lesson concepts.

Additional Differentiated Learning Options

Reading Street Response to Intervention Kit

- Focused intervention lessons on the five critical areas of reading: phonemic awareness, phonics, vocabulary, comprehension, and fluency

My Sidewalks on Reading Street

- Intensive intervention for struggling readers.

STEP 2 Monitor Progress

Don't Wait Until Friday

Use these tools during lesson teaching to **monitor student progress.**

- **Skill and Strategy** instruction during reading
- **Don't Wait Until Friday** boxes to check word reading, retelling, fluency, and oral vocabulary
- **Weekly Assessment** on Day 5 to check phonics and fluency
- **Reader's and Writer's Notebook** pages at point of use
- **Weekly Tests** to assess target skills for the week
- **Fresh Reads for Comprehension and Fluency**

Weekly Tests

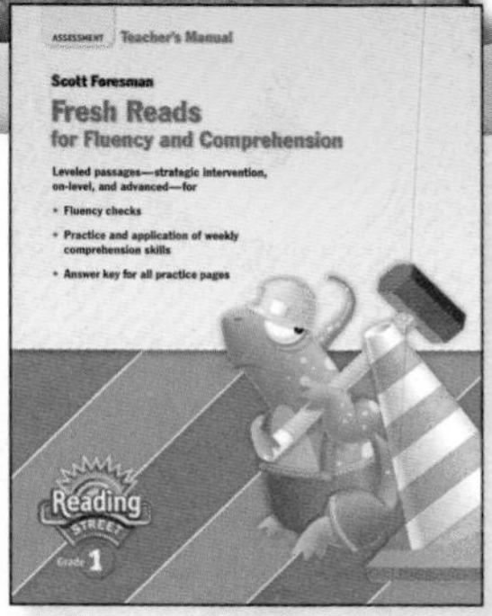

Fresh Reads for Fluency and Comprehension

STEP 3 Assess and Regroup

Use these tools during lesson teaching assess and regroup.

- **Weekly Assessments** Record results of weekly assessments in retelling, phonics, and fluency to track student progress.
- **Unit Benchmark Test** Administer this test to check mastery of unit skills.
- **Regroup** We recommend the first regrouping to be at the end of Unit 1. Use weekly assessment information and Unit Benchmark Test performance to inform regrouping decisions. Then regroup at the end of each subsequent unit.

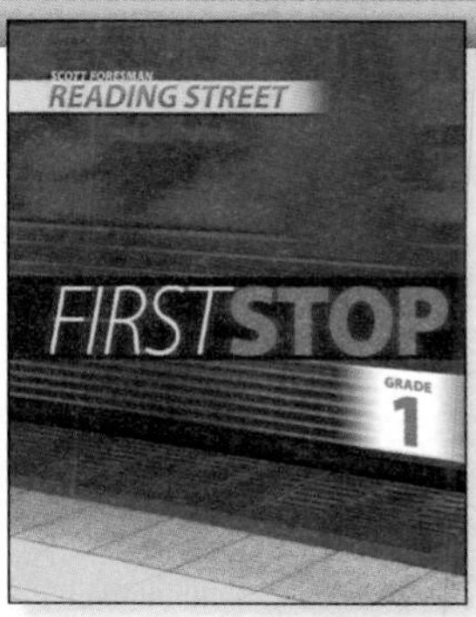

First Stop on Reading Street Assessment Chart

Outside assessments, such as DRA, TPRI, and DIBELS, may recommend regrouping at other times during the year.

STEP 4 Summative Assessment

Use these tools after lesson teaching to assess students.

- **Unit Benchmark Tests** Use to measure a student's mastery of unit skills.
- **End-of-Year Benchmark Test** Use to measure a student's mastery of program skills covered in all six units.

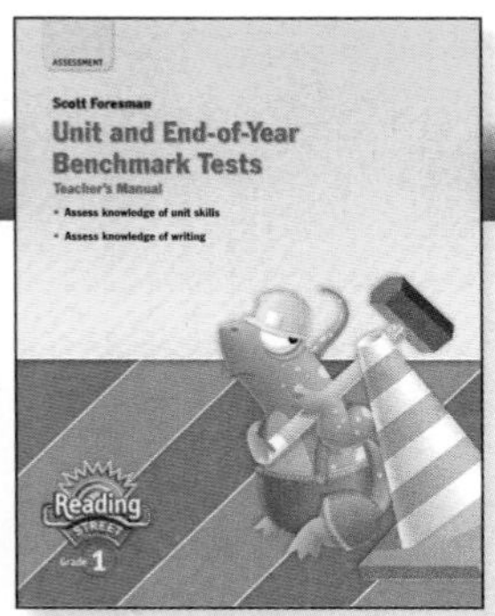

Unit and End-of-Year Benchmark Tests

Concept Launch

Understanding By Design
Grant Wiggins, Ed. D.
Reading Street Author

"Big ideas are the building material of understandings. They can be thought of as the meaningful patterns that enable one to connect the dots of otherwise fragmented knowledge."

Changes

Reading Street Online
www.ReadingStreet.com
- Big Question Video
- eSelections
- Envision It! Animations
- Story Sort

What is changing in our world?

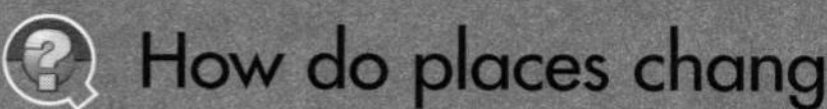

A Place to Play REALISTIC FICTION

How do places change?

Paired Selection
My Neighborhood, Then and Now AUTOBIOGRAPHY

Ruby in Her Own Time ANIMAL FANTASY

What do we learn as we grow and change?

Paired Selection
The Ugly Duckling FAIRY TALE

The Class Pet EXPOSITORY TEXT

What can we learn about animals as they grow and change?

Paired Selection
Belling the Cat FABLE

Frog and Toad Together ANIMAL FANTASY

What changes happen in a garden?

Paired Selection
Growing Plants HOW-TO ARTICLE

I'm a Caterpillar LITERARY NONFICTION

What changes can be seen in nature?

Paired Selection
My Computer 21ST CENTURY SKILLS

Where Are My Animal Friends? DRAMA

connect to SCIENCE

What do animals do when the seasons change?

Paired Selection
"This Tooth," "Tommy," and "Where Do Fish Go in Winter?" POETRY

Small Group Time

Flexible Pacing Plans

Small Group Time

Sometimes you have holidays, programs, assemblies, or other interruptions to the school week. This plan can help you make Small Group Time decisions if you have less time during the week.

Key

- SI Strategic Intervention
- OL On-Level
- A Advanced
- ELL ELL

5 Day Plan

DAY 1	• Phonemic Awareness • Phonics • Reading Practice
DAY 2	• Phonemic Awareness • Phonics • Reading Practice
DAY 3	• Phonics • Leveled Reader
DAY 4	• High-Frequency Words • Reading Practice
DAY 5	• Phonics • Comprehension

4 Day Plan

DAY 1	• Phonemic Awareness • Phonics • Reading Practice
DAY 2	• High-Frequency Words • Leveled Reader
DAY 3	• Phonics • Leveled Reader
DAY 4	• High-Frequency Words • Reading Practice

3 Day Plan

DAY 1	• Phonemic Awareness • Phonics • Reading Practice
DAY 2	• Phonics • Leveled Reader
DAY 3	• High-Frequency Words • Reading Practice

5 Day Plan

DAY 1	• Frontload Concept • Preteach Skills • Conventions and Writing
DAY 2	• Review Concept and Skills • Frontload and Read Main Selection • Conventions and Writing
DAY 3	• Review Concept and Skills • Reread Main Selection • Conventions and Writing
DAY 4	• Review Concept and Skills • Read ELL or ELD Reader • Conventions and Writing
DAY 5	• Review Concept and Skills • Read ELL or ELD Reader • Conventions and Writing

4 Day Plan

DAY 1	• Frontload Concept • Preteach Skills • Conventions and Writing
DAY 2	• Review Concept and Skills • Frontload and Read Main Selection • Conventions and Writing
DAY 3	• Review Concept and Skills • Reread Main Selection • Conventions and Writing
DAY 4	• Review Concept and Skills • Read ELL or ELD Reader • Conventions and Writing

3 Day Plan

DAY 1	• Frontload Concept • Preteach Skills • Conventions and Writing
DAY 2	• Review Concept and Skills • Frontload and Read Main Selection • Conventions and Writing
DAY 3	• Review Concept and Skills • Read ELL or ELD Reader • Conventions and Writing

Grade 1 • Unit 3 • Week 4
Frog and Toad Together
118j–149k

Common Core Standards
Weekly Planning Guide

Selection: Frog and Toad Together
Genre: Animal Fantasy

Alignment of the Common Core Standards with This Week's Skills and Strategies

This Week's Common Core Standards for English Language Arts	Instructional Summary
Reading Standards for Literature	
Literature 4. Ask and answer questions about key details in a text.	In this lesson, children identify the **author's purpose,** or reason, for writing the Listening Comprehension selection "Carlee's Garden" and the main selection *Frog and Toad Together*. Children use illustrations and details to help them **visualize** characters and events. In the genre study for animal fantasy, they **compare and contrast** characters in *Frog and Toad Together* and *Ruby in Her Own Time.*
Literature 7. Use illustrations and details in a story to describe its characters, setting, or events.	
Literature 9. Compare and contrast the adventures and experiences of characters in stories.	
Foundational Skills Standards	
Foundational Skills 2.c. Isolate and pronounce initial, medial vowel, and final sounds (phonemes) in spoken single-syllable words.	The lesson has activities for segmenting, blending, and reading single-syllable words with ***r*-controlled *ar*** and **two-syllable words.** Children focus on reading with **appropriate expression and intonation** for fluency.
Foundational Skills 4.b. Read on-level text orally, with accuracy, appropriate rate, and expression on successive readings.	
Writing Standards	
Writing 2. Write informative/explanatory texts in which they name a topic, supply some facts about the topic, and provide some sense of closure.	In the lesson's Writing section, children work through the **writing process** as they **write a list** telling what Toad did to help his garden grow. With teacher guidance and peer review, they prepare a final draft. In the Research and Inquiry section, the teacher helps children **identify a topic** and **prepare a diagram** illustrating the topic.
Writing 8. With guidance and support from adults, recall information from experiences or gather information from provided sources to answer a question.	
Speaking and Listening Standards	
Speaking/Listening 4. Describe people, places, things, and events with relevant details, expressing ideas and feelings clearly.	For the speaking and listening activities in the lesson, children practice **reading poetry aloud,** using rhythm, rhyme, and punctuation as a guide. In the Research and Inquiry section, children prepare a diagram to use in their **presentation** about plant parts.
Speaking/Listening 5. Add drawings or other visual displays to descriptions when appropriate to clarify ideas, thoughts, and feelings.	
Language Standards	
Language 1.e. Use verbs to convey a sense of past, present, and future (e.g., *Yesterday I walked home; Today I walk home; Tomorrow I will walk home*).	In the Conventions section, children identify and use verbs in the **present, past, and future tense forms.** Children also work with the different types of sentences.
Language 1.j. Produce and expand complete simple and compound declarative, interrogative, imperative, and exclamatory sentences in response to prompts.	

Additional Support for a Common Core Standard This Week

Use the following instruction to supplement the teaching of one of this week's Common Core Standards.

Common Core Standard: **Language 1.j.**
Write the following sentences on the board, and define each type as you read its example.
Declarative sentence (tells about something): Frog planted flower seeds.
Interrogative sentence (asks a question): What kind of flowers did he plant?
Imperative sentence (tells someone to do something): Don't pick the flowers.
Exclamatory sentence (shows strong feeling): What beautiful flowers those are!

- Identify the punctuation at the end of each sentence type. Explain that commands can end with periods or exclamation points.
- Work with children to write one or two examples of each type of sentence.

ISBN-13: 978-0-328-64370-7 ISBN-10: 0-328-64370-X

Grade 1 • Unit 3 • Week 4

Frog and Toad Together

Unit 3

What is changing in our world?

Week 1

A Place to Play

Question of the Week

How do places change?

Concept Talk Guide children as they discuss questions such as:

- What are some ways your neighborhood has changed?

connect to SOCIAL STUDIES

Writing Think about a place to play that you think is interesting. Now write a made-up story about children playing at that place.

Week 2

Ruby in Her Own Time

Question of the Week

What do we learn as we grow and change?

connect to SOCIAL STUDIES

Concept Talk Guide children as they discuss questions such as:

- What can you do now that you could not do when you were younger?

Writing Look at the pictures in *Ruby in Her Own Time*. Think about what Ruby does. Write sentences that tell two things Ruby does that you like.

Week 3

The Class Pet

Question of the Week

What can we learn about animals as they grow and change?

connect to SCIENCE

Concept Talk Guide children as they discuss questions such as:

- Think about different animals. How are the babies different from the adults?

Writing Write a summary of *The Class Pet*. Tell the most important events and ideas.

Common Core Standards and Concept Development

- Introduce and explore this unit's weekly concepts through rich, structured conversations
- Develop complex content knowledge and vocabulary
- Expand on a single concept with engaging literature and nonfiction
- Build better readers in all content areas

Align instruction to **Common Core Anchor Standards**

Week 6

Where Are My Animal Friends?

Question of the Week

What do animals do when the seasons change?

connect to SCIENCE

Concept Talk Guide children as they discuss questions such as:

- Why do you think squirrels gather and hide nuts in the fall?

Writing Think about Raccoon and Squirrel in *Where Are My Animal Friends?* What would they say if they could call Goose on a phone? Write a play scene showing what they would say.

Week 5

I'm a Caterpillar

Question of the Week

What changes can be seen in nature?

connect to SCIENCE

Concept Talk Guide children as they discuss questions such as:

- How do different kinds of animals change as they grow?

Writing Think of changes in nature. Plants and animals grow. Seasons change. Draw two pictures to show one way a plant or animal changes. Write captions about your pictures.

You Are Here: Week 4

Frog and Toad Together

Question of the Week

What changes happen in a garden?

As children answer this unit's Big Question and this week's Question of the Week, they will address:

Reading 9. Analyze how two or more texts address similar themes or topics in order to build knowledge or to compare the approaches the authors take. **(Also Reading 7.)**

Concept Talk Guide children as they discuss questions such as:

- What do seeds look like when you first plant them? Then what happens?

As children answer this week's Concept Talk questions, they will address:

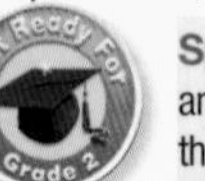

Speaking/Listening 4. Present information, findings, and supporting evidence such that listeners can follow the line of reasoning and the organization, development, and style are appropriate to task, purpose, and audience.

Writing Think of actions Toad tried to help his garden grow. Write a list telling what Toad did that really helped the garden grow. In another list, tell his actions that did not help.

connect to SCIENCE

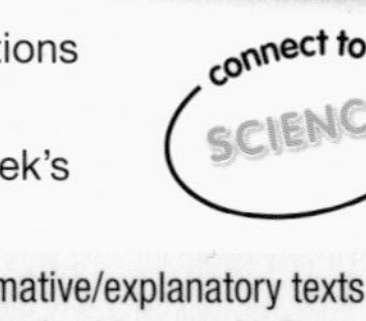

As children write about this week's prompt, they will address:

Writing 2. Write informative/explanatory texts to examine and convey complex ideas and information clearly and accurately through the effective selection, organization, and analysis of content.

Listening and Speaking On page 148, children learn to add expression to their voice when they recite a poem. By doing so, they address:

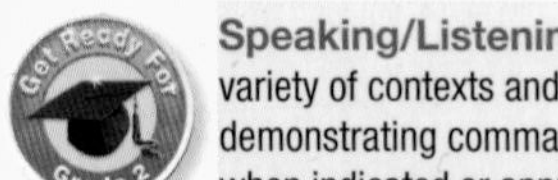

Speaking/Listening 6. Adapt speech to a variety of contexts and communicative tasks, demonstrating command of formal English when indicated or appropriate. **(Also Speaking/Listening 4.)**

This Week's ELL Overview

Grade 1 • Unit 3 • Week 4
Frog and Toad Together
118a–149l and DI•75–DI•84

ELL Handbook

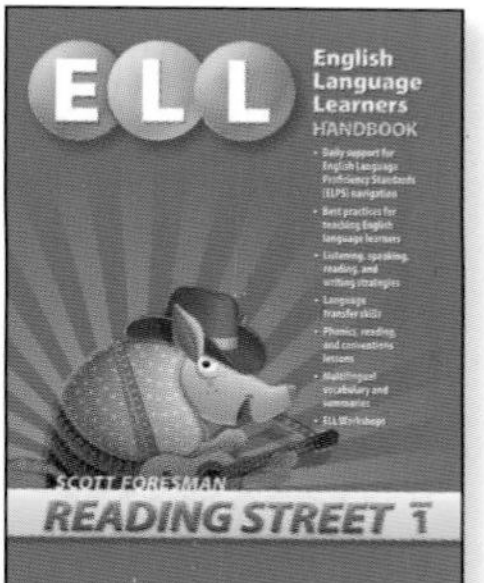

- Maximize Literacy and Cognitive Engagement
- Research Into Practice
- Full Weekly Support for Every Selection

  Frog and Toad Together
  - Multi-Lingual Summaries in Five Languages
  - Selection-Specific Vocabulary Word Cards
  - Frontloading/Reteaching for Comprehension Skill Lessons
  - ELD and ELL Reader Study Guides
- Transfer Activities
- Professional Development

Daily Leveled ELL Notes

ELL notes appear throughout this week's instruction and ELL Support is on the DI pages of your Teacher's Edition. The following is a sample of an ELL note from this week.

English Language Learners

Beginning/Early Intermediate After reading, point out several words with the /är/ sound, such as *park, farm, stars,* and *cars.* Say each word and have children repeat it. Then have children find each object the word names in the illustrations, point to it, and say the word again.

Intermediate After reading, have children search for words with the /är/ sound spelled *ar.* Have children say the words as they write them in a list. Then ask questions that require children to use the words. For example: *When do we see the stars?* (We see the stars at night.)

Early Advanced/Advanced After reading, have children look for /är/ words spelled *ar* and say them aloud. Then have children make up riddles for the words and have other children guess the answer. For example: *I am a place where children play. What am I?* (park) Monitor children's pronunciations and meaning.

Advanced High After reading, organize children into rows or a circle. Tell them you are going to create a class story. Have one child tell a sentence using a word with /är/. The next child will use that sentence to make another with an *ar* word, and so on.

ELL by Strand

The ELL lessons on this week's Support for English Language Learners pages are organized by strand. They offer additional scaffolding for the core curriculum. Leveled support notes on these pages address the different proficiency levels in your class. See pages DI•75–DI•84.

ELL Guy
Dr. Jim Cummins

The Three Pillars of ELL Instruction

ELL Strands	Activate Prior Knowledge	Access Content	Extend Language
Vocabulary p. DI•79	Preteach	Teach/Model	Practice
Reading Comprehension p. DI•80	Preteach	Reteach/Practice	Leveled Practice Activities
Phonics, Spelling, and Word Analysis pp. DI•76–DI•77	Preteach	Listen and Write	Leveled Practice Activities
Listening Comprehension p. DI•78	Prepare for the Read Aloud	First Listening	Second Listening
Conventions and Writing pp. DI•83–DI•84	Preteach/Introduce Terms	Practice/Model	Leveled Practice Activities/ Leveled Writing Activities
Concept Development p. DI•75	Activate Prior Knowledge	Develop Concepts	Review Concepts and Connect to Writing

This Week's Practice Stations Overview

Six Weekly Practice Stations with Leveled Activities can be found at the beginning of each week of instruction. For this week's Practice Stations, see pp. 118h–118i.

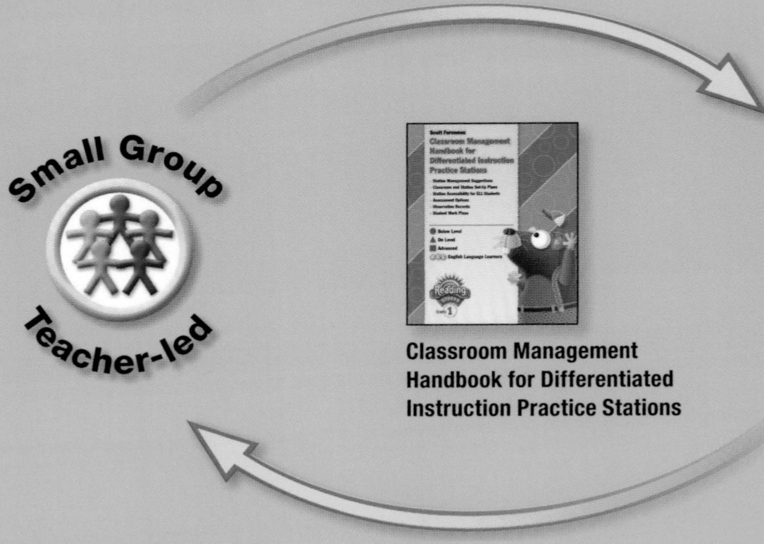

Classroom Management Handbook for Differentiated Instruction Practice Stations

Practice Stations

Daily Leveled Center Activities

- Below
- Advanced
- On-Level
- 

Practice Stations Flip Charts

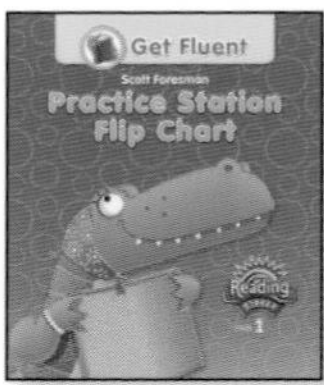

	Listen Up	Word Work	Words to Know	Let's Write	Read for Meaning	Get Fluent
Objectives	• Identify words with *r*-controlled vowel /ôr/.	• Build and write words with ending *-es*, plural *-es*. • Build and write words with *r*-controlled vowel *or, ore*.	• Identify high-frequency words *very, car, away, our, house, school, friends*.	• Write sentences using verbs that do not add *-s*.	• Identify facts and opinions in a selection.	• Read aloud with appropriate phrasing.
Materials	• *Listen Up* Flip Chart Activity 16	• *Word Work* Flip Chart Activity 16 • Letter Tiles • paper • pencils	• *Words to Know* Flip Chart Activity 16 • High-Frequency Word Cards for Unit 3, Week 3 • paper • pencils • crayons	• *Let's Write* Flip Chart Activity 16 • paper • pencils	• *Read for Meaning* Flip Chart Activity 16 • Leveled Readers • paper • pencils	• *Get Fluent* Flip Chart Activity 16 • Leveled Readers

Week 4

This Week on Reading Street!

Changes

Question of the Week

What changes happen in a garden?

Daily Plan

Whole Group

- Adding Endings
- Vowels: *r*-Controlled *ar*
- Author's Purpose
- Fluency
- Vocabulary

MONITOR PROGRESS Success Predictor

Day 1	Day 2	Day 3	Day 4	Day 5
Check Word Reading	Check Word Reading	Check High Frequency Words/Retelling	Check Fluency	Check Oral Vocabulary

Small Group

Teacher-Led

- Reading Support
- Skill Support
- Fluency Practice

Practice Stations

Independent Activities

Customize Literacy More support for a Balanced Literacy approach, see CL•1–CL•47.

Customize Writing More support for a customized writing approach, see CW•11–CW•20.

Whole Group

- Writing: Lists
- Conventions: Verbs for Past and for Future

Assessment

- Weekly Tests
- Day 5 Assessment
- Fresh Reads

This Week's Reading Selections

Main Selection
Genre: **Animal Fantasy**

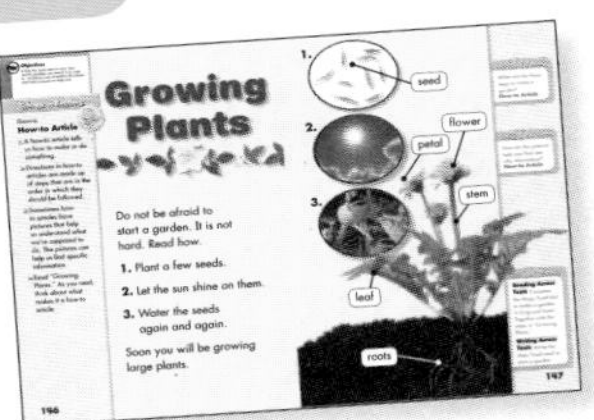

Paired Selection

Decodable Practice Readers

Leveled Readers

ELL and ELD Readers

Resources on Reading Street!

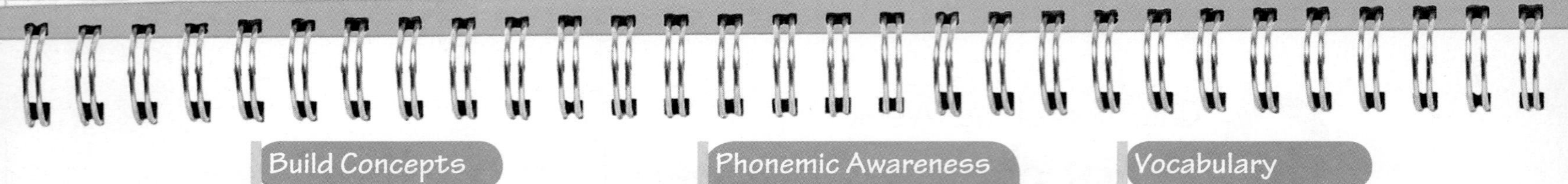

	Build Concepts	Phonemic Awareness and Phonics	Vocabulary
Whole Group	 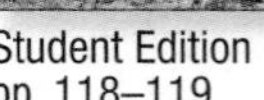 Student Edition pp. 118–119;  Sing with Me	 Student Edition pp. 120–121; Sound-Spelling Cards	 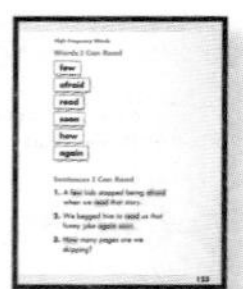 Student Edition p. 123
 Go Digital	• Concept Talk Video • Sing with Me Animations	• Interactive Sound-Spelling Cards • Decodable eReaders	• Vocabulary Activities • Journal Word Bank
Small Group and Independent Practice	 Practice Station Flip Chart;  Leveled Readers;  ELL and ELD Readers	 Practice Station Flip Chart;  Decodable Practice Readers	 Practice Station Flip Chart; 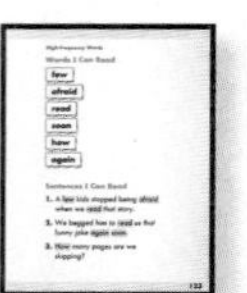 Student Edition p. 123
 Go Digital	• eReaders	• Decodable eReaders • Letter Tile Drag and Drop	• Journal Word Bank • Vocabulary Activities
Customize Literacy	• Leveled Readers	• Decodable Practice Readers	• High-Frequency Word Cards
 Go Digital	• Concept Talk Video • Big Question Video • eReaders	• Interactive Sound-Spelling Cards • Decodable eReaders	• Sing with Me Animations • Vocabulary Activities

Question of the Week

What changes happen in a garden?

Week 4

Comprehension	Fluency	Conventions and Writing
 Student Edition pp. 126–141	 Decodable Practice Readers	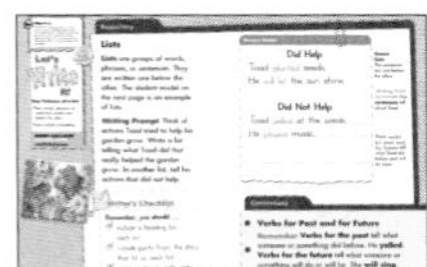 Student Edition pp. 144–145
• Envision It! Animations • eSelections	• eSelections • eReaders	• Grammar Jammer
 Practice Station Flip Chart  Leveled Readers  ELL and ELD Readers	 Practice Station Flip Chart  Decodable Practice Readers	 Practice Station Flip Chart 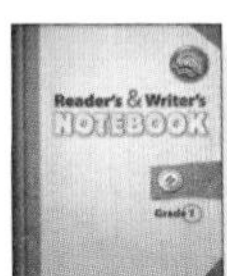 Reader's and Writer's Notebook
• eReaders • Story Sort	• Decodable eReaders	• Grammar Jammer
• Envision It! Skills and Strategies Handbooks • Leveled Readers	• Leveled Readers	• Reader's and Writer's Notebook
• Envision It! Animations • eReaders	• eReaders	• Grammar Jammer

My 5-Day Planner for Reading Street!

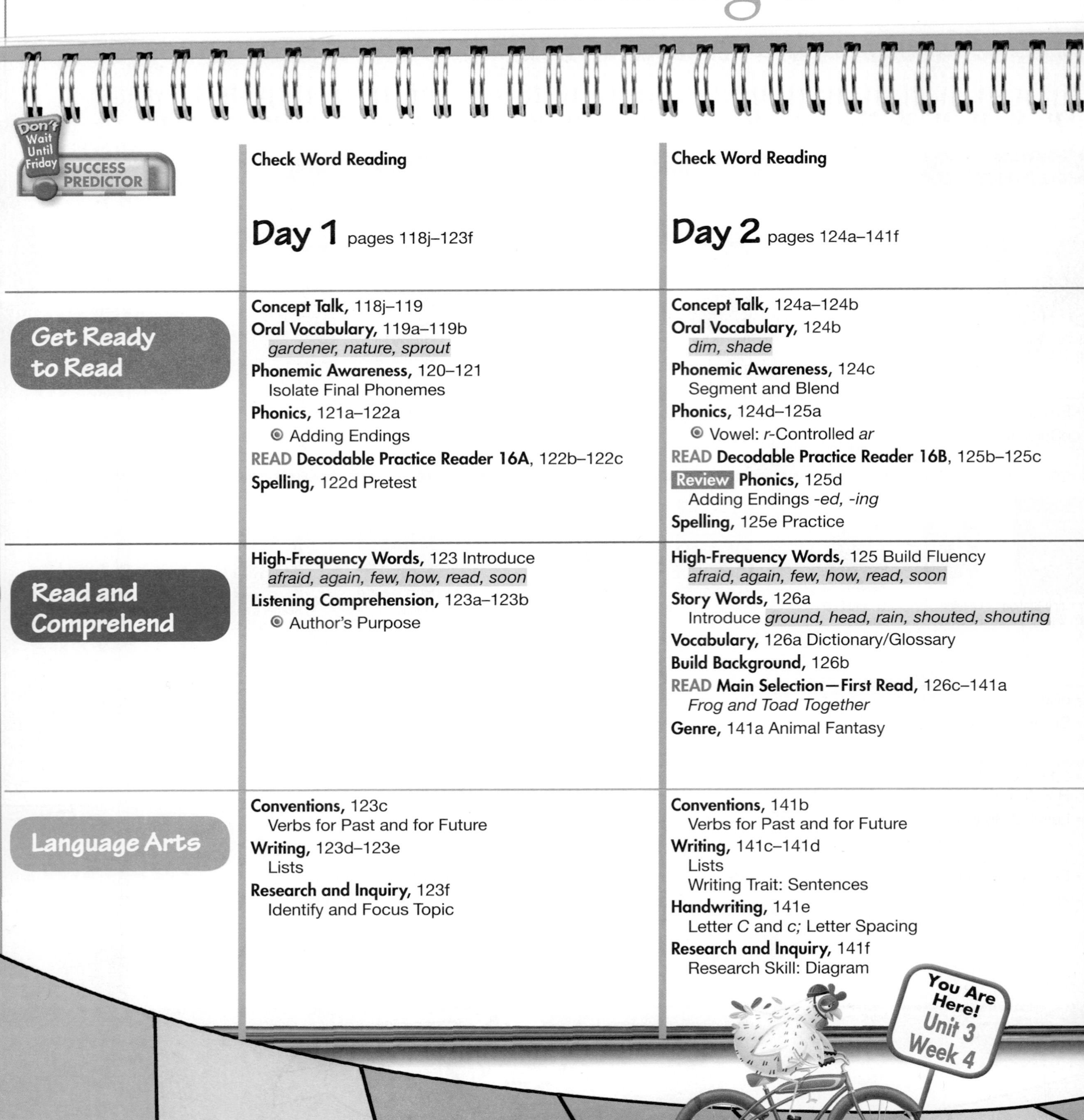

Don't Wait Until Friday SUCCESS PREDICTOR	Check Word Reading **Day 1** pages 118j–123f	Check Word Reading **Day 2** pages 124a–141f
Get Ready to Read	**Concept Talk,** 118j–119 **Oral Vocabulary,** 119a–119b *gardener, nature, sprout* **Phonemic Awareness,** 120–121 Isolate Final Phonemes **Phonics,** 121a–122a ◎ Adding Endings READ **Decodable Practice Reader 16A,** 122b–122c **Spelling,** 122d Pretest	**Concept Talk,** 124a–124b **Oral Vocabulary,** 124b *dim, shade* **Phonemic Awareness,** 124c Segment and Blend **Phonics,** 124d–125a ◎ Vowel: *r*-Controlled *ar* READ **Decodable Practice Reader 16B,** 125b–125c Review **Phonics,** 125d Adding Endings *-ed, -ing* **Spelling,** 125e Practice
Read and Comprehend	**High-Frequency Words,** 123 Introduce *afraid, again, few, how, read, soon* **Listening Comprehension,** 123a–123b ◎ Author's Purpose	**High-Frequency Words,** 125 Build Fluency *afraid, again, few, how, read, soon* **Story Words,** 126a Introduce *ground, head, rain, shouted, shouting* **Vocabulary,** 126a Dictionary/Glossary **Build Background,** 126b READ **Main Selection—First Read,** 126c–141a *Frog and Toad Together* **Genre,** 141a Animal Fantasy
Language Arts	**Conventions,** 123c Verbs for Past and for Future **Writing,** 123d–123e Lists **Research and Inquiry,** 123f Identify and Focus Topic	**Conventions,** 141b Verbs for Past and for Future **Writing,** 141c–141d Lists Writing Trait: Sentences **Handwriting,** 141e Letter *C* and *c;* Letter Spacing **Research and Inquiry,** 141f Research Skill: Diagram

Question of the Week

What changes happen in a garden?

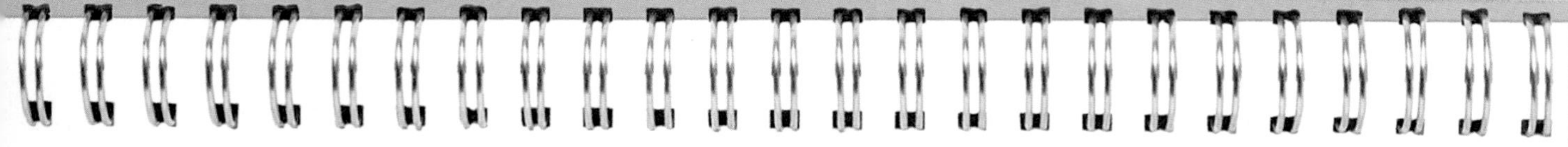

Day 3 pages 142a–145c	Day 4 pages 146a–147f	Day 5 pages 148a–149k
Check High-Frequency Words **Check Retelling**	**Check Fluency**	**Check Oral Vocabulary**
Concept Talk, 142a–142b **Oral Vocabulary,** 142b *sprinkling* **Phonemic Awareness,** 142c Add Phonemes **Phonics,** 142d–142e ◎ Adding Endings ◎ Vowel: *r*-Controlled *ar* **Spelling,** 142f Dictation	**Concept Talk,** 146a–146b **Oral Vocabulary,** 146b *destroy, humongous* **Phonological Awareness,** 146c Review **Phonics,** 146d Ending *-es* and Plural *-es;* *r*-Controlled *or, ore* READ **Decodable Practice Reader 16C,** 146e–146f Review **Fluent Word Reading,** 146g **Spelling,** 146h Partner Review	**Concept Wrap Up,** 148a Review **Oral Vocabulary,** 148b **Phonological Awareness,** 148c Generate Rhyming Words Review **Phonics,** 148c ◎ Adding Endings ◎ Vowel: *r*-Controlled *ar* **Spelling,** 148d Test
Review **High-Frequency Words,** 142g *afraid, again, few, how, read, soon* Review **Story Words,** 142g *ground, head, rain, shouted, shouting* READ **Main Selection—Second Read,** 126–141, 142h–143a **Fluency,** 143b Expression and Intonation	**Science in Reading,** 146i READ **Paired Selection,** 146–147 "Growing Plants" **Fluency,** 147a–147b Expression and Intonation	**Listening and Speaking,** 148–149 Poetry Presentation **Vocabulary,** 149a Dictionary/Glossary **Fluency,** 149a Expression Review **Comprehension,** 149b ◎ Author's Purpose Review **Vocabulary,** 149b High Frequency and Story Words **Procedural Text,** 149c How-to Article **Assessment,** 149d–149f Monitor Progress
Conventions, 144a–145a Verbs for Past and for Future **Writing,** 144–145a Lists Writer's Craft: Tell Characters' Actions **Listening and Speaking,** 145b Poetry Presentation **Research and Inquiry,** 145c Gather and Record Information	**Conventions,** 147c Verbs for Past and for Future **Writing,** 147d–147e Lists Revising Strategy **Research and Inquiry,** 147f Review and Revise Topic	Review **Conventions,** 149g Verbs for Past and for Future **Writing,** 149h–149i Lists Writer's Craft: Verbs for Past and Future **Research and Inquiry,** 149j Communicate **Wrap Up Your Week,** 149k What changes happen in a garden?

Week 4

Grouping Options for Differentiated Instruction
Turn the page for the small group time lesson plan.

Planning Small Group Time on Reading Street!

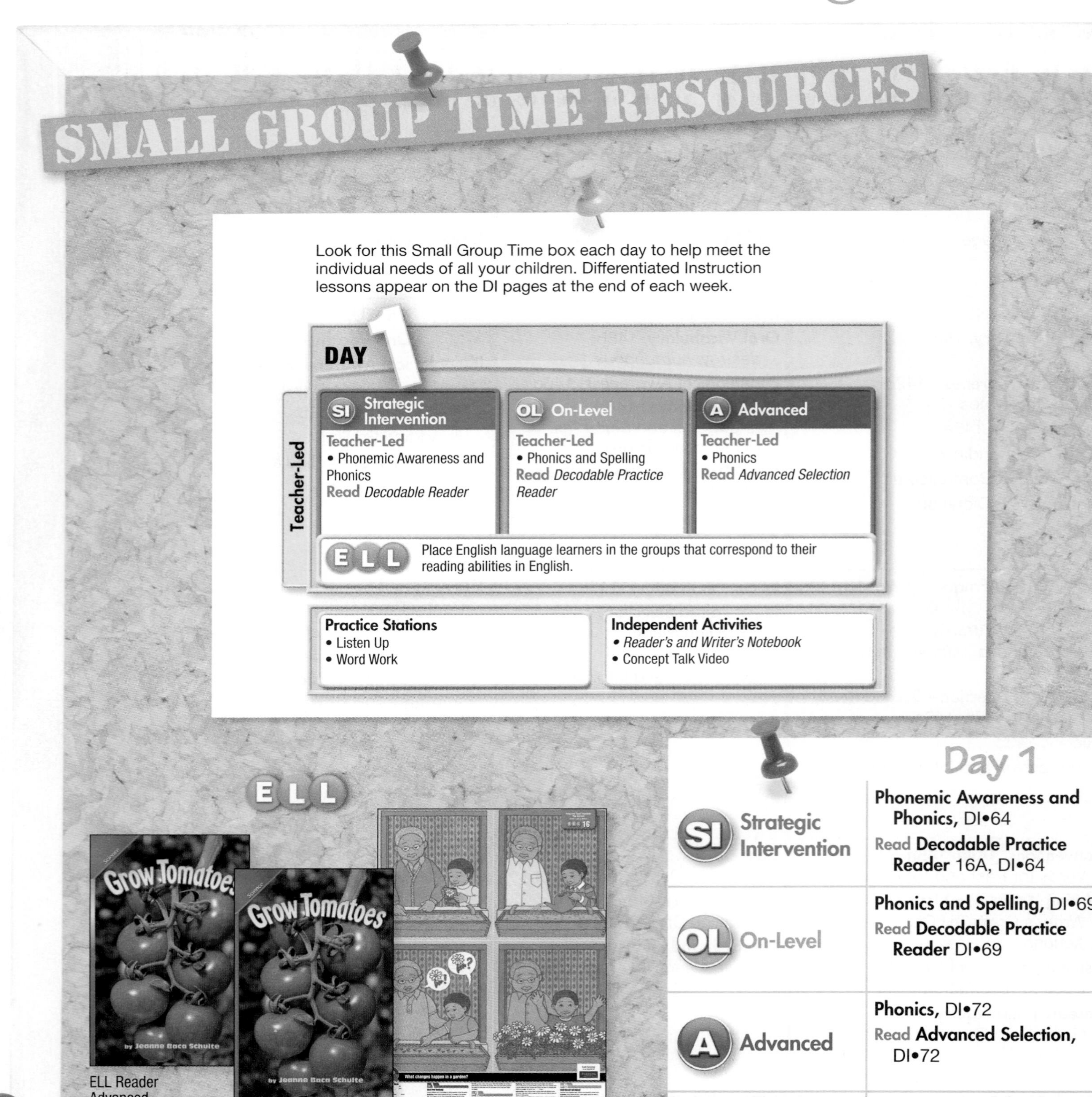

ELL Reader Advanced Advanced-High

ELD Reader Beginning Intermediate

ELL Poster

	Day 1
SI Strategic Intervention	**Phonemic Awareness and Phonics,** DI•64 Read **Decodable Practice Reader** 16A, DI•64
OL On-Level	**Phonics and Spelling,** DI•69 Read **Decodable Practice Reader** DI•69
A Advanced	**Phonics,** DI•72 Read **Advanced Selection,** DI•72
ELL English Language Learners	DI•75–DI•84 **Frontload Concept** **Preteach Skills** **Writing**

You Are Here! Unit 3 Week 4

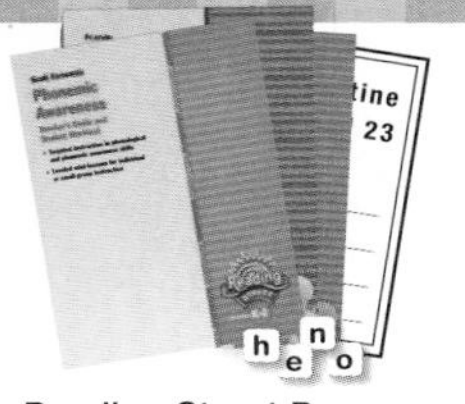

Reading Street Response to Intervention Kit

Reading Street Leveled Practice Stations Kit

Question of the Week

What changes happen in a garden?

SI Strategic Intervention

Below-Level Reader

Decodable Practice Readers

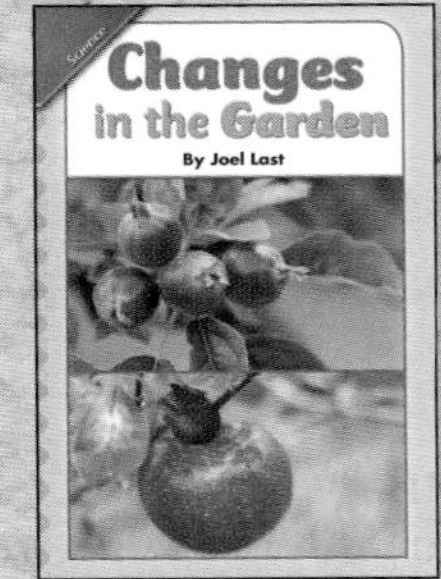

Concept Literacy Reader

OL On-Level

On-Level Reader

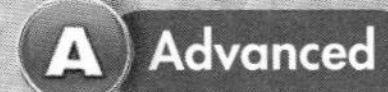

A Advanced

Advanced Reader

Whipped and Flipped

Advanced Selection

Small Group Weekly Plan

Day 2	Day 3	Day 4	Day 5
Phonemic Awareness and Phonics, DI•65 Read **Decodable Practice Reader 16B,** DI•65	**Phonemic Awareness and Phonics,** DI•66 Read **Concept Literacy Leveled Reader,** DI•66	**High-Frequency Words,** DI•67 Read **Decodable Practice Reader 16C,** DI•67	**Phonics Review,** DI•68 Read **Below-Level Leveled Reader,** DI•68
Phonics and High-Frequency Words, DI•69 Read **Decodable Practice Reader 17B,** DI•69	Read **On-Level Leveled Reader,** DI•70	**Conventions,** DI•71 Reread **Main Selection,** DI•711	**Phonics Review,** DI•71 Reread **On-level Leveled Reader,** DI•71
Phonics and Comprehension, DI•72 Read **Main Selection,** DI•72	Read **Advanced Leveled Reader,** DI•73	**Comprehension,** DI•74 Read **Paired Selection,** DI•74 Reread **Leveled Reader,** DI•74	**Fluency and Comprehension,** DI•74 Reread **Advanced Selection,** DI•74
DI•75–DI•84 **Review Concepts** **Practice Skills** **Frontload Main Selection** **Writing**	DI•75–DI•84 **Review Concepts** **Practice Skills** **Reread Main Selection** **Writing**	DI•75–DI•84 **Review Concepts** **Practice Skills** **Read ELL or ELD Reader** **Writing**	DI•75–DI•84 **Review Concepts** **Review Skills** **Writing**

Week 4

Practice Stations for Everyone on Reading Street!

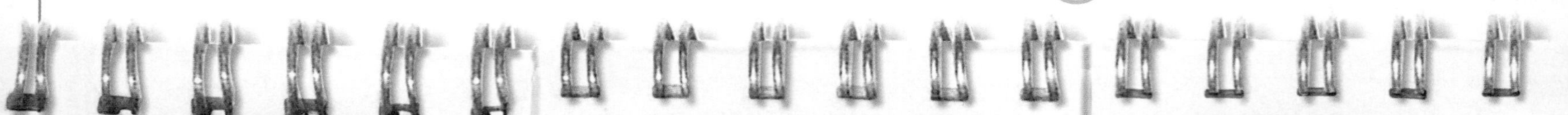

Listen Up!

Generate rhyming words.

Objectives

- Identify words with r-controlled vowel /ôr/.

Materials

- *Listen Up!* Flip Chart Activity 16

Differentiated Activities

● Say the words *shore, port,* and *torn.* Think of words that rhyme with these words. Say them to a partner. Where do you hear the *r*-controlled vowel?

▲ Say the words *shore, port,* and *torn.* Think of words that rhyme with these words. Say them to a partner. Where do you hear the *r*-controlled vowel? Now think of other words with *r*-controlled vowels.

■ Say the words *shore, port,* and *torn.* Think of words that rhyme with these words. Say them to a partner. Where do you hear the *r*-controlled vowel? Now think of other words with *r*-controlled vowels. Say more rhyming words.

Technology

- Interactive Sound-Spelling Cards

Word Work

Ending *-es;* plural *-es; r*-controlled *or, ore*

Objectives

- Build and write words with ending *-es,* plural *-es.*
- Build and write words with *r*-controlled vowel *or, ore.*

Materials

- *Word Work* Flip Chart Activity 16
- Letter Tiles
- paper
- pencils

Differentiated Activities

● Use Letter Tiles. Build the words *batch, mess, wish, fox.* Now add *-es* to each word. What are the new words? Next, build the words *corn* and *short.* Change the last letter in each word to an *e.* What are the new words?

▲ Use Letter Tiles. Build the words *batch, mess, wish, fox.* Now add *-es* to each word. What are the new words? Next, build the words *corn* and *short.* Change the last letter in each word to an *e.* What are the new words? Write all the words on your paper.

■ Use Letter Tiles. Build words that end in *sh, tch, ss,* and *x.* Now add *-es* to each word. What are the new words? Next, build words that contain *or* and *ore.* Write all the words on your paper.

Technology

- Interactive Sound-Spelling Cards

Words To Know

Practice high-frequency words.

Objectives

- Identify high-frequency words *very, car, away, our, house, school, friends.*

Materials

- *Words to Know* Flip Chart Activity 16
- High–Frequency Word Cards for Unit 3, Week 3
- paper
- pencils
- crayons

Differentiated Activities

- A noun names a person, place, animal, or thing.

● Use the Word Cards. Sort the words into two piles: words that are nouns and words that are not nouns. Choose some of the nouns and draw pictures of the words. Label your pictures.

▲ Use the Word Cards. Write these sentences on drawing paper:

> **We got in our car and drove very far away. We will live in a new house. We will go to a new school and make new friends.**

Underline the Words to Know. Draw a picture to go with the sentences.

■ Use the Word Cards. Write sentences using the words. Underline the Words to know. Draw pictures to go with the sentences.

Technology

- Online Tested Vocabulary Activities

You Are Here! Unit 3 Week 4

Use this week's materials from the Reading Street Leveled Practice Stations Kit to organize this week's stations.

Key

Below-Level Activities

On-Level Activities

Advanced Activities

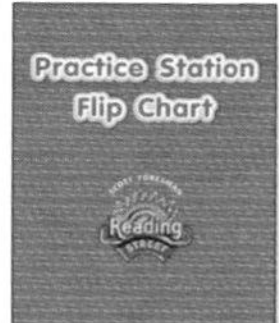

Practice Station Flip Chart

Let's Write!

Use verbs in writing.

Objectives

- Write sentences using verbs that do not add *-s.*

Materials

- *Let's Write!* Flip Chart Activity 16
- paper
- pencils

Differentiated Activities

Think about *The Class Pet.* Make believe you are a baby mouse. Use these sentence frames to tell about how you and your brothers and sisters change and grow: **I** ________ . **We** ________ . Be sure not to add *-s* to the verbs you use. Write as many sentences as you can.

Think about *The Class Pet.* Make believe you are a baby mouse. Write about what you do and about what you and your brothers and sisters do. Be sure not to add -*s* to the verbs you use. Write as many sentences as you can. Underline the verbs.

Think about *The Class Pet.* Make believe you are a baby mouse. Write about what you do and about what you and your brothers and sisters do. Be sure not to add -*s* to the verbs you use. Write as many sentences as you can. Underline the verbs.

Read For Meaning

Identify fact and opinion.

Objectives

- Identify facts and opinions in a selection.

Materials

- *Read for Meaning* Flip Chart Activity, 16
- Leveled Readers
- paper
- pencils

Differentiated Activities

- A **fact** is something that can be proved true.
- An **opinion** is what someone believes.

Read *Gus the Pup.* Talk to a partner about the facts in the book. Now talk about the opinions.

Read *Big Wishes and Her Baby.* Talk to a partner about the facts you find in the book. Now talk about the opinions. Write the facts and the opinions on paper and label them.

Read *Britton Finds a Kitten.* Look for facts and opinions in the book. On your paper, write the facts and opinions. Now share your paper with a partner. Have your partner label the sentences you wrote. Are the labels correct?

Technology

- Leveled eReaders

Get Fluent

Practice fluent reading.

Objectives

- Read aloud with appropriate phrasing.

Materials

- *Get Fluent* Flip Chart Activity 16
- Leveled Readers

Differentiated Activities

Work with a partner. Take turns reading pages from *Gus the Pup.* As you read, look at how words are grouped and read with appropriate phrasing. Punctuation can help you read with appropriate phrasing. Give your partner feedback.

Work with a partner. Take turns reading pages from *Big Wishes and Her Baby.* As you read, look at how words are grouped and read with appropriate phrasing. Punctuation can help you read with appropriate phrasing. Give your partner feedback.

Work with a partner. Take turns reading pages from *Britton Finds a Kitten.* As you read, look at how words are grouped and read with appropriate phrasing. Punctuation can help you read with appropriate phrasing. Give your partner feedback.

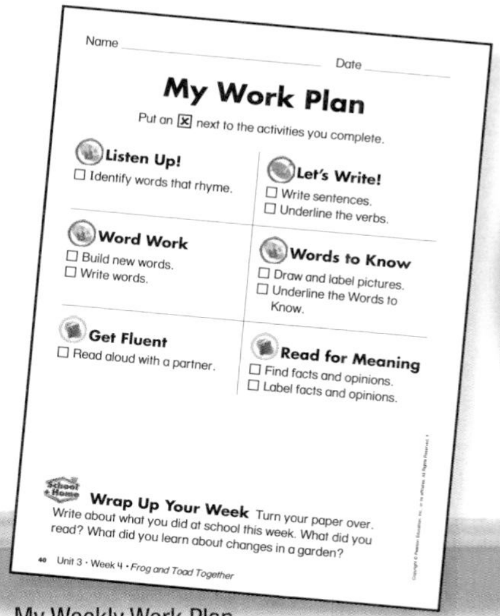

Name ________ Date ________

My Work Plan

Put an ☒ next to the activities you complete.

Listen Up!
☐ Identify words that rhyme.

Let's Write!
☐ Write sentences.
☐ Underline the verbs.

Word Work
☐ Build new words.
☐ Write words.

Words to Know
☐ Draw and label pictures.
☐ Underline the Words to Know.

Get Fluent
☐ Read aloud with a partner.

Read for Meaning
☐ Find facts and opinions.
☐ Label facts and opinions.

Wrap Up Your Week Turn your paper over. Write about what you did at school this week. What did you read? What did you learn about changes in a garden?

48 Unit 3 • Week 4 • Frog and Toad Together

My Weekly Work Plan

Week 4

40–45 min.

Objectives

- Introduce concepts: what changes happen in a garden.
- Share information and ideas about the concept.

Today at a Glance

Oral Vocabulary
gardener, nature, sprout

Phonemic Awareness
Isolate Final Phonemes

Phonics and Spelling
◎ Adding Endings

Fluency
Oral Reading

High-Frequency Words
afraid, again, few, how, read, soon

Comprehension
◎ Author's Purpose

Conventions
Verbs for Past and for Future

Writing
Lists: Introduce

Research and Inquiry
Identify and Focus on Topic

Concept Talk

Question of the Week

What changes happen in a garden?

Introduce the concept To build concepts and focus children's attention, tell them that this week they will talk, sing, read, and write about the changes that happen in a garden. Write the Question of the Week and track the print as you read it.

ROUTINE **Activate Prior Knowledge** Team Talk

1. **Think** Have children think for a minute about the changes that happen in a garden.
2. **Pair** Have pairs of children discuss the question.
3. **Share** Have children share information and their ideas with the group. Remind them to ask questions to clarify information. Guide discussion and encourage elaboration with prompts such as: What do seeds look like when you first plant them? Then what happens?

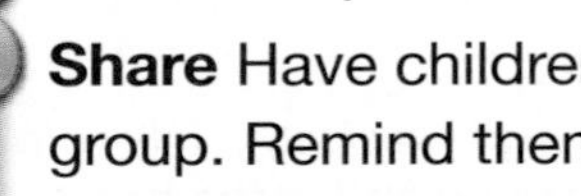

Routines Flip Chart

Anchored Talk

Develop oral language Have children turn to pages 118–119 in their Student Edition. Read the title and look at the photos. Use these questions to guide discussion and create the "What changes happen in a garden?" concept map (shown on the next page).

- What are all the people in this picture doing? (They are helping plants to grow.) Let's add *People can help plants grow* to our map.
- Point to the woman on page 119. How is the woman helping the plants to grow? (She is watering them.) Let's add *We can water plants* to our map.
- Where are the plants she is watering? (In a greenhouse.) A greenhouse lets in sunlight. Let's add *We can keep plants in a sunny place* to our map.

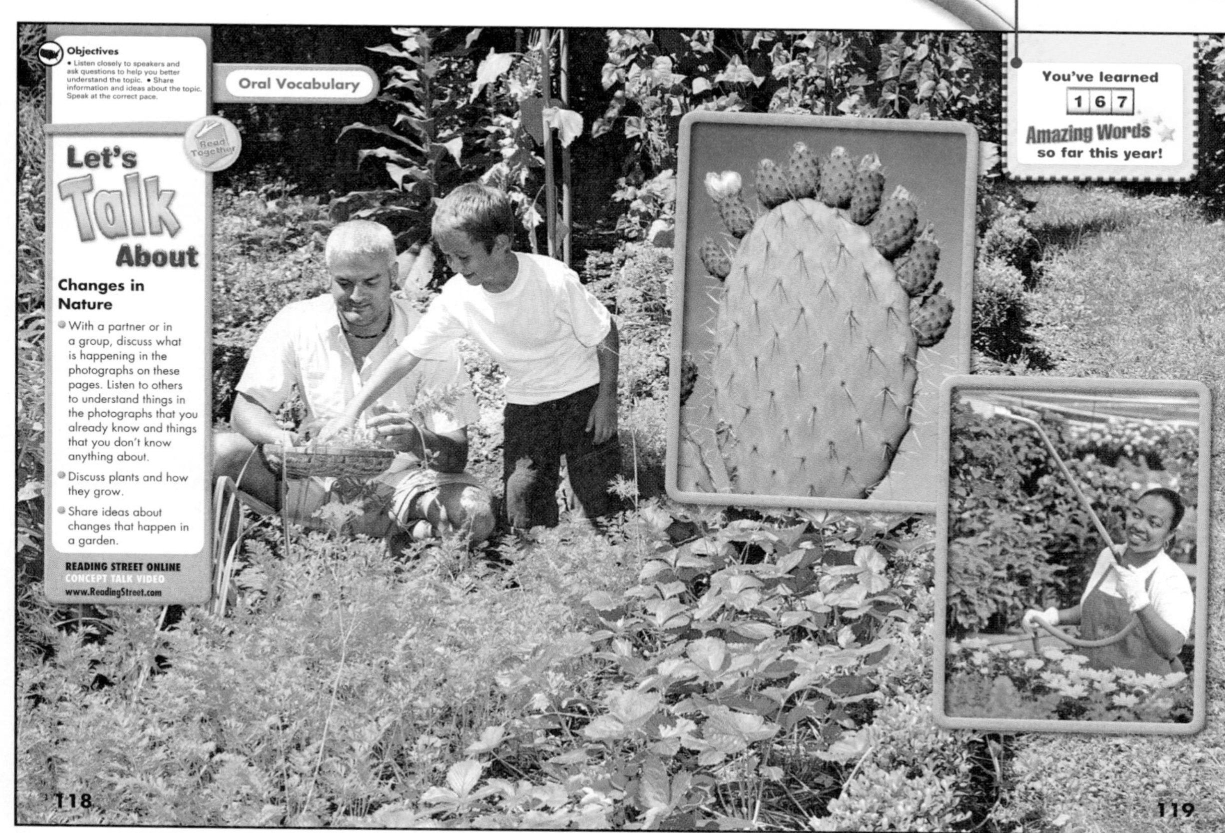

Student Edition pp. 118–119

Connect to reading Explain that this week, children will read about how Toad plants a garden and nature helps it grow. Let's add *Nature helps plants grow* to our map.

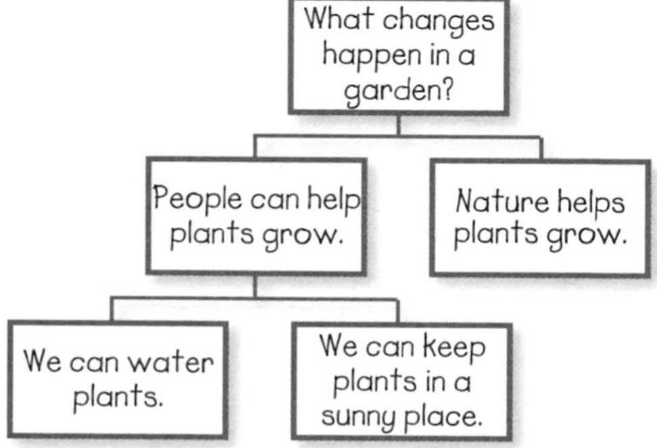

 **Preteach Concepts** Use the Day 1 instruction on ELL Poster 16 to assess and build background knowledge, develop concepts, and build oral vocabulary.

ELL Poster 16

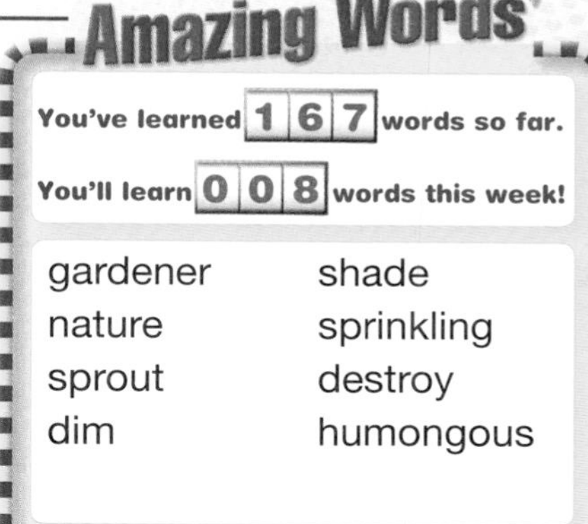

Writing on Demand

Develop Writing Fluency
Ask children to write about what they know about changes that happen in a garden. Have them write for two or three minutes. Children should write as much as they can. Tell them to try to do their best writing. You may want to discuss what children wrote during writing conferences.

ELL

English Language Learners

Listening Comprehension
English learners will benefit from additional visual support to understand the key terms in the concept map. Use the pictures on pp. 118–119 to scaffold understanding. For example, when talking about watering plants, point to the picture of the woman with the hose.

ELL Support Additional ELL support and modified instruction are provided in the *ELL Handbook* and in the ELL Support lessons on pp. DI•75–DI•84.

Objectives

- Build oral vocabulary.
- Discuss the concept to develop oral language.
- Share information and ideas about the concept.

Oral Vocabulary
Amazing Words

Introduce Amazing Words

Display page 16 of the *Sing with Me* Big Book. Tell children they are going to sing "Sprout! It's a Garden," which is about growing a garden. Ask them to listen for the Amazing Words *gardener, nature,* and *sprout* as you sing. Sing the song again and have children join you.

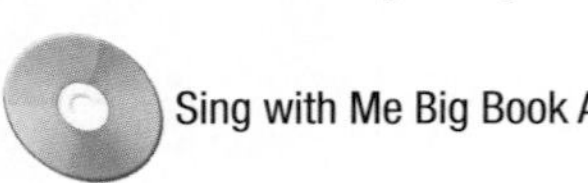

Sing with Me Big Book Audio

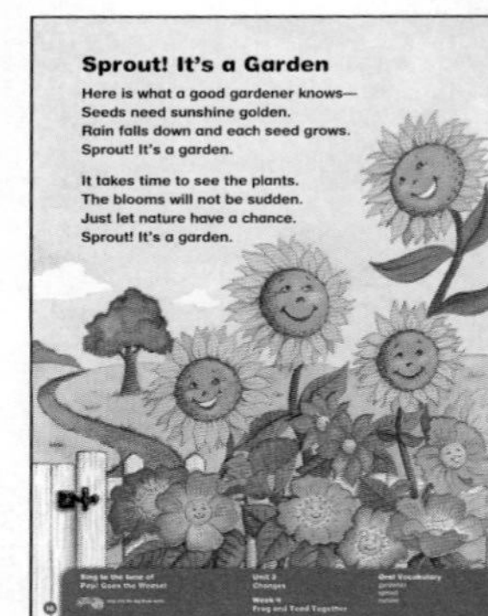

Sing with Me Big Book p. 16

Use the Routine below to develop meaning for the words *gardener, nature,* and *sprout*.

Teach Amazing Words

Amazing Words Oral Vocabulary Routine

1. **Introduce the Word** Relate the word *gardener* to the song. The song says that a *gardener* knows what makes a garden grow. Supply a child-friendly definition: A *gardener* is someone who grows plants. Have children say the word.
2. **Demonstrate** Provide examples to show meaning: A *gardener* decides what to plant in the spring. A *gardener* can grow flowers, vegetables, or trees.
3. **Apply** Have children demonstrate their understanding: Tell me something a *gardener* knows about how to grow plants and take care of them.

See p. OV•1 to teach *nature* and *sprout.*

Routines Flip Chart

Check understanding of Amazing Words

Have children look at the picture on page 16. A *gardener* planted those flowers. What else could a *gardener* plant? Use *gardener* in your answer. (Possible response: A gardener could plant vegetables.)

Flowers are a part of *nature*. What other things are a part of *nature*? Use *nature* in your answer. (Possible response: Trees, the sky, and animals are part of nature.)

What does a plant look like when it *sprouts*? Is it big or small? What color is it? Use *sprout* in your answer. (Possible response: A plant is tiny and green when it sprouts.)

Apply Amazing Words

Have children demonstrate their understanding of the Amazing Words by completing these sentences orally.

If I were a **gardener**, I would ________ .

When I'm outside, one thing I enjoy about **nature** is ________ .

When a seed **sprouts**, it becomes a ________ .

Corrective feedback

If... children have difficulty using the Amazing Words, **then...** remind them of the definitions and provide opportunities for children to use the words in sentences.

Preteach Academic Vocabulary

Write the following on the board:

- **author's purpose**
- **animal fantasy**
- **verbs for past and for future**

Have children share what they know about this week's Academic Vocabulary. Use children's responses to assess their prior knowledge. Preteach the Academic Vocabulary by providing a child-friendly description, explanation, or example that clarifies the meaning of each term. Then ask children to restate the meaning of the Academic Vocabulary in their own words.

Amazing Words

gardener	shade
nature	sprinkling
sprout	destroy
dim	humongous

English Language Learners

Build Oral Vocabulary Work with children to create a hand-play for "Sprout! It's a Garden," including motions for "sunshine golden," "rain falls down," and "Sprout!"

DAY 1 Get Ready to Read

Objectives

- Segment and blend words with the final sounds /ing/, /t/, /d/, and /əd/.
- ◎ Associate the sounds /ing/, /t/, /d/, and /əd/ with the spellings *-ing*, *-d*, and *-ed*.

Skills Trace

◎ **Adding Endings**

Introduce U3W4D1; U4W2D2; U5W3D2

Practice U3W4D3; U3W4D4; U4W2D3; U4W2D4; U5W3D3; U5W3D4

Reteach/Review U3W4D5; U3W5D4; U4W2D5; U4W3D4; U5W3D5; U5W4D4

Assess/Test Weekly Test U3W4

Benchmark Tests U3; U4; U5

KEY:

U=Unit W=Week D=Day

Student Edition pp. 120–121

Phonemic Awareness
Isolate Final Phonemes

Introduce Look at the woman near the barn. What is she doing with the postcard? (putting it in the mailbox) Listen to the sounds at the end of the word *putting:* /i//ng/. Have children look at the picture to identify other actions that end with /i//ng/. (strumming, sitting, spinning) The boy with the tomatoes doesn't look very happy. What happened? (He dropped a tomato.) The last sound I hear in *dropped* is /t/. Have children look again at the picture to find actions that end with the /t/, /d/, or /əd/ sounds. (stopped, begged, painted)

Model Listen to the sounds in the word *putting:* /p/ /u̇/ /t/ /i/ /ng/. Let's blend these sounds to make a word: /p/ /u̇/ /t/ /i/ /ng/, *putting*. Continue modeling with *dropped*.

Guide practice Guide children as they segment and blend these words from the picture: *sitting, spinning, stopped,* and *begged.*

Corrective feedback **If...** children make an error,
then... model by segmenting the word, and have them repeat the segmenting and blending of the word.

Phonics—Teach/Model

Adding Endings

Sound-Spelling Card 121

Sound-Spelling Card 127

ROUTINE Word Parts Strategy

1. **Connect** Write *thinking*. Point out to children that they have already studied words like this, a base word and ending. Ask them to read the word and identify the base word and ending. Explain that today they will learn about words whose spellings change before adding the ending *-ed* or *-ing*.
2. **Use Sound-Spelling Cards** Display Card 121. Point to the word *flipped*. *Flipped* is made from the base word *flip* and the ending *-ed*. Write *flip*. For many words that end with the consonant-vowel-consonant pattern, the last consonant is doubled before adding *-ed* or *-ing*. Demonstrate adding *p* to *flip* and then adding the *-ed* ending. The *-ed* ending can be pronounced /t/, /d/, or /əd/. In *flipped*, it's pronounced /t/, *flipped*. Have children say *flipped* several times. Then repeat this process for *swimming*, using Card 127.
3. **Model** Write *spotted*. *Spotted* is made from the base word *spot* and the ending *-ed*. The final *t* in *spot* is doubled before adding *-ed*.

   When I see a long word, it might be a base word and ending. I look for the base word first: *spot*. Then I read the base word and ending together: *spotted*.
4. **Guide Practice** Have children read *spotted* with you. Write the words below. Have the group read the words with you. Then have children identify the base word, ending, and doubled consonant in each word.

batting	**ripped**	**hopping**	**dotted**
shutting	**stepped**	**digging**	**tagged**

5. **Review** What do you know about reading words that have a base word and ending? (Look for the base word first. Its final consonant might be doubled. Then read the base word and ending together.)

Routines Flip Chart

Differentiated Instruction

 Advanced

More Challenging Words Write the following words on the board: *omitted, omitting, occurred, occurring, starred, starring, knotted, knotting, preferred, preferring*. Read the words aloud and discuss their meanings. Have children write each word, underline the base word, underline the ending, and circle the letter that is doubled. Then have partners choose words to use in a sentence.

Vocabulary Support

You may wish to explain the meaning of this word.

dotted marked with or made up of small spots

English Language Learners

Pronounce *-ing* Children of various backgrounds may not hear the difference between *-ing* and *-in*, so they may say, for example, *hoppin* rather than *hopping*. Help children practice enunciating the *ng* sound in words such as *ripping, petting,* and *swimming*.

Objectives

- Blend and read words with endings *-ed* and *-ing*.
- Decode words in context and in isolation.

Check Word Reading
SUCCESS PREDICTOR

Phonics—Build Fluency

Adding Endings

Model

Have children turn to page 122 in their Student Edition. Look at the pictures on this page. The word in the first picture is *swimming*. When I say *swimming,* I hear the base word *swim* and the ending *-ing. Swim* ends in consonant-vowel-consonant, so the last letter of *swim, m,* is doubled before the ending is added. The word in the second picture is *flipped*. In *flipped*, I hear the base word *flip* and the ending *-ed*. The sound of *-ed* in *flipped* is /t/. *Flip* ends in consonant-vowel-consonant, so the last letter of *flip, p,* is doubled before the ending is added.

Envision It!

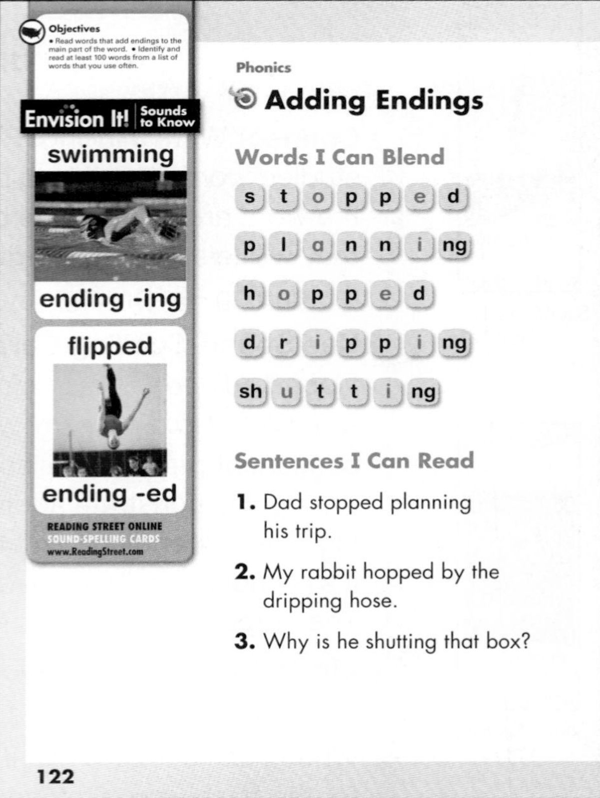

Student Edition p. 122

Guide practice

For each word in "Words I Can Blend," have children identify the base word and ending. Then have children blend the two word parts. Ask which consonant is doubled in each word.

Corrective feedback

If... children have difficulty blending a word,
then... model blending the word, and then ask children to blend it with you.

Blend and Read

Decode words in isolation

After children can successfully segment and blend the words, point to words in random order and ask children to read them naturally.

Decode words in context

Have children read each of the sentences. Have them find the words with an *-ed* or *-ing* and identify the base word. Ask them which letter of the base word was doubled before the ending was added.

Team Talk Pair children and have them take turns reading each of the sentences aloud.

On their own

Use *Reader's and Writer's Notebook* p. 361.

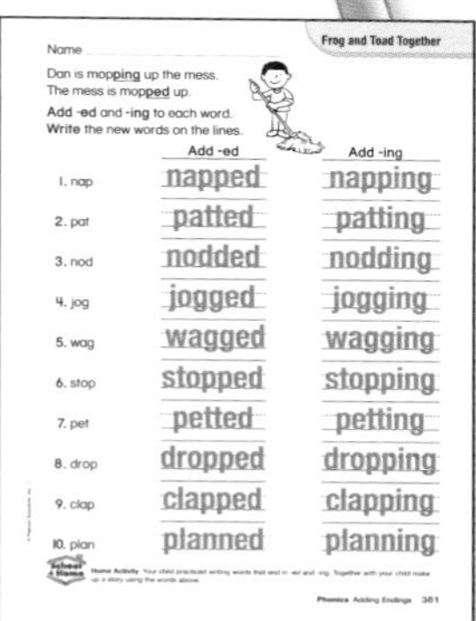
Frog and Toad Together

Name

Dan is mopping up the mess.
The mess is mopped up.

Add -ed and -ing to each word.
Write the new words on the lines.

	Add -ed	Add -ing
1. nap	napped	napping
2. pat	patted	patting
3. nod	nodded	nodding
4. jog	jogged	jogging
5. wag	wagged	wagging
6. stop	stopped	stopping
7. pet	petted	petting
8. drop	dropped	dropping
9. clap	clapped	clapping
10. plan	planned	planning

Phonics Adding Endings 361

Reader's and Writer's Notebook, p. 361

Don't Wait Until Friday

MONITOR PROGRESS — Check Word Reading — Adding Endings

Write the following words and have the class read them. Notice which words children miss during the group reading. Call on individuals to read some of the words.

tapping	**sipped**	**jogging**	**running**	**pinned**	Spiral Review
tripped	**ringing**	**clapping**	**hummed**	**asked**	Row 2 contrasts endings *-ed* and *-ing* with and without spelling changes.
fixes	**getting**	**yelled**	**wishes**	**zipped**	Row 3 reviews endings *-ed*, and *-ing* with and without spelling changes and ending *-es*.

If... children cannot read words with endings *-ed* and *-ing* at this point,
then... use the Small-Group Time Strategic Intervention lesson, p. DI•64, to reteach words with inflected endings *-ed* and *-ing*. Continue to monitor children's progress using other instructional opportunities during the week. See the Skills Trace on pp. 120–121.

Day 1	Day 2	Day 3	Day 4	Day 5
Check Word Reading	Check Word Reading	Check High-Frequency Words/Retelling	Check Fluency	Check Vocabulary

Success Predictor

Differentiated Instruction

SI Strategic Intervention

If children have difficulty identifying the base word in words with *-ed* and *-ing*, write the words and draw a circle around the base word and the ending. Point out the doubled letter between the two circles in words with spelling changes. Then write these words: *stepping, grabbed, tugging, shopped.* Have children copy the words and circle the base words and endings.

Spelling Patterns

Adding Endings For many words that end in consonant-vowel-consonant, the last consonant is doubled before an ending is added.

ELL

English Language Learners

Verb Ending and Tense
In Chinese, Hmong, and Vietnamese, verbs do not change to show the tense. Instead, adverbs or expressions of time indicate when an action has taken place. Explain to children that the *-ed* ending shows that something happened in the past. Write these sentences: *I kick the ball. I kicked the ball. We clap. We clapped.* Have children tell which sentence tells about now and which tells about the past.

Objectives

- Apply knowledge of sound-spellings to decode unknown words when reading.
- Decode and read words in context and in isolation.
- Practice fluency with oral rereading.

Decodable Practice Reader 16A

Adding Endings

Decode words in isolation

Have children turn to page 217. Have children decode each word.

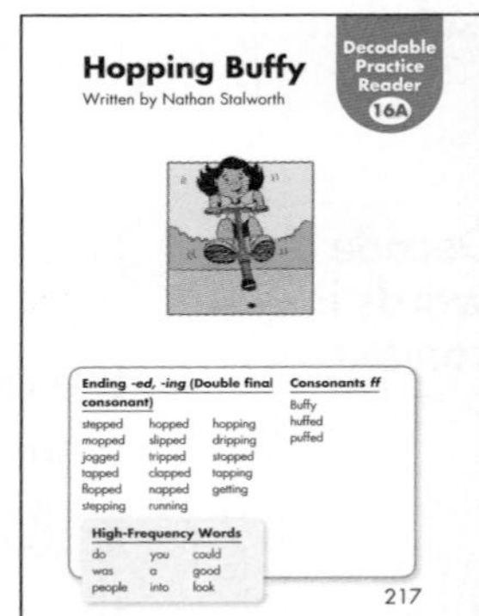

Hopping Buffy

Written by Nathan Stalworth

Decodable Practice Reader 16A

Ending *-ed, -ing* (Double final consonant)			Consonants *ff*
stepped	hopped	hopping	Buffy
mopped	slipped	dripping	huffed
jogged	tripped	stopped	puffed
tapped	clapped	tapping	
flopped	napped	getting	
stepping	running		

High-Frequency Words		
do	you	could
was	a	good
people	into	look

217

Decodable Practice Reader 16A

Review High-frequency words

Review the previously taught words *could, good, into, look, people, was, a, do,* and *you*. Have children read each word as you point to it on the Word Wall.

Preview Decodable Reader

Have children read the title and preview the story. Tell them they will decode words that have a base word and the ending *-ed* or *-ing*.

Decode words in context

Pair children for reading and listen as they decode. One child begins. Children read the entire story, switching readers after each page. Partners reread the story. This time the other child begins.

Buffy came.
Do you think she stepped?
No, Buffy hopped!

218

Buffy could not stop hopping.
She was like a frog.
That was not good.

219

When Buffy mopped and hopped,
she slipped and fell.
Then she was dripping!

220

When Buffy jogged,
she could not stop hopping.
Buffy tripped and stopped.

221

Decodable Practice Reader 16A

Buffy tapped, and people clapped.
Tapping was a lot like hopping!

222

Buffy huffed and puffed!
Buffy flopped into bed.
Buffy napped for a while.

223

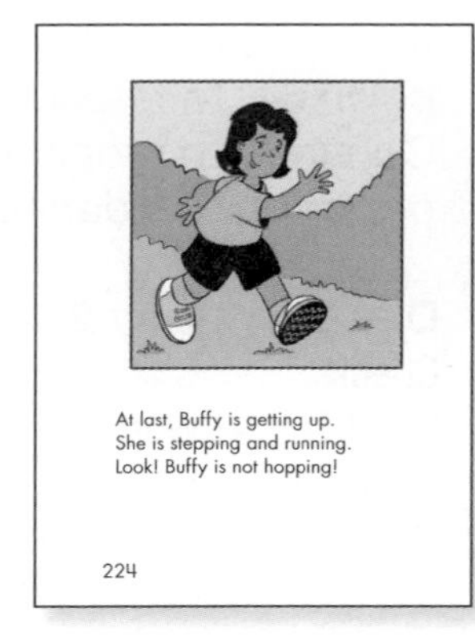

At last, Buffy is getting up.
She is stepping and running.
Look! Buffy is not hopping!

224

Corrective feedback

If... children have difficulty decoding a word,
then... refer them to the Sound-Spelling Cards to identify the sounds in the word. Then prompt them to blend the word.

- What is the new word?
- Is the new word a word you know?
- Does it make sense in the story?

Check decoding and comprehension

Have children retell the story to include characters, setting, and events. Then have children find words with the ending *-ed* or *-ing* in the story. Children should supply *stepped, hopped, hopping, mopped, slipped, dripping, jogged, tripped, stopped, tapped, clapped, tapping, flopped, napped, getting, stepping* and *running.*

Reread for Fluency

Have children reread Decodable Practice Reader 16A to develop automaticity decoding words with inflected endings *-ed* and *-ing*.

ROUTINE **Oral Rereading** Team Talk

1. **Read** Have children read the entire book orally.
2. **Reread** To achieve optimal fluency, children should reread the text three or four times.
3. **Corrective Feedback** Listen as children read. Provide corrective feedback regarding their fluency and decoding.

Routines Flip Chart

Differentiated Instruction

Strategic Intervention

Retelling If children have difficulty retelling the story, do a picture walk-through. Give sentence starters about key events and have children finish the sentences. For example, *Holly could not stop...what?*

English Language Learners

Beginning/Early Intermediate After reading, lead children through *Hopping Buffy* again. Have children tell what Buffy is doing in each picture, using the sentence frame: *Buffy is* ____ .

Intermediate After reading, have children find words that end in *-ed* or *-ing*. Have children use each word in a sentence, for example: *The children jogged around the track.*

Early Advanced/Advanced After reading, have children identify the *-ed* and *-ing* words that rhyme: *hopped, mopped, stopped, flopped; slipped, tripped; tapped, clapped, napped.*

DAY 1 Get Ready to Read

Objectives

- Spell words with inflected ending *-ed.*
- Read high-frequency words.

Spelling Pretest
Words with *-ed*

Dictate spelling words Dictate the spelling words and read the sentences. Have children write the words. If needed, segment the words for children, clarify the pronunciations, and give meanings of words. Have children check their pretests and correct misspelled words.

1. **plan** I **plan** to go to the library.
2. **planned** We **planned** to have a picnic, but it rained.
3. **help** Jill will **help** by setting the table.
4. **helped** Grandpa **helped** me with my homework.
5. **drop** Be careful not to **drop** that glass.
6. **dropped** The plate **dropped** and broke.
7. **call** Sometimes my friends **call** me on the phone.
8. **called** I raised my hand and the teacher **called** on me.
9. **ask** I will **ask** Mom if my friends can come over.
10. **asked*** Paul **asked** his dad to take him to the park.

* Words marked with asterisks come from the selection *Frog and Toad Together.*

On their own Use Let's Practice It! p. 150 on the *Teacher Resource DVD-ROM.*

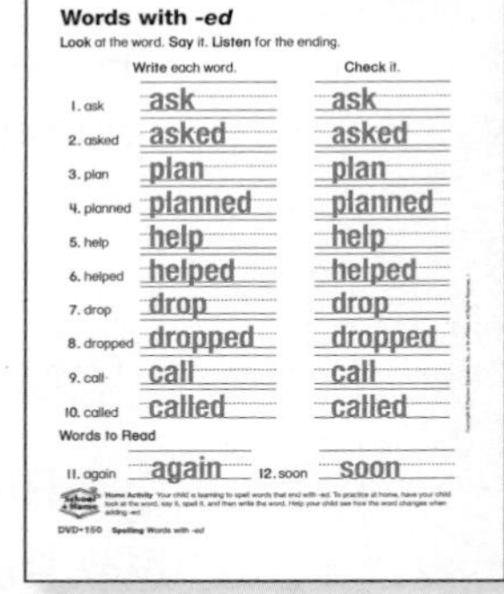

Name ____________ Frog and Toad Together

Words with *-ed*

Look at the word. **Say** it. **Listen** for the ending.

	Write each word.	Check it.
1. ask	ask	ask
2. asked	asked	asked
3. plan	plan	plan
4. planned	planned	planned
5. help	help	help
6. helped	helped	helped
7. drop	drop	drop
8. dropped	dropped	dropped
9. call	call	call
10. called	called	called

Words to Read

11. again again 12. soon soon

DVD•150 Spelling Words with -ed

Let's Practice It! TR DVD•150

Small Group Time

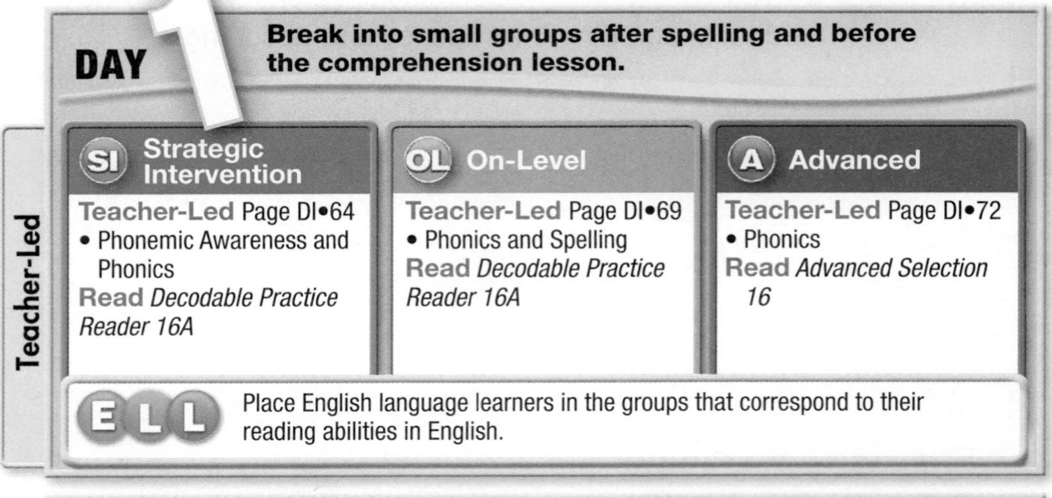

DAY 1 **Break into small groups after spelling and before the comprehension lesson.**

Teacher-Led	SI Strategic Intervention	OL On-Level	A Advanced
	Teacher-Led Page DI•64 • Phonemic Awareness and Phonics Read *Decodable Practice Reader 16A*	Teacher-Led Page DI•69 • Phonics and Spelling Read *Decodable Practice Reader 16A*	Teacher-Led Page DI•72 • Phonics Read *Advanced Selection 16*

ELL Place English language learners in the groups that correspond to their reading abilities in English.

Practice Stations
- Listen Up
- Word Work

Independent Activities
- Read independently/Reading Log on *Reader's and Writer's Notebook* p. RR4
- Concept Talk Video

High-Frequency Words

Introduce

ROUTINE Nondecodable Words

1. **Say and Spell** Look at p. 123. Some words we have to learn by remembering the letters rather than saying the sounds. We will say and spell the words to help learn them. Point to the first word. This word is *few*. The letters in *few* are *f-e-w*, *few*. Have children say and spell each word, first with you, and then without you.
2. **Identify Familiar Letter-Sounds** Point to the first letter in *few*. This letter stands for its own sound. What is this letter and what is its sound? (*f*, /f/)
3. **Demonstrate Meaning** Tell me a sentence using the word *few*.

Repeat this routine with the other Words I Can Read.

Routines Flip Chart

Read words in isolation Have children read the words on p. 123 aloud. Add the words to the Word Wall.

Read words in context Have children read the sentences aloud. Have them identify this week's High-Frequency Words in the sentences.

On their own Use *Reader's and Writer's Notebook* p. 362.

Name

Frog and Toad Together

Circle a word to finish each sentence. Write it on the line.

how few
1. We have a few to take back.

afraid read
2. We read them all and came for new ones.

again few
3. Can we get some again?

soon how
4. We can read how to plant flowers.

afraid few
5. I am afraid this is not the best one.

afraid soon
6. My mom will be here soon.

362 High-Frequency Words

Reader's and Writer's Notebook, p. 362

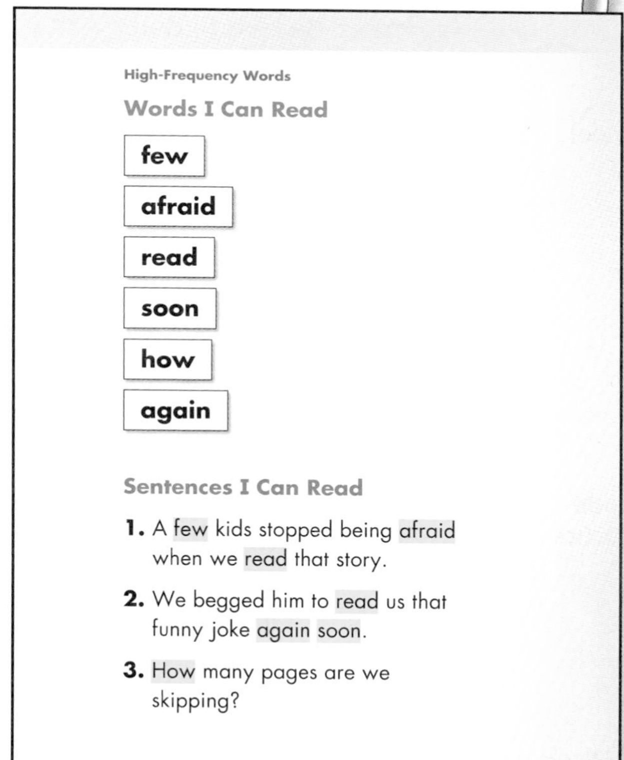
High-Frequency Words

Words I Can Read

few

afraid

read

soon

how

again

Sentences I Can Read

1. A few kids stopped being afraid when we read that story.
2. We begged him to read us that funny joke again soon.
3. How many pages are we skipping?

123

Student Edition p. 123

Differentiated Instruction

Advanced

Extend Spelling Challenge children who spell words correctly to spell more difficult words such as: *snagged*, *trimmed*, *chatted*, *crammed*, *skidded*, and *spotted*.

Phonics/Spelling Generalization

Some spelling words end in *-ed*, pronounced /d/.

English Language Learners

High-Frequency Words Have children use the words *how* and *again* in their own sentences.

Frontload Read Aloud Use the modified Read Aloud in the *ELL Support* pages to prepare children to listen to "Carlee's Garden" (page 123b).

DAY 1 Read and Comprehend

Objectives

- ◎ Make inferences about the author's purpose based on textual evidence.

Skills Trace

◎ **Author's Purpose**
Introduce U2W3D1; U2W5D1; U3W4D1
Practice U2W3D2; U2W3D3; U2W3D4; U2W5D2; U2W5D3; U2W5D4; U3W4D2; U3W4D3; U3W4D4
Reteach/Review U2W3D5; U2W5D5; U2W6D2; U3W1D2; U3W4D5
Assess/Test Weekly Tests U2W3; U2W5; U3W4
Benchmark Tests U2; U3

KEY:
U=Unit W=Week D=Day

Listening Comprehension
◎ Author's Purpose

Introduce

Envision It!

Good readers figure out an author's purpose, or reason, for writing as they read. If the writing is full of facts or useful things to know, the author's purpose is to *inform*—to teach or explain something. If the writing is a funny or exciting story, the author's purpose is to *entertain*—to give readers something to enjoy. Knowing the author's purpose helps you understand your reading.

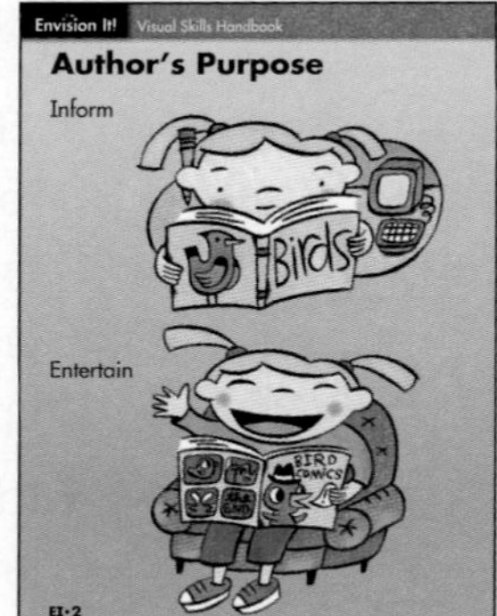

Student Edition p. EI•2

Have children turn to p. EI•2 in their Student Edition. 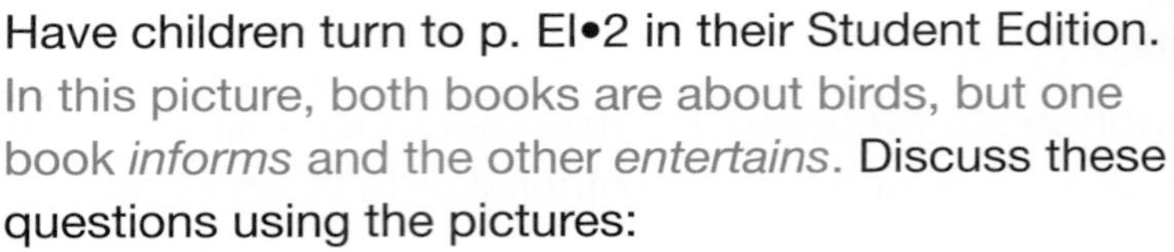 In this picture, both books are about birds, but one book *informs* and the other *entertains*. Discuss these questions using the pictures:

- What might you find in the book that informs? (facts about birds)
- What might you find in the book that entertains? (a funny story about make-believe birds)

Model

Today we will read a story about a vegetable garden. Read "Carlee's Garden" and model how to recognize the author's purpose.

I want to know the author's purpose for writing this story, so I think about what the story is like. As I read, I see that the author is telling me a lot of useful things about where to plant a garden and how to take care of it. I use the evidence I find in the text of the story to decide the author's purpose—to inform me about gardening.

Guide practice

After reading, ask children what details in the story show that the author's purpose was to inform them about gardening. (Possible response: The story shows a real way to keep rabbits out of a vegetable garden. It tells the materials to use for a fence and how to build it so that rabbits can't dig beneath it.)

On their own

Use *Reader's and Writer's Notebook* p. 363.

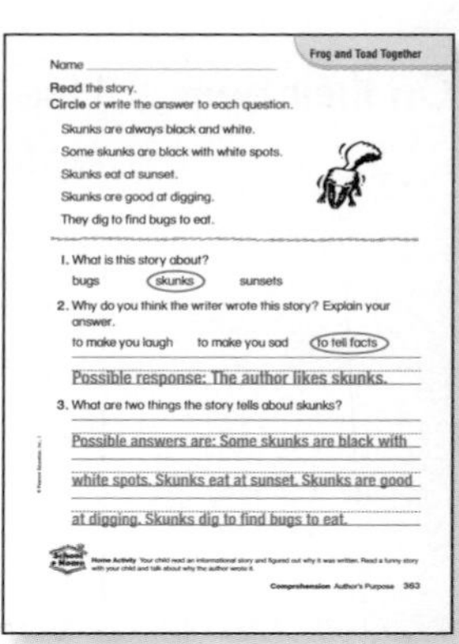

Frog and Toad Together

Name ______________

Read the story.
Circle or write the answer to each question.

Skunks are always black and white.
Some skunks are black with white spots.
Skunks eat at sunset.
Skunks are good at digging.
They dig to find bugs to eat.

1. What is this story about?
bugs (skunks) sunsets
2. Why do you think the writer wrote this story? Explain your answer.
to make you laugh to make you sad (to tell facts)
Possible response: The author likes skunks.
3. What are two things the story tells about skunks?
Possible answers are: Some skunks are black with white spots. Skunks eat at sunset. Skunks are good at digging. Skunks dig to find bugs to eat.

School + Home **Home Activity** Your child read an informational story and figured out why it was written. Read a funny story with your child and talk about why the author wrote it.

Comprehension Author's Purpose 363

Reader's and Writer's Notebook p. 363

Carlee's Garden

"This garden is hard work," Carlee told her dad. They had been digging and planting all morning, and Carlee was hot and tired.

"It will be worth it," her dad said. "If we are good gardeners, then we will grow many plants to eat!"

"All I see is dirt and seeds," Carlee grumbled. But she kept working, and soon the garden had been planted.

For the next few weeks, Carlee and her dad watered the garden every day. It was in a wonderful, sunny location, and soon sprouts began popping up all over. Carlee felt very hungry thinking about the tasty meal they would have once the plants were ready to be picked.

Then one morning Carlee went out to check on the garden. She was surprised to see nibble marks on the lettuce, peas, and beets.

"Dad!" she called. "Something has been nibbling on my plants!"

"Uh-oh," Carlee's dad said. "We must have rabbits living nearby. They love to sneak into gardens and eat plants."

"What will we do?" Carlee asked. "If the rabbits eat all our plants, there won't be any left for us!"

"Don't worry," Carlee's dad answered. "We'll put up a fence."

Carlee and her dad went to the store and bought some chicken wire and wooden posts. Then Carlee's dad built a fence around their garden, burying the bottom part of the chicken wire under the ground so the rabbits couldn't dig their way in.

"I hope this works," Carlee said as they went inside for the night.

The next morning Carlee ran outside to check on their garden. Nothing new had been eaten.

"You were right, Dad," Carlee said. "The fence kept the rabbits out and our plants safe! I hope the rabbits can find other food, though."

"They can find food in nature," her dad told her. "And we'll find food right here in our garden. Come on! It's time to pick our dinner!"

Academic Vocabulary

author's purpose the reason an author writes

Objectives

- Understand and use past and future tense verbs correctly.
- Understand and recognize the features of lists.

MINI-LESSON

5 Day Planner
Guide to Mini-Lessons

DAY 1	Read Like a Writer
DAY 2	Sentences
DAY 3	Tell Characters' Actions
DAY 4	Revising Strategy: Deleting a Word
DAY 5	Proofread for Verbs

Conventions
Verbs for Past and for Future

Model

Remind children that a **verb** is the word in a sentence that shows the action. A verb can tell what happened in the **past** or what will happen in the **future.**

Display Grammar Transparency 16. Read aloud the explanation and the two examples. Point out the *-ed* ending and the helping verb *will* in the examples. Then read the directions and model number 1.

- Time clue words and verbs In a sentence can tell when something happens. In *Last month frog _____ some seeds,* the words *last month* tell about the past.
- So, I will write the verb *planted.* The *-ed* ending tells that the action happened in the past.

Verbs for Past and for Future

Verbs tell what happened in the past. Some verbs that tell about the past end with ***-ed.*** The verb **worked** is **past tense.**

Frog **worked.** (past)

Verbs tell what will happen in the future. Some verbs that tell about the future add ***will.*** The verb **will work** is **future tense.**

Frog **will work.** (future)

Complete each sentence. **Write** the correct verb on the line.

1. Last month Frog planted some seeds. (plants, planted)
2. Now Frog will plant more seeds. (plant, planted)
3. Last week Frog watered the plants. (waters, watered)
4. Today Frog waters the plants. (waters, watered)
5. Now Frog picks flowers again. (picks, picked)
6. Tomorrow Frog will pick many flowers. (pick, picked)

Unit 3 Frog and Toad Together — Grammar 16

Grammar Transparency 16
TR DVD

Guide practice

Continue with items 2–6, having children identify the correct form of the verb for each sentence.

Connect to oral language

Have the class complete these sentence frames orally using the correct past or future form of the verb *play.*

Last week I ________ at the playground.
Yesterday I ________ in my yard.
Tomorrow I ________ with my friend.
In a few days I ________ in the pool.

On their own

Team Talk Write and read aloud the verbs *jump, wish,* and *call.* Have children use the correct form of these verbs in sentences that begin with *Yesterday* or *Tomorrow.*

Writing—Lists
Introduce

MINI-LESSON

Read Like a Writer

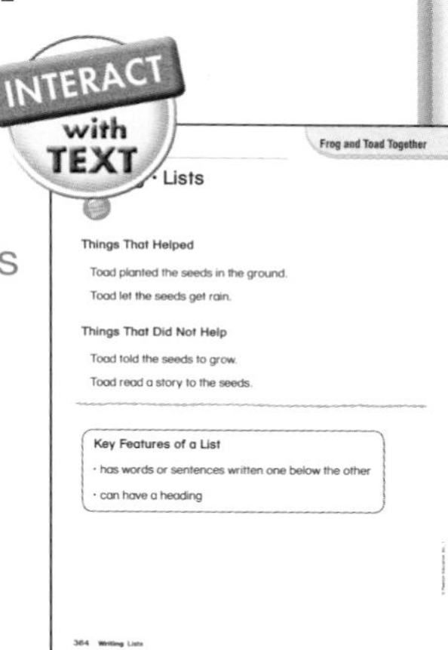

Reader's and Writer's Notebook p. 364

- **Introduce** This week you will write lists. Lists have words or sentences written one below the other. Sometimes lists have headings to tell what ideas will be written.

Prompt	Think of actions Toad tried to help his garden grow. Write a list telling what Toad did that really helped the garden grow. In another list, tell his actions that did not help.
Trait	Sentences
Mode	Expository

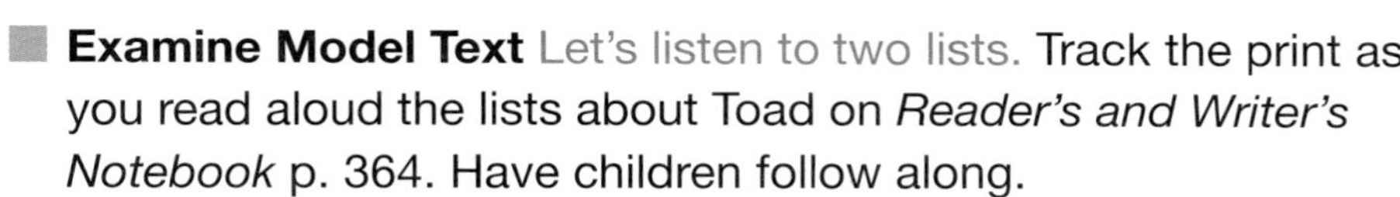

- **Examine Model Text** Let's listen to two lists. Track the print as you read aloud the lists about Toad on *Reader's and Writer's Notebook* p. 364. Have children follow along.

- **Key Features** What is the heading of the first list? (*Things That Helped*) Help children find and circle the heading. Ask children what kinds of ideas they expect to find in that list. Reread the listed items to confirm their answers. Ask children to identify the heading of the second list. (*Things That Did Not Help*) Help children find and circle the heading. Point out that the headings come at the beginning of the list. Explain that the headings give readers clues about what will be in the list.

  These lists have headings. The headings come at the beginning. They tell what will be in the lists.

  The lists are made up of sentences. Each sentence tells something Toad did that helped or did not help his seeds grow.

Write Guy
Jeff Anderson

What Do You Notice?

When children are examining the model text, ask, "What do you notice?" By giving children the responsibility of commenting on what they find effective in the text, they build self-confidence and often begin to notice features of the writing they might not have otherwise. Eventually they will start trying the features in their writing. Relish children's movement toward correctness and beauty.

Academic Vocabulary

past verb a verb that tells something that happened before

future verb a verb that tells something that will happen later

Daily Fix-It

1. Dan helpped me plant my seeds
   Dan helped me plant my seeds.
2. They will be litle plants son.
   They will be little plants soon.

Discuss the Daily Fix-It corrections with children. Review the spelling of past verbs with *-ed,* the double *t* in *little* and *o* in *soon,* and sentence punctuation.

English Language Learners

Conventions To provide students with practice on past and future verbs, use the modified grammar lessons in the *ELL Handbook.*

Language Arts

Objectives

- Understand and recognize the features of a list.
- Develop an understanding of contents of a list.
- Identify a topic connected to this week's concept.
- Narrow the focus of the topic by formulating inquiry questions related to the topic.
- Explore changes in nature.

Writing—Lists
Introduce, continued

Review key features Review key features of a list with children. You may want to post these key features in the classroom to allow children to refer to them as they work on their lists.

Key Features of a List

- has words or sentences written one below the other
- can include a heading

Connect to familiar texts Ask children whether their parents have ever written a list of things for them to do, or recall a list of homework you have assigned to children. Point out that often the list will have a heading, or title, such as *Wednesday's Homework.* The items under the title will tell them what Wednesday's homework will be.

Look ahead Tell children that tomorrow they will plan their own lists.

ROUTINE Quick Write for Fluency Team Talk

1. **Talk** Read the question aloud, and have children list two details in response.

   What are two things we did this morning?

2. **Write** Have children write short sentences in list form to answer the question. Make sure students use past verbs in their sentences.
3. **Share** Partners can read their answers to one another.

Routines Flip Chart

Research and Inquiry
Identify and Focus Topic

Teach Display and review the concept map that explores this week's question: *What changes happen in a garden?* What else would you like to know about how plants grow? Have children suggest ideas. Explain that they can find out what they would like to know by doing **research**. First, they must choose one question to answer.

Model Think Aloud One thing I think is very interesting about plants is that they have many different parts. So a question I would like to answer by doing research is "What are the different parts of a plant?"

Guide practice Have children create a note-taking chart like the one shown. Have them record what they already know about their plant topic. Tell them that tomorrow they will begin doing research to learn more.

Academic Vocabulary

research the study of a topic by gathering information from different sources

What are the different parts of a plant?	
What I Know	What I Learned
leaves stem	

Graphic Organizer Flip Chart 4

Wrap Up Your Day

- ✔ **Phonics: Adding Endings** Write *hopping*. What are the base word and ending? (*hop, -ing*) Elicit that *hop* has one *p* but *hopping* has two. Review that when a word ends with consonant-vowel-consonant, the last consonant is usually doubled before an ending.
- ✔ **Spelling: Words with -ed** Have children spell *plan*. Then have them spell *planned*. Repeat for *help* and *helped*. Discuss why the doubling rule above applies to *plan* but not *help*.
- ✔ **Build Concepts** Ask children to recall what happened in the Read Aloud, "Carlee's Garden." What did Carlee learn about how to keep a garden growing? (Possible response: She learned that a fence can protect the plants from being eaten by animals.)
- ✔ **Homework** Send home this week's Family Times Newsletter from Let's Practice It! pp. 145–146 on the *Teacher Resource DVD-ROM*.

Let's Practice It! TR DVD•145–146

Preview DAY 2

Tell children that tomorrow they will read about a toad who tries out some funny ways to make his garden grow.

Objectives

- Discuss the concept to develop oral language.
- Build oral vocabulary.

Today at a Glance

Oral Vocabulary
dim, shade

Phonemic Awareness
Segment and Blend

Phonics and Spelling
◎ Adding Endings
◎ Vowel: *r*-Controlled *ar*

Fluency
Paired Reading

High-Frequency Words

Story Words
ground, head, rain, shouted, shouting

Comprehension
◎ Author's Purpose
◎ Visualize

Vocabulary
Dictionary/Glossary

Conventions
Verbs for Past and for Future

Writing
Lists

Handwriting
Letter *Cc*/Letter Spacing

Research and Inquiry
Research Skill: Diagram

Concept Talk

Question of the Week

What changes happen in a garden?

Build Concepts To reinforce concepts and to focus children's attention, have children sing "Sprout! It's a Garden" from the *Sing with Me* Big Book. What does the song mean when it says, "It takes time to see the plants"? (The seeds don't sprout right away. You have to wait.)

Sing with Me Big Book Audio

Introduce Amazing Words Display the Big Book, *What Makes the Seasons?* Read the title and identify the author. Explain that in the selection, the author uses the words *dim* and *shade*. Have children listen to the story to find out in what season plants turn a beautiful *shade* of green and in what season the sun begins to grow *dim*.

Use the Oral Vocabulary routine on the next page to teach *shade* and *dim*.

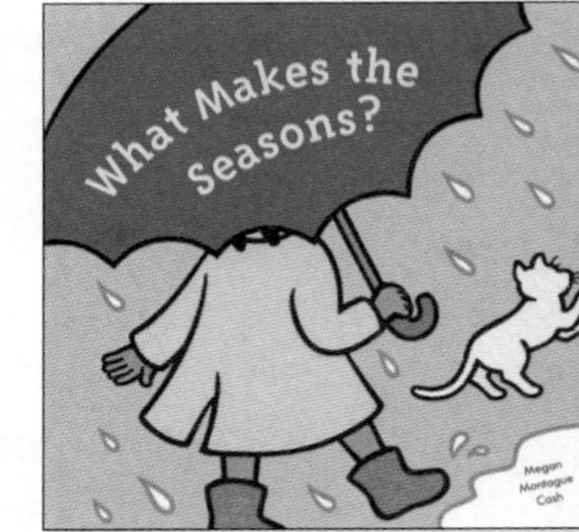

Big Book

ELL Reinforce Vocabulary Use the Day 2 instruction on ELL Poster 16 to reinforce the meanings of high-frequency words.

ELL Poster 16

Oral Vocabulary
Amazing Words

Teach Amazing Words

Amazing Words Oral Vocabulary Routine

1. **Introduce the Word** Relate the word *dim* to the book. The sun grows *dim* when summer turns to autumn. Supply a child-friendly definition. When something is *dim*, it is not very bright. Have children say the word.
2. **Demonstrate** Provide examples to show meaning. When we closed the curtain, the room became *dim*. We made the lights *dim* so that we could watch the movie.
3. **Apply** Have children demonstrate their understanding. What can you do to make the light inside a room *dim*?

See p. OV•1 to teach *shade*.

Routines Flip Chart

Anchored Talk

Add to the concept map

Discuss how nature and people help gardens grow.

- What does the song tell us about how nature waters a garden? (Gardens can get water from rain.) Let's add *Rain waters plants* to our map.
- What else does the song tell us about how nature helps a garden grow? (Plants need sunshine, which comes from nature.) Let's add *The sun helps plants grow* to our map.
- In yesterday's Read Aloud, "Carlee's Garden," rabbits were eating Carlee's plants. How did her dad protect the plants so they could keep growing? (He put up a fence to keep the rabbits out.) Let's add *We can build fences to protect plants* to our map.

Amazing Words

gardener	shade
nature	sprinkling
sprout	destroy
dim	humongous

Differentiated Instruction

Advanced

Using Amazing Words Tell children that *dim* and *bright* are opposites. Read these phrases and ask children if they describe something dim or bright: *a sunny day, a cloudy day, a room at night with lots of lights on, a room a night with just one candle, the inside of a cave, the words on a freshly painted sign, the words on an old and faded sign*.

English Language Learners

Visual Support Demonstrate *dim* by turning off the lights or pulling down the window shades. Demonstrate *shade* by pointing to different shades of the same color and asking, for example, "Which *shade* of blue is lighter? Which *shade* of green do you like better?" Throughout the day, look for more opportunities to reinforce these words by making visual connections.

Objectives

- Segment and blend the sounds in words with /är/.
- ◎ Associate the sound /är/ with *ar*.
- ◎ Blend and read words with /är/.

Skills Trace

◎ **Vowel: *r*-Controlled *ar***
Introduce U3W4D2
Practice U3W4D3; U3W4D4
Reteach/Review U3W4D5; U3W5D4
Assess/Test Weekly Test U3W4
Benchmark Test U3

KEY:
U=Unit W=Week D=Day

Phonemic Awareness
Segment and Blend Phonemes

Model isolating sounds

Have children look at the picture on pages 120–121 in their Student Edition. I see a *farm* in the picture. *Farm* has the /är/ sound. I hear three sounds in the word *farm*. The first sound I hear is /f/. The second sound is /är/. The last sound I hear in *farm* is /m/.

Student Edition pp. 120–121

Model segmenting and blending

Listen to the sounds in the word *barn*: /b/ / /är/ /n/. There are three sounds in *barn*. Let's blend those sounds to make a word: /b/ /är/ /n/, *barn*. Continue modeling with *yard, guitar,* and *postcard.*

Guide practice

Guide children as they segment and blend these words from the picture: *car, arm, jar, star, garden,* and *harvest*.

Corrective feedback

If... children make an error,
then... model by segmenting the word, and have them repeat the segmenting and blending of the word.

On their own

Have children segment and blend the following words.

/h/ /är/ /d/ **hard**	/y/ /är/ /n/ **yarn**	/s/ /t/ /är/ /t/ **start**
/m/ /är/ /k/ **mark**	/ch/ /är/ /t/ **chart**	/p/ /är/ /k/ **park**
/d/ /är/ /t/ **dart**	/f/ /är/ **far**	/k/ /är/ /d/ **card**

Phonics—Teach/Model

Vowel: *r*-Controlled *ar*

Sound-Spelling Card 55

ROUTINE Blending Strategy

1. **Connect** Write *cat* and *had*. You studied words like these already. What do you know about the vowel sound in these words? (The vowel sound is /a/, spelled *a*.) Today you will learn about the sound of *a* when it is followed by *r*.
2. **Use Sound-Spelling Card** Display Card 55. The sound you hear at the beginning of *artist* is /är/. The sound /är/ is spelled *ar*. Have children say /är/ several times as you point to *ar*.
3. **Model** Write *hard*. This word has the letters *ar*, which spell the sound /är/. This is how I blend this word. Segment and blend *hard*. Follow this procedure to model blending *far* and *barn*.
4. **Guide Practice** Continue the process in step 3. This time have children blend with you.

mark	yarn	harp	star	chart	card
car	smart	march	tar	park	charm

5. **Review** What do you know about reading these words? (The letters *ar* can spell the sound /är/.)

Routines Flip Chart

Differentiated Instruction

 Advanced

More Challenging Words Write and read aloud the following words: *target, darkness, charming, charcoal, sparkle, partner, marble.* Discuss the meaning of each word. Then have children copy each word, underline the letters that spell /är/, and use the word in an oral sentence.

Vocabulary Support

You may wish to explain the meaning of these words.

charm the power to please or delight

harp a tall musical instrument that is shaped like a triangle and has strings that are plucked

tar a dark, thick, oily substance that was once used to pave roads

English Language Learners

Visual Support Model isolating sounds while using the pictures on pp. 120–121 of the Student Edition as visual support. For example: /s/ /t/ /är/, *star*. Who can point to the star on the barn? Now let's say the sounds of *star* together: /s/ /t/ /är/.

Objectives

- ◎ Blend and read words with *r*-controlled *ar.*
- ◎ Associate the sound /är/ with *ar.*
- Decode words in context and in isolation.

Check Word Reading
SUCCESS PREDICTOR

Phonics—Build Fluency
Vowel: *r*-Controlled *ar*

Model

Have children turn to page 124 in their Student Edition.

Envision It!

Look at the picture on this page. The word in the picture is *artist*. When I say *artist*, I hear the /är/ sound. The /är/ sound in *artist* is spelled *ar*.

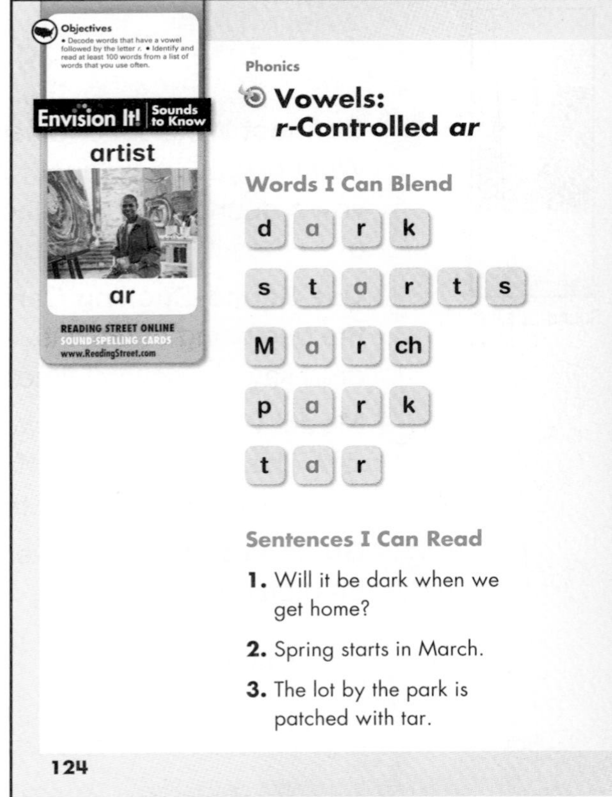

Student Edition p. 124

Guide practice

For each word in "Words I Can Blend," ask for the sound of each letter or group of letters. Make sure that children identify the correct sound for *ar*. Then have children blend the whole word.

Corrective feedback

If... children have difficulty blending a word,
then... model blending the word, and ask children to blend it with you.

Blend and Read

Decode words in isolation After children can successfully segment and blend the words, ask them to read the words naturally.

Decode words in context Have children read each of the sentences. Have them identify words in the sentences with /är/ spelled *ar*.

Team Talk Pair children and have them take turns reading each of the sentences aloud.

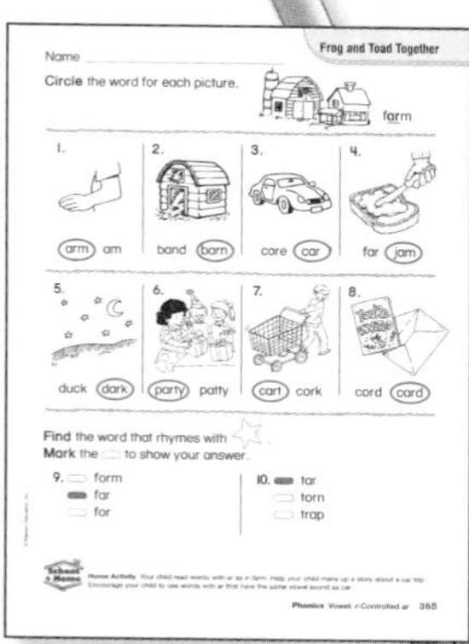
Reader's and Writer's Notebook p. 365

On their own Use *Reader's and Writer's Notebook* p. 365.

Don't Wait Until Friday

MONITOR PROGRESS Check Word Reading r-Controlled *ar*

Write the following words and have the class read them. Notice which words children miss during the group reading. Call on those individuals to read some of the words.

jar	**yard**	**dark**	**hard**	**sharp**
sort	**more**	**scarf**	**porch**	**start**
cat	**cart**	**ham**	**harm**	**bark**

Spiral Review
Row 2 contrasts *r*-controlled *ar* words with *r*-controlled *or and ore* words.
Row 3 contrasts *r*-controlled *ar* words with short *a* words.

If... children cannot blend words with /är/ spelled *ar*,
then... use the Small Group Time Strategic Intervention lesson, p. DI•65, to reteach /är/ spelled *ar*. Continue to monitor children's progress using other instructional opportunities during the week. See the Skills Trace on p. 124c.

Day 1	Day 2	Day 3	Day 4	Day 5
Check Word Reading	**Check Word Reading**	Check High-Frequency Words/Retelling	Check Fluency	Check Vocabulary

Success Predictor

Differentiated Instruction

SI Strategic Intervention

Extra Practice If children are having difficulty reading words with /är/, provide extra practice. Write the following words: *jar, dart, scar, scarf, darn, start, lark, barn, far, harsh.* Point to each spelling as children say the sound. Then run your hand under the word as children say the whole word.

Spelling Patterns

ar The sound /är/ is spelled *ar.*

ELL

English Language Learners

Pronounce /är/ Although *r* is pronounced differently in Spanish, there are similarities in the way some words with *ar* are pronounced in English and Spanish. Point out similarities in words such as *arte/art* and *parte/part*. Have children practice saying these words.

Get Ready to Read

Objectives

- Apply knowledge of sound-spellings to decode unknown words when reading.
- Decode and read words in context and in isolation.
- Practice fluency with oral rereading.

Decodable Practice Reader 16B

Vowel: *r*-Controlled *ar*

Decode words in isolation Have children turn to page 225. Have children decode each word.

Review High-frequency words Review the previously taught words *to, they, from, live, a, the, very, could, look, every,* and *have*. Have children read each word as you point to it on the Word Wall.

Preview Have children read the title and preview the story. Tell them they will read words with the /är/ sound spelled *ar*.

Day at the Farm
Written by Jason Dee
Decodable Practice Reader 16B

Vowels: *r*-Controlled *ar*
farm barn hard harm
cart yard smart bark
dark star car

Syllable Pattern CV
baby she
go

Consonant Patterns *ng, nk*
Frank honks wings thing

Word Family -onk
honks

High-Frequency Words
to they live
a the very
could look every
have from

225

Decodable Practice Reader 16B

Decode words in context Pair children for reading and listen as they decode. One child begins. Children read the entire story, switching readers after each page.

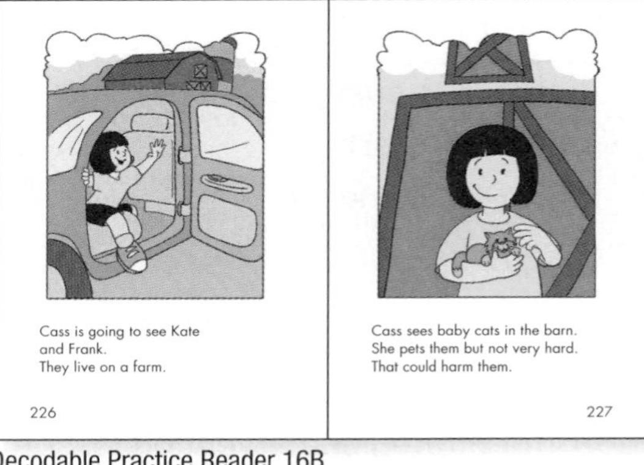
Cass is going to see Kate
and Frank.
They live on a farm.

226

Cass sees baby cats in the barn.
She pets them but not very hard.
That could harm them.

227

Decodable Practice Reader 16B

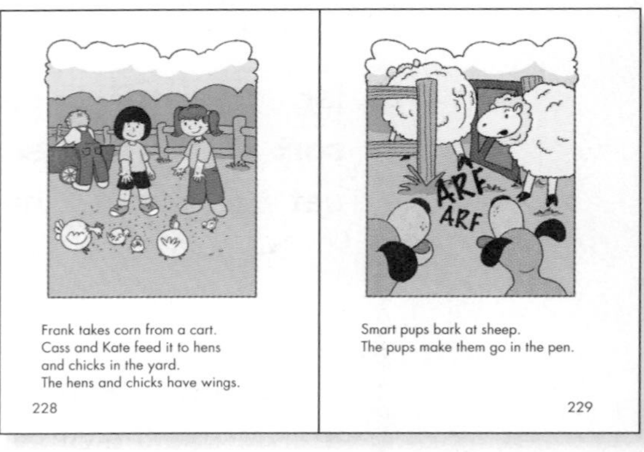
Frank takes corn from a cart.
Cass and Kate feed it to hens
and chicks in the yard.
The hens and chicks have wings.

228

Smart pups bark at sheep.
The pups make them go in the pen.

229

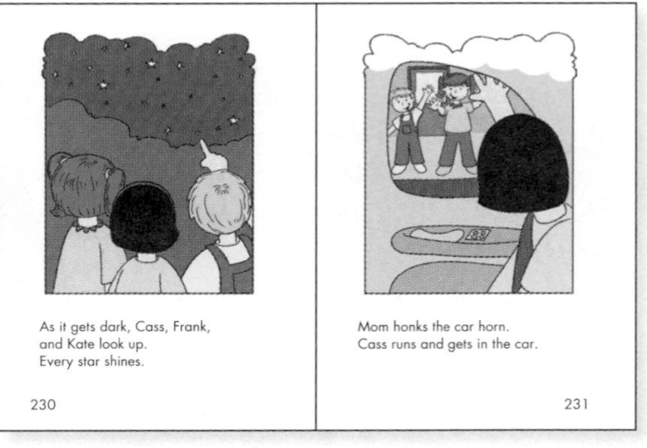
As it gets dark, Cass, Frank,
and Kate look up.
Every star shines.

230

Mom honks the car horn.
Cass runs and gets in the car.

231

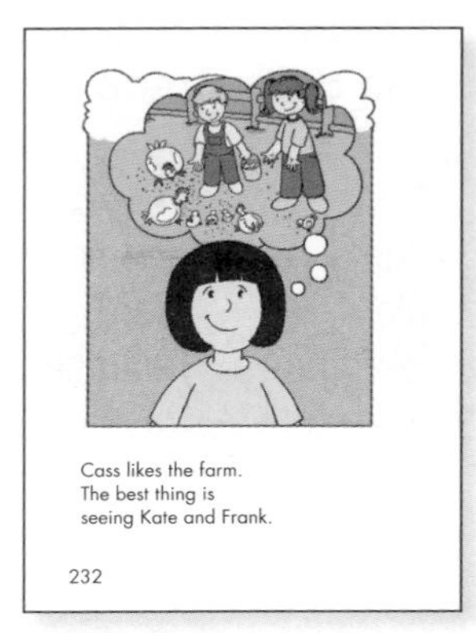
Cass likes the farm.
The best thing is
seeing Kate and Frank.

232

Corrective feedback

If... children have difficulty decoding a word, **then...** refer them to the Sound-Spelling Cards to identify the sounds in the word. Then prompt them to blend the word.

- What is the new word?
- Is the new word a word you know?
- Does it make sense in the story?

Check decoding and comprehension

Have children retell the story to include characters, setting, and events. Then have children find /är/ words in the story. Children should supply *farm*, *barn, hard, harm, cart, yard, smart, bark, dark, star,* and *car*.

Reread for Fluency

Have children reread Decodable Practice Reader 16B to develop automaticity decoding words with /är/ spelled *ar*.

ROUTINE Paired Reading

 **Reread** To achieve optimal fluency, have partners reread the text three or four times.

 **Corrective Feedback** Listen as children read. Provide corrective feedback regarding their fluency and decoding.

Routines Flip Chart

Differentiated Instruction

 Strategic Intervention

Reading Words with *ar* If children are having trouble reading words with /är/, make word cards for *farm*, *barn, hard, harm, cart, yard, smart, bark, dark, star,* and *car*. Segment and blend each word with children and have them practice reading the words two or three times. Then have them reread the story.

English Language Learners

Beginning/Early Intermediate Before children read, lead them through *Day at the Farm*. Have children tell what kinds of animals live on a farm. Point out /är/ words and have children say them aloud

Intermediate After reading, have children find pairs of rhyming words with the /är/ sound and read them aloud. For example, *farm, harm; hard, yard; cart, smart; bark, dark;* and *star, car*. Then have them think of another rhyming word for each pair.

Early Advanced/Advanced After reading, have children find words in the story with the /är/ sound and ask questions that use those words. For example: *Why do the dogs bark at the sheep?* Have children answer.

Objectives

- Read words with inflectional endings *-ed* and *-ing.*
- Spell words with ending *-ed.*

Phonics Review

Adding Endings *-ed, -ing*

Review word parts

Review that some words have a base word and the ending *-ed* or *-ing*. Remind children that when a word ends in consonant-vowel-consonant, the final consonant is usually doubled before adding *-ed* or *-ing*. Use Sound-Spelling Cards 121, 126, and 127.

Decode words in isolation

Display these words. Have the class blend the words. Then point to the words in random order and ask children to decode them quickly.

dipped	**sinking**	**kicked**	**letting**
wishing	**planning**	**napped**	**thanking**
tagged	**listed**	**banged**	**digging**

Corrective feedback

Model blending decodable words and then ask children to blend them with you.

Decode words in context

Display these sentences. Have the class read the sentences.

Team Talk Have pairs take turns reading the sentences naturally.

Nat **slipped** on the ice.

He **kissed** and **hugged** his mom.

Kim likes **batting** and **pitching.**

Spelling
Words with *-ed*

Guide practice

Tell children that you will segment the sounds in each spelling word. They should repeat the sounds in each word as they write the word. Check the spelling of each word before saying the next word.

1. /a/ /s/ /k/ **ask**
2. /a/ /s/ /k/ /t/ **asked**
3. /h/ /e/ /l/ /p/ **help**
4. /h/ /e/ /l/ /p/ /t/ **helped**
5. /d/ /r/ /o/ /p/ **drop**
6. /d/ /r/ /o/ /p/ /t/ **dropped**
7. /c/ /ȯ/ /l/ **call**
8. /c/ /ȯ/ /l/ /d/ **called**
9. /p/ /l/ /a/ /n/ **plan**
10. /p/ /l/ /a/ /n/ /d/ **planned**

On their own

Use *Reader's and Writer's Notebook* p. 366.

Name

Frog and Toad Together

Words with *-ed*

Write the list word to finish the chart.

	Base Word	-ed Word
1.	ask	asked
2.	drop	dropped
3.	help	helped
4.	plan	planned

Spelling Words: ask, asked, plan, planned, help, helped, drop, dropped, call, called

Read the clues. Write the list word.

It rhymes with It starts with pl. 5. plan

It rhymes with It starts with c. 6. call

It rhymes with It starts with dr. 7. drop

Write the list word that tells what happened in the past.

8. We can ask for paper. We asked for paper.
9. I will call my friends. I called my friends.
10. He can help. He helped

366 Spelling Words with -ed

Reader's and Writer's Notebook, p. 366

Small Group Time

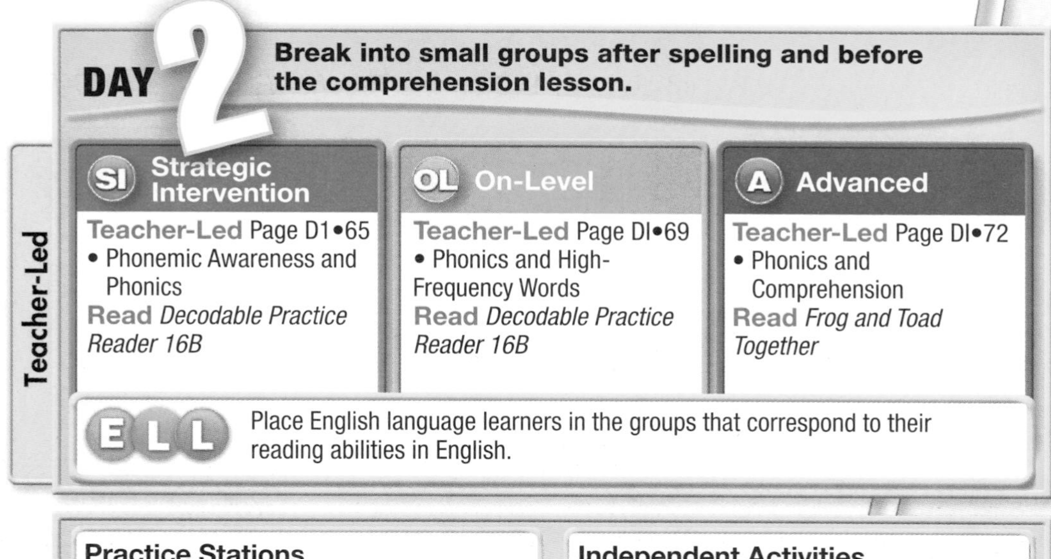
DAY 2 Break into small groups after spelling and before the comprehension lesson.

Teacher-Led

SI Strategic Intervention
Teacher-Led Page D1•65
• Phonemic Awareness and Phonics
Read *Decodable Practice Reader 16B*

OL On-Level
Teacher-Led Page DI•69
• Phonics and High-Frequency Words
Read *Decodable Practice Reader 16B*

A Advanced
Teacher-Led Page DI•72
• Phonics and Comprehension
Read *Frog and Toad Together*

ELL Place English language learners in the groups that correspond to their reading abilities in English.

Practice Stations
• Listen Up
• Word Work

Independent Activities
• Read independently/Reading Log on *Reader's and Writer's Notebook* p. RR4
• AudioText of Main Selection

Differentiated Instruction

Strategic Intervention

Doubling Final Consonants Remind children that when a word ends with consonant-vowel-consonant, the last consonant is usually doubled before adding *-ed.* Ask: Do we double the *p* in *helped?* (no) Why? (because *help* ends with two consonants, *lp*) Do we double the *p* in *dropped?* (yes) Why? (because *drop* ends with consonant-vowel-consonant)

English Language Learners

Pronouncing *-ed* Some children may not pronounce the final /t/ sound in *asked* or the final /d/ sound in *planned*, so the past tense may sound the same as the present. Say each word slowly, emphasizing the final /t/ or /d/ sound. Then have children repeat each word several times.

Objectives
- Learn story words: *ground, head, rain, shouted, shouting.*
- Review high-frequency words.
- Use a dictionary and glossary.

High-Frequency Words
Build Fluency

Read words in isolation Remind children that there are some words we learn by remembering the letters, rather than by saying the sounds. Then have them read each of the highlighted high-frequency words aloud.

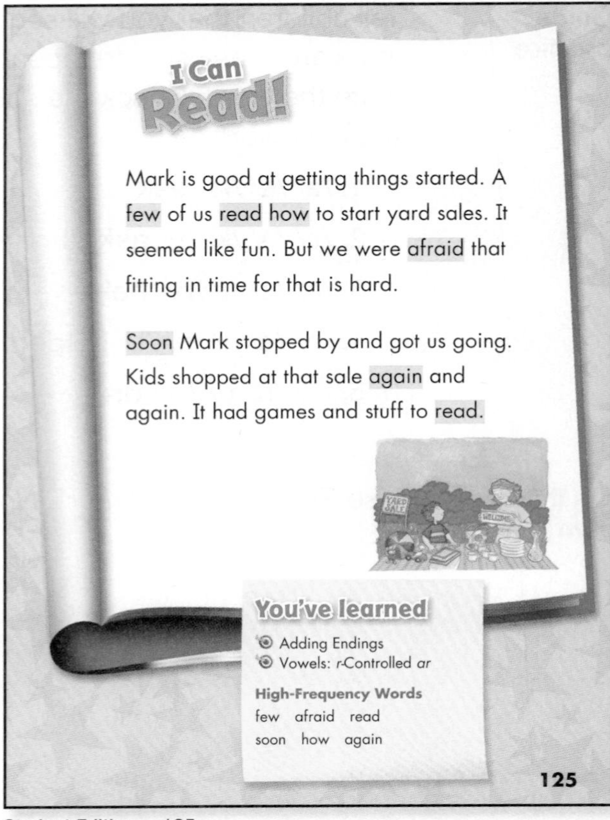

I Can Read!

Mark is good at getting things started. A few of us read how to start yard sales. It seemed like fun. But we were afraid that fitting in time for that is hard.

Soon Mark stopped by and got us going. Kids shopped at that sale again and again. It had games and stuff to read.

You've learned
- Adding Endings
- Vowels: *r*-Controlled *ar*

High-Frequency Words
few afraid read
soon how again

125

Student Edition p. 125

Read words in context Chorally read the "I Can Read!" passage along with the children. Then have them read the passage aloud to themselves. When they are finished, ask children to reread the high-frequency words.

Team Talk Have children choose two high-frequency words and give them time to create a sentence in which both words are used properly. Then have them share their sentence with a partner.

On their own Use Let's Practice It! p. 149 on the *Teacher Resource DVD-ROM.*

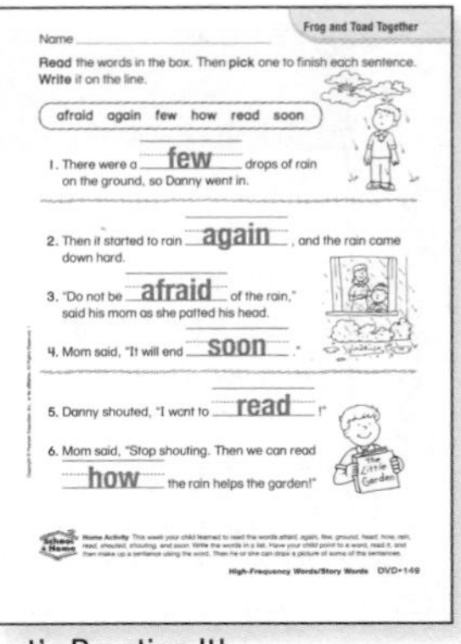

Frog and Toad Together

Name ____________

Read the words in the box. Then **pick** one to finish each sentence. **Write** it on the line.

afraid again few how read soon

1. There were a few drops of rain on the ground, so Danny went in.
2. Then it started to rain again, and the rain came down hard.
3. "Do not be afraid of the rain," said his mom as she patted his head.
4. Mom said, "It will end soon."
5. Danny shouted, "I want to read!"
6. Mom said, "Stop shouting. Then we can read how the rain helps the garden!"

High-Frequency Words/Story Words DVD•149

Let's Practice It!
TR DVD•149

Story Words
Frog and Toad Together

Introduce story words

Use Vocabulary Transparency 16 to introduce this week's story words. Read each sentence as you track the print. Frame each underlined word and explain its meaning.

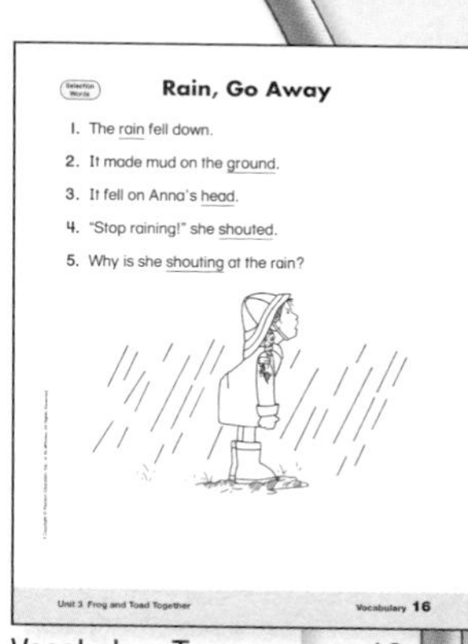

Rain, Go Away

1. The rain fell down.
2. It made mud on the ground.
3. It fell on Anna's head.
4. "Stop raining!" she shouted.
5. Why is she shouting at the rain?

Unit 3 Frog and Toad Together — Vocabulary 16

Vocabulary Transparency 16
TR DVD

- **rain** water that falls in drops from the clouds
- **ground** the soil or dirt on the surface of the earth
- **head** the top part of your body or the front part of most animals' bodies
- **shouted** called out or yelled loudly
- **shouting** calling or yelling

Have children read each sentence with you.

Vocabulary
Dictionary/Glossary

Model using a dictionary or glossary

Draw a T-chart or use Graphic Organizer 4. Label the columns as shown. Explain that a **dictionary** or **glossary** can help you find a word's meaning. Demonstrate using the glossary in the Student Edition.

Word	Meaning
ground	the soil or dirt on the surface of the earth

Graphic Organizer Flip Chart 4

Think Aloud I can find the word *ground* in our glossary because the words are listed in alphabetical order. *Ground* begins with *g*, so I go past the words that begin with *a, b, c, d, e,* and *f* until I come to the *g* words. When I find *ground*, I see its meaning beside it. Read the definition of *ground*. Then add the word and its meaning to the chart.

Guide practice

Write *rain, shouted,* and *head* on the board. In what order will we find these words in our glossary? (*head, rain, shouted*) Add the words in alphabetical order to the chart. Look up *head* and *rain* as a class, and add the definitions.

On their own

Have children work in groups to find the definition of *shouted*. Add the definition to the chart.

Differentiated Instruction

Strategic Intervention

Phonics Support If children have trouble reading the story words, help them identify familiar letter-sounds and word parts: *rain* (/r/r/, n/n/, *ground* (consonant blends *gr, nd*), *head* (/h/h/, d/d/), *shouted* and *shouting* (digraph *sh,* small word *out*, endings *-ed, -ing*). Then have them read the sentences again.

Academic Vocabulary

dictionary a book that explains the meanings of words

glossary a list of special words and their meanings, usually found at the back of a book

English Language Learners

Multilingual Vocabulary Lists Children can apply knowledge of their home language to acquire new English vocabulary by using the Multilingual Vocabulary Lists (*ELL Handbook* pp. 465–476).

DAY 2 Read and Comprehend

Objectives

- Build background on gardening.
- Visualize story events to monitor and adjust comprehension.
- Preview and predict.
- Determine whether a story is true or fantasy.
- Set a purpose for reading text.

Build Background

Background Building Audio

Have children listen to the CD. Tell them to listen to find out how to plant and take care of a garden.

Background Building Audio

Discuss gardening

Team Talk Have children turn to a partner and use these questions for discussion:

- What kinds of plants can grow in gardens?
- What do you do to start a garden?
- What do gardeners do to take care of their plants?

Organize information in a web

Draw a web or display Graphic Organizer 17. Have children recall what they learned from the CD about how to plant and take care of a garden. Record their responses.

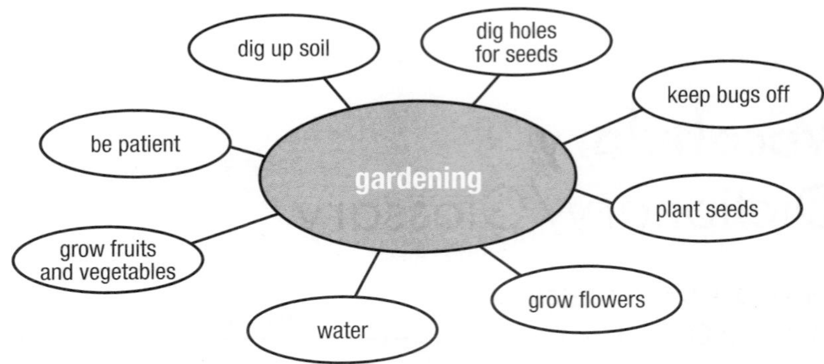

Graphic Organizer Flip Chart 17

Connect to selection

Sometimes people try different ways to grow plants in their garden. Toad is a character in the story we are about to read. His garden is not growing the way he thinks it should. We'll find out how Toad tries to help his seeds grow, and we'll see if anything ever comes up in his garden.

Student Edition, pp. 126–127

Main Selection—First Read

Frog and Toad Together

Practice the skill

Author's Purpose Remind children that knowing an author's purpose helps readers understand a story. Authors write some stories to entertain. These stories may be funny or exciting. Other stories are meant to inform. They contain facts about real things.

Introduce the strategy

Visualize Explain that good readers make pictures in their mind as they read. They picture the characters, the places, and the things that are happening in the story. Have the children turn to page EI•21 in their Student Edition.

Student Edition EI•21

Think Aloud Look at this picture. What is the boy doing as his mother reads to him? (He is making pictures in his mind about the story.) As I read *Frog and Toad Together*, I will try to picture the characters and what they are doing, as well as the setting. This will help me understand the story.

Introduce genre

Let's Read Together An animal fantasy is a made-up story with animal characters that do things real animals can't do. As they read *Frog and Toad Together*, ask children to look for things Frog and Toad do that real frogs and toads cannot.

Preview and predict

Have children identify the title of the story and the author. Read aloud the name of the author, and have children describe his two roles. Help children activate prior knowledge by asking them to look through the story and use the illustrations to predict events in the story.

Set a purpose

Good readers read for a purpose. Setting a purpose helps us to think and understand more as we read. Guide children to set a purpose for reading the story.

Tell children that today they will read *Frog and Toad Together* for the first time. Use the Day 2 Guide Comprehension notes to help children develop their comprehension of the selection.

First Read

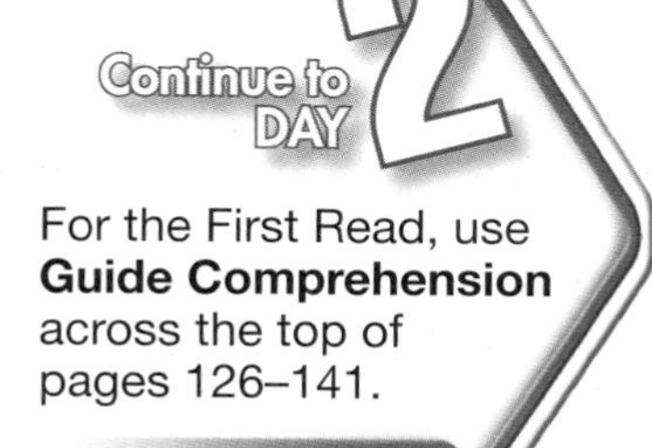

For the First Read, use **Guide Comprehension** across the top of pages 126–141.

INTERACT with TEXT

Strategy Response Log

Background Knowledge Before reading, have children use p. RR28 of their *Reader's and Writer's Notebook* to draw a picture of a seed and a flower. Then have children write a sentence telling one thing a gardener can do to help the seed become a flower.

Academic Vocabulary

author's purpose the reason the author wrote the text

visualize to picture in one's mind what is happening in the text

English Language Learners

Build Background Before children listen to the CD, build background and elicit prior knowledge. On the CD, you will hear about what a boy does to plant and take care of his garden. What do you think he does?

Frontload Main Selection Ask children what they already know about gardening using the picture on p. 128. Then do a picture walk of the selection so children can talk about what Toad does to try to get his garden to grow.

Objectives

- ◎ Make inferences about the author's purpose.
- ◎ Monitor and adjust comprehension by visualizing.
- Determine word meaning and use newly acquired vocabulary.
- Discuss ideas related to but not expressed in the literature.

DAY 2

Guide Comprehension

Skills and Strategies

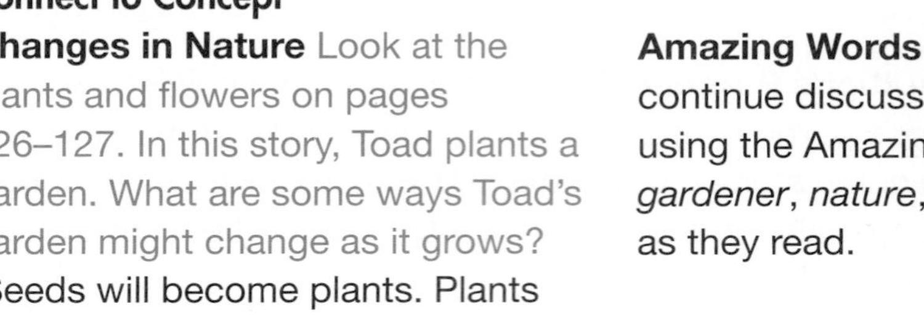

Connect to Concept

Changes in Nature Look at the plants and flowers on pages 126–127. In this story, Toad plants a garden. What are some ways Toad's garden might change as it grows? (Seeds will become plants. Plants will grow leaves and flowers.)

Amazing Words Have children continue discussing the concept using the Amazing Words *dim*, *gardener*, *nature*, *shade*, and *sprout* as they read.

Frog and Toad Together

by Arnold Lobel

The Garden

In an **animal fantasy,** animals say and do things that people might say and do. Next you will read about two friends, Frog and Toad, who act a lot like people.

Question of the Week

What changes happen in a garden?

126 127

Student Edition pp. 126–127

DAY 3

Extend Thinking

Think Critically

Connect to Science

Plant Needs All living things need certain things to survive. Help children identify the things plants need: water, light, air, food from soil, and space to grow.

Skills

Author's Purpose Do you think the author wrote this story to inform or to entertain? Why? (I think he wrote it to entertain because the pictures are funny and Frog and Toad talk like people.)

Vocabulary

Story Words Have children locate the story word *ground* on page 129. Frog says the seeds should be planted in the *ground*. What is the *ground*? (The ground is the earth.)

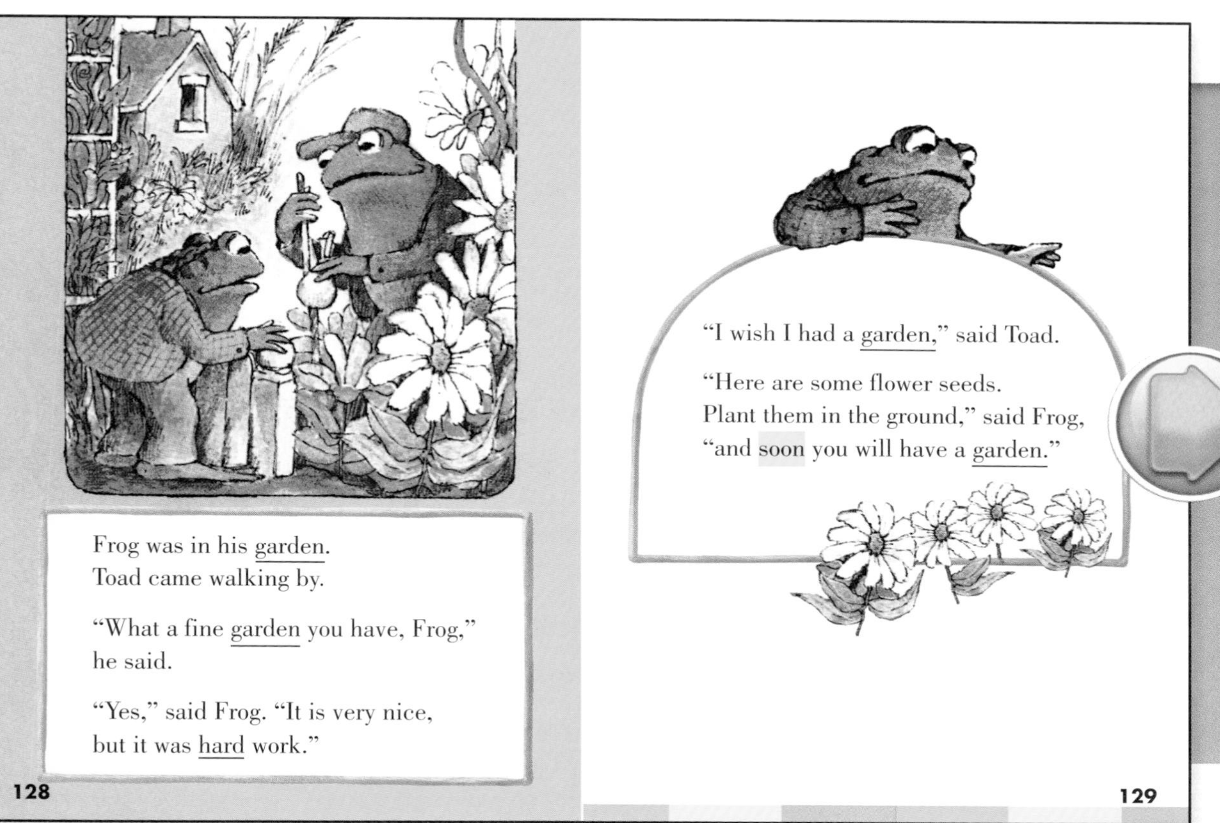
Frog was in his garden.
Toad came walking by.

"What a fine garden you have, Frog," he said.

"Yes," said Frog. "It is very nice, but it was hard work."

128

"I wish I had a garden," said Toad.

"Here are some flower seeds.
Plant them in the ground," said Frog,
"and soon you will have a garden."

129

Student Edition pp. 128–129

Higher-Order Thinking Skills

Analysis What details in the story and pictures tell you that Frog is a very good gardener? (The picture shows lots of flowers in Frog's garden. Frog tells Toad that he has worked hard on his garden.)

Higher-Order Thinking Skills

Synthesis Frog says gardening is hard work. What are some jobs that gardeners do? (Gardeners plant seeds, water them, pull weeds, and put up fences to keep animals out.)

Skills and Strategies, continued

Strategies

Visualize As we read, we make pictures in our mind about the story. Close your eyes and try to see Toad planting the seeds. Describe what you see him doing. (I see Toad digging holes in the ground, putting in seeds, and covering them up with soil.)

Vocabulary

High-Frequency Words Point out the words *how*, *soon*, and *few*. Have children practice reading these words.

"How soon?" asked Toad.

"Quite soon," said Frog.

Toad ran home.
He planted the flower seeds.

"Now seeds," said Toad, "start growing."

Toad walked up and down a few times. The seeds did not start to grow.

130

Toad put his head close to the ground and said loudly,

"Now seeds, start growing!"

131

Student Edition pp. 130–131

Thinking Critically, continued

Higher-Order Thinking Skills

Synthesis Toad is worried because his seeds don't start growing right away. Do you think there is something wrong with his seeds? Why or why not? (No. Seeds just need time to sprout.)

If... children don't know if there is something wrong with the seeds because they don't grow right away,
then... sing the song "Sprout! It's a Garden." Ask them to explain what it means when the song says, "It takes time to see the plants."

Vocabulary

Story Words Have children locate the story word *shouted* on page 132. What is the difference between talking and shouting? (When you shout, your voice is very loud.)

Word Reading

Decoding Have children check their reading of new words using these questions:

- Did I blend the sounds to read the words?
- Did I put the new words in the sentence to make sure it made sense?
- Did I look for word parts to help me understand the word?

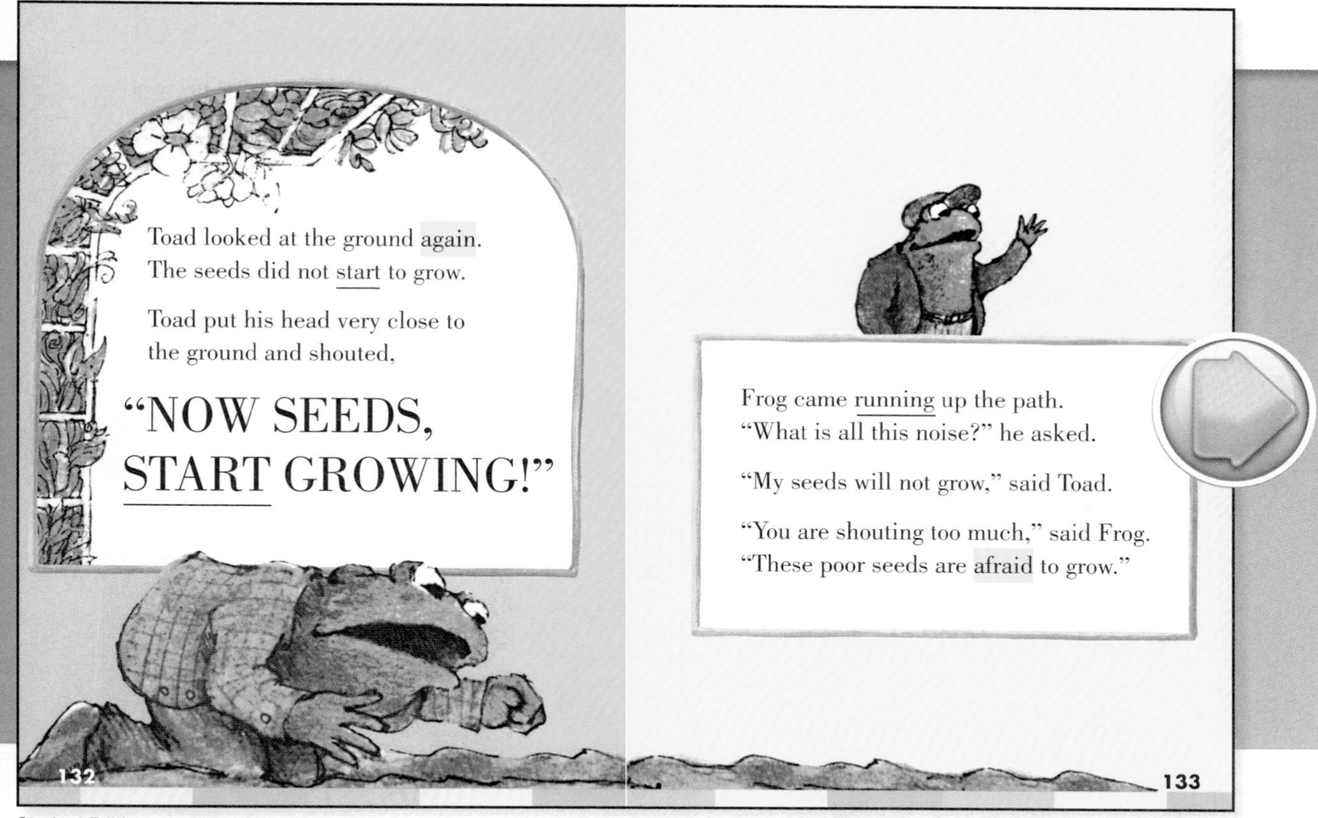

Student Edition pp. 132–133

Higher-Order Thinking Skills

Analysis What is funny about the things Toad and Frog do and say on pages 132–133? (Toad and Frog think seeds are like people or animals that can hear shouting and feel afraid.)

If... children don't know what is funny about the things Frog and Toad say and do,
then... ask children, "Can seeds hear, the way people and animals can? Do you think seeds have feelings, like being afraid?"

Skills and Strategies, continued

DAY 2

Vocabulary

Dictionary/Glossary A dictionary or glossary tells what words mean. The words are in alphabetical order. Look at *rain* on page 134. What letter would I look for in a dictionary or glossary to find this word? (*r*) Demonstrate for children.

If... children don't know what letter to look for to find *rain*,
then... remind children that alphabetical order means that words beginning with *a* come first, *b* words come next, and so on. Ask what letter *rain* begins with.

"My seeds are afraid to grow?" asked Toad.

"Of course," said Frog.
"Leave them alone for a few days.
Let the sun shine on them,
let the rain fall on them.
Soon your seeds will start to grow."

134

That night Toad looked out of his window.

"Drat!" said Toad. "My seeds have not started to grow. They must be afraid of the dark." Toad went out to his garden with some candles.

135

Student Edition pp. 134–135

Think Critically, continued

DAY 3

Higher-Order Thinking Skills

Evaluation On page 134, which things that Frog says are smart, and which are not very smart? (It's smart when Frog says that the seeds need sun, rain, and time to grow. It's not smart when he says the seeds are afraid to grow.)

If... children don't know which things that Frog says are smart and not smart,
then... ask children what they have learned about the things plants need in order to grow. Then go through the page line by line with children to see which things Frogs says are true.

Word Reading

High-Frequency Words Point out the words *read* and *afraid*. Have children practice reading these words.

Strategies

Visualize As we read, we see pictures in our mind. We also hear sounds. Close your eyes and try to see and hear Toad singing to his seeds. Is his voice sweet or croaky? Loud or soft? What kind of song is he singing? (Toad is singing a happy song in a loud, croaky voice.)

Student Edition pp. 136–137

Review Plot

Evaluation We know that the plot of a story includes a problem that the main character tries to solve. What is Toad's problem? (His seeds won't grow.) Do you think he found a smart way to solve this problem? (No. Seeds don't get scared like people and animals. Stories, songs, and poems will not help them grow.)

If... children are not able to identify Toad's problem, **then...** ask children why Toad was worried after he planted his seeds.

Skills and Strategies, continued

DAY 2

Skills

Author's Purpose Earlier, you guessed whether the author's purpose was to inform or entertain. Were you right? Why? (I was right that it was to entertain, because Toad did silly things like shouting at his seeds and reading to them.)

Strategies

Visualize What do you think Toad saw when he looked at his garden? Close your eyes and make a picture in your mind. Describe what you see. (I see little green plants growing.)

Toad looked at the ground.
The seeds still did not start to grow.

"What shall I do?" cried Toad.
"These must be the most frightened seeds in the whole world!"

138

Then Toad felt very tired, and he fell asleep.

"Toad, Toad, wake up," said Frog. "Look at your garden!"

Toad looked at his garden.

139

Student Edition pp.138–139

Thinking Critically, continued

DAY 3

Higher-Order Thinking Skills

Synthesis Why do you think Toad's seeds finally started to grow? (The seeds had sunshine, rain, and enough time to grow.)

If... children don't know why Toad's seeds finally grew,
then... have children look back at the pictures of the sun and rain on pages 134 and 136. Have them reread the bottom half of page 134.

Strategy Self-Check

Visualize Now that we've finished the story, how can we use the pictures that we made in our minds to help us remember the story? (We can close our eyes and see the pictures again to remember what Frog and Toad did and said.)

If... children have trouble visualizing events in the story,
then... ask children to read through a page, then close their eyes and think about what the scene looked like, smelled like, and what they could hear.

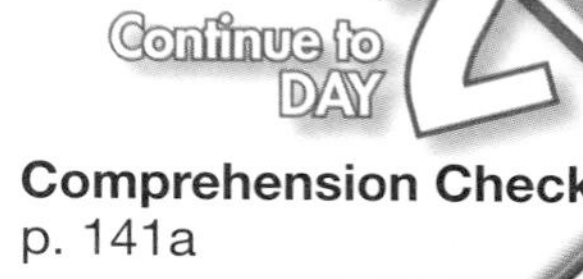
Continue to DAY 2
Comprehension Check
p. 141a

Little green plants were coming up out of the ground.

"At last," shouted Toad, "my seeds have stopped being afraid to grow!"

140

"And now you will have a nice garden too," said Frog.

"Yes," said Toad, "but you were right, Frog. It was very hard work."

141

Student Edition pp. 140–141

Higher-Order Thinking Skills

Analysis Do you think Toad understands what really made his seeds grow? What details on pages 140–141 make you think so? (No, Toad doesn't understand what really made his seeds grow. He says they stopped being afraid and that "It was very hard work.")

If... children don't know if Toad understands why his seeds finally grew,
then... ask children what Toad means by "hard work" on page 141. Ask them if they think this hard work really helped the seeds grow.

Continue to DAY 3
Think Critically
pp. 142–143

DAY 2 Read and Comprehend

Objectives

- Compare and contrast two animal fantasies.
- Use verbs for past and for future.

Comprehension Check

Have children discuss each question with a partner. Ask several pairs to share their responses.

☑ **Animal fantasy** What do Frog and Toad do that a real frog and toad cannot do? (Possible response: Frog and Toad wear clothes, talk, walk, and plant gardens. A real frog and toad could not do these things.)

☑ **Confirm predictions** Which of your predictions about the story were right? How did you know this would happen? (Possible response: I predicted that Toad would play music in his garden because a picture showed him doing that.)

☑ **Connect text to world** Toad was impatient for his seeds to grow, but Frog knew that seeds take time to become plants. What other changes in nature happen slowly? (Possible responses: The weather slowly changes with the seasons.)

Genre
Animal Fantasy

Compare and contrast two animal fantasies Remind children that an animal fantasy is a story in which the characters are animals who do things that real animals don't do. We know that *Frog and Toad Together* is an animal fantasy. Another animal fantasy we have read is *Ruby in Her Own Time*. Tell children that today they will compare and contrast these two stories to see how they are alike and different.

Guide practice Display Graphic Organizer 5. Add the headings shown below. Fill in the chart as children answer the questions.

- How are the characters in both stories alike? How are they different?
- In which story are the setting and actions more true to life? Why?

On their own Have partners think of other ways the two stories are alike and different. Add their ideas to the chart.

Frog and Toad Together	BOTH	Ruby in Her Own Time
Characters are a frog and toad. Setting and actions less real—garden, reading, singing.	Characters are animals that talk.	Characters are ducks. Setting and actions more real—pond, swimming, flying.

Conventions
Verbs for Past and for Future

Model verbs for past and for future Write *He turned* and *He will turn* on the board. Point to each word as you read it. Recall that *turn* is a verb because it shows action. Which sentence tells about what already happened—the past? (*He turned.*) Which tells about what is going to happen—the future? (*He will turn.*) Some verbs use the ending *-ed* to tell about the past. Other verbs use the helping verb *will* to tell about the future.

Guide practice Write the following sentences on the board. Have children read each sentence and say whether it tells about the past or the future. Ask them to explain how they know.

1. Tim petted his cat.
2. She will kick the ball.
3. Dad honked his horn.
4. We will call Beth.

Connect to oral language Have the class complete these sentence frames orally using the correct form of the verb *plant.*

1. Yesterday he ________ flowers.
2. Tomorrow I ________ carrots.
3. Last year we ________ a tree.
4. Next spring we ________ some grass.

On their own Use *Reader's and Writer's Notebook* p. 367.

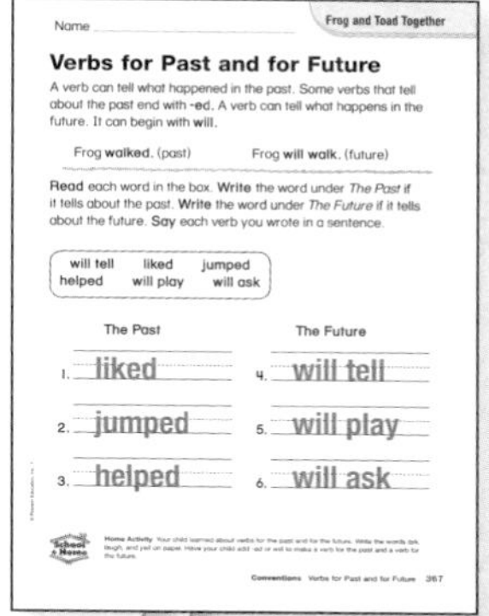
Name ________ Frog and Toad Together

Verbs for Past and for Future

A verb can tell what happened in the past. Some verbs that tell about the past end with **-ed.** A verb can tell what happens in the future. It can begin with **will.**

Frog **walked.** (past) Frog **will walk.** (future)

Read each word in the box. **Write** the word under *The Past* if it tells about the past. **Write** the word under *The Future* if it tells about the future. **Say** each verb you wrote in a sentence.

will tell liked jumped helped will play will ask

The Past	The Future
1. liked	4. will tell
2. jumped	5. will play
3. helped	6. will ask

Conventions Verbs for Past and for Future 367

Reader's and Writer's Notebook, p. 367

Daily Fix-It

3. I plantted seeds last spring
I planted seeds last spring.

4. next year I will do it agan.
Next year I will do it again.

Discuss the Daily Fix-It corrections with children. Review sentence capitalization and punctuation, doubling of final consonants before adding an ending, and the spelling of *again.*

English Language Learners

Future Tense Spanish, Haitian Creole, and Hmong speakers may use the present tense where English calls for the future tense. Give children extra practice completing sentence frames beginning with time clues indicating the future such as *Tomorrow, Later today,* and *Next week.*

Objectives
- Generate list ideas.
- Recognize features of a list.
- Use sentences in a list.

Writing—Lists
Writing Trait: Sentences

Introduce the prompt

Review with children the key features of a list. Point out that *Frog and Toad Together* tells several things that Toad does to make his garden grow. Explain that today children will plan their lists of things that Toad does. They will list things that worked and things that did not work. Read aloud the writing prompt.

Writing Prompt

Think of actions Toad tried to help his garden grow. Write a list telling what Toad did that really helped the garden grow. In another list, tell his actions that did not help.

Sharing the Writing

Today we will plan our lists of sentences. First, we have to think about what we will tell in our sentences. We can start by writing all the things Toad did.

Help children generate list ideas

Guide children in identifying all of the things that Toad does in the story. Record the responses, and keep the chart so that children can refer to it as they plan and draft their stories.

planted	sang
yelled	read poems
took candles	played music
read a story	left them alone

Have each child review the list and choose two things that worked and two things that didn't. Circulate to guide them.

MINI-LESSON

Sentences

INTERACT with TEXT

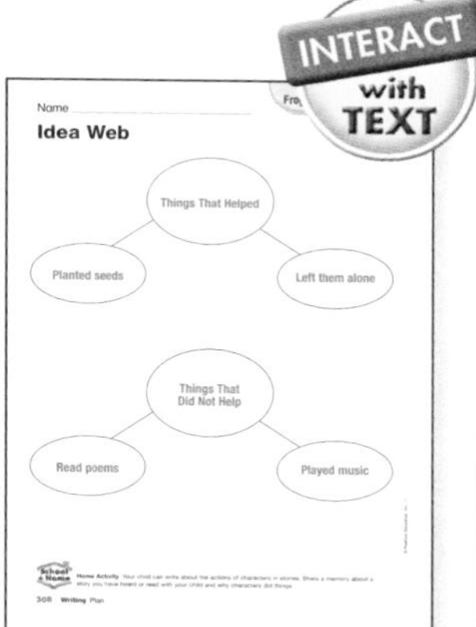

Reader's and Writer's Notebook p. 368

- **Introduce** Use *Reader's and Writer's Notebook* p. 368 to model planning a list of sentences. To plan a list, I can use an idea web. I know I need two lists. I will write what I want to list in the first web—*Things That Helped.* Now I can write two things in the outside circles that helped Toad's garden grow.

- **Model** To finish the first plan for a list, I will look at the ideas we wrote down about Toad. I will think about all the things he did. The seeds would not grow if he didn't plant them. So the first thing I will include in the list is *Planted seeds.* I look at the other things he did. When he fell asleep and left them alone, they grew. I will write *Left them alone* in the second circle. I will use these notes to help me write complete sentences about Toad. Each note tells an action, so I will just need to tell who took the action in my sentences. Now I will fill out the second web to help me plan my list of things that didn't work. You can use your webs to make your plans now. Circulate to guide and assist children.

Write Guy
Jeff Anderson

Two words: subject, verb!

Let's help children gain confidence in composing sentences. Guide partners as they make up fun two-word sentences: *Rex howled! Kathy giggled. Lions growl.* Then let the children continue creating sentences, checking to make sure each includes a subject and a verb. Another activity is to challenge children to find favorite sentences in books and then to whittle them to the simple subject and the verb. This paves the way for grammar to support children's writing.

Differentiated Instruction

SI Strategic Intervention

Planning Lists If children find it difficult to complete their charts, help them copy the actions from the class list.

ROUTINE

Quick Write for Fluency

Team Talk

1. **Talk** Have children take two minutes to tell what they will list to their partners.

2. **Write** Each child briefly writes a sentence about one of the items.

3. **Share** Each child reads the sentence to the partner.

Routines Flip Chart

Objectives

- Write with evenly spaced letters.
- Understand the purpose and features of a diagram.
- Use a diagram to find facts.
- Create a diagram as part of an inquiry project.

Handwriting
Letter *C* and *c*/Letter Spacing

Model letter formation Display upper- and lower-case letters: *Cc.* Use the stroke instructions pictured below to model proper letter formation.

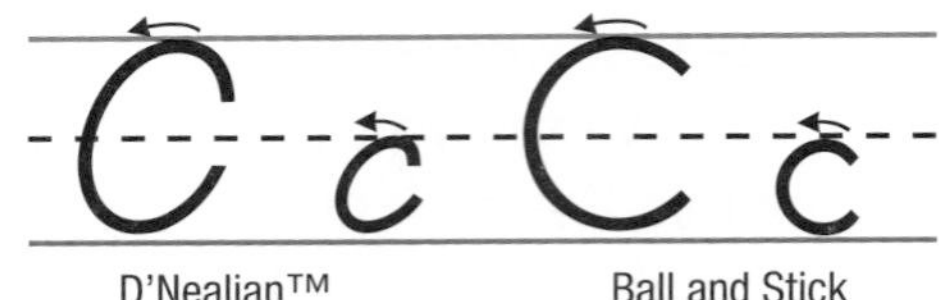

Model letter spacing Explain that when we write a word, all the letters in that word should be evenly spaced. Write the word *card* using correct spacing. When I write the letters in a word, I need to pay attention to the spaces between the letters. Write the word *card* again with the letters too close to each other. The letters should not be so close together that they touch each other. Write *card* a third time with the letters too far from each other. They should not be so far apart that it's hard to tell they spell out a word. By correctly spacing letters in words, I make it easier for others to understand what I write. Ask children which of the three writing examples is easiest to read and have them explain why.

Guide practice Write the following sentence, spacing the letters in some words too tightly and in other words too loosely.

Can a cat chase mice?

Team Talk Have children work in pairs to discuss what is wrong with the sentence and how it needs to be fixed. Have them share with the class.

On their own Use the *Reader's and Writer's Notebook* p. 369.

Name
Frog and Toad Together
C c
Copy the words. Leave the correct space between your letters.

Carl	Carl	Cal	Cal
car	car	cape	cape
barn	barn	harm	harm
start	start	jar	jar
chart	chart	star	star
part	part	bark	bark
card	card	dark	dark

Did you leave the correct space between your letters? Yes No

Reader's and Writer's Notebook, p. 369

Research and Inquiry
Research Skill: Diagram

Teach Display the diagram of a tree on Research Transparency 16. Explain that a **diagram** is a picture of something that has labels naming its different parts. Tell children that when they do research, a diagram can sometimes provide useful facts. Children can also make their own diagram to record what they learn.

Model Think Aloud Yesterday I decided to do research to answer the question, "What are the different parts of a plant?" This diagram shows me the different parts of a tree and shows the names of each part. Point out each label and the arrow that shows which part it names.

Guide practice Have children use the diagram to answer the questions below it. Then have them sketch and label a diagram in the *What I Learned* column of the note-taking chart they began yesterday.

Academic Vocabulary

diagram a picture that has labels naming the different parts of something and that often shows how the parts work

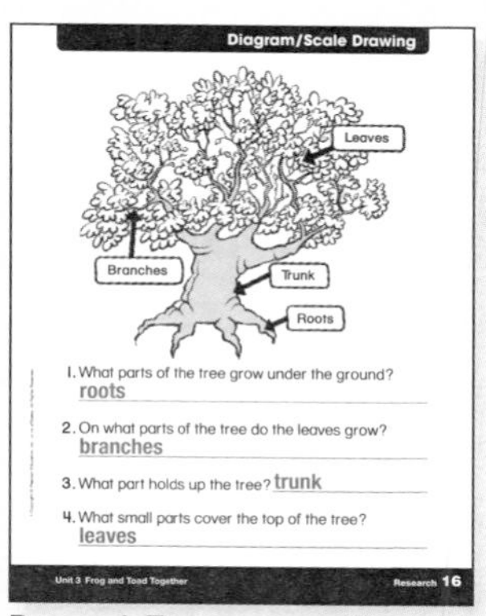
Diagram/Scale Drawing

1. What parts of the tree grow under the ground? roots
2. On what parts of the tree do the leaves grow? branches
3. What part holds up the tree? trunk
4. What small parts cover the top of the tree? leaves

Unit 3 Frog and Toad Together Research 16

Research Transparency 16
TR DVD

Wrap Up Your Day

- **Vowel: *r*-Controlled *ar*** Say *far*. How is the /är/ sound in *far* spelled? (ar) Write *far, part, start, hard,* and *march*. Have children read the words aloud.
- **High-Frequency Words** Point to these words on the Word Wall: *few, afraid, read, soon, how,* and *again*. Have children read each word and use it in a sentence.
- **Build Concepts** Monitor children's use of oral vocabulary as they respond. Recall "Carlee's Garden" and *Frog and Toad Together.* Ask: Do good gardeners expect their plants to sprout right away? (No, good gardeners know that plants take time to sprout.) We know that plants need lots of sunshine to grow. In what season does the sun set early? In what season does the sun set later in the day? (It sets early in winter and late in summer.)

Tell children that tomorrow they will reread *Frog and Toad Together.*

Objectives

- Build oral vocabulary.
- Identify details in text.
- Share information and ideas about the concept.

Today at a Glance

Oral Vocabulary
sprinkling

Phonemic Awareness
Add Phonemes

Phonics and Spelling
◎ Adding Endings
◎ Vowel: *r*-Controlled *ar*

High-Frequency Words
afraid, again, few, how, read, soon

Story Words
ground, head, rain, shouted, shouting

Comprehension
Review Plot

Fluency
Expression and Intonation

Conventions
Verbs for Past and for Future

Writing
Lists
Writer's Craft: Tell Characters' Actions

Listening and Speaking
Poetry Presentation

Research and Inquiry
Gather and Record Information

Concept Talk

Question of the Week

What changes happen in a garden?

Build concepts To reinforce concepts and to focus children's attention, have children sing "Sprout! It's a Garden" from the *Sing with Me* Big Book. What different kinds of weather help gardens grow? (Sunny days and rainy days help gardens grow.)

Sing with Me Big Book Audio

Monitor listening comprehension Display the Big Book *What Makes the Seasons?* As children listen to the story, have them think about what season is the best time of year to plant a garden and why. Then read the book aloud.

Big Book

- What season is the best time of year to plant a garden? Why? (spring, because the ground is warm and the rain helps the plants sprout and grow)
- If we plant flowers in the spring, when will the blossoms appear? (The blossoms will appear in the summer.)
- Do flowers grow quickly or slowly? How can you tell? (slowly, because you have to wait from spring until summer)

ELL Expand Vocabulary Use the Day 3 instruction on ELL Poster 16 to help children expand vocabulary.

ELL Poster 16

Oral Vocabulary
Amazing Words

Amazing Words Oral Vocabulary Routine

Teach Amazing Words

1. **Introduce the Word** Relate the word *sprinkling* to the book. The *sprinkling* rain wakes the girl in the story. Supply a child-friendly definition. A *sprinkling* is a small amount of something, scattered around. Have children say the word.
2. **Demonstrate** Provide examples to show meaning. I like a *sprinkling* of cheese on top of my pasta. My mom put a *sprinkling* of sugar in her iced tea.
3. **Apply** Have children demonstrate their understanding. What does a *sprinkling* of rain feel like?

Routines Flip Chart

Anchored Talk

Add to the concept map

Use these questions to discuss how gardeners and nature make changes happen in a garden as you add to the concept map.

- In *Frog and Toad Together,* what does Toad notice when he wakes up? (His seeds have sprouted.) Let's add *Seeds grow into plants* to our concept map.
- Show children the picture on page 128 of the Student Edition. What might Toad's seeds grow into? (flowers) Let's add *Plants can grow flowers* to our map, too.

Amazing Words

gardener	shade
nature	sprinkling
sprout	destroy
dim	humongous

English Language Learners

Vocabulary Have children practice using the word *sprinkling* by completing these sentence frames: *I like a sprinkling of salt on my _____. I like a sprinkling of sugar on my _____.*

Objectives

- Add a final sound to create a new word.
- Build words with /är/ spelled *ar*.
- ◎ Read words with a doubled consonant before *-ed* or *-ing* and words with /är/ spelled *ar*.

Phonemic Awareness
Add Phonemes

Model adding phonemes

Have children turn to the picture on pp. 120–121 in their Student Edition. Today we are going to add sounds to words to make new words. Look at the picture and find a car. Listen as I say the sounds in *car*: /k/ /är/ . If I add the sound /t/ to the end of *car*, I make a new word: car /t/, *cart*.

Student Edition pp. 120–121

Guide practice

Help children add the sound shown below to the end of each word to make a new word. Then have them point to the matching picture in their Student Edition.

far /m/ (farm) **bar /n/** (barn) **are /m/** (arm)

On their own

Have children add the final sounds shown below to these words to make new words.

ten /t/ (tent)	**star /t/** (start)	**for /k/** (fork)
shore /t/ (short)	**car /d/** (card)	**bar /k/** (bark)

Team Talk Have partners think of sounds they could add to the end of *see* to make new words (*seat, seed, seek, seal*). Ask children to share their words.

Phonics

Build Words

Model word building Now we are going to build words with /är/ spelled *ar*. Write *art* and blend it. Watch me add /k/ to the beginning of *art*. Model blending the new word, *cart*.

Guide practice Have children spell *cart* with letter tiles. Monitor children's work as they build words.

- Change the /k/ in *cart* to /p/. Say the new word together.

- Change the /t/ in *part* to /k/. Say the new word together.

- Add /s/ the beginning of *park*. Say the new word together.

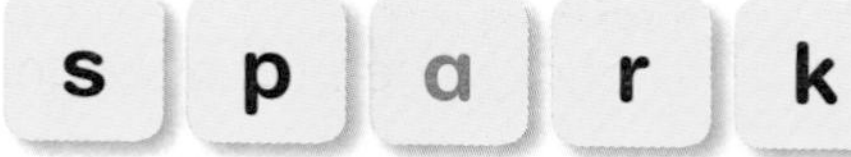

- Change /s//p/ to /sh/. Say the new word together.

Corrective feedback For corrective feedback, model the correct spelling and have children correct their tiles.

Fluent Word Reading

Model Write *dark*. I know the sounds for *d, ar,* and *k*. I blend them and read the word *dark*. Write *clapping*. I know how to read words with base words and endings. The base word is *clap* and the ending is *-ing*. I blend them and read the word *clapping*. Point out that the *p* in *clap* was doubled before the ending was added.

Guide practice Write the words below. Say the sounds in your head for each spelling you see. Look for word parts you know. When I point to the word, we'll read it together. Allow one second per sound-previewing time for the first reading.

fibbing mark fanned farm start plugged snapping

On their own Have children read the list above three or four times, until they can read one word per second.

Differentiated Instruction

 Advanced

Build *ar* Words If children are able to build the words in the class activity easily and independently, have them use letter tiles to build these more difficult words with *ar: charm, charge, large, barge, marble.*

Professional Development

Phonemic Awareness and Phonics Some children may have difficulty with phonics instruction because they haven't developed the necessary phonemic awareness skills that other children have gained through years of exposure to rhymes, songs, and storybooks. However, studies have shown that phonemic awareness can be taught and that such teaching has important effects on children's ability to master reading skills.

English Language Learners

Pronounce Final Phonemes In Spanish, words often end in vowels, and they cannot end in consonant blends. As a result, Spanish speakers may delete or substitute consonant sounds when pronouncing English words with final consonant blends (*car* for *card; pan* for *pant*). Point out these differences in English and Spanish and have children practice pronouncing the words in this lesson with final consonant blends such as *start.*

DAY 3 Get Ready to Read

Objectives

- ◎ Correctly pronounce CVC words with double-consonant endings, and associate the sound /är/ with the spelling *ar.*
- Blend and read CVC words with double-consonant endings and words with /är/ spelled *ar.*
- Decode words in context and isolation.
- Spell words with *-ed*.

Blend and Read

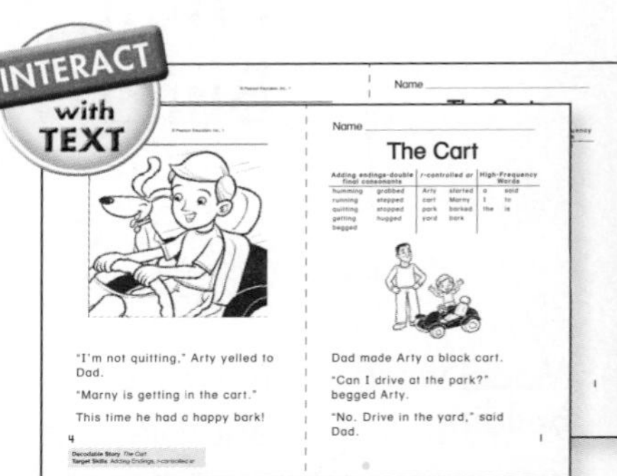

Reader's and Writer's Notebook, pp. 371–372

Decode words in isolation

Have children turn to pages 371–372 in the *Reader's and Writer's Notebook* and find the first two lists of words. Each word in these lists has either a double consonant ending or the sound /är/ spelled *ar*. Let's blend and read these words. Be sure that children identify the correct sounds in words that have a double consonant ending or the sound /är/ spelled *ar.*

Next, have children read the high-frequency words.

Decode words in context

Chorally read the story along with the children. Have children identify words in the story that have a double consonant ending or the sound /är/ spelled *ar.*

Team Talk Pair children and have them take turns reading the story aloud to each other. Monitor children as they read to check for proper pronunciation and appropriate pacing.

On their own

To further develop automaticity, have children take the story home to reread.

Spelling
Words with *-ed*

Spell high-frequency words Write *again* and *soon* and point them out on the Word Wall. Have children say and spell the words with you and then without you.

Dictation Have children write these sentences. Say each sentence. Then repeat it slowly, one word at a time.

1. **Jenny dropped the ball again.**
2. **Mom asked Clark to be home soon.**
3. **Sam called us to plan a trip to the farm.**

Proofread and correct Write each sentence, spelling words one at a time. Have children circle and rewrite any misspelled words.

On their own Use *Reader's and Writer's Notebook* p. 373.

Reader's and Writer's Notebook, p. 373

Spelling Words

Words with *-ed*

1. ask	6. helped
2. asked	7. drop
3. plan	8. dropped
4. planned	9. call
5. help	10. called

High-Frequency Words

11. again **12. soon**

Small Group Time

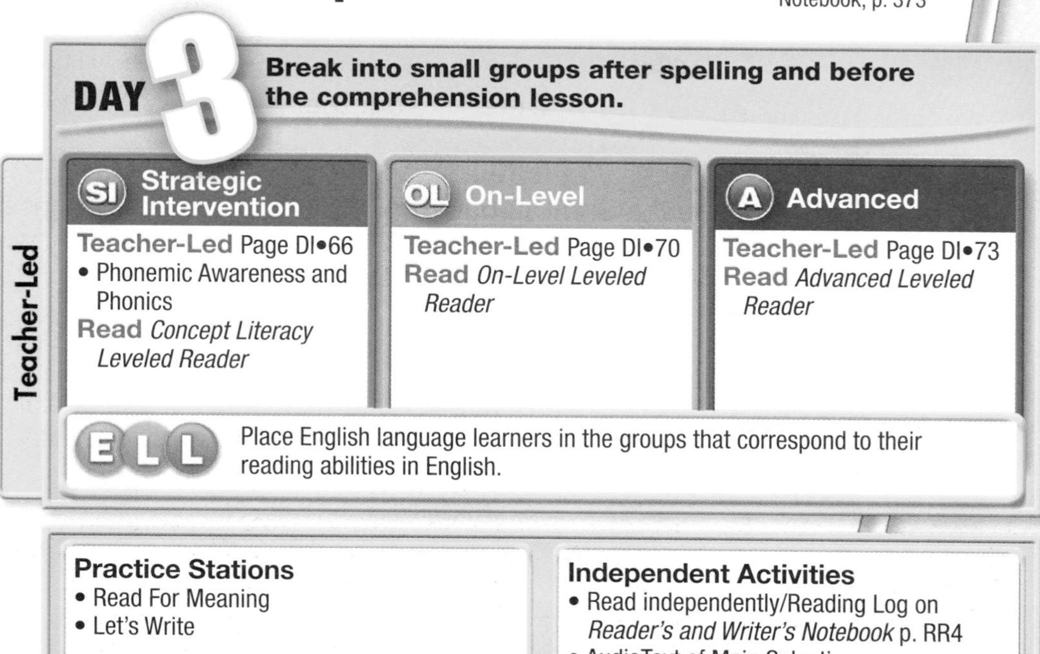

DAY 3 Break into small groups after spelling and before the comprehension lesson.

Teacher-Led

SI Strategic Intervention	OL On-Level	A Advanced
Teacher-Led Page DI•66 • Phonemic Awareness and Phonics Read *Concept Literacy Leveled Reader*	Teacher-Led Page DI•70 Read *On-Level Leveled Reader*	Teacher-Led Page DI•73 Read *Advanced Leveled Reader*

ELL Place English language learners in the groups that correspond to their reading abilities in English.

Practice Stations
- Read For Meaning
- Let's Write

Independent Activities
- Read independently/Reading Log on *Reader's and Writer's Notebook* p. RR4
- AudioText of Main Selection

English Language Learners

Spelling Dictation Children will benefit from hearing each dictated sentence read three times. First, have children listen to understand the sentence. The second time, they should write what they hear. The third time, they can check their work.

Objectives

- Read high-frequency words.
- Establish purpose for reading text.
- Review key features of animal fantasy.

Check High-Frequency Words
SUCCESS PREDICTOR

High-Frequency and Story Words

Read words in isolation

Display and review this week's high-frequency words and story words. Have children read the words aloud.

Read words in context

Display the following sentence frames. Have children complete the sentences using high-frequency and story words. Have children read each completed sentence with you.

1. ***Soon* the _____ will start falling. (rain)**
2. ***How* can I sleep with so much _____ going on? (shouting)**
3. **"He got the ball *again*!" we ____. (shouted)**
4. **I _____ that story a *few* times. (read)**
5. **Don't be *afraid* to pet my cat on his _____. (head)**
6. **The mice dug holes in the _____. (ground)**

Don't Wait Until Friday **MONITOR PROGRESS**

Check High-Frequency Words

Point to these words on the Word Wall and have the class read them. Listen for children who miss words during the reading. Call on those children to read some of the words individually.

again	soon	afraid	how	**Spiral Review** Row 3 reviews previously taught high-frequency words. ←
few	read			
work	very	were	together	

If... children cannot read these words,
then... use the Small Group Time Strategic Intervention lesson, p. DI•67, to reteach the words. Monitor children's fluency with these words during reading and provide additional practice.

Day 1	Day 2	Day 3	Day 4	Day 5
Check Word Reading	Check Word Reading	Check High-Frequency Words/ Retelling	Check Fluency	Check Oral Vocabulary

Success Predictor

Main Selection— Second Read

Frog and Toad Together

Review Plot

Recall this week's main selection, *Frog and Toad Together*. Tell children that today they will read the story again. Remind children that the **plot** of a story is all the events that happen at the beginning, middle, and end, and that most plots are about a problem a character or characters must solve. Understanding the plot makes the story interesting. What is Toad's problem in this story? (His seeds won't grow.) How does he try to solve it? (He shouts at the seeds, then reads, plays music, and sings to them.)

Review Genre: animal fantasy

Let's Read Together Remind children that an animal fantasy is a made-up story with animals that do things real animals can't do. Have children recall things that Frog and Toad do that real frogs and toads can't do. (They talk, wear clothes, plant gardens, and read.)

Set a purpose

Remind children that good readers read for a purpose. Guide children to set a new purpose for reading *Frog and Toad Together* today, perhaps to notice how Frog and Toad are alike and how they are different.

Extend thinking

Tell children they will now read *Frog and Toad Together* for the second time. Use the Day 3 Extend Thinking notes to encourage children to use higher order thinking skills to go beyond the details of the story.

Second Read

For the Second Read, use **Extend Thinking** across the bottom of pages 126–141.

Story Words

rain water that falls in drops from the clouds

ground the soil or dirt on the surface of the earth

head the top part of your body or the front part of most animals' bodies

shouted called out or yelled loudly

shouting calling or yelling

Academic Vocabulary

plot the events that happen at the beginning, middle, and end of a story, usually involving a problem and a solution

English Language Learners

Words in Context To help children complete the sentence frames, offer hints about the missing words by asking questions. For example, for sentence 1, you might ask, *What do you call water when it falls from the sky?* Use gestures and sound effects as additional clues. Once children identify the correct word, have them read aloud the completed sentence frame.

Objectives

- Retell a narrative.
- Identify the author's purpose.
- Visualize a story.
- Write clear, coherent sentences.

Check Retelling
SUCCESS PREDICTOR

Objectives
- Retell a story's beginning, middle, and end in the order in which the events happened.
- Read on your own for a period of time.

Envision It! Retell

READING STREET ONLINE
STORY SORT
www.ReadingStreet.com

Think Critically

1. What do plants need to help them grow? Text to World
2. Why do you think the author made some words in big letters? Think Like an Author
3. Why do you think Arnold Lobel wrote this story? Author's Purpose
4. What picture came to your mind when you read about Toad playing music for his plants? How did that help you understand what you were reading? Visualize
5. **Look Back and Write** Look back at page 134. What advice does Frog give to Toad? Write about it. TEST PRACTICE Extended Response

142

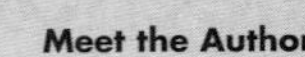

Meet the Author

Arnold Lobel

When Arnold Lobel first wrote about Frog and Toad, there were not many books for beginning readers that were fun to read. Mr. Lobel used easy words, and children love those good friends Frog and Toad!

As a boy, Mr. Lobel liked to draw silly animal pictures for his friends. When he grew up, he wrote and illustrated almost one hundred books!

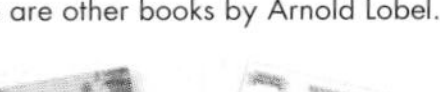

Here are other books by Arnold Lobel.

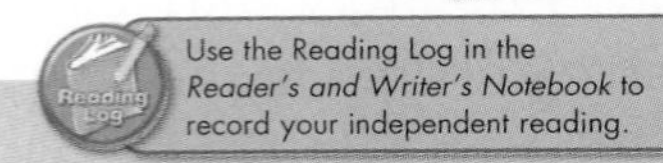

Use the Reading Log in the *Reader's and Writer's Notebook* to record your independent reading.

143

Student Edition pp. 142–143

Retelling

Envision It! Have children work in pairs, retelling the story to one another. Remind children that their partners should include the characters, setting, and events from the beginning, middle, and end of the story. Children should use the retelling strip in the Student Edition as they retell. Monitor children's retelling.

Scoring rubric

Top-Score Response A top-score response makes connections beyond the text, elaborates on the author's purpose, and describes in detail the characters, setting, and plot.

MONITOR PROGRESS **Check Retelling**

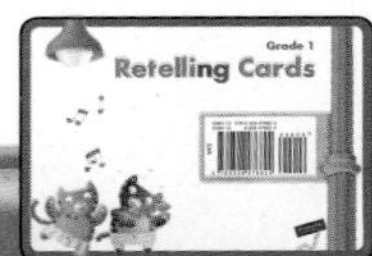

If... children have trouble retelling the story,

then... use Story Sequence Graphic Organizer Flip Chart 23, and the Retelling Cards, and work with the group to scaffold their retelling.

Day 1	Day 2	Day 3	Day 4	Day 5
Check Word Reading	Check Word Reading	Check High-Frequency Words/Retelling	Check Fluency	Check Oral Vocabulary

Think Critically

Text to World

1. Possible response: Plants need soil, sunlight, and water.

Think Like an Author

2. Possible response: The author wanted to show that Toad was shouting.

Author's Purpose

3. Possible response: I think Arnold Lobel wrote this story to make his readers laugh.

Visualize

4. Possible response: The picture that came to mind was someone playing music to an audience. This helped me understand that Toad thought the plants would enjoy his music just like an audience of people would.

5. **Look Back and Write** For writing fluency, assign a five-minute time limit. As children finish, encourage them to reread their response and proofread for errors.

Scoring rubric

> **Top-Score Response** A top-score response gives specific details from the text to tell what advice Frog gave Toad. For example:
>
> Frog told Toad to stop shouting at the seeds. He said to let the sun and rain help the seeds grow.

Meet the author/illustrator Read aloud page 143 as children follow along. Ask children how Arnold Lobel first got interested in writing and illustrating books for children.

Read independently After children enter their independent reading into their Reading Logs, have them paraphrase a portion of the text they have just read. Tell children that when we paraphrase, we express the meaning of what we have read using our own words.

Differentiated Instruction

A Advanced

Look Back and Write Ask children who show proficiency with the writing prompt to tell which character they think is a better gardener, Frog or Toad, and to explain why they think so.

INTERACT with TEXT

Strategy Response Log

Visualize Have children use p. RR28 in their *Reader's and Writer's Notebook* to add a page to the story. Have them draw a picture of Toad in his garden once it has bloomed. Have them write a sentence telling how Toad feels about his garden.

Plan to Assess Retelling

- [ ] Week 1: Strategic Intervention
- [ ] Week 2: Advanced
- [ ] Week 3: Strategic Intervention
- [x] This week: Assess On Level Children.
- [ ] Week 5: Strategic Intervention
- [ ] Week 6: Assess any children not yet checked during this unit.

Objectives

- Read aloud fluently with expression and correct intonation.
- Understand verbs (past) in the context of reading and writing.
- Use verbs (past) when speaking.
- Understand verbs (future) in the context of reading and writing.
- Use verbs (future) when speaking.

Model Fluency
Expression and Intonation

Model fluent reading Have children turn to Student Edition page 130. Point to the quotation marks. Quotation marks show that someone is talking. I try to read the part in quotation marks the way the character would say it.

Guide practice Have children read the page with you. Then have them reread the page as a group until they read with appropriate expression and intonation. Encourage them to read with expression. Continue in the same way with pages 131–132.

Corrective feedback

If... children have difficulty reading with appropriate expression and intonation,
then... prompt:

- Find the marks that tell someone is speaking.
- Who is speaking? How do they feel? How should they sound?

Reread for Fluency

ROUTINE Choral Reading

 **Select a Passage** For *Frog and Toad Together*, use pp. 134–135.

 **Model** First, have children track the print as you read.

 **Guide Practice** Then have children read along with you.

 **Corrective Feedback** Have the class read aloud without you. Monitor progress and provide feedback. For optimal fluency, children should reread three to four times.

Routines Flip Chart

Check comprehension Why did Toad bring candles to the garden? (Possible response: It was nighttime and Toad thought the plants were afraid of the dark.)

Conventions
Verbs for Past and for Future

Review
Verbs for past and for future

Remind children that some verbs use the ending *-ed* to tell what happened in the past. Verbs use the helping verb *will* to tell what will happen in the future.

Guide practice

Write these sentences on the board and have children read them aloud.

1. Jen will open the box.

2. We slipped on the ice.

Which sentence tells about the past? The future? How do you know?

Team Talk Have children change the first sentence to tell about the past and the second sentence to tell about the future.

Connect to oral language

Have children use the sentence starters below to make up oral sentences using the correct form of these verbs: *jump, paint, talk, fix.*

1. Yesterday ________.

2. Tomorrow ________.

3. Next year ________.

4. Two days ago ________.

On their own

Use *Reader's and Writer's Notebook* p. 374.

Verbs for Past and for Future

Possible answer: I crawled. I stayed in a crib. I played with baby toys.

Possible answer: I will read. I will talk with friends. I will play baseball.

Reader's and Writer's Notebook, p. 374

Options for Oral Rereading

Use *Frog and Toad Together* or one of this week's Decodable Practice Readers.

Daily Fix-It

5. I put thre seeds in one pot?
I put three seeds in one pot.

6. then I gave them watter.
Then I gave them water.

Discuss the Daily Fix-It corrections with children. Review sentence capitalization and punctuation, the *ee* spelling of /ē/, and the spelling of *water.*

English Language Learners
Oral Language Brainstorm weekend activities, such as *play, visit, sleep, see, read, buy.* Ask: *What will you do this weekend?* Have children answer, starting with *I will* or *We will.* Invite children to pantomime actions.

Objectives

- Write a draft of two lists.
- Use sentences in writing.

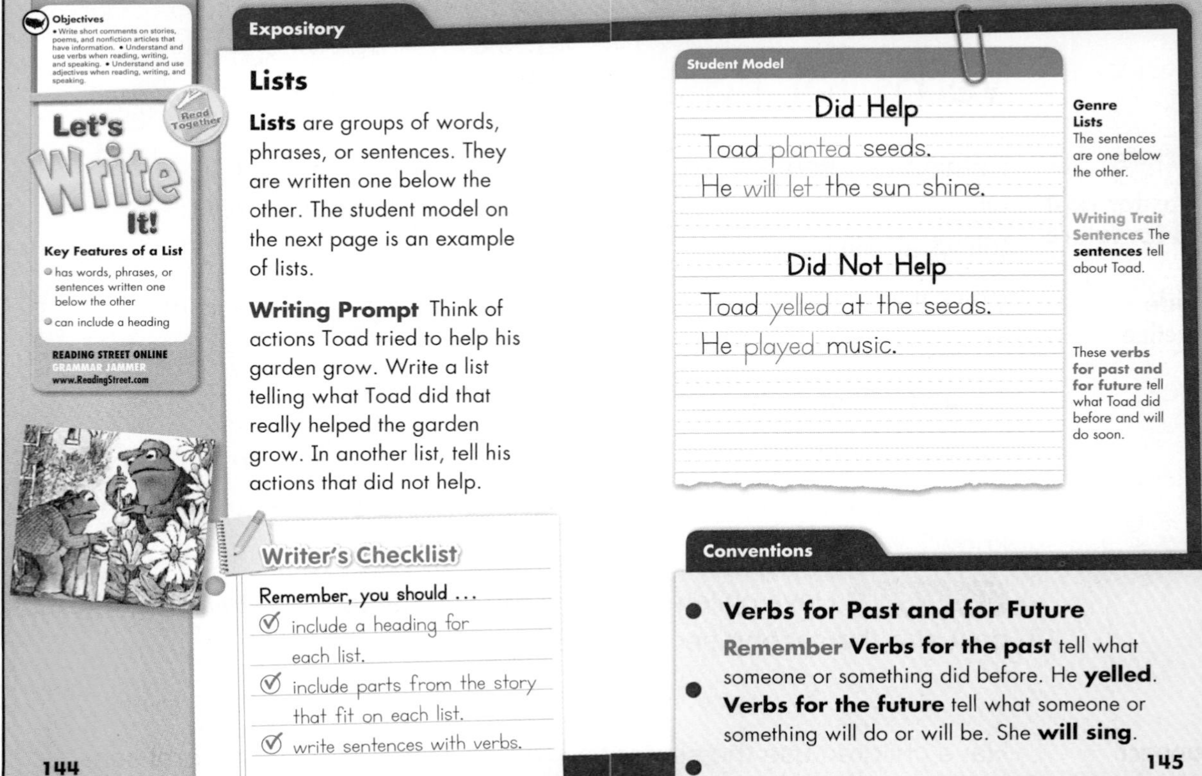

Objectives
• Write short comments on stories, poems, and nonfiction articles that have information. • Understand and use verbs when reading, writing, and speaking. • Understand and use adjectives when reading, writing, and speaking.

Read Together

Let's Write It!

Key Features of a List

- has words, phrases, or sentences written one below the other
- can include a heading

READING STREET ONLINE
GRAMMAR JAMMER
www.ReadingStreet.com

Expository

Lists

Lists are groups of words, phrases, or sentences. They are written one below the other. The student model on the next page is an example of lists.

Writing Prompt Think of actions Toad tried to help his garden grow. Write a list telling what Toad did that really helped the garden grow. In another list, tell his actions that did not help.

Writer's Checklist

Remember, you should ...
- include a heading for each list.
- include parts from the story that fit on each list.
- write sentences with verbs.

144

Student Model

Did Help
Toad planted seeds.
He will let the sun shine.

Did Not Help
Toad yelled at the seeds.
He played music.

Genre Lists The sentences are one below the other.

Writing Trait Sentences The **sentences** tell about Toad.

These **verbs for past and for future** tell what Toad did before and will do soon.

Conventions

- **Verbs for Past and for Future**

Remember Verbs for the past tell what someone or something did before. He **yelled**. **Verbs for the future** tell what someone or something will do or will be. She **will sing**.

145

Student Edition pp. 144–145

Let's Write It! — Lists

Teach Use pages 144–145 in the Student Edition. Read aloud the Key Features of a List and the definition of lists. Help children better understand the Writing Prompt by reading it aloud and discussing the Writer's Checklist with children.

Review the student model Then read the lists on page 145 to children. Point out the heading on each of the lists. Read the content and discuss how the ideas fit each heading. Read aloud and briefly discuss the side notes about Genre, the Writing Trait, and Verbs for Past and for Future to help children understand how an author writes a list.

Scoring rubric

> **Top-Score Response** Help children understand that a top-score response has a list of things that helped and a list of those that didn't, including headings and sentences one below the other. For a complete rubric see Writing Rubric 16 from the Teacher Resource DVD-ROM.

Connect to conventions Read to children the Conventions note about Verbs for Past and for Future. Point out verbs in the model list *(planted, will let, yelled, played).*

Writing—Lists
Writer's Craft: Tell Characters' Actions

MINI-LESSON

Tell Characters' Actions

- **Introduce** Use your idea web from yesterday and Writing Transparency 16A to model writing sentences that tell characters' actions. When I write my lists, I will use my web. Yesterday I wrote in my first web *Things That Helped.* I will start by writing that heading for the list. Now I will read the verbs I wrote in my chart. I will use these verbs to write sentences that tell about Toad's actions. The first thing I wrote is *planted seeds.* I will tell who planted seeds. The first thing in my list is *Toad planted seeds in the ground.* Read aloud the draft on the Transparency to show how to use sentences with vivid verbs to tell characters' actions.

Writing Transparency 16A
TR DVD

- Explain how children can use ideas they recorded yesterday to draft their two lists. Today's goal is to write the lists but not to rewrite each word perfectly. They can edit later to correct the words.

Guide list writing

Now it is time to write your lists. Tell what Toad did that helped his garden grow. Then tell what he did that did not help. Have children use their idea webs as bases for sentences that tell characters' actions. Then guide children as they draft the lists.

ROUTINE **Quick Write for Fluency** Team Talk

1. **Talk** Have partners share an item from their idea webs.
2. **Write** Each child writes a sentence about that action.
3. **Share** Partners read one another's sentences.

Routines Flip Chart

Write Guy
Jeff Anderson

Powerful Words, Powerful Verbs

If children have trouble distinguishing complete sentences from fragments, have them ask this question: "Who or what did something? What did they do?" If there is no answer to the question, they know their words may be a fragment. Children can have fun making a complete statement by adding together subjects *(David)* and powerful verbs *(laughed, talked, punched): David laughed.*

Differentiated Instruction

Advanced

Describing Action Challenge children to choose vivid verbs and precise words to describe Toad's actions in detail in their lists.

Objectives

- Recite poetry, accenting the rhythm and rhyme, pausing where appropriate, and speaking slowly and clearly.
- Listen to poetry.
- Use a diagram to find facts.
- Create a diagram as part of an inquiry project.

Listening and Speaking
Poetry Presentation

Teach poetry presentation

Tell children that reciting a poem is a lot like singing a song. Like a song, a poem has a beat, or **rhythm.** It also has words that **rhyme,** like *frog* and *log.*

- Good speakers read a poem quietly to themselves first.
- Good speakers make sure they understand the words.
- Good readers and good listeners pay attention to the rhythm and the words that rhyme.
- They pay attention to punctuation marks.
- When they recite the poem, they speak slowly and clearly.

Model

Have children turn to the Unit 2 poem "Night Song" on page 199. Use the passage below to model preparing for a poetry presentation. Alternatively, you may choose to present another poem from the classroom library.

Before I recite this poem, I'm going to read it quietly to myself. Read the first stanza in a soft voice. I see that *come* and *hum* rhyme, and I can feel the rhythm—each line has two beats. Repeat the stanza, clapping out the rhythm. The second line ends with a comma, so I paused a little there. The last line ends with a period, so I came to a full stop and used my voice to show that a sentence had ended. Now I'll practice saying this part of the poem more smoothly, speaking slowly and clearly.

Guide practice

Have the class read the rest of the poem softly together. Have them listen carefully for the rhythm and clap it out as they read. Also have them listen for the rhyming words and raise their hands as they hear them. Discuss the meanings of any words children may not know.

On their own

Have children practice reciting the entire poem to a partner. Tell them to take turns practicing until they can read it smoothly, speaking slowly and clearly. Remind children to listen carefully and politely as their partners read.

Research and Inquiry
Gather and Record Information

Teach

Tell children that when they do research, they can find facts in different places. For example, they can talk to an expert or look in a book. Recall the diagram they used yesterday. Point out that diagrams can often be found in books. Have them turn to the flower diagram on page 147 of the Student Edition. Explain that they will read this selection tomorrow.

Model

Think Aloud: Here's another diagram that can help me answer my research question, "What are the different parts of a plant?" This diagram shows the parts of a flower and what each part is called. I see that this flower has petals, stems, leaves, and roots.

Guide practice

Have children look at the diagram of a storm on *Reader's and Writer's Notebook* p. 370. Read aloud the name of each part. Then read aloud the directions, and complete the page as a class. After children have completed the page, have them sketch a storm and label its parts in the *What I Learned* column of their note-taking chart. Provide another sheet of paper if needed.

Wrap Up Your Day

- ✔ **Author's Purpose** Remind children that an author's purpose may be to inform or to entertain. What is the author's purpose for writing a science book? A funny animal story? How do you know?
- ✔ **Visualize** As you listened to "Carlee's Garden," what pictures did you see in your mind when Carlee discovered that animals had nibbled her vegetables? Discuss how visualizing makes reading more fun and interesting.

Differentiated Instruction

SI Strategic Intervention

Using a Diagram to Take Notes If children are unable to sketch and label a storm, draw a simple diagram on chart paper and label the parts together.

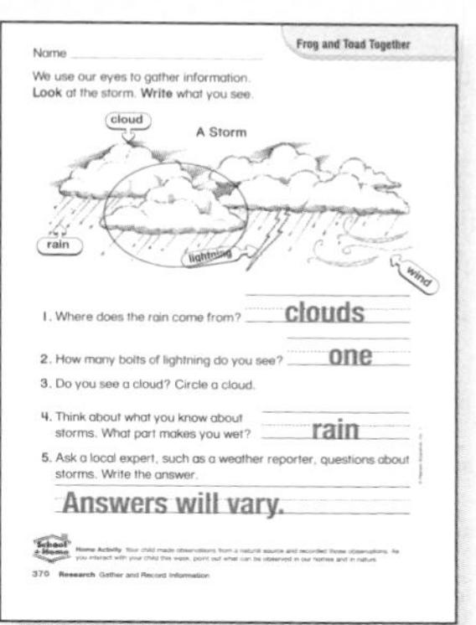
Frog and Toad Together

Name ____________

We use our eyes to gather information.
Look at the storm. **Write** what you see.

A Storm

cloud
rain
lightning
wind

1. Where does the rain come from? clouds
2. How many bolts of lightning do you see? one
3. Do you see a cloud? Circle a cloud.
4. Think about what you know about storms. What part makes you wet? rain
5. Ask a local expert, such as a weather reporter, questions about storms. Write the answer.
Answers will vary.

370 Research Gather and Record Information

Reader's and Writer's Notebook, p. 370

Tell children that tomorrow they will read about how to start their own garden from seeds.

Objectives
- Discuss the concept to develop oral language.
- Build oral vocabulary.
- Identify details in text.

Today at a Glance

Oral Vocabulary
destroy, humongous

Phonological Awareness
Segment and Blend Syllables

Phonics and Spelling
Review Ending *-es;* Plural *-es*
Review *r*-Controlled *or, ore*

High-Frequency Words
Review

Comprehension
◉ Author's Purpose

Fluency
Expression and Intonation

Conventions
Verbs for Past and for Future

Writing
Lists: Revise

Research and Inquiry
Review and Revise Topic

Concept Talk

Question of the Week

What changes happen in a garden?

Build concepts To reinforce concepts and to focus children's attention, have children sing "Sprout! It's a Garden" from the *Sing with Me* Big Book. What does the song tell us about what seeds need before they can become plants? (They need sunshine, rain, and time to grow.)

Sing with Me Big Book Audio

Review Genre: animal fantasy Have children tell the key features of an animal fantasy: it is a made-up story with animals that do things real animals can't do. Tell children that today they will read about a boy whose magic bean seeds grow to be a plant that does things real plants can't do.

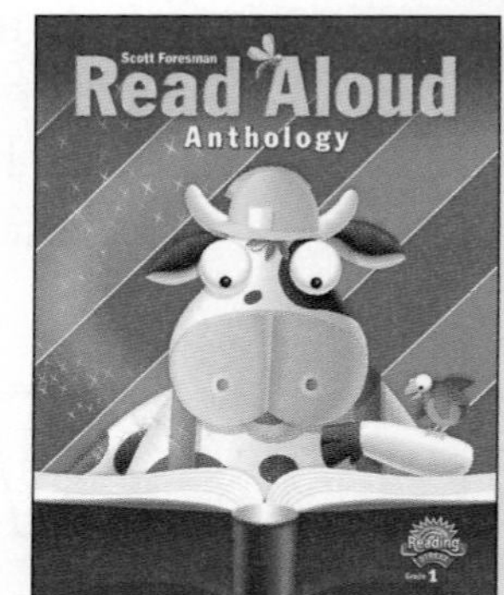

"Jack and the Beanstalk"

Monitor listening comprehension Recall that in the story about Toad's garden, Toad waited quite a long time for his seeds to sprout. Have children listen to "Jack and the Beanstalk" to find out what is amazing about the beans that Jack plants. Read the selection.

ELL **Produce Oral Language** Use the Day 4 instruction on ELL Poster 16 to extend and enrich language.

ELL Poster 16

Oral Vocabulary
Amazing Words

Amazing Words Oral Vocabulary Routine

Teach Amazing Words

1. **Introduce the Word** Relate the word *humongous* to the story. Jack's beanstalk was so *humongous* that he could not even see the top. Supply a child-friendly definition. When something is *humongous,* it is very, very large. Have children say the word.
2. **Demonstrate** Provide examples to show meaning. The *humongous* cake was enough to serve one hundred people. Her *humongous* dog could hardly fit inside the car.
3. **Apply** Have children demonstrate their understanding. What is something *humongous* that you have seen?

See p. OV•1 to teach *destroy*.

Routines Flip Chart

Anchored Talk

Add to the concept map

Discuss how plants grow and change.

- In "Jack and the Beanstalk," we read about a make-believe plant. How was the way Jack's plant grew different from the way real plants grow? (Jack's plant grew much more quickly and much taller than a real plant.)
- Real plants never grow as tall as Jack's beanstalk, but real plants do grow to be different sizes. What kinds of plants grow very tall? (trees) What are some kinds of plants that stay small? (grass, dandelions) Where can we add *Plants grow to be different sizes* to the concept map?

Amazing Words

gardener	shade
nature	sprinkling
sprout	destroy
dim	humongous

Differentiated Instruction

 Advanced

Amazing Words For children who demonstrate understanding of the word *humongous,* write the words *small, large,* and *humongous* on the board. Have children draw a picture to illustrate each size and label their pictures with the appropriate word.

English Language Learners

Frontload Listening Use ELL Poster 16 to review how plants grow from seeds. Before reading have children describe what is happening in each picture of the poster.

Objectives

- Segment and blend words with two syllables.
- Read words with ending *-es,* plural *-es,* and *r*-controlled *or, ore.*

Phonological Awareness
Segment and Blend Syllables

Model This week we read about how Toad planted a garden. Listen as I say the two syllables in garden. Slowly model the syllables: /gär/ • /dn/. Now I will blend the two syllables together to say the word: /gär/ • /dn/, garden. We're going to practice saying and blending two syllables to make a word.

Guide practice I will say two syllables. Repeat them after me. Then blend the syllables to make a word from the story. Say each syllable pair below. Have children say and then blend the syllables to form a word.

Corrective feedback If children make an error, model the correct response. Return to the word later in the practice.

/wȯk/ • /ing/ (walking)	**/flou/ • /ər/** (flower)	**/loud/ • /lē/** (loudly)
/grō/ • /ing/ (growing)	**/ə/ • /frād/** (afraid)	**/myü/ • /zik/** (music)

On their own Have children segment and blend the following two-syllable words.

/plant/ • /əd/ (planted)	**/stôr/ • /ē/** (story)	**/kum/ • /ing/** (coming)
/ə/ • /lōn/ (alone)	**/kan/ • /dl/** (candle)	**/ə/ • /slēp/** (asleep)

Phonics Review
Ending -*es* and Plural -*es*; *r*-Controlled *or, ore*

Review Sound-spellings

To review last week's first phonics skill, write *fixes.* You studied words like this last week. What is the base word? (*fix*) What is the ending? (-*es*) Blend the base word and ending. What is the word? (*fixes*) Repeat with *foxes.* What does it mean when you add -*es* to the name of an animal or thing? (more than one)

Corrective feedback

If children are unable to answer your questions about words with -*es,* refer them to Sound-Spelling Cards 124 and 139.

Review *r*-Controlled *or, ore*

To review last week's second phonics skill, write *corn*. You also studied words like this. What sound do the letters *or* stand for in this word? (They stand for /ôr/.) What's the word? (*corn)* Repeat for the letters *ore* in *chore.*

Guide practice

Draw a T-chart or use Graphic Organizer Flip Chart 4. When I say a word, raise your hand if you hear /ôr/. Write each word in the appropriate column. Have children read the lists and identify words with -*es.*

Words With *or, ore*	Words Without *or, ore*
porches	mixes
born	rushes
shore	buzzes
sport	tosses

On their own

Use Let's Practice It! on pp. 147–148 on the *Teacher Resource DVD-ROM.*

Name

Frog and Toad Together

Add -**s** or -**es** to each verb.
Write the new verb on the line.

1. fix fixes
2. kiss kisses
3. run runs
4. wish wishes
5. help helps
6. catch catches

Add -**es** to each word.
Write the new word on the line.
Draw a picture of the word.

7. box boxes
8. Children's artwork should show more than one box.
9. glass glasses
10. Children's artwork should show more than one drinking glass or eyeglass pair.

Phonics Endings -es; Plural -es Review DVD•147

Let's Practice It!
TR DVD•147

Name

Frog and Toad Together

Circle a word to finish each sentence.
Write it on the line.

horn

1. Todpoles were born (born / bond)
2. I see more than three! (most / more)
3. It will form legs. (form / fond)
4. Then a storm came. I saw a head pop out. (store / storm)
5. The frog swam to shore (shot / shore)

DVD•148 Phonics r-Controlled or, ore Review

Let's Practice It!
TR DVD•148

English Language Learners

Plurals Children who speak Spanish will be familiar with the use of plural endings -*s* and -*es,* as in *plantas* and *flores*. Point out this similarity between Spanish and English to them. In other languages, including Chinese, Hmong, and Vietnamese, nouns do not have plural forms. The plural is indicated with an adjective. Give children who speak these languages extra practice saying phrases such as one pen, two pens; one box, two boxes. Use props to enhance understanding.

DAY 4 Get Ready to Read

Objectives

- Apply knowledge of sound-spellings to decode unknown words when reading.
- Decode words in context and in isolation.
- Practice fluency with oral rereading.

Decodable Practice Reader 16C

Adding Endings; Vowels: *r*-Controlled *ar*

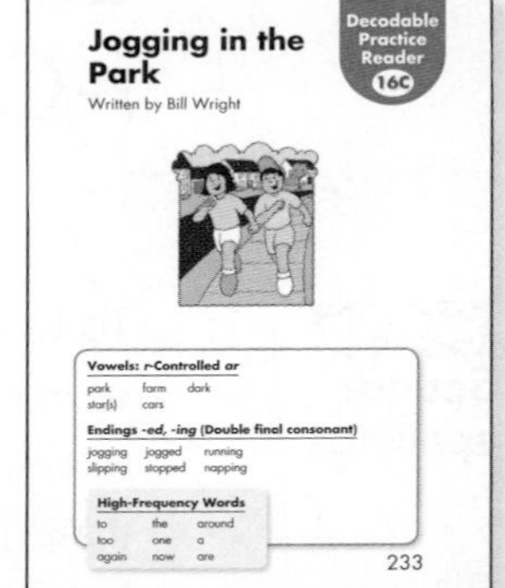

Jogging in the Park

Written by Bill Wright

Decodable Practice Reader 16C

Vowels: r-Controlled ar

park farm dark
star(s) cars

Endings -ed, -ing (Double final consonant)

jogging jogged running
slipping stopped napping

High-Frequency Words

to the around
too one a
again now are

233

Decodable Practice Reader 16C

Decode words in isolation Have children turn to page 233. Have children decode each word.

Review High-frequency words Review the previously taught words *to, the, now, are, around, too, one, a,* and *again.* Have children read each word as you point to it on the Word Wall.

Preview Have children read the title and preview the story. Tell them they will read words with endings *-ed* and *-ing* and words with /är/ spelled *ar.*

Decode words in context Pair children for reading and listen as they decode. One child begins. Children read the entire story, switching readers after each page. Partners reread the story. This time the other child begins.

We like to jog and run.
It makes us feel fine.

234

We go jogging in the park.
We jogged and jogged in the park.

235

We go running at the farm.
We ran and ran at the farm.

236

We go jogging around the track.
We jogged and jogged around the track.

237

Decodable Practice Reader 16C

It is too dark to go jogging.
We see stars in the sky.
One star is slipping.

238

We go jogging in a race.
The cars stopped for the race.
We jogged and jogged.

239

We like jogging.
We will jog again, but now we are napping.

240

Corrective feedback

If... children have difficulty decoding a word, **then...** refer them to the Sound-Spelling Cards to identify the sounds in the word. Then prompt them to blend the word.

- What is the new word?
- Is the new word a word you know?
- Does it make sense in the story?

Check decoding and comprehension

Have children retell the story to include characters, setting, and events. Then have children find words with endings *-ed* and *-ing* and words with /är/ spelled *ar* in the story. Children should supply *jogging, napping, slipping, jogged, running, stopped, park, farm, dark, star(s),* and *cars.*

Reread for Fluency

Have children reread Decodable Practice Reader 16C to develop automaticity decoding words with endings *-ed* and *-ing* and words with /är/ spelled *ar.*

ROUTINE Oral Rereading

1. **Read** Have children read the entire book orally.
2. **Reread** To achieve optimal fluency, children should reread the text three or four times.
3. **Corrective Feedback** Listen as children read. Provide corrective feedback regarding their fluency and decoding.

Routines Flip Chart

English Language Learners

Beginning/Early Intermediate After reading, point out several words with the /är/ sound, such as *park, farm, stars,* and *cars.* Say each word and have children repeat it. Then have children find each object the word names in the illustrations, point to it, and say the word again.

Intermediate After reading, have children search for words with the /är/ sound spelled *ar.* Have children say the words as they write them in a list. Then ask questions that require children to use the words. For example: *When do we see the stars?* (We see the stars at night.)

Early Advanced/Advanced After reading, have children look for /är/ words spelled *ar* and say them aloud. Then have children make up riddles for the words and have other children guess the answer. For example: *I am a place where children play. What am I?* (park) Monitor children's pronunciations and meanings.

Objectives

- Read words fluently in context and in isolation.
- Spell words with *-ed*.
- Spell high-frequency words.

Fluent Word Reading

Spiral Review

Read words in isolation

Display these words. Tell children that they can blend some words on this list and others are Word Wall words.

Have children read the list three or four times until they can read at the rate of two to three seconds per word.

school	**their**	**some**	**fixes**	**house**
old	**Mort**	**away**	**our**	**store**
sorts	**very**	**shore**	**Ford**	**drums**
porches	**other**	**horns**	**people**	**friends**

Word Reading

Corrective feedback

If... children have difficulty reading whole words,
then... have them use sound-by-sound blending for decodable words, or have them say and spell high-frequency words.

If... children cannot read fluently at a rate of two to three seconds per word,
then... have pairs practice the list until they can read it fluently.

Read words in context

Display these sentences. Call on individuals to read a sentence. Then randomly point to review words and have children read them. To help you monitor word reading, high-frequency words are underlined and decodable words are italicized.

Ford fixes and sorts **<u>the</u>** ***horns and drums.***

<u>Their</u> <u>very</u> <u>old</u> <u>house</u> ***has*** **<u>two</u>** ***porches.***

<u>Our</u> <u>friends</u> ***shopped at*** **<u>the</u> <u>school</u>** ***store.***

Mort went **<u>away</u> <u>to</u> <u>the</u>** ***shore*** **<u>with</u> <u>some</u> <u>other</u> <u>people</u>.**

Sentence Reading

Corrective feedback

If... children are unable to read an underlined high-frequency word,
then... read the word for them and spell it, having them echo you.

If... children have difficulty reading an italicized decodable word,
then... guide them in using sound-by-sound blending.

Spelling
Words with *-ed*

Partner Review

Supply pairs of children with index cards on which the spelling words have been written. Have one child read a word while the other writes it. Then have children switch roles. Have them use the cards to check their spelling and correct any misspelled words.

On their own

Use *Reader's and Writer's Notebook* p. 375.

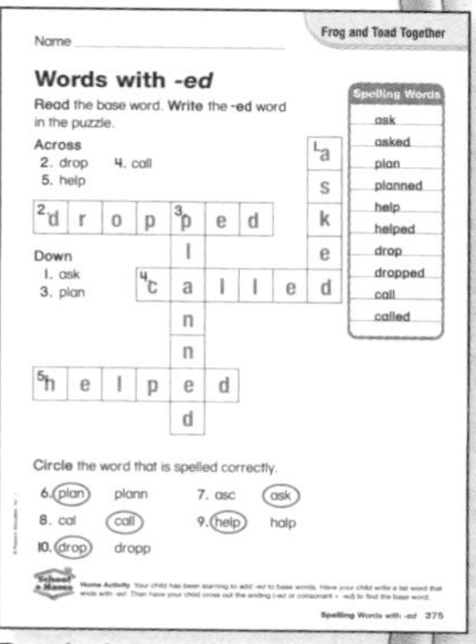

Reader's and Writer's Notebook p. 375

Spiral Review

These activities review

- previously taught high-frequency words *away, friends, house, old, other, our, people, school, some, their, very.*
- /ôr/ spelled *or* and *ore,* digraphs *ch* and *sh,* initial and final consonant blends, and plural endings *-s* and *-es.*

Small Group Time

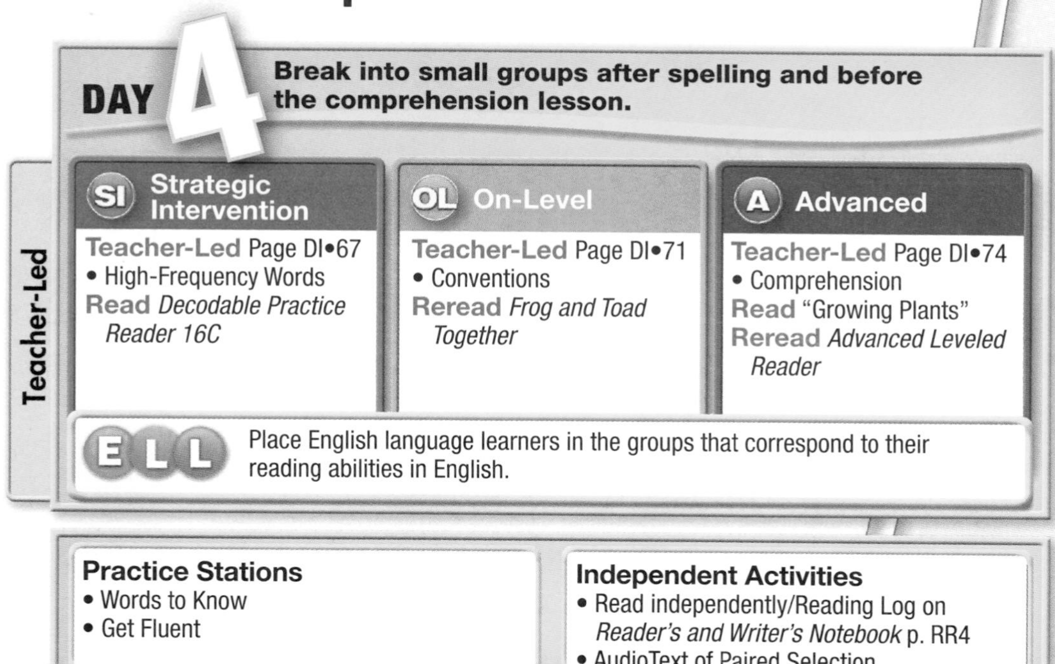

DAY 4 Break into small groups after spelling and before the comprehension lesson.

Teacher-Led

SI Strategic Intervention	OL On-Level	A Advanced
Teacher-Led Page DI•67 • High-Frequency Words Read *Decodable Practice Reader 16C*	Teacher-Led Page DI•71 • Conventions Reread *Frog and Toad Together*	Teacher-Led Page DI•74 • Comprehension Read "Growing Plants" Reread *Advanced Leveled Reader*

ELL Place English language learners in the groups that correspond to their reading abilities in English.

Practice Stations
- Words to Know
- Get Fluent

Independent Activities
- Read independently/Reading Log on *Reader's and Writer's Notebook* p. RR4
- AudioText of Paired Selection

English Language Learners

Fluent Word Reading Have children take turns reading the words aloud to a partner. Have partners read the sentences together several times.

Objectives

- Follow multi-step directions.
- Recognize structure and elements of a how-to article.
- Relate prior knowledge to new text.
- Set purpose for reading.

Science in Reading

Preview and predict Read the title and the first sentence of the selection. Have children look through the selection and predict what they might learn. (Possible response: They might learn about how to grow plants.) Ask them what clues helped them make that prediction. (Possible response: They might say the title of the selection, a list of directions, or the pictures.)

Let's Think About Genre **How-to Article** Review the key features of a how-to article: it tells how to make or do something. It has directions that tell steps to follow in order. Sometimes, it has pictures to help readers understand what to do.

Activate prior knowledge Ask children to recall what they already know about growing plants. (Plants grow from seeds in the ground. Plants need water and sunlight to grow.)

Set a purpose **Let's Read Together** As children read, have them pay attention to the sequence of the directions. Point out that the steps tell what to do in an exact order.

Let's Think About... How-to Article

As you read "Growing Plants" together, use Let's Think About in the Student Edition to help children focus on the features of a how-to article.

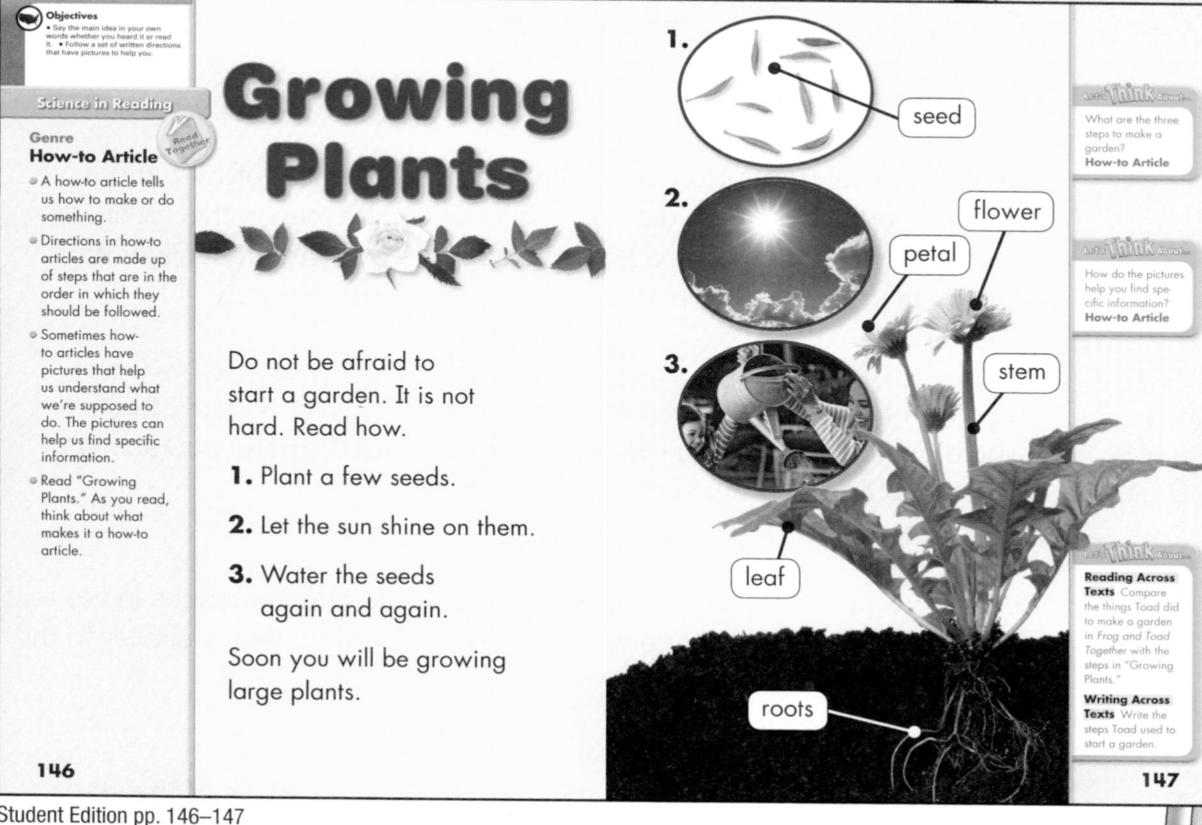
Objectives
• Say the main idea in your own words whether you heard it or read it. • Follow a set of written directions that have pictures to help you.

Science in Reading

Genre
How-to Article

Read Together

- A how-to article tells us how to make or do something.
- Directions in how-to articles are made up of steps that are in the order in which they should be followed.
- Sometimes how-to articles have pictures that help us understand what we're supposed to do. The pictures can help us find specific information.
- Read "Growing Plants." As you read, think about what makes it a how-to article.

Growing Plants

Do not be afraid to start a garden. It is not hard. Read how.

1. Plant a few seeds.
2. Let the sun shine on them.
3. Water the seeds again and again.

Soon you will be growing large plants.

146

Let's Think About...
What are the three steps to make a garden?
How-to Article

Let's Think About...
How do the pictures help you find specific information?
How-to Article

Let's Think About...
Reading Across Texts Compare the things Toad did to make a garden in *Frog and Toad Together* with the steps in "Growing Plants."

Writing Across Texts Write the steps Toad used to start a garden.

147

Student Edition pp. 146–147

Academic Vocabulary

author a person who writes

Science Vocabulary

seed a part of a plant that can grow into a new plant

Guide Comprehension

Following Multi-Step Directions

Guide practice

Think Aloud I think a how-to article has steps to follow in order. When I read *Growing Plants*, I see that the first page has three steps that tell me how to grow plants. One: I need to plant seeds. Two: I need to let sun shine on them. Three: I need to water them again and again.

Author's Purpose

Think Aloud Good readers look for clues about the author's purpose for writing. As I read *Growing Plants*, I see directions that tell me how to grow plants. I also see pictures that give more clues about how to grow plants. I think the author's purpose for writing this article is to teach readers how to grow plants.

Let's Think About... How-to Article

Possible response: The pictures and their labels help me find specific names of the parts of a plant. For example, I can see from the picture that the roots are underground.

Objectives

- Make an inference based on textual evidence.
- Use personal experience and knowledge to connect to text.
- Read aloud grade-level appropriate text fluently.

Check Fluency: WCPM
SUCCESS PREDICTOR

Guide Comprehension, continued

Confirm predictions Do you predict that a seed would grow without sunlight and water? How did you use what you learned in this article to answer this question? No, a seed would not grow without sunlight and water. I learned that plants need water and sunlight to grow.

Connect to self What steps would you follow to grow a plant? First, I would plant a seed. Next, I would make sure that the seed had sunlight. Then, I would water the seed again and again.

Reading Across Texts Have children find words and sentences in the text of *Frog and Toad Together* and identify what Toad did that is similar to the steps in “Growing Plants.”

Writing Across Texts Children might write a numbered list of the steps Toad used for growing his garden.

Fluency
Expression and Intonation

Guide practice

- Have children turn to page 132 in *Frog and Toad Together*.
- Have children follow along as you read the page with appropriate expression and intonation.
- Have the class read the page with you and then reread the page as a group without you until they read with appropriate expression and intonation. To provide additional fluency practice, pair nonfluent readers with fluent readers.

ROUTINE **Paired Reading**

1. **Select a Passage** For *Frog and Toad Together*, use pp. 128-129.
2. **Model** First, have children track the print as you read.
3. **Guide Practice** Then have children read along with you.
4. **On Their Own** For optimal fluency, have partners reread three or four times.

Routines Flip Chart

MONITOR PROGRESS **Check Fluency WCPM**

As children reread, monitor their progress toward their individual fluency goals. Current Goal: 25–35 words correct per minute. End-of-Year Goal: 60 words correct per minute.

If... children cannot read fluently at a rate of 25–35 words correct per minute,

then... have children practice with text at their independent level.

Day 1	Day 2	Day 3	Day 4	Day 5
Check Word Reading	Check Word Reading	Check High-Frequency Words/Retelling	Check Fluency	Check Oral Vocabulary

Success Predictor

Differentiated Instruction

A Advanced

WCPM If children already read at 60 words correct per minute, allow them to read independently.

Fluency Assessment Plan

Do a formal fluency assessment with 8 to 10 children every week. Assess 4 to 5 children on Day 4 and 4 to 5 children on Day 5. Use the reproducible fluency passage, Teacher's Edition, page 149f.

Options for Oral Rereading

Use *Frog and Toad Together* or one of this week's Decodable Practice Readers.

Objectives

- Use past- and future-tense verbs correctly.
- Revise a draft by deleting a word.

Conventions
Verbs for Past and for Future

Test practice Use *Reader's and Writer's Notebook* p. 376 to help children understand past- and future-tense verbs in test items. Recall that a verb with the ending *-ed* tells about the past and that a verb with the helping verb *will* tells about the future: *looked, will look.* Model identifying the appropriate verb form by writing these sentences on the board, choosing the correct one, and explaining why the others are not correct.

Last week we fish in the lake.
Last week we will fish in the lake.
Last week we fished in the lake.

Then read the *Reader's and Writer's Notebook* p. 376 directions. Guide children as they mark the answer for number 1.

On their own Use *Reader's and Writer's Notebook* p. 376.

Connect to oral language After children mark the answers to numbers 1–6, review the correct choices aloud. Have children read each sentence, emphasizing the past- or future-tense verb.

Connect to writing Have children choose one incorrect sentence from *Reader's and Writer's Notebook* p. 376 and write it correctly using the past tense. Then have children choose another incorrect sentence on that page and write it correctly using the future tense.

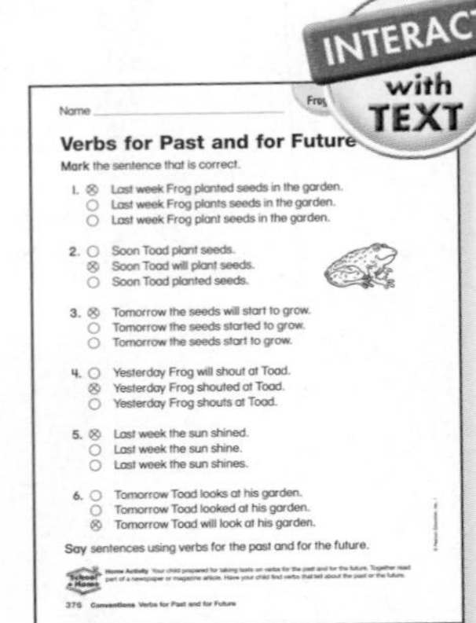

Reader's and Writer's Notebook, p. 376

Writing—Lists
Revising Strategy

MINI-LESSON

Revising Strategy: Deleting a Word

- Yesterday we wrote lists of the things Toad did that helped his garden grow and the things he did that did not help his garden grow. Today we will revise our lists. We can make the ideas clearer or more interesting. We can take away a word that does not make sense or does not help.

Revising Marks

Take Out		Move	
Add	^	Period	⊙

Things That Helped

Toad plantted seeds in the ground.

Toad left the seeds alone.

Things That Did Not Help

Toad read poems to the seeds

toad played ~~some~~ music for the seeds.

Unit 3: Frog and Toad Together — Writing: Revise 16B

Writing Transparency 16B
TR DVD

- Display the Revising Tips. Explain that this is a time for making the list clear for anyone who will read it. Tomorrow children will proofread to correct any errors such as misspellings, missing capital letters, or missing periods.

Revising Tips

- ☐ Make sure your sentences tell what the character does.
- ☐ Delete words that don't make sense or don't help.

- Use Writing Transparency 16B to model deleting a word. When I revise, I make sure my sentences tell what the character does. Each word should help readers understand. The word *some* doesn't help readers. The sentence is clearer without it. Delete *some* from the last item. Tell children that they can delete words as they revise.

Peer conferencing

Peer Revision Have groups of three take turns reading the items in their lists. Have all three children read and compare the items in the first list. Allow three minutes for children to discuss the word choice in the sentences and make suggestions for deletions in revision. Remind children that the purpose of revision is to clarify ideas. Then have children repeat the process for the second list. Allow children time to incorporate their revisions.

Differentiated Instruction

SI Strategic Intervention

Deleting Words Guide children in deleting unnecessary words. Explain that the goal is to express ideas clearly.

Daily Fix-It

7. They ned sunn.
They need sun.

8. I am hapy when they gro.
I am happy when they grow.

Discuss the Daily Fix-It corrections with children. Review the ee spelling of long *e* and the spelling of *sun, happy,* and *grow.*

English Language Learners

Verbs for Past and for Future Be sure children understand that verbs for future are made up of the helping verb *will* and the verb for the present with no *-s.*

Objectives

- Revise a list.
- Review answers to inquiry questions.

Writing
Lists, continued

Guide practice Have children revise their lists. For those not sure how to revise, have children refer to the Revising Tips or the Key Features of Lists.

Corrective feedback Circulate to monitor and conference with children as they write. Remind them that they will have time to proofread and edit tomorrow. Today they can make changes to their lists by deleting words that don't make sense or don't help readers understand.

ROUTINE Quick Write for Fluency — Team Talk

1. **Talk** Read these sentences aloud, and have children tell which sentence is better.

   Toad read a really, really long story to his seeds.

   Toad read a long story to his seeds.

2. **Write** Have children write a sentence telling why the second is better.
3. **Share** Partners can read their explanations to one another.

Routines Flip Chart

Research and Inquiry
Review and Revise Topic

Teach Tell children that after doing some research, the next step is to look over your notes to see if you have found the facts you needed to answer your research question. Explain that sometimes your research may lead you to choose a different or smaller topic.

Model We've been doing research to answer the question, "What are the different parts of a plant?" By looking at different diagrams, one thing we learned is that different plants have different parts. For example, a tree has a trunk but a flower has a stem. With so many different kinds of plants in the world, it would take us too long to learn and write about the parts of *all* plants. So let's change our research question to make it smaller. For instance, we could change our question to "What are the different parts of a flower?"

Guide practice Have children look over their notes from Days 2 and 3 and decide how they want to narrow the focus of their research question. Have them choose between a flower and a tree or, if you wish, suggest specific kinds of flowers or trees for which information is available. Finally, tell children that tomorrow they will make their own diagram to share what they have learned.

Differentiated Instruction

Advanced

Expert Sources If children know about specific kinds of plants from their own experience, invite them to share their information with the class. For example, some children may be familiar with the parts of a corn plant, such as the stalk, leaves, ears, kernels, tassel, and silk.

Wrap Up Your Day

- ✔ **Phonics** Write these words: *winning, sleeping, thanked, rubbed*. Have children identify the base word, ending, and any consonants that were doubled before adding the ending.
- ✔ **Fluency** Write *Did Tom watch that football game? Jan thinks football is fun!* Have the class reread the sentences until they can do so with appropriate expression and intonation.

Remind children that they heard about a boy who grew an amazing beanstalk. Tomorrow they will hear about the boy and his beanstalk again.

Objectives

- Review the concept: what changes happen in a garden.
- Build oral vocabulary.
- Identify details in text.

Today at a Glance

Oral Vocabulary
Review

Phonics
◎ Review Adding Endings
◎ Review Vowel: *r*-Controlled *ar*

Comprehension
◎ Author's Purpose

Story Words
Review

High-Frequency Words
Review

Conventions
Verbs for Past and for Future

Writing
Lists

Research and Inquiry
Communicate

Check Oral Vocabulary
SUCCESS PREDICTOR

Concept Wrap Up

Question of the Week

What changes happen in a garden?

Review Concept

This week we have read and listened to stories about changes that happen in a garden. One change is the way seeds sprout and the tiny young plants grow bigger. Today you will listen to find out how Jack's beanstalk is like a real plant and how it is different. Read the story.

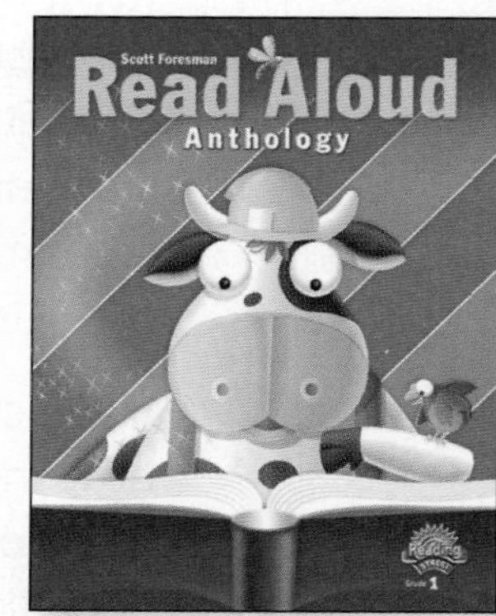

"Jack and the Beanstalk"

- How is Jack's beanstalk like a real plant? How is it different? (Possible response: Jack's beanstalk is like a real plant because it grows out of the ground from seeds and has a stalk and leaves. It is not like a real plant because it grows overnight and reaches higher than the clouds.)

Review Amazing Words

Orally review the meaning of this week's Amazing Words. Then display this week's concept map. Have children use Amazing Words such as *gardener, sprout,* and *sprinkling,* as well as the concept map, to answer the question "What changes happen in a garden?"

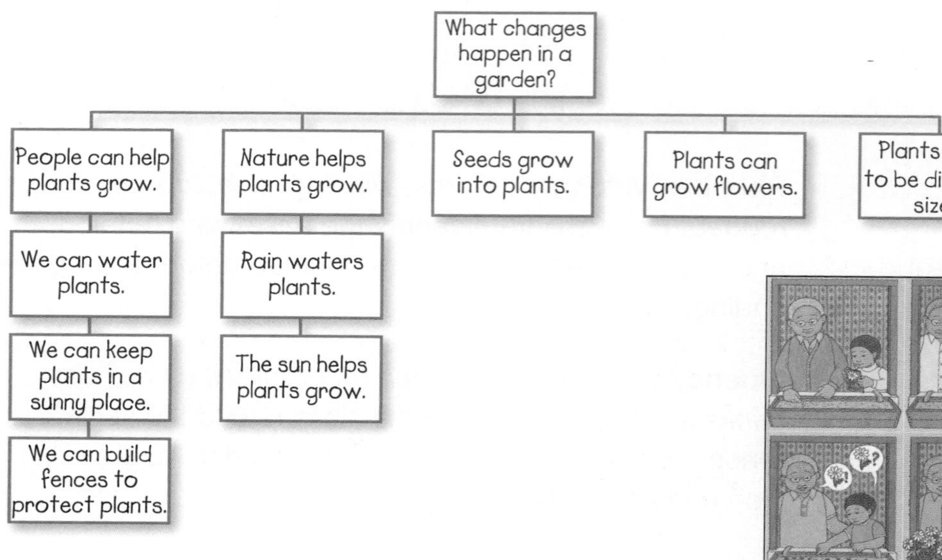

ELL **Check Concepts and Language** Use the Day 5 instruction on ELL Poster 16 to monitor children's understanding of the lesson concept.

ELL Poster 16

Oral Vocabulary
Amazing Words

Connect to the Big Question

Team Talk Pair children and have them discuss how the Question of the Week connects to this unit's Big Question, "What is changing in our world?" Tell children to use the concept map and what they've learned from this week's Anchored Talks and reading selections to form an Amazing Idea—a realization or "big idea" about **change**. Then ask each pair to share their Amazing Idea with the class.

Amazing Ideas might include these key concepts:

- Gardens change as plants sprout and grow.
- Plants grow in spring and summer; they rest in fall and winter.

It's Friday

MONITOR PROGRESS Check Oral Vocabulary

Call on individuals to use this week's Amazing Words to talk about changes that happen in a garden. Prompt discussion with the questions below. Monitor children's ability to use the Amazing Words and note which words children are unable to use.

- **Why do *gardeners* give their plants a *sprinkling* of water?**
- **What things outside our window are a part of *nature*?**
- **In what seasons do you see new plants *sprout*?**
- **Do gardeners plant where the light is bright or *dim*? Why?**
- **When do some leaves turn *shades* of yellow and red?**
- **What could *destroy* a garden?**
- **What does a *humongous* pumpkin look like?**

If... children have difficulty using the Amazing Words,
Then... reteach the unknown words using the Oral Vocabulary Routines, pp. 119a, 124b, 142b, and 146b.

Day 1	Day 2	Day 3	Day 4	Day 5
Check Word Reading	Check Word Reading	Check High-Frequency Words/Retelling	Check Fluency	Check Oral Vocabulary

Success Predictor

Amazing Words

gardener	shade
sprout	sprinkling
nature	destroy
dim	humongous

Differentiated Instruction

Advanced
If children can easily answer the vocabulary questions, ask them to make up their own sentences for the words.

English Language Learners
Amazing Words Create sentence starters for children to help them use the words in sentences. For example:

If a pumpkin keeps growing and growing and growing, it will soon be ________.

When you plant a seed, you must wait many days before it will ________.

Success Predictor

DAY 5 Wrap Up your Week

Objectives

- Generate rhyming words.
- ◎ Review words with *-ed* and *-ing*.
- ◎ Review words with *r*-controlled *ar*.
- Spell high-frequency words.
- Spell verbs with and without *-ed* endings.

Assess

- Read words with *-ed* and *-ing*.
- Spell high-frequency words.

Phonological Awareness
Generate Rhyming Words

Review Rhyming words

Have children orally generate words starting with consonant blends that rhyme with the following words. If children make an error, model a correct response. Return to the word later in the practice. Sample answers are given.

part (start, smart)	**call** (stall, small)
ant (plant, slant)	**feet** (sweet, sleet, treat)
dim (swim, trim, brim, slim)	**rose** (glows, snows, close, froze)

Review Target phonics skills

Phonics
◎ Adding Endings; *r*-Controlled *ar*

Write the following sentences on the board. Have children read each one, first quietly to themselves and then aloud as you track the print.

1. **Clark tripped on a sharp rock in the yard.**
2. **Running around a large park is fun.**
3. **We stopped to look at the stars in the dark sky.**
4. **A shark is swimming in deep water.**

Team Talk Have children discuss with a partner which words have /är/ spelled *ar* and which words have a base word and *-ed* or *-ing.* Have them also identify the consonant that was doubled before adding the ending. Then call on individuals to share with the class.

Spelling Test
Words with *-ed*

Dictate spelling words

Say each word, read the sentence, repeat the word, and allow time for children to write the word.

1. call	**Call** me to come home.
2. helped	Gram **helped** me plant a seed.
3. ask	May I **ask** for a drink?
4. planned	We **planned** to go last week.
5. drop	**Drop** the letter into the mailbox.
6. called	Pete **called** his mom.
7. help	Will you **help** me with this homework?
8. dropped	Katie **dropped** the ball.
9. plan	Who will **plan** the trip?
10. asked	Jane **asked** for two new T-shirts.

High-Frequency Words

11. again	May we march around the room **again**?
12. soon	We'll eat very **soon**.

Small Group Time

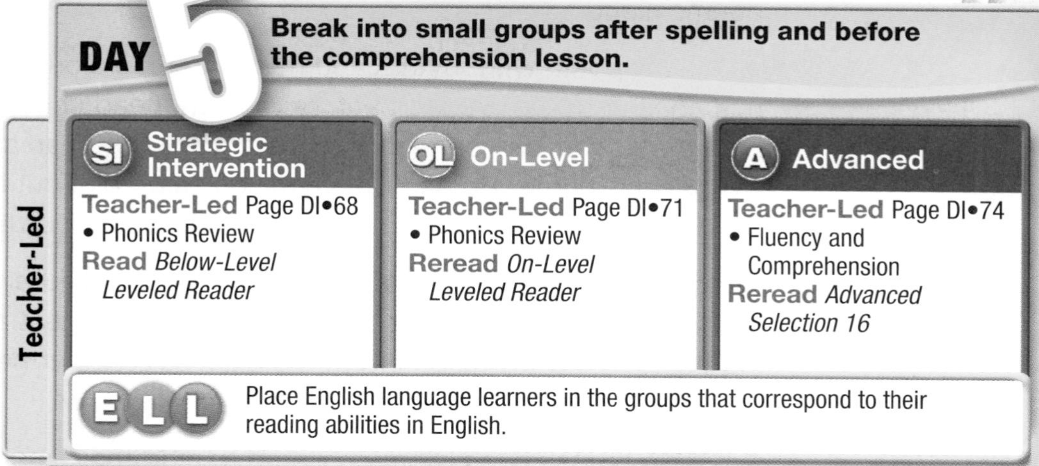
DAY 5 **Break into small groups after spelling and before the comprehension lesson.**

Teacher-Led

SI Strategic Intervention	OL On-Level	A Advanced
Teacher-Led Page DI•68 • Phonics Review **Read** *Below-Level Leveled Reader*	**Teacher-Led** Page DI•71 • Phonics Review **Reread** *On-Level Leveled Reader*	**Teacher-Led** Page DI•74 • Fluency and Comprehension **Reread** *Advanced Selection 16*

ELL Place English language learners in the groups that correspond to their reading abilities in English.

Practice Stations
- Words to Know
- Read for Meaning

Independent Activities
- Read independently/Reading Log on *Reader's and Writer's Notebook* p. RR4
- Concept Talk Video

Differentiated Instruction

SI Strategic Intervention

Review Base Words and *-ed* Before testing, review that when *-ed* is added to a base word, sometimes you hear /ed/, as in *patted*, but other times you hear only /d/ as in *called* or /t/ as in *asked*. Have children orally add *-ed* to *help, plan,* and *drop* and say which sound they hear. Remind them to spell the ending *ed* even when they can only hear /d/ or /t/.

Advanced

Extend Spelling If children easily spelled the words correctly on the test, dictate sentences containing two or three of the words each. For example: Mom *called* and *asked* me to *help* her. Have children write the complete sentences.

English Language Learners

Spelling Dictation Be sure to pronounce the *-ed* ending words clearly so that English learners can discern the difference between each base word and its inflected form.

DAY 5 Wrap Up your Week

40–45 min.

Objectives

- Recite poetry, paying attention to the pattern of words and speaking with expression.
- Listen attentively.
- Read aloud fluently with expression and intonation.
- Alphabetize words to the first letter.
- Use a glossary to find definitions.

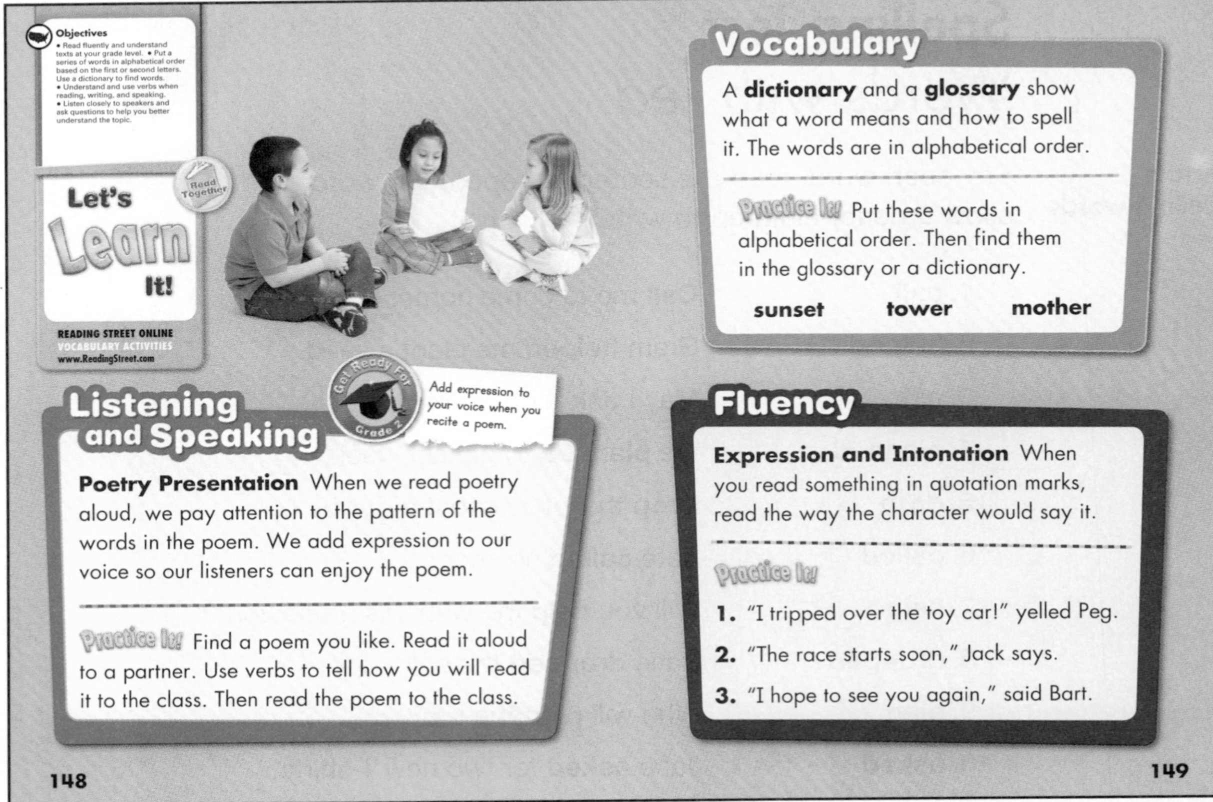

Objectives

- Read fluently and understand texts at your grade level.
- Put a series of words in alphabetical order based on the first or second letters. Use a dictionary to find words.
- Understand and use verbs when reading, writing, and speaking.
- Listen closely to speakers and ask questions to help you better understand the topic.

Let's Learn It! Read Together

READING STREET ONLINE
VOCABULARY ACTIVITIES
www.ReadingStreet.com

Vocabulary

A **dictionary** and a **glossary** show what a word means and how to spell it. The words are in alphabetical order.

Practice It! Put these words in alphabetical order. Then find them in the glossary or a dictionary.

sunset **tower** **mother**

Listening and Speaking

Get Ready For Grade 2 — Add expression to your voice when you recite a poem.

Poetry Presentation When we read poetry aloud, we pay attention to the pattern of the words in the poem. We add expression to our voice so our listeners can enjoy the poem.

Practice It! Find a poem you like. Read it aloud to a partner. Use verbs to tell how you will read it to the class. Then read the poem to the class.

Fluency

Expression and Intonation When you read something in quotation marks, read the way the character would say it.

Practice It!

1. "I tripped over the toy car!" yelled Peg.
2. "The race starts soon," Jack says.
3. "I hope to see you again," said Bart.

148 149

Student Edition pp. 148–149

Listening and Speaking

Poetry Presentation

Teach Have children turn to page 148 of the Student Edition. Explain that they will choose a poem to read. Remind children that good speakers pay attention to the pattern of words when they read poems aloud.

Analyze model Choose a poem with rhythm and rhyme to read aloud together. In this poem, you can hear a beat, or **rhythm**. Lead children in clapping the rhythm as you read the poem again. You can also hear words that **rhyme**. Reread the rhyming lines. Point out the words that rhyme. Reread the next rhyming lines. Which words rhyme?

Introduce prompt Read the Practice It! prompt with the class. Tell children to read their poem quietly to themselves, tapping out the beat and finding the rhyming words before they read it to their partner. Remind partners to listen attentively.

Team Talk Ask two or three children to read their poem aloud. Have the class listen carefully for rhythmic patterns and tap them out. Also, have children listen for rhyming words as the other children read.

Vocabulary
Dictionary/Glossary

Teach Read and discuss the Vocabulary lesson on page 149 of the Student Edition. Demonstrate how to look up the word *precious* in the glossary on p. 222.

Model A dictionary or glossary can help you spell words and learn their meanings. I'm going to look up *precious* in our glossary. What's the first letter in *precious*? *P. P* comes after *a, b, c, d, e, f, g, h, i, j, k, l, m, n* and *o.* So I open the glossary and turn past the words that begin with those letters until I come to the *p* words. And there I find *precious*. I didn't know that *precious* was spelled like that. The *ci* makes the same sound of *sh* as in *shoes.*

Guide practice Read the instructions for the Vocabulary Practice It! Activity. Read the three words aloud and then have children read them with you.

To put these words in alphabetical order, I look at the first letter of each word. *M* comes before *s* and *t* in the alphabet, so *mother* goes first.

On their own Have children alphabetize the rest of the words with a partner. Then have partners look up each word in the glossary and take turns reading the definition aloud.

Corrective feedback Circulate around the room and observe as children look up the words and read the definitions. Provide assistance as needed.

Fluency
Expression and Intonation

Teach Read and discuss the Fluency instructions.

Read words in context Give children a moment to look at the sentences. Then have them read each sentence three or four times until they can read the quotations with good expression and intonation.

Differentiated Instruction

 **Advanced**

If children demonstrate proficiency in alphabetizing words to the first letter, tell them that when the first two letters are the same, they need to look at the second letter. Have them alphabetize these words and then look them up in their glossary: *spring, brown, beautiful, shiver, butterfly.*

Poetry Presentation

In addition to using expression and paying attention to the pattern of words when reciting poetry, children at Grade 2 should be able to change their volume and rate to fit the mood of the poem, and to look at the audience from time to time when reading.

English Language Learners

Poetry Presentation For the Practice It! activity, provide an assortment of short, simple poems containing concrete language for children to choose from. Read the poems aloud, using gestures, pantomime, and illustrations if available to make the meaning clear.

DAY 5 Wrap Up your Week

Objectives

- ◎ Determine the author's purpose based on textual evidence.
- Review high-frequency and story words.
- Identify the features of a how-to article.

Comprehension

Author's Purpose

Review Author's purpose

Remember that good readers figure out whether an author's purpose is to entertain them with something funny or exciting, or to inform them with facts. Have children identify the purpose of books in the classroom.

To check understanding of author's purpose, read aloud the following story paragraph and have children answer the questions that follow.

> Milly McGill was an amazing gardener. She didn't just grow flowers and vegetables. If she broke a china plate, she scattered the pieces in her garden, and in a few weeks, not just one plate but a whole new set would spring up. If she lost a button from her sweater, she pulled off another one and planted it. Soon she had a bush full of matching buttons.

1. Did the author write this story to entertain or to inform? How can you tell? (to entertain; the events are funny and could not really happen)
2. Suppose the author wanted to inform readers about planting a real garden. What are some things she might have written? (She might have explained how to grow a garden by planting seeds in a sunny place, watering them, weeding, and building a fence to keep animals out.)

Vocabulary

High Frequency and Story Words

Review High-frequency words

Review this week's high-frequency words: *few, afraid, read, soon, how,* and *again*. Use one of the words in a sentence about one of the stories the class read this week. For example: Jack climbed up the beanstalk again.

Team Talk Have partners write the words on cards. Have them take turns picking a card and using the word in a sentence about one of the week's stories.

Review Story words

Write the words *ground, head, rain, shouted,* and *shouting*. Read them aloud together. Then have children tell what each word means.

Corrective feedback

If... children cannot tell what the story words mean,
then...review the definitions on page 126a.

Procedural Text
How-to Article

Review Genre Review with children that a **how-to article** tells the reader how to make or do something, giving step-by-step instructions. Sometimes the steps are numbered. Often, pictures help explain what to do.

Teach Have children turn to pages 146–147 in the Student Edition. This is a how-to article. The title, "Growing Plants," tells readers what they will learn how to do. The numbered sentences tell what steps to follow and in what order. In this article, there is also a numbered picture that goes with each step and helps explain how to do it.

Model Think Aloud Suppose I want to use this how-to article to grow my own plant. First, I would read the whole article and look carefully at the pictures to make sure I understand what things I need and what steps I must follow. Then I would gather together all the things I need. Finally, I would reread each step and follow it in the right order.

Guide practice Read the article aloud with children. Point out the picture that goes with each step and discuss what it shows. Then ask the following questions.

- If we wanted to follow these directions, what things would we need to have ready? (Possible response: seeds, a sunny place to plant them, soil, water)
- What would our first step be? Our last step? (Possible response: The first step would be to plant seeds. The last step would be to water them often.)

On their own Why do you think it's important to read a how-to article carefully? (Possible response: If you don't read it carefully, you might not have all the things you need, or you might skip a step and accidently spoil what you are trying to do.)

Differentiated Instruction

SI Strategic Intervention
If children have difficulty explaining why it's important to read a how-to article carefully, scaffold the questioning. For example: What would happen if I didn't read step 3? (The seeds wouldn't grow because they need water. Suppose I was using a how-to article to make pancakes, but I didn't read the step that said to add salt? (The pancakes wouldn't taste right.)

Academic Vocabulary

how-to article an article that gives step-by-step instructions in how to make or do something

English Language Learners
Visual Support After reading each step, point out the corresponding picture and repeat the main word that the picture illustrates (*seeds, sun, water*). Then act out the step.

Wrap Up your Week

Assess

- Adding Endings: Double Final Consonant
- Vowel: *r*-Controlled *ar*
- High-Frequency Words
- Fluency: WCPM
- Author's Purpose

Fluency Goals

Set individual fluency goals for children to enable them to reach the end-of-year goal.

- Current Goal: 25-35 WCPM
- End-of-Year Goal: 60 WCPM

Assessment
Monitor Progress

For a written assessment for adding endings *-ed* and *-ing* with double final consonants, *r*-Controlled *ar,* high-frequency words, and author's purpose, use Weekly Test 16, pages 127–132.

Assess words in context

Sentence reading Use the following reproducible page to assess children's ability to read words in context. Call on children to read two sentences aloud. Start over with sentence one if necessary.

MONITOR PROGRESS **Sentence Reading**

If... children have trouble reading words with endings and double final consonants and words with *r*-Controlled *ar,*
then... use the Reteach Lessons on pp. 215–216 of *First Stop.*

If... children cannot read all the high-frequency words,
then... mark the missed words on a high-frequency word list and have the child practice reading the words with a fluent reader.

Assess

Fluency Take a one-minute sample of children's oral reading. Have children read the fluency passage on page 149f.

Comprehension Have the child read the entire passage. If the child has difficulty with the passage, you may read it aloud. Then have the child identify the author's purpose.

MONITOR PROGRESS **Fluency and Comprehension**

If... a child does not achieve the fluency goal on the timed reading,
then... copy the passage and send it home with the child for additional fluency practice, or have the child practice with a fluent reader.

If... a child cannot understand author's purpose,
then... use the Reteach Lesson on p. 253 of *First Stop.*

Monitor accuracy

Record scores Have children monitor their accuracy by recording their scores using the Sentence Reading Chart and by recording the number of words read correctly per minute on the Fluency Progress Chart in *First Stop.*

Name ______________________________

Read the Sentences

1. Kim dropped a few cards.

2. Soon Bill jogged to the barn.

3. Meg is getting to be afraid in this dark cave.

4. How well is Mark hitting the ball?

5. Luke napped as Jack read in the yard.

6. We met Liz running in this park at lunch time again.

7. We will read the beginning part.

MONITOR PROGRESS

- Fluency
- Adding Endings
- *r*-Controlled *ar*
- High-frequency Words

Name ____________________

Read the Story

How to Fix Up a Yard

Try these five ways to make a yard nice. 9
One way is by planting plenty of trees. Trees make 19
spots of shade, so you can rest if the sun is hot. Pine 32
trees have a nice fresh smell. 38
Make flower beds in lots of places. I planted pink 48
and red roses on all sides of my yard. Roses smell so 60
sweet! 61
Be wise and cut the grass as it starts to get tall, or it 75
will soon look messy. Cutting it again in a week or so 87
will keep it short. 91
Get rid of weeds! Weeds grow fast in summer and 101
make a yard look bad. It can be hard to dig them up, 114
but you will be glad you did. 121
Did you do all these jobs? Then it is time for the last 134
task. Set a bench under a tree so you can sit and chat 147
with pals. That is the best part of keeping a fine yard! 159

MONITOR PROGRESS

- Check Fluency
- Author's Purpose

Objectives

- Use past- and future-tense verbs correctly in reading, writing, and speaking.

Conventions
Verbs for Past and for Future

Review Remind children that a verb with the ending *-ed* tells about the past, and that a verb with the helping verb *will* tells about the future. Have them form the past and future tense of these verbs: *bark, stop, push.*

Guide practice Write the following sentence frames and verbs. Have children write the correct past or future form of the verb.

1. Next week Ken ________ my bike. (fix)
2. Last summer Mom ________ corn. (plant)
3. Tomorrow Jane ________ this job. (finish)
4. Three days ago we ________ at that store. (shop)

Connect to oral language Have children use the sentence starters below to make up oral sentences using the correct form of these verbs: *start, play, call, work.*

Yesterday I ________.
Tomorrow I ________.

On their own Use Let's Practice It! p. 151 on the *Teacher Resource DVD-ROM.*

Let's Practice It!
TR DVD•151

Daily Fix-It

9. he planted the seds.
He planted the seeds.

10. Jan and I waters the garden
Jan and I water the garden.

Discuss the Daily Fix-It corrections with children. Review capitalization and punctuation of sentences, /ē/ spelled *ee*, and subject-verb agreement.

30–35 min.

Objectives

- Edit a draft for spelling, punctuation, and capitalization.
- Create final draft and present.

Writing—Lists
Writer's Craft: Verbs for Past and Future

Review Revising Remind children that yesterday they revised their lists. They may have deleted a word that didn't make sense or didn't help. Today they will proofread their lists.

MINI-LESSON

Proofread for Verbs

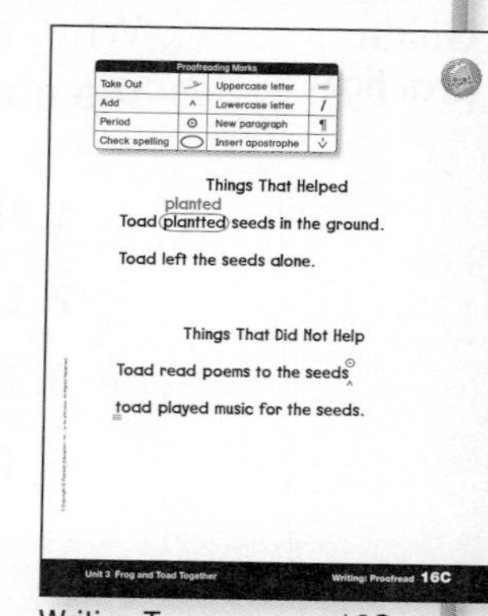
Writing Transparency 16C
TR DVD

- **Teach** Mistakes in spelling, punctuation, and capitalization make it hard for readers to understand what we mean. When we edit, we correct these kinds of mistakes. This will help readers understand us. It will make our writing fun and easy to read.
- **Model** Let's look at my lists about Toad. Display Writing Transparency 16C. Explain that you will look at the verbs for the past and the future. In my first sentence, the verb for the past, *planted,* doesn't look right. I think I added an extra *t.* Show how you would delete the extra *t.* Continue with the editing process. Model how you would change a letter at the beginning of a sentence if it were not capitalized, or add a period if one were missing at the end of a sentence.

Proofread Display the Proofreading Tips or your own rubric for editing. Have children proofread their lists to correct any misspellings, missing capital letters, or errors with periods. Circulate to assist children with verbs for the past and future.

Proofreading Tips

- ✓ Are my verbs spelled correctly? Check a dictionary.
- ✓ Did I use the right verbs for the past and for the future?
- ✓ Do my sentences begin with a capital letter?
- ✓ Did I use periods correctly?

Present

Have children make a final draft of their lists, with their revisions and proofreading corrections. Help as appropriate.

Choose an option for children to present their lists.

Illustrate their lists and post them in the classroom	Combine their lists to make one long class list

When they have finished, help them complete a Self-Evaluation form.

ROUTINE **Quick Write for Fluency** Team Talk

1. **Talk** Have partners take one minute to find a past or future verb in their lists.
2. **Write** Each child writes a new short sentence using one of the verbs.
3. **Share** Partners trade sentences and read them aloud.

Routines Flip Chart

Teacher Note

Self-Evaluation Make copies of the Self-Evaluation form from the Teacher Resource DVD-ROM, and hand them out to children.

English Language Learners

Support Editing Review the spelling rules for forming verbs with *–ed.* Remind children that they do not always need to double the final consonant before adding *–ed.*

Objectives

- Review concept: the changes that happen in a garden.
- Organize information.
- Present results of a research project.

Research and Inquiry
Communicate

Teach

Tell children that they will use their research notes to create a poster showing a diagram of a plant. Remind children that they have learned about the parts of different kinds of plants by looking at diagrams, drawing sketches, and taking notes. They have also narrowed their topic to one kind of plant.

Model

Think Aloud — Demonstrate making a diagram of a rose. To make a diagram of a rose, I'll start with a clean sheet of poster paper. At the top I'll write the title, Rose. Next, I'll draw the flower with all its parts. The research notes I wrote remind me that a rose has a stem with thorns, flowers, leaves, and buds. Now I'll add labels. I'll draw an arrow from each label to the part it names.

Guide practice

Review children's topic choices and notes. Work with them to draw and label the plant they have chosen.

On their own

Divide children into small groups. If possible, group children whose diagrams show different plants. Then instruct them to pretend to be biologists and explain their diagrams to the group, pointing out the different parts of the plants. Remind them how to be good speakers and listeners:

- Good speakers pronounce their words clearly and speak loudly enough to be heard.
- Good listeners pay attention to the speaker. When the speaker is finished, they politely ask questions about anything they don't understand.

Wrap Up Your Week!

Amazing Words

You've learned 008 words this week!

You've learned 175 words this year!

Question of the Week
What changes happen in a garden?

Think Aloud This week we explored the changes that gardeners observe as their seeds sprout and the small new plants develop leaves and blossoms. In the story *Frog and Toad Together*, we saw that Toad had to wait many days for his seeds to sprout. The selection "Growing Plants" gave us step-by-step instructions in how to start a garden. In both selections, we learned that plants need soil, water, sunshine, and time to grow. Have children recall their Amazing Ideas about gardens. Then have children use these ideas to help them demonstrate their understanding of the Question of the Week.

ELL

English Language Learners

Poster Preview Prepare children for next week by using Week 5, ELL Poster 17. Read the Poster Talk-Through to introduce the concept and vocabulary. Ask children to identify and describe objects and actions in the art.

Selection Summary Send home the summary of *I'm a Caterpillar* in English and the child's home language if available. Children can read the summary with family members.

Preview NEXT WEEK

Tell children that next week they will read about the amazing changes that happen to some animals in nature.

Assessment Checkpoints for the Week

Weekly Assessment

Use pp. 127–132 of *Weekly Tests* to check:

- ✔ **Phonics** Adding Endings
- ✔ **Phonics** Vowel: *r*-Controlled *ar*
- ✔ **Comprehension Skill** Author's Purpose
- ✔ **High-Frequency Words**

afraid	how
again	read
few	soon

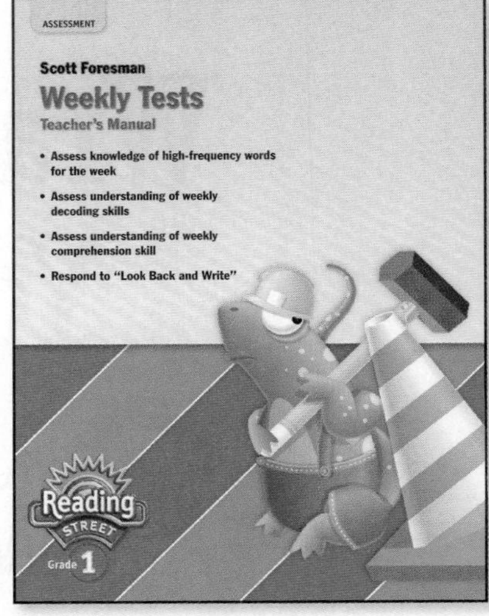

Weekly Tests

Differentiated Assessment

Advanced

On-Level

Strategic Intervention

Use pp.127–132 of *Fresh Reads for Fluency and Comprehension* to check:

- ✔ **Comprehension Skill** Author's Purpose
- ✔ Review **Comprehension Skill** Plot
- ✔ **Fluency** Words Correct Per Minute

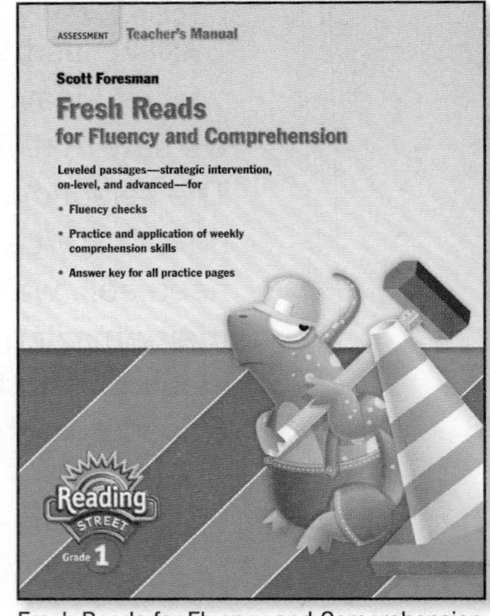

Fresh Reads for Fluency and Comprehension

Managing Assessment

Use *Assessment Handbook* for:

- ✔ **Weekly Assessment Blackline Masters for Monitoring Progress**
- ✔ **Observation Checklists**
- ✔ **Record-Keeping Forms**
- ✔ **Portfolio Assessments**

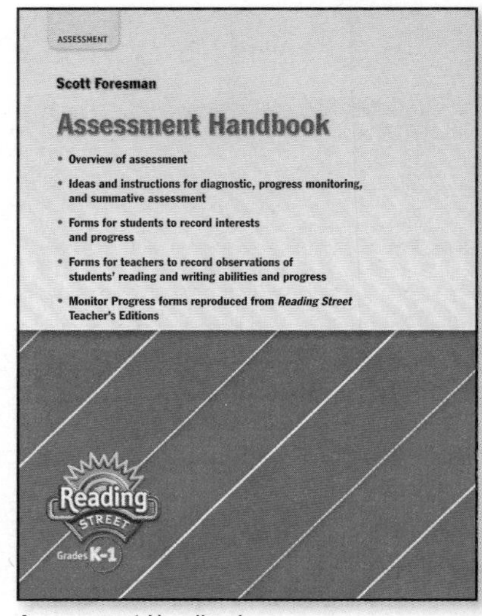

Assessment Handbook

Whipped and Flipped

What are clouds? Clouds are made up of drops of water and bits of ice. When there is a lot of water in a cloud, the water will fall. It may fall as rain or snow.

Have you ever spotted shapes in clouds? One cloud might look like a rabbit hopping. Another might look like a tiger running.

Have you stopped to look at clouds for another reason? They can tell you about the weather. Some clouds mean a nice day. Some mean rain or snow.

One type of cloud is high and thin. Imagine that a giant dipped a paintbrush in white paint. He dragged the brush across the sky. These clouds look like those streaks. They mean weather will change soon.

Here is another type of cloud. Imagine that a cook whipped cream. She flipped the fluffy white puffs into the sky. If you see these clouds in warm weather, it might rain.

Some clouds come near the ground. This is fog. When you walk in fog, you feel as if you are wrapped in a damp blanket.

Look up at the sky. What type of clouds can you see today?

Advanced Selection 16 **Vocabulary:** streaks, whipped

Pacing Small Group Instruction

5 Day Plan

DAY 1	• Phonemic Awareness/ Phonics • Decodable Reader
DAY 2	• Phonemic Awareness/ Phonics • Decodable Reader
DAY 3	• Phonemic Awareness/ Phonics • Leveled Reader
DAY 4	• High-Frequency Words • Decodable Reader
DAY 5	• Phonics Review • Leveled Reader

3 or 4 Day Plan

DAY 1	• Phonemic Awareness/ Phonics • Decodable Reader
DAY 2	• Phonemic Awareness/ Phonics • Decodable Reader
DAY 3	• Phonemic Awareness/ Phonics • Leveled Reader
DAY 4	• High-Frequency Words • Decodable Reader

3 Day Plan: Eliminate the shaded box.

SI Strategic Intervention — DAY 1

Phonemic Awareness • Phonics

■ **Segment and Blend Phonemes** Reteach pp. 120–121 of the Teacher's Edition. Model segmenting and blending these words. Then have children practice segmenting and blending on their own.

landed /l/ /a/ n/ /d/ /ə/ /d/	**hugging** /h/ /u/ /g/ /i/ /ng/
batted /b/ /a/ t/ /ə/ /d/	**drinking** /d/ /r/ /i/ /nk/ /i/ /ng/

■ **Adding Endings** Reteach p. 121a of the Teacher's Edition. Then write the words below. Have children read the words, identify the endings, and frame the base words. If children have difficulty reading a base word, have them cover the added consonant and the ending to blend the base word.

sipping	**quitting**	**winning**	**flipped**	**sunning**	**gripped**
tapped	**hopped**	**begged**	**stepping**	**rubbing**	**clapped**

Decodable Practice Reader 16A

■ **Review** Review words with *-ed* and *-ing* endings and the high-frequency words *do, you, could, was, a, good, people, into, look*. Then have children blend and read these words from the story: *while, frog, when, flopped, jogged, mopped*.

> **If...** children have difficulty with any of these words,
> **then...** reteach the word by modeling. Have children practice the words, with feedback from you, until they can read them independently.

Have children reread the text orally. To achieve optimal fluency, children should reread the text three or four times.

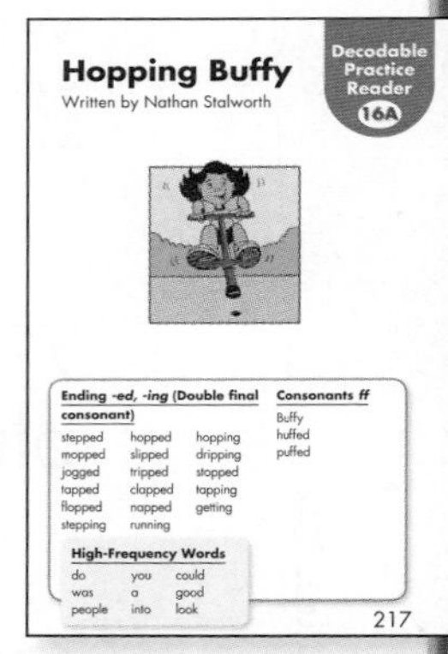

Decodable Practice Reader 16A

Objectives
- Read base words with inflectional endings.
- Read aloud grade-level appropriate text with fluency.

DAY 2

Phonemic Awareness • Phonics

- **Segment and Blend Phonemes** Reteach p. 124c of the Teacher's Edition. Model segmenting and blending these words. Then have children practice segmenting and blending on their own.

chart /ch/ /är/ /t/ **hard** /h/ /är/ /d/ **sharp** /sh/ /är/ /p/

- ***r*-Controlled *ar*** Reteach p. 124d of the Teacher's Edition. Then have children spell *bar* using letter tiles. Monitor their work.

- Add *n* to the end of *bar*. What is the new word? b a r n
- Change the *n* in *barn* to *k*. What is the new word? b a r k
- Change the *b* in *bark* to *d*. What is the new word? d a r k

Decodable Practice Reader 16B

- **Review** Review words with *r*-controlled *ar* and the high-frequency words *to, they, live, a, the, very, could, look, every, have*. Then have children blend and read these words from the story: *chicks, honks, shines, sheep, corn, Frank*.

  If... children have difficulty with any of these words, **then...** reteach the word by modeling. Have children practice the words, with feedback from you, until they can read them independently.

Have children reread the text orally. To achieve optimal fluency, children should reread the text three or four times.

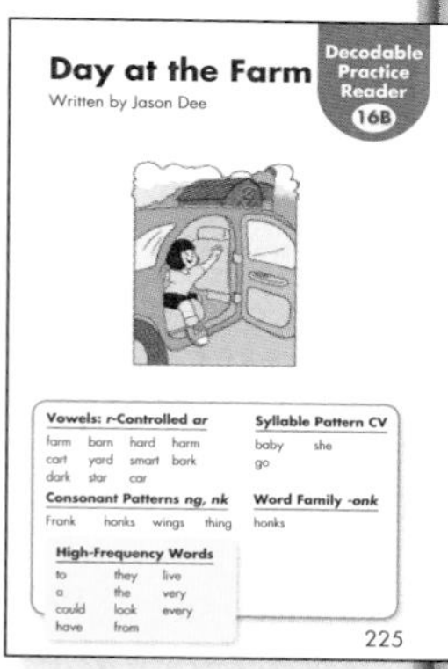

Decodable Practice Reader 16B

More Reading

Use Leveled Readers or other text at children's instructional level to develop fluency.

Objectives

- Use common syllabication patterns to decode words, including: *r*-controlled vowel sounds, including *ar*.
- Read aloud grade-level appropriate text with fluency.

Phonemic Awareness • Phonics

Add Phonemes Model adding a sound to the end of a word to make a new word. Say the word *far* and have children repeat it. Now listen as I add the sound /m/ to the end of *far*: *far* /m/. What is the new word? (farm)

Have children add the final sound shown to each word below to make a new word.

car /d/ **card**	are /k/ **ark**	star /t/ **start**

- **Adding Endings and *r*-Controlled *ar*** Reteach p. 142e of the Teacher's Edition. Have children blend and read these additional words to help them practice the target phonics skills.

running	**park**	**getting**	**sharp**	**tapped**	**yard**	**flopping**

For a complete literacy instructional plan and additional practice with this week's target skills and strategies, see the **Leveled Reader Teaching Guide.**

Concept Literacy Leveled Reader

- **Preview and Predict** Read the title and the author's name. Have children look at the cover and ask them to describe what they see. Help children activate their prior knowledge by asking them to look through the selection and to use the photos to predict things that might take place.
- **Set a Purpose** Remind children that setting a purpose for reading can help them better understand what they read. Guide children to pay attention to the changes that happen to seeds and plants.
- **Read** Provide corrective feedback as children read the selection orally. During reading, ask them if they were able to confirm any of the predictions they made prior to reading.

If... children have difficulty reading the selection individually,
then... read a sentence aloud as children point to each word. Then have the group reread the sentences as they continue pointing. Continue reading in this way until children read individually.

- **Retell** Have children take turns retelling the selection. To help them recall the kinds of changes that happen to plants, point to each page and ask, What kind of plant do we see here? How has it changed in the second picture?

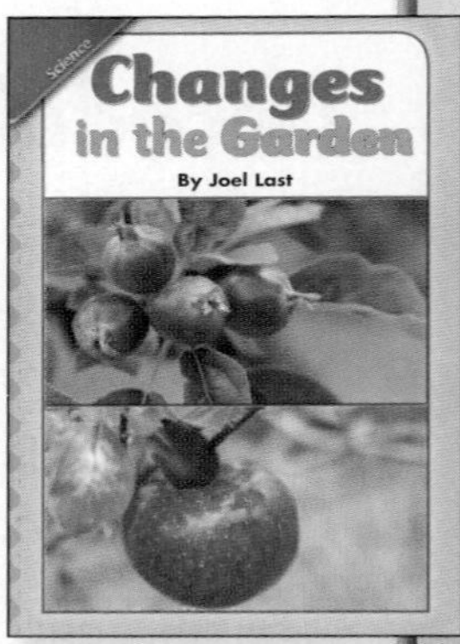

Concept Literacy

Objectives
- Use common syllabication patterns to decode words, including: *r*-controlled vowel sounds, including *ar*.
- Read words with inflectional endings.

eReaders 

High-Frequency Words

- **Review** Write *few, afraid, read, soon, how, again* on the board. Model saying each word. Then have children read each word, spell each word as you point to each letter, and have them say each word again. Allow time for children to practice reading these high-frequency words using the word cards.

Decodable Practice Reader 16C

- **Review** Use the word lists to review words with *-ed*, *-ing* endings and *r*-controlled *ar*. Remind children that in many words ending with CVC, the final consonant is doubled before adding an ending. Also be sure they understand that the letters *ar* often spell the sound /är/. Then have children blend and read the two different groups of words.

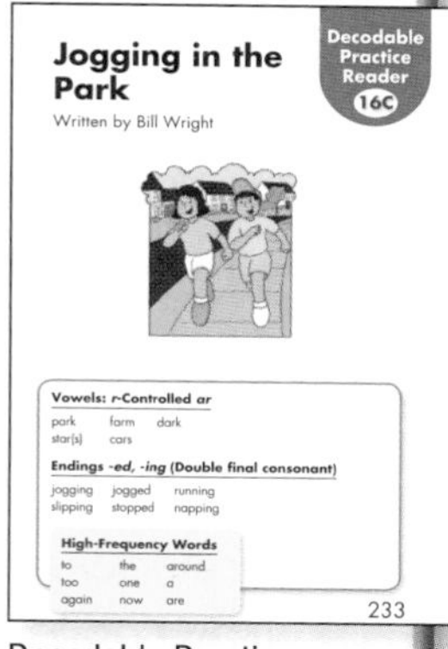

Decodable Practice Reader 16C

If... children have difficulty reading the story individually, **then...** read a sentence aloud as children point to each word. Then have the group reread the sentences as they continue pointing. Continue reading in this way until children read individually.

Check comprehension by having children retell the story including the characters, plot, and setting. Have children locate words in the story with *-ed*, *-ing* endings and *r*-controlled *ar*. List the words children identify. Then have children sort the words in a chart with columns labeled *ar*, *-ed*, and *-ing*.

ar	-ed	-ing
park	jogged	jogging
farm	stopped	running
dark		slipping
stars		napping
star		
cars		

More Reading

Use Leveled Readers or other text at children's instructional level.

Objectives

- Use common syllabication patterns to decode words, including: *r*-controlled vowel sounds, including *ar*.
- Read at least 100 high-frequency words from a commonly used list.

More Reading

Use Leveled Readers or other text at children's instructional level.

Phonics Review

- **Adding Endings and *r*-Controlled *ar*** Write these sentences on the board. Have children read them aloud as you track the print. Then call on individuals to blend and read the underlined words.

We jogged past the barn.

Dad was clapping as my band marched.

I hit my arm on a sharp stick.

The hard part is winning the game.

For a complete literacy instructional plan and additional practice with this week's target skills and strategies, see the **Leveled Reader Teaching Guide.**

Below-Level Leveled Reader

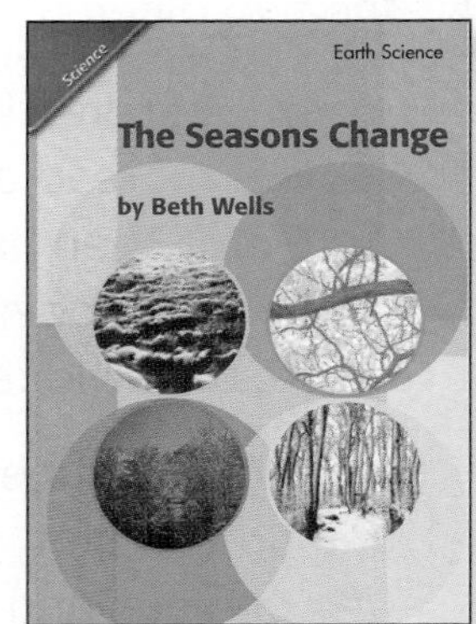

Below-Level Reader

Preview and Predict Read the title and the author's name. Have children look at the cover and ask them to describe what they see. Help children activate their prior knowledge by asking them to look through the selection and to use the photos to predict things that might take place.

- **Set a Purpose** Remind children that setting a purpose for reading can help them better understand what they read. Tell children to read to find out what changes happen outside as each new season arrives.
- **Read** Provide corrective feedback as children read the selection orally. During reading, ask them if they were able to confirm any of the predictions they made prior to reading.

  If... children have difficulty reading the selection individually,
  then... read each sentence aloud as children point to each word. Then have the group reread the sentences as they continue pointing.

- **Author's Purpose** Ask children to tell what they think the author wanted them to learn from this selection.

Objectives

- Make inferences about text.
- Establish purpose for reading selected texts.

DAY 1

Phonics • Spelling

- **Adding Endings** Write the following words on the board and have children practice reading words with endings *-ed* and *-ing*.

  flipping **chatted** **dragging** **hummed**

  Then have children identify the base word and the consonant that was doubled before adding the ending.

- **Words with *-ed*** Remind children that some of the spelling words have the ending *-ed*. Clarify the pronunciation and meaning of each word. For example, say: If you have *planned* something, you have decided how you will do it. Ask children whether the final consonant of the base word was doubled before adding the ending in these words: *planned, helped, dropped, called, asked.*

Objectives
- Read words with inflectional endings.
- Spell base words with inflectional endings.

OL On-Level

DAY 2

Phonics • High-Frequency Words

- ***r*-Controlled *ar*** Write the following words on the board and have children practice reading words with the /är/ sound.

  arch **Clark** **yard** **smart**

  Then have children identify the letters that spell the /är/ sound.

- **High-Frequency Words** Hold up this week's High-Frequency Word Cards *(afraid, again, few, how, read, soon)* and review proper pronunciation. Continue holding the cards and have children chorally read each word. To help children demonstrate their understanding of the words, provide them with oral sentence frames such as: I know ___ to swim. (how)

High-Frequency Word Cards for Grade 1

Objectives
- Use common syllabication patterns to decode words, including: *r*-controlled vowel sounds, including *ar*.
- Identify at least 100 high-frequency words from a commonly used list.

Pacing Small Group Instruction

20–30 min.

5 Day Plan

DAY 1	• Phonics • Spelling • Decodable Reader
DAY 2	• Phonics • High-Frequency Words • Decodable Reader
DAY 3	• Leveled Reader
DAY 4	• Conventions • Main Selection
DAY 5	• Phonics Review • Leveled Reader

3 or 4 Day Plan

DAY 1	• Phonics • Spelling • Decodable Reader
DAY 2	• Phonics • High-Frequency Words • Decodable Reader
DAY 3	• Leveled Reader
DAY 4	• Conventions • Main Selection

3 Day Plan: Eliminate the shaded box.

Decodable Practice Readers

For a complete literacy instructional plan and additional practice with this week's target skills and strategies, see the **Leveled Reader Teaching Guide.**

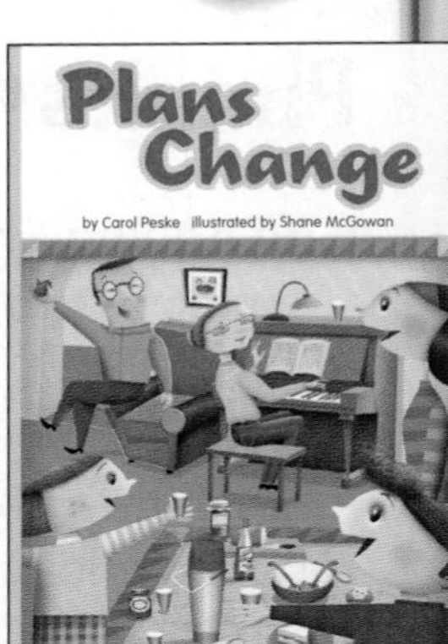

On-Level

On-Level Leveled Reader

- **Preview and Predict** Read the title and the names of the author and illustrator. Have children look at the cover and ask them to describe in detail what they see. Help children preview the selection by looking through the story and using the pictures to predict things that might take place.
- **Author's Purpose** Before reading, remind children that setting a purpose for reading can help them better understand a story. As children begin reading, tell them to think about the author's purpose. What does the author want us to learn about what we can do when we have to change our plans?
- **Read** During reading, monitor children's comprehension by providing higher-order thinking questions. Ask:
  - How do Mom and Dad surprise Jen and Mark?
  - What do you think the author wants us to learn from this story?

To help children gain a better understanding of the text, build upon their responses with a group discussion.

- **Visualize** Have partners take turns telling about the pictures they made in their minds to help them understand the story. Use these questions.
  - What picture did you make in your mind when you read that the family was planning a picnic?
  - What picture did you make in your mind when Mom said it would rain?
- **Text to Self** Help children make personal connections to the story. Ask:
  - Tell about a time when you had to change your plans because of the weather.

Objectives

- Monitor comprehension.
- Make inferences about text.

DAY 4

Conventions

- **Verbs for Past and for Future** Remind children that verbs can tell what happened in the past or what will happen in the future.
  - Some verbs use the ending *-ed* to tell about the past. Write *Yesterday I walked to the park*. Read the sentence aloud. Point to the *-ed* in *walked*.
  - Verbs use the helping verb *will* to tell about the future. Write *Tomorrow I will walk to the park*. Read the sentence aloud. Point to *will* in *will walk*.

Have the class complete these sentence frames orally using the correct form of the verb *visit*.

Yesterday he ____ his grandma.	**Tomorrow I _____ my friend.**
Last Monday we _____ the zoo.	**Next year we _____ Mexico.**

Objectives

- Understand and use verbs (past) in the context of reading, writing, and speaking.
- Use and understand verbs (future) in the context of reading, writing, and speaking.

More Reading

Use Leveled Readers or other text at children's instructional level to develop fluency.

OL On-Level

DAY 5

Phonics Review

- **Adding Endings and *r*-Controlled *ar*** Have children practice blending and reading words that contain this week's target phonics skills. Write the following words on the board, and say and sound out each word with the children.

snapped	**harp**	**shark**	**plugged**	**ripping**
harm	**swimming**	**trotted**	**fanning**	**chart**

Then have children sort into separate groups the words that have *-ed*, *-ing*, or /är/ spelled *ar*.

Objectives

- Use common syllabication patterns to decode words, including: *r*-controlled vowel sounds, including *ar*.
- Read words with inflectional endings.

Small Group Time

Pacing Small Group Instruction

20–30 mins.

5 Day Plan

DAY 1	• Phonics • Advanced Selection
DAY 2	• Phonics • Comprehension • Main Selection
DAY 3	• Leveled Reader
DAY 4	• Comprehension • Paired Selection
DAY 5	• Fluency • Comprehension • Advanced Selection

3 or 4 Day Plan

DAY 1	• Phonics • Advanced Selection
DAY 2	• Phonics • Comprehension • Main Selection
DAY 3	• Leveled Reader
DAY 4	• Comprehension • Paired Selection

3 Day Plan: Eliminate the shaded box.

A Advanced — DAY 1

Phonics • Advanced Selection

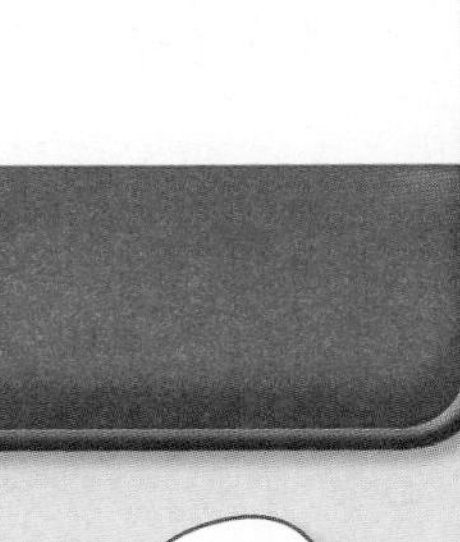

Advanced Selection 16

- **Adding Endings** Have children practice with longer words containing endings *-ed* and *-ing*. Discuss the meaning of unfamiliar words. Have children write the words and identify the base word, the ending, and the doubled final consonant. Then have them choose two or three words to use in sentences.

omitted **omitting** **occurred** **occurring**

starred **starring** **permitted** **permitting**

- **Advanced Selection 16** Before reading, have children identify these story words: *streaks* and *whipped*. Provide oral sentences with the words in context to help children determine their meaning. After reading, have children recall the two most important ideas of the story.

Objectives

- Read words with inflectional endings.

A Advanced — DAY 2

Phonics • Comprehension

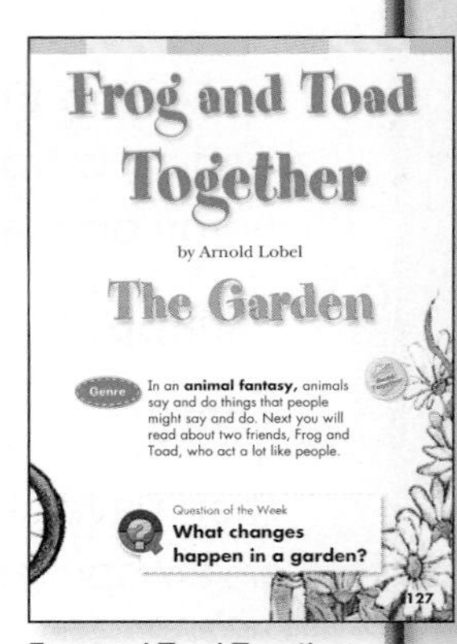

Frog and Toad Together

- ***r*-Controlled *ar*** Have children practice with longer words containing the /är/ spelled *ar*. Discuss the meaning of unfamiliar words. Have children write each word and circle the letters that spell the /är/ sound.

target **darkness** **charming** **starter**

charcoal **sparkle** **partner** **marble**

- **Comprehension** Have children silently read this week's main selection, *Frog and Toad Together*. Have them retell the story, identifying characters, setting, and sequence of events. Discuss what makes the story an animal fantasy. Point out that in real life, animals do not speak, wear clothes, plant gardens, read, and play musical instruments.

Objectives

- Use common syllabication patterns to decode words, including: *r*-controlled vowel sounds, including *ar*.

Advanced
DAY 3

For a complete literacy instructional plan and additional practice with this week's target skills and strategies, see the **Leveled Reader Teaching Guide.**

Advanced Leveled Reader

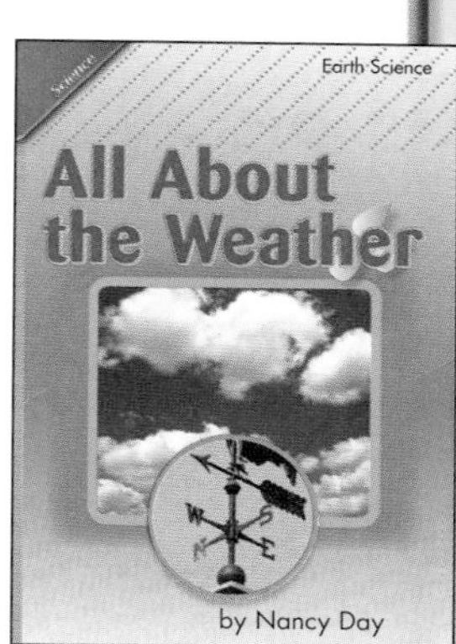

Advanced Reader

- **Activate Prior Knowledge** Read the title and the author's name. Have children look at the cover and describe in detail what they see. Remind them that the *temperature* of something is how hot or cold it is. Then activate children's prior knowledge by asking them to describe the temperature of the air outside in summer and winter.
- **Author's Purpose** Before reading, remind children that setting a purpose for reading can help them better understand what they read. Tell children to read this selection to find out what main ideas the author wants us to learn about the weather.
- **Read** During reading, monitor children's comprehension by providing higher-order thinking questions. Ask:
  - What is one main idea that the author wants us to learn in this selection?
  - Why are sayings and rhymes about the weather useful to people?

  Build on children's answers to help them gain a better understanding of the text.
- **Visualize** Have partners take turns describing the pictures they made in their minds to help them understand this selection. Use questions like these.
  - What did you picture in your mind when you read "Birds flying low, expect rain and a blow"?
  - What did you picture when you read "If a dog whines for no reason, look for a storm"?
- **Text to World** Help children make connections to the story. Ask:
  - We read that sailors need to be able to predict the weather. In what other kinds of jobs is the weather important?

Objectives
- Monitor comprehension.
- Make inferences about text.

More Reading
Use Leveled Readers or other text at children's instructional level.

More Reading

Use Leveled Readers or other text at children's instructional level.

Comprehension

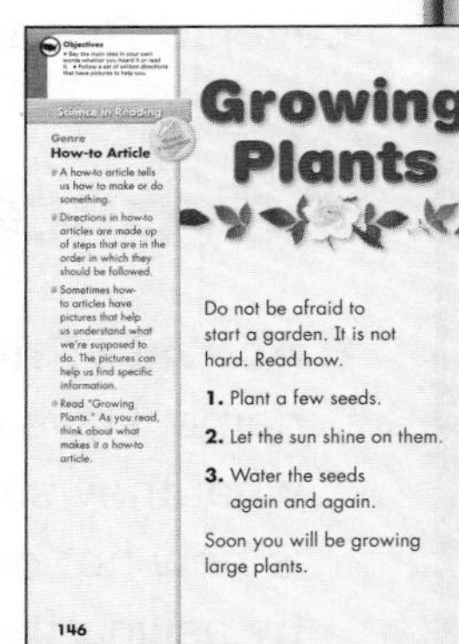

Genre
How-to Article
- A how-to article tells us how to make or do something.
- Directions in how-to articles are made up of steps that are in the order in which they should be followed.
- Sometimes how-to articles have pictures that help us understand what we're supposed to do. The pictures can help us find specific information.
- Read "Growing Plants." As you read, think about what makes it a how-to article.

Growing Plants

Do not be afraid to start a garden. It is not hard. Read how.

1. Plant a few seeds.
2. Let the sun shine on them.
3. Water the seeds again and again.

Soon you will be growing large plants.

146

Growing Plants

- **Comprehension** Have children silently read this week's paired selection, "Growing Plants." Then have them retell the steps in starting a garden.

  Talk about what makes "Growing Plants" an example of a how-to article. Be sure children understand that a how-to article explains how to make or do something, describing each step in the right order and often using pictures to help.

- **Text to World** Have children identify other activities for which people need directions. (how to play a game, how to bake cookies, how to make a puppet)

Objectives
- Follow written multi-step directions with picture cues.

Fluency • Comprehension

Whipped and Flipped

Advanced Selection 16

- **Fluency** Using the first few sentences of Advanced Selection 16, model reading with expression and intonation. Then have children read the selection to a partner as you listen to their reading. Provide corrective feedback as needed.

- **Comprehension** After they have finished reading the selection, have children summarize the selection by retelling the main ideas. Then, on the back of the selection page, have them write three sentences that tell interesting facts they learned about clouds.

Objectives
- Read aloud grade-level appropriate text with fluency (expression).

ELL English Language Learners

The ELL lessons are organized by strands. Use them to scaffold the weekly lesson curriculum or during small-group time.

Concept Development

What changes happen in a garden?

- **Activate Prior Knowledge** Write the Question of the Week and read it aloud. Underline the word *changes* and have children say it with you. The word *changes* mean that things are different than they were before. Display a picture of a new plant and a mature plant. New plants start small. How do they change as they grow? (they get bigger, they grow more leaves)
- **Connect to New Concept** Have children turn to pages 118–119 in the Student Edition. Read the title and have children track the print as you read it. Point to the pictures one at a time and use them to guide a discussion about how plants change and grow. For example, point to the flowers. What are these? (flowers) Flowers start as seeds. They grow and change into plants.
- **Develop Concepts** Show this week's Concept Talk Video and ask children to name some kinds of weather. (snowy, rainy, sunny, snowy) How does the weather change? During a second viewing, stop at appropriate places to show children different kinds of weather. Use the leveled prompts below to assess understanding and build oral language.

Beginning Ask yes/no questions, such as Do you need an umbrella when it rains? Are there warm days in the summer?

Intermediate Provide sentence frames to help children talk about the video. *On a rainy day, I see ______. On a sunny day, I see ______.*

Advanced/Advanced-High Have children answer the Question of the Week by giving specific examples from the video and from their own experiences.

- **Review Concepts and Connect to Writing** Review children's understanding of the concept at the end of the week. Ask them to write in response to these questions: How do plants change? What English words did you learn this week? Write and display key ideas from the discussion.

Objectives

- Understand the general meaning, main points, and important details of spoken language ranging from situations in which topics, language, and contexts are familiar to unfamiliar.
- Listen to and derive meaning from a variety of media such as audiotape, video, DVD, and CD ROM to build and reinforce concept and language attainment.

Content Objectives

- Describe plants and how they grow and change.

Language Objectives

- Share information orally.
- Use basic vocabulary for describing plants and gardens.

Daily Planner

DAY 1	• **Frontload Concepts** • **Preteach** Comprehension Skill, Vocabulary, Phonemic Awareness/ Phonics, Conventions/ Writing
DAY 2	• **Review** Concepts, Vocabulary, Comprehension Skill • **Frontload Main Selection** • **Practice** Phonemic Awareness/Phonics, Conventions/Writing
DAY 3	• **Review** Concepts, Comprehension Skill, Vocabulary, Conventions/ Writing • **Reread Main Selection** • **Practice** Phonemic Awareness/Phonics
DAY 4	• **Review Concepts** • **Read ELL/ELD Readers** • **Practice** Phonemic Awareness/Phonics, Conventions/Writing
DAY 5	• **Review** Concepts, Vocabulary, Comprehension Skill, Phonemic Awareness/ Phonics, Conventions/ Writing • **Reread ELL/ELD Readers**

*See the ELL Handbook for ELL Workshops with targeted instruction.

ELL Poster 16

Build concept understanding and oral vocabulary throughout the week by using the daily activities on ELL Poster 16.

Language Objectives

- Add phonemes.
- Add endings: double final consonant.

Transfer Skills

Inflected endings and spelling changes may be difficult for English language learners to master. Languages such as Chinese, Hmong, and Vietnamese do not use inflected endings. Children may need help understanding that adding *-ed* to a word indicates that the action happened in the past. They may also need help learning the rules for spelling changes.

ELL Teaching Routine

For more practice with word endings, use the Sound-by-Sound Blending Routine (*ELL Handbook*, page 493).

ELL English Language Learners

Phonemic Awareness: Add Phonemes

■ **Preteach** the sound /är/

- Have children open to pages 120–121. Point to the man's arm. What is this? (arm) We can add a sound to *arm* make a new word. Point to the barn. The people are visiting a *farm*. Say the word *farm* slowly. Listen for the first and last sounds. /f/ /är/ /m/ The first sound I hear is /f/. The last sound I hear is /m/. What sound did we add to make a new word? (/f/)
- Point to the car. What is this? (a car) Let's add /t/ to the word *car*. Say the word *cart* slowly. Listen for the first and last sounds. /k/ /är/ /t/ The last sound I hear is /t/. Which sound did we add to *car* to make a new word? (/t/) Point to the cart behind the tractor. What is the new word? (cart)
- Point to the hat and say *hat* aloud. What sounds can we add to *at* to make a new word? Have children look at the pictures for help. Write their answers on the board and pronounce them all. (Possible Answers: bat, mat, sat, cat)

■ **Practice** Have children add these phonemes to the following words: *for* /k/, *star* /t/, /s/ *it*. Have them say the original word, the additional sound, and the new word. Point to pictures on pages 120–121 for support.

Phonics: Add Endings—Double Final Consonant

■ **Preteach** Display Sound-Spelling Cards 121 and 127. This is someone swimming. The word *swimming* has the ending *-ing* added to the end of the word *swim*. Use your finger to underline *swim* and *-ing*. The letter *m* is a consonant. When we add *-ing* to a word that ends in a consonant, we double the consonant. Point to and say the word again. Then, point to the word *flipped*. The word *flip* has the ending *-ed* added to the word *flip* at the end. The letter *d* is a consonant. When we add *-ed* to a word that ends in a consonant, we double the consonant. Point to and say the word again.

■ **Listen and Write** Distribute Write and Wipe Boards. Write the words *sledding* and *hopped* on the board. Point to and read each word. Copy these words. Underline the endings *-ing* and *-ed*. Circle the final consonant. Have children repeat the words.

Objectives

- Learn relationships between sounds and letters of the English language and decode (sound out) words using a combination of skills such as recognizing sound-letter relationships and identifying cognates, affixes, roots and base words.

ELL English Language Learners

■ **Reteach and Practice** Write the following words on the board and have children read them aloud and act them out with you: *clapping, hopping, clapped, hopped*. Segment and blend each word with children. Point out the base words and the endings. Remind children that the consonant is doubled when adding *-ing* and *-ed*. Leave the words on the board, but erase the endings. Have children add *-ing* and *-ed* to each word and tell you the correct spelling. Write the correct spelling for each word as children restate the rule: double the final consonant before adding the ending. Use the word *stopped* on p. 140 of the Student Edition as an example of how to use the rule.

Beginning Have children read the words aloud and point to the endings. Ask them what happens to the final consonant when adding *-ing* or *-ed*.

Intermediate Have children read the words aloud and tell you the endings. Have them point to the final consonant and explain the rule.

Advanced/Advanced-High Have children read the words aloud, tell you the endings, and explain the rule. Then have children say and spell *sitting* and *stopped*.

Phonics: *r*-Controlled *ar*

■ **Preteach** Have children turn to Envision It! on page 124 of the Student Edition.

- The word in the picture is *artist*. What sound do you hear at the beginning of *artist*? (/är/) Say it with me: /är/. Have children repeat the word *artist*.
- Which letters in the word *artist* make the /är/ sound? (a,r)

■ **Practice** Distribute the Letter Tiles *a, r, d, k, s, t,* and *p*.

- Blend the sounds in *park* and have pairs spell *park* with their tiles. /p/ /är/ /k/.
- Take away the *p*. Spell /d/ /är/ /k/.
- Take away the *d* and the *k*. Spell /s/ /t/ /är/.
- Take away the *s*. Spell /t/ /är/.

Objectives

- Learn relationships between sounds and letters of the English language and decode (sound out) words using a combination of skills such as recognizing sound-letter relationships and identifying cognates, affixes, roots and base words.
- Spell familiar English words with increasing accuracy.

Language Objectives

- Add endings: double final consonant.
- Read words with *r*-controlled *ar*.
- Correctly spell words following a spelling rule.

Catch Up

Remind children that *r* controls how we pronounce other sounds such as *or* and *ore*.

Transfer Skills

The /r/ sound is flapped or rolled in languages such as Spanish, Polish, Farsi, and Arabic, so speakers of these languages may have difficulty pronouncing words with *r*-controlled vowels, especially in words such as *part*, when the *r* is followed by a consonant.

Practice Page

ELL Handbook page 313 provides additional practice for this week's skill.

Content Objectives

- Monitor and adjust oral comprehension.

Language Objectives

- Discuss oral passages.
- Use a graphic organizer to take notes.

ELL Teacher Tip

Have partners work together to identify the problem and solution using prompts such as *What happened to the plants? What did Carlee and her dad do to keep the rabbits out?*

ELL Workshop

As you give directions for using the graphic organizer, you might use *Follow Directions (ELL Handbook*, pages 432–433) to support children in comprehending increasingly complex spoken directions.

ELL English Language Learners

Listening Comprehension

No Rabbits

The sun was shining. Carlee was hot. She was tired. Carlee and her Dad were planting a garden. They dug in the dirt. They put seeds in the ground. They watered the seeds.

"Dad, why are we planting seeds?"

"Carlee, the seeds will grow into plants.

"What kind of plants?"

"The plants are vegetables. They are lettuce, peas, and beets. They need water to grow. They grow bigger every day."

The next day Carlee went outside. She looked at the plants. She saw nibble marks on the leaves. Something ate the leaves!

"Dad, something ate the leaves!" she yelled.

Dad laughed. "Rabbits like our garden. They ate the leaves. Let's build a fence. A fence keeps rabbits out of the garden."

The fence kept the rabbits out. The plants grew bigger and bigger.

Prepare for the Read Aloud The modified Read Aloud above prepares children for listening to the oral reading "Carlee's Garden" on page 123b.

- **First Listening: Listen to Understand** Write the title of the Read Aloud on the board. Have you ever planted a garden? Did animals eat the plants in the garden? I am going to read a story about someone who plants a garden and something that eats the plants. What do you think might eat the plants in the garden? Listen to find out what eats the plants. After reading, ask children to recall the names of the characters and the events. Who plants a garden? (Carlee and her dad) What eats the plants? (rabbits) How do Carlee and her dad keep the rabbits out? (They build a fence.)
- **Second Listening: Listen to Check Understanding** Using the Problem and Solution graphic organizer (*ELL Handbook*, page 513), work with children to identify the problem and the solution in the story. Ask questions to prompt answers as you fill in the graphic organizer.

Objectives

- Demonstrate listening comprehension of increasingly complex spoken English by following directions, retelling or summarizing spoken messages, responding to questions and requests, collaborating with peers, and taking notes commensurate with content and grade-level needs.

ELL English Language Learners

High-Frequency Words

- **Preteach** Distribute copies of this week's Word Cards (*ELL Handbook*, p. 155). Have children point to or hold up the corresponding card when you say a word in a sentence or make a gesture. When appropriate, use opposites to reinforce meaning.
  - If you are scared, you are *afraid*. Show a look of fear on your face. *afraid*
  - Open a book and *read* a sentence aloud. I can *read* a book.
  - *Soon* means in a short time. Point to a watch or clock. It will be lunchtime *soon*.
  - *Again* tells about something that happens one more time. Turn in a circle. I turned around. Turn again. I turned *again*.
  - Put your hand up to your head, measuring your height. *How* tall am I?
  - If you have *few* of something, you do not have many. Hold two pencils in your hand. I have a *few* pencils.
- **Practice** Briefly repeat each clue. Have children hold up and read the corresponding Word Card.
- **Speaking/Writing with High-Frequency Words**
  - **Teach/Model** Give each child two Word Cards. Say each word aloud and have children repeat. Monitor for pronunciation.
  - **Practice** Have the children sit in a circle. Then write the following story starter on the board: *This is a story about a sudden thunderstorm*. Explain that each child will add to the story by making up a sentence using his or her words.

Beginning Go around the circle and have each child add to the story using his or her Word Cards. Offer help or allow children to help each other add simple phrases or create sentences.

Intermediate Have each child add a complete sentence to the story using his or her Word Cards.

Advanced/Advanced-High Have each child add a complete sentence to the story using his or her Word Cards. Tell each child to write his or her sentence down. Offer help to ensure correct spelling.

Objectives

- Use strategic learning techniques such as concept mapping, drawing, memorizing, comparing, contrasting, and reviewing to acquire basic and grade-level vocabulary.

Language Objectives

- Use accessible language to learn new and essential language.
- Use high-frequency English words.
- Develop basic sight vocabulary.

Mini-Lesson: Use Sight Vocabulary

Turn to p. 123 of the Student Edition. Ask children to look at the words on the cards at the top of the page and point to those words in the sentences. Have them work with partners to read the sight words. Then they can point to and read the sight words with you as you read the sentences aloud.

Content Objectives

- Identify the author's purpose.
- Identify the author's purpose to aid comprehension.

Language Objectives

- Discuss the main topic and the author's purpose.
- Retell the main topic of the reading.
- Write the main topic and the author's purpose.
- Understand environmental print.

Mini-Lesson: Environmental Print

Have children focus on the environmental print on El•2 by pointing out the book covers. What kind of information can children glean from the covers of books? Talk about covers of all sorts of reading materials as environmental print and ask children what they can learn from looking at the cover of a text.

ELL English Language Learners

Guide Comprehension
Author's Purpose

- **Preteach** Model by pantomiming as you define author's purpose. The author's purpose is the reason an author wrote a reading. Authors write to inform. They tell us about facts. They tell us how to do something. They might inform us about animals or plants. They also write to entertain us. They tell us funny stories that make us laugh.
- **Practice** Have children turn to Envision It! on page El•2 in the Student Edition. Discuss the pictures with children. Have them point to the picture that shows *inform*. Have them point to the picture that shows *entertain*. Repeat having children say *inform* and *entertain*.
- **Reteach/Practice** Distribute copies of the Picture It! (*ELL Handbook*, p. 156). Read the title aloud. Ask students what they think the reading will be about. Then, read the Picture It! aloud. (**Answers** 1. a. 2. c.)

Leveled Support

Beginning Ask for student volunteers. Read the paragraph aloud. As you read each sentence, have a different child act it out.

Intermediate Reread the paragraph. Have children number the sentences in the order they should be performed. Then, ask if they feel they could grow a tomato plant with these *instructions*.

Advanced Ask students to name something they do well. Then, ask them to verbally explain how to do it. Guide the children to see that the author wrote because she wanted to explain how to do something, just as they did verbally.

Advanced-High Have children complete the same activity as above, but ask them to write their explanation, rather than give it verbally.

MINI-LESSON

Give Instructions

Instructions tell you how to do something. Listen as I tell you how to draw a house. *First, draw a square. Then, draw a triangle on top of the square for the roof. Last, draw a rectangle inside of the square for the door.* Have children suggest other activities. Craft instructions for one of their activities. Finally, have children practice giving instructions to each other.

Objectives

- Understand the general meaning, main points, and important details of spoken language ranging from situations in which topics, language, and contexts are familiar to unfamiliar.

Reading Comprehension
Frog and Toad Together

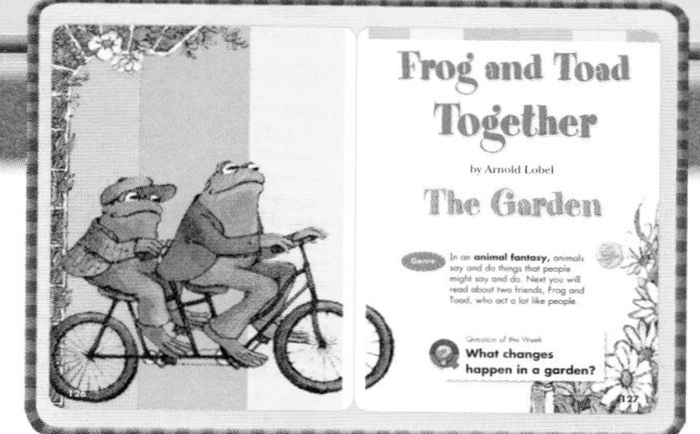

Student Edition pp. 126–127

Frontloading

- **Background Knowledge** Read the title aloud and discuss it. Have you ever planted seeds? Have you seen a garden? Do you have a garden?
- **Preview** Guide children on a picture walk through the story, asking them to identify people, places, and actions. Reteach these words using visuals in the Student Edition: *garden* (p. 128), *seeds* (p. 129), *growing* (p. 130).
- **Predict** What do you think will happen to the seeds in the story?

Sheltered Reading Ask questions such as the following to guide children's comprehension:

- p. 128: Point to the garden. Where is Frog? (in his garden) Point to Toad. Who walks by? (Toad)
- pp. 130–132: Point to Toad. What does Toad tell the seeds? (start growing) How does Toad tell the seeds to start growing? Is he quiet or loud? (loud)
- p. 134: Point to the sunshine. What does Frog tell Toad the seeds need to grow? (sunshine and rain)
- pp. 135–137: Point to Toad. Why does Toad think his seeds aren't growing? (They are afraid.) What does he do? (takes candles outside, reads to them, sings songs to them)

Fluency: Read with Expression and Intonation Remind children that reading with expression means to read like you are speaking when you talk to a friend. Reading with intonation means to stress certain words in sentences. Read page 131, modeling the frustration in your voice when you read "Now seeds start growing!" Point out that the exclamation point gives a clue how to read expressively. Make sure you also read with appropriate intonation. Have pairs read page 132. Have children read expressively and with appropriate intonation as their partners listen and offer feedback. For more practice, use the Fluency: Oral Rereading Routine (*ELL Handbook*, page 497).

After Reading Help children summarize the text with the Retelling Cards. Ask questions that prompt children to summarize the important parts of the text.

Objectives

- Speak using learning strategies such as requesting assistance, employing non-verbal cues, and using synonyms and circumlocution (conveying ideas by defining or describing when exact English words are not known).
- Distinguish sounds and intonation patterns of English with increasing ease.

Content Objectives

- Monitor and adjust comprehension.
- Make and adjust predictions.

Language Objectives

- Read grade-level text with expression and appropriate intonation.
- Summarize text using visual support.
- Use visual support to comprehends language.
- Express feelings.

Audio Support

Children can prepare for reading *Frog and Toad Together* by using the eSelection or the AudioText CD.

Mini-Lesson: Expressing Feelings

Have children express their feelings about different parts of the story. Provide sentence models such as *I liked* ______. *I was happy was* ______. Turn to p. 131 in the Student Edition and ask what feelings Toad might express. Have children role-play Toad on that page.

ELL English Language Learners

For additional leveled instruction, see the **ELL/ELD Reader Teaching Guide.**

Comprehension: *Grow Tomatoes*

ELL Reader

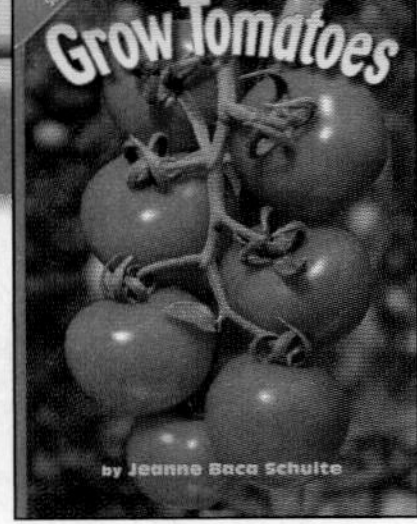

ELD Reader

- **Before Reading** Distribute copies of the ELL and ELD Readers, *Grow Tomatoes*, to children at their reading level.
  - **Preview** Read the title to children and allow time for them to look through the pages. This is a story about growing tomatoes. Activate prior knowledge. The story in our book was about growing plants. This story is about growing plants too. What kinds of plants have you planted? Have you ever planted tomato plants?
  - **Set a Purpose for Reading** Let's read to find out how to grow tomatoes.
- **During Reading** Follow this Reading Routine for both reading groups.

1. Read the entire Reader aloud slowly as children follow along and finger point.
2. Reread the Reader, having children choral read with you.

- **After Reading** Use the exercises on the inside back cover of *Grow Tomatoes* and invite children to share drawings and writing. In a whole-group discussion, ask children how we grow tomatoes. Encourage children to identify each step in order. Children can point to the steps in the book.

ELD Reader Beginning/Intermediate

- **pp. 2–4** Point to the pots. What is the first thing you put in the pots? What do you do next? What do you do last?
- **pp. 7–8** Point to the dirt. What do plants need to grow?

Writing Have children work in pairs and draw pictures to describe the steps for growing a tomato. Pairs should label their pictures. Have pairs share their pictures with the class.

ELL Reader Advanced/Advanced-High

- **pp. 2–4** What do you need to grow a tomato garden? How do you plant a tomato garden?
- **pp. 5–8** What happens to the yellow flowers? What happens next?

Study Guide Distribute copies of the ELL Reader Study Guide (*ELL Handbook*, page 160). Scaffold comprehension by having children point to the sentences that tell what happens at the beginning, middle, and end and using that information for their pictures. Review their responses together. (**Answers** See *ELL Handbook*, pp. 245–248.)

Objectives

- Share information in cooperative learning interactions.

eReaders

ELL English Language Learners

Conventions

Past and Future Tense Verbs

- **Preteach** Perform these actions and say *I walk to the board. I write on the board.* The words *walk* and *write* are verbs. They tell what is happening. Present tense verbs tell what is happening now. The verbs *walk* and *write* tell what I am doing now. If the verb talks about one other person or thing, we add *-s*. Write *She walks. He writes.* Point to children as you say the sentences. Underline the *-s* in *walks* and *writes*. We can also talk about what will happen in the future. Pantomime and say *What will I do after school? I will go home. I will ride my bike.* To talk about things that happen in the future we use verbs in future tense. Write *I will ride a bike*. Underline *will*. We use the helping verb *will* to talk about what will happen in the future.

- **Practice** Ask children to leaf through the Student Edition to call attention to Frog and Toad's actions. Have children do the exercises below.

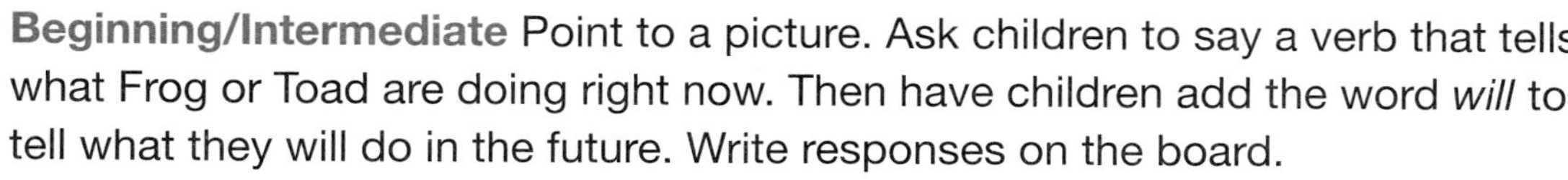

Leveled Support

Beginning/Intermediate Point to a picture. Ask children to say a verb that tells what Frog or Toad are doing right now. Then have children add the word *will* to tell what they will do in the future. Write responses on the board.

Advanced/Advanced-High Have children create sentences in the present tense and future tense to tell about a picture. Ask them to identify which sentence is present tense and which sentence is future tense.

- **Reteach**
  - Write *Frog plants seeds* and *Frog will water the seeds tomorrow* on the board. Underline *plants* and *will water.* Which sentence tells what Frog is doing now? Which sentence tells what frog will do tomorrow?
  - Write *Frog* on an index card. On other index cards write *will sing, reads, waters, will sing,* etc. Then work with children to create sentences in the present and future. Have children identify the tense of each sentence.

- **Practice** Have children do the exercises below.

Leveled Support

Beginning/Intermediate Have partners tell each other what they are doing right now and what they will do after school. Have them write the verb in the correct tense.

Advanced/Advanced-High Help children write sentences about what they are doing now and what they will do after school. Have partners edit each others' sentences for correct verb tense.

Objectives

- Adapt spoken language appropriately for formal and informal purposes.

Content Objectives

- Identify and use past and future tense verbs.
- Correctly use past and future tense verbs in sentences.

Language Objectives

- Speak using past and future tense verbs.
- Write phrases and sentences with past and future tense verbs.

Transfer Skills

Present Tense English verb endings differ from verb endings in languages such as Spanish and Polish, which use different endings for person and number. However, children may need practice adding *-s* or *-es* to present-tense verbs with third-person singular subjects.

Future Tense Spanish, Haitian Creole, and Hmong speakers may use present tense in places where English calls for future tense. Help children practice verbs in statements such as *I will read later* and *After we hear the story, we will write a new story.*

Content Objectives

- Identify lists.
- Identify sentences.
- Identify sentences that tell what characters did in lists.

Language Objectives

- Write lists with sentences.
- Share feedback for editing and revising.
- Retelling or summarizing spoken messages.
- Write and speak with connecting words.

Mini-Lesson: Retelling

Tell children that a list is one way to jot down notes to retell or summarize a spoken message. Have children take notes to retell or summarize a spoken message. Read the list of directions for growing plants on p. 146 of the Student Edition. Ask children to take notes as you read, perhaps by drawing pictures or writing down key words. Then children can retell the steps.

Conventions

As children list, they might write sentences rather than numbered lists. Have them use commas and connecting words in lists. They can speak as you write so that they can copy the sentences. Model the conventions of commas and connecting words.

ELL English Language Learners

Write Lists

- **Introduce Terms** Write *list* on the board and explain the word as you point to it. A *list* tells you things you need to buy at the store. Lists can also tell you what you need to make something. Lists can also tell you what someone did in a story that you read.
- **Introduce** Explain that sentences are complete thoughts. We can use sentences to tell what characters do in a story. Write this paragraph on the board:

Juan's Garden

Juan wants to plant a garden. First, he puts holes in the ground. Then, he puts seeds in the holes. He carefully covers the seeds. Finally, he waters the seeds. Juan can't wait to see his garden grow.

- **Model** Make a numbered list from 1 to 4. Engage children in listing what Juan did to make his garden. Write sentences for each item in the list.
- **Write** Have children copy the list topic: *Summer Vacation*. Have them number their paper 1 to 4. Write the following paragraph on the board.

Summer Vacation

Lily was going to read a lot of books during her summer vacation. She went to the library. She checked out several books. She packed her books in her backpack. She went home. She began reading the first book.

Have partners work together to create a list to describe what Lily did.

Leveled Support

Beginning Number your paper 1 to 4. Think of what Lily did to get ready. Draw four things she did. Have children tell about their pictures. Supply the sentences. Have children copy the sentences in their list.

Intermediate Guide children's writing. What did Lily do first? What else did she do? Help children with sentence construction.

Advanced/Advanced-High Have children make a list using words and phrases as their prewriting. Then have them write their list with sentences.

Objectives

- Understand the general meaning, main points, and important details of spoken language ranging from situations in which topics, language, and contexts are familiar to unfamiliar.
- Express opinions, ideas, and feelings ranging from communicating single words and short phrases to participating in extended discussions on a variety of social and grade-appropriate academic topics.

Common Core Standards
Weekly Planning Guide

Grade 1 • Unit 3 • Week 5
I'm a Caterpillar
150j–181k

Selection: I'm a Caterpillar
Genre: Literary Nonfiction

Alignment of the Common Core Standards with This Week's Skills and Strategies

This Week's Common Core Standards for English Language Arts	Instructional Summary
Reading Standards for Informational Text	
Informational Text 3. Describe the connection between two individuals, events, ideas, or pieces of information in a text. **Informational Text 4.** Ask and answer questions to help determine or clarify the meaning of words and phrases in a text. **Informational Text 7.** Use the illustrations and details in a text to describe its key ideas.	In this lesson, children identify **facts and opinions** in the Listening Comprehension selection and the main selection. They use the Envision It! page to identify the **text structure** of sequence and apply what they learn to the main selection. In addition, children use the text details and illustrations to trace the life cycle of a caterpillar.
Foundational Skills Standards	
Foundational Skills 3. Know and apply grade-level phonics and word analysis skills in decoding words. **Foundational Skills 4.b.** Read on-level text orally, with accuracy, appropriate rate, and expression on successive readings.	Children apply phonics skills as they decode **words with *r*-controlled *er, ir,*** and ***ur*** and words with **contractions** with ***'s, 've,*** and ***'re.*** The fluency activities help children focus on reading with **appropriate expression and intonation.**
Writing Standards	
Writing 2. Write informative/explanatory texts in which they name a topic, supply some facts about the topic, and provide some sense of closure. **Writing 5.** With guidance and support from adults, focus on a topic, respond to questions and suggestions from peers, and add details to strengthen writing as needed.	In the Writing section, children draw pictures about something in nature that changes and **write captions** that show and tell about the drawings. In the Research and Inquiry section, children choose a **topic** and **gather and record information** on a chart.
Speaking and Listening Standards	
Speaking/Listening 1.a. Follow agreed-upon rules for discussions (e.g., listening to others with care, speaking one at a time about the topics and texts under discussion). **Speaking/Listening 3.** Ask and answer questions about what a speaker says in order to gather additional information or clarify something that is not understood.	In the Listening and Speaking section, children review **attributes of good speakers,** and they share information about favorite games. They are encouraged to ask questions and add ideas about a speaker's topic. They review **speaking and listening rules** in the Research and Inquiry section.
Language Standards	
Language 1.c. Use singular and plural nouns with matching verbs in basic sentences (e.g., *He hops; We hop*). **Language 2.d.** Use conventional spelling for words with common spelling patterns and for frequently occurring irregular words.	In the Conventions section, children match **linking verbs** to singular and plural subjects and use the correct tense of the linking verbs. The **Spelling** section focuses on high-frequency words and words with *er, ir,* and *ur.*

Additional Support for a Common Core Standard This Week

Use the following instruction to supplement the teaching of one of this week's Common Core Standards.

Common Core Standard: **Foundational Skills 4.b.**
Have children turn to pages 162–165 of the main selection *I'm a Caterpillar.*

- Tell children that punctuation and positions of words provide clues to how lines in a selection should be read.
- Point out how the words in the second sentence on page 162 are staggered. Demonstrate how to read the sentence, dragging out the word *wait* and pausing at the commas for effect.
- Point out the exclamation point in the last sentence on page 163. Tell children that this punctuation mark is a signal to read the sentence with emphasis. Model how to read the sentence.
- Point to the question mark at the end of the last sentence on page 165 and explain that we raise our voices at the end of questions. Model how to read the question.
- Then have children take turns reading the pages with appropriate expression and intonation.

ISBN-13: 978-0-328-64370-7 ISBN-10: 0-328-64370-X

Grade 1 • Unit 3 • Week 5

I'm a Caterpillar

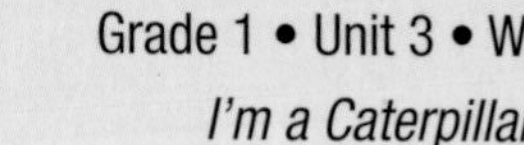

Unit 3

What is changing in our world?

Common Core Standards and Concept Development

- Introduce and explore this unit's weekly concepts through rich, structured conversations
- Develop complex content knowledge and vocabulary
- Expand on a single concept with engaging literature and nonfiction
- Build better readers in all content areas

Align instruction to **Common Core Anchor Standards**

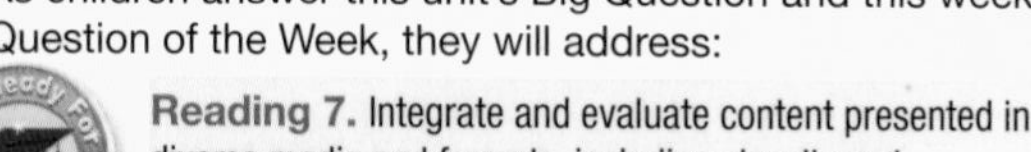

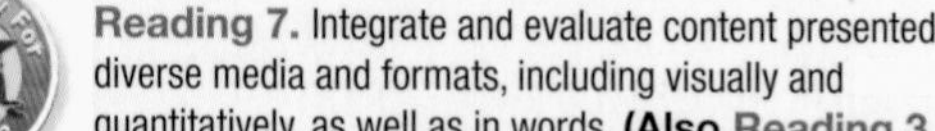

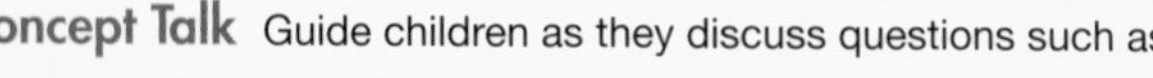

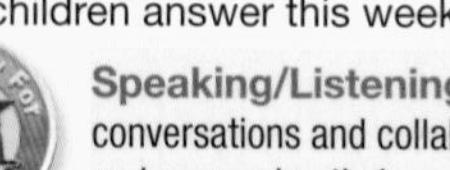

Week 1

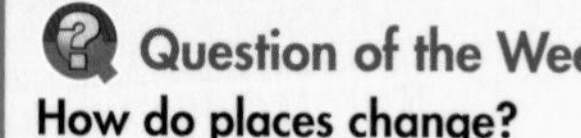

A Place to Play

Question of the Week

How do places change?

connect to SOCIAL STUDIES

Concept Talk Guide children as they discuss questions such as:

- What are some ways your neighborhood has changed?

Writing Think about a place to play that you think is interesting. Now write a made-up story about children playing at that place.

Week 2

Ruby in Her Own Time

Question of the Week

What do we learn as we grow and change?

connect to SOCIAL STUDIES

Concept Talk Guide children as they discuss questions such as:

- What can you do now that you could not do when you were younger?

Writing Look at the pictures in *Ruby in Her Own Time*. Think about what Ruby does. Write sentences that tell two things Ruby does that you like.

Week 3

The Class Pet

Question of the Week

What can we learn about animals as they grow and change?

connect to SCIENCE

Concept Talk Guide children as they discuss questions such as:

- Think about different animals. How are the babies different from the adults?

Writing Write a summary of *The Class Pet*. Tell the most important events and ideas.

Week 4

Frog and Toad Together

Question of the Week

What changes happen in a garden?

connect to SCIENCE

Concept Talk Guide children as they discuss questions such as:

- What do seeds look like when you first plant them? Then what happens?

Writing Think of actions Toad tried to help his garden grow. Write a list telling what Toad did that really helped the garden grow. In another list, tell his actions that did not help.

You Are Here: Week 5

I'm a Caterpillar

Question of the Week

What changes can be seen in nature?

connect to SCIENCE

As children answer this unit's Big Question and this week's Question of the Week, they will address:

Reading 7. Integrate and evaluate content presented in diverse media and formats, including visually and quantitatively, as well as in words. **(Also Reading 3.)**

Concept Talk Guide children as they discuss questions such as:

- How do different kinds of animals change as they grow?

As children answer this week's Concept Talk question, they will address:

Speaking/Listening 1. Prepare for and participate effectively in a range of conversations and collaborations with diverse partners, building on others' ideas and expressing their own clearly and persuasively.

Writing Think of changes in nature. Plants and animals grow. Seasons change. Draw two pictures to show one way a plant or animal changes. Write captions about your pictures.

As children write about this week's prompt, they will address:

Writing 2. Write informative/explanatory texts to examine and convey complex ideas and information clearly and accurately through the effective selection, organization, and analysis of content. **(Also Writing 5.)**

Listening and Speaking On page 180, children learn to follow agreed-upon rules for discussion. By doing so, they address:

Speaking/Listening 1. Prepare for and participate effectively in a range of conversations and collaborations with diverse partners, building on others' ideas and expressing their own clearly and persuasively.

Week 6

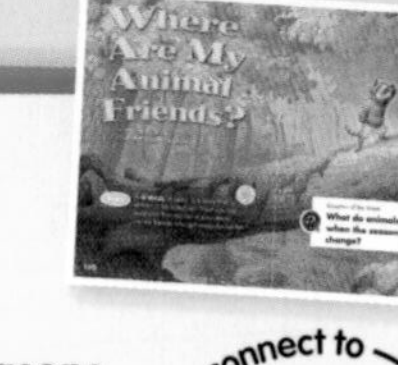

Where Are My Animal Friends?

Question of the Week

What do animals do when the seasons change?

connect to SCIENCE

Concept Talk Guide children as they discuss questions such as:

- Why do you think squirrels gather and hide nuts in the fall?

Writing Think about Raccoon and Squirrel in *Where Are My Animal Friends?* What would they say if they could call Goose on a phone? Write a play scene showing what they would say.

This Week's ELL Overview

Grade 1 • Unit 3 • Week 5
I'm a Caterpillar
150a–181l
and DI•96–DI•105

ELL Handbook

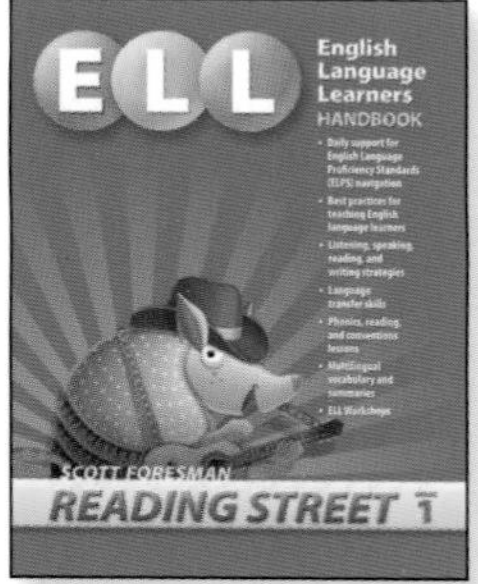

- Maximize Literacy and Cognitive Engagement
- Research Into Practice
- Full Weekly Support for Every Selection

I'm a Caterpillar
- Multi-Lingual Summaries in Five Languages
- Selection-Specific Vocabulary Word Cards
- Frontloading/Reteaching for Comprehension Skill Lessons
- ELD and ELL Reader Study Guides

- Transfer Activities
- Professional Development

Daily Leveled ELL Notes

ELL notes appear throughout this week's instruction and ELL Support is on the DI pages of your Teacher's Edition. The following is a sample of an ELL note from this week.

English Language Learners

Beginning Point out sentences with contractions in *She's Flying!* Help children restate the sentences, substituting the two words the contraction is made from.

Intermediate Have children find the four sentences that contain contractions and read them aloud. Have children identify the two words each contraction is made from and the letter(s) that are replaced by the apostrophe.

Advanced Have children make up new dialogue for the birds, using the contractions *you're, they're, she's* and *we've.*

Advanced High After reading, make a 3-column chart labeled *Pronoun, Verb,* and *Contraction.* Help children complete the chart with pronouns and verbs and the contractions made from each pair.

ELL by Strand

The ELL lessons on this week's Support for English Language Learners pages are organized by strand. They offer additional scaffolding for the core curriculum. Leveled support notes on these pages address the different proficiency levels in your class. See pages DI•96–DI•105.

The Three Pillars of ELL Instruction

ELL Strands	Activate Prior Knowledge	Access Content	Extend Language
Vocabulary p. DI•100	Preteach	Teach/Model	Practice
Reading Comprehension p. DI•101	Preteach	Reteach/Practice	Leveled Practice Activities
Phonics, Spelling, and Word Analysis pp. DI•97–DI•98	Preteach	Listen and Write	Leveled Practice Activities
Listening Comprehension p. DI•99	Prepare for the Read Aloud	First Listening	Second Listening
Conventions and Writing pp. DI•104–DI•105	Preteach/Introduce Terms	Practice/Model	Leveled Practice Activities/ Leveled Writing Activities
Concept Development p. DI•96	Activate Prior Knowledge	Develop Concepts	Review Concepts and Connect to Writing

This Week's Practice Stations Overview

Grade 1 • Unit 3 • Week 5
I'm a Caterpillar
150a–181l

Six Weekly Practice Stations with Leveled Activities can be found at the beginning of each week of instruction. For this week's Practice Stations, see pp. 150h–150i.

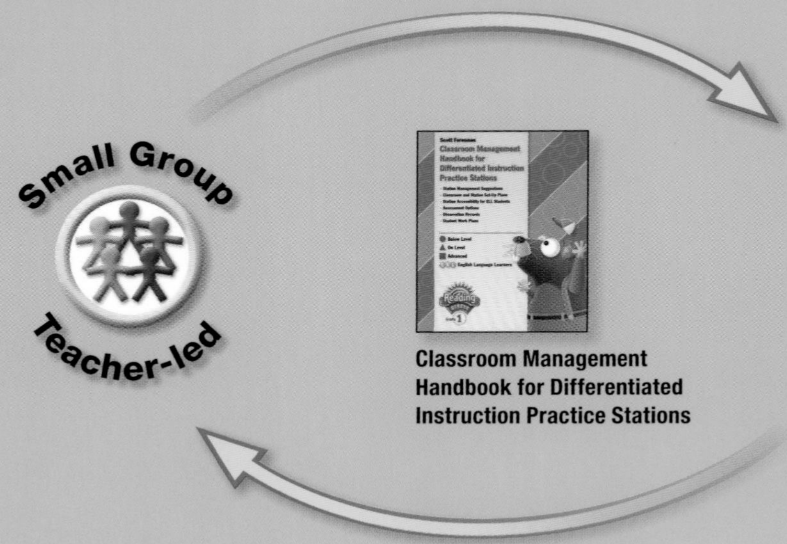

Classroom Management Handbook for Differentiated Instruction Practice Stations

Practice Stations

Daily Leveled Center Activities

● Below ■ Advanced
▲ On-Level 

Practice Stations Flip Charts

	 Listen Up	 Word Work	 Words to Know	 Let's Write	 Read for Meaning	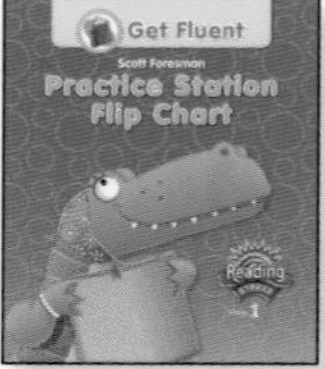 Get Fluent
Objectives	• Identify words with *r*-controlled /är/.	• Build and write words with endings, doubling final consonant. • Build and write words with *r*-controlled vowel *ar.*	• Identify high-frequency words *few, afraid, read, soon, how, again.* • Use a dictionary.	• Write sentences using verbs for the past. • Write sentences using verbs for the future.	• Identify a selection's topic. • Identify the author's purpose for writing the selection.	• Read aloud with expression and intonation.
Materials	• *Listen Up* Flip Chart Activity 17 • six or seven Picture Cards, including *garden, starfish, yarn*	• *Word Work* Flip Chart Activity 17 • Letter Tiles • paper • pencils	• *Words to Know* Flip Chart Activity 17 • High-Frequency Word Cards for Unit 3, Week 4 • children's dictionary • paper • pencils	• *Let's Write* Flip Chart Activity 17 • paper • pencils	• *Read for Meaning* Flip Chart Activity 17 • Leveled Readers • paper • pencils	• *Get Fluent* Flip Chart Activity 17 • Leveled Readers

This Week on Reading Street!

Question of the Week

What changes can be seen in nature?

Daily Plan

Whole Group

- ◎ Vowels: *r*-Controlled *er, ir, ur*
- ◎ Contractions *'s, 've, 're*
- ◎ Fact and Opinion
- Fluency
- Vocabulary

MONITOR PROGRESS Success Predictor

Day 1	Day 2	Day 3	Day 4	Day 5
Check Word Reading	Check Word Reading	Check High Frequency Words/Retelling	Check Fluency	Check Oral Vocabulary

Small Group

Teacher-Led

- Reading Support
- Skill Support
- Fluency Practice

Practice Stations

Independent Activities

Customize Literacy More support for a Balanced Literacy approach, see CL•1–CL•47.

Customize Writing More support for a customized writing approach, see CW•11–CW•20.

Whole Group

- Writing: Captions and Pictures
- Conventions: Verbs *Am, Is, Are, Was, and Were*

Assessment

- Weekly Tests
- Day 5 Assessment
- Fresh Reads

This Week's Reading Selections

Main Selection
Genre: **Literary Nonfiction**

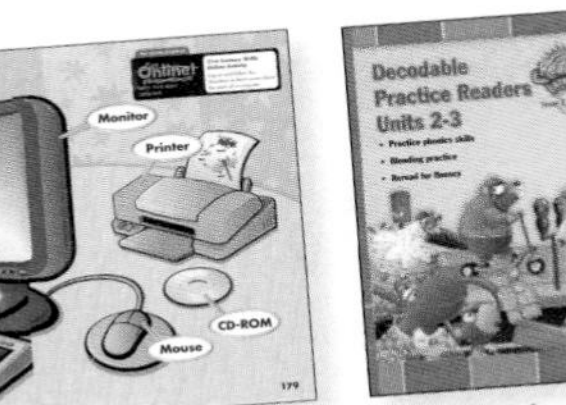

Paired Selection

Decodable Practice Readers

Leveled Readers

ELL and ELD Readers

Resources on Reading Street!

	Build Concepts	Phonemic Awareness and Phonics	Vocabulary
Whole Group	 Student Edition pp. 150–151;  Sing with Me	 Student Edition pp. 152–153;  Sound-Spelling Cards	 Student Edition p. 155
Go Digital	• Concept Talk Video • Sing with Me Animations	• Interactive Sound-Spelling Cards • Decodable eReaders	• Vocabulary Activities • Journal Word Bank
Small Group and Independent Practice	 Practice Station Flip Chart;  Leveled Readers;  ELL and ELD Readers	 Practice Station Flip Chart;  Decodable Practice Readers	 Practice Station Flip Chart;  Student Edition p. 155
Go Digital	• eReaders	• Decodable eReaders • Letter Tile Drag and Drop	• Journal Word Bank • Vocabulary Activities
Customize Literacy	• Leveled Readers	• Decodable Practice Readers	• High-Frequency Word Cards
Go Digital	• Concept Talk Video • Big Question Video • eReaders	• Interactive Sound-Spelling Cards • Decodable eReaders	• Sing with Me Animations • Vocabulary Activities

Question of the Week

What changes can be seen in nature?

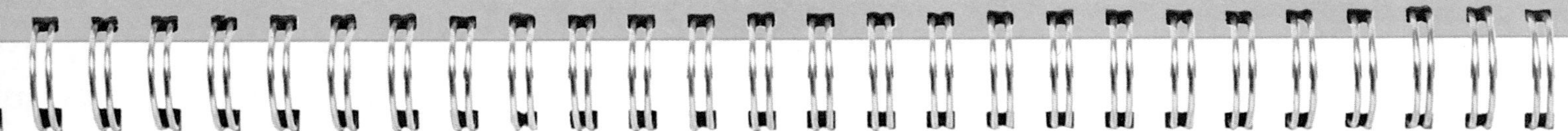

Comprehension	Fluency	Conventions and Writing
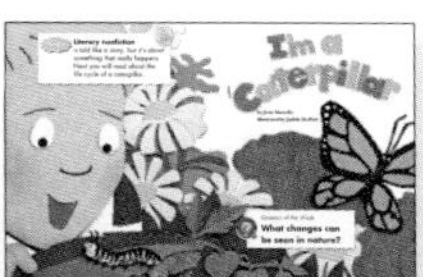 Student Edition pp. 158–173	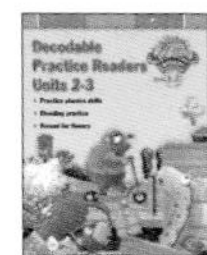 Decodable Practice Readers	Student Edition pp. 176–177
• Envision It! Animations • eSelections	• eSelections • eReaders	• Grammar Jammer
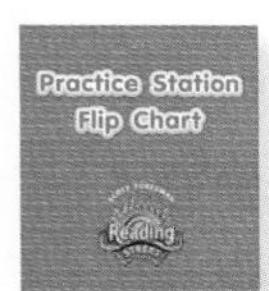 Practice Station Flip Chart  Leveled Readers  ELL and ELD Readers	 Practice Station Flip Chart  Decodable Practice Readers	 Practice Station Flip Chart 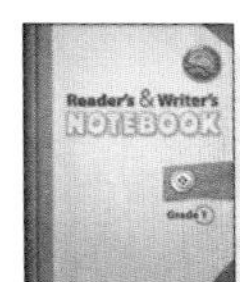 Reader's and Writer's Notebook
• eReaders • Story Sort	• Decodable eReaders	• Grammar Jammer
• Envision It! Skills and Strategies Handbooks • Leveled Readers	• Leveled Readers	• Reader's and Writer's Notebook
• Envision It! Animations • eReaders	• eReaders	• Grammar Jammer

Week 5

My 5-Day Planner for Reading Street!

Don't Wait Until Friday SUCCESS PREDICTOR

	Check Word Reading **Day 1** pages 150j–155f	Check Word Reading **Day 2** pages 156a–173f
Get Ready to Read	**Concept Talk,** 150j–151 **Oral Vocabulary,** 151a–151b *cycle, develop, insect* **Phonemic Awareness,** 152–153 Isolate Medial and Final Phonemes **Phonics,** 153a–154a ◉ Vowels: *r*-Controlled *er, ir, ur* READ **Decodable Practice Reader 17A,** 154b–154c **Spelling,** 154d Pretest	**Concept Talk,** 156a–156b **Oral Vocabulary,** 156b *rearrange* **Phonemic Awareness,** 156c Isolate Medial and Final Phonemes **Phonics,** 156d–157a ◉ Contractions with *'s, 've, 're* READ **Decodable Practice Reader 17B,** 157b–157c Review **Phonics,** 157d *r*-Controlled /ėr/ *er, ir, ur* and /är/ *ar* **Spelling,** 157e Practice
Read and Comprehend	**High-Frequency Words,** 155 Introduce *done, know, push, visit, wait* **Listening Comprehension,** 155a–155b ◉ Fact and Opinion	**High-FrequencyWords,** 157 Build Fluency *done, know, push, visit, wait* **Story Words,** 158a Introduce *caterpillar, chrysalis, crawl, pupa, shiver* **Vocabulary,** 158a Dictionary/Glossary **Build Background,** 158b READ **Main Selection—First Read,** 158c–173a *I'm a Caterpillar* **Literary Nonfiction,** 173a True Story or Fantasy
Language Arts	**Conventions,** 155c Verbs *Am, Is, Are, Was,* and *Were* **Writing,** 155d–155e Captions and Pictures **Research and Inquiry,** 155f Identify and Focus Topic	**Conventions,** 173b Verbs *Am, Is, Are, Was,* and *Were* **Writing,** 173c–173d Captions and Pictures Writing Trait: Focus/Ideas **Handwriting,** 173e Letter *V* and *v;* Left-to-Right Progression **Research and Inquiry,** 173f Technology: My Computer

You Are Here! Unit 3 Week 5

Question of the Week

What changes can be seen in nature?

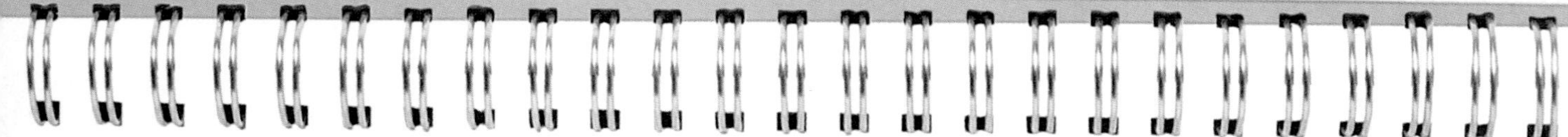

Check High-Frequency Words Check Retelling **Day 3** pages 174a–177c	Check Fluency **Day 4** pages 178a–179f	Check Oral Vocabulary **Day 5** pages 180a–181k
Concept Talk, 174a–174b **Oral Vocabulary,** 174b *flurries* **Phonemic Awareness,** 174c Add Phonemes **Phonics,** 174d–174e ◎ Vowels: *r*-Controlled *er, ir, ur* ◎ Contractions with *'s, 've, 're* **Spelling,** 174f Dictation	**Concept Talk,** 178a–178b **Oral Vocabulary,** 178b *emerge, fragile, vessel* **Phonological Awareness,** 178c Review **Phonics,** 178d Endings *-ed, -ing;* *r*-Controlled *ar* READ **Decodable Practice Reader 17C,** 178e–178f Review **Fluent Word Reading,** 178g **Spelling,** 178h Partner Review	**Concept Wrap Up,** 180a Review **Oral Vocabulary,** 180b **Phonological Awareness,** 180c Generate Rhyming Words Review **Phonics,** 180c ◎ *r*-Controlled *er, ir, ur* ◎ Contractions *'s, 've, 're* **Spelling,** 180d Test
Review **High-Frequency Words,** 174g *done, know, push, visit, wait* Review **Story Words,** 174g *caterpillar, chrysalis, crawl, pupa, shiver* READ **Main Selection—Second Read,** 158–173, 174h–175a **Fluency,** 175b Expression and Intonation	**21st Century Skills,** 178i READ **Paired Selection,** 178–179 "My Computer" **Fluency,** 179b Expression and Intonation	**Listening and Speaking,** 180–181 **Vocabulary,** 181a Dictionary/Glossary **Fluency,** 181a Expression, Intonation Review **Comprehension,** 181b ◎ Fact and Opinion Review **Vocabulary,** 181b High Frequency and Story Words **Literary Nonfiction,** 181c Author's Craft **Assessment,** 181d–181f Monitor Progress
Conventions, 176a–177a Verbs *Am, Is, Are, Was,* and *Were* **Writing,** 176–177a Captions and Pictures Writer's Craft: Details **Listening and Speaking,** 177b Share Information and Ideas **Research and Inquiry,** 177c Gather and Record Information	**Conventions,** 179c Verbs *Am, Is, Are, Was,* and *Were* **Writing,** 179d–179e Captions and Pictures Revising Strategy **Research and Inquiry,** 179f Review and Revise Topic	Review **Conventions,** 181g Verbs *Am, Is, Are, Was,* and *Were* **Writing,** 181h–181i Captions and Pictures Writer's Craft: Verbs **Research and Inquiry,** 181j Communicate **Wrap Up Your Week,** 181k What changes can be seen in nature?

Grouping Options for Differentiated Instruction
Turn the page for the small group time lesson plan.

Week 5

Planning Small Group Time on Reading Street!

Look for this Small Group Time box each day to help meet the individual needs of all your children. Differentiated Instruction lessons appear on the DI pages at the end of each week.

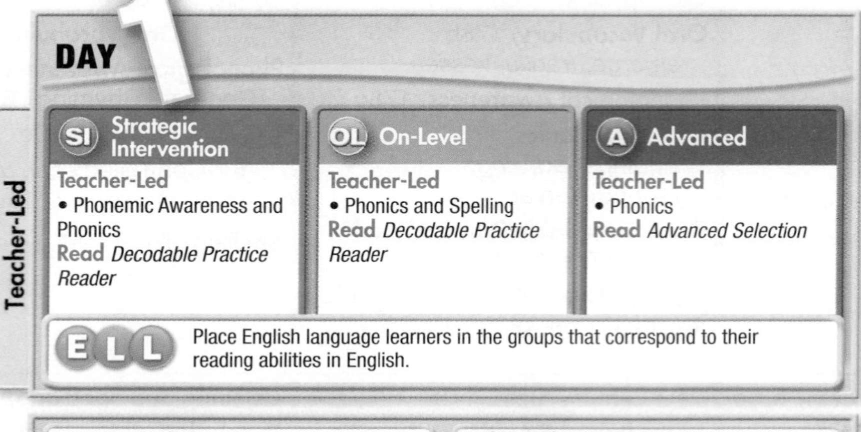

Practice Stations
- Listen Up
- Word Work

Independent Activities
- *Reader's and Writer's Notebook*
- Concept Talk Video

ELL

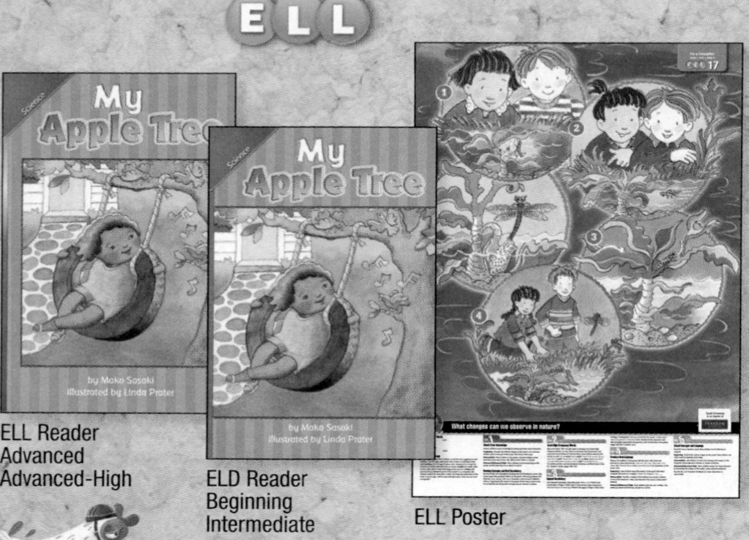

ELL Reader Advanced Advanced-High

ELD Reader Beginning Intermediate

ELL Poster

	Day 1
SI Strategic Intervention	**Phonemic Awareness and Phonics,** DI•85 Read **Decodable Practice Reader 17A,** DI•85
OL On-Level	**Phonics and Spelling,** DI•90 Read **Decodable Practice Reader 17A,** DI•90
A Advanced	**Phonics,** DI•93 Read **Advanced Selection,** DI•93
ELL English Language Learners	DI•96–DI•105 **Frontload Concept** **Preteach Skills** **Writing**

You Are Here! Unit 3 Week 5

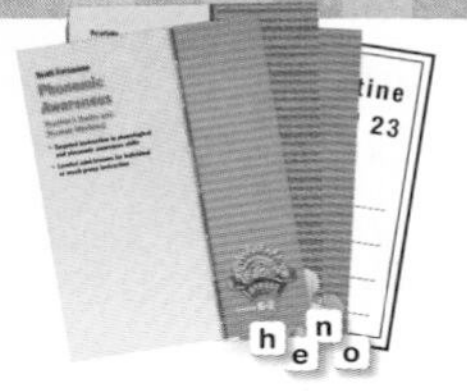

Reading Street Response to Intervention Kit

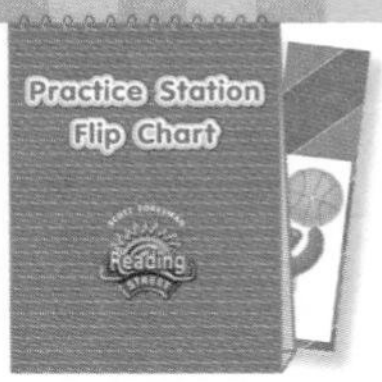

Reading Street Leveled Practice Stations Kit

Question of the Week

What changes can be seen in nature?

Below-Level Reader

Decodable Practice Readers

Concept Literacy Reader

On-Level Reader

A Advanced

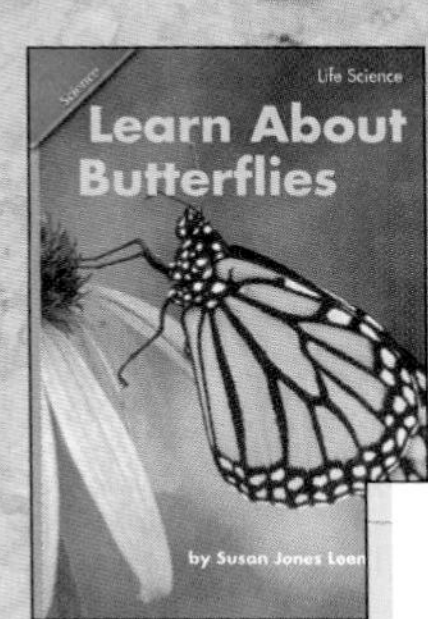

Advanced Reader

The Caterpillar and the Fawn

Advanced Selection

Small Group Weekly Plan

Day 2	Day 3	Day 4	Day 5
Phonemic Awareness and Phonics, DI•86 Read **Decodable Practice Reader 17B,** DI•86	**Phonemic Awareness and Phonics,** DI•87 Read **Concept Literacy Leveled Reader,** DI•87	**High-Frequency Words,** DI•88 Read **Decodable Practice Reader 17C,** DI•88	**Phonics Review,** DI•89 Read **Below-Level Leveled Reader,** DI•89
Phonics and High-Frequency Words, DI•90 Read **Decodable Practice Reader 17B,** DI•90	Read **On-Level Leveled Reader,** DI•91	**Conventions,** DI•92 Reread **Main Selection,** DI•92	**Phonics Review,** DI•92 Reread **On-level Leveled Reader,** DI•92
Phonics and Comprehension, DI•93 Read **Main Selection,** DI•93	Read **Advanced Leveled Reader,** DI•94	**Comprehension,** DI•95 Read **Paired Selection,** DI•95 Reread **Leveled Reader,** DI•95	**Fluency and Comprehension,** DI•95 Reread **Advanced Selection,** DI•95
DI•96–DI•105 **Review Concept** **Practice Skills** **Frontload Main Selection** **Writing**	DI•96–DI•105 **Review Concept** **Practice Skills** **Reread Main Selection** **Writing**	DI•96–DI•105 **Review Concept** **Practice Skills** **Read ELL or ELD Reader** **Writing**	DI•96–DI•105 **Review Concept** **Review Skills** **Writing**

Week 5

Practice Stations for Everyone on Reading Street!

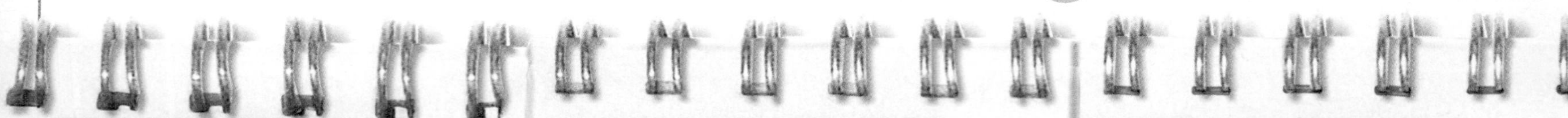

Listen Up!

Match sounds and pictures.

Objective s

- Identify words with r-controlled /är/.

Materials

- *Listen Up!* Flip Chart Activity 17
- Six or seven Picture Cards, including *garden, starfish, yarn*.

Differentiated Activities

● Find Picture Cards that contain the sound you hear at the beginning of *artist.* Say the words.

▲ Find Picture Cards that contain the sound you hear at the beginning of *artist.* Say the words. Now say other words that contain that sound.

■ Find Picture Cards that contain the sound you hear at the beginning of *artist.* Say the words. Now say other words that contain that sound.

Technology

- Interactive Sound-Spelling Cards

Word Work

Adding endings; *r*-controlled vowel *ar*

Objectives

- Build and write words with endings, doubling final consonant.
- Build and write words with *r*-controlled vowel *ar.*

Materials

- *Word Work* Flip Chart Activity 17
- Letter Tiles
- paper
- pencils

Differentiated Activities

● Use Letter Tiles. Build the words *step, chat, jog, swim.* Add *-ed* to the first two words and *-ing* to the second two. Don't forget to double the final consonant. What are the new words? Next, build the words *park* and *car*. Build other words that contain *ar*.

▲ Use Letter Tiles. Build the words *step, chat, jog, swim.* Add *-ed* to the first two words and *-ing* to the second two. Don't forget to double the final consonant. What are the new words? Next, build words that contain *ar*. Write all the words on your paper.

■ Use Letter Tiles. Build the words *step, chat, jog, swim.* Add *-ed* to the first two words and *-ing* to the second two. Don't forget to double the final consonant. What are the new words? Next, build words that contain *ar*. Write sentences using these words. Underline the words with endings and the *ar* words.

Technology

- Interactive Sound-Spelling Cards

Words To Know

Practice high-frequency words.

Objectives

- Identify high-frequency words *few, afraid, read, soon, how, again.*
- Use a dictionary.

Materials

- *Words to Know* Flip Chart Activity 17
- High-Frequency Word Cards for Unit 3, Week 4
- children's dictionary
- paper
- pencils

Differentiated Activities

- A **dictionary** lists words, their definitions, and their pronunciations.

● Use the Word Cards. Write the Words to Know on your paper. Choose one of the words and find it in the dictionary. Write the definition next to it.

▲ Use the Word Cards. Write the Words to Know on your paper. Choose some of the words and find them in the dictionary. Write the definitions next to the words.

■ Use the Word Cards. Write the Words to Know on your paper. Find the words in the dictionary. Write the definitions next to the words.

Technology

- Online Tested Vocabulary Activities

Use this week's materials from the Reading Street Leveled Practice Stations Kit to organize this week's stations.

Key

- ● Below-Level Activities
- ▲ On-Level Activities
- ■ Advanced Activities

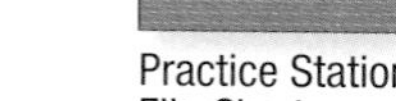
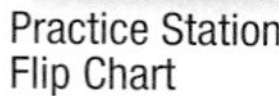
Practice Station Flip Chart

Let's Write!

Use verbs in writing.

Objectives

- Write sentences using verbs for the past.
- Write sentences using verbs for the future.

Materials

- *Let's Write!* Flip Chart Activity 17
- paper
- pencils

Differentiated Activities

● Think about something you did yesterday. Write a sentence about it. Now think about something you will do later or tomorrow. Write a sentence about that too, remembering to include the word *will* in your sentence. Circle the verbs you used.

▲ Think about something you did yesterday. Write a sentence about it. Now think about something you will do later or tomorrow. Write a sentence about that too. Circle the verbs you used.

■ Write a paragraph about something you did yesterday. Circle the verbs for the past you used. Now write a paragraph about something you plan to do later or tomorrow. Circle the verbs for the future you used.

Read For Meaning

Identify author's purpose.

Objectives

- Identify a selection's topic.
- Identify the author's purpose for writing the selection.

Materials

- *Read for Meaning* Flip Chart Activity 17
- Leveled Readers
- paper
- pencils

Differentiated Activities

- The **author's purpose** is the reason the author wrote a selection.

● Read *The Seasons Change.* What is the topic? What do you think the author's purpose is? Write a sentence or two to answer.

▲ Read *Plans Change.* Write a paragraph telling the topic and author's purpose. Use details to support your answer.

■ Read *All About the Weather.* Write two paragraphs explaining the topic and author's purpose. Support your answer with details from the selection.

Technology

- Leveled eReaders

Get Fluent

Practice fluent reading.

Objectives

- Read aloud with expression and intonation.

Materials

- *Get Fluent* Flip Chart Activity 17
- Leveled Readers

Differentiated Activities

● Work with a partner. Take turns reading pages from *The Seasons Change.* Read with expression and intonation. Pay attention to punctuation. Give your partner feedback.

▲ Work with a partner. Take turns reading pages from *Plans Change.* Read with expression and intonation. Pay attention to punctuation. Give your partner feedback.

■ Work with a partner. Take turns reading pages from *All About the Weather.* Read with expression and intonation. Pay attention to punctuation. Give your partner feedback.

Technology

- Reading Street Readers CD-ROM

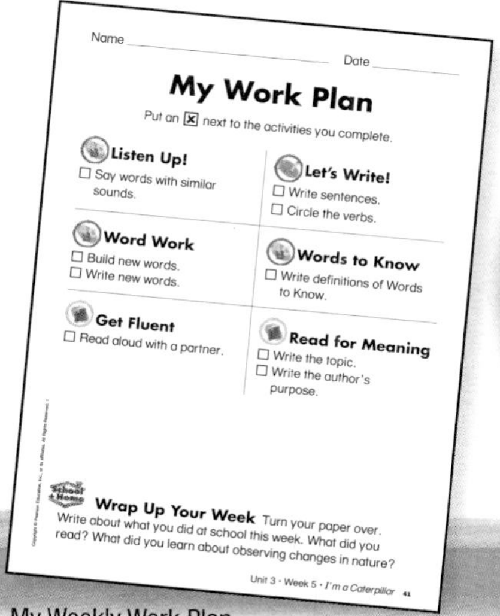
Name ______ Date ______

My Work Plan

Put an ☒ next to the activities you complete.

Listen Up!
☐ Say words with similar sounds.

Let's Write!
☐ Write sentences.
☐ Circle the verbs.

Word Work
☐ Build new words.
☐ Write new words.

Words to Know
☐ Write definitions of Words to Know.

Get Fluent
☐ Read aloud with a partner.

Read for Meaning
☐ Write the topic.
☐ Write the author's purpose.

Wrap Up Your Week Turn your paper over. Write about what you did at school this week. What did you read? What did you learn about observing changes in nature?

Unit 3 • Week 5 • I'm a Caterpillar

My Weekly Work Plan

Week 5

Objectives

- Introduce concepts: changes we can observe in nature.
- Share information and ideas about the concept.

Today at a Glance

Oral Vocabulary
cycle, develop, insect

Phonemic Awareness
Isolate Medial and Final Phonemes

Phonics and Spelling
◎ Vowels: r-Controlled *er, ir, ur*

Fluency
Oral Rereading

High-Frequency Words
done, know, push, visit, wait

Comprehension
◎ Fact and Opinion

Conventions
Verbs *am, is, are, was, were*

Writing
Captions and Pictures: Introduce

Research and Inquiry
Identify and Focus Topic

Concept Talk

Question of the Week

What changes can be seen in nature?

Introduce the concept To build concepts and to focus children's attention, tell them that this week they will talk, sing, read, and write about changes that can be seen in nature. Write the Question of the Week and track the print as you read it.

ROUTINE Activate Prior Knowledge **Team Talk**

Think Have children think for a minute about what changes can be seen in nature.

Pair Have pairs of children discuss the question.

Share Have children share information and their ideas with the group. Remind them to ask questions to clarify information. Guide discussion and encourage elaboration with prompts such as: How do different kinds of animals change as they grow?

Routines Flip Chart

Anchored Talk

Develop oral language Have children turn to pages 150–151 in their Student Edition. Read the title and look at the photos. Use these questions to guide discussion and create the "What changes can be seen in nature?" concept map.

- We know that people develop from babies into adults. *Develop* means "to grow." Where does a baby bird start to develop? (in an egg) The eggs hatch. Then the babies grow up and lay more eggs. The changes that happen as a living thing is born, grows, and then dies are its life cycle. Let's add these ideas to our map.
- The insect on the branch has an interesting life cycle. It once lived under the water. Later it came to live on land and developed into a creature with wings. Can you tell what it is? (a dragonfly)

Student Edition pp. 150–151

Connect to reading

Explain that this week, children will read about how a caterpillar develops into a butterfly. Let's add *The Life Cycle of a Butterfly* to our map.

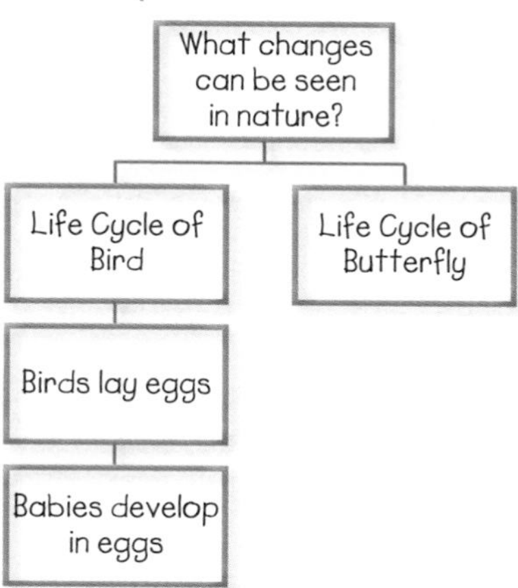

ELL Preteach Concepts Use the Day 1 instruction on ELL Poster 17 to assess and build background knowledge, develop concepts, and build oral vocabulary.

Poster 17

Develop Writing Fluency
Ask children to write about what they know about changes they can see in nature. Have them write for two or three minutes. Children should write as much as they can. Tell them to try to do their best writing. You may want to discuss what children wrote during writing conferences.

ELL

English Language Learners

Listening Comprehension
English learners will benefit from additional visual support to understand the key terms in the concept map. Use the pictures on pp. 150–151 to scaffold understanding. For example, when talking about the way a bird develops, point to the pictures of the eggs and the baby bird.

ELL Support Additional ELL support and modified instruction is provided in the *ELL Handbook* and in the *ELL Support Lessons* on pp. DI•96–DI•105.

Objectives

- Build oral vocabulary.
- Discuss the concept to develop oral language.
- Share information and ideas about the concept.

Oral Vocabulary
Amazing Words

Introduce Amazing Words

Display page 17 of the *Sing with Me* Big Book. Tell children they are going to sing about how a caterpillar changes into a butterfly. Ask children to listen for the Amazing Words *cycle*, *develop*, and *insect* as you sing. Sing the song again and have children join you.

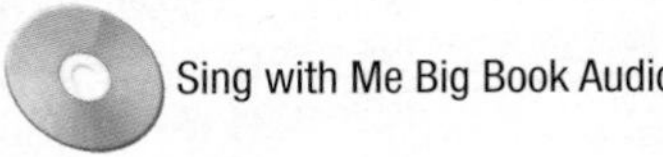
Sing with Me Big Book Audio

Sing with Me Big Book, p. 17

Teach Amazing Words

Amazing Words Oral Vocabulary Routine

1. **Introduce the Word** Relate the word *cycle* to the song. In the song, a caterpillar changes into a butterfly. Then the butterfly lays eggs to make new caterpillars so that the *cycle* can start all over again. Supply a child-friendly definition: A *cycle* is something that keeps starting over again. Have children say the word.
2. **Demonstrate** Provide examples to show meaning: A bird's life is a *cycle* because baby birds hatch from eggs, grow up, and lay their own eggs to produce new baby birds. A sunflower's life is a *cycle* because it sprouts from seeds, grows up, and makes its own seeds to produce new sunflowers.
3. **Apply** Have children demonstrate their understanding: Explain why the life of a cat is a *cycle*.

See p. OV•2 to teach *develop* and *insect*.

Routines Flip Chart

Check understanding of Amazing Words

Have children look at the picture on page 17. What two kinds of *insects* do you see? (caterpillars and butterflies) What other kinds of animals are *insects*? Use *insect* in your answer. (Possible response: Flies, bees, ladybugs, and mosquitoes are insects.)

A caterpillar *develops* into a butterfly. What does a tadpole *develop* into? What does an apple seed *develop* into? Use *develop* in your answers. (Possible response: A tadpole develops into a frog. An apple seed develops into an apple tree.)

What happens in the life *cycle* of a chicken? How does the *cycle* start over again? (Possible response: A chicken lays eggs. Chicks hatch and develop into chickens. The cycle starts over again when the new chickens lay eggs.)

Apply Amazing Words

Have children demonstrate their understanding of the Amazing Words by completing these sentences orally.

> The kinds of **insects** I often see are ________.
>
> As a ________ grows, it **develops** into a ________.
>
> One thing that happens in the life **cycle** of a bird is ________.

Corrective feedback

If... children have difficulty using the Amazing Words,
then... remind them of the definitions and provide opportunities for children to use the words in sentences.

Preteach Academic Vocabulary

Write the following on the board:

- fact and opinion
- literary nonficton
- verbs *am, is, are, was,* and *were*

Have children share what they know about this week's Academic Vocabulary. Use children's responses to assess their prior knowledge. Preteach the Academic Vocabulary by providing a child-friendly description, explanation, or example that clarifies the meaning of each term. Then ask children to restate the meaning of the Academic Vocabulary in their own words.

Amazing Words

cycle	flurries
develop	emerge
insect	fragile
rearrange	vessel

English Language Learners

Build Oral Vocabulary Help children understand the song "Life Cycle" by using pantomime as you sing the words *hatches, hides,* and *flies,* and by pointing to the appropriate parts of the picture as you sing the words *insect, leaves, shell,* and *butterfly*.

DAY 1 Get Ready to Read

Objectives

- Isolate medial and final phonemes.
- Segment and blend words with *r*-controlled /ėr/.
- ◎ Associate the sound /ėr/ with the spellings *er, ir,* and *ur.*

Skills Trace

◎ **Vowels: *r*-Controlled *er, ir, ur***
Introduce U3W5D1
Practice U3W5D3; U3W5D4
Reteach/Review U3W5D5; U3W6D4
Assess/Test Weekly Test U3W5 Benchmark Test U3

KEY:
U=Unit W=Week D=Day

Student Edition pp. 152–153

Phonemic Awareness
Isolate Medial and Final Phonemes

Introduce Read together the first bulleted point on pages 152–153 of the Student Edition. I see a tree with a nest. What is in the nest? (a bird) The middle sound I hear in *bird* is /ėr/. Have children find four other items in the picture with the middle sound /ėr/. (Possible responses: dirt, skirt, girl, squirrel, curl, herd) The last sound I hear in curl is /l/. What else in the picture has the middle sound /ėr/ and the last sound /l/? (girl)

Model Listen to the sounds in the word herd: /h/ /ėr/ /d/, herd. The middle sound is /ėr/. The last sound is /d/.

Guide practice Guide children as they segment and blend these words and identify the middle and last sound: *bird, dirt, skirt, girl, curl.*

Corrective feedback **If...** children make an error,
then... model by segmenting and blending the word and identifying the middle and last sounds. Then have children repeat the process.

Phonics—Teach/Model

Vowels: r-Controlled *er, ir, ur*

Sound-Spelling Card 67

Sound-Spelling Card 72

Sound-Spelling Card 104

ROUTINE Blending Strategy

1. **Connect** Write the words *for* and *far*. Have children say the words. Remind them that they already know that the letters *or* can stand for the sound /ôr/ and the letters *ar* can stand for the sound /är/. Explain that today they will learn how to spell and read words that have the sound /ėr/.
2. **Use Sound-Spelling Cards** Display Card 67. Point to *er*. The letters *er* can stand for the sound /ėr/. Have children say /ėr/ several times as you point to *er*. Display Card 72. Point to *ir*. The letters *ir* can also stand for the sound /ėr/. Have children say /ėr/ several times as you point to *ir*. Display Card 104. Point to *ur*. The letters *ur* can stand for the sound /ėr/ too. Have children say /ėr/ several times as you point to *ur*.
3. **Model** Write *her*. In this word, the letters *er* stand for the sound /ėr/. Segment and blend *her*; then have children blend with you: /h/ /ėr/, *her*. Follow this procedure to model *bird* and *turn*.
4. **Guide Practice** Continue the process in step 3. This time have children blend with you. Remind children that *er, ir,* and *ur* can spell the sound /ėr/.

verb	**sir**	**curl**	**third**	**perch**	**stir**
fern	**surf**	**thirst**	**verse**	**burn**	**dirt**

5. **Review** What do you know about reading these words? (The letters *er, ir,* and *ur* can spell the sound /ėr/.)

Routines Flip Chart

Professional Development

Final Consonants Final consonants can be difficult to isolate even when they are pronounced clearly. Many speakers tend to omit them because of habit or dialect. For these reasons, find time to give extra help and practice to those who need it.

Vocabulary Support

You may wish to explain the meaning of these words.

perch a branch or rod on which a bird can sit; to sit on a perch

surf the waves of the ocean as they break on the shore

verb a word that names an action

verse words put together with rhythm and rhyme; one part of a poem or song

English Language Learners

Pronounce /ėr/ Spanish does not have a sound equivalent to /ėr/, so Spanish speakers may pronounce *dirt* as *deert*. Have children practice saying and writing words such as *her, bird,* and *turn.*

Objectives

- ◎ Associate the sound /ėr/ with the spellings *er, ir, ur.*
- Blend and read words with *r*-controlled *er, ir, ur.*
- Decode words in context and isolation.

Check Word Reading
SUCCESS PREDICTOR

Phonics—Build Fluency
◎ *r*-Controlled *er, ir, ur*

Model

Envision It!

Have children turn to page 154 in their Student Edition. Look at the pictures on this page. I see a picture of a fern, a girl, and curtains. When I say each of these words, I hear the /ėr/ sound: *fern, girl, curtains*. Look at the word above each picture. In *fern*, /ėr/ is spelled *er*. In *girl*, /ėr/ is spelled *ir*. In *curtains*, /ėr/ is spelled *ur*.

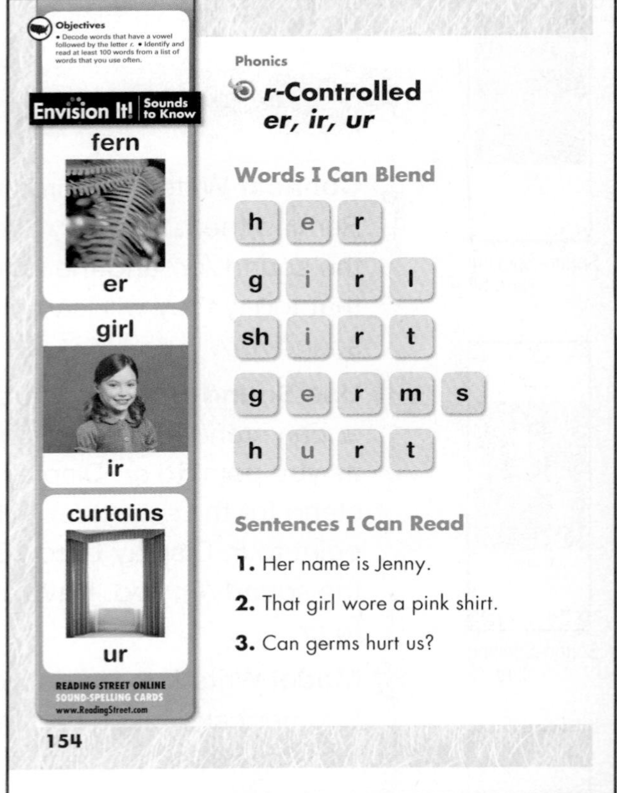

Student Edition p. 154

Guide practice

For each word in "Words I Can Blend," ask for the sound of each letter or group of letters. Make sure that children identify the correct sound for *er, ir,* and *ur*. Then have children blend the whole word.

Corrective feedback

If... children have difficulty blending a word,
then... model blending the word, and then ask children to blend it with you.

Blend and Read

Decode words in isolation

After children can successfully segment and blend the words, point to words in random order and ask children to read them naturally.

Decode words in context

Have children read each of the sentences. Have them identify words in the sentences that have the /ėr/ sound.

Team Talk Pair children and have them take turns reading each of the sentences aloud.

On their own

Use *Reader's and Writer's Notebook* p. 377.

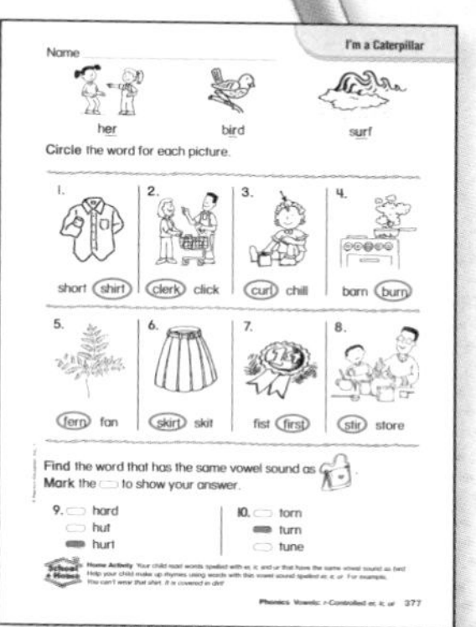

Reader's and Writer's Notebook p. 377

Don't Wait Until Friday

MONITOR PROGRESS

Check Word Reading r-Controlled *er, ir, ur*

Write the following words and have the class read them. Notice which words children miss during the group reading. Call on individuals to read some of the words.

ferns	**swirl**	**curb**	**chirp**	**nurse**	**Spiral Review**
smart	**turn**	**shore**	**thirty**	**fork**	Row 2 contrasts *or, ore, ar* with *ir, ur.*
pigpen	**jerk**	**curve**	**skirt**	**spun**	Row 3 contrasts short vowels *e, i, u* with *er, ir, ur.*

If... children cannot blend words with *er, ir, ur* at this point,

then... use the Small-Group Time Strategic Intervention lesson, p. DI•85, to reteach /ėr/ spelled *er, ir,* and *ur*. Continue to monitor children's progress using other instructional opportunities during the week. See the Skills Trace on pp. 152–153.

Day 1	**Day 2**	**Day 3**	**Day 4**	**Day 5**
Check Word Reading	Check Word Reading	Check High-Frequency Words/Retelling	Check Fluency	Check Oral Vocabulary

Success Predictor

Differentiated Instruction

A Advanced

More Challenging Words Have children blend and read these words: *gardener, circle, surprise, turkey, birthmark, yesterday, thirsty, silver, purpose, thirteen, furnace, kernel, confirm, injury, furniture.* Have children copy the words on cards and sort them according to the *er, ir,* or *ur* spelling of the /ėr/ sound. Then have children use several of the words in sentences.

Spelling Patterns

er, ir, ur The sound /ėr/ may be spelled *er, ir,* or *ur*.

ELL

English Language Learners

Pronunciation Tip Help Spanish-speaking children distinguish between the pronunciation of /ėr/ and /ē/r by modeling the following pairs of words. Have children repeat after you: *her/hear, fur/fear, purr/peer, stir/steer*.

Objectives

- Apply knowledge of sound-spellings to decode unknown words when reading.
- Decode and read words in context and isolation.
- Practice fluency with oral rereading.

Decodable Practice Reader 17A

Vowels: *r*-Controlled *er, ir, ur*

Decode words in isolation Have children turn to page 241. Have children decode each word.

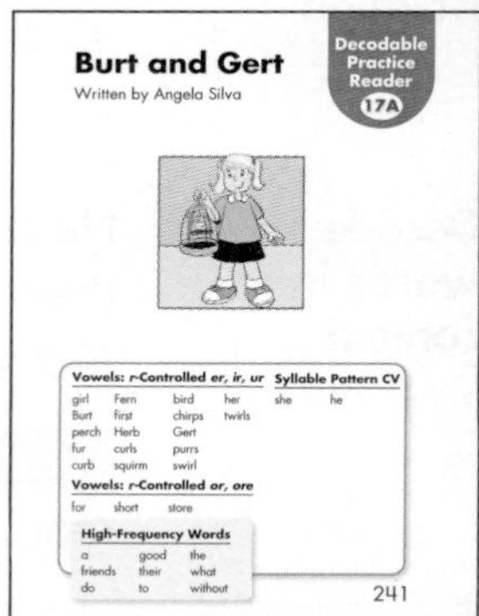
Burt and Gert

Written by Angela Silva

Decodable Practice Reader 17A

Vowels: *r*-Controlled *er, ir, ur*

girl Fern bird her

Burt first chirps twirls

perch Herb Gert

fur curls purrs

curb squirm swirl

Syllable Pattern CV

she he

Vowels: *r*-Controlled *or, ore*

for short store

High-Frequency Words

a good the

friends their what

do to without

241

Decodable Practice Reader 17A

Review High-frequency words Review the previously taught words *friends, a, do, the, good, their, to, what,* and *without*. Have children read each word as you point to it on the Word Wall.

Preview Have children read the title and preview the story. Tell them they will read words that have the /ėr/ sound spelled *er, ir,* and *ur* in this story.

Decode words in context Pair children for reading and listen carefully as they decode. One child begins. Children read the entire story, switching readers after each page. Partners reread the story. This time the other child begins.

This girl is Fern.
She has a bird.
Her bird is Burt.

242

Burt is a good pet.
First he chirps and sings.
Then he twirls on his perch.

243

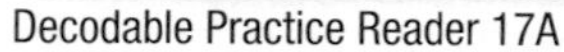
Decodable Practice Reader 17A

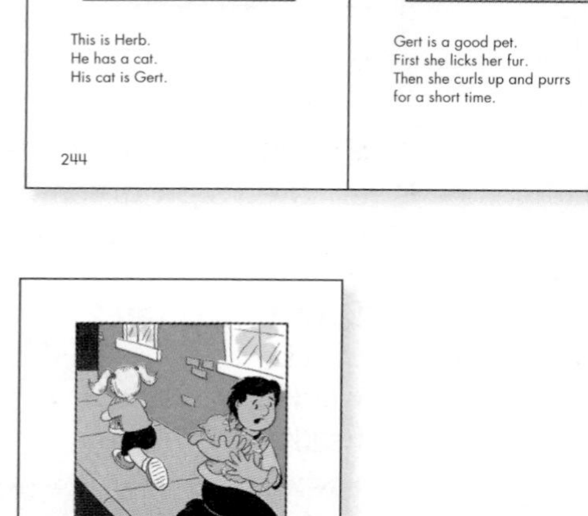
This is Herb.
He has a cat.
His cat is Gert.

244

Gert is a good pet.
First she licks her fur.
Then she curls up and purrs
for a short time.

245

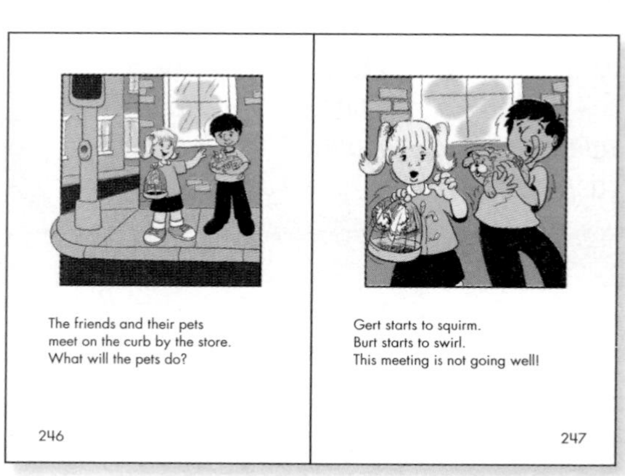
The friends and their pets
meet on the curb by the store.
What will the pets do?

246

Gert starts to squirm.
Burt starts to swirl.
This meeting is not going well!

247

Next time Fern and Herb will meet
without pets!

248

Corrective feedback

If. . . children have difficulty decoding a word,

then. . . refer them to the Sound-Spelling Cards to identify the sounds in the word. Then prompt them to blend the word.

- What is the new word?
- Is the new word a word you know?
- Does it make sense in the story?

Check decoding and comprehension

Have children retell the story to include characters, setting, and events. Then have children locate words that have /ėr/ words spelled *er, ir,* and *ur* in the story. List words that children name. Children should supply *girl, Fern, bird, her, Burt, first, chirps, twirls, perch, Herb, Gert, fur, curls, purrs, curb, squirm,* and *swirl*. Ask children how they know these words have the /ėr/ sound. (They all have the letters *er, ir,* or *ur*.)

Reread for Fluency

Have children reread Decodable Reader 17A to develop automaticity decoding words with the /ėr/ sound.

ROUTINE Oral Rereading

1. **Read** Have children read the entire book orally.
2. **Reread** To achieve optimal fluency, children should reread the text three or four times.
3. **Corrective Feedback** Listen as children read. Provide corrective feedback regarding their fluency and decoding.

Routines Flip Chart

Differentiated Instruction

 Advanced

Parts of Speech After reading, have partners write the following /ėr/ words from the story on separate cards: *girl, Fern, bird, Burt, chirps, purrs, fur, swirl, perch,* and *twirls*. Have them say each word and sort the cards into two piles: nouns (naming words) and verbs (action words).

English Language Learners

Vowels: *r*-Controlled *er, ir, ur*

Beginning Before children read, lead them through Burt and Gert, identifying the characters. In addition to the characters' names, point out /ėr/ words such as *girl, her, bird, curls,* and *curb*. Have children say them aloud.

Intermediate After reading, have children find /ėr/ words and use them in sentences. For example: *The cat curls up and takes a nap*. Monitor children's pronunciation.

Advanced/Advanced High After reading, have children describe how Gert squirms and Burt swirls. Then have children make up their own sentences for *squirm* and *swirl*.

Get Ready to Read

Objectives
- Read words with *er, ir, ur*.
- Read high-frequency words.

Spelling Pretest
Words with *er, ir, ur*

Dictate spelling words

Dictate the spelling words and read the sentences. Have children write the words. If needed, segment the words for children, clarify the pronunciations, and give meanings of words. Have children check their pretests and correct misspelled words.

1. her	The cat and **her** kittens are asleep.
2. first	May I be **first** in line?
3. bird*	The **bird** made a nest in our tree.
4. girl	There is a new **girl** in our class.
5. burn	We **burn** wood in our fireplace.
6. were	The bears **were** asleep all winter.
7. shirt	We got Dad a **shirt** for his birthday.
8. fur	My dog has soft **fur**.
9. hurt	I **hurt** my knee when I fell off my bike.
10. sir	The soldier said, "Yes **sir**" to the general.

* The word marked with an asterisk comes from the selection *I'm a Caterpillar.*

On their own

Use Let's Practice It! p. 158 on the *Teacher Resource DVD-ROM.*

Let's Practice It! TR DVD•158

Small Group Time

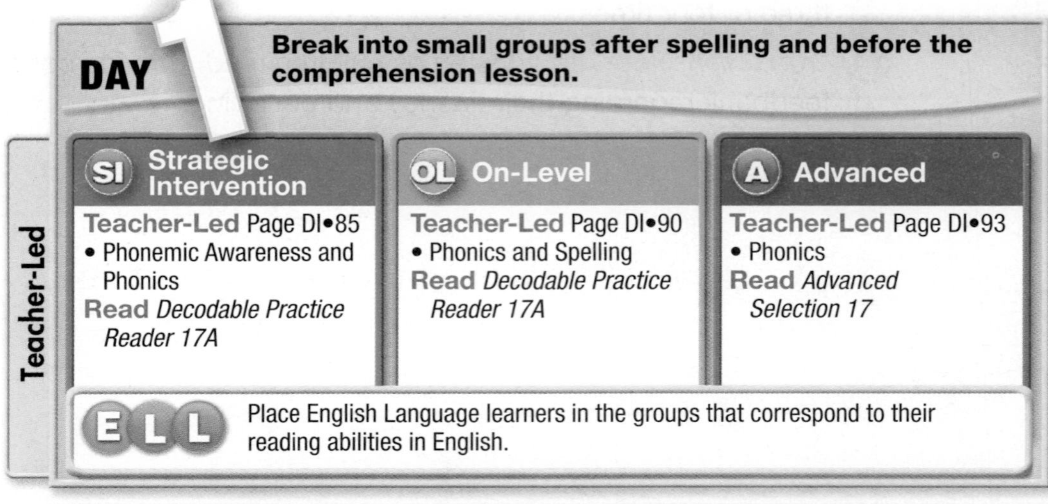
DAY 1 **Break into small groups after spelling and before the comprehension lesson.**

Teacher-Led

SI Strategic Intervention	OL On-Level	A Advanced
Teacher-Led Page DI•85 • Phonemic Awareness and Phonics **Read** *Decodable Practice Reader 17A*	**Teacher-Led** Page DI•90 • Phonics and Spelling **Read** *Decodable Practice Reader 17A*	**Teacher-Led** Page DI•93 • Phonics **Read** *Advanced Selection 17*

ELL Place English Language learners in the groups that correspond to their reading abilities in English.

Practice Stations
- Listen Up
- Word Work

Independent Activities
- Read independently/Reading Log on *Reader's and Writer's Notebook* p. RR4
- Concept Talk Video

High-Frequency Words

Introduce

ROUTINE Nondecodable Words

1. **Say and Spell** Look at p. 155. Some words we have to learn by remembering the letters rather than saying the sounds. We will say and spell the words to help learn them. Point to the first word. This word is *know*. The letters in *know* are *k-n-o-w*, *know*. Have children say and spell each word, first with you, and then without you.
2. **Demonstrate Meaning** Tell me a sentence using the word *know*. Repeat this routine with the other Words I Can Read.

Routines Flip Chart

Read words in isolation Have children read the words on p. 155 aloud. Add the words to the Word Wall.

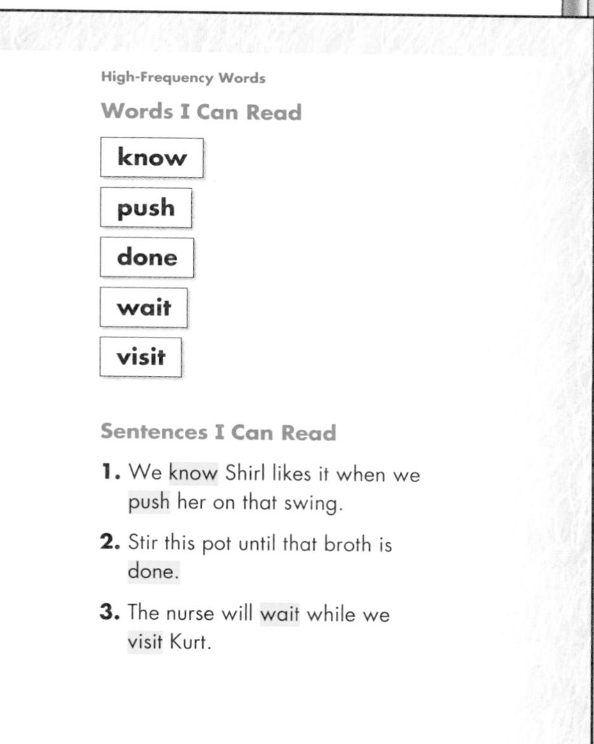

High-Frequency Words

Words I Can Read

know

push

done

wait

visit

Sentences I Can Read

1. We know Shirl likes it when we push her on that swing.
2. Stir this pot until that broth is done.
3. The nurse will wait while we visit Kurt.

155

Student Edition p. 155

Read words in context Have children read the sentences aloud. Have them identify this week's High-Frequency Words in the sentences.

On their own Use *Reader's and Writer's Notebook* p. 378.

Name

I'm a Caterpillar

Read the words in the box.
Pick a word to finish each sentence.
Write the words in the puzzles.

push visit wait

done know

Reader's and Writer's Notebook, p. 378

Differentiated Instruction

A Advanced

Extend Spelling Challenge children who spell words correctly to spell more difficult words such as: *furnish, murky, disturb, further, thirteen, and expert.*

Phonics/Spelling Generalization

Each spelling word has the letters *er, ir,* or *ur,* which spell the sound /ėr/.

English Language Learners

Survival Vocabulary Pantomime the meanings of some of the high-frequency words and/or spelling words, and have children repeat your gestures and say the words.

Frontload Read Aloud Use the modified Read Aloud in the *ELL Support* pages to prepare children to listen to "Fern's Wild Job" (page 155b).

DAY 1 Read and Comprehend

30–35 min.

Objectives

◎ Distinguish facts from opinions in text.

Skills Trace

◎ **Fact and Opinion**

Introduce U3W3D1; U3W5D1

Practice U3W3D2; U3W3D3; U3W3D4; U3W5D2; U3W5D3; U3W5D4

Reteach/Review U3W3D5; U3W5D5; U4W3D2

Assess/Test Weekly Tests U3W3; U3W5

Benchmark Tests U3

KEY:

U=Unit W=Week D=Day

Listening Comprehension

◎ Fact and Opinion

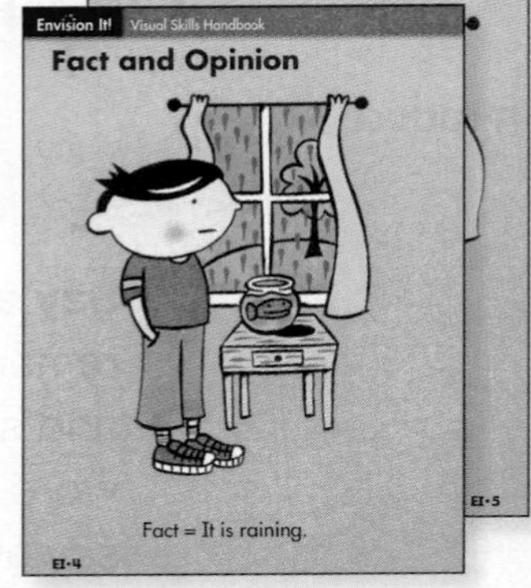

Student Edition EI•4–EI•5

Introduce

Envision It!

A **fact** tells something that can be proved true by observing, checking in a book, or asking an expert. An **opinion** tells someone's idea or feeling about something. It cannot be proved true or false.

Have children turn to pp. EI•4–5 in their Student Editions. The pictures and sentences show a fact and an opinion. Discuss these questions using the words and pictures:

- Why is the sentence "It is raining" a fact? (It can be proved true by observing. The picture shows rain.)
- Why is the sentence "Rainy days are fun" an opinion? (It just tells how the girl feels. It can't be proved true or false. Someone else might feel that rainy days are no fun at all.)

Model

Today we will read a story about an interesting job. Read "Fern's Wild Job." Draw a T-chart or use Graphic Organizer 4 to model fact and opinion.

Think Aloud Knowing the difference between facts and opinions helps me understand what I read. When Mrs. Beal says, "Many animals eat foods that people eat," that's a fact I could prove by observing or looking in a nature book. When Fern says, "Nuts are delicious!" that's just her opinion—it tells me how she feels about nuts. I might feel the same way, or I might feel differently.

Fact	Opinion
Many animals eat foods that people eat.	Nuts are delicious.

Guided practice

After reading the story, give children other facts and opinions from it. Discuss why each is a fact or an opinion, and add it to the appropriate column in the chart. Then choose topics of interest to children and have them state facts and opinions about them. Add those to the chart as well.

On their own

Use *Reader's and Writer's* Notebook p. 379.

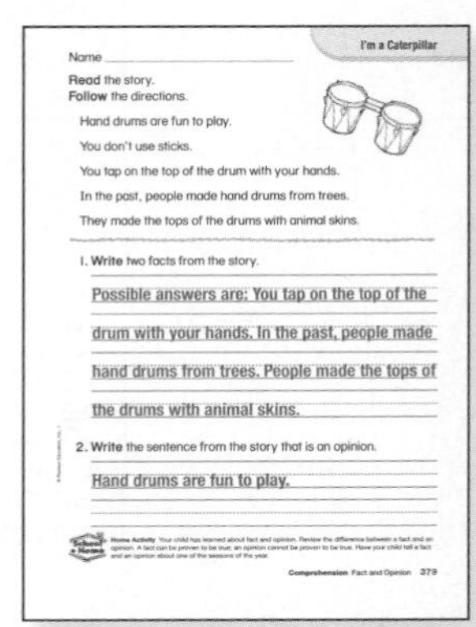
Name

I'm a Caterpillar

Read the story.
Follow the directions.

Hand drums are fun to play.
You don't use sticks.
You tap on the top of the drum with your hands.
In the past, people made hand drums from trees.
They made the tops of the drums with animal skins.

1. **Write** two facts from the story.

Possible answers are: You tap on the top of the drum with your hands. In the past, people made hand drums from trees. People made the tops of the drums with animal skins.

2. **Write** the sentence from the story that is an opinion.

Hand drums are fun to play.

Comprehension Fact and Opinion 379

Reader's and Writer's Notebook p. 379

Read Aloud

Fern's Wild Job

Fern stepped into Mrs. Beal's garden shed.

"Hi, Fern!" Mrs. Beal said. "Are you ready for work?"

Fern nodded excitedly. "Taking care of animals is the best kind of job!" she said.

Mrs. Beal smiled. "I think so too," she said. All year long, Mrs. Beal fed the birds, squirrels, chipmunks, and rabbits that lived in her yard. Now she was going on vacation for two weeks, and she had hired Fern to feed the animals while she was away.

Fern looked around the shed. She saw gardening tools and flower pots. She also saw a shelf full of boxes and bags.

Mrs. Beal said, "This shelf is where I keep the animal food." Fern saw that one large bag said Sunflower Seeds, another said Peanuts, and another said Walnuts.

"Nuts are delicious!" Fern said. "I eat them for snacks myself."

"Yes," Mrs. Beal said. "Many animals eat foods that people eat. Some birds eat fruit, such as raisins and pieces of apple or orange. I'll give you a bag of fruit to keep fresh in your refrigerator, so you can bring some to the birds every day."

Mrs. Beal took Fern around the yard. "Rabbits look for food on the ground. Many birds look for food in feeders," she explained. She showed Fern how to fill each feeder and where to scatter food. Before long, blue jays, cardinals, and robins flew in for a meal. Squirrels, chipmunks, and a big rabbit nibbled food on the ground. The squirrels raced around, trying to steal each other's peanuts.

"The most interesting part of this job is watching the animals," said Mrs. Beal. "The squirrels are the funniest!"

"I wish I could do this job all year," Fern said.

"Well, you can," said Mrs. Beal. "Pet stores sell feeders. You can put a feeder in your own yard."

Fern clapped her hands together. "That's what I'll buy with the money I earn!" she said. She could hardly wait to begin her new job.

Academic Vocabulary

fact piece of information that can be proved to be true

opinion the way someone thinks or feels about something

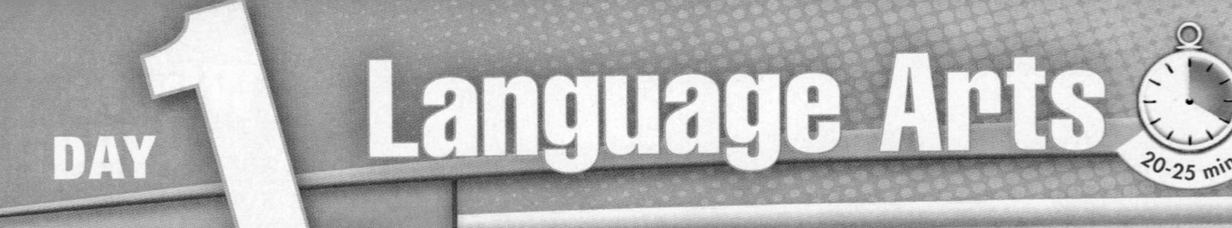

Objectives

- Use verbs *am, is, are, was,* and were with correct subject-verb agreement.
- Understand the features of captions about pictures.

MINI-LESSON

5 Day Planner
Guide to Mini-Lessons

DAY 1	Read Like a Writer
DAY 2	Focus/Ideas
DAY 3	Details to Show and Tell
DAY 4	Revising Strategy: Adding a Sentence
DAY 5	Proofread for Verbs

Conventions
Verbs *Am, Is, Are, Was,* and *Were*

Model

Explain that some **verbs** help tell how things are or were. *Am, is, are, was,* and *were* are verbs. Tell children that the verbs *am, is,* and *are* tell about now. The verbs *was* and *were* tell about the past.

Display Grammar Transparency 17. Read the explanations and examples aloud. Then read the directions and model number 1.

- *Am* is the verb in sentence one.
- *Am* tells about now, so I will write the word *now* on the line.

Verbs: Am, Is, Are, Was, Were

The words **am, is,** and **are** tell about now. Use **am** or **is** to tell about one. Use **are** to tell about more than one.

I **am** big. It **is** small. They **are** small.

The words **was** and **were** tell about the past. Use **was** to tell about one. Use **were** to tell about more than one.

It **was** hungry. They **were** hungry.

Circle the verb in each sentence. **Write** *Now* if the sentence tells about now. **Write** *Past* if the sentence tells about the past.

1. I am a butterfly. Now
2. I was a caterpillar. Past
3. Leaves were my food. Past
4. Butterflies are on the flowers. Now
5. The nectar is sweet. Now

Unit 3 I'm a Caterpillar — Grammar 17

Grammar Transparency 17
TR DVD

Also, teach children that when you ask a question using *am, is, are, was,* and *were,* those words often come first. Write the following questions on the board and read them aloud: *Are you feeling well? Were the boots on the mat?* Have children come up to the board and circle the first word of the question.

Guide practice

Continue working on transparency items 2–5, having children identify which verbs tell about now and which verbs tell about the past.

Connect to oral language

Have the class complete these sentence frames orally.

1. They _______ late for school.
2. _______ we in first grade?
3. I _______ six years old.

On their own

Team Talk Pair children and have them talk about qualities that they and other people that they know have. Have them use *am, is, are, was,* and *were.* Then have them identify which verbs tell about now and which tell about the past.

Writing—Captions and Pictures
Introduce

MINI-LESSON

Read Like a Writer

Reader's and Writer's Notebook p. 380

- **Introduce** This week you will write captions to go with pictures you draw. Captions usually are below pictures. They tell about the pictures they are with. Many captions are sentences.

Prompt Think of changes in nature. Plants and animals grow. Seasons change. Draw two pictures to show one way a plant or animal changes. Write captions about your pictures.

Trait Focus/Ideas

Mode Descriptive

- **Examine Model Text** Let's listen to some captions. Track the print as you read aloud the captions and students view the pictures on *Reader's and Writer's Notebook* p. 380. Have children follow along.

- **Key Features** What is in the first picture? (A yellow bird) When is the bird yellow? (summer) Help children find and circle the information in the caption. Ask how the bird changes in winter. (It turns brown.) Help children underline the information in the second caption. Explain that the second picture and caption show and tell this information.

These pictures have captions below them. The captions tell about the birds in the pictures.

The captions are complete sentences. They have subjects and verbs. They tell a complete thought.

Write Guy
Jeff Anderson

Let's Use Books

Let's use books to solve problems! If a child wants to write dialogue, she can look at how the author of a recently read story wrote dialogue. Have the child ask herself, "What do I like about how these characters speak?" Young writers need models—and the books in your classroom are brimming with lessons to learn.

Daily Fix-It

1. The gurl saw a bug
   The girl saw a bug.
2. it was on hur shirt.
   It was on her shirt.

Discuss the Daily Fix-It corrections with children. Review sentence capitalization, punctuation, and the spellings of *r*-controlled vowels in *girl* and *her*.

English Language Learners

Options for Convensions Support To provide children with practice on verbs *am, is, are, was,* and *were,* use the modified grammar lessons in the *ELL Handbook.*

Objectives

- Understand and recognize the features of captions and pictures.
- Develop an understanding of focus and ideas in captions and pictures.
- Identify a topic connected to this week's concept.
- Narrow the focus of the topic by formulating inquiry questions related to the topic.
- Explore changes in nature.

Writing—Captions and Pictures
Introduce, continued

Review key features Review key features of captions and pictures with children. You may want to post these key features in the classroom to allow children to refer to them as they work on their captions and pictures.

Key Features of Captions and Pictures

- Captions tell about what pictures show.
- Many captions are sentences.

Connect to familiar texts Use examples from *Life in the Forest* (Unit 2) or another expository text that includes captions and photographs. In *Life in the Forest,* the text is augmented with photographs and captions that show elements and events in nature. The captions tell what is pictured and give more information about the pictures and the topic.

Look ahead Tell children that tomorrow they will plan their own captions and pictures.

ROUTINE Quick Write for Fluency **Team Talk**

1. **Talk** Read these questions aloud, and have children respond with ideas about change in nature.
   How do animals change when they grow?
   What happens when seasons change?
2. **Write** Have children write a short sentence to answer one of the questions.
3. **Share** Partners can read their answers to one another.

Routines Flip Chart

Research and Inquiry
Identify and Focus Topic

Teach Display and review the concept map that explores this week's question: *What changes can be seen in nature?* What are some changes in nature that you have seen? Ask children to share their ideas.

Model Think Aloud I'm going to ask you some questions that might help you remember some changes in nature that you have seen. What are some places in nature that you like to visit? (my backyard) What are some plants and animals you see at these places? (grass, flowers, ants) Do you remember any changes in any of these things? (the grass grows and needs to be mowed; flowers bloom in spring)

Guide practice Have children think of answers and then record them in a chart.

Place in Nature	What did you see there?	What changes did you see?
My backyard	grass, flowers, ants	The grass grows and has to be mowed. The flowers bloom in spring.

Wrap Up Your Day

- ✔ **Phonics: *r*-Controlled *er, ir, ur*** Write *her, bird,* and *burn.* Ask children how the sound /ėr/ is spelled in *her, bird,* and *burn.* (The sound /ėr/ is spelled *er* in *her, ir* in *bird,* and *ur* in *burn.*)
- ✔ **Spelling: Words with *er, ir, ur*** Have children name the spelling for each sound in *first.* Write the spelling as children write the letters in the air. Continue with *were, fur,* and *shirt.*
- ✔ **Build Concepts** Ask children to recall what happened in the Read Aloud, "Fern's Wild Job." How does feeding the birds and animals show an example of change in nature? (Possible response: Animals and birds need food in order to grow and change.)
- ✔ **Homework** Send home this week's Family Times Newsletter from Let's Practice It! pp. 153–154 on the *Teacher Resource DVD-ROM.*

Let's Practice It!
TR DVD•153–154

Differentiated Instruction

SI Strategic Intervention

Selecting a Topic If children have trouble remembering places in nature that they have been, then provide them with a list that may jog their memory: *a park, backyard, nature center, hiking trail, the beach.* They may select a place they have been or visited from your list.

Preview DAY 2

Tell children that tomorrow they will read about a caterpillar that grows and changes.

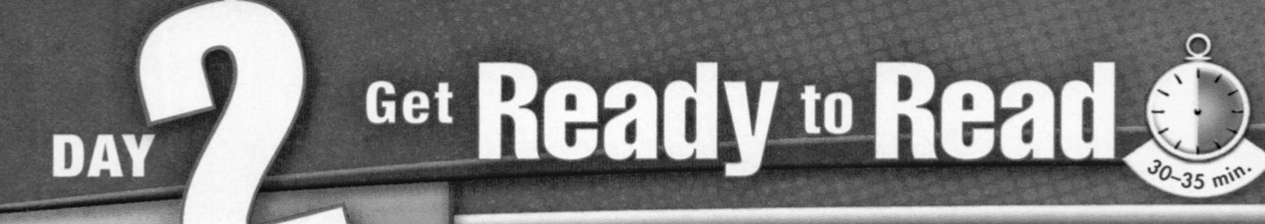

Objectives

- Discuss the concept to develop oral vocabulary.
- Build oral vocabulary.

Today at a Glance

Oral Vocabulary
rearrange

Phonemic Awareness
Isolate Medial and Final Phonemes

Phonics and Spelling
◉ *r*-Controlled *er, ir, ur*
◉ Contractions

Fluency
Paired Reading

High-Frequency Words

Story Words
caterpillar, chrysalis, crawl, pupa, shiver

Comprehension
◉ Fact and Opinion
◉ Text Structure

Vocabulary
Dictionary/Glossary

Conventions
Verbs *am, is, are, was, were*

Writing
Captions and Pictures

Handwriting
Letter V and v; Left-to-Right Progression

Research and Inquiry
Research Skill: Technology

Concept Talk

Question of the Week

What changes can be seen in nature?

Build concepts

To reinforce concepts and to focus children's attention, have them sing "Life Cycle" from the *Sing with Me* Big Book. In what season does the insect develop in her shell? (winter) In what season does she come out as a butterfly? (summer)

Sing with Me Big Book Audio

Introduce Amazing Words

Display the Big Book, *What Makes the Seasons?* Read the title and identify the author. Explain that in the story, the author uses the word *rearrange*. Have children listen as you read the story to find out how the seasons rearrange themselves in different parts of the world.

Use the Oral Vocabulary routine on the next page to teach the word *rearrange*.

Big Book

ELL Reinforce Vocabulary Use the Day 2 instruction on ELL Poster 17 to reinforce meanings of high-frequency words.

ELL Poster 17

Oral Vocabulary
Amazing Words

Amazing Words

cycle
develop
insect
rearrange
flurries
emerge
fragile
vessel

Teach Amazing Words

Amazing Words Oral Vocabulary Routine

1. **Introduce the Word** Relate the word *rearrange* to the book. We learned that when it's winter in one half of the Earth, it's summer in the other half. The seasons *rearrange* themselves by changing places. Supply a child-friendly definition. When you *rearrange* things, you move them around. Have children say the word.
2. **Demonstrate** Provide examples to show meaning. You could *rearrange* furniture to make a room look different. If we *rearrange* our school day, we do things in a different order.
3. **Apply** Have children demonstrate their understanding. What are some things you have *rearranged*?

Routines Flip Chart

Differentiated Instruction

SI Strategic Intervention

Using Amazing Words If children have difficulty using the word *rearrange,* provide sentence starters like this: *I can rearrange my (desk, hair, hockey cards) by* ________.

Anchored Talk

Add to the concept map

Discuss cycles of change we can observe in nature.

- Yesterday we learned that a cycle is something that happens and then starts all over again. Why are the seasons a kind of cycle? (Possible response: The four seasons happen each year and then start over.) Let's add *The Cycle of Seasons* to our map.
- Draw a circle on the board and write *spring, summer, fall, winter* at quarter points around it. Have children say the seasons aloud with you as you point to them. What happens next when spring, summer, fall, and winter have all passed? (It's spring again.) Let's add this idea to our map.

ELL

English Language Learners

Demonstrate Meaning Display a row of number or letter cards. Ask children to *rearrange* the cards in a different order.

Objectives

- Isolate medial and final phonemes in contractions.
- ◎ Blend and read contractions with *'s, 've,* and *'re.*

Skills Trace

◎ **Contractions**

Introduce U2W4D2; U3W5D2

Practice U2W4D3; U2W4D4; U3W5D3; U3W5D4

Reteach/Review U2W4D5; U2W5D4; U3W5D5; U3W6D4

Assess/Test Weekly Test U2W4; U3W5

Benchmark Tests U3

KEY:

U=Unit W=Week D=Day

Phonemic Awareness

Isolate Medial and Final Phonemes

Model isolating sounds Have children look at the picture on pages 152–153 in their Student Edition. I see a girl in the picture. She's walking by the pond. When I say *she's,* the middle sound I hear is /ē/. The last sound I hear in *she's* is /z/. I see some tadpoles in the pond. They've started turning into frogs. When I say *they've*, the middle sound I hear is /ā/. The last sound I hear in *they've* is /v/.

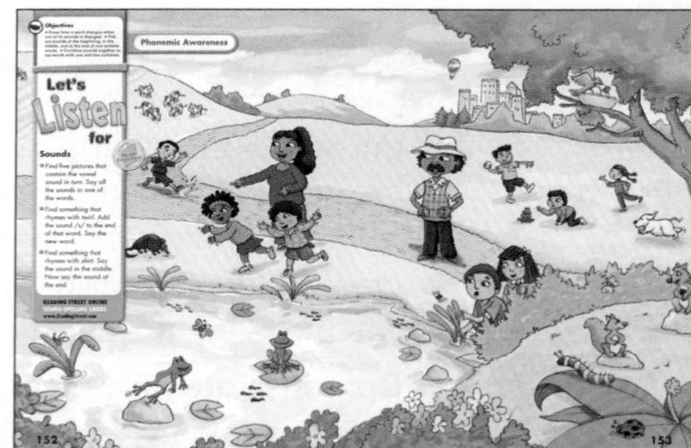

Student Edition pp. 152–153

Model segmenting and blending Listen to the sounds in the word *he's*: /h/ /ē/ /z/. There are three sounds in *he's*. Let's blend those sounds to make a word: /h/ /ē/ /z/, *he's*. Continue modeling with *they're, you've,* and *who's*.

Guide practice Guide children as they segment and blend these contractions: *we've, we're, it's, what's, I've,* and *you're*.

Corrective feedback **If...** children make an error,
then... model by segmenting the word, and have them repeat the segmenting and blending of the word.

On their own Have children segment and blend the following contractions.

/i/ /t/ /s/ **it's**	/h/ /ü/ /z/ **who's**
/sh/ /ē/ /z/ **she's**	/y/ /ü/ /r/ **you're**
/w/ /ē/ /v/ **we've**	/ī/ /v/ **I've**

Phonics—Teach/Model
Contractions with *'s, 've, 're*

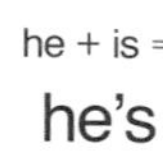
he + is =
he's

Sound-Spelling Card 114

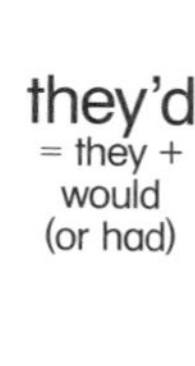
they'd
= they + would (or had)

Sound-Spelling Card 115

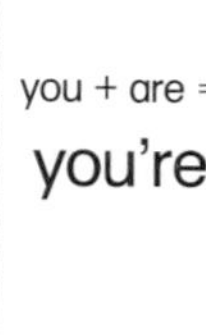
you + are =
you're

Sound-Spelling Card 113

ROUTINE Word Parts Strategy

1. **Connect** Connect today's lesson to previous learning. Write *aren't* and *she'll*. Point out to children that they have already studied words like these. What do we call words like these? (contractions) Remind children that a contraction is a short way of writing two words. Ask them to read *aren't* and *she'll*. What two words make up *aren't*? (are not) *She'll*? (she will) Explain that today they will learn about other contractions.
2. **Use Sound-Spelling Cards** Display Card 114. Point to *he's*. On the board, write *he is*. *He's* is a short way of writing *he is*. Point to the apostrophe. The apostrophe takes the place of the letter *i* that is left out. Have children say *he is* and *he's* several times as you point first to *he is* and then to *he's*. Repeat this process for *they'd* and *you're* using Cards 115 and 113.
3. **Model** Write *they've*. Beneath it write *they have*. The contraction *they've* is made from the words *they* and *have*.

   When I see a word with an apostrophe, it might be a contraction. I read the word that comes before the apostrophe, *they*, and the letters that come after it, *ve*. Then I read them together as one word: *they've*.
4. **Guide Practice** Have children read *they've* with you. Write the contractions below. Have the group read them with you. Then have them identify the words that make up each contraction.

   she's **you're** **we've** **that's** **we're** **I've**
5. **Review** What do you know about reading contractions? (Contractions are a short way of writing two words. The apostrophe takes the place of the letter or letters that are left out.)

Routines Flip Chart

Differentiated Instruction

SI Strategic Intervention

Contractions Have children write the contractions. Below each contraction, have them write the two words that form it. Then have them circle the apostrophe in the contraction. In the words below it, have them circle the letter(s) that the apostrophe stands for.

ELL

English Language Learners

Visual Support Model isolating sounds while using the pictures on pp. 152–153 of the Student Edition as visual support. For example: Look at the caterpillar. It's crawling up the tree. Let's say the sounds in *it's*: /i/ /t/ /s/, *it's*.

Objectives

- ◎ Identify contractions and the words that form them.
- Blend and read contractions with *'s, 've, 're.*
- Decode words in context and in isolation.

Check Word Reading
SUCCESS PREDICTOR

Phonics—Build Fluency
◎ Contractions with *'s, 've, 're*

Model

Envision It!

Have children turn to page 156 in their Student Editions. Look at the white word boxes on this page. The word after each equal sign is a contraction. A contraction is a short way of writing two words. The word in the second white box is *he's*. *He's* is a contraction for *he is*. The apostrophe takes the place of the *i* that has been left out of *is*. To read *he's*, I blend the word that comes before the apostrophe with the sound of the letter that comes after the apostrophe. I read them as one word: *he* /z/, *he's*. Repeat this process for *we've* and *you're*.

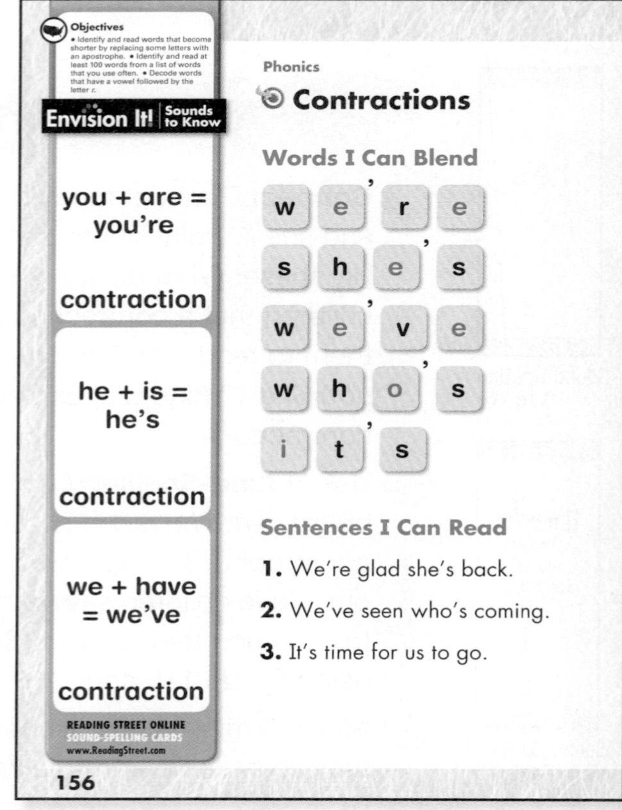

Student Edition p. 156

Guide practice

For each word in "Words I Can Blend", identify the two words that form the contraction. Have children pronounce the word that comes before the apostrophe and the sound that comes after. Make sure children pronounce each part of the contraction correctly. Then have them blend the whole word.

Corrective feedback

If... children have difficulty blending a word,
then... model blending the word, and ask children to blend it with you.

Blend and Read

Decode words in isolation

After children can successfully segment and blend the words, ask them to read the words naturally.

Decode words in context

Have children read each of the sentences. Have them identify each contraction and the two words that form it.

Team Talk Pair children and have them take turns reading each of the sentences aloud.

On their own

Use *Reader's and Writer's Notebook* p. 381.

Name

I'm a Caterpillar

Pick a word from the box that means the same as each pair of words. Write it on the line.

She is tall. She's tall.

he's	it's	I've	that's	they're
they've	we're	we've	you're	you've

1. I + have — I've
2. we + are — we're
3. it + is — it's
4. that + is — that's
5. you + have — you've
6. they + have — they've
7. we + have — we've
8. he + is — he's
9. they + are — they're
10. you + are — you're

Reader's and Writer's Notebook p. 381

MONITOR PROGRESS — Check Word Reading ⟲ Contractions

Write the following words and have the class read them. Notice which children miss words during the group reading. Call on those individuals to read some of the words.

he's	**you've**	**it's**	**I've**	**we're**	Spiral Review
isn't	**they're**	**I'm**	**they'll**	**what's**	Row 2 and 3 include review of contractions
you'll	**she's**	**didn't**	**we've**	**wasn't**	with *n't, 'm, 'll.*

If... children cannot blend contractions,

then... use the Small Group Time Strategic Intervention lesson, p. DI•86, to reteach contractions. Continue to monitor children's progress using other instructional opportunities during the week. See the Skills Trace on p. 156c.

Day 1	**Day 2**	Day 3	Day 4	Day 5
Check Word Reading	**Check Word Reading**	Check High-Frequency Words/Retelling	Check Fluency	Check Oral Vocabulary

Success Predictor

Differentiated Instruction

SI Strategic Intervention

Letter Tiles Use letter tiles to form the two words that make up contractions. Have children say the two words. Then push the two words together and replace the appropriate letters with an apostrophe. (If no apostrophe tile is available, cover any tile with a sticky note and write an apostrophe on it.) Have children read the contraction they have just formed.

Spelling Patterns

Contraction A contraction is a shortened form of two words. An apostrophe appears where letters have been dropped from the original words.

English Language Learners

Recognize Contractions Some other languages also include contractions. If possible, provide examples of contractions in the home language. In Spanish, *de* + *el* = *del*; in Portuguese, *por* + *os* = *pelos*. Point out that English contractions use an apostrophe to replace missing letter(s).

Objectives

- Apply knowledge of sound-spellings to decode unknown words when reading.
- Decode words in context and isolation.
- Practice fluency with oral rereading.

Decodable Practice Reader 17B

Contractions

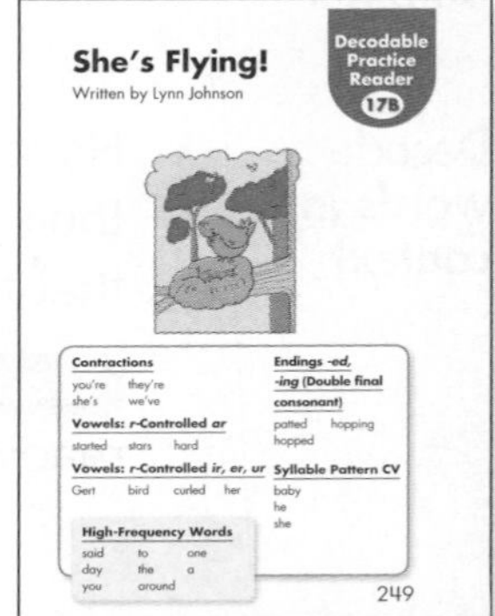

She's Flying!

Written by Lynn Johnson

Decodable Practice Reader 17B

Contractions

you're they're
she's we've

Vowels: *r*-Controlled *ar*

started stars hard

Vowels: *r*-Controlled *ir, er, ur*

Gert bird curled her

Endings *-ed, -ing* (Double final consonant)

patted hopping
hopped

Syllable Pattern CV

baby
he
she

High-Frequency Words

said to one
day the a
you around

249

Decodable Practice Reader 17B

Decode words in isolation Have children turn to page 249. Have children decode each word.

Review High-frequency words Review the previously taught words *said, one, the, you, to, day, a,* and *around*. Have children read each word as you point to it on the Word Wall.

Preview Have children read the title and preview the story. Tell them they will read contractions in this story.

Decode words in context Pair children for reading and listen carefully as they decode. One child begins. Children read the entire story, switching readers after each page. Partners reread the story. This time the other child begins.

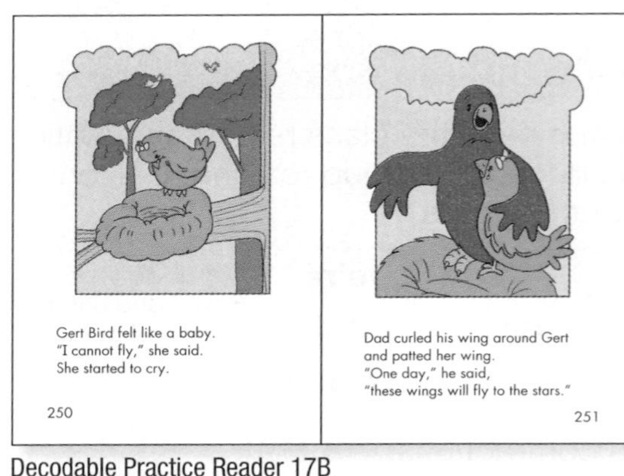

Gert Bird felt like a baby.
"I cannot fly," she said.
She started to cry.

250

Dad curled his wing around Gert and patted her wing.
"One day," he said,
"these wings will fly to the stars."

251

Decodable Practice Reader 17B

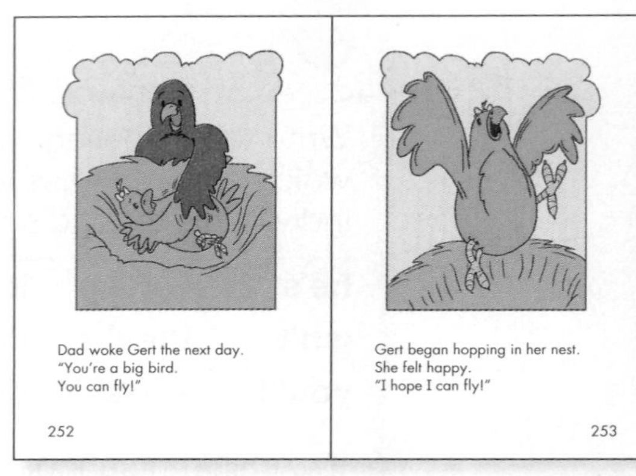

Dad woke Gert the next day.
"You're a big bird.
You can fly!"

252

Gert began hopping in her nest.
She felt happy.
"I hope I can fly!"

253

Mom came with Gert and Dad.
"Hop off with those fine feet, Gert.
They're so strong," Mom called.

254

Gert hopped off the branch.
The wind lifted her up.
"She's flying!" Dad yelled.

255

"She's flying!" Mom said.
"We've seen Gert try hard."

256

Corrective feedback

If. . . children have difficulty decoding a word,

then. . . refer them to the Sound-Spelling Cards to identify the sounds in the word. Then prompt them to blend the word.

- What is the new word?
- Is the new word a word you know?
- Does it make sense in the story?

Check decoding and comprehension

Have children retell the story to include characters, setting, and events. Then have children locate contractions in the story. List the contractions children name. Children should supply *you're, they're, she's,* and *we've*. Ask children how they know these words are contractions. (Each word has an apostrophe that takes the place of one or more letters that are left out. Each is a short way of writing two words.) Have the children name the two words that make up each contraction in the story. List the word pair next to the matching contraction.

Reread for Fluency

Have children reread Decodable Practice Reader 17B to develop automaticity decoding words that are contractions.

ROUTINE **Paired Reading**

1. **Reread** To achieve optimal fluency, children should reread the text three or four times.

2. **Corrective Feedback** Listen as children read. Provide corrective feedback regarding their fluency and decoding.

Routines Flip Chart

Differentiated Instruction

Strategic Intervention

Retelling If children have difficulty retelling the story, ask them questions regarding events in the story.

English Language Learners
Contractions

Beginning Point out sentences with contractions in *She's Flying!* Help children restate the sentences, substituting the two words the contraction is made from.

Intermediate Have children find the sentences that contain contractions and read them aloud. Have children identify the two words each contraction is made from and the letter(s) that are replaced by the apostrophe.

Advanced/Advanced-High Have children make up new dialog for the birds, using the contractions *you're, they're, she's* and *we've*.

Objectives

- Apply knowledge of letter-sound correspondences and *r*-controlled vowel sounds to decode words in context and in isolation.
- Spell words with /ėr/ spelled *er, ir, ur.*

Phonics Review

r-Controlled /ėr/ *er, ir, ur* and /är/ *ar*

Review Sound-Spellings

Review the *er, ir,* and *ur* spellings of /ėr/ and the *ar* spelling of /är/ using Sound-Spelling Cards 67, 72, 104, and 55.

Decode words in isolation

Display these words. Have the class blend the words. Then point to the words in random order and ask children to decode them quickly.

hurt	**smart**	**curls**
yarn	**first**	**term**
party	**third**	**curb**

Corrective feedback

Model blending decodable words and then ask children to blend them with you.

Decode words in context

Display these sentences. Have the class read the sentences.

Team Talk Have pairs take turns reading the sentences naturally.

A **girl** went into the **barn**.

Burt planted some green **ferns**.

We fed **birds** in the **park**.

Spelling
Words with *er, ir, ur*

Guide practice

Tell children that you will segment the sounds in each spelling word. They should repeat the sounds in each word as they write the word. Check the spelling of each word before saying the next word. Point out the silent *e* in *were*.

1. /h/ /ėr/ **her**	**6.** /w/ /ėr/ **were**
2. /f//ėr//s//t/ **first**	**7.** /sh/ /ėr/ /t/ **shirt**
3. /b/ /ėr/ /d/ **bird**	**8.** /f/ /ėr/ **fur**
4. /g/ /ėr/ /l/ **girl**	**9.** /h/ /ėr/ /t/ **hurt**
5. /b/ /ėr//n/ **burn**	**10.** /s/ /ėr/ **sir**

On their own

Use *Reader's and Writer's Notebook* p. 382.

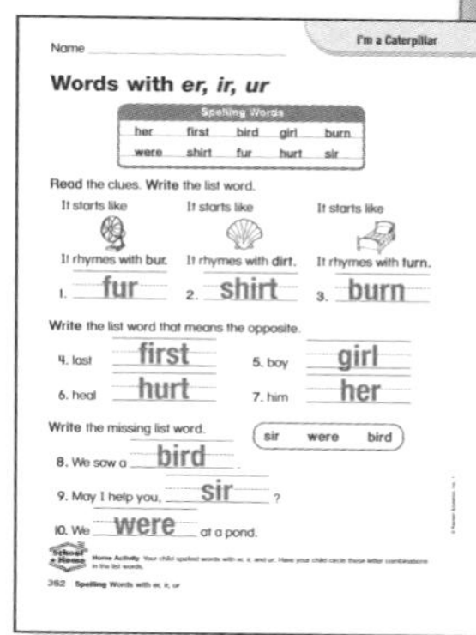
Name

I'm a Caterpillar

Words with *er, ir, ur*

Spelling Words				
her	first	bird	girl	burn
were	shirt	fur	hurt	sir

Read the clues. **Write** the list word.

It starts like ... It rhymes with bur. 1. fur

It starts like ... It rhymes with dirt. 2. shirt

It starts like ... It rhymes with turn. 3. burn

Write the list word that means the opposite.

4. last first
5. boy girl
6. heal hurt
7. him her

Write the missing list word. (sir were bird)

8. We saw a bird.
9. May I help you, sir?
10. We were at a pond.

382 Spelling Words with er, ir, ur

Reader's and Writer's Notebook p. 382

Small Group Time

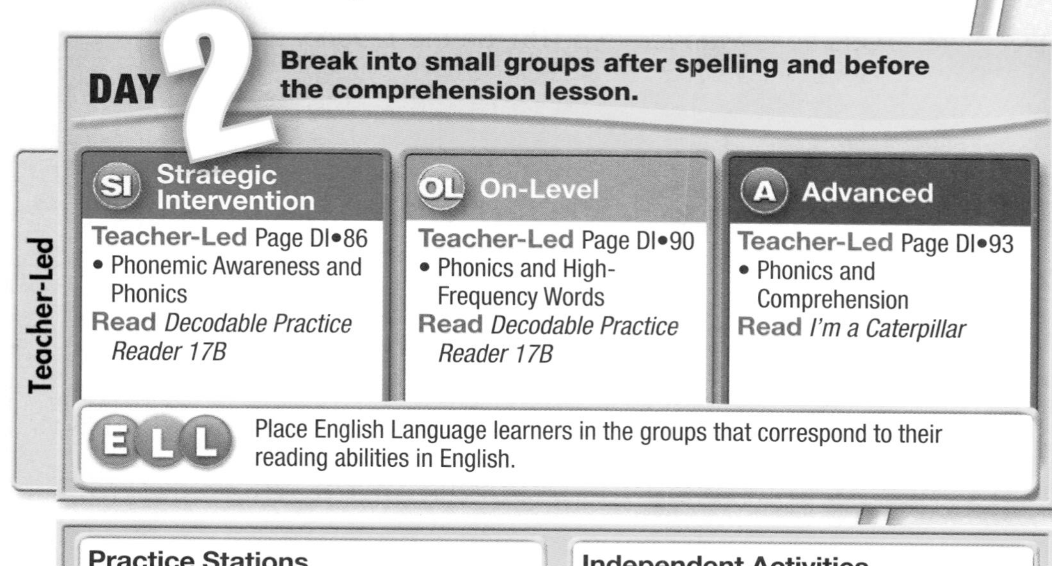
DAY 2 **Break into small groups after spelling and before the comprehension lesson.**

Teacher-Led

SI Strategic Intervention	OL On-Level	A Advanced
Teacher-Led Page DI•86 • Phonemic Awareness and Phonics **Read** *Decodable Practice Reader 17B*	**Teacher-Led** Page DI•90 • Phonics and High-Frequency Words **Read** *Decodable Practice Reader 17B*	**Teacher-Led** Page DI•93 • Phonics and Comprehension **Read** *I'm a Caterpillar*

ELL Place English Language learners in the groups that correspond to their reading abilities in English.

Practice Stations
- Listen Up
- Word Work

Independent Activities
- Read independently/Reading Log on *Reader's and Writer's Notebook* p. RR 4
- AudioText of Main Selection

English Language Learners

/ėr/ Spelled er, ir, ur Clarify the pronunciation and meaning of each spelling word. Explain that first can mean "coming before all others," as in *He is first*. It can also mean "the beginning," as in *At first, I was hurt.*

Objectives

- Learn story words: *caterpillar, chrysalis, crawl, pupa, shiver.*
- Review high-frequency words.
- Use a dictionary and glossary.

High-Frequency Words
Build Fluency

Read words in isolation Remind children that there are some words we learn by remembering the letters, rather than by saying the sounds. Then have them read each of the highlighted high-frequency words aloud.

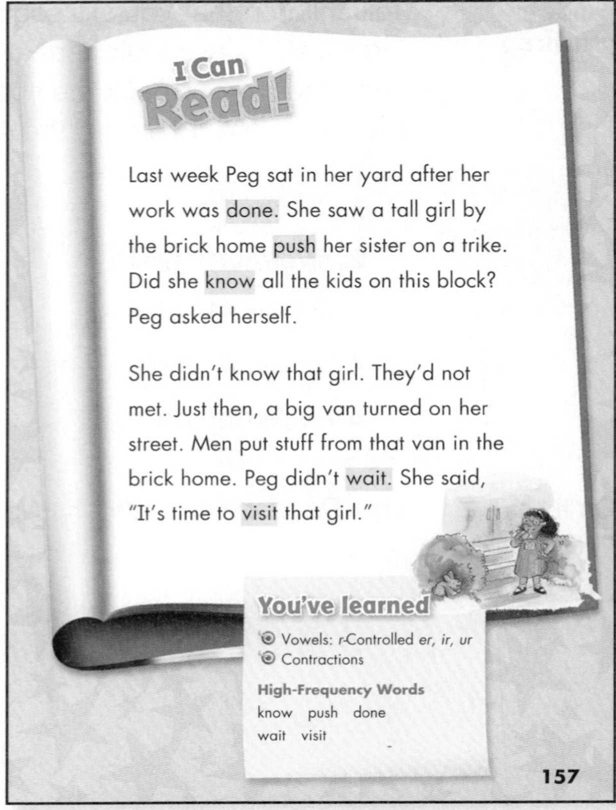

Student Edition p. 157

Read words in context Chorally read the "I Can Read!" passage along with the children. Then have them read the passage aloud to themselves. When they are finished, ask children to reread the high-frequency words.

Team Talk Have children choose two high-frequency words and give them time to create a sentence in which both words are used properly. Then have them share their sentence with a partner.

On their own Use *Let's Practice It!* p. 157 on the *Teacher Resource DVD-ROM.*

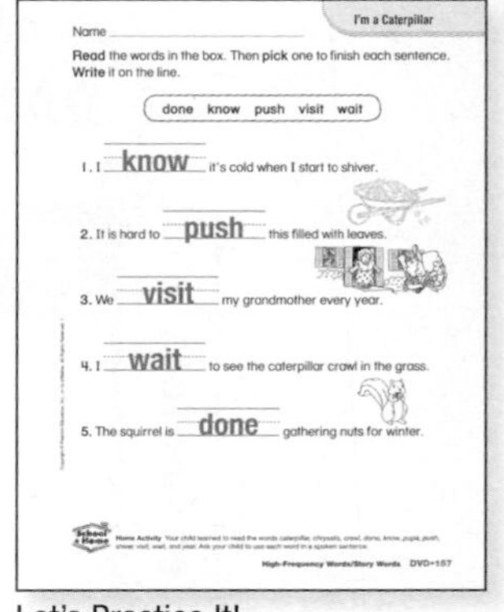

Let's Practice It!
TR DVD•157

Story Words
I'm a Caterpillar

Introduce story words

Use Vocabulary Transparency 17 to introduce this week's story words. Read each sentence as you track the print. Frame each underlined word and explain its meaning.

caterpillar	an insect that changes into a moth or butterfly
crawl	to move on your hands and knees or with your body close to the ground
chrysalis	forms from the body of a caterpillar and has a hard shell that protects the caterpillar as it changes into a butterfly
pupa	the form of an insect while it is changing from a wormlike larva into an adult
shiver	to shake

A Butterfly Grows

1. First a butterfly is a caterpillar.
2. A caterpillar can crawl.
3. Then it makes a shell that is a chrysalis.
4. It is a pupa inside.
5. It must shiver to get out of the shell.

Vocabulary Transparency 17
TR DVD

Have children read each sentence with you.

Vocabulary
Dictionary/Glossary

Model using a dictionary or glossary

Remind children that they can find the spelling and meaning of words in a **dictionary** or **glossary**. Review the difference between a dictionary and glossary. Remind children that the words are listed in alphabetical order. Model how to use a children's dictionary or the glossary on page 219 of the Student Edition.

Let's say I don't know what *chrysalis* means. *Chrysalis* begins with *c*. I know that *c* comes after *b* in the alphabet, so I turn past the *a* and *b* words until I come to the *c* words. And there I find *chrysalis*. I didn't know *chrysalis* had an *h* or a *y* in it. Now I can spell it correctly. Read aloud the definition.

Guide practice

Write *father, art, tower, mouse*. Have children help you put them in alphabetical order. Then say *butterfly*. Have children use the glossary to check the spelling.

On their own

Have groups of children work together to look up the meaning of each word in the glossary of their Student Edition.

Differentiated Instruction

SI Strategic Intervention

To help children understand *chrysalis* and *pupa*, draw simple pictures to illustrate the life cycle of a butterfly. Point to each picture as you discuss the life cycle. Explain that a caterpillar forms the chrysalis and becomes a pupa. Inside the chrysalis, the pupa slowly turns into a butterfly. When the butterfly has completely formed, it comes out of the chrysalis.

Academic Vocabulary

dictionary a book that explains the meanings of words

glossary a list of special words and their meanings, usually found at the back of a book

English Language Learners

Multilingual Vocabulary Lists Children can apply knowledge of their home languages to acquire new English vocabulary by using the *Multilingual Vocabulary Lists* (*ELL Handbook* pp. 465–476).

Objectives

- Build background about the life cycle of a butterfly.
- Preview and predict.
- Use key structure and elements of literary nonfiction to improve understanding of text.
- Set a purpose for reading text.

Build Background
I'm a Caterpillar

Background-Building Audio

Have children listen to the CD. Tell them to listen to find out how a caterpillar changes into a butterfly.

Background Building Audio

Discuss the life cycle of a butterfly

Team Talk Have children turn to a partner and use these questions for discussion:

- Where do butterflies lay their eggs, and why?
- What kind of animal hatches from a butterfly egg? What is this animal like?
- How does a caterpillar slowly turn into a butterfly?

Organize information in a cycle chart

Draw a 5-part cycle chart or display Graphic Organizer 30. Have children recall what they learned from the CD about the life cycle of a butterfly. Record their responses.

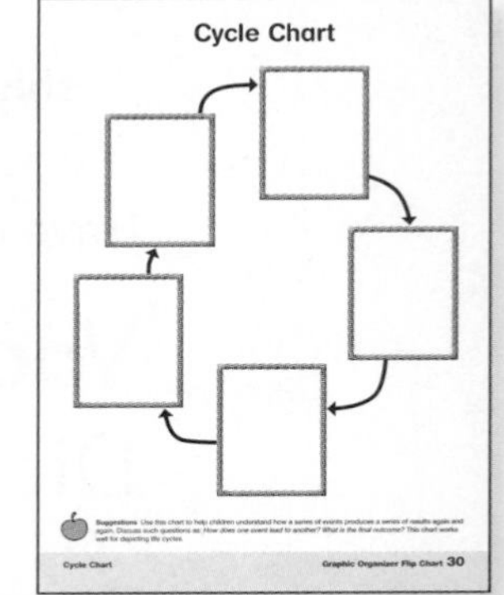

Graphic Organizer Flip Chart 30

Connect to selection

We learned how caterpillars hatch from butterfly eggs and then slowly become butterflies themselves. In the story we're about to read, *I'm a Caterpillar*, we'll learn more about the steps a caterpillar goes through to become a butterfly.

Student Edition pp. 158–159

Main Selection—First Read

I'm a Caterpillar

Practice the skill

Fact and Opinion Remind children that a fact tells something that can be proved to be true by observing, checking in a book, or asking an expert. Example: *Caterpillars hatch from butterfly eggs.* An opinion tells someone's idea of feeling. It cannot be proved true or false. Example: *Caterpillars are the cutest insects.*

Introduce the strategy

Text Structure Explain that good readers pay attention to the order, or **sequence**, in which things happen in their reading. This helps them understand and remember what they have learned. Have children turn to page EI•20 in their Student Edition.

Envision It!

Think Aloud: Look at the life cycle of a frog. How does a tadpole turn into a frog? Tell the steps in sequence. (First, a tadpole has no legs. Next, it grows legs. Finally, it becomes a frog.) Repeat for the life cycle of a plant. As I read *I'm a Caterpillar*, I will pay attention to the sequence of the steps a caterpillar goes through as it changes.

Student Edition EI•20

Introduce genre

Let's Read Together Literary nonfiction tells about real people or animals, real places, and true events. As they read *I'm a Caterpillar*, tell children to look for things that really happen in nature.

Preview and predict

Have children read the title of the story. Read the names of the author and illustrator, and have children describe the role of each. Help children activate prior knowledge by looking through the story and using the illustrations to predict what will happen.

Set a purpose

Good readers read for a purpose. Setting a purpose helps us to think and understand more as we read. Guide children to set a purpose for reading the selection.

Tell children that today they will read *I'm a Caterpillar* for the first time. Use the Day 2 Guide Comprehension notes to help children develop their comprehension of the selection.

First Read

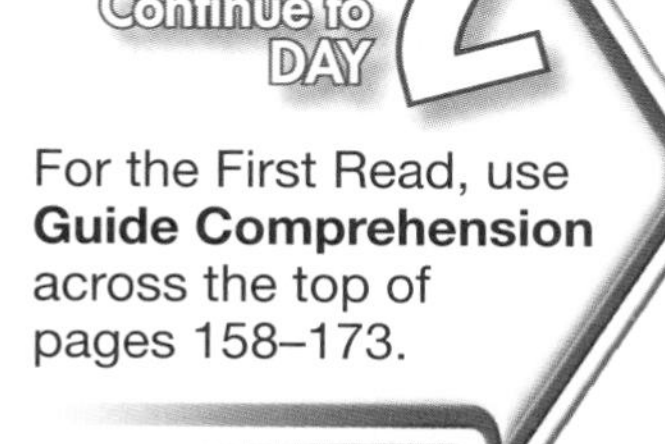

For the First Read, use **Guide Comprehension** across the top of pages 158–173.

Strategy Response Log

Genre Have children use p. RR 29 in their *Reader's and Writer's Notebook* to identify the characteristics of literary nonfiction.

Academic Vocabulary

fact piece of information that can be proved to be true

opinion the way someone thinks or feels about something

sequence the order of events in a selection, or the order of the steps in which something is done

English Language Learners

Build Background Activate children's prior knowledge by asking them what they know about butterflies and caterpillars. Then take a picture walk to frontload the selection.

Objectives

- Determine word meaning and use newly acquired vocabulary.
- ◎ Distinguish facts from opinions in text.
- ◎ Use illustrations to understand and remember a sequence of events.

DAY 2

Guide Comprehension

Skills and Strategies

Connect to Concept

Changes in Nature Look at the picture on pages 158–159. What two animals do you see? (a caterpillar and a butterfly) What do you know about the connection between caterpillars and butterflies? (A caterpillar changes into a butterfly.)

Amazing Words

Have children continue discussing the concept using the Amazing Words *insect, develop, cycle,* and *rearrange* as they read.

Student Edition pp. 158–159

DAY 3

Extend Thinking

Think Critically

Higher-Order Thinking Skills

Evaluation The caterpillar and butterfly are in a garden. Is this a good place for them? Why? (Yes. The caterpillar can eat the leaves and then find a stem to hang from. The butterfly can sip nectar from the flowers and lay eggs on leaves.)

If... children are unable to explain why a garden is a good place for caterpillars and butterflies,
then... ask questions such as, *What do caterpillars eat? Are there leaves in a garden? What do butterflies eat? Are there flowers in a garden?*

Vocabulary

Story Words Have children locate the story word *caterpillar* on page 160. Who is saying "I'm a caterpillar?" Have children point to the picture of the caterpillar. Describe what a caterpillar looks like. (It is shaped like a worm and has many short legs. It has antennas on its head. This kind of caterpillar is yellow with black markings.)

Skills

Fact and Opinion Is the sentence "I'm getting bigger" a fact or an opinion? Why? (fact; it can be proved true by observing) Does the caterpillar think leaves taste good? (yes) Why do you think so? (It keeps munching them.) Is "Leaves taste good" a fact or opinion? (opinion)

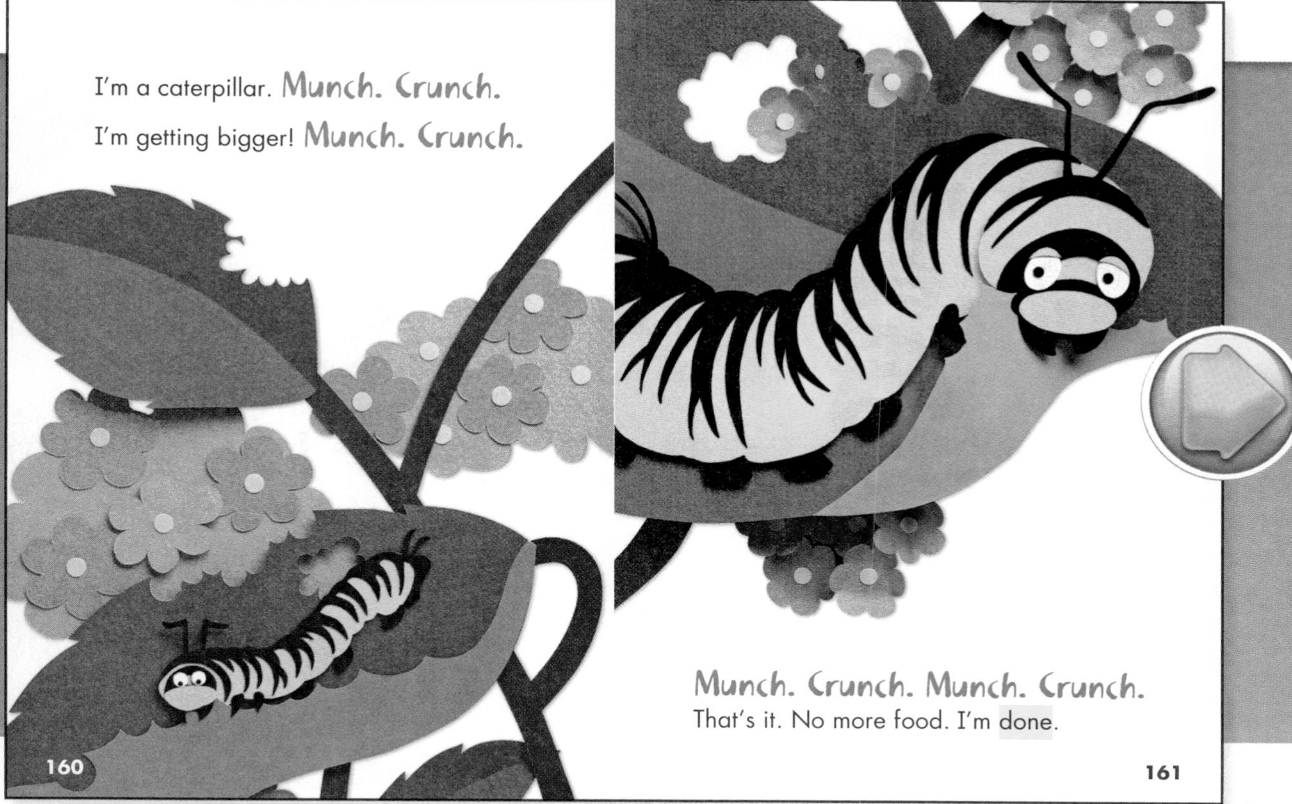

Student Edition pp. 160–161

Higher-Order Thinking Skills

Analysis Sometimes authors choose words for their sounds. Which words on these pages help you hear the sound of caterpillars eating? *(munch, crunch)*

Synthesis On our CD, we heard that as a caterpillar eats and grows bigger, its skin gets too tight and it molts. It keeps eating and growing until it has molted 4–6 times. Then it forms a chrysalis. So, why do you think the caterpillar in this story is ready to stop eating? (It has been growing and has molted its skin 4–6 times. Now it is big enough to form a chrysalis.)

Skills and Strategies, continued

Vocabulary

Dictionary/Glossary Where could we find the meaning of *shiver*? (in a dictionary or glossary) Would *shiver* come before or after *caterpillar*? (after) Before or after *pupa*? (after) Before or after *tower*? (before) Have children look up *shiver* in their Student Edition glossary.

If... children have trouble determining the alphabetical order of the words,
then... have them recite the alphabet, or write it on the board.

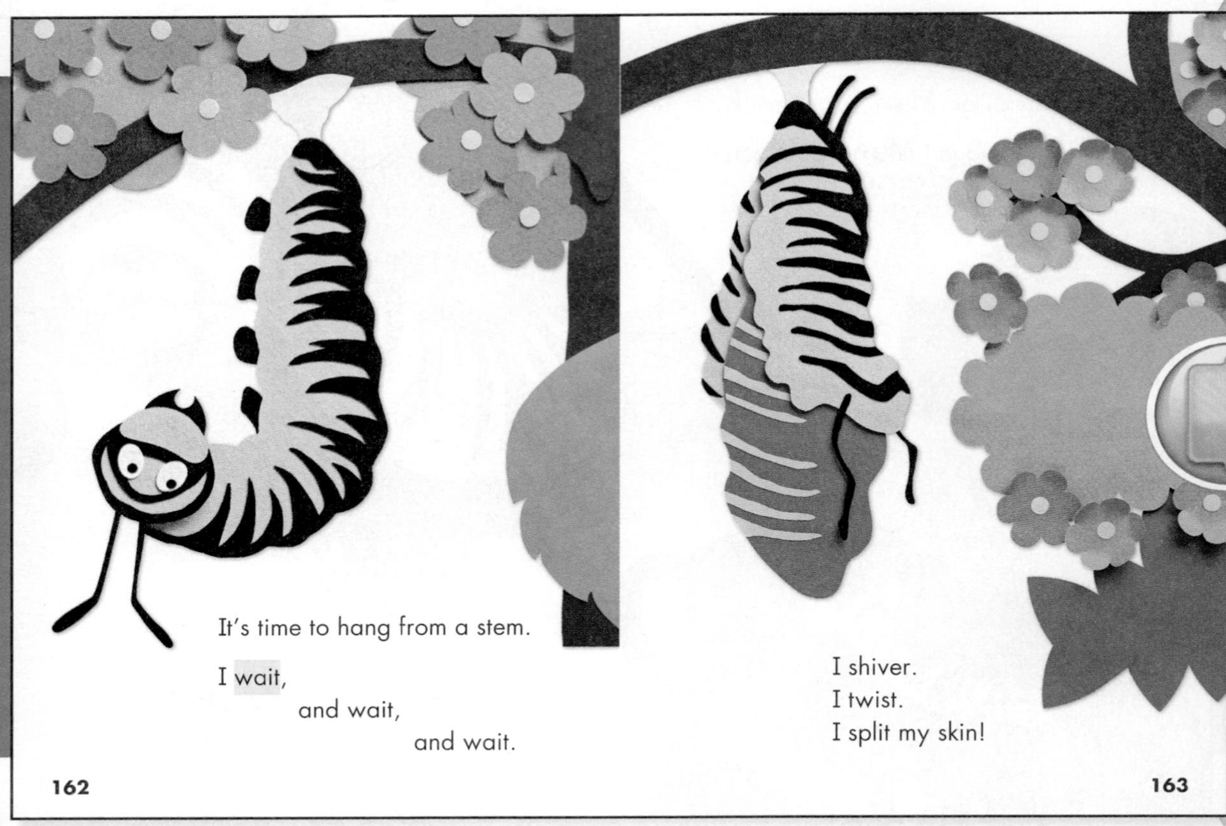

Student Edition pp. 162–163

Think Critically, continued

Higher-Order Thinking Skills

Analysis After the caterpillar hangs from a stem, it has to wait before it can split its skin. Does it wait for a short time or a long time? How can you tell? (It waits for a long time. The word *wait* is repeated three times.)

Evaluation Does the picture on page 163 help you understand what is happening to the caterpillar? (yes) What can you see? (You can see how the skin split in half, and you can see the pupa that was inside.)

Strategies

Text Structure Remind children that good readers pay attention to the sequence, or order, of things that happen in their reading. What is the sequence of steps the caterpillar goes through to become a butterfly? Look back at pictures to help you remember. (The caterpillar eats leaves, hangs from a stem, splits its skin, forms a chrysalis, and changes into a butterfly.)

Skills

Fact and Opinion Is the sentence "I am now a chrysalis" a fact or an opinion? (It is a fact.) How do you know? (It can be proved true by observing. We have also learned in class that a caterpillar changes to a chrysalis.)

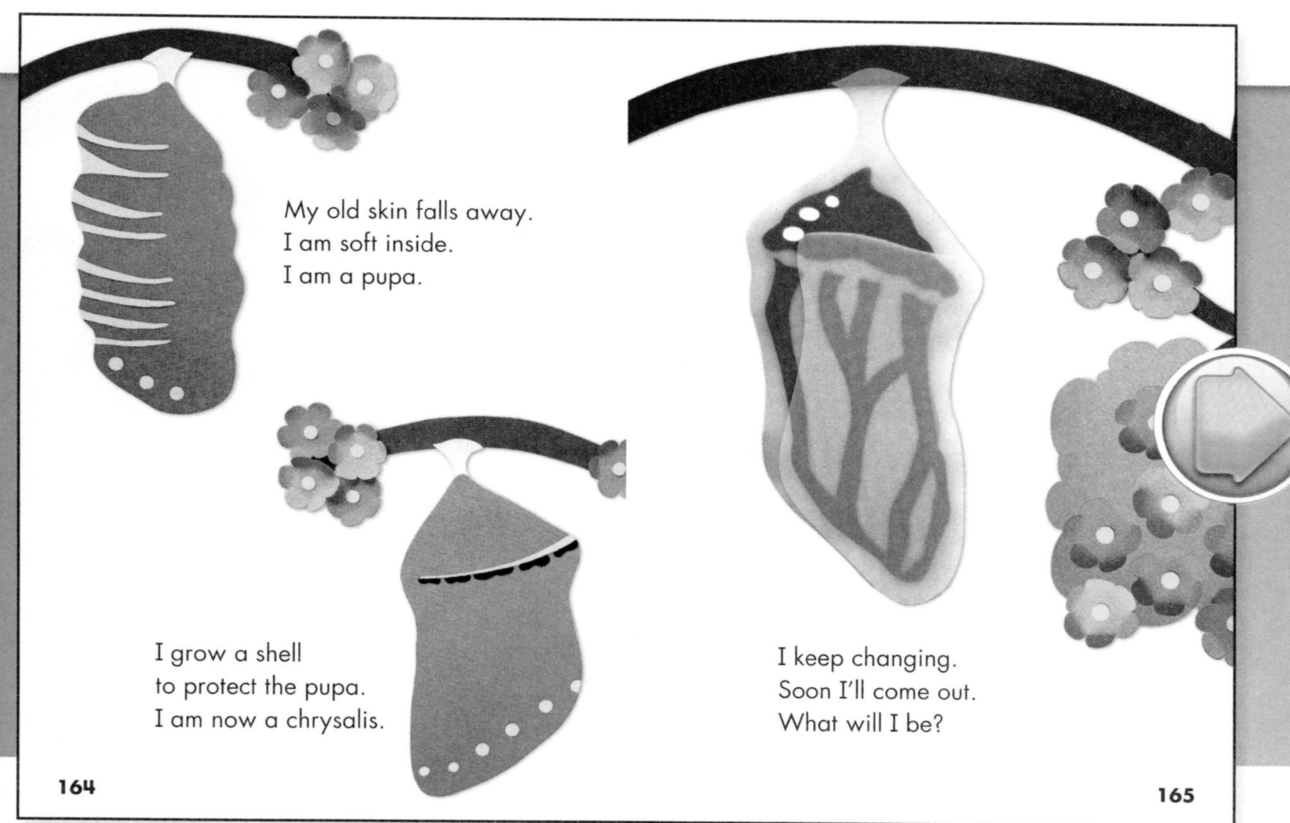

Student Edition pp. 164–165

Higher-Order Thinking Skills

Analysis Why does the chrysalis need a shell that protects the pupa? (The pupa is soft, so it could be easily hurt.)

If... children have difficulty evaluating the importance of the shell,
then... have them reread the top part of page 164. Ask: What can happen to something that is very soft? How could a shell protect it?

Skills and Strategies, continued

DAY 2

Skills

Fact and Opinion Would it be more fun to be a chrysalis or a butterfly? Is your answer a fact or opinion? Why? (An opinion; it's just the way I feel—I can't prove it.) What text in the story might make you think being a butterfly is fun? ("Wow! I'm free!"; "I can fly!")

If... children have difficulty understanding the difference between a fact and an opinion,
then... provide simple facts and opinions, such as *This pen is red. Red is the best color.* Discuss how people may disagree about opinions but not about facts.

Student Edition pp. 166–167

Think Critically, continued

Higher-Order Thinking Skills

Synthesis In *Ruby in Her Own Time*, Ruby couldn't fly until her feathers grew out and her wings grew broad. How is a new butterfly like a baby duck? (Its wings aren't ready to fly right away.)

Word Reading

Decoding Have children check their reading of new words using these guidelines:

- Did I blend the sounds to read the word?
- Did I put the new word in the sentence to make sure it made sense?
- Did I look for word parts to help me understand the word?

Vocabulary

Dictionary/Glossary Where could we find the meaning of *nectar*? (in a dictionary or glossary) Would *nectar* come before or after *forest*? (after) Before or after *squirrel*? (before) Before or after *leaves*? (after) Have children look up *nectar* in a children's dictionary.

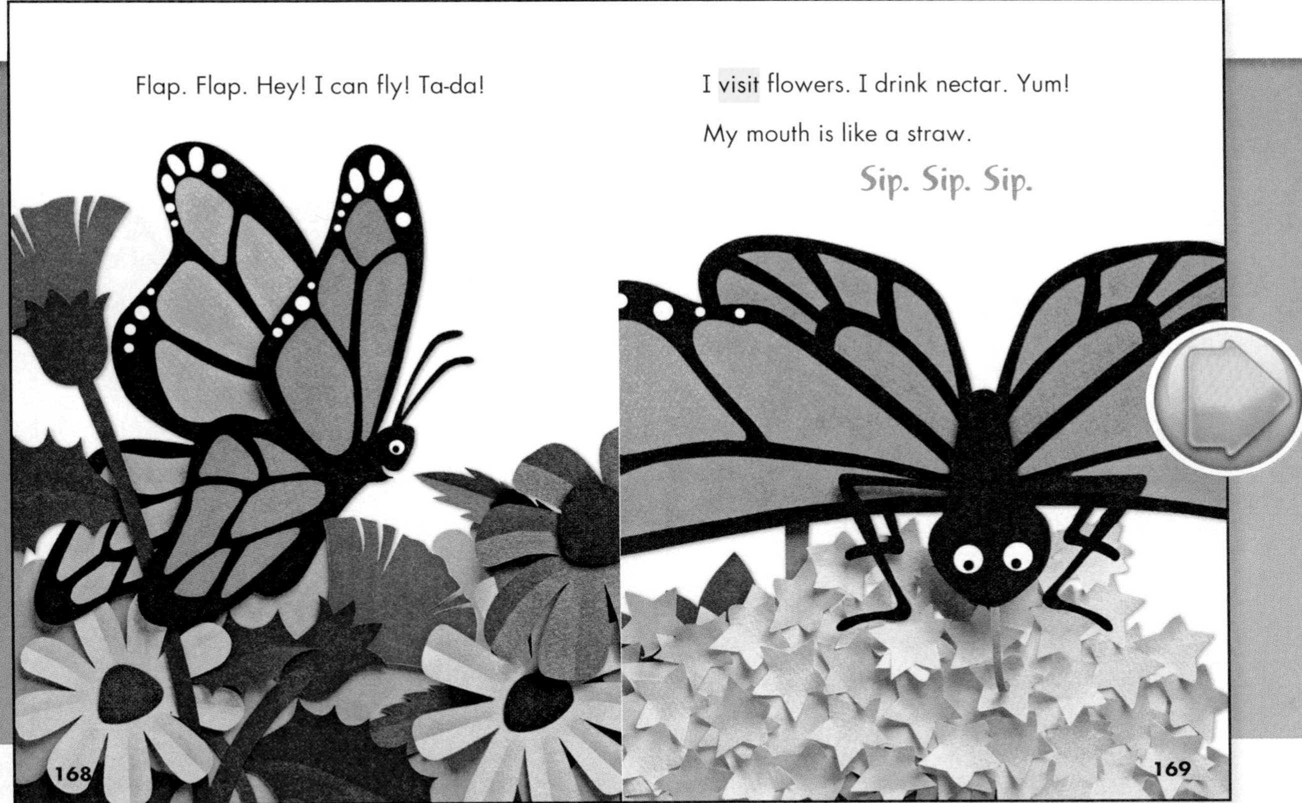

Student Edition pp. 168–169

Higher-Order Thinking Skills

Analysis What does the caterpillar mean when it says "My mouth is like a straw"? (Its mouth is long, thin, and hollow. The butterfly sucks liquid through it.)

If... children have difficulty explaining how the butterfly's mouth is like a straw,
then... ask children what a straw looks like and how it is used. Point out the picture of the butterfly's mouth and the words "Sip. Sip. Sip." on page 169.

Skills and Strategies, continued

DAY 2

Strategies

Text Structure After a butterfly comes out of the chrysalis, what steps does it go through to complete its life cycle? Use the pictures to help you remember. (It dries its wings, flies to flowers, sips nectar, gets a mate, and lays eggs.)

Word Reading

High-Frequency Words Point out the words *visit* and *know*. Have children practice reading these words.

Student Edition pp. 170–171

Think Critically, continued

DAY 3

Connect to Science

Adaptations Animals have special parts that help or protect them. We call these adaptations. For instance, anteaters have long tongues to reach into anthills to eat ants.

Team Talk Have partners discuss adaptations that help butterflies eat and stay safe.

Higher-Order Thinking Skills

Synthesis What other animals do you know of that have special adaptations? (Possible responses: Turtles have shells to hide in; giraffes have long necks for reaching high leaves; hummingbirds have long, thin beaks for sipping nectar.)

Vocabulary

Story Words We know that a caterpillar is shaped like a worm and has very short legs. So when we read "Baby caterpillars crawl out," what can we guess about the meaning of *crawl*? (It means that the caterpillar moves with its body close to the ground, like a worm.)

Strategy Self-Check

Text Structure See if you can tell all the steps in the life cycle of a butterfly in the right sequence. Look back at the pictures and use the diagram on page 173 to help you. (The caterpillar eats leaves, hangs from a stem, splits its skin, forms a chrysalis, changes into a butterfly, dries its wings, flies to flowers, sips nectar, gets a mate, and lays eggs. The eggs hatch into new caterpillars.)

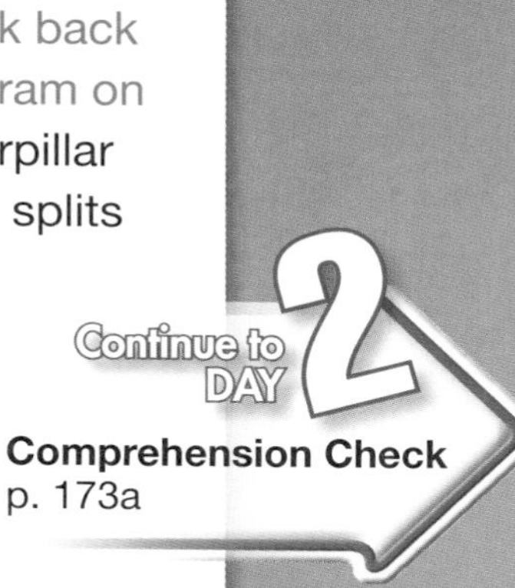
Continue to DAY 2
Comprehension Check
p. 173a

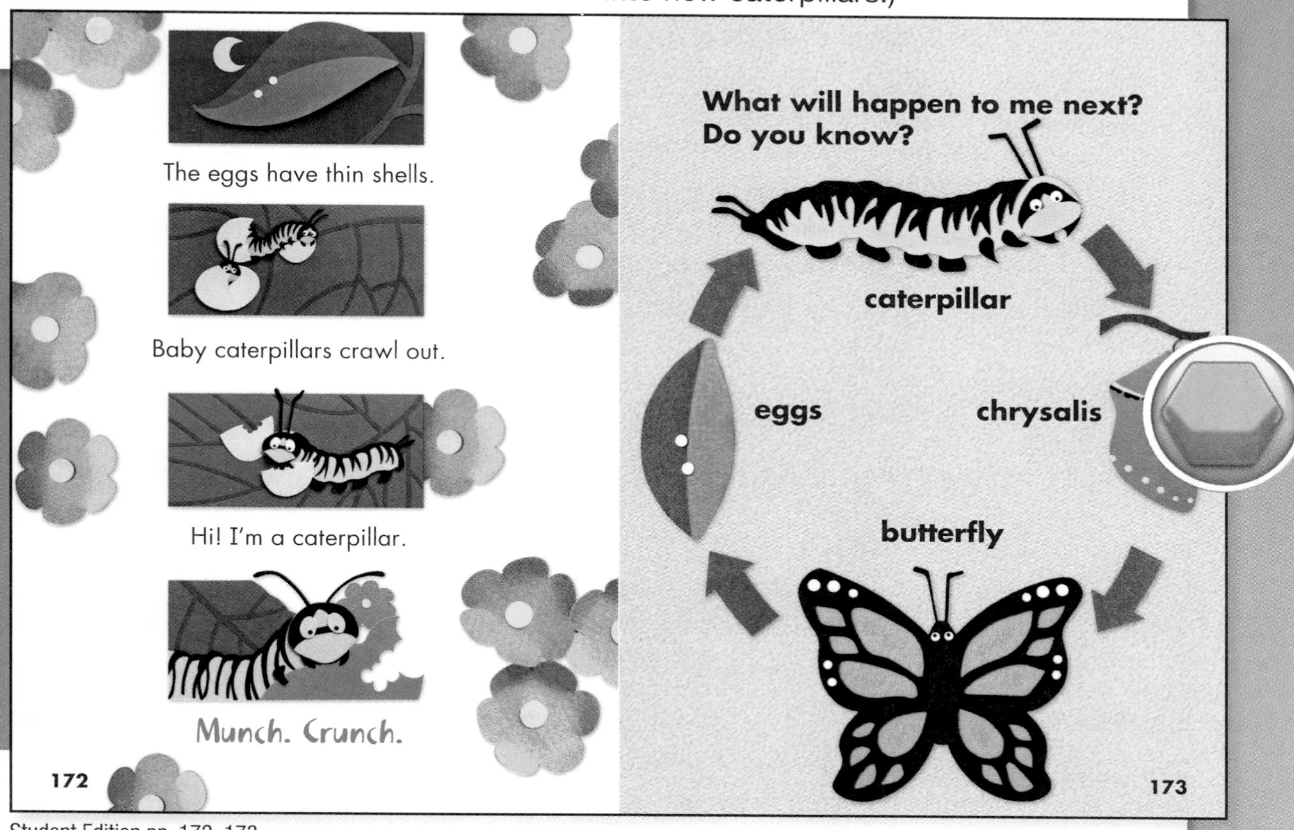

Student Edition pp. 172–173

Review Sequence

Synthesis Yesterday we learned about the life cycle of frogs. Frogs' eggs hatch into tadpoles. Then what happens? (They grow legs and change to frogs.) How is this like and unlike a butterfly's life cycle? Use the diagram and the words on page 173. (In both, eggs hatch then turn into a grown-up animal. But tadpoles don't make a chrysalis.)

If... children have difficulty comparing and contrasting the sequence of events in the life cycles of frogs and butterflies, **then...** have them turn to page EI•20 in their Student Edition to review the life cycle of a frog.

Continue to DAY 3
Think Critically
p. 174–175

DAY 2 Read and Comprehend

Objectives

- Determine whether a story is true or fantasy.
- Use verbs *am, is, are, was, were* with correct subject-verb agreement in statements and questions.

Comprehension Check

Have children discuss each question with a partner. Ask several pairs to share their responses.

☑ **Literary nonfiction** Literary nonfiction tells about things that are true. What is true in this story? (Possible response: The way the caterpillar changes into a butterfly is true.)

☑ **Confirm prediction** How did you use the pictures and things you already knew to predict what would happen next in the story? (Possible response: I knew that caterpillars turn into butterflies, so when I saw the caterpillar starting to make a chrysalis, I knew it would turn into a butterfly.)

☑ **Connect text to text** Think about what you learned in *Honey Bees* in Unit 2. How are bees and butterflies alike and different? (Possible response: *Alike:* Both are insects, can fly, drink nectar. *Different:* Bees work in big groups, sting, make honey; butterflies start out as caterpillars; have big, colorful wings.)

Literary Nonfiction

True Story or Fantasy

Distinguish between a true story and a fantasy

Use *I'm a Caterpillar* and last week's story *Frog and Toad Together* to contrast a true story with a fantasy.

- We know that *I'm a Caterpillar* is a true story. How is a true story different from a fantasy? (In a true story, real things happen. In a fantasy, things happen that can't happen in real life.)
- Is *Frog and Toad Together* a true story or a fantasy? (fantasy) Tell one thing that happens that could not happen in real life. (Possible response: A toad plants a garden.)

Guide practice

Draw a T-chart or use Graphic Organizer 4. Have children list what is true in *I'm a Caterpillar* and what is fantasy in *Frog and Toad Together*.

True	Fantasy

Graphic Organizer Flip Chart 4

On their own

Divide children into small groups, and assign each group a previously read selection from the Student Edition. Tell them to figure out whether the story is true or a fantasy, and why. Have them share their ideas with the class.

Conventions

Verbs *Am, Is, Are, Was,* and *Were*

Model verbs *am, is, are, was,* and *were*

Write *am* and *was* on the board. Point to each word as you read it. Use each in a sentence about your school. Ask children to identify the word that tells about now (*am*) and the word that tells about the past (*was*). Point out that *are* and *were* can be used with *you* and with plural subjects. Continue with *are* and *were*. *Am, is,* and *are* tell about now. *Was* and *were* tell about the past. Which of these words can tell about one? (*am, is, are, was, were*) Which words tell about more than one? (*are, were*)

Remind children that when you ask a question using *am, is, are, was,* and *were,* those words often come first.

Guide practice

Have children identify the correct words for these sentences. Write the words in the blank spaces.

1. ________ he five years old last year? (*was*)

2. Today she ________ six. (*is*)

3. Now I ________ six years old. (*am*)

4. Last year the kittens ________ little. (*were*)

5. ________ the kittens big now? (*are*)

Connect to oral language

Have the class complete these sentence frames orally.

1. I ________ a first grader.

2. She ________ my sister.

On their own

Use *Reader's and Writer's Notebook* p. 383.

Reader's and Writer's Notebook p. 383

Differentiated Instruction

 **Strategic Intervention**

Verbs in Sentences Write this sentence on the board: *Today I am at home.* Read it aloud. Tell children that in this sentence, the verb *am* tells about one person and it tells about the present. Write this sentence: *Yesterday I was in school.* Read it aloud. Tell children that in this sentence, the verb *was* tells about one person and tells about the past. Continue modeling in the same way with *is/was* and *are/were.*

Daily Fix-It

3. She did not want to hert it?
She did not want to hurt it.

4. she pickked it up.
She picked it up.

Discuss the Daily Fix-It corrections with children. Review sentence capitalization and punctuation, and the three spellings of the sound /ėr/.

English Language Learners

Forms of *to be* In Chinese, Hmong, and Haitian Creole, *to be* is not required in some sentences. If children say *I happy*, practice with sentences such as *I am happy* and *We are tired*.

Objectives

- Generate picture and caption ideas.
- Recognize features of pictures and captions.
- Use focus and ideas to plan pictures and captions.

Writing—Captions and Pictures

Writing Trait: Focus/Ideas

Introduce the prompt

Review with children the key features of captions and pictures. Point out that *I'm a Caterpillar* tells about the way an insect changes. Tell them that the pictures they draw will show how something in nature changes. Explain that today children will plan their captions and pictures. Read aloud the writing prompt.

Writing Prompt

Think of changes in nature. Plants and animals grow. Seasons change. Draw two pictures to show one way a plant or animal changes. Write captions about your pictures.

Sharing the Writing

Help children generate caption and picture ideas

Let's think about things in nature that change. We can list a few things and tell how they change. Display a T-chart. I'll start with *apple trees*.

Guide children in identifying several plants and animals and how they change. Possible ideas are shown. Record the responses, and keep the chart so that children can refer to it as they plan and draft their captions and pictures.

Things in Nature	How They Change
apple trees	flowers turn into apples
baby birds	grow feathers and fly
flowers	have big blooms and then turn brown in the winter

Have each child choose a topic for the pictures. Circulate to guide them. Have them tell what kind of change they will show and describe.

MINI-LESSON

Focus/Ideas

Introduce Use *Reader's and Writer's Notebook* p. 384 to model planning captions and pictures. I can use a chart to plan my pictures and captions. My chart can tell what I will put in my first picture and caption and in my second picture and caption. Then I can look at my chart when I draw my pictures and write my captions.

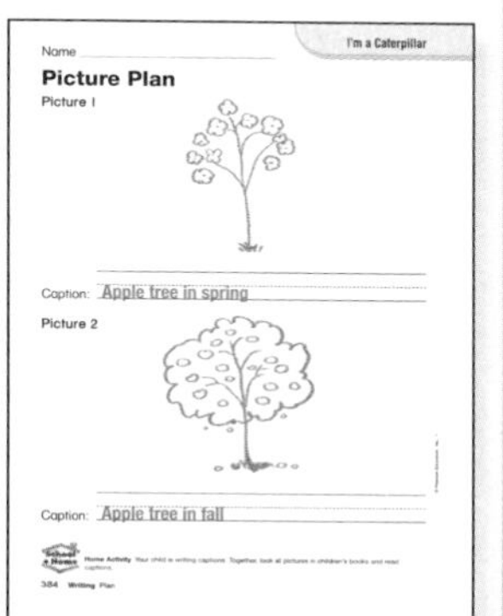
Name ____ I'm a Caterpillar
Picture Plan
Picture 1
Caption: Apple tree in spring
Picture 2
Caption: Apple tree in fall

Reader's and Writer's Notebook p. 384

Model I am going to draw pictures of an apple tree. I will show how it changes. My first picture will be an apple tree with lots of flowers. I will write that in my chart. I will tell in the caption that it is spring. In my second picture, I will draw an apple tree with loads of apples. I will write that in my chart. I will tell in my caption that the apple tree has apples in the fall. Now plan for your pictures and captions. Circulate to guide and assist children.

ROUTINE

Quick Write for Fluency

Team Talk

1. **Talk** Have children take two minutes to tell partners what they will draw.
2. **Write** Each child briefly writes about the pictures he or she will draw.
3. **Share** Each child reads the ideas to the partner.

Routines Flip Chart

Write Guy
Jeff Anderson

Let Me Check My List

Encourage children to keep lists of words they come across that are exciting or interesting to them. They can use their lists to increase their vocabulary and incorporate them in their own writing. This is a great way to improve vocabulary and word choice.

Differentiated Instruction

SI Strategic Intervention

Showing and Telling If children have difficulty telling what they will draw, have them close their eyes and orally tell what they imagine. Help them record their ideas in their charts.

English Language Learners

Support Prewriting

Beginning Encourage children to describe in words their pictures, and allow them to make rough drawings of their planned pictures.

Intermediate Have children describe orally their pictures to partners. Then, have them record short phrases in their charts.

Advanced/Advanced High Have children draw pictures and write short sentences in their charts. As they share the plan with partners, children can clarify and add ideas.

Objectives

- Write with consistent left-to-right progression.
- Understand how to use a computer to create a word-processed document.
- Apply knowledge of computers to an inquiry project.

Handwriting

Letter *V* and *v*/ Left-to-Right Progression

Model letter formation Display upper- and lower-case letters: *Vv*. Use the stroke instructions pictured below to model proper letter formation.

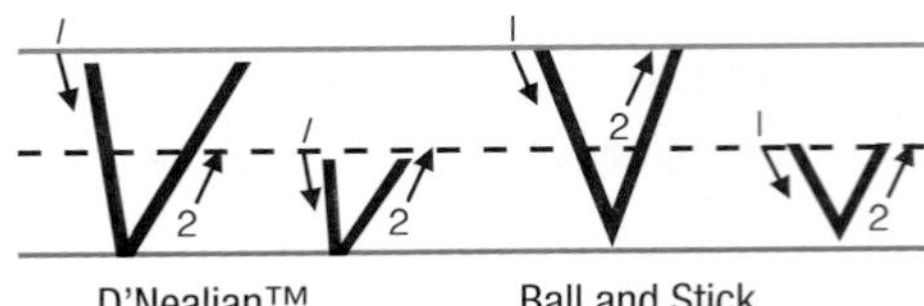

Model left-to-right progression Remind children that when we write words, we begin on the left and move to the right. Write the words *insect, develop,* and *cycle* on the board. When you are done, draw an arrow underneath each word that points from left to right. Model how to write the words by writing them again underneath the arrows as you say: When I am writing, I always start on the left and move to the right. Repeat this action for each word. Then write the letters *Vv* on the board to model how to write a series of letters from left to right.

Guide practice As you write the following words, go slowly and say, As I write, I go left to right!

change **nature** **volcano** **caterpillar**

Team Talk Have children work in pairs and practice writing the words from *Guide practice* slowly and from left to right.

On their own Use *Reader's and Writer's Notebook* p. 385.

Reader's and Writer's Notebook p. 385

Research and Inquiry
Research Skill: My Computer

Teach

Tell children that you can do many different things on a computer. You can create documents, do math problems, and even play games. You can use a computer to help you do research. A computer's **hard drive** stores all of the computer's information.

Model

Think Aloud — Display Research Transparency 17. Explain that the screen, or **monitor,** shows the work being done on the computer. Words are typed in using keys on the **keyboard.** A **mouse** lets you point to a place on the screen and highlight words to be changed. A blinking line on the screen, called the **cursor,** shows where you are typing. A **file** is a document that you create and save under its own **file name.** Let's answer the questions on the transparency.

Technology: My Computer

MyTrip.doc

My Summer Trip

Last summer I went on a fun trip with my family. We drove to see my Aunt Sally. She lives in Texas. It is hot in Texas! We saw

1. What work is being done on the computer? A document is being created.
2. What words have been highlighted, or selected? We saw
3. What part of the computer is used to select words? the mouse
4. What is the filename of the document? MyTrip.doc
5. Where will this file be stored once it is saved? on the hard drive

Unit 3 I'm a Caterpillar — Research 17

Research Transparency 17
TR DVD

Guide practice

Help children answer the questions on the transparency. Review the information after you have recorded their responses.

Academic Vocabulary

hard drive where all of a computer's information is stored

monitor the screen showing the work being done on the computer

keyboard where you type words and numbers

mouse a device that lets you point to a place on the computer screen

cursor a blinking line that shows where you are typing

file a document you create

file name the name you give to a document you create

Wrap Up Your Day

- ✔ **Contractions** Write the words *we've, he's,* and *you're*. Have children identify the two words that make up each contraction.
- ✔ **High-Frequency Words** Point to these words on the Word Wall: *done, know, push, wait,* and *visit*. Have children read each word and use it in a sentence.
- ✔ **Build Concepts** Monitor children's use of oral vocabulary as they respond. Recall the Big Book *What Makes the Seasons?* Ask: What "makes weather rearrange"? (The Earth's yearly trip around the sun makes the seasons and weather change.) During what season do plants grow best? Why? (Plants grow best in the summer because the days are long and bright.)

Tell children that tomorrow they will reread *I'm a Caterpillar.*

Objectives

- Build oral vocabulary.
- Identify details in text.
- Share information and ideas about the concept.

Today at a Glance

Oral Vocabulary
flurries

Phonemic Awareness
Add Phonemes

Phonics and Spelling
◎ Vowels: *r*-Controlled *er, ir, ur*
◎ Contractions with *'s, 've, 're*

High-Frequency Words
done, know, push, visit, wait

Story Words
caterpillar, chrysalis, crawl, pupa, shiver

Comprehension
Review Sequence

Fluency
Expression and Intonation

Conventions
Verbs *am, is, are, was* and *were*

Writing
Captions and Pictures
Writer's Craft: Details to Show and Tell

Listening and Speaking
Share Information and Ideas

Research and Inquiry
Gathering and Recording Information

Concept Talk

Question of the Week

What changes can be seen in nature?

Build concepts

To reinforce concepts and to focus children's attention, have children sing "Life Cycle" from the *Sing with Me* Big Book. The song says that when the butterfly lays eggs, the cycle starts over again. In what way does it start over again? (Possible response: Caterpillars hatch from the eggs, and then they slowly change into butterflies.)

Sing with Me Big Book Audio

Monitor listening comprehension

Display the Big Book *What Makes the Seasons?* Remind children that the seasons are another kind of cycle. As you read the selection, have children notice the changes that happen in the weather and other parts of nature as one season turns to the next.

- What changes happen in nature as summer turns to fall? (The days turn darker; the wind grows colder; leaves change color and fall off.)
- What changes happen as fall turns to winter? (Snow falls; plants rest; many animals hibernate; the days grow very short.)

Big Book

ELL Poster 17

ELL Expand Vocabulary Use the Day 3 instruction on ELL Poster 17 to expand children's use of English Vocabulary to communicate about lesson concepts.

Oral Vocabulary
Amazing Words

Amazing Words Oral Vocabulary Routine

Teach Amazing Words

1. **Introduce the Word** Relate the word *flurries* to the book. In many places, winter brings snow *flurries*. Supply a child-friendly definition: Snow *flurries* are light snowfalls. Have children say the word.
2. **Demonstrate** Provide examples to show meaning. The snow *flurries* never turned into a big snowstorm. The snow *flurries* did not leave behind enough snow to build a snowman.
3. **Apply** Have children demonstrate their understanding. What do snow *flurries* look like?

Routines Flip Chart

Anchored Talk

Add to the concept map

Use these questions to discuss the changes that happen in the life cycle of a butterfly as you add to the concept map.

- In *I'm a Caterpillar*, we read about the changes that happen as a caterpillar becomes a butterfly. Where do baby caterpillars come from? (butterfly eggs) Let's add that to our map.
- After a caterpillar grows big, what changes happen to it? (It forms a chrysalis and turns into a butterfly.) Let's add those ideas to the map.
- How does the new butterfly start the cycle all over again? (It lays eggs that hatch into caterpillars.) Let's add that to our map.

Amazing Words

cycle	flurries
develop	emerge
insect	fragile
rearrange	vessel

English Language Learners

Visual Support Tell children that a lot of snow is called a snow-storm and a little snow is called a snow flurry. Draw two small houses on different parts of the board. Using white chalk marks, indicate a snowstorm around one house and a snow flurry around the other. Point to each picture and have children say *snowstorm* or *snow flurry*.

Objectives

- Recognize the change in a spoken word when a phoneme is added.
- Sort contractions with *'s, 've, 're.*
- Read words with /ėr/ spelled *er, ir, ur* and contractions with *'s, 've, 're.*

Phonemic Awareness
Add Phonemes

Model adding phonemes Read together the second bullet point on pp. 152–153 of the Student Edition. Today we're going to use this picture to help us add a new sound to the end of word a word to make a new word. The directions tell us to find something in the picture that rhymes with *twirl* and add the /z/ sound to it. I see a squirrel in the picture. *Squirrel* rhymes with *twirl*. When I add /z/ to *squirrel*, I make a different word: *squirrel /z/, squirrels.*

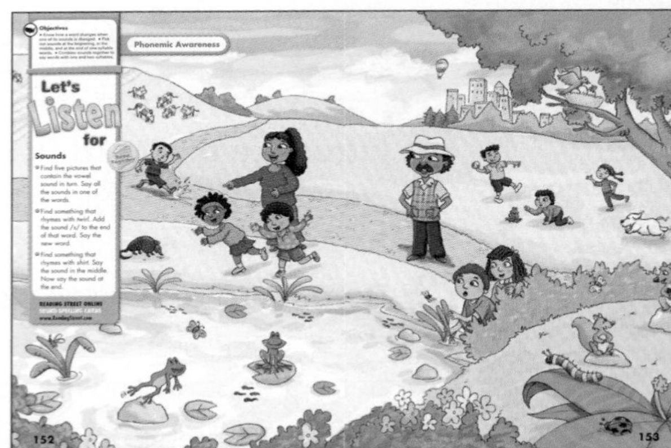

Student Edition pp. 152–153

Guide practice What else in the picture rhymes with *twirl*? (girl, curl). Have children add the /z/ sound to each word. Then have them find something in the picture that matches each word below. Have them say the word and then add the sound indicated to the end of it to make a new word.

tree /t/ (treat)	**ball /d/** (bald)	**fur /n/** (fern)

On their own Have children add /p/ to the end of the following words to make new words.

lamb (lamp)	**plum** (plump)	**why** (wipe)
gray (grape)	**she** (sheep)	**who** (hoop)

Team Talk Have partners think of words they can make by adding different sounds to the end of *be*. *(bead, beef, beak, beam, bean, beep, beat, bees, beach)*

Phonics
Sort Words

Model word building Draw a three-column chart or use Graphic Organizer 5. Now we're going to sort contractions with *is, have,* and *are*. Write *you've* and read it aloud. *You've* is made from the words *you* and *have*, so it goes in the *have* column.

Guide practice Write on the board in random order contractions with *is, have,* and *are*. Have children read each contraction, identify the two words it is made from, and add it to the appropriate column of the chart.

is	have	are
he's	you've	you're
she's	they've	they're
it's	we've	we're
who's	I've	

Corrective feedback For corrective feedback, read the contraction aloud, name the two words it is made from, and identify the letter or letters replaced by the apostrophe. Then have children add it to the correct column.

Fluent Word Reading

Model Write *hurt*. I know the sounds for *h, ur,* and *t*. I blend them and read the word *hurt*.

Write *you'll*. The apostrophe tells me this word is a contraction. I know the Word Wall word *you*, and I know the sound for *l*. I blend them and read the contraction *you'll*.

Guide practice Write the words below. Say the sounds in your head for each spelling you see. When I point to the word, we'll read it together. Allow one second per sound previewing time for the first reading.

jerk **you're** **third** **we've** **curb** **it's**

On their own Have children read the list above three or four times, until they can read one word per second.

Differentiated Instruction

A Advanced

More Challenging Contractions If children are able to identify the words that make up each contraction and sort them easily, write these contractions: *could've, there's, should've, would've, must've*. Read them aloud. Have children write the contractions on cards and sort them by ending. Then have them write the two words that make up each contraction.

Academic Vocabulary

contraction a short way of writing two words. An apostrophe replaces the letters that have been left out.

English Language Learners

Practice Contractions Haitian Creole does not include contractions. If children who speak Haitian Creole or another language need extra practice, have them build and read contractions using letter tiles and a piece of elbow macaroni as the apostrophe.

Get Ready to Read

Objectives

- ◎ Associate the sound /ėr/ with the spellings *er, ir,* and *ur,* and pronounce contractions correctly.
- Blend and read contractions and words with /ėr/ spelled *er, ir,* or *ur.*
- Decode words in context and isolation.
- Spell words with *er, ir,* and *ur.*

Blend and Read

Decode words in isolation

Have children turn to pages 387–388 in the *Reader's and Writer's Notebook* and find the first list of words. Each word in this list is either a contraction or a word with the sound /ėr/ spelled *er, ir,* or *ur.* Let's blend and read these words. Be sure that children identify the correct sounds in contractions and words that have /ėr/ spelled *er, ir,* or *ur.*

Reader's and Writer's Notebook pp. 387–388

Next, have children read the high-frequency words.

Decode words in context

Chorally read the story along with the children. Have children identify words in the story that are contractions or have /ėr/ spelled *er, ir,* or *ur.*

Team Talk Pair children and have them take turns reading the story aloud to each other. Monitor children as they read to check for proper pronunciation and appropriate pacing.

On their own

To further develop automaticity, have children take the story home to reread.

Spelling
Words with *er, ir, ur*

Spell high-frequency words Write *visit* and *done* and point them out on the Word Wall. Have children say and spell the words with you and then without you.

Dictation Have children write these sentences. Say each sentence. Then repeat it slowly, one word at a time.

1. **Kim will visit her friend soon.**
2. **Tell me when you are done with the mop.**
3. **My shirt is red.**

Proofread and correct Write each sentence, spelling words one at a time. Have children circle and rewrite any misspelled words.

On their own Use *Reader's and Writer's Notebook* p. 389.

Name ____ I'm a Caterpillar

Words with *er, ir, ur*

Circle the word that is spelled correctly. **Write** it.

1. I like your ___.
shert (shirt) shurt — shirt
2. I knew where you ___.
(were) wir wure — were
3. Meet the new ___.
gerl (girl) gurl — girl
4. Let the candle ___.
bern birn (burn) — burn
5. Judy said, "Yes, ___."
ser (sir) sur — sir
6. Look at the ___.
berd (bird) burd — bird
7. Can I be ___?
ferst (first) furst — first
8. His dog has black ___.
fer fure (fur) — fur
9. Are you ___?
dun dune (done) — done
10. Let's ___ our friends.
(visit) visot visat — visit

Spelling Words: her, first, bird, girl, burn, were, shirt, fur, hurt, sir

High-Frequency Words: visit, done

Spelling Words with er, ir, ur 389

Reader's and Writer's Notebook p. 389

Small Group Time

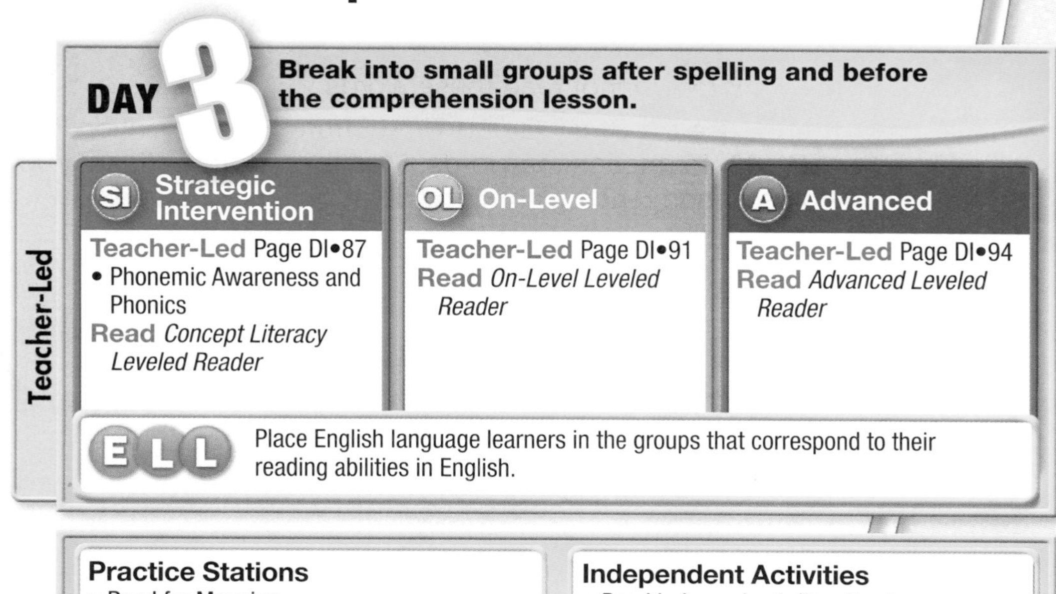
DAY 3 Break into small groups after spelling and before the comprehension lesson.

Teacher-Led

SI Strategic Intervention	OL On-Level	A Advanced
Teacher-Led Page DI•87 • Phonemic Awareness and Phonics **Read** *Concept Literacy Leveled Reader*	**Teacher-Led** Page DI•91 **Read** *On-Level Leveled Reader*	**Teacher-Led** Page DI•94 **Read** *Advanced Leveled Reader*

ELL Place English language learners in the groups that correspond to their reading abilities in English.

Practice Stations
- Read for Meaning
- Let's Write

Independent Activities
- Read independently/Reading Log on *Reader's and Writer's Notebook* p. RR4
- AudioText of Main Selection

Spelling Words

Words with *er, ir, ur*

1. her	**6. were**
2. first	**7. shirt**
3. bird	**8. fur**
4. girl	**9. hurt**
5. burn	**10. sir**

High-Frequency Words

11. visit	**12. done**

ELL

English Language Learners

Pronouncing /ėr/ Some children may not pronounce the *r* in /ėr/ words such as *burn* and *shirt*. Say each word slowly and emphasize the *r*-controlled vowel. Then have children repeat each word several times.

Objectives

- Read high-frequency words.
- Establish purpose for reading text.
- Review key features of literary nonfiction.

Check High-Frequency Words
SUCCESS PREDICTOR

High-Frequency and Story Words

Read words in isolation

Display and review this week's high-frequency words and story words. Have children read the words aloud.

Read words in context

Display the following sentence frames. Have children complete the sentences using high-frequency and story words. Have the children read each completed sentence with you.

1. **This ________ has a hard shell to keep its *pupa* safe. (chrysalis)**
2. **We ________ as we *wait* for the bus in the chilly wind. (shiver)**
3. **A ________ can *crawl* up a thin stem. (caterpillar)**
4. **If he gets his chores *done*, he can ________ Rob and Dale. (visit)**
5. **I *know* that Kate likes me to ________ her on the swing. (push)**

Don't Wait Until Friday

MONITOR PROGRESS — Check High-Frequency Words

Point to these words on the Word Wall and have the class read them. Listen for children who miss words during the reading. Call on those children to read some of the words individually.

push	**visit**	**wait**	**done**	**know**	Spiral Review
food	**from**	**afraid**	**now**	**soon** ←	Rows 2 and 3 review previously taught high-frequency words.
come	**have**	**out**	**what**	**away** ←	

If... children cannot read these words,

then... use the Small Group Time Strategic Intervention lesson, p. DI•88, to reteach the words. Monitor children's fluency with these words during reading and provide additional practice.

Day 1	Day 2	Day 3	Day 4	Day 5
Check Word Reading	Check Word Reading	Check High-Frequency Words/Retelling	Check Fluency	Check Oral Vocabulary

Success Predictor

Main Selection—Second Read
I'm a Caterpillar

Review Sequence

Recall this week's main selection, *I'm a Caterpillar*. Tell children that today they will read the story again. Remind children that the order in which things happen is their **sequence**. As we read, paying attention to the sequence of events helps us understand and remember what we are learning. What is the first thing a caterpillar does after it hatches? (Possible response: It eats leaves.) What happens next? (Possible response: It grows bigger; it makes a chrysalis.)

Review Genre: literary nonfiction

Let's Read Together Remind children that literary nonfiction is about real people or animals, real places, and true events. Have children recall events in *I'm a Caterpillar* that really happen in nature. (Caterpillars really hatch from butterfly eggs, eat leaves, make chrysalises, and turn into butterflies.)

Set a purpose

Remind children that good readers read for a purpose. Guide children to set a new purpose for reading *I'm a Caterpillar* today, perhaps to see how well they can remember and predict what will happen next after each event.

Extend thinking

Tell children they will now read *I'm a Caterpillar* for the second time. Use the Day 3 Extend Thinking notes to encourage children to use higher order thinking skills to go beyond the details of the selection.

Second Read

Continue to DAY 3

For the Second Read, use **Extend Thinking** across the bottom of pages 158–173.

Story Words

caterpillar an insect that changes into a moth or butterfly

crawl to move on your hands and knees or with your body close to the ground

chrysalis forms from the body of a caterpillar and has a hard shell that protects the caterpillar as it changes into a butterfly

pupa the form of an insect while it is changing from a wormlike larva into an adult

shiver to shake

Academic Vocabulary

sequence the order of events in a selection

English Language Learners

Words in Context To help children understand unfamiliar words in the context sentences, use gestures or draw quick sketches on the board. Then have children practice reading the sentences with a partner.

DAY 3 Read and Comprehend

Objectives

- Retell a nonfiction selection.
- Identify fact and opinion.
- Identify text structure.
- Write clear, coherent sentences.

Check Retelling
SUCCESS PREDICTOR

Objectives
• Show where in the selection you found the answer. • Read on your own for a period of time.

Envision It! Retell

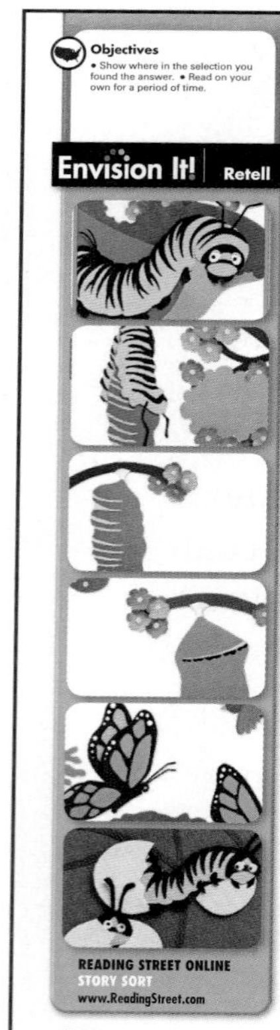

Think Critically

1. What other animals have you read about that change? Text to Text
2. Why do you think the author ends the selection the same way it starts? Think Like an Author
3. Name one fact you learned about caterpillars. Fact and Opinion
4. How does the order the author used to write this selection help you understand it better? Text Structure
5. **Look Back and Write** Why aren't the butterflies in this selection afraid of birds? Look back at page 170 and take notes. Then use your notes to write about why they aren't afraid of birds. TEST PRACTICE Extended Response

174

Meet the Author

Jean Marzollo

Jean Marzollo was a high school teacher and a magazine editor. Now she has written more than one hundred books for children! She writes about science, and she writes poetry, made-up stories, and *I Spy* books.

Ms. Marzollo likes to sew and work in her garden. She says writing is creative in the same way. It is hard and fun.

Here are other books by Jean Marzollo.

Use the Reading Log in the *Reader's and Writer's Notebook* to record your independent reading.

175

Student Edition pp. 174–175

Retelling

Have children work in pairs, retelling the selection to one another. Remind children that their partners should include the topics, main ideas, and what they learned from the reading. Children should use the retelling strip in the Student Edition as they retell. Monitor children's retelling.

Scoring rubric

Top-Score Response A top-score response makes connections beyond the text, elaborates on the topics, main ideas, and what children learned from the reading.

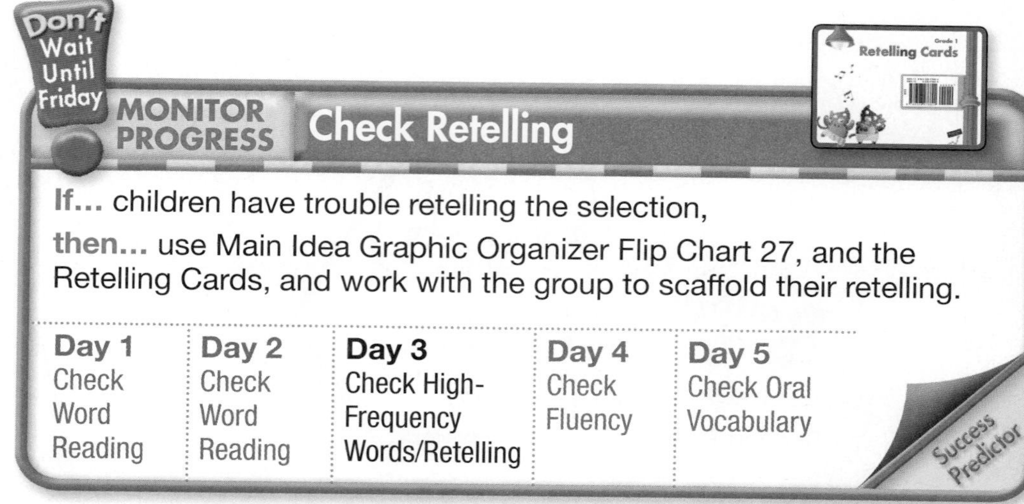

Don't Wait Until Friday **MONITOR PROGRESS** **Check Retelling**

If... children have trouble retelling the selection,
then... use Main Idea Graphic Organizer Flip Chart 27, and the Retelling Cards, and work with the group to scaffold their retelling.

Day 1	Day 2	Day 3	Day 4	Day 5
Check Word Reading	Check Word Reading	Check High-Frequency Words/Retelling	Check Fluency	Check Oral Vocabulary

Success Predictor

Think Critically

Text to Text 1. Possible response: Baby birds grow feathers and learn to fly. Tadpoles grow legs and change into frogs.

Think Like an Author 2. Possible response: The author wants us to learn that the life cycle of a butterfly starts over again when a caterpillar hatches and begins to eat.

Fact and Opinion 3. Possible response: A caterpillar makes a chrysalis and changes into a butterfly inside the chrysalis.

Text Structure 4. Possible response: Reading about the events in order helped me learn the life cycle of a butterfly.

Writing on Demand 5. **Look Back and Write** For writing fluency, assign a 5-minute time limit. As children finish, encourage them to reread their response and proofread for errors.

Scoring rubric

> **Top-Score Response** A top-score response uses facts from the text and inference to tell why these butterflies aren't afraid of birds. For example:
>
> These butterflies aren't afraid of birds because birds will not eat these butterflies. The birds know that these butterflies taste awful.

Meet the author Read aloud page 175 as children follow along. Ask children what different kinds of books Jean Marzollo likes to write.

Read independently After children enter their independent reading into their Reading Logs, have them paraphrase a portion of the text they have just read. Tell children that when we paraphrase, we express the meaning of what we have read using our own words.

Differentiated Instruction

A Advanced

Look Back and Write Ask children who show proficiency with the writing prompt to explain why butterflies lay their eggs on leaves.

INTERACT with TEXT

Strategy Response Log

Text Structure Have children use p. RR29 in their *Reader's and Writer's Notebook* to draw pictures of three things that happen in the life cycle of a butterfly. Have them number their pictures to show the sequence of events.

Plan to Assess Retelling

- ☐ Week 1: Strategic Intervention
- ☐ Week 2: Advanced
- ☐ Week 3: Strategic Intervention
- ☐ Week 4: On-Level
- ☑ This week: Assess Strategic Intervention children.
- ☐ Week 6: Assess any children you have not yet checked during this unit.

Retelling Success Predictor

Objectives

- Read aloud fluently, attending to punctuation.
- Speak in complete sentences with correct subject-verb agreement.
- Ask questions with appropriate subject-verb inversion.

Model Fluency
Expression and Intonation

Model fluent reading Have children turn to Student Edition pages 160–161. Have children identify the various end marks. Discuss what each end mark means. As I read these pages, I'll look for end marks that tell me to stop, to read in an excited way, or to read as if I'm asking a question.

Guide practice Have children read the pages with you. Then have them reread the pages as a group until they read with appropriate expression and intonation. Continue in the same way with pages 166–167.

Corrective feedback **If...** children have difficulty reading with appropriate expression and intonation,
then... prompt:

- What do the end marks tell you about the way each sentence should be read?
- Try to make your voice sound as if the characters are speaking.

Reread for Fluency

ROUTINE **Choral Reading**

1. **Select a Passage** For *I'm a Caterpillar*, use pp. 168–169.

2. **Model** First, have children track the print as you read.

3. **Guide Practice** Then have children read along with you.
4. **Corrective Feedback** Have the class read aloud without you. Monitor progress and provide feedback. For optimal fluency, children should reread three to four times.

Routines Flip Chart

Check comprehension How do you think the butterfly feels about its change? (Possible response: Happy that it can fly.)

Conventions
Verbs *Am, Is, Are, Was,* and *Were*

Review verbs *am, is, are, was,* and *were*

Remind children that when talking about one thing or person, *am, is, are, was* or *were* can be used. When talking about more than one thing or person, only *are* or *were* are used. *Am, is,* and *are* tell about now, while *was* and *were* tell about the past. Read the following sentences aloud: *The girl was running.* (one person, past event) *The leaves are falling.* (more than one person, event is happening now) When asking a question, the words *am, is, are, was,* and *were* often come at the beginning.

Guide practice

Write these sentences on the board and have children use *am, is, are, was,* and *were* to provide answers.

How old are you today?

How old were you last year?

What are your parents' names?

Where were the stars last night?

Team Talk Have children give their responses to the questions using *am, is, are, was,* and *were.*

Connect to oral language

Have children complete these sentence frames orally.

1. Apples ________ good to eat.

2. ________ they up late last night?

3. He ________ sleepy when he woke up.

On their own

Use *Reader's and Writer's Notebook* p. 390.

Verbs: *Am, Is, Are, Was, Were*

Possible answer: I am looking at a picture. Some leaves are there. One bird is on a leaf. The bird was flying. Were other birds in the tree?

That is a bird.

Reader's and Writer's Notebook p. 390

Options for Oral Rereading

Use *I'm a Caterpillar* or one of this week's Decodable Practice Readers.

Daily Fix-It

5. The bug yelow wings had.
The bug had yellow wings.

6. what kind of bug was it.
What kind of bug was it?

Discuss the Daily Fix-It corrections with children. Review sentence capitalization and punctuation, the *ll* spelling of /l/, and word order in sentences.

ELL

English Language Learners

Forms of *to be* Tell Spanish speakers that English speakers say *We are hungry* rather than *We have hunger*, and *I am six years old* rather than *I have six years*.

Objectives

- Write a draft of pictures and captions.
- Use details that show and tell.

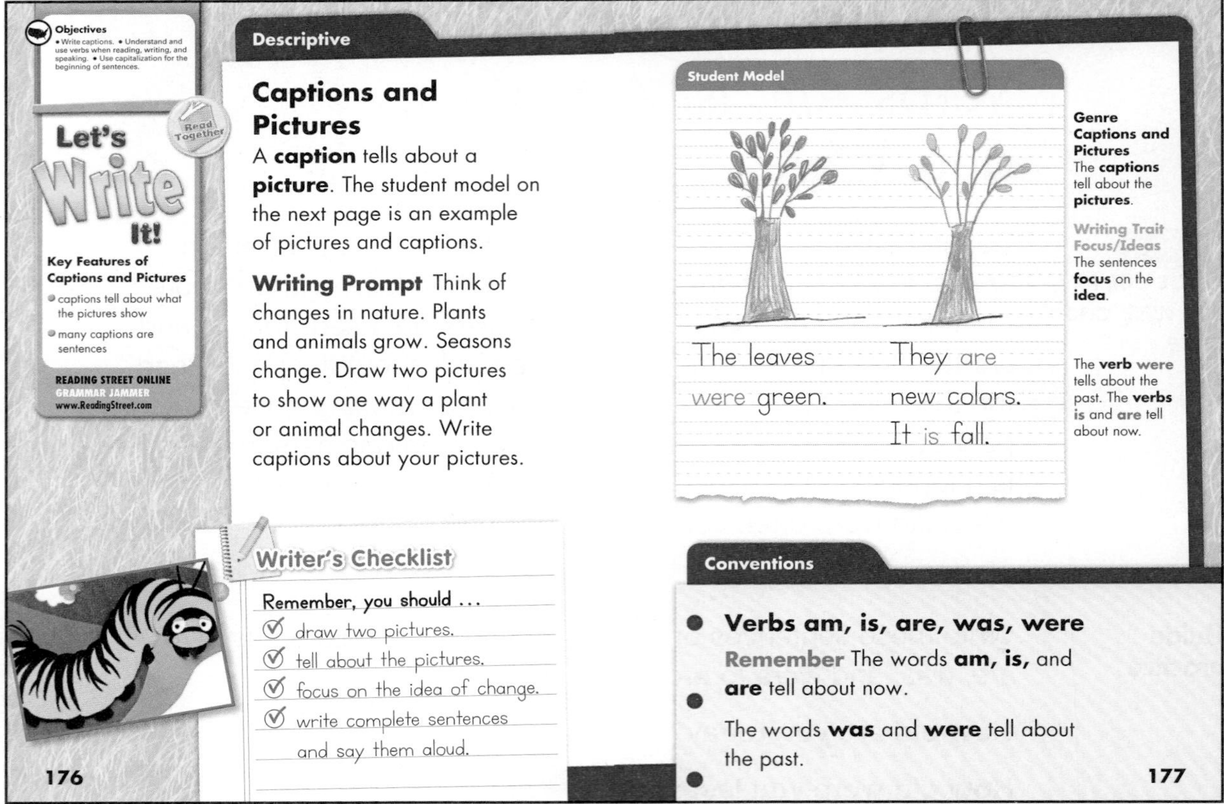

Student Edition pp. 176–177

Let's Write It!

Teach

Use pages 176–177 in the Student Edition. Read aloud the Key Features of Captions and Pictures and the definition of captions and pictures. Help children better understand the Writing Prompt by reading it aloud and discussing the Writer's Checklist with children.

Review the student model

Then read the student model on page 177 to children. Point out the changes in the pictures. Ask children to identify the changes. (The leaves changed colors.) Discuss how the time of year has changed, identifying the season in the second caption. Read aloud and briefly discuss the side notes about Genre, the Writing Trait, and Verbs to help children understand how an author writes a caption.

Scoring rubric

Top-Score Response Help children understand that a top-score response has pictures that show a change and captions that tell about the pictures. For a complete rubric see Writing Rubric 17 from the Teacher Resource DVD-ROM.

Connect to conventions

Read to children the Conventions note about Verbs *Am, Is, Are, Was,* and *Were*. Point out verbs in the model *(were, are, is)*.

Writing—Captions and Pictures

Writer's Craft: Details

MINI-LESSON

Details to Show and Tell

- **Introduce** Use your chart from yesterday and Writing Transparency 17A to model captions that show and tell. Yesterday, I wrote my plan for my pictures and captions. Today I will draw my pictures and write my captions. My first picture is of an apple tree covered in blossoms. Now I need to write a caption that helps people learn about the tree. I will tell when the picture is and what the tree is like. Read aloud the draft on the Transparency to show how to use details to show and tell.

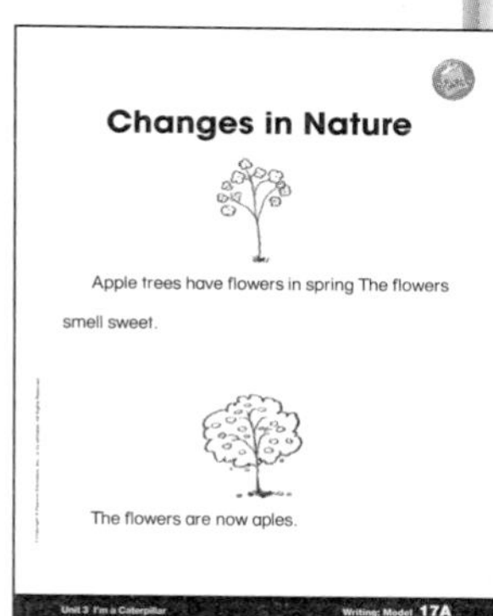

Writing Transparency 17A
TR DVD

- Explain how children can use their charts from yesterday to draw their pictures and write their captions. Today's goal is to write the captions but not to rewrite each word perfectly. They can edit later to correct the words.

Guide caption writing Now it is time to draw your pictures and write your captions. Use details to help your readers learn about things. Have children use their charts. Guide children as they draft the captions.

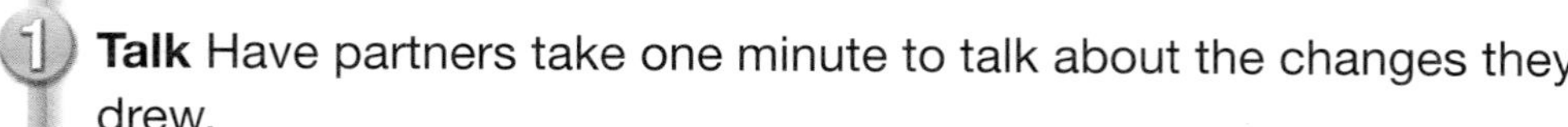

ROUTINE **Quick Write for Fluency** Team Talk

1. **Talk** Have partners take one minute to talk about the changes they drew.
2. **Write** Each child writes a sentence about the change.
3. **Share** Partners point out detail words in the others' sentences.

Routines Flip Chart

Differentiated Instruction

A Advanced

Vary Sentence Beginnings Challenge advanced children to vary the beginnings of the captions using time phrases, such as *in the spring, in fall, in winter.*

Write Guy *Jeff Anderson*

Nice Big, Long, Pointless, Listy Adjective Strings

As children learn to write, many love to "improve" sentences with adjectives—big adjectives, little adjectives, many adjectives. We don't want to encourage strings of adjectives. On the other hand, this is a problem that can correct itself. Show a sample of a sentence with too many adjectives (not written by the child). Ask which *one* adjective might be unnecessary.

Objectives

- Share ideas and information about how nature changes.
- Listen carefully to others while they are speaking.
- Share appropriate ideas when contributing to a discussion.
- Gather and record information for an inquiry project.

Listening and Speaking
Share Information and Ideas

Teach sharing information and ideas

Explain that people share information and ideas in order to help others learn about a topic. Remind children that an idea is a thought. When people share information and ideas, it helps if they raise their hand before they speak and wait to be called on. It also helps if they listen to others when they speak.

- Good speakers raise their hand.
- Good speakers do not speak without being called on.
- Good speakers listen to others.
- Good speakers share ideas that have to do with the topic.

Model

I will share what I know about changes that happen in nature. There are four seasons in each year. After winter is over, the four seasons start over again, beginning with spring. Birds lay eggs that hatch into new birds.

Guide practice

Briefly discuss other ideas about how nature changes. Have children share what they know and tell their ideas. You may wish to guide them in consulting their concept charts or in rereading the main selection to get ideas.

On their own

Have children work in pairs and tell each other about some changes they have observed in nature. Monitor children to be sure they are using good speaking and listening skills.

Research and Inquiry
Gather and Record Information

Teach Tell children that today they will gather facts about a topic. They will fill in more of their chart.

Model Team Talk Display the chart the class created on Day 1. Let's gather some information so we can fill in more of our chart. Let's go outside and observe nature in the area around our school. Take your charts with you and record what you see and what changes you either can see or imagine happening in the future.

Guide practice Go outside and guide children as they observe nature. Encourage them to look down, up, and around them. Have them record their observations in their chart.

Place in Nature	What did you see there?	What changes did you see?
My backyard	grass, flowers, ants	The grass grows and has to be mowed. The flowers bloom in spring
My school playground	ants, sidewalk	Ants build an anthill. Grass is growing through cracks in the pavement.

On their own Use *Reader's and Writer's Notebook*, p. 386.

Wrap Up Your Day

- ✔ **Fact and Opinion** Have children reread *I'm a Caterpillar.* Are there any opinions in the selection? What are they?
- ✔ **Text Structure** Remind children that the text structure, or illustrations and the way the text is shown on a page, can help you understand what the text is about.

Differentiated Instruction

SI Strategic Intervention

Taking Notes Some children may not know where to begin once they are outside. You may go around and suggest key words that may stimulate their imagination and observation skills: *tree, grass, pavement, sidewalk, weeds, grow, fall, leaves, ants, insects, season, snow, flowers.* From there, they should be able to come up with observations and potential changes.

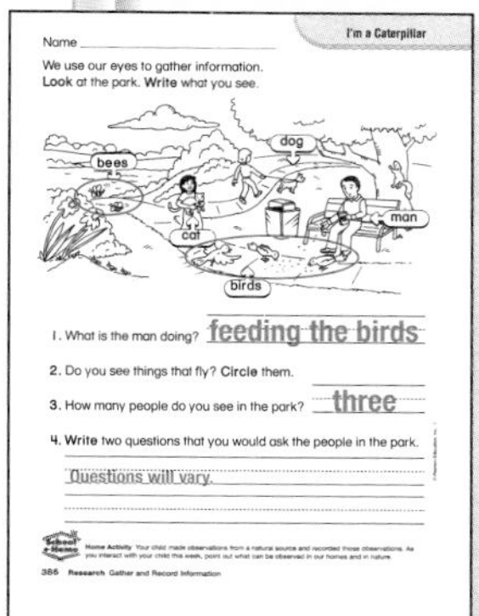

Reader's and Writer's Notebook p. 386

Tell children that tomorrow they will read about a girl who learns about insects.

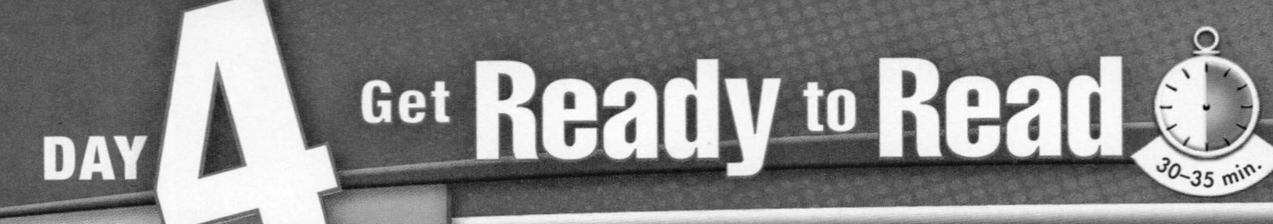

Objectives

- Discuss the concept to develop oral language.
- Build oral vocabulary.
- Identify details in text.

Today at a Glance

Oral Vocabulary
emerge, fragile, vessel

Phonological Awareness
Blend and Segment Syllables

Phonics and Spelling
Review *r*-Controlled *ar*
Review Endings *-ed, ing*

High-Frequency Words
Review

Comprehension
Text Structure

Fluency
Expression and Intonation

Conventions
Verbs *am, is, are, was, were*

Writing
Captions and Pictures: Revise

Research and Inquiry
Review and Revise Topic

Concept Talk

Question of the Week

What changes can be seen in nature?

Build concepts

To reinforce concepts and to focus children's attention, have children sing "Life Cycle" from the *Sing with Me* Big Book. We've learned a lot about the life cycle of a butterfly since we first sang this song. What facts can we add to what the song tells us? (Possible response: The caterpillar hangs upside down and splits its skin to form the shell. The shell is called a chrysalis.)

Sing with Me Big Book Audio

Review Genre: Literary nonfiction

Have children tell the key features of literary nonfiction: it tells about real people or animals, real places, and true events. Explain that today they will hear about another kind of insect in "Song of the Cicada," by Tristin Toohil.

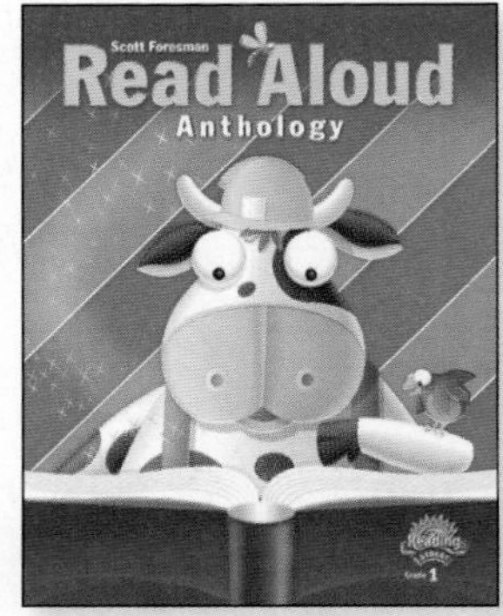

Read Aloud Anthology
"Song of the Cicada"

Monitor listening comprehension

Recall that in the life cycle of a butterfly, a wingless insect, the caterpillar, turns into an insect that can fly. Have children listen to "Song of the Cicada" to find out how a cicada's life cycle is like that of a butterfly.

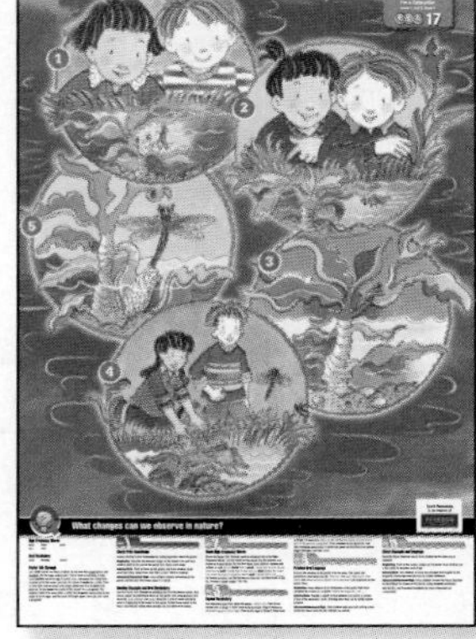
ELL Poster 17

ELL Produce Oral Language Use the Day 4 instruction on ELL Poster 17 to extend and enrich language.

Oral Vocabulary
Amazing Words

Teach Amazing Words

Amazing Words Oral Vocabulary Routine

1. **Introduce the Word** Relate the word *fragile* to the story. The shells that the cicadas left behind were *fragile*. Supply a child-friendly definition. When something is *fragile*, it breaks easily. Have children say the word.
2. **Demonstrate** Provide examples to show meaning. A glass is *fragile*. If you drop something that is *fragile*, it will probably break.
3. **Apply** Have children demonstrate their understanding. How would you carry something that is fragile?

See p. OV•2 to teach *emerge* and *vessel*.

Routines Flip Chart

Anchored Talk

Add to the concept map

Discuss the changes that happen in the life cycle of a cicada.

- Cicadas have wings, but the insects that hatch from their eggs have no wings. How is this like the life cycle of a butterfly? (Butterflies have wings, but the caterpillars that hatch from their eggs have no wings.) Let's add the information about cicadas to our map.
- A winged cicada grows inside the wingless insect. Then what happens? (The back of the insect splits open and the winged cicada climbs out.) Let's add these ideas to our map.
- How do you think the life cycle of the cicada starts over again? (The new cicada lays eggs that hatch into wingless insects.) Let's add this idea to our map.

Amazing Words

cycle	flurries
develop	emerge
insect	fragile
rearrange	vessel

Differentiated Instruction

SI Strategic Intervention

Amazing Words To enhance understanding, ask children the following questions. Have them answer in full sentences using the vocabulary word.

- Why is a spider web *fragile*?
- Why is an egg *fragile*?
- What could *emerge* from the ground?
- What could *emerge* from a pond?

English Language Learners

Frontload Listening Using pictures from *I'm a Caterpillar* and ELL Poster 17, help children describe the changes that happen in the life cycle of each insect. Tell children you will read to them about a cicada, another insect that changes.

Objectives

- Segment and blend words with two syllables.
- Read words with endings *-ed, -ing* and words with *r*-controlled *ar*.

Phonological Awareness
Segment and Blend Syllables

Model This week we read about the changes that happen in the life cycle of insects. Listen as I say the two syllables in *insect*. Slowly model the syllables: /in/ /sekt/. Now I will blend the two syllables together to say the word: /in/ /sekt/, *insect*.

Guide practice I will say two syllables. Repeat them after me. Then we will blend the syllables to make a word from the story. Say each syllable pair below. Have children repeat them. Together, blend the syllables to form a word.

Corrective feedback If children make an error, model the correct response. Return to the word later in the practice.

/big/ /ər/ (bigger)	**/shiv/ /ər/** (shiver)	**/flou/ /ər/** (flower)
/viz/ /it/ (visit)	**/nek/ /tər/** (nectar)	**/ȯ/ /fəl/** (awful)

On their own Say the two syllables in each word. Have children repeat the syllables and blend the word independently.

/sum/ /ər/ (summer)	**/win/ /tər/** (winter)	**/ôr/ /inj/** (orange)
/s ī/ /kəl/ (cycle)	**/gär/ /dn/** (garden)	**/fin/ /ish/** (finish)

Phonics Review

Endings *-ed, -ing;* *r*-Controlled *ar*

Review endings *-ed, -ing*

To review last week's first phonics skill, write *patted*. You studied words like this last week. You can read this word because you know how to blend the base word and the *-ed* ending when the final consonant is doubled. What is the base word? (*pat*) Blend the base word and the *-ed* ending. What's the word? (*patted*) Repeat this process for *stopping*.

Review *r*-controlled *ar*

To review last week's second phonics skill, write *mark*. You also studied words like this. What sound does ar stand for in this word? (/är/) What's the word? (*mark*)

Corrective feedback

If children are unable to answer your question about the /är/ sound, refer them to Sound-Spelling Card 55.

Guide practice

Draw a T-chart. I'm going to write some words. As I write each word, I want you to read the word and name the base word and ending. Write the words shown below one at a time in random order. Have children tell whether or not the final consonant of the base word was doubled before adding the ending. Then have children identify the words with /är/ spelled *ar*. (*barked, harmed, parking, marching*)

-ed	-ing
flipped	parking
barked	jogging
harmed	marching
dropped	stepping

On their own

Use Let's Practice It! pp. 155–156 on the *Teacher Resource DVD-ROM*.

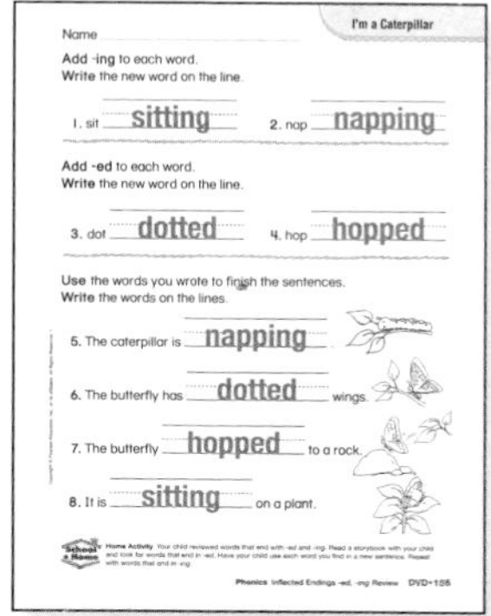
I'm a Caterpillar

Name

Add -ing to each word.
Write the new word on the line.

1. sit sitting 2. nap napping

Add -ed to each word.
Write the new word on the line.

3. dot dotted 4. hop hopped

Use the words you wrote to finish the sentences.
Write the words on the lines.

5. The caterpillar is napping.
6. The butterfly has dotted wings.
7. The butterfly hopped to a rock.
8. It is sitting on a plant.

Phonics Inflected Endings -ed, -ing Review DVD•155

Let's Practice It! TR DVD•155

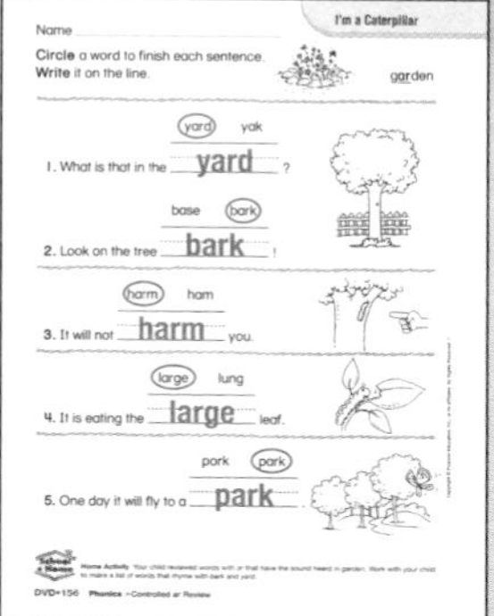
I'm a Caterpillar

Name

Circle a word to finish each sentence.
Write it on the line.

garden

1. What is that in the yard? (yard, yak)
2. Look on the tree bark! (base, bark)
3. It will not harm you. (harm, ham)
4. It is eating the large leaf. (large, lung)
5. One day it will fly to a park. (pork, park)

DVD•156 Phonics r-Controlled ar Review

Let's Practice It! TR DVD•156

English Language Learners

Multi-Syllable Words Speakers of monosyllabic languages such as Cantonese, Hmong, Khmer, Korean, and Vietnamese may pronounce the syllables of a multi-syllable word as separate words. Give children who speak these languages extra practice saying multi-syllable words.

DAY 4 Get Ready to Read

Objectives

- Apply knowledge of sound-spellings to decode unknown words when reading.
- Decode words in context and isolation.
- Practice fluency with oral rereading.

Decodable Practice Reader 17C

Vowels: *r*-Controlled /ėr/ *er, ir, ur;* Contractions

Decode words in isolation Have children turn to page 257. Have children decode each word.

Review High-frequency words Review the previously taught words *a, what, to, done, the, put, look,* and *said*. Have children read each word as you point to it on the Word Wall.

We've Made Shirts
Written by Karen Finch
Decodable Practice Reader 17C

Contractions
she's they're
it's we've

Vowels: *r*-Controlled *ir, er, ur*
Fern shirts stirs
churning her turn
twirls swirls

Long *i*: *i*
Vi hi

High-Frequency Words
a what to the
put look said done

257

Decodable Practice Reader 17C

Preview Decodable Reader Have children read the title and preview the story. Tell them they will read some words that have the /ėr/ sound and those that are contractions.

Decode words in context Pair children for reading and listen carefully as they decode. One child begins. Children read the entire story, switching readers after each page. Partners reread the story. This time the other child begins.

Decodable Practice Reader 17C

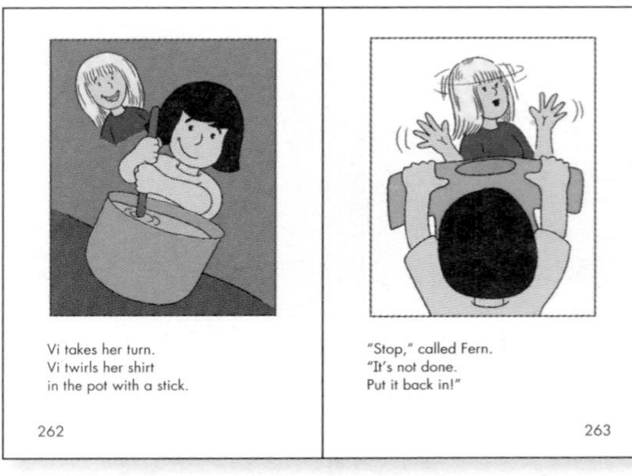

Corrective feedback

If. . . children have difficulty decoding a word,

then. . . refer them to the Sound-Spelling Cards to identify the sounds in the word. Then prompt them to blend the word.

- What is the new word?
- Is the new word a word you know?
- Does it make sense in the story?

Check decoding and comprehension

Have children retell the story to include characters, setting, and events. Then point to the words in the story that are contractions and those with the /ėr/ sound spelled *er, ir,* and *ur*. Ask children to say the words. List the words that children name. Children should supply *we've, shirts, Fern, they're, she's, first, stirs, churning, turn, twirls, it's,* and *swirls*. Ask them how they know these words are contractions or have the /ėr/ sound. (Some of the words have apostrophes between the letters and some words have the letters *ir, ur,* and *er*.)

Reread for Fluency

Have children reread Decodable Practice Reader 17C to develop automaticity decoding words that have the /ėr/ sound and those words that are contractions.

ROUTINE Oral Rereading

1. **Read** Have children read the entire book orally.
2. **Reread** To achieve optimal fluency, children should reread the text three or four times.
3. **Corrective Feedback** Listen as children read. Provide corrective feedback regarding their fluency and decoding.

Routines Flip Chart

English Language Learners

Contractions

Decodable Practice Reader

Beginning Before reading, have children say each contraction and its corresponding word pair. Have them identify the words with the /ėr/ sound. Monitor their pronunciation.

Intermediate After reading, have children use contractions to answer the following questions: *What are Vi and Fern going to make? (They're) Can you describe something that we have made in class? (We've)*

Advanced/Advanced-High After reading, have children list the words with the /ėr/ sound and the words that are contractions.

Objectives

- Read words fluently in context and in isolation.
- Spell words with /ėr/ spelled *er, ir, ur*.
- Spell high-frequency words.

Fluent Word Reading

Spiral Review

Read words in isolation

Display these words. Tell children that they can blend some words on this list and others are Word Wall words.

Have children read the list three or four times until they can read at the rate of two to three seconds per word.

jar	**shark**	**want**	**large**	**hugged**
park	**there**	**who**	**how**	**read**
few	**hopping**	**Clark**	**soon**	**again**
dark	**afraid**	**water**	**kissed**	**swimming**

Word Reading

Corrective feedback

If... children have difficulty reading whole words,
then... have them use sound-by-sound blending for decodable words or have them say and spell high-frequency words.
If... children cannot read fluently at a rate of two to three seconds per word,
then... have pairs practice the list until they can read it fluently.

Read words in context

Display these sentences. Call on individuals to read a sentence. Then randomly point to review words and have children read them. To help you monitor word reading, high-frequency words are underlined and decodable words are italicized.

<u>Who</u> *has* <u>a</u> <u>few</u> *large bugs hopping in his or her jar*?

<u>How</u> *can that shark be swimming* <u>there</u> *in such dark* <u>water</u>?

***Clark felt* <u>afraid</u> <u>to</u> *go, so he kissed and hugged Mom* <u>again</u>.**

***She will* <u>want</u> *us* <u>to</u> <u>read</u> *this park map and get back* <u>soon</u>.**

Sentence Reading

Corrective feedback

If... children are unable to read an underlined high-frequency word,
then... read the word for them and spell it, having them echo you.
If... children have difficulty reading an italicized decodable word,
then... guide them in using sound-by-sound blending.

Spelling
Words with *er, ir, ur*

Partner review Supply pairs of children with index cards on which the spelling words have been written. Have one child read a word while the other writes it. Then have children switch roles. Have them use the cards to check their spelling and correct any misspelled words.

On their own Use *Reader's and Writer's Notebook* p. 391.

Name

I'm a Caterpillar

Words with *er, ir, ur*

Spelling Words				
her	first	bird	girl	burn
were	shirt	fur	hurt	sir

Use this code. **Write** the words.

e f h i r s t u

1. hurt 2. sir 3. shirt
4. her 5. first 6. fur

Draw a line through the word that does not match. Then **write** the word that matches.

7. were ~~where~~ were — were
8. bird bird ~~bid~~ — bird
9. ~~grill~~ girl girl — girl
10. burn ~~turn~~ burn — burn

Spelling Words with er, ir, ur 391

Reader's and Writer's Notebook, p. 391

Spiral Review

These activities review

- previously taught high-frequency words *few, afraid, read, soon, how, again*.
- inflected endings *-ed, -ing*; *r*-controlled *ar*.

Small Group Time

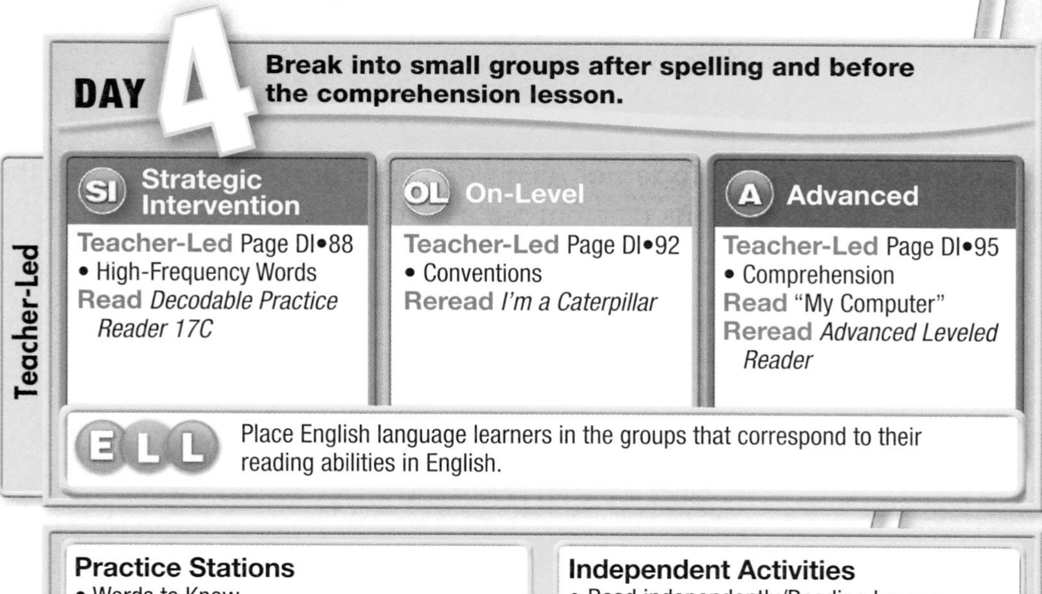
DAY 4 Break into small groups after spelling and before the comprehension lesson.

Teacher-Led

SI Strategic Intervention	OL On-Level	A Advanced
Teacher-Led Page DI•88 • High-Frequency Words Read *Decodable Practice Reader 17C*	Teacher-Led Page DI•92 • Conventions Reread *I'm a Caterpillar*	Teacher-Led Page DI•95 • Comprehension Read "My Computer" Reread *Advanced Leveled Reader*

ELL Place English language learners in the groups that correspond to their reading abilities in English.

Practice Stations
- Words to Know
- Get Fluent

Independent Activities
- Read independently/Reading Log on *Reader's and Writer's Notebook* p. RR4
- AudioText of Paired Selection

English Language Learners

Fluent Word Reading Have children listen to a more fluent reader say the words. Then have them repeat the words.

Objectives

- ◎ Identify text structures and the different ways information is conveyed on a page.
- Learn 21st century skills.
- Relate prior knowledge to new text.
- Set purpose for reading.

21st Century Skills

Introduce the strategy Have children notice the different ways information is displayed on the spread in the Student Edition. "My Computer" is written in big, colorful letters because it is the title. The title tells us what the selection is about. There are also pictures of a computer and its parts. Each picture has a big black word called a *caption*. The captions are in circles that have arrows pointing to the pictures.

Preview and predict Read the title of the selection. Have children look at the selection and predict what they might learn. (Possible response: They might learn about a computer.) Ask them what clue helped them make that prediction. (Possible response: They might say the title of the selection or the pictures.)

Genre **21st Century Skills** Tell children that they will be learning skills that will help them now and as they grow. Being able to work with new technology is one kind of skill. Computers are an example of technology. Technology is always changing. Explain that people use computers in many different ways, for both work and pleasure. Tell them that it is essential that they learn to use computers.

Activate prior knowledge Ask children to recall what they already know about computers. (Some children will have used a computer in the past and may know some of the parts, such as a mouse.)

Set a purpose **Let's Read Together** As children look at the selection, have them pay attention to the different parts of a computer.

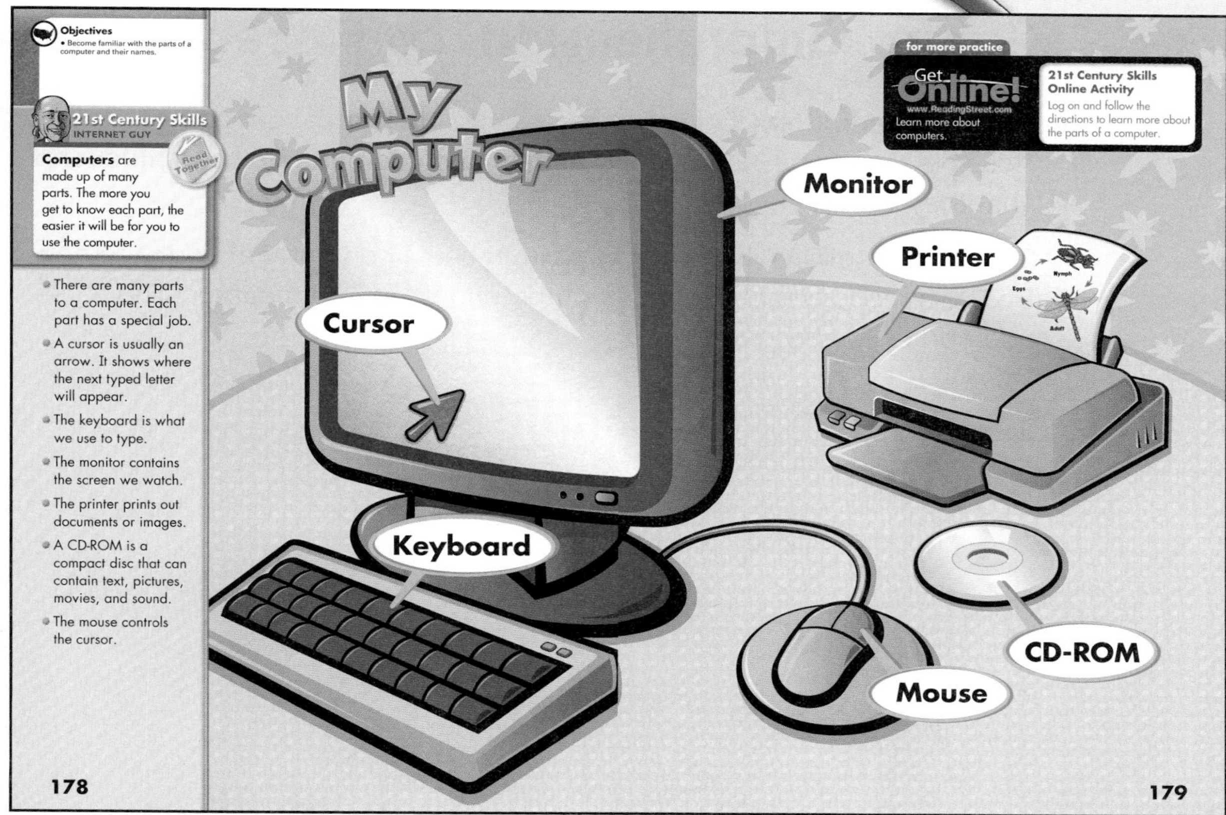

Student Edition pp. 178–179

Science Vocabulary

cursor the blinking or moving symbol on a computer screen that tells you where you are on the screen or in a document

CD-ROM a compact disc that stores a lot of digital data

Guide Comprehension

Guide practice

Think Aloud Good readers look carefully at all the words and pictures on a page. I look at the word *mouse* and see an arrow pointing to a picture. That tells me that the word *mouse* names that part of the computer. I am going to read the rest of the words and notice that they all name parts of a computer.

Objectives

- Learn 21st century skills.
- Read aloud fluently with expression and appropriate intonation.

Check Fluency WCPM
SUCCESS PREDICTOR

Guide Comprehension, continued

Confirm predictions What did the selection tell you about computers? (Possible response: I learned the names of some parts of a computer and what they look like.)

Connect to self In what ways might you use a computer at your age now? (Possible responses: I use a computer to look up information online; I use a computer to play games.)

Fluency
Expression and Intonation

Guide practice

- Have children turn to pp. 160–161 in *I'm a Caterpillar.*
- Have children follow along as you read the pages with appropriate expression and intonation.
- Have the class read the pages with you and then reread the pages as a group without you until they read with appropriate expression and intonation. To provide additional fluency practice, pair nonfluent readers with fluent readers.

ROUTINE Paired Reading

1. **Select a Passage** For *I'm a Caterpillar,* use pp. 163–164.
2. **Model** First, have children track the print as you read.
3. **Guide Practice** Then have children read along with you.
4. **On Their Own** For optimal fluency, have partners reread three or four times.

Routines Flip Chart

MONITOR PROGRESS Check Fluency WCPM

As children reread, monitor their progress toward their individual fluency goals. Current Goal: 25–35 words correct per minute. End-of-Year Goal: 60 words correct per minute.

If... children cannot read fluently at a rate of 25–35 words correct per minute,

then... have children practice with text at their independent level.

Day 1	Day 2	Day 3	Day 4	Day 5
Check Word Reading	Check Word Reading	Check High-Frequency Words/Retelling	Check Fluency	Check Oral Vocabulary

Success Predictor

Differentiated Instruction

Advanced

WCPM If children already read at 60 words correct per minute, allow them to read independently.

Fluency Assessment Plan

Do a formal fluency assessment with 8 to 10 children every week. Assess 4 to 5 children on Day 4 and 4 to 5 children on Day 5. Use the reproducible fluency passage, Teacher's Edition, page 181f.

Options for Oral Rereading

Use *I'm a Caterpillar* or one of this week's Decodable Practice Readers.

Objectives

- Use verbs *am, is, are, was,* and *were* with correct subject-verb agreement.
- Revise captions to make them clear.

Conventions

Verbs *Am, Is, Are, Was,* and *Were*

Test practice Use *Reader's and Writer's Notebook* p. 392 to help children understand the verbs *am, is, are, was,* and *were* in test items. Remind children that *am, is,* or *was* can be used when talking about one thing or person. *Are* or *were* are used when talking about more than one thing or person. *Are* and *were* also are used with the subject *you*. *Am, is,* and *are* tell about now, while *was* and *were* tell about the past. When using one of these verbs to ask a question, the verb often appears at the beginning of the sentence.

Then read the Reader's and Writer's Notebook p. 392 directions. Guide children as they mark the answer for number 1.

On their own Use *Reader's and Writer's Notebook* p. 392.

Connect to oral language After children mark the answers to numbers 1–6, review the correct choices aloud, and have children read each sentence aloud, emphasizing the verbs *am, is, are, was,* and *were.*

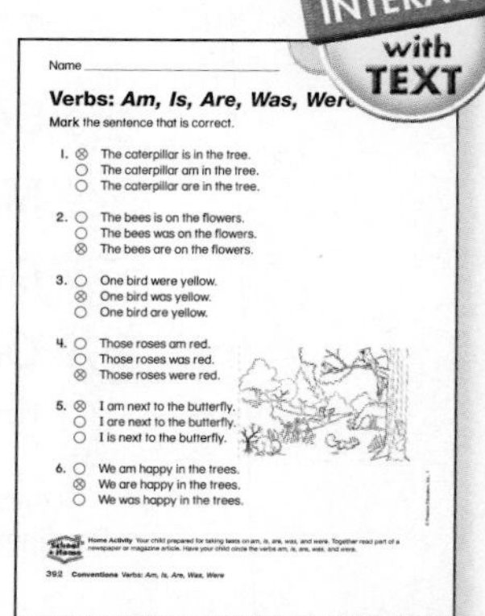

Name ____________

Verbs: *Am, Is, Are, Was, Were*

Mark the sentence that is correct.

1. ⊗ The caterpillar is in the tree.
   ○ The caterpillar am in the tree.
   ○ The caterpillar are in the tree.
2. ○ The bees is on the flowers.
   ○ The bees was on the flowers.
   ⊗ The bees are on the flowers.
3. ○ One bird were yellow.
   ⊗ One bird was yellow.
   ○ One bird are yellow.
4. ○ Those roses am red.
   ○ Those roses was red.
   ⊗ Those roses were red.
5. ⊗ I am next to the butterfly.
   ○ I are next to the butterfly.
   ○ I is next to the butterfly.
6. ○ We am happy in the trees.
   ⊗ We are happy in the trees.
   ○ We was happy in the trees.

School + Home **Home Activity** Your child prepared for taking tests on am, is, are, was, and were. Together read part of a newspaper or magazine article. Have your child circle the verbs am, is, are, was, and were.

392 **Conventions** Verbs: Am, Is, Are, Was, Were

Reader's and Writer's Notebook p. 392

Writing—Captions and Pictures
Revising Strategy

MINI-LESSON

Revising Strategy: Adding a Sentence

- Yesterday we drew pictures and wrote captions for them. Today we will revise our captions. We can help people who look at the pictures. We can make sure our captions give the information people need. If we need to, we can add a sentence to the caption.

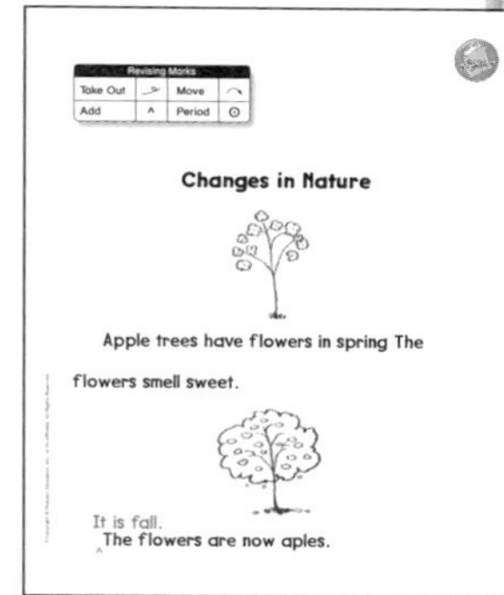

Writing Transparency 17B
TR DVD

- Display the Revising Tips. Explain that this is a time for making the captions clear for readers. Tomorrow children will proofread to correct any errors such as misspellings, missing capital letters, or missing periods.

Revising Tips

- ☐ Make sure your captions are complete sentences.
- ☐ Add a sentence to make your caption clear.

- Use Writing Transparency 17B to model adding a sentence. I want to make the captions clear for readers. The caption for the second picture doesn't tell when the flowers become apples. I will add a sentence. Add *It is fall* to the caption.

- Tell children that they can add a sentence to their captions as they revise.

Peer conferencing

Peer Revision Have pairs of children exchange captions and pictures. Have children look at the pictures and read the captions. Then have them take turns asking questions that come up, such as *When does this happen? Why does this change happen?* Children can add sentences to answer their partners' questions.

Differentiated Instruction

SI Strategic Intervention

Identifying Missing Information Tell children that a key to making sure ideas are clear is to pretend they are looking at someone else's writing. Have them imagine they know little or nothing about their topic and then look at the pictures and captions. They can consider whether the captions give enough information from this perspective.

Daily Fix-It

7. It can fli veree high.
It can fly very high.

8. She saw it fly awae?
She saw it fly away.

Discuss the Daily Fix-It corrections with children. Review the spelling of words that end in *y,* the *ay* spelling of long *a,* and end punctuation.

English Language Learners

Verbs *Am, Is, Are, Was, Were* Give children the following chart to consult as they practice forms of the verb *be*.

I am. You are. He/She/It is. I was. You were. He/She/It was.	We are. You are. They are. We were. You were. They were.

Objectives

- Revise a draft for clarity.
- Review answers to inquiry questions.

Writing
Captions and Pictures, continued

Guide practice Have children revise their captions and pictures. For those not sure how to revise, have children refer to the Revising Tips or the Key Features of Captions and Pictures.

Corrective feedback Circulate to monitor and conference with children as they write. Remind them that they will have time to proofread and edit tomorrow. Today they can make changes in captions to make them clearer. Help them understand the benefits of adding a sentence to clarify their explanations.

ROUTINE Quick Write for Fluency Team Talk

1. **Talk** Have children talk about what their chosen plant or animal was like and what it is like after the change.
2. **Write** Have children write two short sentences about the plant using a past and a present form of *be.*
3. **Share** Partners can read the sentences to one another.

Routines Flip Chart

Research and Inquiry
Review and Revise Topic

Teach Tell children that the next step in the inquiry project is to review our topic to see if we have the information we set out to find. Or, did our answers lead to a different topic?

Model We wanted to answer this week's question: *What changes can be seen in nature?* We came up with some changes that we have seen ourselves. Display the chart. Now we have some changes that we have seen here at school. We also have some ideas about changes we have seen at home and at the park. These ideas answer the original question: *What changes can be seen in nature?* So, we have answered our original topic and it does not need to change.

Guide practice Have children look at the information they gathered on Day 3. Then instruct them to work with a partner to discuss the entire chart. Does the information tell them about changes they can see in nature? They may want to go back outside (in small groups supervised by a teaching aide or parental helper) to gather more information. Finally, tell children that tomorrow they will organize all the information in order to share it with others.

Wrap Up Your Day

- **Phonics Review** List several contractions. Have children read each word and identify the two words that make up the contraction.
- **Fluency** Write *We're not afraid of birds. They know that we taste awful.* Have the class reread the sentences until they can do so with appropriate expression and intonation.

Differentiated Instruction

Advanced

Extra Research Advanced students may wish to think of another place in nature they have observed change (a zoo or hiking trail, for example). You may wish to organize a field trip to a zoo or nature center.

Remind children that they heard about a cicada that left its shell behind as it grew. Tomorrow they will hear about the cicada again.

Objectives

- Review the concept: changes we can observe in nature.
- Build oral vocabulary.
- Identify details in text.

Today at a Glance

Oral Vocabulary
Review

Phonics
◉ Review *r*-Controlled *er, ir, ur*
◉ Review Contractions with *'s, 've, 're*

Comprehension
◉ Fact and Opinion

Story Words
Review

High-Frequency Words
Review

Conventions
Verbs am, is, are, was, were

Writing
Captions and Pictures

Research and Inquiry
Communicate

Check Oral Vocabulary
SUCCESS PREDICTOR

Concept Wrap Up

Question of the Week

What changes can be seen in nature?

Review Concept

This week we have read and listened to stories about changes we can see in nature. Today you will listen to find out how a young cicada is like a caterpillar. Read the story.

- How is a young cicada like a caterpillar? (Possible response: They are crawling insects. They split their skin or shell to become flying insects.)

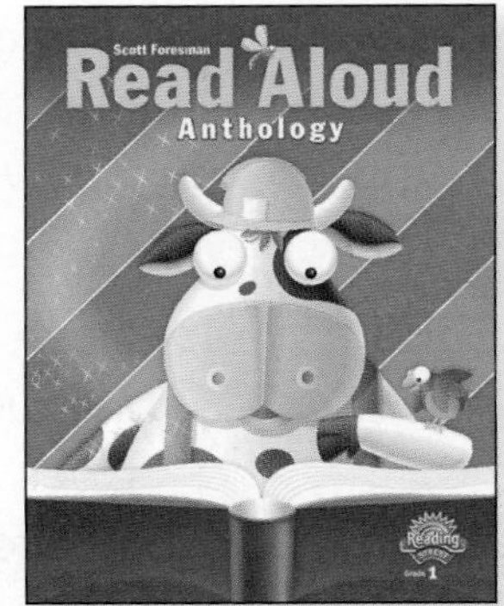

Read Aloud Anthology
"Song of the Cicada"

Review Amazing Words

Orally review the meaning of this week's Amazing Words. Then display this week's concept map. Have children use Amazing Words such as *cycle, insect, develop,* and *emerge,* as well as the concept map, to answer the question, "What changes can be seen in nature?"

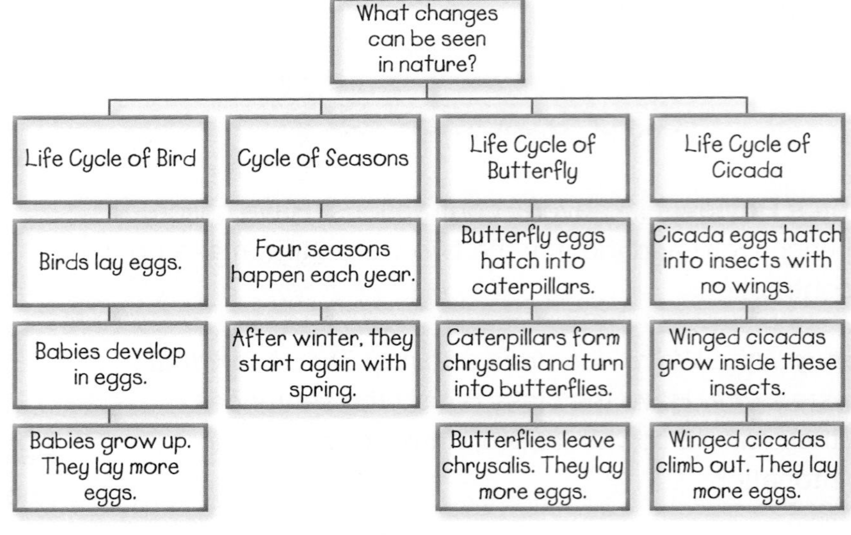

ELL Check Concepts and Language Use the Day 5 instruction on ELL Poster 17 to monitor children's understanding of the lesson concept.

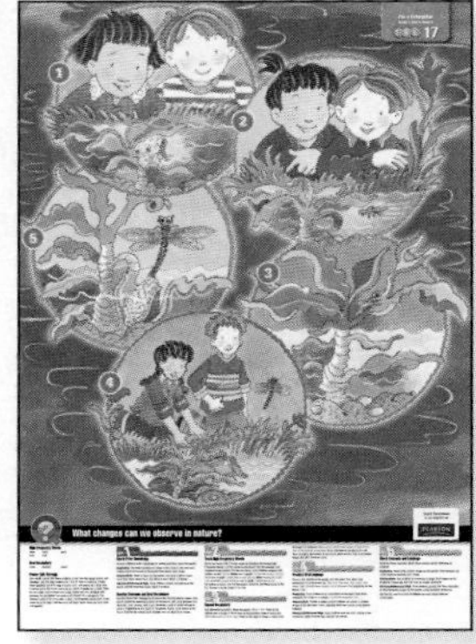
ELL Poster 17

Oral Vocabulary
Amazing Ideas

Connect to the Big Question

Team Talk Pair children and have them discuss how the Question of the Week connects to this unit's Big Question, "What is changing in our world?" Tell children to use the concept map and what they've learned from this week's Anchored Talks and reading selections to form an Amazing Idea—a realization or "big idea" about **Change.** Then ask each pair to share their Amazing Idea with the class.

Amazing Ideas might include these key concepts:

- Some animals change into another kind of animal.
- Things in nature happen in cycles, sequences that start over again, such as the seasons and the way animals develop.

MONITOR PROGRESS Check Oral Vocabulary

Call on individuals to use this week's Amazing Words to talk about changes we can observe in nature. Prompt discussion with the questions below. Monitor children's ability to use the Amazing Words and note which words children are unable to use.

- **How does a caterpillar *develop* into a flying *insect*?**
- **What *emerges* when a cicada splits its back?**
- **Why are a cicada's new wings *fragile*?**
- **How do *vessels* in the new wings change them?**
- **Why are the seasons a kind of *cycle*?**
- **Why might a snowstorm make you *rearrange* your plans?**
- **What's the difference between a snowstorm and *flurries*?**

If... children have difficulty using the Amazing Words,
then... reteach the unknown words using the Oral Vocabulary Routines, pp. 151a, 156b, 174b, 178b.

Day 1	Day 2	Day 3	Day 4	Day 5
Check Word Reading	Check Word Reading	Check High Frequency Words/Retelling	Check Fluency	**Check Vocabulary**

Success Predictor

Amazing Words

cycle	flurries
develop	emerge
insect	fragile
rearrange	vessel

ELL

English Language Learners

Oral Vocabulary The word *fragile* has a cognate in Spanish. The Spanish word *frágil* may help Spanish speakers learn the English word.

DAY 5 Wrap Up your Week

Objectives

- Change initial sounds to create rhyming words.
- ◎ Review words with the *r*-controlled *er, ir, ur.*
- ◎ Review contractions with *'s, 've, 're.*

Assess

- Spell words with *r*-controlled *er, ir, ur.*
- Spell high-frequency words.

Phonological Awareness
Generate Rhyming Words

Review rhyming words

Have children change the initial sound of each word below to make a rhyming word. If children make an error, model a correct response. Return to the word later in the practice. Sample answers are given.

green (clean)	**true** (glue)	**lake** (make)
slip (trip)	**whale** (tail)	**snow** (low)
pack (back)	**look** (book)	**feel** (meal)

Phonics
◎ *r*-Controlled *er, ir, ur;* Contractions *'s, 've, 're*

Review Target phonics skills

Write the following sentences on the board. Have children read each one, first quietly to themselves and then aloud as you track the print.

1. **<u>You've</u> got <u>dirt</u> on that <u>shirt</u>.**
2. **<u>That's</u> a big <u>bird</u> on a small <u>perch</u>.**
3. **<u>We're</u> going to <u>surf</u> in those waves.**
4. **<u>She's</u> a <u>clerk</u> in this garden store.**

Team Talk Have children discuss with a partner which words have /ėr/ spelled *er, ir,* or *ur,* which words are contractions, and what two words each contraction is made from. Then call on individuals to share with the class.

Spelling Test
Words with *er, ir, ur*

Dictate spelling words

Say each word, read the sentence, repeat the word, and allow time for children to write the word.

1. her	She put on **her** red jacket.
2. first	You're in **first** grade.
3. bird	The **bird** will sip the water.
4. girl	That **girl** can run fast.
5. burn	**Burn** the trash in a safe place.
6. were	We **were** sitting with our friends
7. shirt	His **shirt** got wet in the sink.
8. fur	The kitten has gray **fur.**
9. hurt	Be careful not to **hurt** the cat.
10. sir	**Sir,** can I go now?

High-Frequency Words

11. visit	Burt came for a **visit.**
12. done	Have you **done** your homework?

Small Group Time

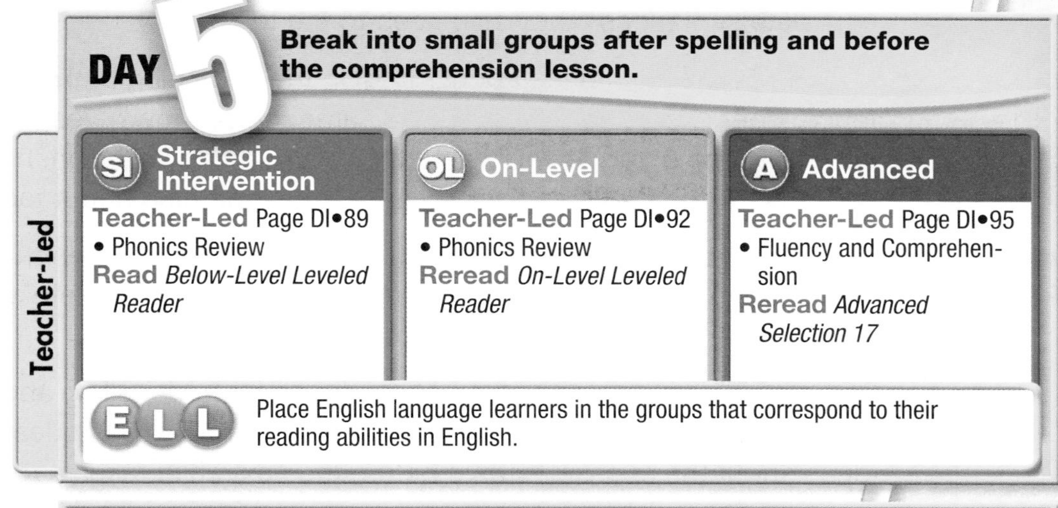

DAY 5 **Break into small groups after spelling and before the comprehension lesson.**

Teacher-Led

SI Strategic Intervention	OL On-Level	A Advanced
Teacher-Led Page DI•89 • Phonics Review **Read** *Below-Level Leveled Reader*	**Teacher-Led** Page DI•92 • Phonics Review **Reread** *On-Level Leveled Reader*	**Teacher-Led** Page DI•95 • Fluency and Comprehension **Reread** *Advanced Selection 17*

ELL Place English language learners in the groups that correspond to their reading abilities in English.

Practice Stations
- Words to Know
- Read for Meaning

Independent Activities
- Read independently/Reading Log on *Reader's and Writer's Notebook* p. RR 4
- Concept Talk Video

Differentiated Instruction

SI Strategic Intervention

Check Spelling To guide practice, have children write the words on white boards. Have children sound out each sound they hear in each of the spelling words. Then have children check their work with partners.

A Advanced

Extend Spelling Have children make up their own sentences using five of the spelling words.

Objectives

- Share information and ideas.
- Speak clearly at an appropriate rate.
- Listen attentively.
- Make appropriate contributions to a discussion.
- Alphabetize words to the first letter.
- Use a glossary to find words.
- Read aloud fluently with expression.

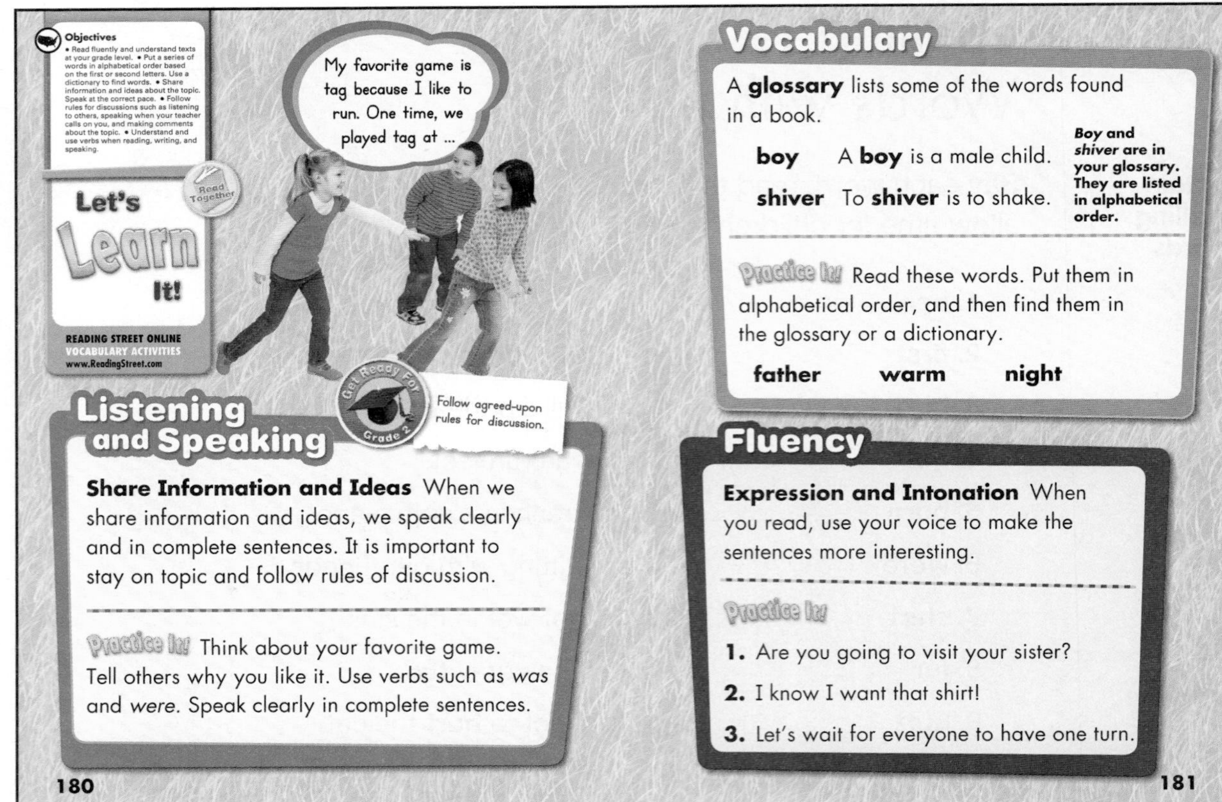

Listening and Speaking

Share Information and Ideas When we share information and ideas, we speak clearly and in complete sentences. It is important to stay on topic and follow rules of discussion.

Practice It! Think about your favorite game. Tell others why you like it. Use verbs such as *was* and *were*. Speak clearly in complete sentences.

Vocabulary

A **glossary** lists some of the words found in a book.

boy A **boy** is a male child.

shiver To **shiver** is to shake.

***Boy* and *shiver* are in your glossary. They are listed in alphabetical order.**

Practice It! Read these words. Put them in alphabetical order, and then find them in the glossary or a dictionary.

father **warm** **night**

Fluency

Expression and Intonation When you read, use your voice to make the sentences more interesting.

Practice It!

1. Are you going to visit your sister?
2. I know I want that shirt!
3. Let's wait for everyone to have one turn.

180 181

Student Edition pp. 180–181

Listening and Speaking
Share Information and Ideas

Teach Have children turn to page 180 of the Student Edition. Read and discuss the information that the speaker is sharing. Remind children that good speakers use the correct form of verbs such as *is* and *are*, and speak in complete sentences. They also keep to the topic.

Analyze model What is the first sentence about? (tag) In the beginning of the second sentence, does the speaker keep to the same topic? How? (yes, by talking about a game of tag) If you wanted to add to this discussion, how would you keep to the topic? (by asking or telling something about tag)

Introduce prompt Read the Practice It! prompt with the class. Remind children that they should keep to the topic. They should also speak in complete sentences and use the verbs *am*, *is*, *are*, *was*, and *were* correctly.

Team Talk Have small groups of children take turns telling about their favorite game. Tell them to listen to each other and to ask questions or add ideas about the speaker's topic before the next child takes a turn.

Vocabulary
Dictionary/Glossary

Teach Read and discuss the Vocabulary lesson on page 181 of the Student Edition. Use the model to explain how words are listed and defined in a dictionary or glossary.

Model Point to the two sample entries. Which word will come first in a dictionary or glossary? Why? (*boy*, because *b* comes before *s* in the alphabet) How could we find the word *boy* in a dictionary or glossary? (by turning past the *a* words until we come to the *b* words)

Guide practice Read the instructions for the Vocabulary Practice It! Activity. With children, determine which word comes first alphabetically, and look it up in the glossary of the Student Edition.

What is the first letter of each word? (*f*, *w*, *n*) Which of these letters comes first in the alphabet? (*f*) So father comes before the other words in a dictionary or glossary. Tell children to turn to their glossary that begins on page 218. Have them find words that begin with *f* and locate *father*. Read the definition together.

On their own Have partners write the rest of the words in alphabetical order, look them up in the glossary, and read the definitions.

Corrective Feedback Circulate around the room as children alphabetize and look up the words. Provide assistance as needed.

Fluency
Expression and Intonation

Teach Read and discuss the Fluency instructions.

Read words in context Give children a moment to look at the sentences. Then have them read each sentence three or four times until they can read each sentence with good expression and intonation.

Differentiated Instruction

Strategic Intervention

Alphabetizing Have pairs of children write the alphabet on a sheet of paper. Then give them a set of letter tiles. One child picks four letters and puts them in order. The other child checks the order against the alphabet and makes any corrections. Then the partners switch roles.

Share Information and Ideas

Along with keeping to the topic when speaking, children at Grade 2 should be able to develop their topic with details that make the information clear and interesting. They should also look at their audience and speak slowly and loudly enough to be understood.

English Language Learners

Dictionary/Glossary For children who have not mastered the English alphabet, write it on the board and have children practice reciting or singing it.

DAY 5 Wrap Up your Week

Objectives

- ◎ Distinguish fact from opinion in text.
- Read high-frequency and story words.
- Understand features of nonfiction.

Comprehension

Fact and Opinion

Review fact and opinion

What do we call a statement that tells something that can be proved true by observing, checking in a book, or asking an expert? (fact) What do we call a statement that tells someone's idea or feeling about something? (opinion)

To check understanding of fact and opinion, read aloud the following paragraph and have children answer the questions that follow.

> My class went to the nature museum. The best part was the insect room. Caterpillars are the most amazing insects. They make a shell called a chrysalis. Inside, they change into a butterfly. We saw different kinds of butterflies. The monarchs were the prettiest. They are orange and black. Everyone should visit the insect room at the nature museum.

1. What are two facts that you heard? (Possible response: They make a shell called a chrysalis. Inside, they change into a butterfly.)
2. What are two opinions that you heard? (Possible response: The best part was the insect room. The monarchs were the prettiest.)

Vocabulary

High-Frequency and Story Words

Review High-frequency words

Review this week's high-frequency words: *done, know, push, visit,* and *wait*. Write each word on a word card. Pick a card, show the word, read it aloud, and use it in a sentence, such as: I *know* interesting facts about caterpillars and tadpoles.

Team Talk Write the high-frequency words on the board. Have partners copy them onto word cards and then take turns picking a card, reading the word aloud, and using it in a sentence.

Review Story words

Write the words *caterpillar, chrysalis, crawl, pupa,* and *shiver*. Read them aloud together. Then have children tell what each word means.

Corrective feedback

If... children cannot tell what the story words mean,
then... review the definitions on page 158a.

Literary Nonfiction
Author's Craft

Review Genre Remind children that literary nonfiction tells about real people or animals, real places, and real events. Recall that the changes that happen to the caterpillar in *I'm a Caterpillar* are things that really happen in nature. Authors who write nonfiction are like teachers. They want us to learn information about their topic, so they present it in ways that make it interesting and easy to understand.

Teach Explain that the author of *I'm a Caterpillar* makes information clear in several different ways. She tells about events in the right sequence. She provides pictures and puts each picture near the text that tells about it. She also includes a chart.

Model  Have children turn to pages 164–165. On page 164, each picture is near the sentences that tell about it. So when I read the sentences, I know which picture to look at for more information. The things that happen on these pages are also arranged in the right sequence, so I can tell what happens first, next, and so on.

Guide practice Ask the following questions to guide children in observing and understanding the purpose of features of nonfiction.

- Let's turn to page 172. What are some different ways the author helps you understand what is happening here? (Possible response: Pictures show what is happening. Each sentence is below the picture it tells about. The pictures and sentences are in the right sequence.)
- Let's look at page 173. Why did the author arrange these words and pictures in the shape of a circle? (Possible response: The circle helps show that the life cycle of a butterfly keeps starting over again.)

On their own Look at the arrows on page 173. What do they show? (Possible response: They show that one thing happens after the other.)

Differentiated Instruction

 Strategic Intervention

Fact and Opinion Have children practice distinguishing between fact and opinion using sentence pairs about things in the room that they can observe and respond to. For example:
This crayon is yellow./Yellow is the best color.
It's raining./Rainy days are boring.
Discuss how each fact can be proved true, and why people might disagree or even change their own minds about each opinion.

Academic Vocabulary

sequence the order of events or steps in a process

Assess

- ◉ Vowels: *r*-Controlled *er, ir, ur*
- ◉ Contractions
- High-Frequency Words
- Fluency: WCPM
- ◉ Fact and Opinion

Fluency Goals

Set individual fluency goals for children to enable them to reach the end-of-year goal.

- Current Goal: 25-35 WCPM
- End-of-Year Goal: 60 WCPM

Assessment
Monitor Progress

For a written assessment of vowels: *r*-controlled *er, ir ur,* contractions, high-frequency words, and fact and opinion, use Weekly Test 17, pages 133–138.

Assess words in context

Sentence reading Use the following reproducible page to assess children's ability to read words in context. Call on children to read two sentences aloud. Start over with sentence one if necessary.

MONITOR PROGRESS — Sentence Reading

If... children have trouble reading vowels: *r*-controlled *er, ir, ur* and contractions,
then... use the Reteach Lessons on page 216–217 in *First Stop*.

If... children cannot read all the high-frequency words,
then... mark the missed words on a high-frequency word list and have the child practice reading the words with a fluent reader.

Assess

Fluency Take a one-minute sample of children's oral reading. Have children read the fluency passage on page 181f.

Comprehension Have the child read the entire passage. If the child has difficulty with the passage, you may read it aloud. Then have the child identify facts and opinions in the passage.

MONITOR PROGRESS — Fluency and Comprehension

If... a child does not achieve the fluency goal on the timed reading,
then... copy the passage and send it home with the child for additional fluency practice, or have the child practice with a fluent reader.

If... a child cannot comprehend fact and opinion,
then... use the Reteach Lesson on page 255 in *First Stop*.

Success Predictor

Monitor accuracy

Record scores Have children monitor their accuracy by recording their scores using the Sentence Reading Chart and by recording the number of words read correctly per minute on the Fluency Progress Chart in *First Stop*.

Name ________________________________

Read the Sentences

1. He's done with his first chore.

2. You've got to wait in line for that clerk.

3. This nurse will know if we're getting sick.

4. They're going to visit places by the shore to surf.

5. I've asked that girl to help me push this cart uphill.

6. I know I got a big fish if it's jerking my fishing rod.

MONITOR PROGRESS

- Fluency
- r-Controlled *er, ir, ur*
- Contractions with *'s, 've, 're*
- High-frequency Words

Name ______________________________

Read the Story

My Bird Pete 3

Birds make the best pets. My bird Pete is green. At 14
times, he sits in his cage. He just naps or eats. Then he 27
hops out and flaps his wings. It's fun to see him fly in my 41
room. He lands on my desk or my lamp. If I sit still, he 55
perches on my head! 59

It's not hard to take care of birds. You feed them 70
seeds and water in cups. Pete takes baths all by himself 81
in his small pink tub. That is so cute! He splashes me a 94
lot with his wings. 98

Pete can talk. He can say "Snack time! Snack time!" 108
If I feed him a bit of grape, he yells "Sweet! Sweet!" No 121
other pet is as smart and funny as my Pete. 131

MONITOR PROGRESS

- Check Fluency
- Fact and Opinion

Objectives

- Use verbs *am, is, are, was,* and *were* with correct subject-verb agreement.

Conventions
Verbs *Am, Is, Are, Was,* and *Were*

Review Remind children that when they talk about one thing or person, *am, is, are, was,* or *were* can be used. When talking about more than one thing or person, only *are* or *were* are used. *Am*, *is*, and *are* tell about now, while *was* and *were* tell about the past. In a question that uses *am*, *is*, *are*, *was*, or *were*, these words often come first.

Guide practice Write the following sentences. Have children write which of the verbs *am*, *is*, *are*, *was*, and *were* make sense.

1. I ________ tall.
2. You ________ funny.
3. ________ the dog old?

Connect to oral language Display and read the following sentence frames. Have children work in pairs to name as many of the verbs *am*, *is*, *are*, *was*, and *were* as could be used to complete the sentence. Then have children share their responses with the class.

1. ________ the cat always noisy?
2. My mom never ________ late.
3. We always ________ playing together.

On their own Use Let's Practice It! p. 159 on the *Teacher Resource DVD-ROM.*

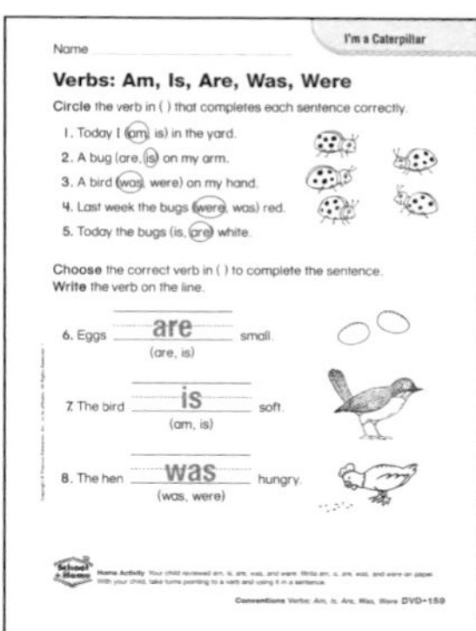
Name ________ I'm a Caterpillar

Verbs: Am, Is, Are, Was, Were

Circle the verb in ( ) that completes each sentence correctly.

1. Today I (am, is) in the yard.
2. A bug (are, is) on my arm.
3. A bird (was, were) on my hand.
4. Last week the bugs (were, was) red.
5. Today the bugs (is, are) white.

Choose the correct verb in ( ) to complete the sentence. **Write** the verb on the line.

6. Eggs are small. (are, is)
7. The bird is soft. (am, is)
8. The hen was hungry. (was, were)

Conventions Verbs: Am, Is, Are, Was, Were DVD•159

Let's Practice It!
TR DVD•159

Daily Fix-It

9. ann watch butterflies.
Ann watches (or watched) butterflies.

10. Its your turn to bat
It's your turn to bat.

Discuss the Daily Fix-It corrections with children. Review sentence capitalization and punctuation, subject-verb agreement, and the spelling of contractions.

Objectives

- Edit a draft for spelling, punctuation, and capitalization.
- Create final draft and present.

Writing—Captions and Pictures

Writer's Craft: Verbs *Am, Is, Are, Was, Were*

Review Revising

Remind children that yesterday they revised their captions. They may have added a sentence to make their ideas clearer. Today they will proofread their captions.

MINI-LESSON

Proofread for Verbs

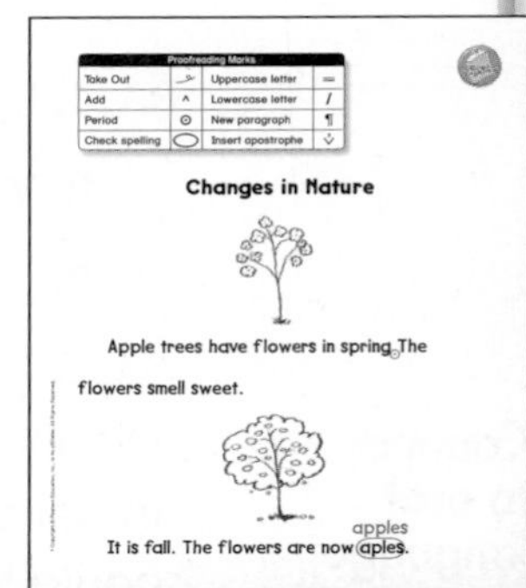

Writing Transparency 17C
TR DVD

- **Teach** Just like in stories and expository paragraphs, we need to spell things correctly in captions. We need to make sure we used the right punctuation and capitalization. All these things will help our readers understand what we mean.
- **Model** Let's look at my captions. I will look at my punctuation first. Display Writing Transparency 17C. I see I am missing a period at the end of my first sentence. Model how you would add a period. I will check my verbs. I see that *is* matches *it*, so I don't have to change that. Now I will check my spelling. I think *apples* is spelled wrong. Model looking up the word *apples* in a dictionary. Then correct the word on the transparency.

Proofread

Display the Proofreading Tips. Have children proofread their stories to correct any misspellings or errors with periods. Circulate to assist children with forms of *be*.

Proofreading Tips

- ✓ Did I use verbs correctly?
- ✓ Are words spelled correctly? Check a dictionary.
- ✓ Do my sentences begin with a capital letter?
- ✓ Did I use periods correctly?

Present

Have children make a final draft of their pictures and captions with their revisions and proofreading corrections. Help as appropriate.

Choose an option for children to present their pictures and captions.

Decorate the classroom or bulletin board with children's pictures and captions	Compile a picture book of changes in nature

When they have finished, help them complete a Self-Evaluation form.

ROUTINE **Quick Write for Fluency** Team Talk

1. **Talk** Have partners identify uses of the verbs *am*, *is*, *are*, *was*, or *were* in their captions.
2. **Write** Each child writes a new short sentence using one of the verbs.
3. **Share** Partners trade sentences and read them aloud.

Routines Flip Chart

Teacher Note

Self-Evaluation Make copies of the Self-Evaluation form from the Teacher Resource DVD-ROM, and hand them out to children.

English Language Learners

Support Editing Remind children to look at their charts of the verbs *am*, *is*, *are*, *was*, and *were* as they edit. If necessary, make the connection between the singular pronouns and any singular nouns that children use in their captions. Repeat the process for plurals.

Objectives

- Review concept: we can see changes in nature.
- Organize information.
- Create a word-processed document on a computer.
- Present results of an inquiry project.

Research and Inquiry
Communicate

Teach Tell children that today they will type a sentence that tells a fact about their topic using a computer. Then they will share the information with others. If they don't have access to a computer, have them write the sentence on paper.

Model Think Aloud Display the chart. I will review my facts and pick the one I think is the most interesting. That will be the fact I will write my sentence about. The fact I think is most interesting is *Roots of trees are breaking through the sidewalk*. I am going to type this sentence into a document on a computer.

Guide practice Review children's favorite facts. Work with them to be sure each fact is stated as a complete sentence.

On their own Have children choose the fact they would like to share with the class and type it into a document on a computer. Have children share their sentences in small groups. Then instruct them to read aloud their sentences to one another. Remind them how to be good speakers and listeners:

- Good speakers talk at a pace that everyone can understand. So, be careful not to talk too fast or too slow.
- Good listeners wait until the speaker has finished speaking before raising their hands to ask a question.

Wrap Up Your Week!

Question of the Week

What changes can be seen in nature?

Think Aloud This week we explored the topic of changes in nature. In *I'm a Caterpillar*, we read about how a caterpillar changes into a butterfly. In *What Makes the Seasons?*, we read how nature changes with each season. All these changes are cycles, because they keep starting over again. The butterfly's life cycle starts over again when it lays eggs that hatch into new caterpillars. The cycle of seasons starts over when winter ends and the warm spring sun gets plants growing again. Have children recall their Amazing Ideas about changes in nature. Then have children use these ideas to help them demonstrate their understanding of the Question of the Week.

English Language Learners

Poster Preview Prepare children for next week by using Week 6, ELL Poster 18. Read the Poster Talk-Through to introduce the concept and vocabulary. Ask children to identify and describe objects and actions in the art.

Selection Summary

Send home the summary of *Where Are My Animal Friends?* in English and the child's home language if available. Children can read the summary with family members.

Preview NEXT WEEK

Tell children that next week they will read about what animals do when the seasons change.

Assessment Checkpoints for the Week

Weekly Assessment

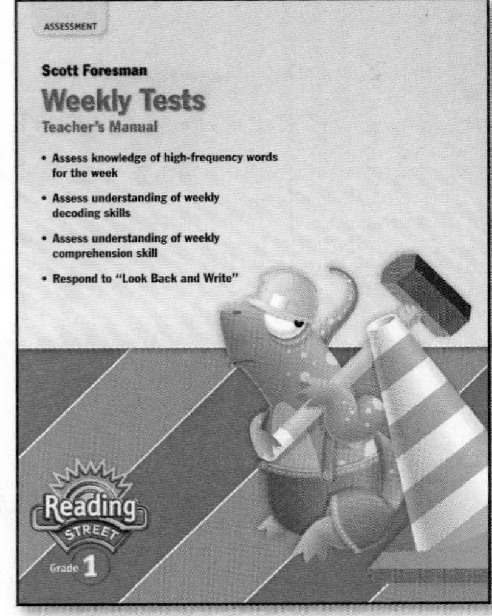

Weekly Tests

Use pp. 133–138 of *Weekly Tests* to check:

✔ **Phonics** Vowels: *r*-Controlled *er, ir, ur*

✔ **Phonics** Contractions

✔ **Comprehension Skill** Fact and Opinion

✔ **High-Frequency Words**

done	visit
know	wait
push	

Differentiated Assessment

Advanced

On-Level

Strategic Intervention

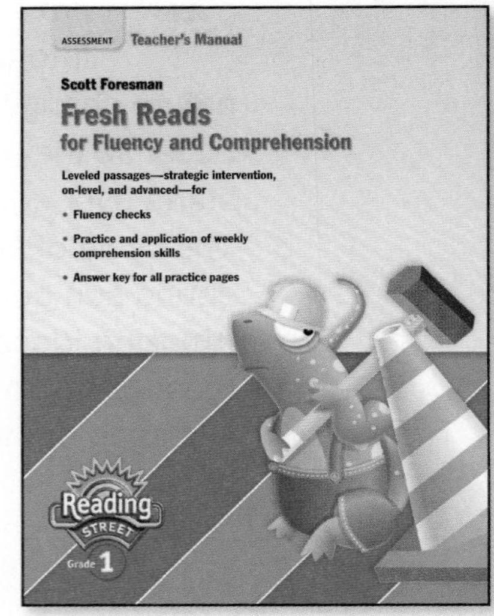

Fresh Reads for Fluency and Comprehension

Use pp. 133–138 of *Fresh Reads for Fluency and Comprehension* to check:

✔ **Comprehension Skill** Fact and Opinion

✔ Review **Comprehension Skill** Author's Purpose

✔ **Fluency** Words Correct Per Minute

Managing Assessment

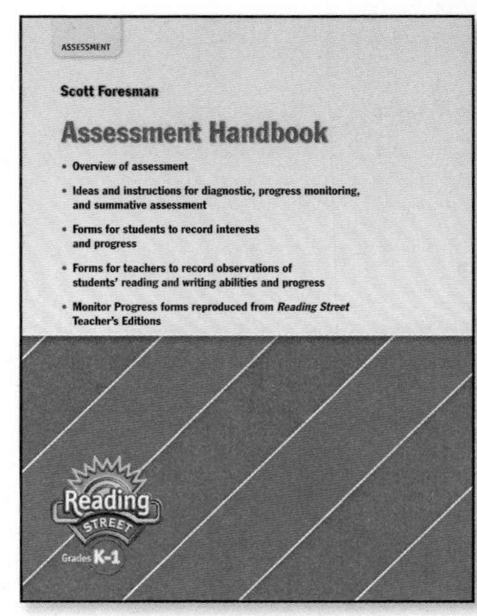

Assessment Handbook

Use *Assessment Handbook* for:

✔ **Weekly Assessment Blackline Masters for Monitoring Progress**

✔ **Observation Checklists**

✔ **Record-Keeping Forms**

✔ **Portfolio Assessments**

The Caterpillar and the Fawn

Once upon a time, two young animals lived in a forest. One was an insect—a little caterpillar. The other was a fawn—a baby deer. Even though they were very different animals, they were good friends.

One day, Caterpillar was too tired to play. She climbed up into a tree, made herself a cozy place to rest, and fell into a deep sleep.

Fawn lay at the base of the tree. She waited and waited, but Caterpillar did not come down. Time passed, and eventually Caterpillar woke up. She wriggled out of her silky resting spot and stretched her body. She felt different, but she wasn't sure exactly how. She looked around for Fawn. She saw a large animal with antlers beginning to grow out of its head and decided to ask that animal if it had seen Fawn. "Excuse me," she said. "I am looking for my friend— "

"That's strange," the large animal interrupted. "I'm also looking for my friend, a small caterpillar."

"But that's me," said Caterpillar.

"You're not a caterpillar. Look at yourself."

Caterpillar looked at her reflection in a puddle of water. She was a moth with big, beautiful wings.

"Fawn?" said the moth. "Is that you? Your fur is different. Your spots are gone."

"I guess we have both changed," said the deer. "But we can still be friends."

Advanced Selection 17 **Vocabulary:** eventually, reflection

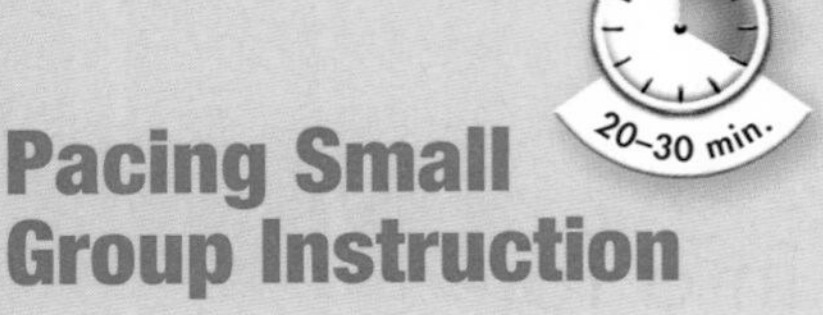

Pacing Small Group Instruction

5 Day Plan

DAY 1	• Phonemic Awareness/ Phonics • Decodable Reader
DAY 2	• Phonemic Awareness/ Phonics • Decodable Reader
DAY 3	• Phonemic Awareness/ Phonics • Leveled Reader
DAY 4	• High-Frequency Words • Decodable Reader
DAY 5	• Phonics Review • Leveled Reader

3 or 4 Day Plan

DAY 1	• Phonemic Awareness/ Phonics • Decodable Reader
DAY 2	• Phonemic Awareness/ Phonics • Decodable Reader
DAY 3	• Phonemic Awareness/ Phonics • Leveled Reader
DAY 4	• High-Frequency Words • Decodable Reader

3 Day Plan: Eliminate the shaded box.

SI Strategic Intervention

DAY 1

Phonemic Awareness • Phonics

- **Isolate Medial and Final Phonemes** Reteach pp. 152–153 of the Teacher's Edition. Model segmenting and blending these words. Have children identify the middle and final sound.

her /h/ /ėr/ **firm** /f/ /ėr/ /m/ **hurt** /h/ /ėr/ /t/

- ***r*-Controlled *er, ir, ur*** Reteach p. 153a of the Teacher's Edition. Then have children spell *bird* using letter tiles. Monitor their work.

  - Change the *b* in *bird* to *th*. What is the new word?

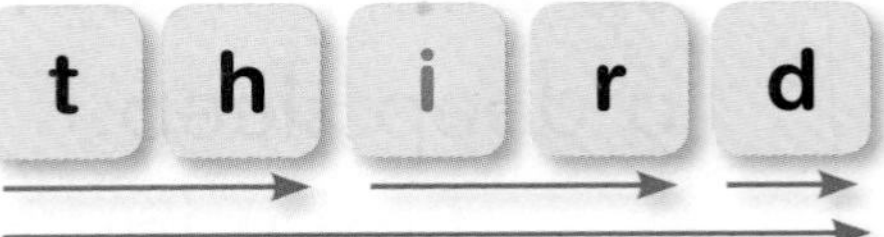

  - Change the *d* in *third* to *st*. What is the new word?

  - Change the *th* in *thirst* to *f*. What is the new word?

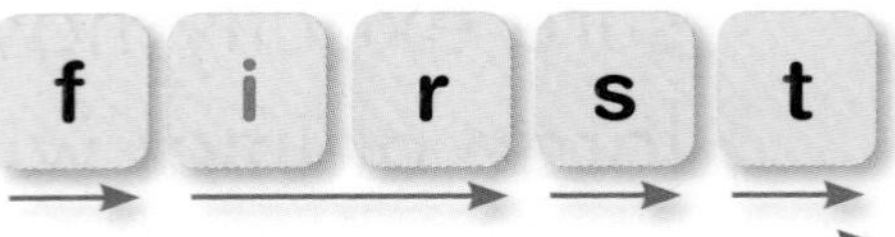

Decodable Practice Reader 17A

- **Review** Review words with *r*-controlled *er, ir, ur* and the high-frequency words *a, good, the, friends, their, what, do, to, without*. Then have children blend and read these words from the story: *short, meet, store, meeting, starts, going, next*.

  If... children have difficulty with any of these words, **then...** reteach the word by modeling. Have children practice the words, with feedback from you, until they can read them independently.

Have children reread the text orally. To achieve optimal fluency, children should reread the text three or four times.

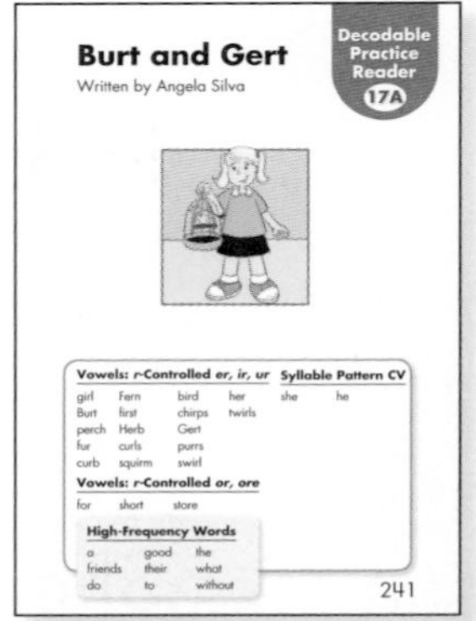

Decodable Practice Reader 17A

Objectives

- Isolate medial sounds in one-syllable spoken words.
- Use common syllabication patterns to decode words, including: *r*-controlled vowel sounds.

DAY 2

Phonemic Awareness • Phonics

- **Isolate Medial and Final Phonemes** Reteach p. 156c of the Teacher's Edition. Model segmenting and blending these words. Have children identify the middle and final sound.

we've /w/ /ē/ /v/	**who's** /h/ /ü/ /z/	**they've** /th/ /ā/ /v/

- **Contractions** Reteach p. 156d of the Teacher's Edition. Then write these contractions. Have children read the first word and blend the sounds of the letters after the apostrophe to read the contractions. Have children name the two words that make up the contraction.

that's	**we're**	**you're**	**he's**
they're	**she's**	**you've**	**I've**

Decodable Practice Reader 17B

- **Review** Review contractions and the high-frequency words *said, said, to, one, day, the, a, you, around*. Then have children blend and read these words from the story: *baby, cannot, flying, began, strong, called, lifted*.

  If... children have difficulty with any of these words, **then...** reteach the word by modeling. Have children practice the words, with feedback from you, until they can read them independently.

  Have children reread the text orally. To achieve optimal fluency, children should reread the text three or four times.

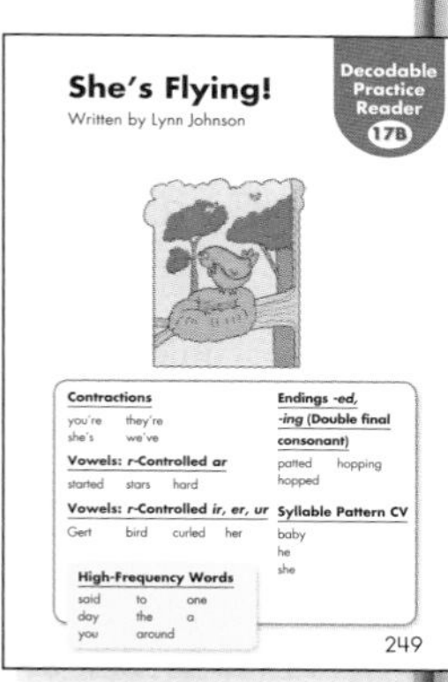

Decodable Practice Reader 17B

More Reading

Use Leveled Readers or other text at children's instructional level to develop fluency.

Objectives

- Use common syllabication patterns to decode words, including: *r*-controlled vowel sounds.
- Read contractions.

Phonemic Awareness • Phonics

Add Phonemes Model adding a sound to the end of a word to make a new word. Say the word *fur* and have children repeat it. Now listen as I add the sound /n/ to the end of *fur*: *fur* /n/. What is the new word? (fern).

Have children add the final sound shown to each word below to make a new word.

her /d/ **herd**	purr /k/ **perk**	fur /m/ **firm**	sir /f/ **surf**

- ***r*-Controlled *er, ir, ur* and Contractions** Reteach p. 174e of the Teacher's Edition. Have children blend and read these additional words to help them practice the target phonics skills.

burn	**she's**	**dirt**	**I've**	**first**	**you're**

For a complete literacy instructional plan and additional practice with this week's target skills and strategies, see the **Leveled Reader Teaching Guide.**

Concept Literacy Leveled Reader

- **Preview and Predict** Read the title and the author's name. Have children look at the cover and ask them to describe what they see. Help children activate their prior knowledge by asking them to look through the selection and to use the photos to predict things that might take place.
- **Set a Purpose** Remind children that setting a purpose for reading can help them better understand what they read. Guide children to pay attention to each change that the caterpillar goes through on its way to becoming a butterfly.
- **Read** Provide corrective feedback as children read the selection orally. During reading, ask them if they were able to confirm any of the predictions they made prior to reading.

If... children have difficulty reading the selection individually,
then... read a sentence aloud as children point to each word. Then have the group reread the sentences as they continue pointing. Continue reading in this way until children read individually.

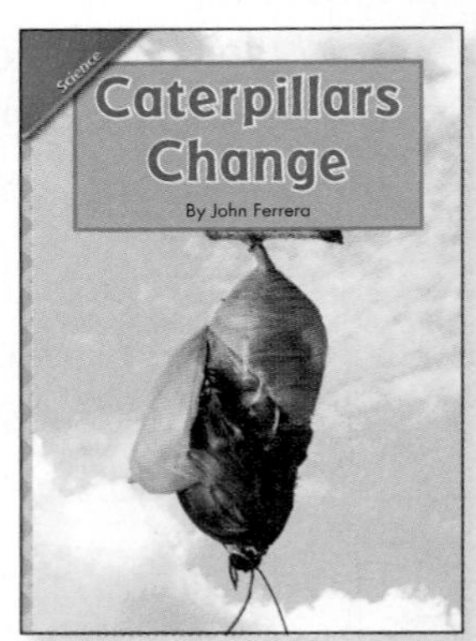

Concept Literacy

- **Retell** Have children take turns retelling the selection. Help them the recall stages of a caterpillar's life cycle by asking questions such as, What tiny thing did the caterpillar start out as? (an egg) After the caterpillar hatched, where did it hide itself? (in a cocoon)

Objectives

- Use common syllabication patterns to decode words, including: *r*-controlled vowel sounds.
- Read contractions.

DAY 4

High-Frequency Words

- **Review** Write *know, push, done, wait, visit* on the board. Model saying each word. Then have children read each word, spell each word as you point to each letter, and have them say each word again. Allow time for children to practice reading these high-frequency words using the word cards.

Decodable Practice Reader 17C

- **Review** Use the word lists to review words with the /ėr/ sounds and contractions. Be sure children understand that /ėr/ can be spelled *er, ir,* or *ur*. Remind them that a contraction is a short way of writing two words and that the apostrophe takes the place of the missing letters. Have children blend and read the words.

  If... children have difficulty reading the story individually, **then...** read a sentence aloud as children point to each word. Then have the group reread the sentences as they continue pointing. Continue reading in this way until children read individually.

Decodable Practice Reader 17C

Check comprehension by having children retell the story including the characters, plot, and setting. Have children locate words in the story that have /ėr/ spelled *er, ir,* or *ur* and words that are contractions. List the words children identify: *Fern, her, shirts, first, stirs, twirls, swirls, churning, turn, they're, she's, it's, we've*. Then have children name the two words that make up each contraction.

Contractions	Word 1	Word 2
they're	they	are
she's	she	is
it's	it	is
we've	we	have

Objectives

- Use common syllabication patterns to decode words, including: *r*-controlled vowel sounds.
- Read at least 100 high-frequency words from a commonly used list.

More Reading

Use Leveled Readers or other text at children's instructional level.

More Reading

Use Leveled Readers or other text at children's instructional level.

Phonics Review

- ***r*-Controlled *er, ir, ur* and Contractions** Write these sentences on the board. Have children read them aloud as you track the print. Then call on individuals to blend and read the underlined words.

It's her turn to stir the pot.

Birds chirp in those birch trees.

I've got a burn that hurts.

We're going to plant a fern.

For a complete literacy instructional plan and additional practice with this week's target skills and strategies, see the **Leveled Reader Teaching Guide.**

Below-Level Leveled Reader

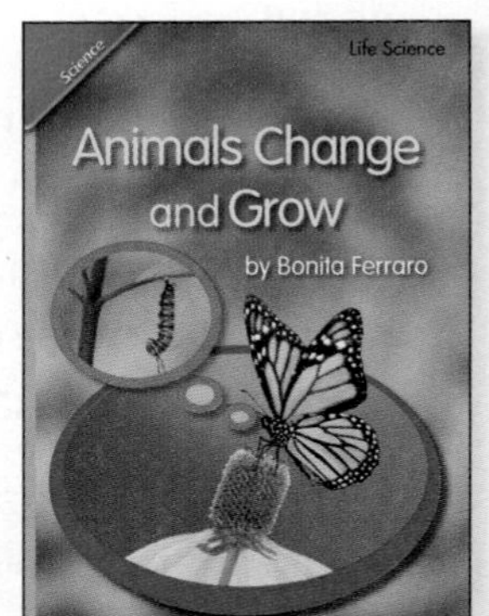

Below-Level Reader

Preview and Predict Read the title and the author's name. Have children look at the cover and ask them to describe what they see. Help children activate their prior knowledge by asking them to look through the selection and to use the photos to predict things that might take place.

- **Set a Purpose** Remind children that setting a purpose for reading can help them better understand what they read. Guide children to notice the ways each animal changes as it grows.
- **Read** Provide corrective feedback as children read the selection orally. During reading, ask them if they were able to confirm any of the predictions they made prior to reading.

  If... children have difficulty reading the selection individually,
  then... read each sentence aloud as children point to each word. Then have the group reread the sentences as they continue pointing.

- **Text Structure** Ask children to explain how the photos and arrows helped them to understand what they read.

Objectives

- Establish purpose for reading selected texts.
- Use text features to locate specific information in text.

On-Level DAY 1

Phonics • Spelling

- ***r*-Controlled *er, ir, ur*** Write the following words on the board and have children practice reading words with *r*-controlled *er, ir, ur*.

thirst **clerk** **spurt** **stir** **churn** **herd**

Then have children tell which letter spell the /ėr/ sound.

- **Words with *er, ir, ur*** Remind children that each spelling word has the /ėr/ sound spelled *er, ir,* or *ur*. Clarify the pronunciation and meaning of each word. For example, say: We call a man *sir* when we want to be very polite. Have children tell whether the /ėr/ sound is spelled *er, ir,* or *ur* in these words: *first, hurt, were, bird, burn, her*.

Objectives
- Use common syllabication patterns to decode words, including: *r*-controlled vowel sounds.
- Use phonological knowledge to match sounds to letters to construct words.

On-Level DAY 2

Phonics • High-Frequency Words

- **Contractions** Write the following contractions on the board and have children practice reading them. Then have children tell what two words make up each contraction.

they've **who's** **we're** **he's**

- **High-Frequency Words** Hold up this week's High-Frequency Word Cards *(done, know, push, visit, wait)* and review proper pronunciation. Continue holding the cards and have children chorally read each word. To help children demonstrate their understanding of the words, provide them with oral sentence frames such as: If dinner isn't ready, you will have to ___. (wait)

High-Frequency Word Cards for Grade 1

Objectives
- Read contractions.
- Identify at least 100 high-frequency words from a commonly used list.

Pacing Small Group Instruction

20–30 min.

5 Day Plan

DAY 1	• Phonics • Spelling • Decodable Reader
DAY 2	• Phonics • High-Frequency Words • Decodable Reader
DAY 3	• Leveled Reader
DAY 4	• Conventions • Main Selection
DAY 5	• Phonics Review • Leveled Reader

3 or 4 Day Plan

DAY 1	• Phonics • Spelling • Decodable Reader
DAY 2	• Phonics • High-Frequency Words • Decodable Reader
DAY 3	• Leveled Reader
DAY 4	• Conventions • Main Selection

3 Day Plan: Eliminate the shaded box.

Decodable Practice Readers

For a complete literacy instructional plan and additional practice with this week's target skills and strategies, see the **Leveled Reader Teaching Guide.**

On-Level Leveled Reader

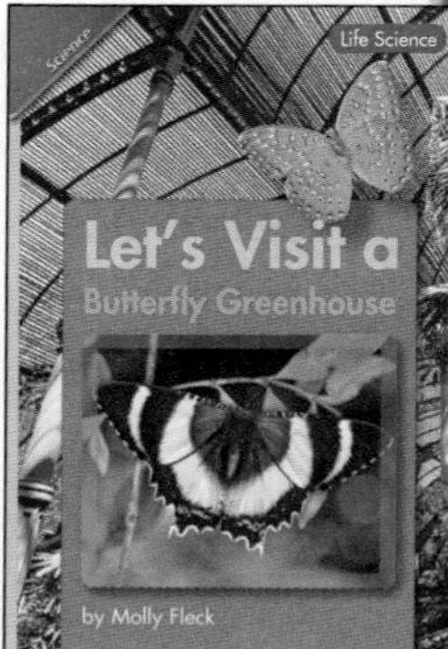

On-Level

- **Preview and Predict** Read the title and the author's name. Have children look at the cover and ask them to describe in detail what they see. Help children preview the story by asking them to look through the selection and to use the photos to predict things that might take place.
- **Fact and Opinion** Before reading, have children set a purpose for reading. Remind them that writing often contains both facts and opinions, and review the difference. Tell children to read this selection to see what facts they learn, and to see if they can find an opinion as well.
- **Read** During reading, monitor children's comprehension by providing higher-order thinking questions. Ask:
  - Why do you think the chrysalis is important to the caterpillar as it changes?
  - The author says that a butterfly greenhouse is an exciting place. Is that a fact or an opinion? Explain.

To help children gain a better understanding of the text, build upon their responses with a group discussion.

- **Text Structure** Discuss with the class how the organization and features of this selection helped them understand it. Ask:
  - The author told about the egg first, then the caterpillar, then the chrysalis, and then the butterfly. Was this a good order to use? Why?
  - Look at the labels on pages 6 and 10. What do they tell you?
- **Text to World** Help children make connections to the selection. Ask:
  - What other animals change a lot over time? Describe the changes.

Objectives

- Make inferences about text.
- Use text features to locate specific information in text.

On-Level

DAY 4

Conventions

- **Verbs *am, is, are, was, were*** Remind children that *am, is,* and *was* can be used with one person or thing, and that *are* and *were* can be used with more than one. *Are* and *were* are used with the subject *you*. Also remind them that *am, is,* and *are* tell about now, and that *was* and *were* tell about the past.
  - Write *Kate _______ happy now. The girls _______ happy yesterday.* Which word is correct in each sentence—*is, are, was* or *were*? Discuss why *is* belongs in the first sentence and *were* belongs in the second sentence.

  Have children continue completing sentence frames with singular and plural subjects. Include past and present time words such as *now* and *yesterday*.

Objectives
- Speak in complete sentences with correct subject-verb agreement.

More Reading
Use Leveled Readers or other text at children's instructional level to develop fluency.

On-Level

DAY 5

Phonics Review

- ***r*-Controlled *er, ir, ur* and Contractions** Have children practice blending and reading words that contain this week's target phonics skills. Write the following words on the board, and say and sound out each word with the children.

swirl	**stern**	**thirst**	**they're**	**burst**
you've	**churn**	**she's**	**clerk**	**we're**

  Then have children sort the words with *er, ir,* and *ur* and the contractions into four separate groups.

Objectives
- Use common syllabication patterns to decode words, including: *r*-controlled vowel sounds.
- Read contractions.

Small Group Time

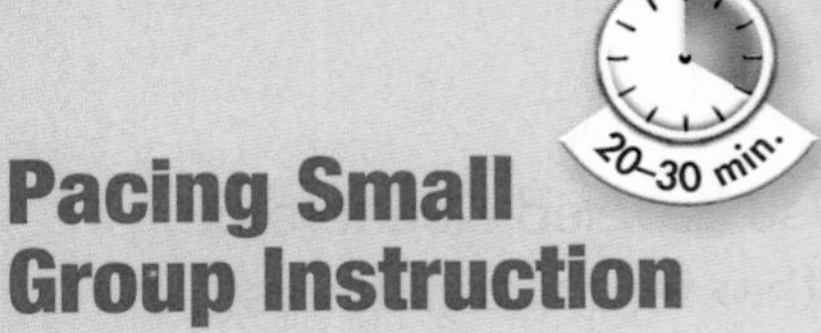

Pacing Small Group Instruction

20–30 min.

5 Day Plan

DAY 1	• Phonics • Advanced Selection
DAY 2	• Phonics • Comprehension • Main Selection
DAY 3	• Leveled Reader
DAY 4	• Comprehension • Paired Selection
DAY 5	• Fluency • Comprehension • Advanced Selection

3 or 4 Day Plan

DAY 1	• Phonics • Advanced Selection
DAY 2	• Phonics • Comprehension • Main Selection
DAY 3	• Leveled Reader
DAY 4	• Comprehension • Paired Selection

3 Day Plan: Eliminate the shaded box.

A 

DAY 1

Phonics • Advanced Selection

- ***r*-Controlled *er, ir, ur*** Have children practice with longer words containing *r*-controlled *er, ir, ur*. Have children write the words on cards and sort them by the spellings of /ėr/. Then have them choose several words to use in sentences.

circle	**birthmark**	**kernel**	**verse**	**surprise**
turkey	**thirsty**	**purpose**	**furnace**	**thirteen**

- **Advanced Selection 17** Before reading, have children identify these story words: *eventually* and *reflection*. Provide oral sentences with the words in context to help children determine their meaning. After reading, have children recall the two most important ideas of the story.

The Caterpillar and the Fawn

Once upon a time, two young animals lived in a forest. One was an insect—a little caterpillar. The other was a fawn—a baby deer. Even though they were very different animals, they were good friends.

One day, Caterpillar was too tired to play. She climbed up into a tree, made herself a cozy place to rest, and fell into a deep sleep.

Fawn lay at the base of the tree. She waited and waited, but Caterpillar did not come down. Time passed, and eventually Caterpillar woke up. She wriggled out of her silky resting spot and stretched her body. She felt different, but she wasn't sure exactly how. She looked around for Fawn. She saw a large animal with antlers beginning to grow out of its head and decided to ask that animal if it had seen Fawn. "Excuse me," she said. "I am looking for my friend—"

"That's strange," the large animal interrupted. "I'm also looking for my friend, a small caterpillar."

"But that's me," said Caterpillar.

"You're not a caterpillar. Look at yourself."

Caterpillar looked at her reflection in a puddle of water. She was a moth with big, beautiful wings.

"Fawn?" said the moth. "Is that you? Your fur is different. Your spots are gone."

"I guess we have both changed," said the deer. "But we can still be friends."

Advanced Selection 17

Objectives

- Use common syllabication patterns to decode words, including: *r*-controlled vowel sounds.

A 

DAY 2

Phonics • Comprehension

- **Contractions** Have children practice with these words. Have children write the contractions and the two words that make up each one. Explain that *'s* after a name can mean *is* or show possession.

might've	**Dan's**	**we're**	**you're**
could've	**who's**	**Jill's**	**they've**

- **Comprehension** Have children silently read this week's main selection, *I'm a Caterpillar*. Have them retell the selection, describing the stages of the caterpillar's life cycle in the correct sequence. Discuss what makes *I'm a Caterpillar* literary nonfiction. Point out that each change the caterpillar goes through is something that really happens in nature.

I'm a Caterpillar

Objectives

- Read contractions.

DAY 3

For a complete literacy instructional plan and additional practice with this week's target skills and strategies, see the **Leveled Reader Teaching Guide.**

Advanced Leveled Reader

- **Activate Prior Knowledge** Read the title and the author's name. Have children look at the cover and describe in detail what they see. Remind them that when something *develops*, it grows and changes. Then activate the children's prior knowledge by asking them how plants develop from seeds.

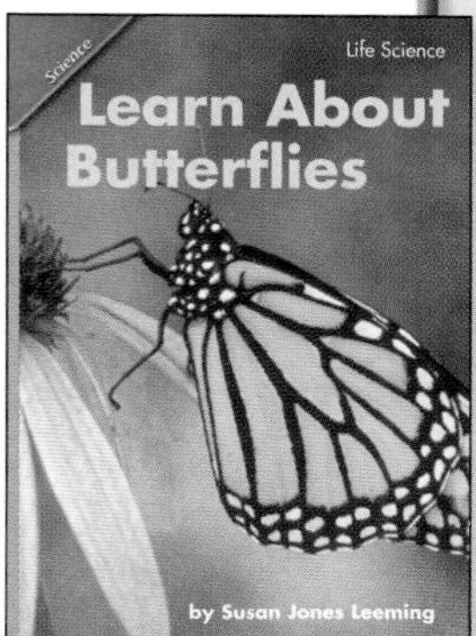

Advanced Reader

- **Fact and Opinion** Before reading, remind children that setting a purpose for reading can make a selection more interesting. Point out to children that this selection contains both facts and opinions. Review the difference. Tell children to read this selection to see what new facts they can learn, and to see if they agree with the author's opinions.
- **Read** During reading, monitor children's comprehension by providing higher-order thinking questions. Ask:
  - The author says that butterflies are beautiful and amazing. Are these facts of opinions? Explain. Do you agree or disagree? Why?
  - How is the life cycle of a butterfly like and different from the life cycle of another animal that you know about?

  Build on children's answers to help them gain a better understanding of the text.
- **Text Structure** Discuss as a class how the text structure of the selection helps make the information clear.
  - On pages 4–6, does the author tell the facts in an order that makes sense? Explain.
  - How do the labels on page 8 and the caption on page 10 help you learn more from the pictures?
- **Text to World** Help children make connections to the story. Ask:
  - You've learned that butterflies have special features that protect them. What special features do other animals have that protect them?

Objectives

- Make inferences about text.
- Use text features to locate specific information in text.

More Reading

Use Leveled Readers or other text at children's instructional level.

More Reading

Use Leveled Readers or other text at children's instructional level.

Comprehension

- **Comprehension** Have children silently read this week's paired selection, "My Computer." Have children summarize what they learned about computers from the selection.

  Talk about why understanding how to use a computer is an important 21st century skill. Ensure that children understand that it is currently the 21st century. A 21st century skill is something that is important to know and understand in this century.

- **Text to Self** Help children make connections to the selection by asking how writing would be harder without a computer.

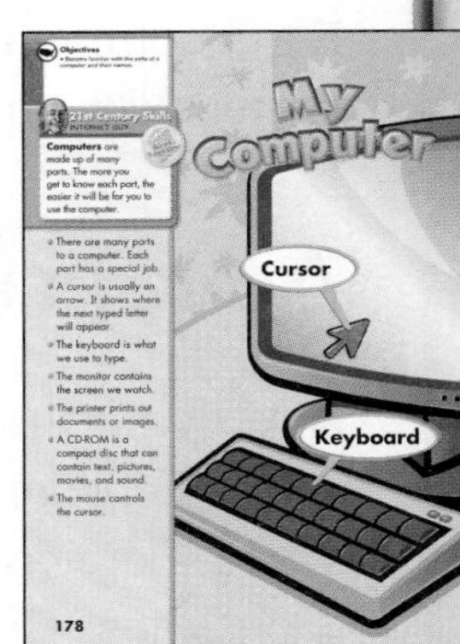

My Computer

Objectives

- Use text features to locate specific information in text.

Fluency•Comprehension

- **Fluency** Using the first few sentences of Advanced Selection 17, model reading with good expression and intonation. Then have children read the selection to a partner as you listen to their reading. Provide corrective feedback as needed.
- **Comprehension** After they have finished reading the selection, have children retell what happened by stating the story events in sequence. Then, on the back of the selection page, have them write three sentences explaining why Caterpillar and Fawn had trouble finding each other.

The Caterpillar and the Fawn

Advanced Selection 17

Objectives

- Read aloud grade-level appropriate text with fluency (expression).

ELL English Language Learners

The ELL lessons are organized by strands. Use them to scaffold the weekly lesson curriculum or during small-group time.

Concept Development

What changes can be seen in nature?

- **Activate Prior Knowledge** Write the Question of the Week and read it aloud. Underline the word *changes* and have children say it with you. Changes means that things are different. Display a picture of a mother cat and kittens. How do cats look when they are very young? (they are tiny; their eyes are closed) Big animals started out as small babies. Other animals grow and change in different ways. Have children use prior knowledge to discuss how other animals change and grow.

- **Connect to New Concept** Have children turn to pages 150–151 in the Student Edition. Read the title and have children track the print as you read it. Use pictures to guide a discussion about how caterpillars and butterflies are related. For example, point to the caterpillar. What is this? (a caterpillar) A caterpillar looks like a worm with lots of legs. What does it eat? (leaves) Point to the butterfly. What is this? (a butterfly) How are the butterfly and the caterpillar related? (Caterpillars turn into butterflies.)

- **Develop Concepts** Show this week's Concept Talk Video and ask children to name the seasons. (winter, spring, summer, fall) What changes when the seasons change? During a second viewing, stop at appropriate places to show children seasonal changes. Use the leveled prompts below to assess understanding and build oral language. Encourage students to seek clarification.

Beginning Ask yes/no questions, such as Do plants get new leaves in the winter? Do you wear different clothes in the summer than in the winter?

Intermediate Ask simple questions for children to answer. What do birds do in the fall? What happens to flowers in the summer?

Advanced/Advanced-High Have children answer the Question of the Week by giving specific examples from the video. Ask them to choose a season and describe it.

- **Review Concepts and Connect to Writing** Review children's understanding of the concept at the end of the week. Ask them to write in response to these questions: What changes do you see in nature? What English words did you learn this week? Write and display key ideas from the discussion.

Objectives

- Use prereading supports such as graphic organizers, illustrations, and pretaught topic-related vocabulary and other prereading activities to enhance comprehension of written text.

Content Objectives

- Describe changes in nature.

Language Objectives

- Share information orally and seek clarification.
- Use basic vocabulary for describing nature.

Daily Planner

DAY	
DAY 1	• **Frontload Concepts** • **Preteach** Comprehension Skill, Vocabulary, Phonemic Awareness/ Phonics, Conventions/ Writing
DAY 2	• **Review** Concepts, Vocabulary, Comprehension Skill • **Frontload Main Selection** • **Practice** Phonemic Awareness/Phonics, Conventions/Writing
DAY 3	• **Review** Concepts, Comprehension Skill, Vocabulary, Conventions/ Writing • **Reread Main Selection** • **Practice** Phonemic Awareness/Phonics
DAY 4	• **Review Concepts** • **Read ELL/ELD Readers** • **Practice** Phonemic Awareness/Phonics, Conventions/Writing
DAY 5	• **Review** Concepts, Vocabulary, Comprehension Skill, Phonemic Awareness/ Phonics, Conventions/ Writing • **Reread ELL/ELD Readers**

*See the ELL Handbook for ELL Workshops with targeted instruction.

ELL Poster 17

Build concept understanding and oral vocabulary throughout the week by using the daily activities on ELL Poster 17.

Language Objectives

- Segment and blend phonemes.

Transfer Skills

The /r/ sound is flapped or rolled in languages such as Spanish, Polish, Farsi, and Arabic, so speakers of these languages may have difficulty pronouncing words with *r*-controlled vowels, especially in words such as *turn*, when *r* is followed by a consonant. Also, Spanish does not have a sound that is equivalent to /ėr/, so Spanish speakers may pronounce *bird* as *beerd* or *later* as *la-tair*.

ELL Teaching Routine

For more practice with *r*-controlled vowels, use the Sound-by-Sound Blending Routine (*ELL Handbook*, page 493).

ELL English Language Learners

Phonemic Awareness: Blend and Segment Phonemes (*er, ir, ur*)

■ **Preteach** the Sound /ėr/

- Have children open to pages 152–153. What is in the tree? (birds) Say the word *bird* slowly. I am going to say the sounds in *bird*. Listen for the middle sound: /b/ /ėr/ /d/. The middle sound I hear is /ėr/. Say /ėr/ with me. Say these words as you point to corresponding pictures: *girl, arm, squirrel, acorn, purple, dirt*. Have children repeat the word and give a thumbs-up if they hear the /ėr/ sound.
- Point to a flower in the picture. What is this? (flower) Listen to the last sound in *flower*. Slowly blend and segment the sounds: /f/ /l/ /ò/ /w/ /ėr/. What is the last sound in *flower*? (/ėr/) Yes, say the last sound in *flower* with me: /ėr/. Have children point out other pictures whose names have the final sound of /ėr/. (runner, teacher, water)

■ **Practice** Listen again as I say all the sounds in *girl*. Stretch the sounds as you say them: /ggg/ /ėr ėr ėr/ /lll/, girl. Now you try. Have children blend sounds to make these words.

/p/ /ėr/ /p/ /l/, purple	/r/ /u/ /n/ /ėr/, runner	/t/ /ē/ /ch/ /ėr/, teacher
/w/ /ò/ /t/ /ėr/, water	/d/ /ėr/ /t/, dirt	/f/ /ėr/, fur

Phonics: *r*-Controlled Vowels (*er, ir, ur*)

■ **Preteach** Display Sound-Spelling Card 67. This is a fern. What sound do you hear in the middle of *fern*? (/ėr/) Say it with me: /ėr/. Point to *er*. The /ėr/ sound is spelled *er* in *fern*. Display Sound-Spelling Card 72. This is a girl. What sound do you hear in the middle of *girl*? (/ėr/) Say it with me: /ėr/. Point to *ir*. The /ėr/ sound is spelled *ir* in girl. Display Sound-Spelling Card 104. These are curtains. What sound do you hear in the middle of *curtains*? (/ėr/) Say it with me: /ėr/. Point to *ur*. The /ėr/ sound is spelled *ur* in *curtains*.

■ **Listen and Write** Distribute Write and Wipe Boards. Write the word *dirt* on the board. Copy this word. As you write *ir*, say the sound to yourself: /ėr/. Now say the sound aloud. (/ėr/) Underline *ir* in *dirt*. The letters *ir* spell /ėr/ in dirt. Repeat the instruction for /ėr/ spelled *er* and *ur* using the words *water* and *fur*.

Objectives

- Learn relationships between sounds and letters of the English language and decode (sound out) words using a combination of skills such as recognizing sound-letter relationships and identifying cognates, affixes, roots and base words.

ELL English Language Learners

■ **Reteach and Practice** Write the following words on the board and have children read them aloud with you: *burn, hunger, first, germ, birth, surf, sister*. Segment and blend each word with children. Have children decide whether the /ėr/ sound is in the middle or at the end of each word. Leave the words on the board, but erase the letters that form the /ėr/ sound from each word and replace them with a blank. Have children tell whether the blank should contain *er, ir,* or *ur*.

Beginning Have children read the word aloud. Monitor for accurate pronunciation. Have them point to the letters for the /ėr/ sound in each word.

Intermediate Have children read the word aloud. Monitor for accurate pronunciation. Ask them to tell the vowel that should come before the *r* in the /ėr/ sound.

Advanced/Advanced-High Have children read the word aloud and name another word that has the /ėr/ sound spelled the same.

Phonics: Contractions

■ **Preteach** Have children turn to Envision It! on page 156 of the Student Edition.

- The word in the first box is *you're*. It is made up of two smaller words, *you* and *are*. The letter *a* was dropped from the word *are*. Contractions that contain the word *are* have *re* after the apostrophe.
- The word in the second box is *he's*. It is made up of the words *he* and *is*. The letter *i* was dropped from the word *is*. Contractions that contain the word *are* have *s* after the apostrophe.
- The word in the third box is *we've*. It is made up of the words *we* and *have*. The letters *ha* were dropped from the word *have*. Contractions that contain the word *have have ve* after the apostrophe.

■ **Practice** Distribute Letter Tiles *e, o, r, u, w,* and *y* to pairs.

- Blend the sounds in *you're* and have pairs spell *you're* with their tiles: /y/ /ėr/.
- Replace the *you*. Spell *we're*.

Objectives

- Spell familiar English words with increasing accuracy, and employ English spelling patterns and rules with increasing accuracy as more English is acquired.

Language Objectives

- Associate the /ėr/ sound with the spellings *er, ir,* and *ur*.
- Read words with contractions.

Catch Up

Remind children that a contraction is a shortened form of two words. An apostrophe appears where letters have been dropped from the original words.

Transfer Skills

Ask children if there are contractions in their home language. (In Spanish, *a* + *el* = *al* and *de* + *el* = *del*; in Portuguese, *de* + *as* = *das*.) Explain that an English contraction uses an apostrophe to replace the missing letters.

Practice Page

ELL Handbook pages 306 and 307 provide additional practice for this week's skill.

Content Objectives

- Monitor and adjust oral comprehension.

Language Objectives

- Discuss oral passages.
- Use accessible language to learn new language.
- Use a graphic organizer to take notes.

ELL Teacher Tip

You might have pairs discuss the most important details of the story before completing the main idea organizer.

ELL English Language Learners

Listening Comprehension

Wild Work

Fern and Mrs. Beal went into the shed. "Are you ready to work?" Mrs. Beal asked.

"I sure am! It will be fun to take care of animals!" she said.

Mrs. Beal fed birds, squirrels, chipmunks, and rabbits in her yard. But she was going away for two weeks. So she paid Fern to feed the animals while she was away.

Mrs. Beal showed Fern the animal food. Fern saw that the bags had sunflower seeds, peanuts, and walnuts.

"I like nuts too," said Fern.

"Yes," said Mrs. Beal, "animals like nuts and fruit, just like people."

Mrs. Beal showed Fern the yard. "Rabbits find food on the ground. Birds find food in feeders," she said. She showed Fern how to fill the feeders and scatter food for the birds. Soon, birds came to eat. Squirrels, chipmunks, and a rabbit came to eat the food on the ground.

"I like to watch the animals. I like the squirrels best," said Mrs. Beal.

"I wish I could do this job all year," Fern said.

"You can," said Mrs. Beal. "You can put a feeder in your yard."

Prepare for the Read Aloud The modified Read Aloud above prepares children for listening to the oral reading "Fern's Wild Job" on page 155b.

- **First Listening: Listen to Understand** Write the title of the Read Aloud on the board. Have you ever had a job to do? I am going to read a story about someone who has a new job. Listen to find out what kind of job she has to do and how she feels about it. After reading, ask children to recall the things Fern had to do as part of her job. What is Fern's job? (feeding Mrs. Beal's animals) How did she feel about it? (She was happy about her new job.)
- **Second Listening: Listen to Check Understanding** Using the Main Idea graphic organizer (*ELL Handbook*, page 510), work with children to recall the main idea and the details from the story. Ask questions to prompt answers as you fill in the graphic organizer.

Objectives

- Use accessible language and learn new and essential language in the process.

High-Frequency Words

- **Preteach** Distribute copies of this week's Word Cards (*ELL Handbook*, p. 161). Have children point to or hold up corresponding cards when you say a word in a sentence or make a gesture. When appropriate, use opposites to reinforce meaning.
  - When you *know* something, you have the facts about it or can do it. Point to your head. I *know* how to read.
  - *Done* means *finished*. Pantomime finishing a drink. I am *done* with my drink.
  - When you *push* something, you move it away from you. Pantomime pushing.
  - *Wait* means to stay where you are or stop doing something until something else happens. I can't *wait* for recess!
  - *Visit* tells about going to see a place or person. I like to *visit* my grandma.
- **Practice** Have children hold up and read each Word Card at the right time as you briefly repeat each clue.
- **Speaking/Writing with High-Frequency Words**
  - **Teach/Model** Use the poster or make a quick drawing on the board to represent each high-frequency word. Have children pronounce each word.
  - **Practice** Play a game of Beanbag Word Toss. Tape the Word Cards to the floor and give each child a chance to throw the beanbag at a word.

Leveled Support

Beginning Tell children to say the word that is closest to where the beanbag lands.

Intermediate Tell children to say the word that is closest to where the beanbag lands. Help each child use the word in a sentence.

Advanced/Advanced-High Tell children to say the word that is closest to where the beanbag lands and to use the word in a complete sentence.

Objectives

- Use strategic learning techniques such as concept mapping, drawing, memorizing, comparing, contrasting, and reviewing to acquire basic and grade-level vocabulary.

Language Objectives

- Use accessible language to learn new and essential language.
- Use high-frequency English words.
- Write using newly acquired vocabulary.

Cognates

For Spanish speakers, point out that the verb for to *visit* is spelled *visitar* in Spanish. Reinforce the concept that these languages share many words that are the same or similar.

Mini-Lesson: Writing

Have children write using the newly-acquired academic vocabulary words. Turn to p. 155 of the Student Edition. Have children copy the sentences on the page, underlining the highlighted words as they write. Then have them dictate sentences with the words. They can copy the dictated sentences.

Content Objectives

- Identify facts and opinions.

Language Objectives

- Write to show facts and opinions.
- Distinguish between formal and informal language.
- Express opinions.
- Expand inferential reading skills.

ELL English Language Learners

Guide Comprehension
Fact and Opinion

- **Preteach** Model by showing facial expressions to indicate opinions. Facts tell about things that are real. Opinions show how we feel about things. It is a fact that fruits are good for my body; it is my opinion that fruits taste good.
- **Practice** Have children turn to Envision It! on page EI•4 in the Student Edition. Discuss the pictures with children. Tap into children's influential skills to have them determine which statement is fact and which is opinion. Have them tell why the first sentence is a fact and the second sentence is an opinion.
- **Reteach/Practice** Distribute copies of the Picture It! (*ELL Handbook*, p. 162). Have children look at the images. Ask them to tell one fact and one opinion about each picture. First read the text under each picture. Ask the children to raise their hand when they hear an opinion. Discuss how they knew it was an opinion. (**Answers** Roses smell the best. The orange and red leaves are pretty. It is hard to make a snowman. Opinions are the thoughts and feelings of the writer and not everyone.)

Beginning Have the children choral read each sentence with you. After each sentence discuss if it is a fact or an opinion.

Intermediate/Advanced/Advanced-High Have the children choral read the paragraph with you. Create a T-chart with facts on one side and opinions on the other. After each sentence discuss if it is a fact or an opinion. Then write it on the chart.

MINI-LESSON

Social Language

Facts tell about things that are real. Opinions tell what someone thinks about something. We use *I know* to tell facts. We use *I think* to tell opinions. Have children express opinions based on the student edition. Turn to p. 166. Ask children what facts are on the page. What opinion could they express about the page. *(I think the butterfly is pretty. I think it's gross when a butterfly comes out of a cocoon.)*

Objectives

- Demonstrate an increasing ability to distinguish between formal and informal English and an increasing knowledge of when to use each one commensurate with grade-level learning expectations.
- Understand the general meaning, main points, and important details of spoken language ranging from situations in which topics, language, and contexts are familiar to unfamiliar.

Reading Comprehension
I'm a Caterpillar

Student Edition pp. 158–159

■ **Frontloading**

- **Background Knowledge** Read the title aloud and discuss it. Have you ever seen a caterpillar? What did it do?
- **Preview** To provide visual prereading supports, guide children on a picture walk through the story, asking them to identify people, places, and actions. Reteach these words using visuals in the Student Edition: *munch* (p. 160), *shiver* (p. 163), *unfold* (p. 167), and *awful* (p. 170).
- **Predict** What do you think will happen to the caterpillar in the story?

Sheltered Reading Ask questions that require students to use visual and contextual support to read this grade-appropriate content area text.

- p. 160: Point to the caterpillar, emphasizing academic vocabulary as you have children name the animal. What is this? (a caterpillar) What is it doing? (eating the leaf)
- p. 164: Where is the caterpillar? (Use academic vocabulary: in the chrysalis)
- p. 166: Point to the butterfly. What is this? (a butterfly) Where did it come from? (the chrysalis)
- p. 169: What is the butterfly doing? (drinking) How does it drink? (It sips like a straw.) Lead children to pantomime drinking from a straw.
- p. 173: What will happen to the caterpillar first? (It will form a chrysalis.) Lead children to point to each step and say the word. As children are able, introduce the questions in the Student Edition. Provide the questions on Student Edition p. 174 to have students respond.

■ **Fluency: Expression and Intonation** Remind children that we use a different tone of voice for different words. Read page 169, modeling the excitement in your voice when you read "Yum!" Point out that the exclamation point tells us to read with expression. Have pairs share the reading, taking turns reading page 166 expressively as their partners listen and offer feedback.

After Reading Help children summarize the text by asking questions to prompt them to tell the important parts of the text.

Objectives

- Distinguish sounds and intonation patterns of English with increasing ease.
- Use visual and contextual support and support from peers and teachers to read grade-appropriate content area text, enhance and confirm understanding, and develop vocabulary, grasp of language structures, and background knowledge needed to comprehend increasingly challenging language.

Content Objectives

- Monitor and adjust comprehension.
- Make and adjust predictions.
- Use teacher support to confirm understanding.
- Learn academic vocabulary.

Language Objectives

- Read grade-level text with expression.
- Summarize text using visual support.
- Participate in shared reading.
- Respond to questions.
- Use prereading supports.

Mini-Lesson: Visual and Contextual Support

Help children see how they can use visuals such as illustrations or photos and contextual support. Explain that when you don't know the meaning of a word, other words in the sentence can help you figure out what the word means. Sometimes a photo or picture can also give you clues as to the meaning of challenging language.

ELL English Language Learners

For additional leveled instruction, see the **ELL/ELD Reader Teaching Guide.**

Comprehension: *My Apple Tree*

- **Before Reading** Distribute copies of the ELL and ELD Readers, *My Apple Tree,* to children at their reading level.
  - **Preview** Read the title aloud with children and allow time for them to look through the pages. This is a story about a girl who has a tree in her yard. The tree changes with the seasons. What changes happen when the seasons change? What changes in nature have you seen around your home?
  - **Set a Purpose for Reading** Let's read to find out how the tree changes with the seasons.
- **During Reading** Follow this Reading Routine for both reading groups.

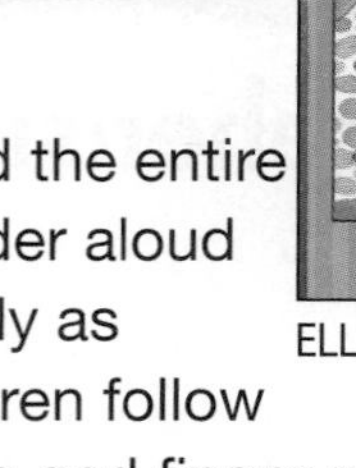

ELL Reader

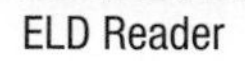

ELD Reader

1. Read the entire Reader aloud slowly as children follow along and finger point.
2. Reread the Reader one sentence at a time, having children echo read after you.

- **After Reading** Use the exercises on the inside back cover of *My Apple Tree* and invite children to share drawings and writing. In a whole-group discussion, ask children to name ways the tree changed with the seasons. Encourage children to identify one change that took place during each season. Children can point to examples in the book of the changes in each season. Keep both readers available for children to read independently during independent reading time.

ELD Reader Beginning/Intermediate

- **p. 4** Point to the tree. How does the tree look in spring? (It has flowers.)
- **p. 6** Point to the leaves. What color are the leaves on the tree in fall?

Writing Draw a picture of the tree in one season. Write the season under the picture. Ask children to work in pairs and share their pictures with the whole class. Have them compare the differences in their pictures and tell how the tree changes.

ELL Reader Advanced/Advanced-High

- **p. 2** Point to the tree. What kind of tree is it? (an apple tree)
- **pp. 2–7** Where does the author sit to enjoy the tree? (in her swing)

Study Guide Distribute copies of the ELL Reader Study Guide (*ELL Handbook*, page 166). Scaffold comprehension by having children look back through the Reader and determine the season in each page based on the pictures. Review their responses together. (**Answers** See *ELL Handbook*, pp. 245–248.)

Objectives

- Demonstrate comprehension of increasingly complex English by participating in shared reading, retelling or summarizing material, responding to questions, and taking notes commensurate with content area and grade level needs.

ELL English Language Learners

Conventions
Verbs *am, is, are, was,* and *were*

- **Preteach** Review the verbs *am, is, are, was,* and *were* with the class. Write the following sentences on the board: *I _______ a teacher. You _______ a student.* Have children suggest which verb would best fit each sentence. (am, are)
- **Practice** Write the following incomplete sentences on the board:

I _______/_______ a good student. (am/was)

We _______/_______ good *children*. (are/were)

My brother _______/_______ a good student. (is/was)

They _______/_______ silly. (are/were)

You _______/_______ a good reader. (are/were)

It _______/_______ cold outside. (is/was)

Tell children to complete the sentences using the verbs *am, is, are, was,* and *were*.

Beginning/ Intermediate Have children choose from the present tense verbs *am, is,* and *are* to complete the sentences.

Advanced/Advanced-High Have children write the completed sentences and read them aloud. Tell them to use two verbs for each sentence—one present tense and one past tense.

- **Reteach** Write *Present Tense* and *Past Tense* on the board. Guide children as they suggest which of the verbs *am, is, are, was,* and *were* belong under each heading.
- **Practice** Write the following sentences on the board under the heading *Present Tense*: *It is hot. They are happy. I am a good dancer.* Then write the following sentences under the heading *Past Tense*: *It was cold. They were sad. He was a good artist.* Tell children to rewrite the underlined verbs in the opposite tense.

Beginning/ Intermediate Guide children to rewrite one verb from each tense. Have them point to each verb and read the new sentence aloud. Monitor for accuracy and comprehension.

Advanced/Advanced-High Tell children to rewrite the underlined verbs in the opposite tense. Then have children share their sentences with a partner. Partners should edit for appropriate verb tenses.

Objectives
- Edit writing for standard grammar and usage, including subject-verb agreement, pronoun agreement, and appropriate verb tenses commensurate with grade-level expectations as more English is acquired.

Content Objectives
- Review verbs *am, is, are, was,* and *were*.

Language Objectives
- Write using verbs *am, is, are, was,* and *were*.
- Spell familiar English words.

Transfer Skills
In languages including Chinese and Korean, linking verbs often are not required: *She tired. They sad.* Help children practice English sentences using different tenses of *am, is, are, was,* and *were*.

Mini-Lesson: Subject-Verb Agreement
The subject and verb of a sentence must agree. That means they both mean one or more than one. In the *Pam is my friend, Pam* is one person; *is,* the verb, is used for one person. In the sentence *They are my friends, they* is more than one person; the verb *are* is used for more than one. Have children edit the incorrect sentences to make them correct: *They is my friends. Tad are my friend.* Have children write sentences and check them for subject-verb agreement.

Mini-Lesson: Spelling
Point out that these verbs are common in English. Children should memorize their spellings. Read sentences from the Student Edition and have children spell the verbs.

Content Objectives

- Compose images and details to show and tell an idea.

Language Objectives

- Write captions to explain pictures.
- Write captions about changes in nature using content-based grade-level vocabulary.
- Demonstrating listening comprehension when collaborating with peers.
- Know when to use formal English.

Mini-Lesson: Collaboration

Have children turn to p. 176 in the Student Edition. Read the prompt to children. Then have them collaborate to complete the assignment. Children can work with partners. Each partner can draw a set of pictures and then exchange the pictures. The partners then listen to each other dictate the captions for the pictures as they record what their partners say.

ELL English Language Learners

Captions and Pictures

- **Introduce Terms** Write *caption* on the board. A *caption* tells about a picture. Draw a simple picture of a house. Write under it *The house is small.* Read the sentence aloud. This sentence is a *caption* because it tells about the picture.
- **Explain Captions** Captions help us understand pictures. Draw a face on the board. What is this? (a face) What could we write to help people understand this picture? Have children suggest possible captions. Guide them to use the expression on the face to form the caption. Write the caption under the picture.
- **Model** Using a T-chart, draw a picture of a caterpillar in one column and a butterfly in the second column. Have children suggest captions based on the pictures and their knowledge about caterpillars. Use the first row of the T-chart to write the captions. Have children look through textbooks or other science books with you to find examples of pictures with captions. Point out that captions use formal language and content words but may include one or two words instead of complete sentences. Have children find and read captions in the books to get a feel for the formal language and the use of content-based grade-level vocabulary.
- **Write** Have children draw a T-chart. Have children draw one picture in each column of the T-chart to show how an animal or object in nature changes. Have children write captions at the top of each column. Ask children: What can you write to describe the drawing in the first column? What can you write to describe the drawing in the second column? To help children internalize new English words, tell children to use content-based grade-level vocabulary, such as *seed, tree, cub, bear, kitten, cat, sunny, rainy,* and so on, to write their captions.

Beginning Have children dictate captions for their pictures. Help them write the captions onto the T-chart.

Intermediate Have partners tell each other about their pictures before writing captions. Tell them to choose the most important words from those they used to explain their pictures as the captions.

Advanced/Advanced-High Have children write a sentence for each caption in the T-chart. Then have them read their sentences aloud to a partner and tell what each caption explains about the pictures.

Objectives

- Narrate, describe, and explain with increasing specificity and detail to fulfill content area writing needs as more English is acquired.

Common Core Standards
Weekly Planning Guide

Grade 1 • Unit 3 • Week 6
Where Are My Animal Friends?
182j–217k

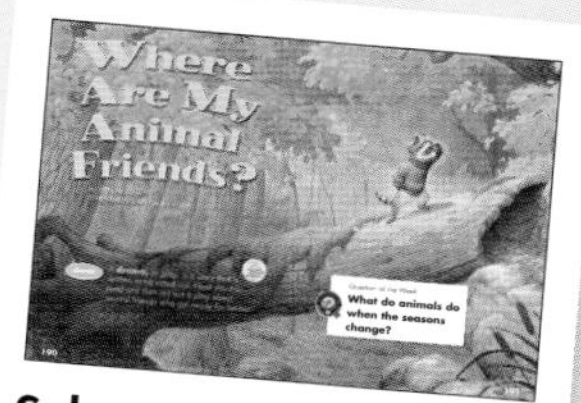

Selection: Where Are My Animal Friends?
Genre: Drama

Alignment of the Common Core Standards with This Week's Skills and Strategies

This Week's Common Core Standards for English Language Arts	Instructional Summary
Reading Standards for Literature	
Literature 1. Ask and answer questions about key details in a text. **Literature 3.** Describe characters, settings, and major events in a story, using key details. **Literature 6.** Identify who is telling the story at various points in a text.	In the lesson, children use story details and what they know to **draw conclusions** about the characters, events, or settings in the Listening Comprehension selection "Home Sweet Home" and the main selection *Where Are My Animal Friends?* As children read, they are encouraged to use their **background knowledge** of animals and seasons to help them understand the play. The play uses small pictures to help children identify speakers.
Foundational Skills Standards	
Foundational Skills 2.d. Segment spoken single-syllable words into their complete sequence of individual sounds (phonemes). **Foundational Skills 4.b.** Read on-level text orally with accuracy, appropriate rate, and expression on successive readings. **Foundational Skills 4.c.** Use context to confirm or self-correct word recognition and understanding, rereading as necessary.	In the phonemic awareness and phonics activities, children segment, blend, and read single-syllable words with the **pattern *dge*.** Children focus on reading with **appropriate expression and intonation** in the fluency activities.
Writing Standards	
Writing 3. Write narratives in which they recount two or more appropriately sequenced events, include some details regarding what happened, use temporal words to signal event order, and provide some sense of closure. **Writing 5.** With guidance and support from adults, focus on a topic, respond to questions and suggestions from peers, and add details to strengthen writing as needed.	Children use the writing process to **write a play scene** in this lesson's Writing section. They plan, draft, revise, edit, and publish their written work. In the Research and Inquiry section, children ask each other what they like to do in the different seasons and use the responses to **prepare a chart.**
Speaking and Listening Standards	
Speaking/Listening 1. Participate in collaborative conversations about *grade 1 topics and texts* with peers and adults in small and larger groups. **Speaking/Listening 6.** Produce complete sentences when appropriate to task and situation. (See grade 1 Language standards 1 and 3 on page 26 for specific expectations.)	In the Listening and Speaking section, children review **rules** for effective listening and speaking and they discuss information to include in an announcement. Children are reminded to use **complete sentences** in announcements they make.
Language Standards	
Language 2.d. Use conventional spelling for words with common spelling patterns and for frequently occurring irregular words. **Language 4.a.** Use sentence-level context as a clue to the meaning of a word or phrase.	The lesson provides explicit **spelling** instruction for high-frequency words and for words with the *dge* pattern. In the lesson's Vocabulary section, children learn to **use context** to identify the meaning of multiple-meaning words.

Additional Support for a Common Core Standard This Week

Use the following instruction to supplement the teaching of one of this week's Common Core Standards.

Common Core Standard: **Literature 6.**
Have children turn to pages 192 and 193 of the main selection *Where Are My Animal Friends?*

- Remind children that this selection is a play. Tell them that in a play, the characters tell the story as they talk.
- Identify the different characters in the play by reviewing their pictures on page 192.
- Read the first line on page 193. Ask children who is saying the line. Then ask how they know which character is saying the line. Help them conclude that Raccoon is saying the line because his picture is in front of the line.
- Point to and read other lines in the play and have children identify the speaker.

ISBN-13: 978-0-328-64370-7 ISBN-10: 0-328-64370-X

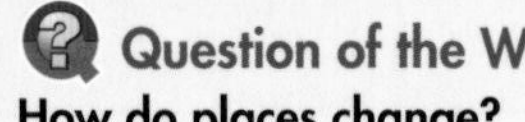

Week 1

A Place to Play

Question of the Week

How do places change?

Concept Talk Guide children as they discuss questions such as:

- What are some ways your neighborhood has changed?

connect to SOCIAL STUDIES

Writing Think about a place to play that you think is interesting. Now write a made-up story about children playing at that place.

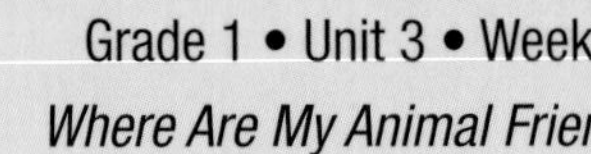

Grade 1 • Unit 3 • Week 6

Where Are My Animal Friends?

Unit 3

What is changing in our world?

You Are Here: Week 6

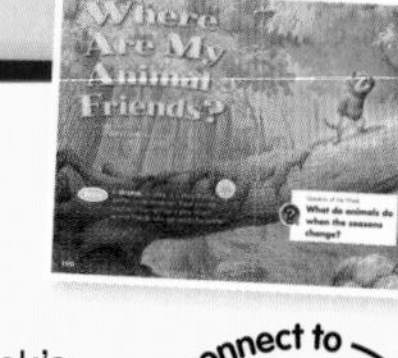

Where Are My Animal Friends?

Question of the Week

What do animals do when the seasons change?

connect to SCIENCE

As children answer this unit's Big Question and this week's Question of the Week, they will address:

Reading 1. Read closely to determine what the text says explicitly and to make logical inferences from it; cite specific textual evidence when writing or speaking to support conclusions drawn from the text.

Concept Talk Guide children as they discuss questions such as:

- Why do you think squirrels gather and hide nuts in the fall?

As children answer this week's Concept Talk question, they will address:

Speaking/Listening 1. Prepare for and participate effectively in a range of conversations and collaborations with diverse partners, building on others' ideas and expressing their own clearly and persuasively.

Writing Think about Raccoon and Squirrel in *Where Are My Animal Friends?* What would they say if they could call Goose on a phone? Write a play scene showing what they would say.

As children write about this week's prompt, they will address:

Writing 3. Write narratives to develop real or imagined experiences or events using effective technique, well-chosen details, and well-structured event sequences. **(Also Writing 5.)**

Listening and Speaking On page 216, children learn to speak clearly and slowly when making an announcement. By doing so, they address:

Speaking/Listening 6. Adapt speech to a variety of contexts and communicative tasks, demonstrating command of formal English when indicated or appropriate. **(Also Speaking/Listening 1.)**

Week 2

Ruby in Her Own Time

Question of the Week

What do we learn as we grow and change?

connect to SOCIAL STUDIES

Concept Talk Guide children as they discuss questions such as:

- What can you do now that you could not do when you were younger?

Writing Look at the pictures in *Ruby in Her Own Time*. Think about what Ruby does. Write sentences that tell two things Ruby does that you like.

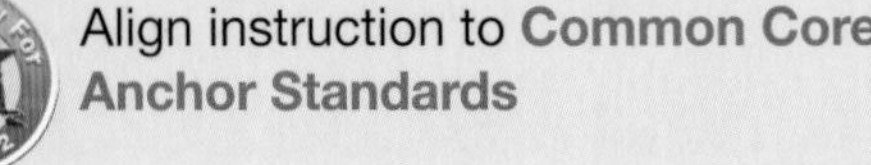

Common Core Standards and Concept Development

- Introduce and explore this unit's weekly concepts through rich, structured conversations
- Develop complex content knowledge and vocabulary
- Expand on a single concept with engaging literature and nonfiction
- Build better readers in all content areas

Align instruction to **Common Core Anchor Standards**

Week 3

The Class Pet

Question of the Week

What can we learn about animals as they grow and change?

connect to SCIENCE

Concept Talk Guide children as they discuss questions such as:

- Think about different animals. How are the babies different from the adults?

Writing Write a summary of *The Class Pet*. Tell the most important events and ideas.

Week 4

Frog and Toad Together

Question of the Week

What changes happen in a garden?

connect to SCIENCE

Concept Talk Guide children as they discuss questions such as:

- What do seeds look like when you first plant them? Then what happens?

Writing Think of actions Toad tried to help his garden grow. Write a list telling what Toad did that really helped the garden grow. In another list, tell his actions that did not help.

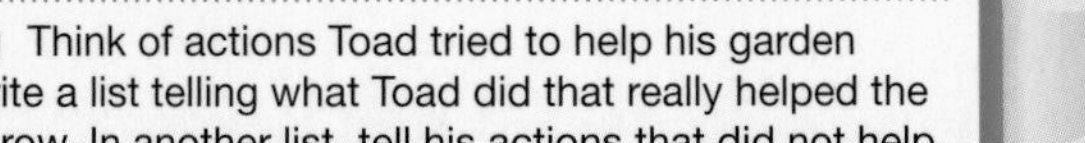

Week 5

I'm a Caterpillar

Question of the Week

What changes can be seen in nature?

connect to SCIENCE

Concept Talk Guide children as they discuss questions such as:

- How do different kinds of animals change as they grow?

Writing Think of changes in nature. Plants and animals grow. Seasons change. Draw two pictures to show one way a plant or animal changes. Write captions about your pictures.

This Week's ELL Overview

Grade 1 • Unit 3 • Week 6
Where Are My Animal Friends?
182a–217n and DI•117–DI•126

ELL Handbook

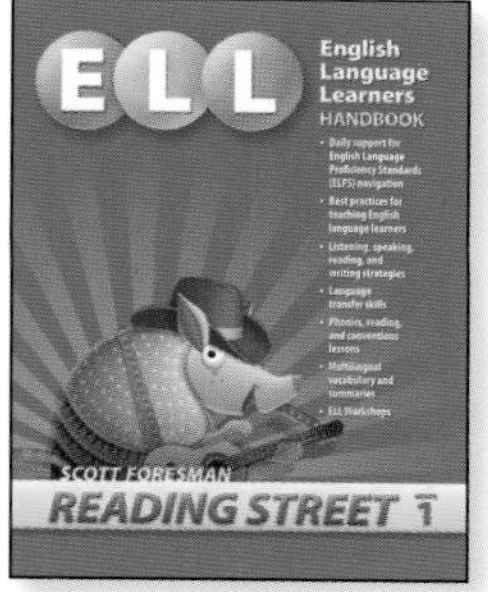

- Maximize Literacy and Cognitive Engagement
- Research Into Practice
- Full Weekly Support for Every Selection

Where Are My Animal Friends?

- Multi-Lingual Summaries in Five Languages
- Selection-Specific Vocabulary Word Cards
- Frontloading/Reteaching for Comprehension Skill Lessons
- ELD and ELL Reader Study Guides

- Transfer Activities
- Professional Development

Daily Leveled ELL Notes

ELL notes appear throughout this week's instruction and ELL Support is on the DI pages of your Teacher's Edition. The following is a sample of an ELL note from this week.

English Language Learners

Beginning Give children starter questions to begin their play scene, such as *Hi, Goose. What are you doing?* or *When are you coming home?*

Intermediate Have partners come up with questions to begin their play scenes. Tell children to consider what Goose or Raccoon and Squirrel might want to know.

Advanced Have children role-play the conversations and record their main lines in the charts.

Advanced High Have children choose whether they like Goose or Raccoon better and discuss their choices. Children may tell what they like about both characters.

ELL by Strand

The ELL lessons on this week's Support for English Language Learners pages are organized by strand. They offer additional scaffolding for the core curriculum. Leveled support notes on these pages address the different proficiency levels in your class. See pages DI•117–DI•126.

ELL Strands	The Three Pillars of ELL Instruction		
	Activate Prior Knowledge	**Access Content**	**Extend Language**
Vocabulary p. DI•121	Preteach	Teach/Model	Practice
Reading Comprehension p. DI•122	Preteach	Reteach/Practice	Leveled Practice Activities
Phonics, Spelling, and Word Analysis pp. DI•118–DI•119	Preteach	Listen and Write	Leveled Practice Activities
Listening Comprehension p. DI•120	Prepare for the Read Aloud	First Listening	Second Listening
Conventions and Writing pp. DI•125–DI•126	Preteach/Introduce Terms	Practice/Model	Leveled Practice Activities/ Leveled Writing Activities
Concept Development p. DI•117	Activate Prior Knowledge	Develop Concepts	Review Concepts and Connect to Writing

This Week's Practice Stations Overview

Grade 1 • Unit 3 • Week 6
Where Are My Animal Friends?
182a–217n

Six Weekly Practice Stations with Leveled Activities can be found at the beginning of each week of instruction. For this week's Practice Stations, see pp. 182h–182i.

Classroom Management Handbook for Differentiated Instruction Practice Stations

Practice Stations

Daily Leveled Center Activities

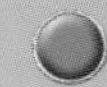 Below
 On-Level
Advanced

Practice Stations Flip Charts

	 Listen Up	 Word Work	 Words to Know	 Let's Write	 Read for Meaning	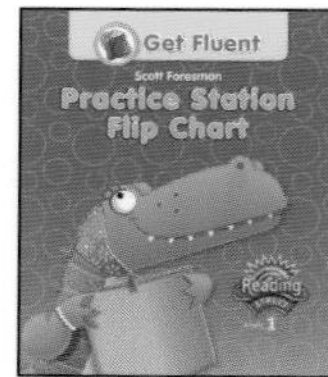 Get Fluent
Objectives	• Identify words with *r*-controlled /ėr/.	• Identify words with *r*-controlled vowels *er, ir,* and *ur.* • Identify contractions.	• Identify high-frequency words *know, done, push, wait, visit.* • Alphabetize to the first letter.	• Write sentences using *am, is, was, are, were.*	• Identify facts and opinions in a selection.	• Read aloud with expression and intonation.
Materials	• *Listen Up* Flip Chart Activity 18 • ten Picture Cards, including *feather, hammer, spider, tiger, zipper*	• *Word Work* Flip Chart Activity 18 • teacher-made Word Cards • 4-column charts • pencils	• *Words to Know* Flip Chart Activity 18 • High-Frequency Word Cards for Unit 3, Week 5 • paper • pencils	• *Let's Write* Flip Chart Activity 18 • paper • pencils	• *Read for Meaning* Flip Chart Activity 18 • Leveled Readers • T-charts • pencils	• *Get Fluent* Flip Chart Activity 18 • Leveled Readers

This Week on Reading Street!

Question of the Week

What do animals do when the seasons change?

Daily Plan

Whole Group

- Comparative Endings *-er, -est*
- Consonant Pattern *-dge*
- Draw Conclusions
- Fluency
- Vocabulary

MONITOR PROGRESS — Success Predictor

Day 1	Day 2	Day 3	Day 4	Day 5
Check Word Reading	Check Word Reading	Check High Frequency Words/Retelling	Check Fluency	Check Oral Vocabulary

Small Group

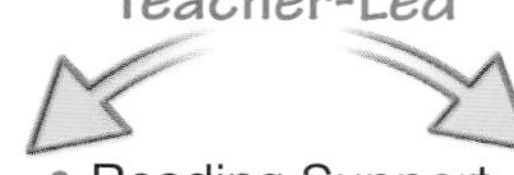

Teacher-Led

- Reading Support
- Skill Support
- Fluency Practice

Practice Stations

Independent Activities

Customize Literacy More support for a Balanced Literacy approach, see CL•1–CL•47.

Customize Writing More support for a customized writing approach, see CW•11–CW•20.

Whole Group

- Writing: Play Scene
- Conventions: Contractions with Not

Assessment

- Weekly Tests
- Day 5 Assessment
- Fresh Reads

This Week's Reading Selections

Main Selection
Genre: **Drama**

Paired Selection

Decodable Practice Readers

Leveled Readers

ELL and ELD Readers

Resources on Reading Street!

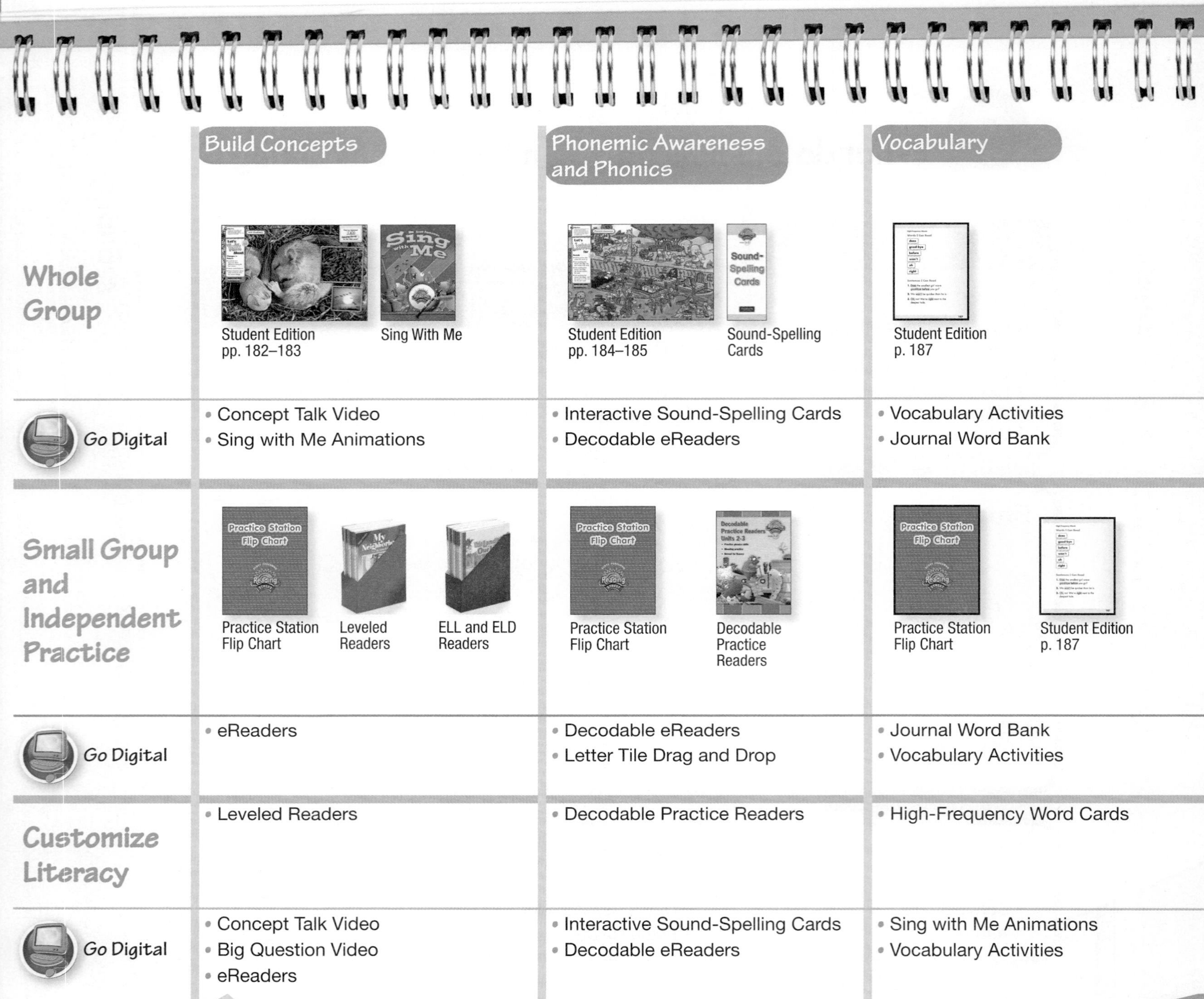

	Build Concepts	Phonemic Awareness and Phonics	Vocabulary
Whole Group	Student Edition pp. 182–183 Sing With Me	Student Edition pp. 184–185 Sound-Spelling Cards	Student Edition p. 187
Go Digital	• Concept Talk Video • Sing with Me Animations	• Interactive Sound-Spelling Cards • Decodable eReaders	• Vocabulary Activities • Journal Word Bank
Small Group and Independent Practice	Practice Station Flip Chart Leveled Readers ELL and ELD Readers	Practice Station Flip Chart Decodable Practice Readers	Practice Station Flip Chart Student Edition p. 187
Go Digital	• eReaders	• Decodable eReaders • Letter Tile Drag and Drop	• Journal Word Bank • Vocabulary Activities
Customize Literacy	• Leveled Readers	• Decodable Practice Readers	• High-Frequency Word Cards
Go Digital	• Concept Talk Video • Big Question Video • eReaders	• Interactive Sound-Spelling Cards • Decodable eReaders	• Sing with Me Animations • Vocabulary Activities

Question of the Week

What do animals do when the seasons change?

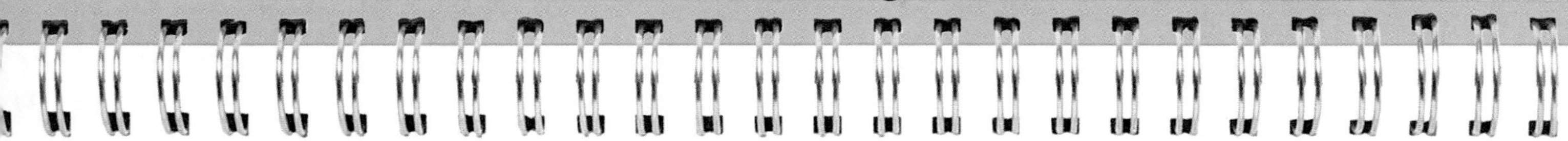

Week 6

Comprehension	Fluency	Conventions and Writing
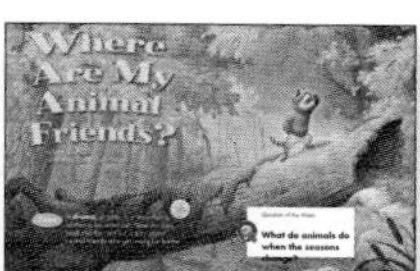 Student Edition pp. 190–207	 Decodable Practice Readers	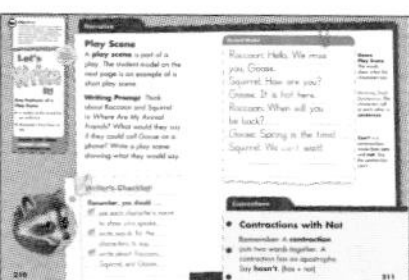 Student Edition pp. 210–211
• Envision It! Animations • eSelections	• eSelections • eReaders	• Grammar Jammer
 Practice Station Flip Chart  Leveled Readers  ELL and ELD Readers	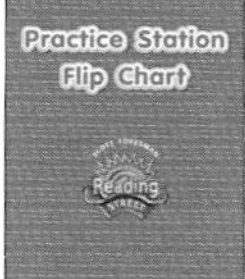 Practice Station Flip Chart  Decodable Practice Readers	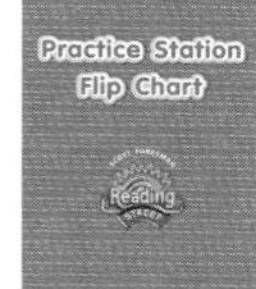 Practice Station Flip Chart 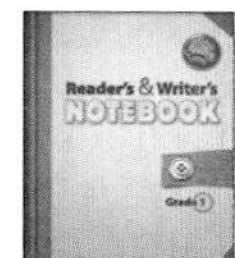 Reader's and Writer's Notebook
• eReaders • Story Sort	• Decodable eReaders	• Grammar Jammer
• Envision It! Skills and Strategies Handbooks • Leveled Readers	• Leveled Readers	• Reader's and Writer's Notebook
• Envision It! Animations • eReaders	• eReaders	• Grammar Jammer

My 5-Day Planner for Reading Street!

Don't Wait Until Friday SUCCESS PREDICTOR

	Check Word Reading **Day 1** pages 182j–187f	Check Word Reading **Day 2** pages 188a–207g
Get Ready to Read	**Concept Talk,** 182j–183 **Oral Vocabulary,** 183a–183b *hibernate, migrate, temperature* **Phonological Awareness,** 184–185 Segment and Blend Words **Phonics,** 185a–186a ◎ Comparative Endings *-er, -est* READ **Decodable Practice Reader 18A,** 186b–186c **Spelling,** 186d Pretest	**Concept Talk,** 188a–188b **Oral Vocabulary,** 188b *autumn* **Phonemic Awareness,** 188c Segment and Blend Phonemes **Phonics,** 188d–189a ◎ Consonant Pattern *-dge* READ **Decodable Practice Reader 18B,** 189b–189c Review **Phonics,** 189d Endings *-er, -est, -ing, -ed* **Spelling,** 189e Practice
Read and Comprehend	**High-Frequency Words,** 187 Introduce *before, does, good-bye, oh, right, won't* **Listening Comprehension,** 187a–187b ◎ Draw Conclusions	**High-Frequency Words,** 189 Build Fluency *before, does, good-bye, oh, right, won't* **Story Words,** 190a Introduce *butterfly, goose, raccoon, spring, warm* **Vocabulary,** 190a Context Clues **Build Background,** 190b READ **Main Selection—First Read,** 190c–207a *Where Are My Animal Friends?* **Genre,** 207b Drama
Language Arts	**Conventions,** 187c Contractions with *Not* **Writing,** 187d–187e Play Scene **Research and Inquiry,** 187f Identify and Focus Topic	**Conventions,** 207c Contractions with *Not* **Writing,** 207d–207e Play Scene Writing Trait: Sentences **Handwriting,** 207f Letter *J* and *j;* Letter Slant **Research and Inquiry,** 207g Research Skill: Picture Graph

You Are Here! Unit 3 Week 6

Question of the Week

What do animals do when the seasons change?

Check High-Frequency Words Check Retelling **Day 3** pages 208a–211c	Check Fluency **Day 4** pages 212a–215e	Check Oral Vocabulary **Day 5** pages 216a–217k
Concept Talk, 208a–208b **Oral Vocabulary,** 208b *freeze* **Phonemic Awareness,** 208c Add Phonemes **Phonics,** 208d–208e ◎ Comparative Endings *-er, -est* ◎ Consonant Pattern *-dge* **Spelling,** 208f Dictation	**Concept Talk,** 212a–212b **Oral Vocabulary,** 212b *bitterly, weary* **Phonemic Awareness,** 212c Change Initial Phonemes Review **Phonics,** 212d *r*-Controlled *er, ir, ur*; Contractions *'s, 've, 're* READ **Decodable Practice Reader 18C,** 212e–212f Review **Fluent Word Reading,** 212g **Spelling,** 212h Partner Review	**Concept Wrap Up,** 216a Review **Oral Vocabulary,** 216b **Phonological Awareness,** 216c Generate Rhyming Words Review **Phonics,** 216c ◎ Comparative Endings *-er, -est* ◎ Consonant Pattern *-dge* **Spelling,** 216d Test
Review **High-Frequency Words,** 208g *before, does, good-bye, oh, right, won't* Review **Story Words,** 208g *butterfly, goose, raccoon, spring, warm* Review **Main Selection—Second Read,** 190–207, 208h–209a **Fluency,** 209b Expression and Intonation	**Poetry,** 212i READ **Paired Selection,** 212–215 Poetry Collection **Fluency,** 215a Expression and Intonation	**Listening and Speaking,** 216–217 **Vocabulary,** 217a Context Clues **Fluency,** 217a Expression and Intonation Review **Comprehension,** 217b ◎ Draw Conclusions Review **Vocabulary,** 217b High-Frequency and Story Words **Literary Text,** 217c Rhyme, Rhythm, and Alliteration **Assessment,** 217d–217f Monitor Progress
Conventions, 210a–211a Contractions with *Not* **Writing,** 210–211a Play Scene Writer's Craft: Strong Verbs **Listening and Speaking,** 211b Give Announcements **Research and Inquiry,** 211c Gather and Record Information	**Conventions,** 215b Contractions with *Not* **Writing,** 215c–215d Play Scene Revising Strategy **Research and Inquiry,** 215e Review and Revise Topic	Review **Conventions,** 217g Contractions with *Not* **Writing,** 217h–217i Play Scene Writers Craft: Contractions **Research and Inquiry,** 217j Communicate **Wrap Up Your Week,** 217k What do animals do when the seasons change?

Week 6

Grouping Options for Differentiated Instruction

Turn the page for the small group time lesson plan.

Planning Small Group Time on Reading Street!

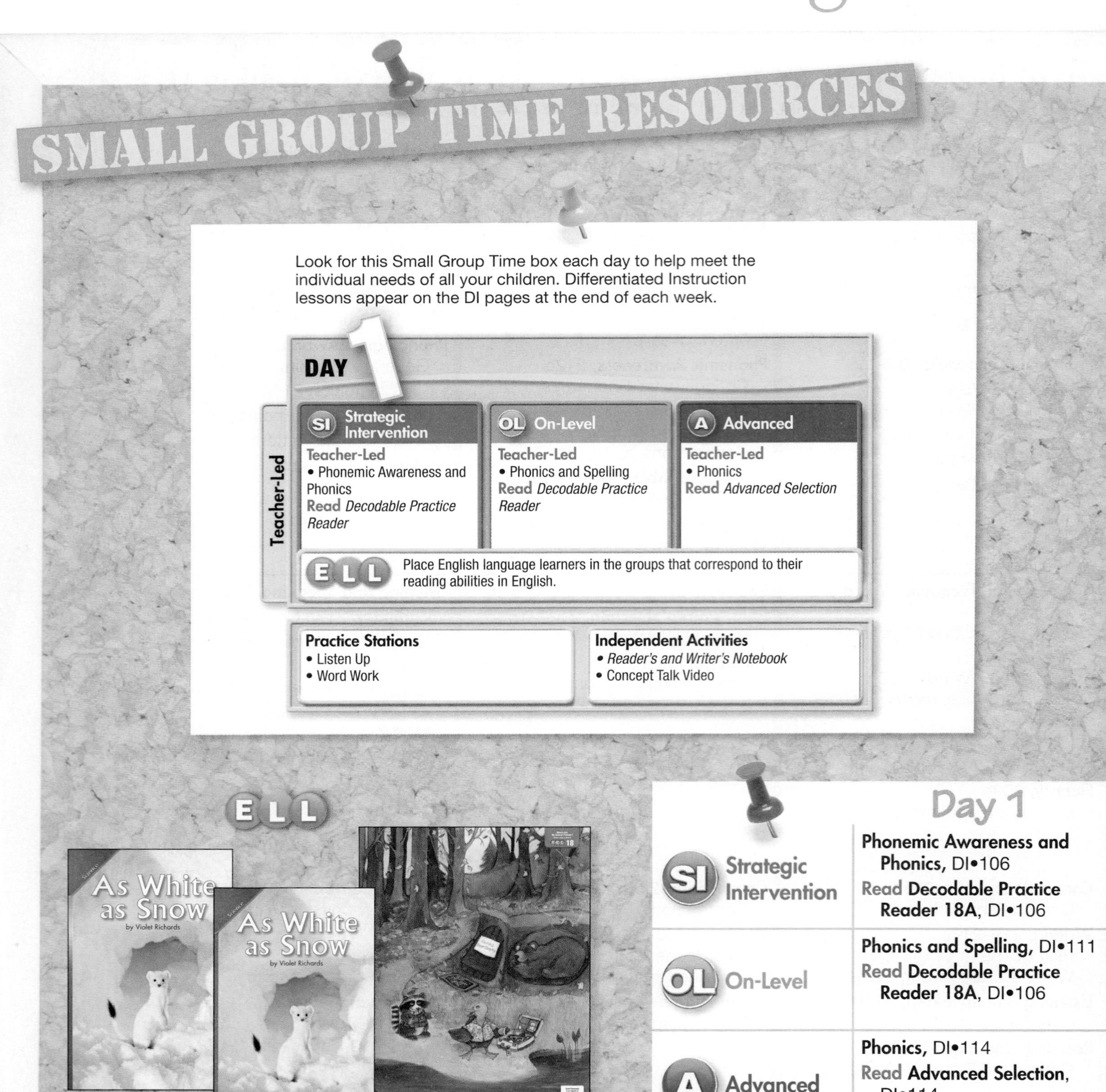

ELL Reader Advanced Advanced-High

ELD Reader Beginning Intermediate

ELL Poster

	Day 1
SI Strategic Intervention	**Phonemic Awareness and Phonics,** DI•106 Read **Decodable Practice Reader 18A,** DI•106
OL On-Level	**Phonics and Spelling,** DI•111 Read **Decodable Practice Reader 18A,** DI•106
A Advanced	**Phonics,** DI•114 Read **Advanced Selection,** DI•114
ELL English Language Learners	DI•117–DI•126 **Frontload Concept** **Preteach Skills** **Writing**

You Are Here! Unit 3 Week 6

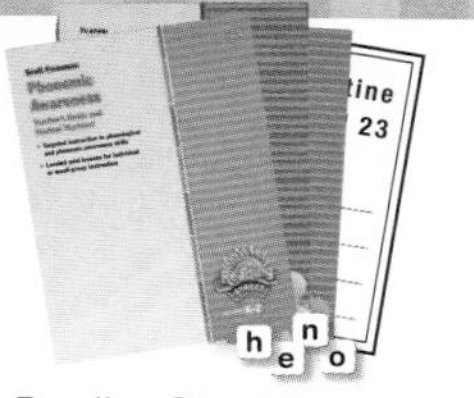

Reading Street Response to Intervention Kit

Reading Street Leveled Practice Stations Kit

Question of the Week

What do animals do when the seasons change?

Below-Level Reader

Decodable Practice Readers

Concept Literacy Reader

On-Level Reader

A Advanced

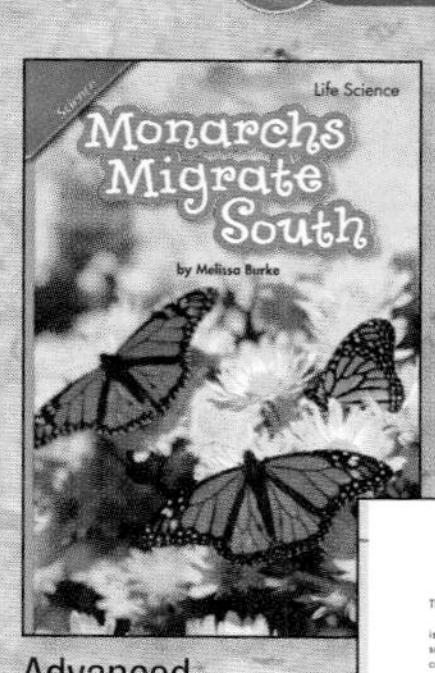

Advanced Reader

The Hardest Job

Advanced Selection

Small Group Weekly Plan

Day 2	Day 3	Day 4	Day 5
Phonemic Awareness and Phonics, DI•107 Read **Decodable Practice Reader 18B,** DI•107	**Phonemic Awareness and Phonics,** DI•108 Read **Concept Literacy Leveled Reader,** DI•108	**High-Frequency Words,** DI•109 Read **Decodable Practice Reader 18C,** DI•109	**Phonics Review,** DI•110 Read **Below-Level Leveled Reader,** DI•110
Phonics and High-Frequency Words, DI•111 Read **Decodable Practice Reader 18B,** DI•111	Read **On-Level Leveled Reader,** DI•112	**Conventions,** DI•113 Reread **Main Selection,** DI•113	**Phonics Review,** DI•113 Reread **On-Level Leveled Reader,** DI•116
Phonics and Comprehension, DI•114 Read **Main Selection** DI•114	Read **Advanced Leveled Reader,** DI•115	**Comprehension,** DI•116 Read **Paired Selection,** DI•116 Reread **Leveled Reader,** DI•116	**Fluency and Comprehension,** DI•116 Reread **Advanced Selection,** DI•116
DI•117–DI•126 **Review Concept** **Practice Skills** **Frontload Main Selection** **Writing**	DI•117–DI•126 **Review Concept** **Practice Skills** **Reread Main Selection** **Writing**	DI•117–DI•126 **Review Concept** **Practice Skills** **Read ELL or ELD Reader** **Writing**	DI•117–DI•126 **Review Concept** **Review Skills** **Writing**

Week 6

Practice Stations for Everyone on Reading Street!

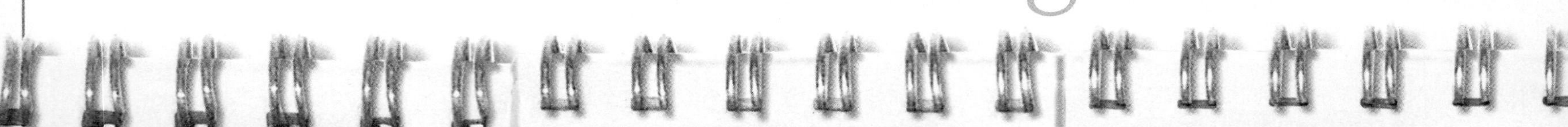

Listen Up!

Match sounds and pictures.

Objectives

- Identify words with *r*-controlled /ėr/.

Materials

- *Listen Up!* Flip Chart Activity 18
- Ten Picture Cards, including *feather, hammer, spider, tiger, zipper*

Differentiated Activities

● Find Picture Cards that contain the sound you hear at the end of *fur.* Say the words.

▲ Find Picture Cards that contain the sound you hear at the end of *fur.* Say the words. Now say other words that contain that sound.

■ Find Picture Cards that contain the sound you hear at the end of *fur.* Say the words. Now take turns with a partner saying words that have the sound in the beginning, in the middle, and at the end.

Technology

- Interactive Sound-Spelling Cards

Word Work

r-Controlled vowels *er, ir, ur;* contractions

Objectives

- Identify words with the *r*-controlled vowels *er, ir,* and *ur.*
- Identify contractions.

Materials

- *Word Work* Flip Chart Activity 18
- teacher-made word cards
- 4-column charts
- pencils

Differentiated Activities

● Label the columns on your chart *er, ir, ur, Contractions.* Look at the word cards. Write the words in the correct columns.

▲ Label the columns on your chart *er, ir, ur, Contractions.* Look at the word cards. Write the words in the correct columns. Add other words to the columns.

■ Label the columns on your chart *er, ir, ur, Contractions.* Look at the word cards. Write the words in the correct columns. Add other words to the columns. Now write sentences using some of the words.

Technology

- Interactive Sound-Spelling Cards

Words To Know

Practice high-frequency words.

Objectives

- Identify high-frequency words *know, done, push, wait, visit.*
- Alphabetize to the first letter.

Materials

- *Words to Know* Flip Chart Activity 18
- High-Frequency Word Cards for Unit 3, Week 5
- paper
- pencils

Differentiated Activities

● Use the Word Cards. Put them in alphabetical order. Write them in alphabetical order on your paper.

▲ Use the Word Cards. Put them in alphabetical order. Write them in alphabetical order on your paper. Write a sentence using one or more of the words.

■ Use the Word Cards. Put them in alphabetical order. Write them in alphabetical order on your paper. Write sentences using the words. Underline the Words to Know.

Technology

- Online Tested Vocabulary Activities

You Are Here! Unit 3 Week 6

Use this week's materials from the Reading Street Leveled Practice Stations Kit to organize this week's stations.

Key

● Below-Level Activities

▲ On-Level Activities

■ Advanced Activities

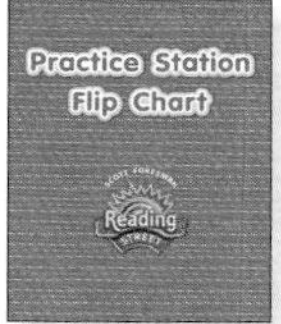

Practice Station Flip Chart

Let's Write!

Use verbs in writing.

Objectives

- Write sentences using *am, is, was, are, were.*

Materials

- *Let's Write!* Flip Chart Activity 18
- paper
- pencils

Differentiated Centers

● Complete these sentence frames using *am, is, was, are,* or *were:*

I _____ a caterpillar.

This leaf _____ tasty.

My wings _____ wet.

▲ Write sentences about a caterpillar using the verbs *am, is, was, are,* and *were.* Underline the verbs.

■ Write a story about a caterpillar using the verbs *am, is, was, are,* and *were.* Underline the verbs.

Read For Meaning

Identify fact and opinion.

Objectives

- Identify facts and opinions in a selection.

Materials

- *Read for Meaning* Flip Chart Activity 18
- Leveled Readers
- T-charts
- pencils

Differentiated Activities

- A **fact** is a statement that can be proved true.
- An **opinion** is a statement of what someone believes.

● Read *Animals Change and Grow.* Look for facts and opinions. Share what you've found with a partner.

▲ Read *Let's Visit a Butterfly Greenhouse.* Label the columns on your chart "Facts" and "Opinions." Find statements in the book that are facts and opinions and write them in the correct columns. Which column contains the most statements?

■ Read *Learn About Butterflies.* Label the columns on your chart "Facts" and "Opinions." Find statements in the book that are facts and opinions and write them in the correct columns. Now add your own opinions to the "Opinions" column.

Technology

- Leveled eReaders

Get Fluent

Practice fluent reading.

Objectives

- Read aloud with expression and intonation.

Materials

- *Get Fluent* Flip Chart Activity 18
- Leveled Readers

Differentiated Activities

● Work with a partner. Take turns reading pages from *Animals Change and Grow.* Read with expression and intonation. Pay attention to punctuation. Give your partner feedback.

▲ Work with a partner. Take turns reading pages from *Let's Visit a Butterfly Greenhouse.* Read with expression and intonation. Pay attention to punctuation. Give your partner feedback.

■ Work with a partner. Take turns reading pages from *Learn About Butterflies.* Read with expression and intonation. Pay attention to punctuation. Give your partner feedback.

Technology

- Reading Street Readers CD-ROM

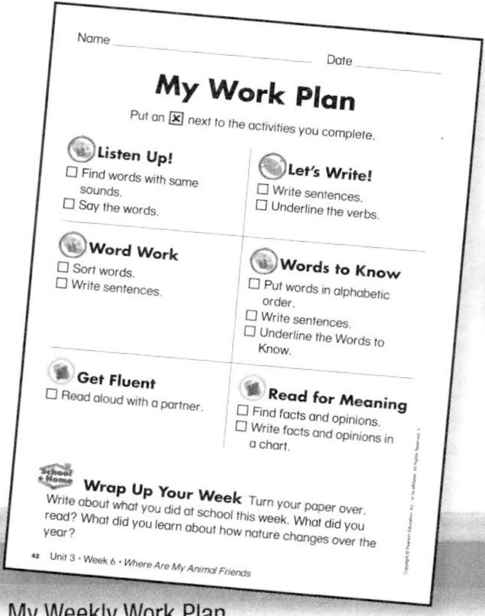
Name _______ Date _______

My Work Plan

Put an ☒ next to the activities you complete.

Listen Up!
☐ Find words with same sounds.
☐ Say the words.

Let's Write!
☐ Write sentences.
☐ Underline the verbs.

Word Work
☐ Sort words.
☐ Write sentences.

Words to Know
☐ Put words in alphabetic order.
☐ Write sentences.
☐ Underline the Words to Know.

Get Fluent
☐ Read aloud with a partner.

Read for Meaning
☐ Find facts and opinions.
☐ Write facts and opinions in a chart.

Wrap Up Your Week Turn your paper over. Write about what you did at school this week. What did you read? What did you learn about how nature changes over the year?

42 Unit 3 • Week 6 • Where Are My Animal Friends?

My Weekly Work Plan

Week 6

Objectives

- Introduce concept: what animals do when the seasons change.
- Share information and ideas about the concept.

Today at a Glance

Oral Vocabulary
hibernate, migrate, temperature

Phonological Awareness
Segment and Blend Words

Phonics and Spelling
◎ Comparative Endings *-er, -est*

Fluency
Oral Rereading

High-Frequency Words
before, does, good-bye, oh, right, won't

Comprehension
◎ Draw Conclusions

Conventions
Contractions with *Not*

Writing
Play Scene: Introduce

Research and Inquiry
Identify and Focus on Topic

Concept Talk

Question of the Week

What do animals do when the seasons change?

Introduce the concept

To build concepts and focus children's attention, tell them that this week they will talk, sing, read, and write about what animals do when the seasons change. Write the Question of the Week and track the print as you read it.

ROUTINE Activate Prior Knowledge **Team Talk**

1. **Think** Have children think for a minute about what they have seen squirrels and birds do at certain times of the year.
2. **Pair** Have pairs of children discuss the question.
3. **Share** Have children share information and their ideas with the group. Remind them to ask questions to clarify information. Guide discussion and encourage elaboration with prompts such as: Why do you think squirrels gather and hide nuts in the fall?

Routines Flip Chart

Anchored Talk

Develop oral language

Have children turn to pages 182–183 in their Student Edition. Read the title and look at the photos. Use these questions to guide discussion and create the "What do animals do when the seasons change?" concept map.

- The pictures show how different animals stay warm in winter. How do the birds stay warm? (Possible response: by flying south in fall) This is called *migrating*. Let's add *Birds migrate to warm places* to our chart.
- How does the little dormouse stay warm? (Possible response: by sleeping all winter) This is called *hibernating*. Let's add *Some animals hibernate* to our chart.
- Why do you think the snakes are curled up together? (Possible response: to stay warmer) Let's add *Some animals gather together* to our chart.

Student Edition pp. 182–183

Connect to reading Explain that this week, children will read a story about what different kinds of animals do when winter is coming. Let's look at our chart and see what we know so far about what animals do in the fall and winter.

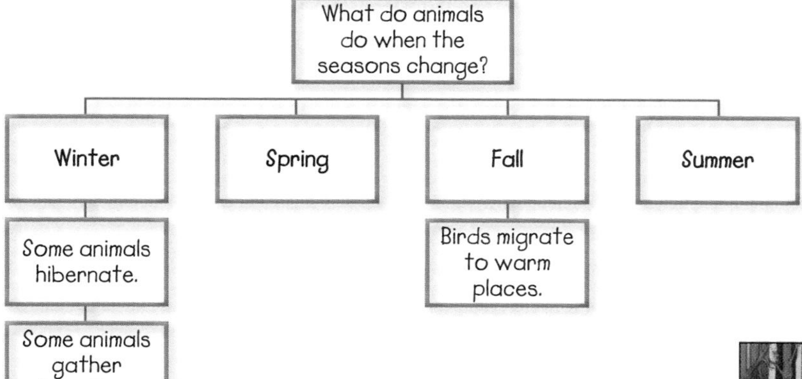

ELL Preteach Concepts Use the Day 1 instruction on ELL Poster 18 to assess and build background knowledge, develop concepts, and build oral vocabulary.

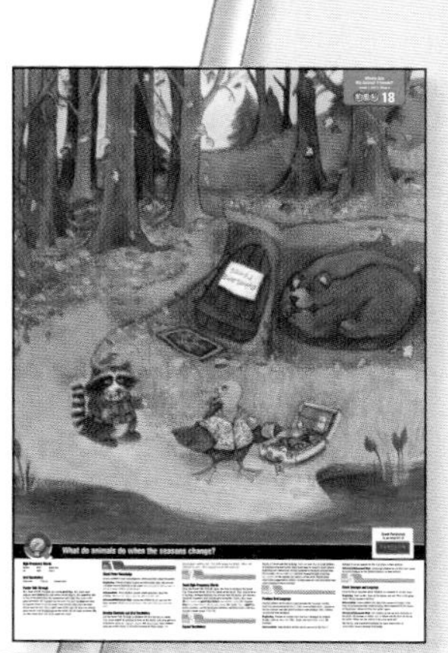
ELL Poster 18

Amazing Words

You've learned 1 8 3 words so far.

You'll learn 0 0 7 words this week!

hibernate	freeze
migrate	bitterly
temperature	weary
autumn	

Writing on Demand

Develop Writing Fluency

Ask children to write about what they know about what animals do when the seasons change. Have them write for two or three minutes. Children should write as much as they can. Tell them to try to do their best writing. You may want to discuss what children wrote during writing conferences.

ELL

English Language Learners

Activate Prior Knowledge Have children name the different animals and seasons shown in the pictures in their home language and in English.

ELL Support Additional ELL support and modified instruction are provided in the *ELL Handbook* and in the ELL Support Lessons on pp. DI•117–DI•126.

Objectives
- Build oral vocabulary.
- Discuss the concept to develop oral language.
- Share information and ideas about the concept.

Oral Vocabulary
Amazing Words

Introduce Amazing Words

Display p. 18 of the *Sing with Me* Big Book. Tell children they are going to sing about what animals do when the winter is coming. Ask children to listen for the Amazing Words *hibernate*, *migrate*, and *temperature* as you sing. Sing the song again and have children join you.

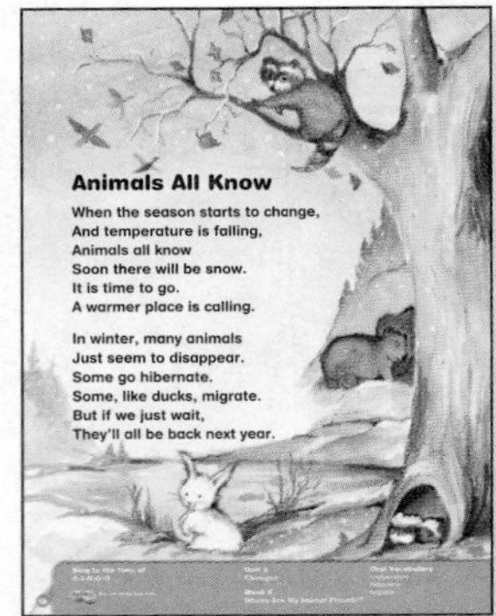

Sing with Me Big Book, p. 18

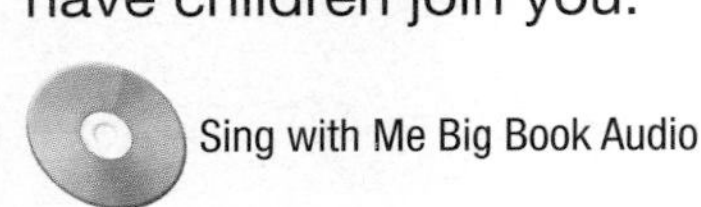
Sing with Me Big Book Audio

Teach Amazing Words

Amazing Words Oral Vocabulary Routine

1. **Introduce the Word** Relate the word *hibernate* to the song. Many animals seem to disappear in winter. Some of them *hibernate*. Supply a child-friendly definition: *Hibernate* means "to spend the winter sleeping." Have children say the word.
2. **Demonstrate** Provide examples to show meaning: Some bats *hibernate*, or sleep all winter long in caves. Some frogs *hibernate* by burying themselves in mud.
3. **Apply** Have children demonstrate their understanding: Where do you think bears go when they *hibernate*? Why?

See p. OV•3 to teach *migrate* and *temperature*.

Routines Flip Chart

Oral Vocabulary
Amazing Words

Check understanding of Amazing Words

Have children look at the picture on p. 18. What good places do you see for an animal to *hibernate*? Use *hibernate* in your answer. (Possible response: An animal could hibernate in the cave or tree hollow.)

What clues in the picture tell you what the *temperature* is like? Use *temperature* in your answer. (Possible response: The snow and bare branches show that the temperature is low, or cold.)

Why are the birds *migrating*? Use *migrate* in your answer. (Possible response: The birds are migrating to a warmer place because they can't live where the weather is very cold.)

Apply Amazing Words

Have children demonstrate their understanding of the Amazing Words by completing these sentences orally.

When animals **hibernate,** they ________.

Many ________ **migrate** by flying south.

When the **temperature** is low, it is ________ outside.

Corrective feedback

If... children have difficulty using the Amazing Words,
then... remind them of the definitions and provide opportunities for children to use the words in sentences.

Preteach Academic Vocabulary

Write the following on the board:

- draw conclusions
- drama
- contractions with *not*

Have children share what they know about this week's Academic Vocabulary. Use children's responses to assess their prior knowledge. Preteach the Academic Vocabulary by providing a child-friendly description, explanation, or example that clarifies the meaning of each term. Then ask children to restate the meaning of the Academic Vocabulary in their own words.

Amazing Words

hibernate	freeze
migrate	bitterly
temperature	weary
autumn	

Differentiated Instruction

SI Strategic Intervention

Sentence Production As children say the sentences, remind them to enunciate the sound of *er* in *hibernate*, *winter*, and *temperature*.

English Language Learners

Use Cognates Spanish-speaking children may know the Spanish cognates *hibernar* (hibernate) and *temperatura* (temperature). Remind children of these cognates to help them learn the Amazing Words.

Objectives

- Segment and blend words with comparative endings *-er, -est.*
- ◎ Use word analysis to recognize words with comparative endings *-er, -est.*
- Read words with comparative endings *-er, -est.*

Skills Trace

◎ **Comparative Endings *-er, -est***

Introduce U3W6D1

Practice U3W6D3; U3W6D4

Reteach/Review U3W6D5; U4W1D4

Assess/Test Weekly Test U3W6

Benchmark Test U3

KEY:

U=Unit W=Week D=Day

Student Edition pp. 184–185

Phonological Awareness
Segment and Blend Two-Syllable Words

Introduce Have children look at the picture on pages 184–185 in their Student Edition. I see four beavers. Two are *bigger* than the others. The ending I hear in *bigger* is *-er*. What else has the *-er* ending? I see some goats who are *older* than others. One goat is the *oldest*. The ending I hear in *oldest* is *-est*. What else ends with *-est*? I see the *biggest* beaver. Help children name other items in the picture that have *-er* or *-est* endings.

Model Listen to the syllables in the word *bigger*, /big/ /ər/. There are two syllables in *bigger*. Let's blend those syllables to make a word: /big/ /ər/, *bigger*. Continue modeling with *oldest*.

Guide practice Guide children as they segment and blend these words from the picture: *smaller, smallest, biggest, older, faster, fastest, taller,* and *tallest*.

Corrective feedback **If...** children make an error,
then... model by segmenting the word, and have them repeat the segmenting and blending of the word.

Phonics—Teach/Model

Comparative Endings *-er, -est*

Sound-Spelling Card 123

ending -est

Sound-Spelling Card 125

ROUTINE Word Parts Strategy

1. **Connect** Write *think* and *thinking*. Point out to children that they have already studied words like these. Ask them to read the words. Remind them that *think* is a base word and *thinking* is the base word with the ending *-ing*. Explain that today they will learn how to read and spell words with the ending *-er* or *-est*.
2. **Use Sound-Spelling Cards** Display Card 123. Point to *taller*. *Taller* is made up of the base word *tall* and the ending *-er*. We use *-er* to compare two things. Have children say each word part several times as you point to it. Then have them say the whole word. Display Card 125. Point to *smallest*. *Smallest* is made up of the base word *small* and the ending *-est*. We use *-est* to compare three or more things. Have children say each word part several times as you point to it. Then have them say the whole word.
3. **Model** Write *faster*. *Faster* is the base word *fast* with the *-er* ending. *Faster* means "more fast than something else." Write *fastest*. *Fastest* is the base word *fast* with the *-est* ending. *Fastest* means "the most fast of three or more things." When I see a long word, it might be a base word and ending. First, I look for the base word and ending: *fast, -est*. Then I read them together as one word: *fastest*.
4. **Guide Practice** Have children read *faster* and *fastest* with you. Write the words below. Identify the base word and ending in each word. Then have the group read the words with you.

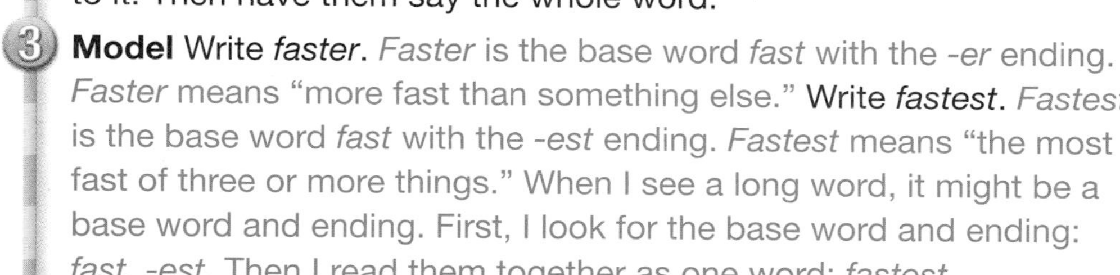

thicker	**thickest**	**bigger**	**biggest**
smarter	**smartest**	**thinner**	**thinnest**

5. **Review** What do you know about reading these words? (You put the base word and ending together. The *-er* ending tells you that two things are being compared. The *-est* ending tells you that three or more things are being compared.)

Routines Flip Chart

Differentiated Instruction

Strategic Intervention

Visual Support Draw two different-sized squares. Ask: Which is bigger? After children identify the bigger one, write *bigger* in it. Have children find the base word and ending and say each part separately as you point to it. Then have them say the whole word. Repeat this process with other words that have the *-er* or *-est* ending.

Spelling Patterns

Endings *-er* and *-est*
Sometimes the final consonant of a base word is doubled when an ending such as *-er* or *-est* is added, as in *bigger* and *thinnest*.

English Language Learners

Pronounce *-er* In Spanish, *-er* is pronounced like *air* in English, so Spanish speakers may pronounce a word like *faster* as *fastair*. Give children extra practice in saying words with the ending *-er*, such as *colder, deeper*, and *longer*.

Objectives

- Read words with comparative endings *-er* and *-est.*
- Decode words in context and isolation.

Check Word Reading
SUCCESS PREDICTOR

Phonics—Build Fluency
Comparative Endings *-er, -est*

Model

Envision It!

Have children turn to page 186 in their Student Edition. Look at the pictures on this page. The word in the first picture is *taller*. When I say *taller*, I hear the base word *tall* and the ending *-er*. The word in the second picture is *smallest*. When I say *smallest*, I hear the base word *small* and the ending *-est.*

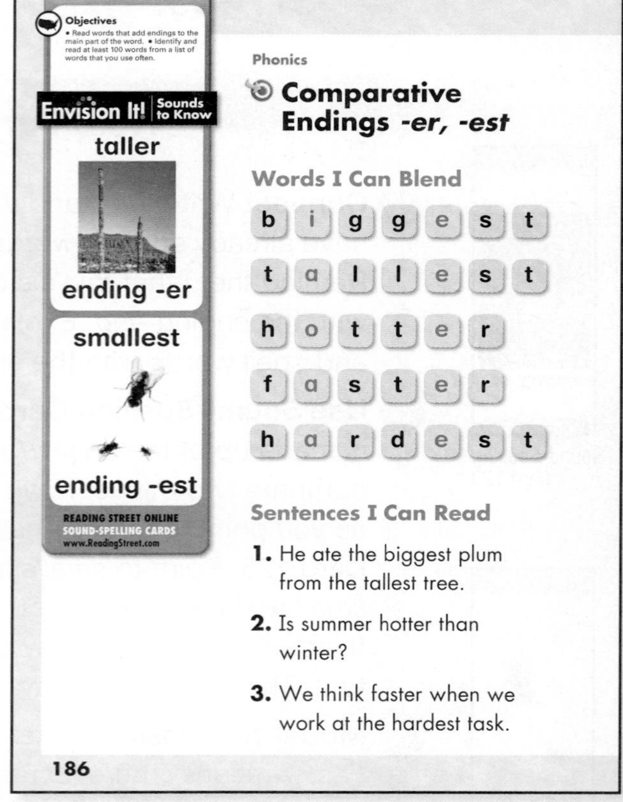

Student Edition p. 186

Guide practice

For each word in "Words I Can Blend," have children find the base word and ending. Make sure they pronounce each word part correctly. Then have children blend the two word parts.

Corrective feedback

If... children have difficulty blending a word,
then... model blending the word, and then ask children to blend it with you.

Blend and Read

Decode words in isolation

After children can successfully segment and blend the words, point to words in random order and ask children to read them naturally.

Decode words in context

Have children read each of the sentences. Have them identify words in the sentences that have the ending *-er* or *-est*.

Team Talk Pair children and have them take turns reading each of the sentences aloud.

On their own

Use *Reader's and Writer's Notebook* p. 393.

Name
Where Are My Friends?
Circle the word for each picture.
small smaller smallest
1. faster fastest
2. bigger biggest
3. taller tallest
4. sweeter sweetest
5. thicker thickest
6. thinner thinnest
Write -er or -est to finish the word in each sentence.
7. The little bird has the few est eggs.
8. The little bird has a long er tail than the big bird.

Reader's and Writer's Notebook p. 393

Don't Wait Until Friday

MONITOR PROGRESS — Check Word Reading: Comparative Endings *-er, -est*

Write the following words and have the class read them. Notice which words children miss during the group reading. Call on individuals to read some of the words.

fewer	**sweeter**	**newest**	**firmest**	**shorter**	
smaller	**taller**	**smallest**	**stalled**	**tallest**	← Spiral Review: Row 2 reviews the sound of *a* in *ball*.
bigger	**hottest**	**skipped**	**thinnest**	**trotting**	← Row 3 reviews doubling the final consonant before endings.

If... children cannot blend *-er* and *-est* words at this point,
then... use the Small-Group Time Strategic Intervention lesson, p. DI•106, to reteach words with *-er* and *-est*. Continue to monitor children's progress using other instructional opportunities during the week. See the Skills Trace on p. 184–185.

Day 1	Day 2	Day 3	Day 4	Day 5
Check Word Reading	Check Word Reading	Check High-Frequency Words/Retelling	Check Fluency	Check Oral Vocabulary

Success Predictor

Differentiated Instruction

Advanced

Extend Blending Provide children who can segment and blend all the words correctly with more challenging words such as: *looser, brighter, cleanest, happiest, bravest, tightest, plainest.*

ELL

English Language Learners

Comparative Forms In Spanish, Korean, and Hmong, comparisons are expressed with phrases rather than with adjectives that change form. In Spanish, for example, *slow/slower/slowest* becomes *lento/más lento/el más lento* (or *lenta* for feminine singular nouns). To provide extra practice with forming comparative adjectives, have children compare the sizes of objects in the classroom, using first their home language and then English.

Objectives

- Apply knowledge of sound-spellings to decode unknown words when reading.
- Decode and read words in context and isolation.
- Practice fluency with oral rereading.

Decodable Practice Reader 18A

Comparative Endings *-er, -est*

Decode words in isolation

Have children turn to page 265. Have children decode each word.

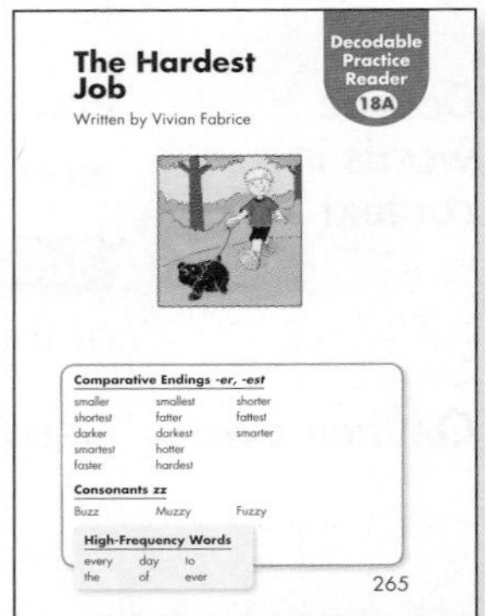

The Hardest Job

Written by Vivian Fabrice

Decodable Practice Reader 18A

Comparative Endings *-er, -est*

smaller smallest shorter
shortest fatter fattest
darker darkest smarter
smartest hotter
faster hardest

Consonants zz

Buzz Muzzy Fuzzy

High-Frequency Words

every day to
the of ever

265

Decodable Practice Reader 18A

Review High-frequency words

Review the previously taught words *every, day, to, the, of,* and *ever*. Have children read each word as you point to it on the Word Wall.

Preview Decodable Reader

Have children read the title and preview the story. Tell them they will read words that have the *-er* or *-est* ending.

Decode words in context

Pair children for reading and listen as they decode. One child begins. Children read the entire story, switching readers after each page. Partners reread the story. This time the other child begins.

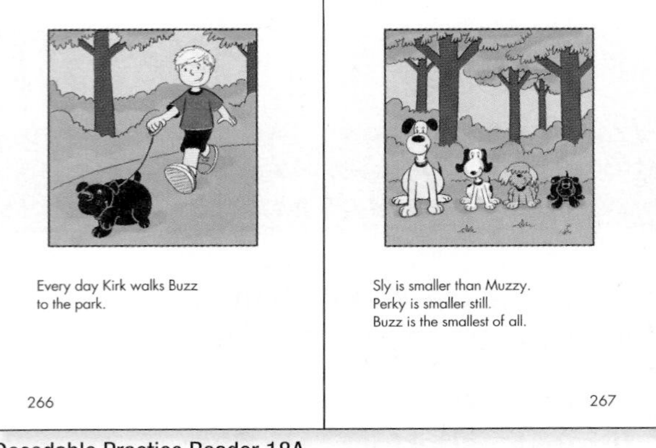

Every day Kirk walks Buzz to the park.

266

Sly is smaller than Muzzy.
Perky is smaller still.
Buzz is the smallest of all.

267

Decodable Practice Reader 18A

Ike is shorter than Lark.
Tig is shorter still.
Buzz is the shortest of all.

268

Wink is fatter than Pal.
Curly is fatter still.
Buzz is the fattest of all.

269

Dee is darker than Ruff.
Sport is darker still.
Buzz is the darkest of all.

270

Fuzzy is smarter than King.
Jinks is smarter still.
Buzz is the smartest of all.

271

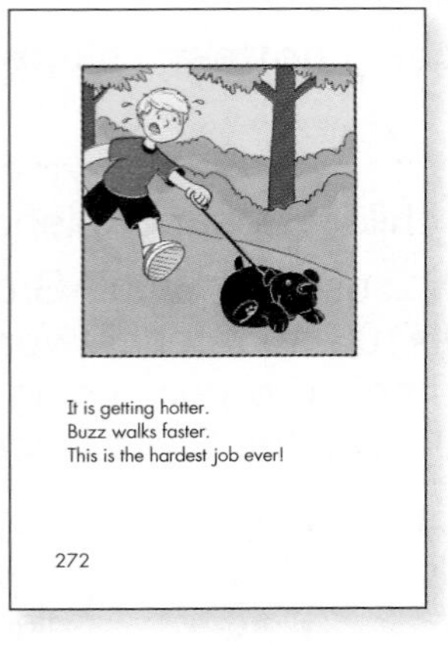

It is getting hotter.
Buzz walks faster.
This is the hardest job ever!

272

Corrective feedback

If... children have difficulty decoding a word, **then...** refer them to the Sound-Spelling Cards to identify the sounds in the word. Then prompt them to blend the word.

- What is the new word?
- Is the new word a word you know?
- Does it make sense in the story?

Check decoding and comprehension

Have children retell the story to include characters, setting, and events. Then have children find words with *-er* and *-est* endings in the story. Children should supply *smaller, smallest, shorter, shortest, fatter, fattest, darker, darkest, smarter, smartest, hotter, faster,* and *hardest*.

Reread for Fluency

Have children reread Decodable Practice Reader 18A to develop automaticity decoding words with the *-er* or *-est* ending.

ROUTINE Oral Rereading

1. **Read** Have children read the entire book orally.
2. **Reread** To achieve optimal fluency, children should reread the text three or four times.
3. **Corrective Feedback** Listen as children read. Provide corrective feedback regarding their fluency and decoding.

Routines Flip Chart

Differentiated Instruction

 Advanced

Extend Comprehension If children are able to read the story fluently, have them draw pictures of three animals of different sizes and colors. Have children name the animals and write sentences comparing them to each other, using comparative words from the story such as *shorter, tallest*, and *darker*. Then have children share their pictures and read their sentences to the class.

ELL

English Language Learners

Comparative Endings *-er, -est*

Beginning/Early Intermediate Write several *-er* and *-est* words from the book on the board. Underline the ending in each word. Say each word aloud, clapping your hands for each syllable. Have children repeat after you.

Intermediate Write the headings *-er* and *-est* on the board. Have children write the *-er* and *-est* words from the book under the correct heading.

Early Advanced/Advanced Have children use the pictures in the book to make up their own sentences about the dogs. Have them use the words *longer, longest, thicker, thickest, thinner,* and *thinnest*.

Objectives

- Spell words with endings *-er, -est.*
- Read high-frequency words.

Spelling Pretest
Comparative Endings *-er, -est*

Dictate spelling words

Dictate the spelling words and read the sentences. Have children write the words. If needed, segment the words for children, clarify the pronunciations, and give meanings of words. Have children check their pretests and correct misspelled words.

1. faster	Ann can run **faster** than her younger brother.
2. fastest	The **fastest** way to travel is by plane.
3. taller	An elephant is **taller** than a horse.
4. tallest	The giraffe is the **tallest** animal in the world.
5. shorter*	Jack is **shorter** than his older sister.
6. shortest	The **shortest** poem in the book is four lines.
7. sadder	Are you **sadder** on rainy days than on sunny days?
8. saddest*	I felt the **saddest** when my best friend moved.
9. bigger	My dog is **bigger** than my cat.
10. biggest	My dog is the **biggest** dog on our block.

* Words marked with asterisks come from the selection *Where Are My Animal Friends?*

Let's Practice It! TR DVD•166

On their own

Use Let's Practice It! p. 166 on the *Teacher Resource DVD-ROM.*

Small Group Time

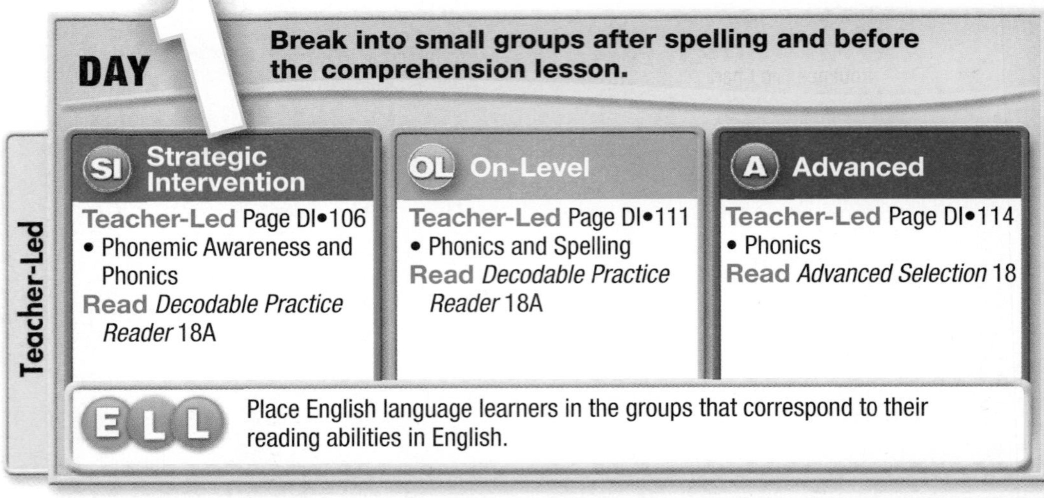

Practice Stations
- Listen Up
- Word Work

Independent Activities
- Read independently/Reading Log on *Reader's and Writer's Notebook* p. RR4
- Concept Talk Video

High-Frequency Words

ROUTINE Nondecodable Words

Introduce

1. **Say and Spell** Look at p. 187. Some words we have to learn by remembering the letters rather than saying the sounds. We will say and spell the words to help learn them. Point to the first word. This word is *does*. The letters in *does* are d-o-e-s, *does*. Have children say and spell each word, first with you, and then without you.
2. **Identify Familiar Letter-Sounds** Point to the first letter in *does*. You know the sound for this letter. What is this letter and what is its sound? (d, /d/)
3. **Demonstrate Meaning** Tell me a sentence using the word *does*. Repeat this routine with the other Words I Can Read.

Routines Flip Chart

Read words in isolation Have children read the words on p. 187 aloud. Add the words to the Word Wall.

Read words in context Have children read the sentences aloud. Have them identify this week's High-Frequency Words in the sentences.

On their own Use *Reader's and Writer's Notebook* p. 394.

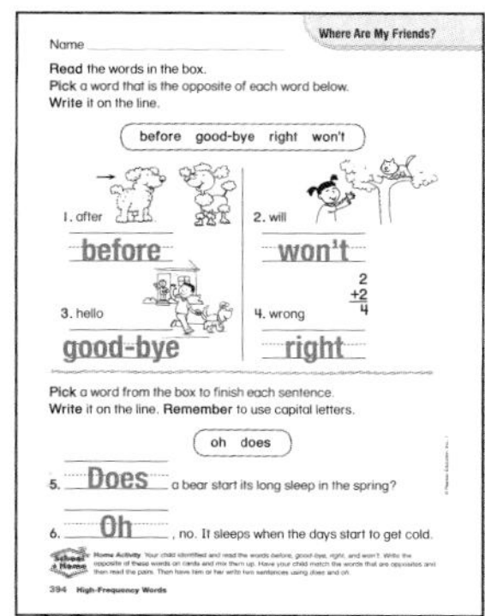
Name

Where Are My Friends?

Read the words in the box.
Pick a word that is the opposite of each word below.
Write it on the line.

before good-bye right won't

1. after before
2. will won't
3. hello good-bye
4. wrong right

Pick a word from the box to finish each sentence.
Write it on the line. Remember to use capital letters.

oh does

5. Does a bear start its long sleep in the spring?
6. Oh, no. It sleeps when the days start to get cold.

394 High-Frequency Words

Reader's and Writer's Notebook p. 394

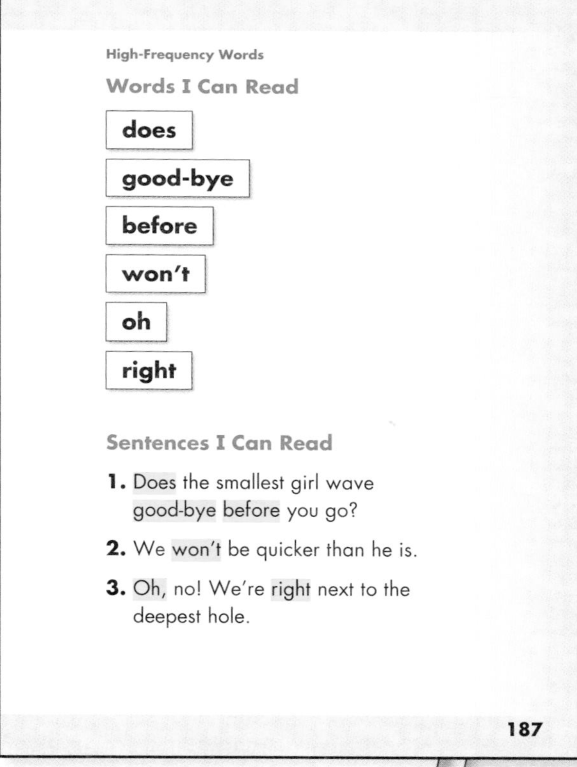
High-Frequency Words

Words I Can Read

does

good-bye

before

won't

oh

right

Sentences I Can Read

1. Does the smallest girl wave good-bye before you go?
2. We won't be quicker than he is.
3. Oh, no! We're right next to the deepest hole.

187

Student Edition p. 187

Differentiated Instruction

Advanced

Extend Spelling Challenge children who spell words correctly to spell more difficult words such as: *steeper, steepest, gladder, gladdest, kinder,* and *kindest.*

Phonics/Spelling Generalization

Each spelling word has the letters *-er* or *-est*.

English Language Learners

Words with *-er* Remind children that when we add the *-er* ending to a base word, we are comparing two things. For example: *A cat is fast, but a cheetah is **faster**.*

Frontload Read Aloud Use the modified Read Aloud in the ELL Support pages to prepare children to listen to "Home Sweet Home" (page 187b).

Objectives

◎ Draw conclusions about a story.

Skills Trace

◎ **Draw Conclusions**

Introduce U3W6D1; U4W1D1; U5W2D1

Practice U3W6D2; U3W6D3; U3W6D4; U4W1D2; U4W1D3; U4W1D4; U5W2D2; U5W2D3; U5W2D4

Reteach/Review U3W6D5; U4W1D5; U4W2D2; U4W5D2; U5W2D5

Assess/Test Weekly Tests U3W6; U4W1; U5W2

Benchmark Tests U3

KEY:

U=Unit W=Week D=Day

Listening Comprehension

◎ Draw Conclusions

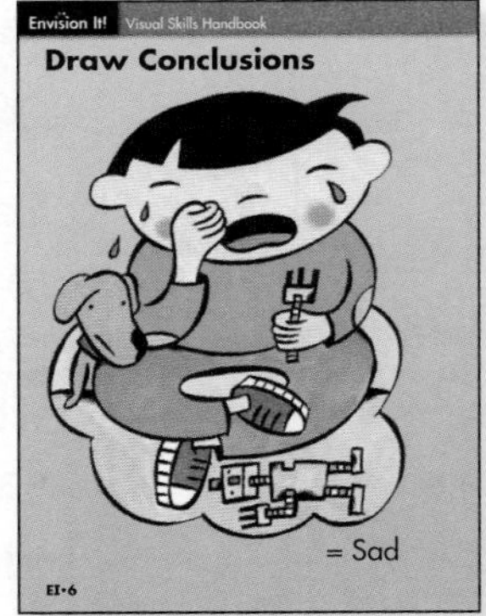

Student Edition EI•6

Introduce Authors don't explain everything that happens in a story. They let us use what we have read and what we know from real life to figure some things out for ourselves. This is called **drawing conclusions**. Good readers and listeners pay careful attention so they can draw the right conclusions.

Envision It!

Have children turn to page EI•6 in their Student Edition. These pictures give some details about what happened. Discuss these questions using the pictures:

- What conclusion can you draw from this picture about who the story is about? (It's about a boy playing with his toys.)
- What can we figure out by looking at the picture? What conclusions can we determine? (The boy was playing with one of his toys and it broke.)

Model Today we will read a story about a robin who must leave her nest. Read "Home Sweet Home" and model how to draw a conclusion.

As I read, I figure some things out for myself by using what I read and what I know from real life. In "Home Sweet Home," I read that Robin did not want to go away with Hummingbird. But the author didn't tell me why, so I had to figure that out myself. I knew from the story that Robin had a very nice nest, and I knew from real life that people and animals are often sad to move way from their home. So I drew the conclusion that Robin wanted to stay because she loved her home and would be sad to leave.

Guide practice After reading, remind children that Hummingbird said life would become hard for Robin if she stayed. What details in the story helped you draw conclusions about what Hummingbird meant? (Leaves were falling and some birds were migrating. This meant winter was coming.) What did you already know about winter and birds that helped you draw conclusions about why life would be hard? (Possible response: In winter, some birds can't keep themselves warm or find enough food.)

On their own Use *Reader's and Writer's Notebook* p. 395.

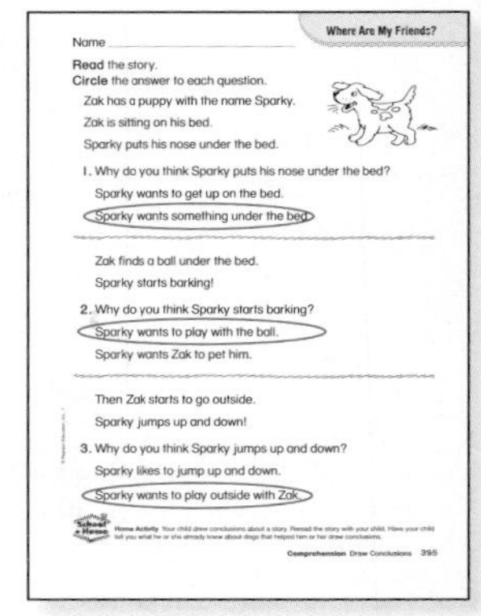

Reader's and Writer's Notebook p. 395

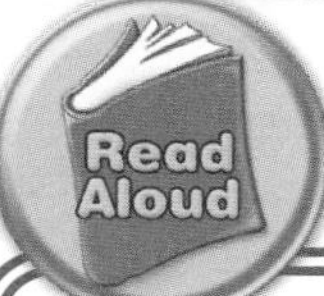

Home Sweet Home

Robin lived in the north. She had a lovely, comfortable nest, which she had made herself, and plenty of insects to eat.

Then one day, Robin noticed that leaves were falling from the trees. Many of her friends were flying away. "Where is everyone going?" Robin asked Hummingbird, who was older and wiser.

"Everyone has decided to migrate," Hummingbird explained. "They are all flying south, where it is warmer. We should leave, too."

"No, no!" Robin said. "I don't want to leave!"

"You must come with me," said Hummingbird. "Life will become very hard for you if you stay. We will build new nests in the south."

So Robin flew south with Hummingbird. When they got to a nice, warm place, they began to build their nests. First, they gathered twigs and stems. Then they wove the twigs and stems together into nests that were round and roomy! Last, they put grass and leaves inside their nests to make them soft and comfortable.

Robin hopped inside her nest. "I love my new home," she said to Hummingbird. "I think I could live here forever!"

Hummingbird laughed. "You can enjoy your new home for now. But in a few months, it will be time to fly back north and build new homes once again."

Academic Vocabulary

draw conclusions to figure out more about what happens in a story by using what you have read and what you know from real life

Objectives

- Use contractions with *not* in sentences.
- Understand and recognize the features of a play scene.

MINI-LESSON

5 Day Planner
Guide to Mini-Lessons

DAY 1	• Read Like a Writer
DAY 2	• Sentences
DAY 3	• Strong Verbs
DAY 4	• Revise: Rearranging Sentences
DAY 5	• Proofread for Contractions with *Not*

Conventions
Contractions with *Not*

Model

Explain that a **contraction** is a way of writing two words as one. *Didn't, isn't,* and *hasn't* are contractions. Write them, and explain that an **apostrophe** is used in place of the letters that have been left out.

Display Grammar Transparency 18. Read the definition aloud. Model combining the two words in each example to form a contraction. Then read the directions and model number 1.

- *Does* and *not* can be put together to form a contraction.
- I will put an apostrophe where the letter *o* used to be in *not*. I will write the contraction *doesn't* on the line.

Contractions with Not

A **contraction** is a short way to put two words together. A **verb** and the word **not** can be put together to make a contraction. An **apostrophe** (') is used in place of one or more missing letters.

are + not = aren't	has + not = hasn't
did + not = didn't	is + not = isn't
do + not = don't	was + not = wasn't
does + not = doesn't	can + not = can't

Write the contraction for the underlined words.

1. A bear <u>does not</u> wake up all winter. doesn't
2. Squirrels <u>do not</u> sleep through the winter. don't
3. The hummingbird <u>did not</u> wait for winter. didn't
4. The geese <u>are not</u> flying south yet. aren't
5. The butterfly <u>is not</u> coming out until spring. isn't

Unit 3 Where Are My Animal Friends? Grammar 18

Grammar Transparency 18
TR DVD

Guide practice

Continue with items 2–5, having children identify the contraction that is formed and the letter that is replaced by an apostrophe.

Connect to oral language

Have the class revise these sentences orally by substituting a contraction for the underlined words.

This <u>is not</u> my hat.

I <u>do not</u> see that girl.

We <u>are not</u> going on the bus. ________.

On their own

Team Talk List *does not, do not, did not, are not,* and *is not* on the board. Have partners take turns putting each word pair together orally to form a contraction. Then have them use the contraction in a sentence.

Writing—Play Scene
Introduce

MINI-LESSON

Read Like a Writer

- **Introduce** This week you will write a play scene. A play scene is written for actors to say aloud for an audience. Each character has lines to say.

Prompt Think about Raccoon and Squirrel in *Where Are My Animal Friends?* What would they say if they could call Goose on a phone? Write a play scene showing what they would say.

Trait Sentences

Mode Narrative

- **Examine Model Text** Let's listen to a play scene. Track the print as you read aloud the play scene on *Reader's and Writer's Notebook* p. 396. Have children follow along.

INTERACT with TEXT

Where Are My Friends?

· Play Scene

A Friendly Phone Call

Goose: Hello?
Raccoon: Hi, Goose! How are you?
Squirrel: We wish you were here!
Goose: I miss my friends. But I can't stand the cold.
Raccoon: It sure is cold here. We went ice skating.
Goose: I went fishing today.
Squirrel: When will you come home?
Goose: I will be back in spring.
Raccoon: We can't wait!
Squirrel: 'Bye, Goose.

Key Features of a Play Scene
- is written to be acted for an audience
- characters have lines to say

396 Writing Play Scene

Reader's and Writer's Notebook p. 396

- **Key Features** Who are the characters in this play scene? (Raccoon, Squirrel, and Goose) Help children find and circle the names. Ask children to describe what happens. Help children understand that Raccoon, Squirrel, and Goose are talking on the phone.

This play scene has three characters. Each character has lines to speak.

The play scene is written for actors to say lines aloud to an audience. Actors would pretend to be talking on the phone in this scene.

Write Guy *Jeff Anderson*

Let's Use Books

Let's use books to solve problems! If a child wants to write dialogue, she can look at how the author of a recently read story wrote dialogue. Have the child ask herself, "What do I like about how these characters speak?" Young writers need models—and the books in your classroom are brimming with lessons to learn.

Academic Vocabulary

contraction a short way of writing two words as one

Daily Fix-It

1. The bigest burd said good-bye first.
   The biggest bird said good-bye first.
2. It was the sadest day?
   It was the saddest day.

Discuss the Daily Fix-It corrections with children. Review sentence punctuation, the spelling of the *r*-controlled vowel in *bird,* and the use of double consonants in superlatives.

English Language Learners

Conventions To provide children with practice on contractions with *not,* use the modified grammar lessons in the *ELL Handbook.*

Objectives

- Understand and recognize the features of a play scene.
- Develop an understanding of sentences in a play scene.
- Identify a topic connected to this week's concept.
- Narrow the focus of the topic by formulating inquiry questions related to the topic.
- Explore changes in nature.

Writing—Play Scene
Introduce, continued

Review key features Review key features of a play scene with children. You may want to post these key features in the classroom to allow children to refer to them as they work on their play scenes.

Key Features of Play Scenes

- is written to be acted for an audience
- characters have lines to say

Connect to familiar texts Use examples from children's favorite television shows or movies. Explain that the actors in these works have lines to say. The lines are written down in a scene. Then the actors memorize these lines. Then they act out the scene in front of a camera.

Look ahead Tell children that tomorrow they will plan their own play scenes.

ROUTINE Quick Write for Fluency **Team Talk**

1. **Talk** Read these questions aloud, and have children respond with answers that use contractions with *not.*
   Why can't you stay for dinner?
   Who doesn't like vegetables?

2. **Write** Have children write short sentences to answer the questions. Make sure their sentences include a contraction with *not.*

3. **Share** Partners can read their answers to one another.

Routines Flip Chart

Research and Inquiry
Identify and Focus Topic

Teach Display and review the concept map that explores this week's question: *What do animals do when the seasons change?* What do people do when the seasons change? Ask children to share their ideas.

Model Think Aloud: First think about what you do when the seasons change. Here are some questions that might help get you started. What do you do when it gets colder? (I wear warmer clothes; my family turns on the heat in our home) What activities do you like to do in the summer? (go on vacation with my family, ride my bike; go to the beach; go to a fair or amusement park)

Guide practice Have children think of their own answers to the question and then record them in a chart.

Spring	Summer	Fall	Winter
Ride my bike	Vacation with my family	Rake leaves	Celebrate holidays

Wrap Up Your Day

- ✔ **Phonics: Comparative Endings *-er, -est*** Write *smaller* and *tallest.* Ask children what the base word is in each case. (The base word in *smaller* is *small* and in *tallest* is *tall.*)
- ✔ **Spelling: Words with *-er, -est*** Have children name the letter that spells each sound in *sadder*. Write the spelling as children write the letters in the air. Continue with *biggest, fastest,* and *shorter.*
- ✔ **Build Concepts** Ask children to recall what happened in the Read Aloud, "Home Sweet Home." What do the birds have to do in the fall? (The birds have to fly where it's warmer and build new nests.)
- ✔ **Homework** Send home this week's Family Times Newsletter from Let's Practice It! pp. 161–162 on the *Teacher Resource DVD-ROM.*

Let's Practice It!
TR DVD•161–162

Differentiated Instruction

SI Strategic Intervention

Selecting a Topic If children have trouble thinking of what people do when the seasons change, remind them of what the seasons are and give them a few key words and phrases that describe each season. For example, you may say for summer, *hot weather, school's not in session.* From there, they can think about what they and others do during the summer. Try this for each season.

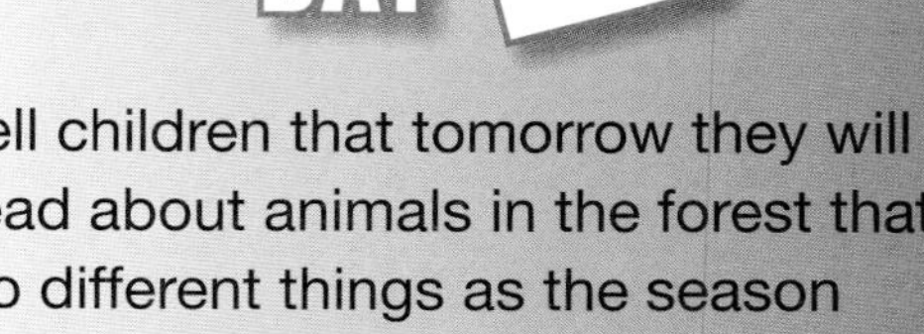
Tell children that tomorrow they will read about animals in the forest that do different things as the season changes.

Objectives

- Discuss the concept to develop oral vocabulary.
- Build oral vocabulary.

Today at a Glance

Oral Vocabulary
autumn

Phonemic Awareness
Segment and Blend Phonemes

Phonics and Spelling
◉ Comparative Endings *-er, -est*
◉ Consonant Pattern *-dge*

Fluency
Paired Reading

High-Frequency Words

Story Words
spring, warm, goose, raccoon, butterfly

Comprehension
◉ Draw Conclusions
◉ Background Knowledge

Vocabulary
Context Clues

Conventions
Contractions with *not*

Writing
Play Scene

Handwriting
Letter *J* and *j*; Letter Slant

Research and Inquiry
Research Skill: Picture Graph

Concept Talk

Question of the Week

What do animals do when the seasons change?

Build concepts

To reinforce concepts and to focus children's attention, have children sing "Animals All Know" from the *Sing with Me* Big Book. What different things do the animals do when winter arrives? (Some hibernate, or sleep all winter; some migrate to a warmer place.)

Sing with Me Big Book Audio

Introduce Amazing Words

Display the Big Book, *What Makes the Seasons?* Read the title and identify the author. Explain that, in the story, the author uses the word *autumn*. Have children listen to the story to find out what the weather is like in the season called autumn.

Use the Oral Vocabulary routine on the next page to teach the word *autumn*.

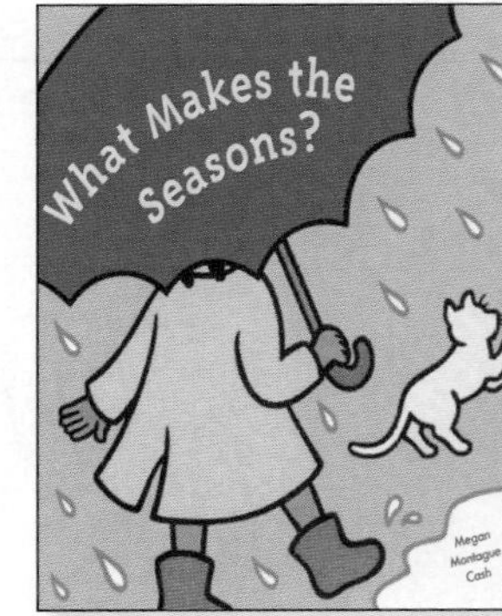

Big Book

ELL Reinforce Vocabulary Use the Day 2 instruction on ELL Poster 18 to reinforce meanings of high-frequency words.

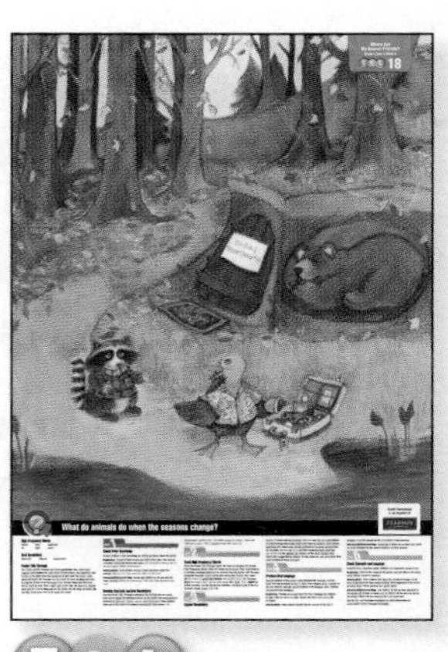
ELL Poster 18

Oral Vocabulary
Amazing Words

Teach Amazing Words

Amazing Words Oral Vocabulary Routine

1. **Introduce the Word** Relate the word *autumn* to the book. *Autumn* is the season that follows summer, when the weather grows cool. Supply a child-friendly definition. *Autumn* is the season between summer and winter. Have children say the word.
2. **Demonstrate** Provide examples to show meaning. In *autumn*, the leaves change color from green to red and gold. Another word for *autumn* is "fall." Thanksgiving is an *autumn* holiday.
3. **Apply** Have children demonstrate their understanding. How do the trees change in autumn where you live? What activities do you enjoy doing in autumn?

Routine Flip Chart

Anchored Talk

Add to the concept map

Discuss why animals do different things in different seasons.

- What happens to the temperature outside in winter? (It gets low; the weather gets cold.)
- In our Read Aloud story from yesterday, "Home Sweet Home," why did Robin and Hummingbird have to migrate south? (Food was getting hard to find in the cold weather.) Let's add *Food gets hard to find* to the Winter box of our chart.
- What will Robin and Hummingbird do in the spring? (They will migrate back north because winter will be over there.) Let's add *Birds migrate by flying north* to the Spring box of our chart.

Amazing Words

hibernate	freeze
migrate	bitterly
temperature	weary
autumn	

Differentiated Instruction

SI Strategic Intervention

Vocabulary Support Help children practice naming the seasons by playing a question-and-answer game, using questions such as *In what season does school begin? What is the hottest season? When do the trees grow new leaves?* When the answer is *autumn* or *fall*, have them use both words.

English Language Learners

Visual Learning Have children draw a picture of something they like to do outdoors in each season. Have them label each picture with the name of the season.

Objectives

- Segment and blend words with consonant pattern *-dge.*
- ◎ Associate the sound /j/ with *-dge.*
- ◎ Blend and read words with consonant pattern *-dge.*

Skills Trace

◎ **Consonant Pattern *–dge***

Introduce U3W6D2
Practice U3W6D3; U3W6D4
Reteach/Review U3W6D5; U4W1D4
Assess/Test Weekly Test U3W6
Benchmark Test U3

KEY:
U=Unit W=Week D=Day

Phonemic Awareness
Segment and Blend Phonemes

Model isolating sounds Have children look at the picture on pages 184–185 in their Student Edition. They are building a *bridge* over the river. In the word *bridge*, I hear four sounds. The first sound I hear is /b/. The second sound is /r/. The third sound is /i/. The last sound I hear in *bridge* is /j/.

Student Edition pp. 184–185

Model segmenting and blending Listen to the sounds in the word *smudge*: /s/ /m/ /u/ /j/. There are four sounds in *smudge*. Let's blend those sounds to make a word: /s/ /m/ /u/ /j/, *smudge*. Continue modeling with *hedge*.

Guide practice Guide children as they segment and blend these words from the picture: *judge, badge, edge, lodge, badger,* and *hedgehog*.

Corrective feedback **If...** children make an error,
then... model by segmenting the word, and have them repeat the segmenting and blending of the word.

On their own Have children segment and blend the following words.

/l/ /e/ /j/ **ledge**	/f/ /u/ /j/ **fudge**
/r/ /i/ /j/ **ridge**	/b/ /r/ /i/ /j/ **bridge**
/b/ /u/ /j/ **budge**	/p/ /l/ /e/ /j/ **pledge**

Phonics—Teach/Model

Consonant Pattern *-dge*

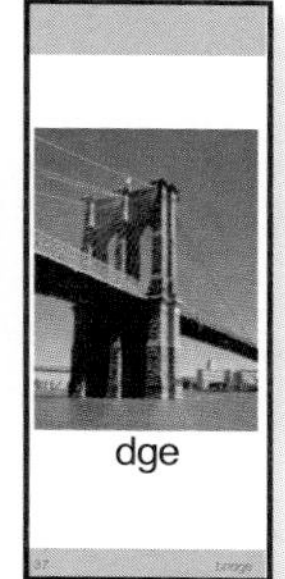

Sound-Spelling Card 37

ROUTINE **Blending Strategy**

1. **Connect** Write the words *gem* and *ginger*. You studied words like these already. What sound is spelled by the letter *g* in these words? (/j/) Today you will learn how to read and spell words with the /j/ sound spelled *-dge*.
2. **Use Sound-Spelling Cards** Display Card 37. Point to *dge*. The sound you hear at the end of *bridge* is /j/. The sound /j/ can be spelled *-dge*. Have children say /j/ several times as you point to *-dge*.
3. **Model** Write *lodge*. In this word, the letters *-dge* stand for the sound /j/. This is how I blend this word. Segment and blend *lodge*. Follow this procedure to model blending *judge* and *ledge*.
4. **Guide Practice** Continue the process in step 3. This time have children blend with you.

ridge	**edge**	**judge**	**pledge**	**sludge**	**ledge**
fudge	**Madge**	**hedge**	**budge**	**lodge**	**grudge**

5. **Review** What do you know about reading these words? (The letters *-dge* spell the sound /j/.)

Routines Flip Chart

Differentiated Instruction

 Advanced

Longer *-dge* Words Write the following words on the board and have children practice reading them: *gadget, fidget, drudgery, ledger, budget, porridge,* and *knowledge*. Have children write the words on cards and underline the letters that stand for /j/. Discuss the meanings of unfamiliar words. Then have partners use several of the words in sentences.

Vocabulary Support

You may wish to explain the meaning of these words.

budge to move a little

grudge a feeling of anger toward someone that lasts for a long time

hedge a row of bushes planted close together to form a fence

pledge to promise

sludge mud or mud-like material

English Language Learners

Visual Support Model isolating sounds while using the pictures on pp. 184–185 of the Student Edition as visual support. For example: /l/ /o/ /j/, *lodge*. Who can point to the beaver lodge? Now let's say the sounds of *lodge* together: /l/ /o/ /j/.

Objectives

- ◎ Blend and read word with consonant pattern *-dge.*
- Associate the sound /j/ with *-dge.*
- Decode words in context and in isolation.

Check Word Reading
SUCCESS PREDICTOR

Phonics—Build Fluency
◎ Consonant Pattern *-dge*

Model

Envision It!

Have children turn to page 188 in their Student Edition. Look at the picture of the bridge on this page. The word in the picture is *bridge*. When I say the word *bridge*, I hear the /j/ sound. In *bridge*, the /j/ sound is spelled *-dge*.

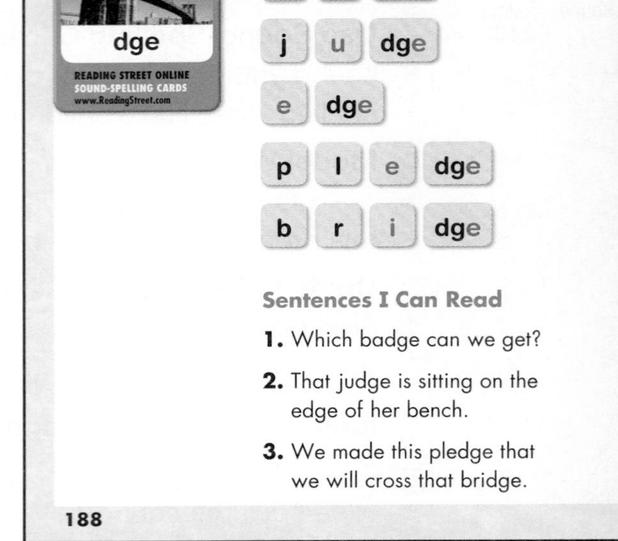

Student Edition p. 188

Guide practice

For each word in "Words I Can Blend," ask for the sound of each letter or group of letters. Make sure that children identify the correct sound for *-dge*. Then have children blend the whole word.

Corrective feedback

If... children have difficulty blending a word,
then... model blending the word, and ask children to blend it with you.

Blend and Read

Decode words in isolation

After children can successfully segment and blend the words, ask them to read the words naturally.

Decode words in context

Have children read each of the sentences. Have them identify words with the /j/ sound spelled *dge*.

Team Talk Pair children and have them take turns reading each of the sentences aloud.

On their own

Use *Reader's and Writer's Notebook* p. 397.

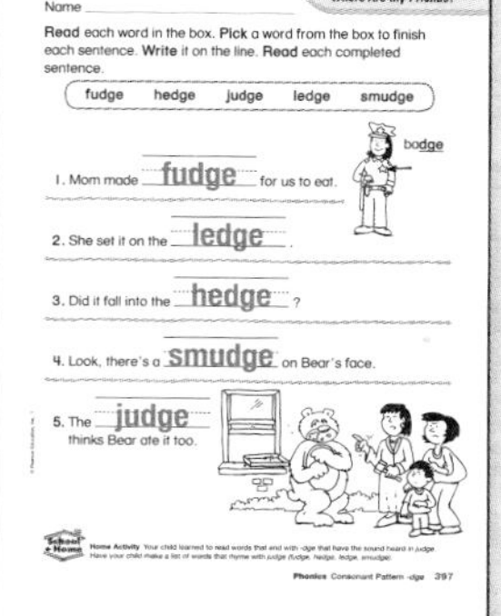
Where Are My Friends?

Name ______

Read each word in the box. **Pick** a word from the box to finish each sentence. **Write** it on the line. **Read** each completed sentence.

fudge hedge judge ledge smudge

badge

1. Mom made fudge for us to eat.
2. She set it on the ledge.
3. Did it fall into the hedge?
4. Look, there's a smudge on Bear's face.
5. The judge thinks Bear ate it too.

Phonics Consonant Pattern -dge 397

Reader's and Writer's Notebook p. 397

MONITOR PROGRESS

Check Word Reading Consonant Pattern *-dge*

Write the following words and have the class read them. Notice which children miss words during the group reading. Call on those individuals to read some of the words.

judge	**lodge**	**pledge**	**bridge**	**smudge**	Spiral Review
gem	**ridge**	**page**	**nudge**	**large** ←	Row 2 contrasts /j/ *dge* words with /j/ *g* words.
game	**fudge**	**gate**	**porridge**	**ginger** ←	Row 3 contrasts /j/ *dge* words with /j/ *g* and /g/ *g* words.

If... children cannot blend words with /j/ spelled *dge*,

then... use the Small Group Time Strategic Intervention lesson, p. DI•107, to reteach words with /j/ spelled *dge*. Continue to monitor children's progress using other instructional opportunities during the week. See the Skills Trace on p. 182c.

Day 1	Day 2	Day 3	Day 4	Day 5
Check Word Reading	Check Word Reading	Check High-Frequency Words/Retelling	Check Fluency	Check Oral Vocabulary

Spelling Patterns

Consonant Pattern The sound /j/ may be spelled *dge* at the end of a word.

English Language Learners

Pronounce /j/ French, Hmong, and Spanish do not have the /j/ sound heard in words such as *edge* and *badge*. Provide additional practice saying and writing words with *dge*.

Objectives

- Apply knowledge of sound-spellings to decode unknown words when reading.
- Decode and read words in context and isolation.
- Practice fluency with oral rereading.

Decodable Practice Reader 18B

Consonant Pattern *-dge*

Decode words in isolation

Have children turn to page 273. Have children decode each word.

Review High-frequency words

Review the previously taught words *find, of, said, see, I, where,* and *your*. Have children read each word as you point to it on the Word Wall.

Preview

Have children read the title and preview the story. Tell them they will read words that have the /j/ sound spelled *dge*.

Decode words in context

Pair children for reading and listen as they decode. One child begins. Children read the entire story, switching readers after each page.

Where Is My Badge?
Written by Erik Perez
Decodable Practice Reader 18B

Consonant Pattern -dge
badge Madge
ledge edge

Word Family -ink
think pink
wink

High-Frequency Words
said to where your I
the of find a see

273

Decodable Practice Reader 18B

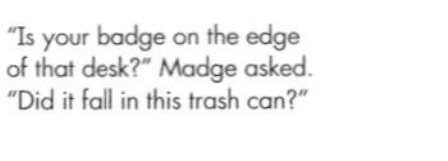

Decodable Practice Reader 18B

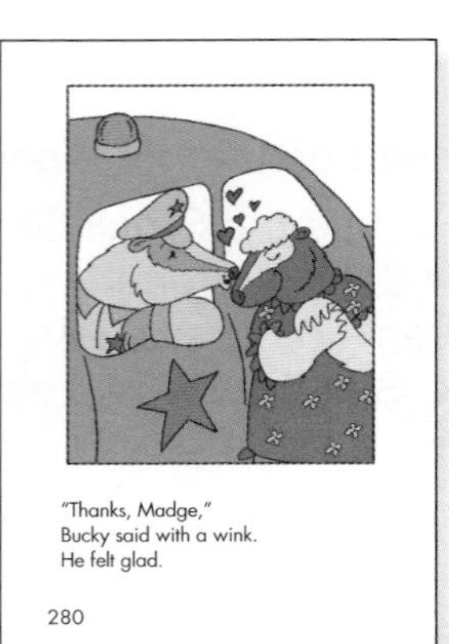

Corrective feedback

If... children have difficulty decoding a word, **then...** refer them to the Sound-Spelling Cards to identify the sounds in the word. Then prompt them to blend the word.

- What is the new word?
- Is the new word a word you know?
- Does it make sense in the story?

Check decoding and comprehension

Have children retell the story to include characters, setting, and events. Then have children find /j/ *dge* words in the story. Children should supply *badge, Madge, ledge,* and *edge.*

Reread for Fluency

Have children reread Decodable Practice Reader 18B to develop automaticity decoding /j/ *dge* words.

ROUTINE Paired Reading

1. **Reread** To achieve optimal fluency, have partners reread the text three or four times.
2. **Corrective Feedback** Listen as children read. Provide corrective feedback regarding their fluency and decoding.

Routines Flip Chart

Differentiated Instruction

SI Strategic Intervention

Retelling If children have difficulty retelling the story, ask questions such as "What did Bucky lose? Who helped him look for it? Where did they look? Where did they finally find it?"

English Language Learners

Words with /j/ Spelled *-dge*

Beginning/Early Intermediate Before children read, lead them through *Where Is My Badge?* Point out words with the /j/ sound spelled *dge*, such as *badge*, *Madge*, and *ledge*. Have children say the words aloud.

Intermediate After reading, have children find the words in the story with /j/ spelled *dge*. Have children use each word in a sentence. Example: *A police officer wears a badge*.

Early Advanced/Advanced High After reading, have children identify the two pairs of rhyming *dge* words: *badge, Madge* and *ledge, edge*.

Objectives

- Apply knowledge of letter-sound correspondences and syllable patterns to decode words in context and in isolation.
- Spell words with endings *-er, -est.*

Phonics Review
Endings *-er, -est, -ing, -ed*

Review Sound-spellings

Review the following endings: *-er, -est, -ing, -ed.* Use Sound-Spelling Cards 123, 125, 121, and 127.

Decode words in isolation

Display these words. Have the class blend the words. Then point to the words in random order and ask children to read them quickly.

shortest	**darker**	**swimming**
hotter	**tripped**	**taller**
biggest	**newer**	**jumping**

Corrective feedback

Model blending decodable words and then ask children to blend them with you.

Decode words in context

Display these sentences. Have the class read the sentences.

Team Talk Have pairs take turns reading the sentences naturally.

That is the **tallest** tree in the yard.
Jill is **running faster** than Jack.
Tim went **fishing** on the **hottest** day in June.

Spelling
Comparative Endings *-er, -est*

Guide practice Tell children you will chunk the spelling words. They should say the parts of each word aloud as they write them. Check the spelling of each word before saying the next word.

1. /fast/ /ər/ **faster**
2. /fast/ /əst/ **fastest**
3. /tȯl/ /ər/ **taller**
4. /tȯl/ /əst/ **tallest**
5. /shôrt/ /ər/ **shorter**
6. /shôrt/ /əst/ **shortest**
7. /sad/ /ər/ **sadder**
8. /sad/ /əst/ **saddest**
9. /big/ /ər/ **bigger**
10. /big/ /əst/ **biggest**

On their own Use *Reader's and Writer's Notebook* p. 398.

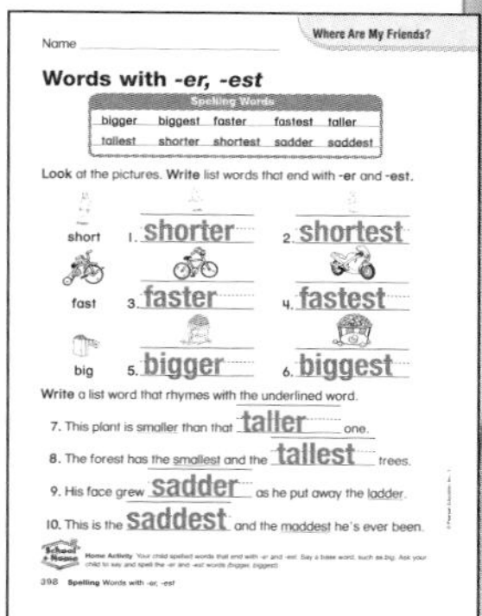

Name ______ Where Are My Friends?

Words with *-er, -est*

Spelling Words				
bigger	biggest	faster	fastest	taller
tallest	shorter	shortest	sadder	saddest

Look at the pictures. **Write** list words that end with **-er** and **-est**.

short 1. shorter 2. shortest

fast 3. faster 4. fastest

big 5. bigger 6. biggest

Write a list word that rhymes with the underlined word.

7. This plant is smaller than that taller one.
8. The forest has the smallest and the tallest trees.
9. His face grew sadder as he put away the ladder.
10. This is the saddest and the maddest he's ever been.

398 **Spelling** Words with -er, -est

Reader's and Writer's Notebook p. 398

Small Group Time

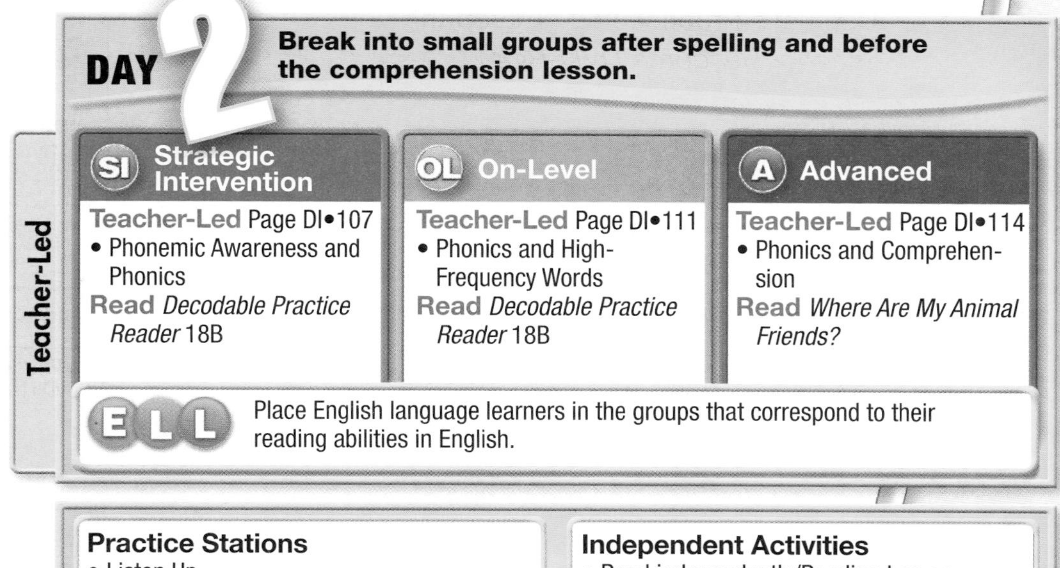

DAY 2 Break into small groups after spelling and before the comprehension lesson.

Teacher-Led

SI Strategic Intervention
Teacher-Led Page DI•107
- Phonemic Awareness and Phonics

Read *Decodable Practice Reader* 18B

OL On-Level
Teacher-Led Page DI•111
- Phonics and High-Frequency Words

Read *Decodable Practice Reader* 18B

A Advanced
Teacher-Led Page DI•114
- Phonics and Comprehension

Read *Where Are My Animal Friends?*

ELL Place English language learners in the groups that correspond to their reading abilities in English.

Practice Stations
- Listen Up
- Word Work

Independent Activities
- Read independently/Reading Log on *Reader's and Writer's Notebook* p. RR4
- AudioText of Main Selection

English Language Learners

Doubling Final Consonant Other languages do not have many words with double consonants. Remind children that a single final consonant that follows a short vowel is often doubled before adding *-er* or *-est*. Provide extra practice spelling words with final consonants that are doubled when these endings are added.

Objectives

- Learn story words: *spring, warm, goose, raccoon, butterfly*
- Review high-frequency words.
- Identify context clues for multiple-meaning words.

High-Frequency Words
Build Fluency

Read words in isolation Remind children that there are some words we learn by remembering the letters, rather than by saying the sounds. Then have them read each of the highlighted high-frequency words aloud.

Read words in context Chorally read the "I Can Read!" passage along with the children. Then have them read the passage aloud to themselves. When they are finished, ask children to reread the high-frequency words.

Have children choose two high-frequency words and give them time to create a sentence in which both words are used properly. Then have them share their sentence with a partner.

I Can Read!

Sally kisses her mom good-bye before lunch. She walks right next to the hedge and calls, "Fluffy, I am the saddest girl in the world. Won't you sit with me and purr?"

Does Fluffy run to Sally? Oh, no! Fluffy runs deeper into the hedge. Why does Fluffy run? Sally squeezes harder than Fluffy likes.

Later Sally makes a pledge to be nice to Fluffy. After that, Fluffy never runs from Sally!

You've learned
- Comparative Endings -er, -est
- Consonant Pattern -dge

High-Frequency Words
does good-bye before
won't oh right

189

Student Edition p. 189

On their own Use Let's Practice It! p. 165 on the *Teacher Resource DVD-ROM*.

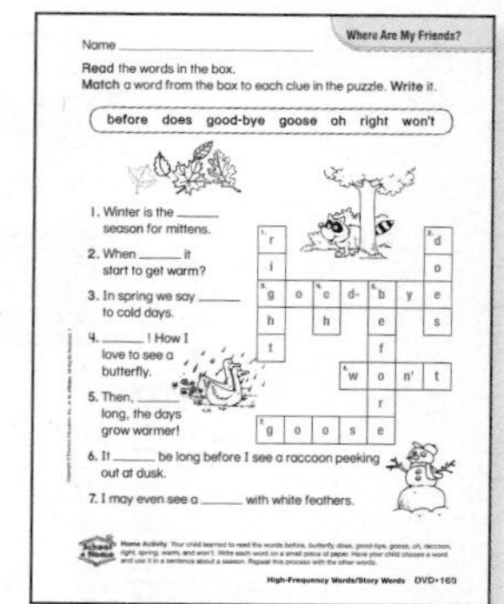
Let's Practice It!
TR DVD•165

Story Words
Where Are My Animal Friends?

Introduce story words

Use Vocabulary Transparency 18 to introduce this week's story words. Read each sentence as you track the print. Frame each underlined word and explain its meaning.

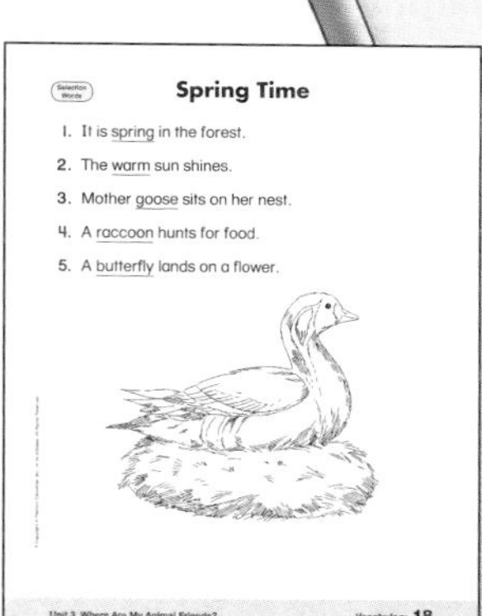

Spring Time

1. It is spring in the forest.
2. The warm sun shines.
3. Mother goose sits on her nest.
4. A raccoon hunts for food.
5. A butterfly lands on a flower.

Vocabulary Transparency 18
TR DVD

spring	the season after winter when plants begin to grow
warm	more hot than cold
goose	a large bird with a long neck
raccoon	a small animal with thick fur whose markings look like rings on its tail and a black mask around its eyes
butterfly	an insect with colored wings

Have children read each sentence with you.

Vocabulary
Context Clues

Model context clues

Explain that when a word has more than one meaning, other words in the sentence can tell you which meaning is right. These words are called **context clues**. Write the words and meanings shown below.

Think Aloud: I know that the word *bear* can mean "a large animal with thick fur" and "to carry or support." In the sentence "A *bear* lives in the woods," the words *lives* and *woods* tell me that the first meaning is right. Repeat this process for the second meaning of *bear*.

Guide practice

Explain two meanings of the word *fall*. Write a sentence for each meaning. Have children tell which meaning is right and what context clues they used. Repeat this process for *spring* and *play*.

On their own

Assign pairs of children one word used in the lesson. Have them make up a sentence for each meaning of the word to tell to the class. Ask the class to say which meaning is right and what context clues they used.

Differentiated Instruction

SI Strategic Intervention

Word Cards Using word cards, have children practice reading *before, does, oh, right, won't, butterfly, spring, warm, raccoon,* and *goose*. Continue until children can read them fluently.

Academic Vocabulary

context clues the words, phrases, or sentences near an unknown word that give the reader clues to the word's meaning

English Language Learners

Multicultural Vocabulary Lists Children can apply knowledge of their home language to acquire new English vocabulary by using the *Multilingual Vocabulary List* (*ELL Handbook* pp. 465–476.)

DAY 2 Read and Comprehend

Objectives

- Build background about what animals do when the seasons change.
- Preview and predict.
- ◎ Use background knowledge to improve understanding of text.
- Set a purpose for reading text.

Build Background
Where Are My Animal Friends?

Background Building Audio

Have children listen to the CD. Tell them to listen for what geese and bears do in winter and spring.

Background Building Audio

Discuss migration and hibernation

Team Talk Have children turn to a partner and use these questions for discussion:

- How does the weather change when winter comes?
- What happens to trees and other plants in winter?
- What do geese do when winter is coming? Why?
- What do bears do when winter is coming? Why?

Organize information in a chart

Have children recall what they learned from the CD about how a forest changes in winter and what geese and bears do. Record their responses.

Connect to selection

We learned that when the weather turns cold, geese migrate south to warmer places and bears hibernate. In the play we're about to read, *Where Are My Animal Friends?*, we'll read more about what these and other animals do when winter is coming.

Student Edition pp. 190–191

Main Selection—First Read
Where Are My Animal Friends?

Practice the skill

Draw Conclusions Remind children that authors don't always tell us everything. Sometimes we must put together facts and details in the story along with other things we know to figure things out for ourselves.

Introduce the strategy

Background Knowledge Explain that good readers connect what they read to things they have read before and things they know from their own experience to help them understand their reading.

Envision It!

Think Aloud: Look at this picture. As the children watch a skier, the girl is remembering something she has done. What is it? (sledding) Thinking about sledding helps her understand what it's like to ski. As I read *Where Are My Animal Friends?*, I'm going to think about what I already know about animals and seasons to help me understand the play.

Student Edition EI•12

Introduce genre

Let's Read Together A **play** is a story to be acted out. The words are said by different characters. As children read *Where Are My Animal Friends?*, point out the small circles with pictures of the animals in them that show which character is speaking.

Preview and predict

Have children identify the title of the story, the author and the illustrator. Have children describe the role of each. Have them activate prior knowledge by looking through the story and predicting what it will be about.

Set a purpose

Good readers read for a purpose. Setting a purpose helps us to think and understand more as we read. Guide children to set a purpose for reading the play.

Tell children that today they will read *Where Are My Animal Friends?* for the first time. Use the Day 2 Guide Comprehension notes to help children develop their comprehension of the play.

First Read

Continue to DAY 2

For the First Read, use **Guide Comprehension** across the top of pages 190–207.

Strategy Response Log

Background Knowledge Before reading, have children use p. RR30 of their *Reader's and Writer's Notebook* to draw a picture of an animal getting ready for winter. Have them label the animal and write a sentence telling what it is doing.

Academic Vocabulary

draw conclusions to figure something out by using what you know from your reading and from your own experience

background knowledge the things you already know when you begin reading

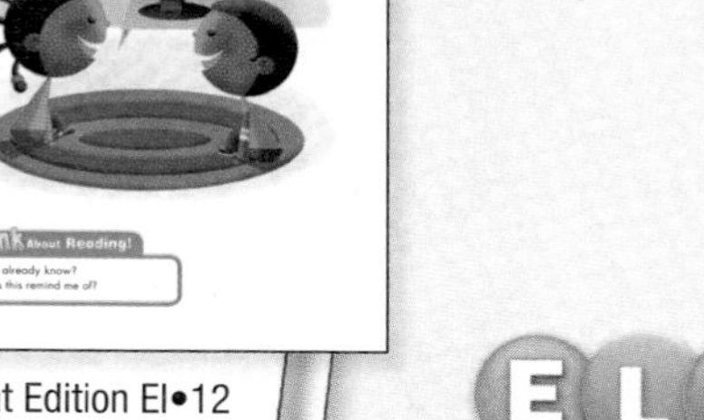

English Language Learners

Build Background Before children listen to the CD, build background and elicit prior knowledge. On the CD, you will hear about what geese and bears do when winter is coming. What is a goose? (a large bird) What did we learn that some birds do when winter is coming? (migrate, or fly to a warmer place) What do some animals that can't fly do? (hibernate, or sleep all winter)

Frontload Main Selection Ask children what they already know about the fall using the picture on pp. 190–191. Then do a picture walk of the selection so that children can talk about the things different animals do when winter is coming.

Objectives

- ◎ Draw conclusions about elements of a play.
- ◎ Use background knowledge to monitor and adjust comprehension.
- Determine word meaning and use newly acquired vocabulary.
- Discuss ideas related to but not expressed in the literature.

DAY 2

Guide Comprehension
Skills and Strategies

Connect to Concept

Changes in Nature Look at the pictures on pages 190 and 191. What season do you think it is? How can you tell? (It is fall. Leaves have turned from green to red, yellow, and orange and are on the ground.)

Amazing Words

Have children continue discussing the concept using the Amazing Words *autumn, freeze, hibernate, migrate,* and *temperature* as they read.

Student Edition pp. 190–191

DAY 3

Extend Thinking
Think Critically

Higher-Order Thinking Skills

Synthesis We see a fall scene here. What season has just passed? What season is coming next? (Summer has just passed. Winter is coming.)

If... children are unable to say what season comes before and after fall, **then...** teach children this cheer: *Say the seasons with the drummer: Fall, winter, spring, and summer!* Use a drum to keep the beat.

Skills

Draw Conclusions Look at page 192. Why do you think a play lists the characters at the beginning? (Possible response: The characters are listed at the beginning to show how many actors are needed and what different parts they will play.)

Strategy

Background Knowledge What you know about reading a play will help you understand this play. Look at page 193. How can you tell which character says which words? (The picture next to the words shows which character says them.)

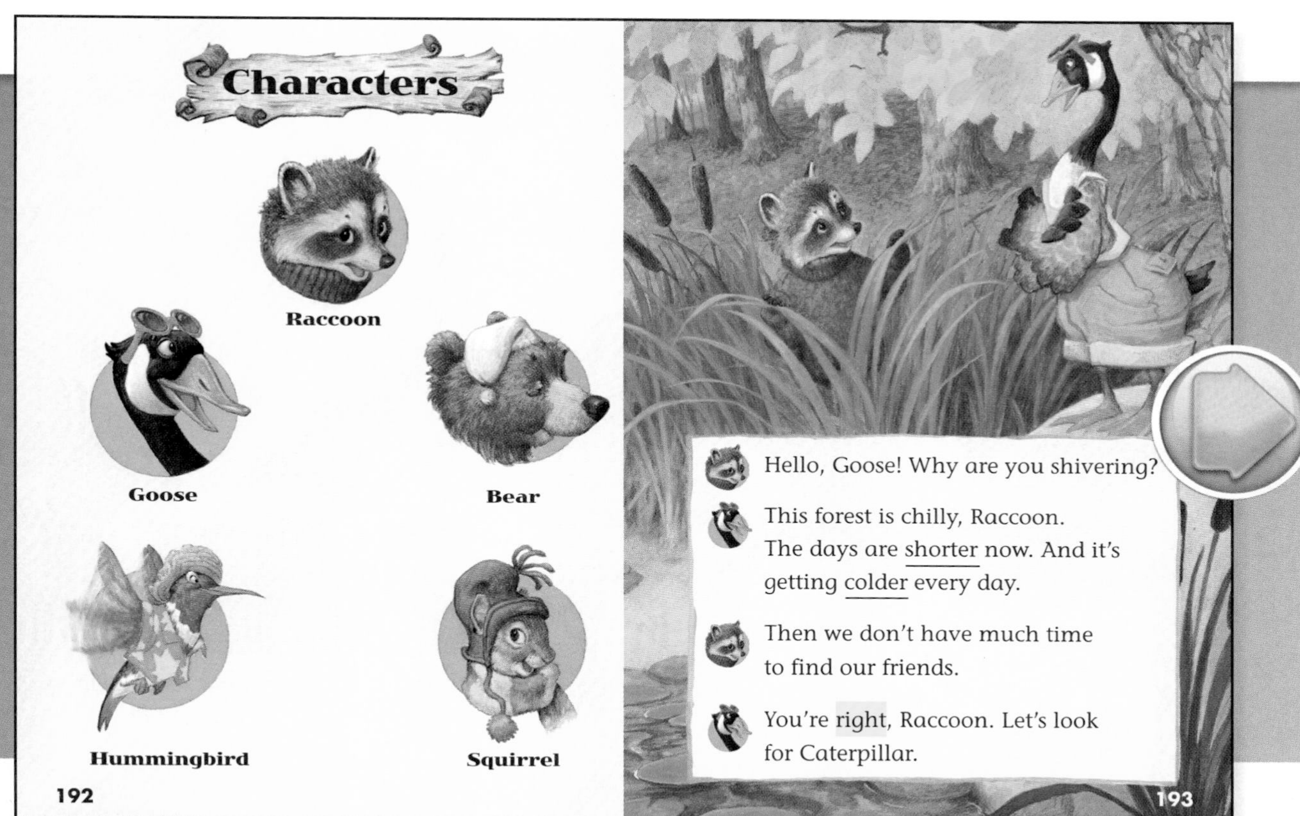

Student Edition pp. 192–193

Higher-Order Thinking Skills

Analysis What does Goose mean when she says, "The days are shorter now"? (Goose means that the sun does not shine for as long. Darkness comes earlier.)

If...children are unable to explain what Goose means by "The days are shorter now,"
then...ask children how day and night are different. (The sun shines during the day.) Then ask if shorter days are days when the sun shines for more time or less time.

Skills and Strategies, continued

DAY 2

Vocabulary

Context Clues Have children reread the second sentence on page 194. The word *leaves* can mean "parts of a plant" or "goes away." What does *leaves* mean in this sentence? What context clue did you use? (It means "parts of a plant." The word *tree* is a context clue.)

Skills

Draw Conclusions Why do you think the leaves are on the ground? (They have fallen off because trees lose their leaves in the fall.)

Student Edition pp. 194–195

Think Critically, continued

DAY 3

Higher-Order Thinking Skills

Analysis Which parts of this play are true-to-life? Which parts are fantasy? (Possible response: The forest and the animals' bodies look real, but real animals don't talk and wear clothes.)

If...children are unable to say which parts are true-to-life or fantasy, **then...**have children examine the pictures. Ask questions such as, "Do real animals wear clothes? Do real raccoons have striped tails and masks?"

Vocabulary

Story Words Have children locate the story word *butterfly* on page 197. What kind of animal is a butterfly? What does it look like? (It is an insect with large, brightly colored wings.)

Word Reading

Decoding Have children check their reading of new words using these questions:

- Did I blend the sounds to read the words?
- Did I put the new word in the sentence to make sure it made sense?
- Did I look for word parts to help me understand the word?

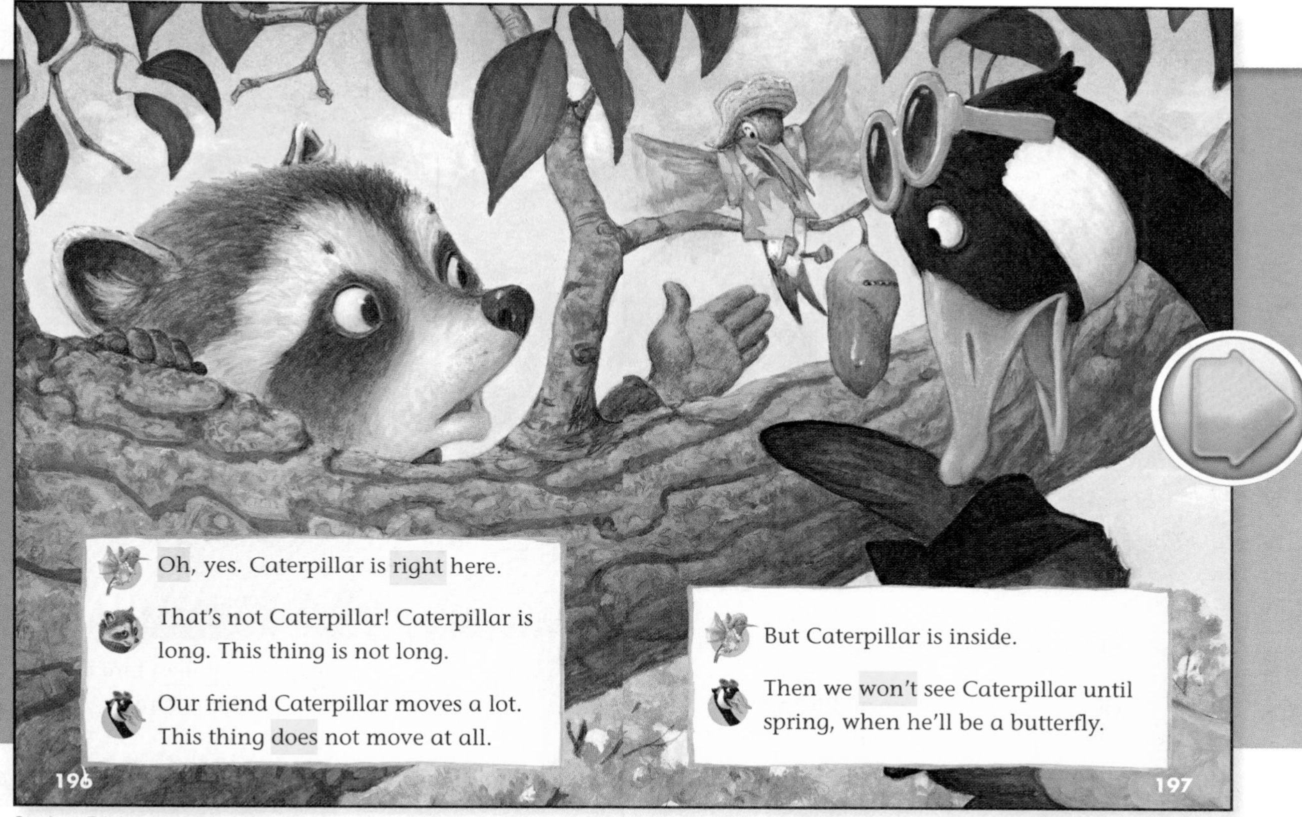

Student Edition pp. 196–197

Higher-Order Thinking Skills

Synthesis What is the "thing" that Raccoon sees? How do you know? (Possible response: It's a chrysalis. I know from the story "I Am a Caterpillar" and from the picture of a chrysalis. I also know because Hummingbird says that Caterpillar is inside and Goose says that he will be a butterfly.)

Evaluation Who seems older and wiser, Raccoon or his friends Goose and Hummingbird? Why? (Possible response: Goose and Hummingbird seem older and wiser. Raccoon asks many questions that his friends can answer. They know where the leaves went and what is happening to Caterpillar.)

Skills and Strategies, continued

Vocabulary

Context Clues Have children reread the sentence that begins "I must fly..." on page 198. *Fly* can mean "an insect" or "to move through the air." What does *fly* mean here? What context clues did you use? (It means "to move through the air." Possible context clues: *I must....away.*)

Strategies

Background Knowledge Look at Raccoon's first words on page 199. How should the actor's voice sound when he says, "Oh, my!" Why? (Possible response: He should sound sad. The actor's voice should sound the way the character is feeling.)

Student Edition pp. 198–199

Think Critically, continued

Connect to Science

Animal Behavior In winter, many animals can't find enough food. Some migrate to find shelter and hibernate.

Team Talk Have children discuss in pairs which animals they know of that migrate and which hibernate.

Higher-Order Thinking Skills

Evaluation What would you like and not like about moving to a warmer place in the winter? (Possible response: I would like being able to swim outdoors. I would not like leaving my friends, and I would miss the snow.)

Skills

 **Draw Conclusions** Why does Bear ask Raccoon if it is spring yet? (Possible response: He has been hibernating. He is mixed up because he did not expect to wake up until spring.)

Word Reading

High-Frequency Words Point out the words *before* and *won't*. Have children practice reading these words.

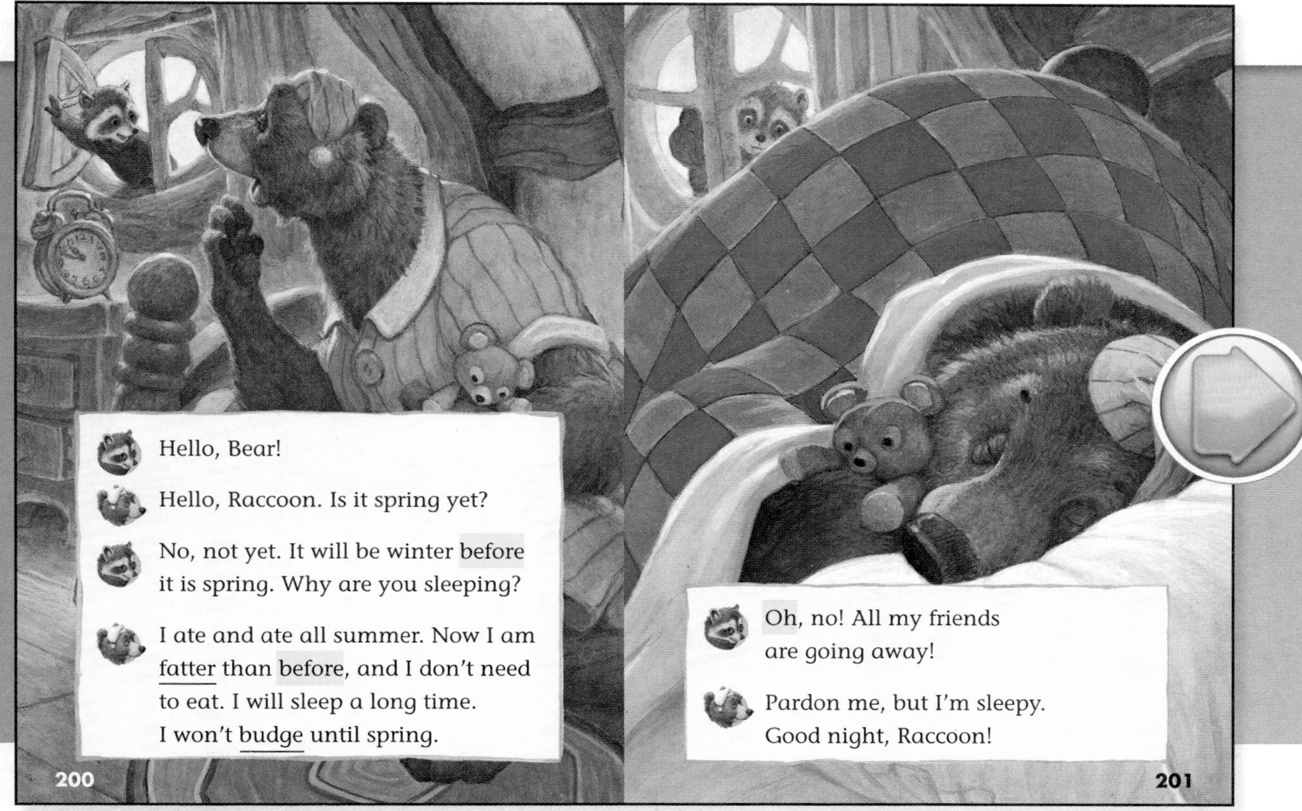

Student Edition pp. 200–201

Higher-Order Thinking Skills

Synthesis Why was Bear able to eat and get fat during the summer? (In summer, there are lots of plants and animals to eat.) What problem would Bear have if he stayed awake in winter? Why? (He would not find enough food. In winter plants lose their leaves and berries and animals that bears eat migrate or hibernate.)

If...children are not able to explain why bears eat a lot during the summer and hibernate in winter, **then...**ask them what kind of weather plants need to grow. Then ask in what seasons the forest would be filled with plants and the animals that eat those plants.

Skills and Strategies, continued

DAY 2

Vocabulary

Story Words Have children locate the story word *raccoon* on page 203. How would you describe a raccoon to someone who has never seen one? (Possible response: A raccoon is an animal with brown fur, a long bushy tail, a mask around its eyes, and black rings around its tail.)

If...children have difficulty describing a raccoon,
then...guide them to notice the details in the picture of Raccoon on page 202.

Student Edition pp. 202–203

Think Critically, continued

Higher-Order Thinking Skills

Analysis What are some clues in the picture that tell you Squirrel will be around in the winter? (Possible response: Squirrel is wearing a hat, vest, and scarf, which are all winter clothes.)

If...children are unable to answer the question,
then...ask them to think about how the weather changes in the winter and the kinds of clothes they wear for winter weather.

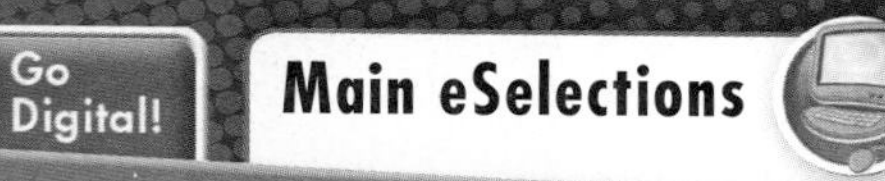

Skills

Draw Conclusions How does Raccoon feel at the end of the play? How do you know? (Possible response: He is happy. He is smiling. He has found a friend who will stay with him all winter.)

Strategy Self-Check

Background Knowledge Ask children what they know about plays that helped them read this play. (Possible response: The words tell what the characters are saying. A name or picture next to the words tells which character is speaking.)

Student Edition pp. 204–205

Higher-Order Thinking Skills

Synthesis Why do you think Squirrel has "lots of food" for the winter? (Possible response: He gathered nuts during the fall and stored them.)

Review Compare and Contrast

Analysis In what ways are Raccoon and Squirrel alike? Different? Have children read from the story to answer the questions. (Possible response: Raccoon and Squirrel both live in the forest all winter. Both have bushy tails. Raccoon is larger than Squirrel.)

Skills and Strategies, continued

Vocabulary

Context Clues Look at the word *Scenery* on page 207. What parts of the sentence below it are clues to the meaning of *scenery*? (Possible response: "show that the play is set in a forest..." is a clue that scenery is the things on a stage that show where the events happen.)

Continue to DAY 2
Comprehension Check
p. 207a

Put On a Play!

What you will need:

Costumes

Costumes can be simple or fancy.

Props

One prop you will need for this play is a chrysalis. Will you need anything else?

Scenery

Simple sets can show that the play is set in a forest in the fall.

An Audience

Practice your parts. Then ask another class to come to the play!

206 207

Student Edition pp. 206–207

Think Critically, continued

Higher-Order Thinking Skills

Evaluation Which character do you think would be most fun to play? Why? (Possible response: I would like most to play Raccoon, because Raccoon had the most lines.)

Comprehension Check

Have children discuss each question with a partner. Ask several pairs to share their responses.

- ☑ **Play** What special things does this play have that a regular story does not? (It has a list of characters. It has pictures to show who is speaking.)
- ☑ **Confirm predictions** What things that you already knew about seasons and animals helped you predict what would happen in this play? (Possible response: I predicted where Caterpillar was because I knew that caterpillars form a chrysalis and become butterflies. I knew that bears hibernate so I predicted that Bear would be sleeping.)
- ☑ **Summarize** What did Raccoon learn about the different things animals do when winter is coming? (Possible response: He learned that birds fly south to warmer places, caterpillars form chrysalises, bears hibernate, and squirrels stay where they are because they have stored up food for the winter.)
- ☑ **Author's Purpose** Do you think the author of this play wants his readers to learn something, to have fun, or both? How can you tell? (Possible response: Both. The play tells many facts about what real animals do, but it is also fun because the animals talk like people and wear clothes.)
- ☑ **Connect text to world** In the area where you live, what different animals do you see in different seasons? (Possible response: I see robins, flies, and bees in spring and summer. I see pigeons and squirrels all year.)

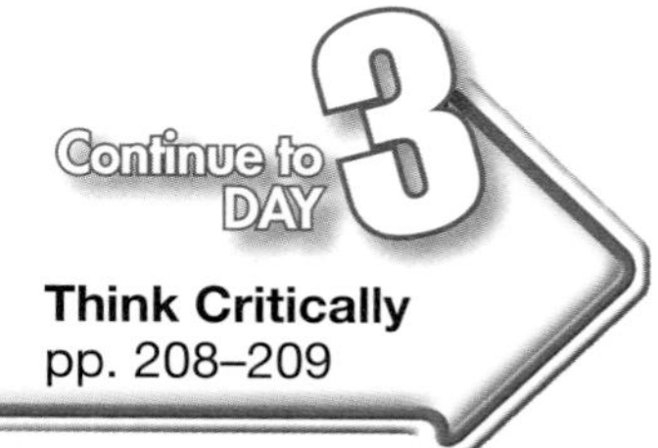

Think Critically
pp. 208–209

English Language Learners
Summarizing To help children summarize what Raccoon learned, prompt them by pointing to a picture of each animal in the play and having them complete this sentence starter: When winter is coming, a goose ________.

Objectives

- Identify the features of drama.
- Read and use contractions with *not* correctly.

Genre
Drama

Identify features of drama

Use the play *Where Are My Animal Friends?* to have children identify the features of drama.

- Why do we call *Where Are My Animal Friends?* a play rather than a story? (It was written to be acted out.)
- In a story, some of the words tell what the characters say, while other words tell what the characters look like or what they do. How is a play different? (In a play, the words don't tell what the characters look like or what they do. The words only tell what the characters say.)
- Why do you think a play begins with a list of the characters? (The list of characters makes it easy to see how many actors are needed and what parts they will play.)

Guide practice

Draw a three-column chart or display Graphic Organizer 5. Have children compare and contrast the features of a play with those of a story.

Play	BOTH	Story
Is meant to be acted out Tells only what characters say Begins with a list of characters	Characters Setting Plot	Is meant to be read Tells what characters say, do, and look like No list of characters

Graphic Organizer Flip Chart 5

On their own

Remind children that at the end of *Where Are My Animal Friends?* there are suggestions for how to put on a play. Divide the play into two-page parts, and assign parts to groups of children. Have the groups practice their parts and then perform for the class.

Conventions
Contractions with *Not*

Model contractions with *not*

Write *aren't* and *hasn't* on the board. Point to each contraction as you read it. A contraction is a short way to put two words together. Below each contraction, write the two words that form it and say them aloud. What letter was left out of each contraction? (*o*) What was used in place of the letter *o*? (an apostrophe)

Guide Practice

Write the following sentences on the board. Have children read each sentence, identify the two words that can form a contraction, and say the contraction. Write the contractions on the board.

1. **Bob has not seen my bike. (hasn't)**
2. **We were not at home. (weren't)**
3. **I was not sitting with Deb. (wasn't)**
4. **Lilly did not get a card. (didn't)**

Connect to oral language

Have children revise these sentences orally by substituting a contraction for the underlined words.

1. **The girls <u>are not</u> playing catch.**
2. **I <u>do not</u> want more juice.**
3. **Mike <u>is not</u> at the park.**

On their own

Use *Reader's and Writer's Notebook* p. 399.

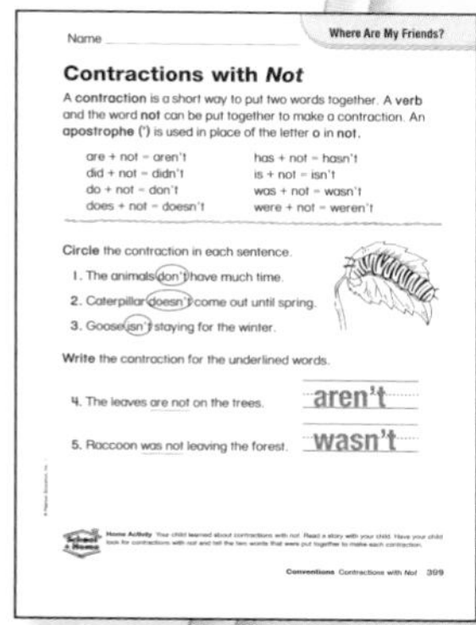

Name ______ Where Are My Friends?

Contractions with *Not*

A **contraction** is a short way to put two words together. A **verb** and the word **not** can be put together to make a contraction. An **apostrophe** (') is used in place of the letter **o** in **not**.

are + not = aren't	has + not = hasn't
did + not = didn't	is + not = isn't
do + not = don't	was + not = wasn't
does + not = doesn't	were + not = weren't

Circle the contraction in each sentence.

1. The animals don't have much time.
2. Caterpillar doesn't come out until spring.
3. Goose isn't staying for the winter.

Write the contraction for the underlined words.

4. The leaves are not on the trees. aren't
5. Raccoon was not leaving the forest. wasn't

Conventions Contractions with *Not* 399

Reader's and Writer's Notebook p. 399

Differentiated Instruction

 **Strategic Intervention**

Contractions Use letter tiles to spell *is not*. Have children say the two words, then push the two words together, remove the *o*, and replace it with an apostrophe. (If no apostrophe tile is available, cover any tile with a sticky note and write an apostrophe on it.) Have children say the contraction they have just spelled. Repeat this process with other verbs plus *not*.

Daily Fix-It

3. jay was the fastest bird.
Jay was the fastest bird.

4. Duck were the slowest bird
Duck was the slowest bird.

Discuss the Daily Fix-It corrections with children. Review sentence capitalization and punctuation, the spelling of words with comparative endings -*er* and -*est*, and subject-verb agreement with *was* and *were*.

English Language Learners

Contractions Some other languages, such as the Romance languages, also include contractions. If possible, provide examples of contractions in the home language. (In Spanish, *a* + *el* = *al;* in Portuguese, *de* + *as* = *das*.) Point out that in English, an apostrophe is used to replace the missing letter(s).

Objectives

- Generate play scene ideas.
- Recognize features of a play scene.
- Use sentences in writing a plan for a play scene.

Writing—Play Scene
Writing Trait: Sentences

Introduce the prompt

Review with children the key features of a play scene. Point out that *Where Are My Animal Friends?* is a play. Tell children they, too, can make up a conversation between animal characters. Explain that today children will plan their own play scene with characters from *Where Are My Animal Friends?* This will express their ideas about the play. Read aloud the writing prompt.

Writing Prompt

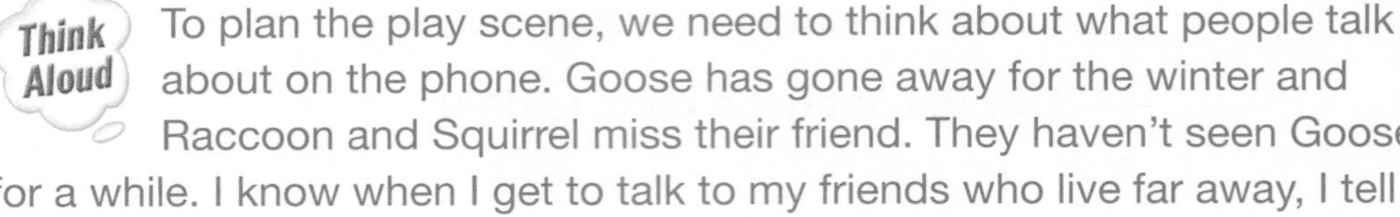

Think about Raccoon and Squirrel in *Where Are My Animal Friends?* What would they say if they could call Goose on a phone? Write a play scene showing what they would say.

Help children generate play scene ideas

Sharing the Writing

Think Aloud To plan the play scene, we need to think about what people talk about on the phone. Goose has gone away for the winter and Raccoon and Squirrel miss their friend. They haven't seen Goose for a while. I know when I get to talk to my friends who live far away, I tell them what I am doing. What else might you say to a far-away friend?

Guide children in identifying topics of conversation, such as missing one another, planning to see one another soon, and catching up after being apart for a while.

Have each child choose a main topic of conversation for the play scene.

MINI-LESSON

Sentences

- **Introduce** Use *Reader's and Writer's Notebook* p. 400 to model play scene planning. I can use an idea web to help me plan my play scene. I will decide the main idea the characters will talk about. I will put that in the middle of the web. Then I can put my characters' words in the outside circles. I will use sentences to tell what they say.

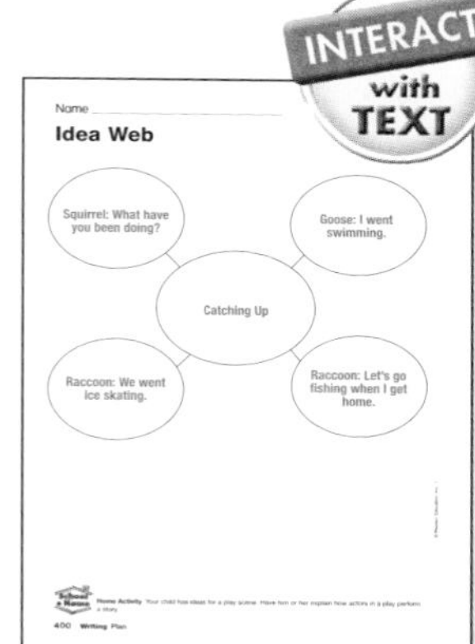

Reader's and Writer's Notebook p. 400

- **Model** I am going to write about the characters catching up. They will tell one another what they have been doing since Goose left for the winter. I will write *Catching Up* in the center circle. Now I have to think about what I will have each character say. I will write the name of each character and things they might say to one another in the outside circles. Now plan for your play scene. Circulate to guide and assist children.

ROUTINE

Quick Write for Fluency

Team Talk

1. **Talk** Have children take two minutes to tell their dialogue ideas to a partner.
2. **Write** Each child briefly writes a line of dialogue for the play scene.
3. **Share** Each child reads the line to the partner.

Routines Flip Chart

Write Guy
Jeff Anderson

The Sunny Side

I like to look for what's *right* in children's writing rather than focusing on things I can edit or fix. Most children don't write flawlessly—who does? However, they will learn what they are doing well if we point it out.

Differentiated Instruction

SI Strategic Intervention

Planning Conversation If children find it difficult to think of lines to write, have them work in groups of three and pretend they are Raccoon, Goose, and Squirrel talking on the phone. Then have them record ideas from their role-play for their play scenes.

English Language Learners

Support Prewriting

Beginning Give children starter questions to begin their play scene, such as *Hi, Goose. What are you doing?* or *When are you coming home?*

Intermediate Have partners come up with questions to begin their play scenes. Tell children to consider what Goose or Raccoon and Squirrel might want to know.

Advanced/Advanced High Have children role-play the conversations and record their main lines in the charts.

Objectives

- Write with correct letter slant.
- Understand the features of a picture graph.

Handwriting
Letter *J* and *j*/Letter Slant

Model letter formation Display upper- and lower-case letters: *Jj*. Use the stroke instructions pictured below to model proper letter formation.

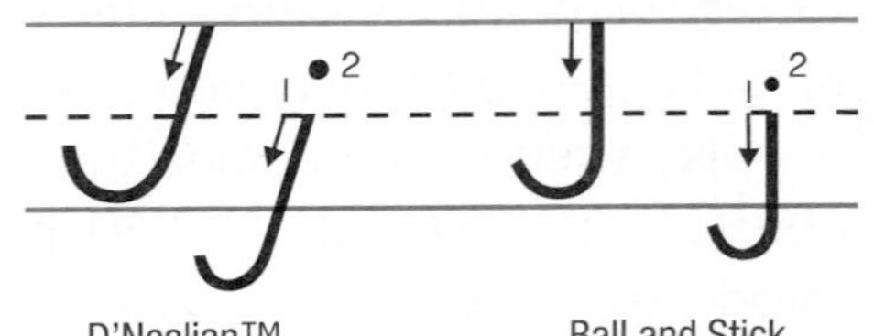

Model consistent letter slant Explain that when we write a word, all the letters in that word should be slanted correctly. Write the word *jelly* two times, first with the letters slanted correctly, then with the letters slanted in different directions. When I write the letters in a word, I need to make sure they all go the correct way. Writing letters with the correct slant makes them easier to read.

Guide practice Write the following words, one slanted correctly and the rest slanted in different directions.

joke **shell** **judge** **sloppy**

Team Talk Have children work in pairs to discuss which word is slanted correctly. Then have them discuss how to correct the other words. Ask them to share with the class.

On their own Use the *Reader's and Writer's Notebook*, p. 401.

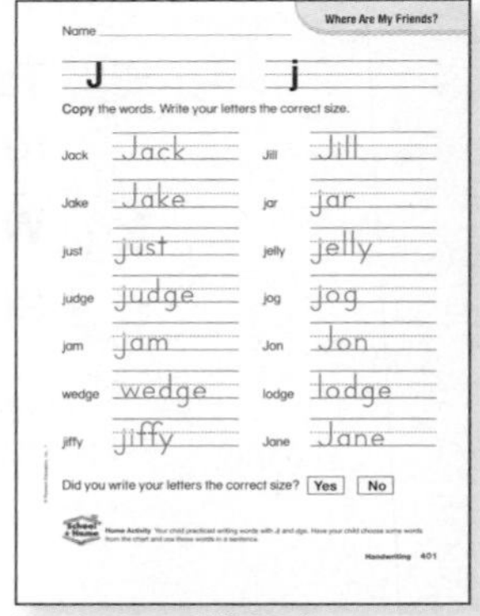

Reader's and Writer's Notebook p. 401

Research and Inquiry

Research Skill: Picture Graph

Teach Tell children that a **picture graph** uses pictures to compare amounts. The pictures may go up and down or across the page. The title tells what the graph is about.

Model Think Aloud Display Research Transparency 18. This picture graph shows how one class voted for their favorite animal from the play, *Where Are My Animal Friends?* Graphs have titles. See the names of the animals along the left side. The picture of the animal's face stands for one vote. The numbers on the bottom stand for the number of votes. Use the transparency to model how to find answers to the questions.

Guide practice Help children answer the questions on the transparency. Review the information after you have recorded their responses.

Academic Vocabulary

picture graph a chart that uses pictures to compare amounts

Picture Graph

Our Favorite Animals

Raccoon, Bear, Squirrel, Hummingbird, Goose

1 2 3 4 5 6 7

1. How many children voted for Raccoon? 7
2. Which two animals got the same number of votes? Bear and Squirrel
3. How many children voted for Goose? 6
4. Which animal got the most votes? Raccoon
5. Which animal got the fewest votes? Hummingbird

Unit 3 Where Are My Animal Friends? Research 18

Research Transparency 18
TR DVD

Wrap Up Your Day

- **Consonant Pattern *-dge*** Write the word *fudge.* Ask children to identify the sound at the end of this word.
- **High-Frequency Words** Write the following sentence: *Oh, won't you say good-bye before you leave?* Have children point to each high-frequency word and say it aloud.
- **Build Concepts** Monitor children's use of oral vocabulary as they respond. Recall the Big Book *What Makes the Seasons?* Ask: What season comes before autumn? (Summer comes before autumn.) What do many creatures do in the winter? (Many creatures hibernate, or sleep until the weather gets warmer.)

Tell children that tomorrow they will reread *Where Are My Animal Friends?*

Objectives

- Build oral vocabulary.
- Identify details in text.
- Share information and ideas about the concept.

Today at a Glance

Oral Vocabulary
freeze

Phonemic Awareness
Add Phonemes

Phonics and Spelling
◎ Comparative Endings *-er. -est*
◎ Consonant Pattern *-dge*

High-Frequency Words
before, does, good-bye, oh, right, won't

Story Words
butterfly, goose, raccoon, spring, warm

Comprehension
Review Compare and Contrast

Fluency
Expression and Intonation

Conventions
Contractions with *not*

Writing
Play Scene
Writer's Craft: Draft

Listening and Speaking
Give Announcements

Research and Inquiry
Gathering and Recording Information

Concept Talk

Question of the Week

What do animals do when the seasons change?

Build concepts

To reinforce concepts and to focus children's attention, have children sing "Animals All Know" from the *Sing with Me* Big Book. Why do some animals disappear in the winter and come back in the spring? (Possible response: They migrate or hibernate in winter because it is too cold and they can't find enough food. They return or wake up in spring because the weather is warm again and there is enough food.)

Sing with Me Big Book Audio

Monitor listening comprehension

Review that yesterday the class read the Big Book, *What Makes the Seasons?,* to find out what the season called autumn is like.
Ask children to listen today to find out how our lives change with the seasons.

- How do our lives change as the seasons change? (We change our activities; we change what we wear.)
- How do the changes that happen in autumn help animals prepare for winter? (Some animals gather the fallen nuts to store for winter and collect fallen leaves to make warm beds. The colder weather tells some animals that it's time to hibernate.)

Big Book

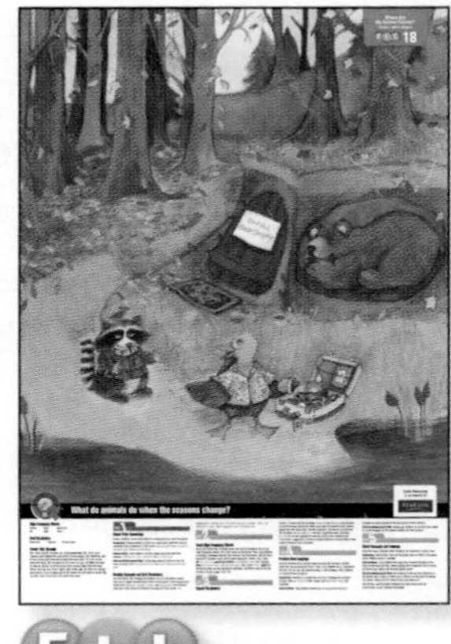
ELL Poster 18

ELL Expand Vocabulary Use the Day 3 instruction on ELL Poster 18 to help children expand vocabulary.

Oral Vocabulary
Amazing Words

Teach Amazing Words

Amazing Words Oral Vocabulary Routine

1. **Introduce the Word** Relate the word *freeze* to the book. When raindrops *freeze*, they turn into snow. Supply a child-friendly definition. When things *freeze*, they turn hard because of the cold. Have children say the word.
2. **Demonstrate** Provide examples to show meaning. The pond will *freeze* when the temperature drops tonight. We will *freeze* the juice to make ice pops.
3. **Apply** Have children demonstrate their understanding. What happens when you *freeze* water?

Routine Flip Chart

Amazing Words

hibernate	freeze
migrate	bitterly
temperature	weary
autumn	

Anchored Talk

Add to the concept map

Use these questions to discuss how different animals prepare for the changing seasons as you add to the concept map.

- In *Where Are My Animal Friends?*, what do Goose and Hummingbird do when winter is coming? (They fly away to a warmer place.) We already have *Birds migrate to warm places* on our chart.
- What does Bear do to prepare for the changing seasons? (He eats a lot in summer. In winter he sleeps, or hibernates.) Let's add what bear does to the chart.
- What do Raccoon and Squirrel do in winter? (They stay in the forest.) They can stay in the forest because in fall they collected food for the winter. Let's add those ideas to our chart.

English Language Learners

Sentence Production Have children answer these questions using the word *freeze. Why might people slip and fall in winter? How do you make ice cubes?*

Objectives

- Add initial sound to create a new word.
- Build words with *-dge.*
- ◎ Read words with *-dge* and comparative endings *-er, -est.*

Phonemic Awareness
Add Phonemes

Student Edition pp. 184–185

Model adding initial phonemes Have children look at the picture on pp. 184–185 in their Student Edition. I see the *edge* of the river. Listen as I say the sounds in *edge*: /e/ /j/. If I add the sound /l/ to the beginning of *edge*, I make a new word: /l/ *edge, ledge.*

Guide practice Help children add an initial sound to each word below to make a new word. Then have them point to the matching picture in their Student Edition.

/h/**edge** (hedge)	/b/**ridge** (bridge)	/s/**tick** (stick)

On their own Have children add initial /t/ to the following words to make new words.

rail (trail)	**or** (tore)	**rap** (trap)
air (tear)	**rain** (train)	**all** (tall)

Team Talk Have partners think of other initial sounds they could add to *all* to make new words (*ball, hall, wall, fall, call*). Ask children to share their words.

Phonics
Build Words

Model word building Now we are going to build words that end with the sound /j/. Write *nudge* and blend it. Watch me change /n/ to /f/. Model blending the new word, *fudge*.

Guide practice Have children spell *fudge* with letter tiles. Monitor children's work as they build words.

- Change /f/ to /b/. Say the new word together. 
- Change the /u/ to /a/. Say the new word together. 
- Change the /a/ to /r/ /i/. Say the new word together. 
- Take away the /b/. Say the new word together. 

Corrective feedback For corrective feedback, model the correct spelling and have children correct their tiles.

Fluent Word Reading

Model Write *dodge*. I know the sounds for *d, o,* and *dge*. I blend them and read the word *dodge*.

Guide practice Write the words below. Say the sounds in your head for each spelling you see. When I point to the word, we'll read it together. Allow one second per sound previewing time for the first reading.

judge	saddest	darker	biggest
grudge	hedge	tallest	

On their own Have children read the list above three or four times, until they can read one word per second.

Differentiated Instruction

Advanced

Build *-dge* Words If children are able to build the words in the class activity easily and independently, have them use letter tiles to build these more difficult words with *dge: badger, pledge, grudge, smudge, sludge,* and *hedgehog*.

English Language Learners

Pronounce *-est* Because Spanish words do not end with *st*, Spanish speakers may drop the *t* from words with comparative ending *-est*, saying *hardes* instead of *hardest*. Give children extra practice saying and writing words that end in *-est*, such as *thinnest, smartest,* and *hottest*.

Objectives

- ◎ Associate the sound /j/ with the spelling *-dge,* and correctly pronounce words with the comparative endings *-er* and *-est.*
- Blend and read words with /j/-*dge* or the comparative endings *-er* or *-est.*
- Decode words in context and isolation.
- Spell words with *-er* and *-est.*

Blend and Read

Decode words in isolation

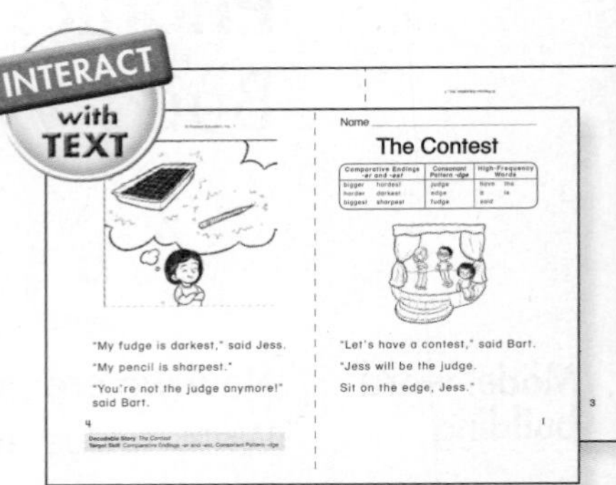

Reader's and Writer's Notebook pp. 403–404

Have children turn to pages 403–404 in the *Reader's and Writer's Notebook* and find the first list of words. Each word in this list has the ending *-er,* the ending *-est,* or the sound /j/ spelled *-dge* at the end of the word. Let's blend and read these words. Be sure that children identify the correct sounds in words that have *-er, -est,* or *-dge.*

Next, have children read the high-frequency words.

Decode words in context

Chorally read the story along with the children.
Have children identify words in the story that have *-er, -est,* or *-dge.*

Team Talk Pair children and have them take turns reading the story aloud to each other. Monitor children as they read to check for proper pronunciation and appropriate pacing.

On their own

To further develop automaticity, have children take the story home to reread.

Spelling
Comparative Endings *-er, -est*

Spell high-frequency words Write *good-bye* and *before* and point them out on the Word Wall. Have children say and spell the words with you and then without you.

Dictation Say each sentence. Then repeat each one slowly, one word at a time, as children write them.

1. **Is a bug taller or shorter than a bird?**
2. **We waved good-bye and sat on the biggest bus.**
3. **He ran faster than Jane before she got bigger.**

Proofread and correct Write each sentence, spelling words one at a time. Have children circle and rewrite any misspelled words.

On their own Use *Reader's and Writer's Notebook* p. 405.

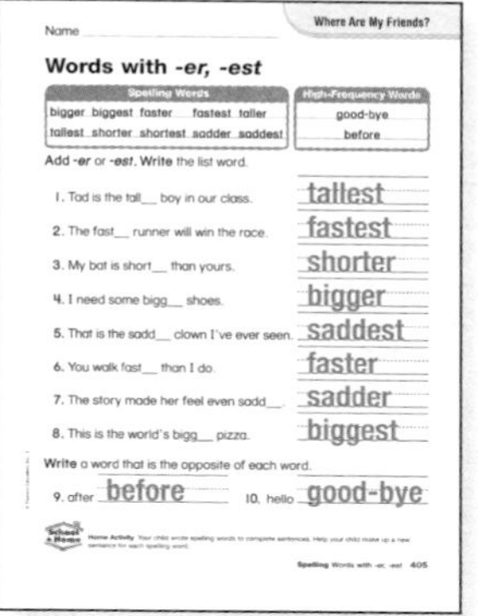
Name ______ Where Are My Friends?

Words with *-er, -est*

Spelling Words					High-Frequency Words
bigger	biggest	faster	fastest	taller	good-bye
tallest	shorter	shortest	sadder	saddest	before

Add ***-er*** or ***-est***. **Write** the list word.

1. Tad is the tall__ boy in our class. tallest
2. The fast__ runner will win the race. fastest
3. My bat is short__ than yours. shorter
4. I need some bigg__ shoes. bigger
5. That is the sadd__ clown I've ever seen. saddest
6. You walk fast__ than I do. faster
7. The story made her feel even sadd__. sadder
8. This is the world's bigg__ pizza. biggest

Write a word that is the opposite of each word.

9. after before 10. hello good-bye

Spelling Words with -er, -est 405

Reader's and Writer's Notebook p. 405

Spelling Words
Comparative Endings *-er, -est*

1. bigger	**6. tallest**
2. biggest	**7. shorter**
3. faster	**8. shortest**
4. fastest	**9. sadder**
5. taller	**10. saddest**

High-Frequency Words

11. before	**12. good-bye**

Small Group Time

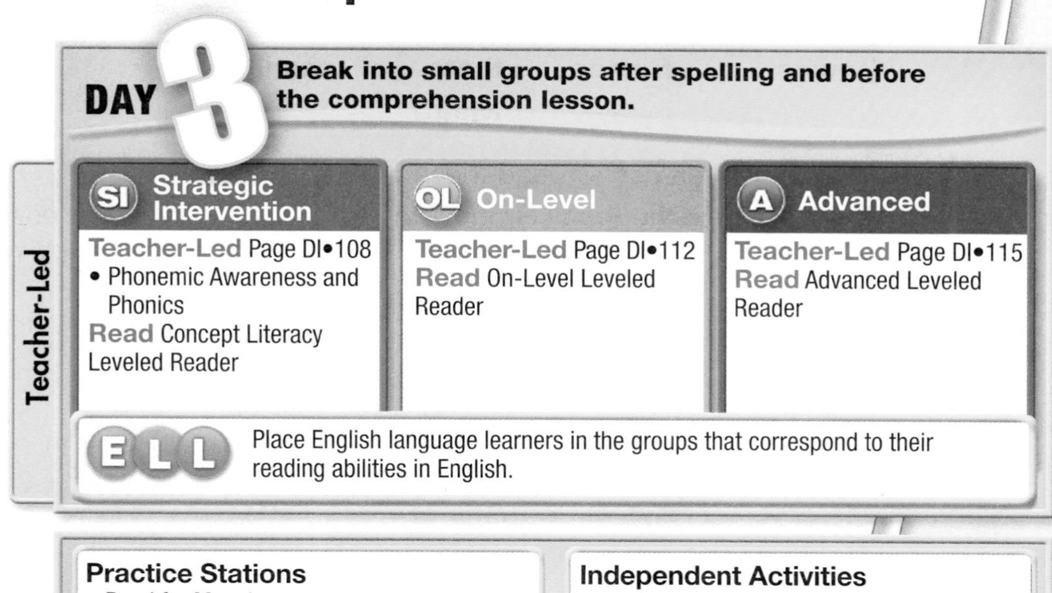
DAY 3 **Break into small groups after spelling and before the comprehension lesson.**

Teacher-Led

SI Strategic Intervention	OL On-Level	A Advanced
Teacher-Led Page DI•108 • Phonemic Awareness and Phonics **Read** Concept Literacy Leveled Reader	**Teacher-Led** Page DI•112 **Read** On-Level Leveled Reader	**Teacher-Led** Page DI•115 **Read** Advanced Leveled Reader

ELL Place English language learners in the groups that correspond to their reading abilities in English.

Practice Stations
- Read for Meaning
- Let's Write

Independent Activities
- Read Independently/Reading Log on *Reader's and Writer's Notebook* pp. RR 4
- AudioText of Main Selection

English Language Learners

Spelling Dictation Children will benefit from hearing each dictated sentence read three times. First, have children listen to understand the sentence. The second time, they should write what they hear. The third time, they can check their work.

Objectives

- Read high-frequency words.
- Establish purpose for reading text.
- Review key features of plays.

Check High-Frequency Words
SUCCESS PREDICTOR

High-Frequency and Story Words

Read words in isolation Display and review this week's high-frequency words and story words. Have children read the words aloud.

Read words in context Display the following sentence frames. Have children complete the sentences using high-frequency and story words. Have the children read each completed sentence with you.

1. **That *goose* will fly to a ________ place. (warm)**
2. **I wave ________ *before* I get in the car. (good-bye)**
3. ***Oh*, a ________ with big wings is sitting on this rose! (butterfly)**
4. **I am sad that he ________ be home till *spring*. (won't)**
5. **She *does* all the math and gets it ________. (right)**
6. **A ________ has a black mask on its face. (raccoon)**

Don't Wait Until Friday **MONITOR PROGRESS** **High-Frequency Words**

Point to these words on the Word Wall and have the class read them. Listen for children who miss words during the reading. Call on those children to read some of the words individually.

does	**right**	**before**	**won't**	**Spiral Review** Rows 3 and 4 review previously taught high-frequency words.
oh	**good-bye**			
who	**friends**	**there**	**small** ←	
inside	**away**	**where**	←	

If... children cannot read these words,

then... use the Small Group Time Strategic Intervention lesson, p. DI•109, to reteach the words. Monitor children's fluency with these words during reading and provide additional practice.

Day 1	Day 2	Day 3	Day 4	Day 5
Check Word Reading	Check Word Reading	**Check High-Frequency Words/Retelling**	Check Fluency	Check Oral Vocabulary

Success Predictor

Main Selection—Second Read
Where Are My Animal Friends?

Review
Compare and contrast

Recall this week's main selection, *Where Are My Animal Friends?* Tell children that today they will read the story again. Remind children that when we tell how things are like each other, we **compare**; when we tell how things are different, we **contrast**. Paying attention to how things are alike and different helps us understand our reading. What do Goose and Hummingbird do that is the same? (Possible response: They both fly to a warmer place.) Bear does something different. What does he do? (Possible response: He stays in the forest and hibernates.)

Review
Genre: play

Let's Read Together Remind children that a play is a story to be acted out, and that it tells the words that each character says. How does the play that we read show which character says which words? (It shows a picture of the character next to the words.)

Set a purpose

Remind children that good readers read for a purpose. Guide children to set a new purpose for reading *Where Are My Animal Friends?* For instance, they might read to find out why some animals leave the forest for the winter and other animals stay.

Extend thinking

Tell children they will now read *Where Are My Animal Friends?* for the second time. Use the Day 3 Extend Thinking notes to encourage children to use higher order thinking skills to go beyond the details of the play.

Second Read

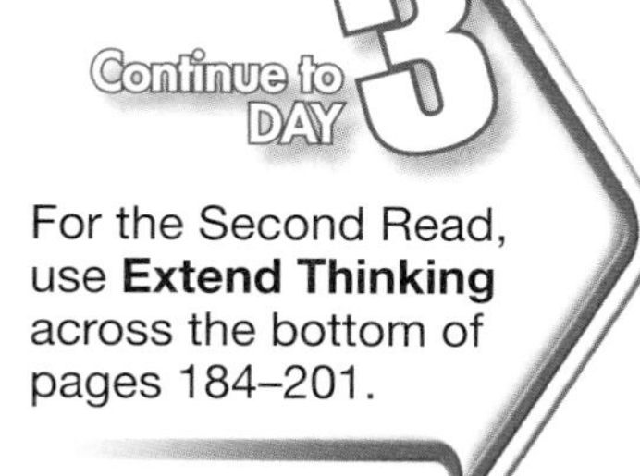

For the Second Read, use **Extend Thinking** across the bottom of pages 184–201.

Story Words

spring the season after winter, when plants begin to grow

warm more hot than cold

goose a large bird with a long neck

raccoon a small animal with thick fur whose markings look like rings on its tail and a black mask around its eyes

butterfly an insect with colored wings

Academic Vocabulary

compare to tell how things are alike
contrast to tell how things are different

English Language Learners

Visual Support When reviewing high-frequency and story words on p. 202g, point to pictures in the selection, use gestures, or draw quick sketches to illustrate meanings.

High-Frequency Words
Success Predictor

Objectives

- Retell a narrative.
- ◎ Draw conclusions.
- ◎ Use background knowledge to better understand a story.
- Write clear, coherent sentences.

Check Retelling
SUCCESS PREDICTOR

Think Critically

1. What do you remember about how a caterpillar changes? Text to Text
2. What does the author want you to learn from this play? Author's Purpose
3. Why are the animals in a hurry to find their friends? ◎ Draw Conclusions
4. How do you know which line to read in a play? ◎ Background Knowledge
5. **Look Back and Write** Look back at pages 198 and 199. Where do animals go when the days turn cold? Write about it. TEST PRACTICE Extended Response

208

Meet the Author

William Chin

William Chin likes the winter. He lives in Chicago, where it gets cold in winter. His daughter is a figure skater. He and his wife skate too.

Mr. Chin sang in musicals in school. Now he is a choir director. He works with a children's choir. He is also a conductor for the Chicago Symphony Chorus.

Here are more books about winter.

Use the Reading Log in the *Reader's and Writer's Notebook* to record your independent reading.

209

Student Edition pp. 208–209

Retelling

Have children work in pairs, retelling the story to one another. Remind children that their partners should include the characters, setting, and events from the beginning, middle, and end of the story. Children should use the retelling strip in the Student Edition as they retell. Monitor children's retelling.

Scoring rubric

Top-Score Response A top-score response makes connections beyond the text, elaborates on the author's purpose, and describes in detail the characters, setting, and plot.

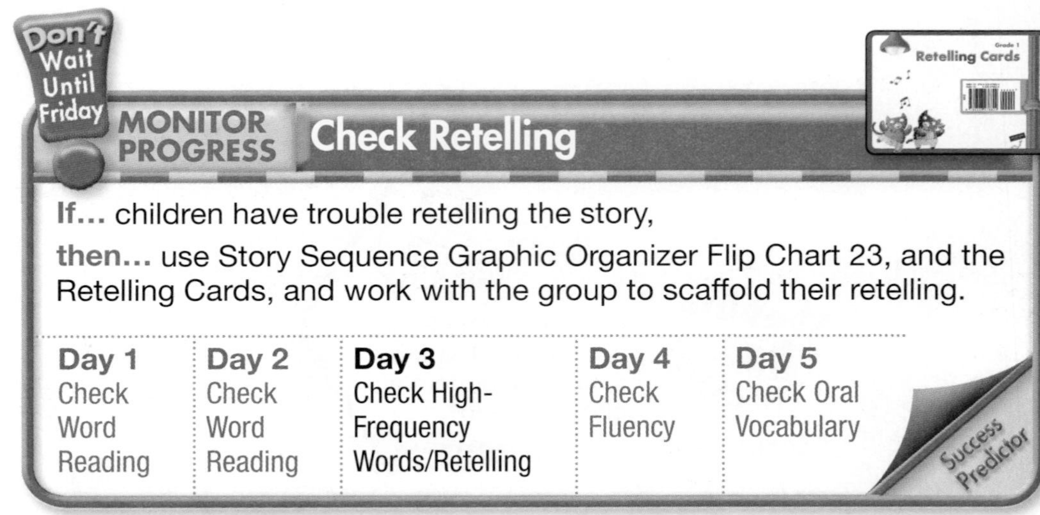

MONITOR PROGRESS **Check Retelling**

If... children have trouble retelling the story,
then... use Story Sequence Graphic Organizer Flip Chart 23, and the Retelling Cards, and work with the group to scaffold their retelling.

Day 1	Day 2	Day 3	Day 4	Day 5
Check Word Reading	Check Word Reading	Check High-Frequency Words/Retelling	Check Fluency	Check Oral Vocabulary

Success Predictor

Think Critically

Text to Text

1. Possible response: A caterpillar hangs from a stem, sheds its skin, and becomes a pupa. The pupa grows a shell to form a chrysalis. Then the pupa inside becomes a butterfly.

Author's Purpose

2. Possible response: The author wants us to learn what different forest animals do when winter comes.

Draw Conclusions

3. Possible response: They know that winter is coming and they won't have much more time to play together.

Background Knowledge

4. The pictures in small circles show which animal is speaking.

Writing on Demand

5. **Look Back and Write** For writing fluency, assign a five-minute time limit. As children finish, encourage them to reread their response and proofread for errors.

Scoring rubric

Top-Score Response A top-score response uses details from the text and the pictures to tell where animals go when the days turn cold. For example:

When the days turn cold, geese and hummingbirds fly to a warmer place. Caterpillars stay inside their chrysalis. Bears sleep in their dens.

Meet the author

Read aloud page 209 as children follow along. Ask children what else William Chin likes to do besides writing for children.

Read Independently

After children enter their independent reading into their Reading Logs, have them paraphrase a portion of the text they have just read. Tell children that when we paraphrase, we express the meaning of what we have just read using our own words.

Differentiated Instruction

A Advanced

Look Back and Write Ask children who show proficiency with the writing prompt to explain why animals that migrate or hibernate are able to return or wake up in the spring.

Strategy Response Log

Genre After reading, have children use p. RR30 of their *Reader's and Writer's Notebook* to tell how a play is different from a story.

Plan to Assess Retelling

- ☐ Week 1: Strategic Intervention
- ☐ Week 2: Advanced
- ☐ Week 3: Strategic Intervention
- ☐ Week 4: On-Level
- ☐ Week 5: Strategic Intervention
- ☑ This week assess any children you have not yet checked during this unit.

Retelling
Success Predictor

Read and Comprehend

Objectives

- Read aloud fluently with expression and intonation.
- Understand verbs (present) in the context of reading and writing.
- Use verbs (present) when speaking.

Model Fluency
Expression and Intonation

Model fluent reading

Have children turn to Student Edition page 193. I'm going to read this page. I want to sound like the different characters talking to each other. I will try to use my voice to sound the way each character might sound.

Guide practice

Have children read the page with you. Then have them reread the page as a group until they read with appropriate expression and intonation. Encourage them to read the way the characters might speak. Continue in the same way with pages 194–195.

Corrective feedback

If... children have difficulty reading with appropriate expression and intonation,
then... prompt:

- Who is the character speaking?
- How does the character feel?
- How do you think the character sounds when he is saying this?

Reread for Fluency

ROUTINE Choral Reading

1. **Select a Passage** For *Where Are My Animal Friends?*, use pp. 200–201.
2. **Model** First, have children track the print as you read.
3. **Guide Practice** Then have children read along with you.
4. **Corrective Feedback** Have the class read aloud without you. Monitor progress and provide feedback. For optimal fluency, children should reread three to four times.

Routines Flip Chart

Check comprehension

How can you use what you know about bears to figure out what Bear is doing? (Possible response: Bear is telling Raccoon that he ate all summer and will sleep until spring. I know that real bears hibernate, or sleep, all winter long, so I think that is what Bear is doing.)

Conventions
Contractions with *Not*

Review Contractions with *not* Remind children that a contraction is a short way to put two words together, and that a letter is replaced by an apostrophe. Write and say: *is not, isn't.*

Guide practice Write *are* + *not, did* + *not, has* + *not,* and *were* + *not*. What contraction can we make by adding *are* plus *not*? (aren't) Draw a line under *are* + *not*. Write *aren't* below it.

are + not
aren't

Have children do "word math" to form contractions for the remaining pairs of words.

Team Talk Have children work in pairs to combine *is* + *not, does* + *not, was* + *not,* and *do* + *not.*

Connect to oral language Have children revise these sentences orally by substituting a contraction for the underlined words.

1. **Tom was not in the kitchen.**
2. **Jill and Ann were not on the porch.**
3. **I do not see them at all.**

On their own Use *Reader's and Writer's Notebook,* p. 406.

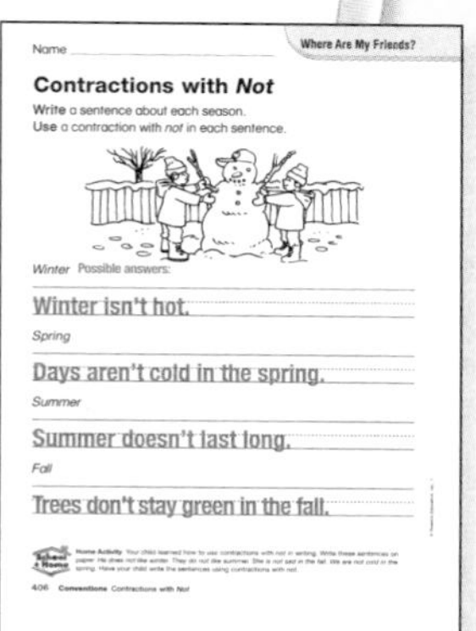

Name ______ Where Are My Friends?

Contractions with *Not*

Write a sentence about each season.
Use a contraction with *not* in each sentence.

Winter Possible answers:
Winter isn't hot.
Spring
Days aren't cold in the spring.
Summer
Summer doesn't last long.
Fall
Trees don't stay green in the fall.

406 Conventions Contractions with *Not*

Reader's and Writer's Notebook p. 406

Options for Oral Reading

Use *Where Are My Animal Friends?* or one of this week's Decodable Practice Readers.

Professional Development

Fluency Help children pay attention to phrasing and expressive reading by having them read and record a familiar story. Collecting several recordings for each child over a period of time can help you assess each child's progress. The recordings can also be shared during parent-teacher conferences.

Daily Fix-It

5. It is cold last week?
   It was cold last week.
6. some birds can not find fod.
   Some birds can not find food.

Discuss the Daily Fix-It corrections with children. Review sentence capitalization and punctuation, verb tense, and the spelling of the high-frequency word *food*.

Objectives

- Write a draft of a play scene.
- Use strong verbs in writing.

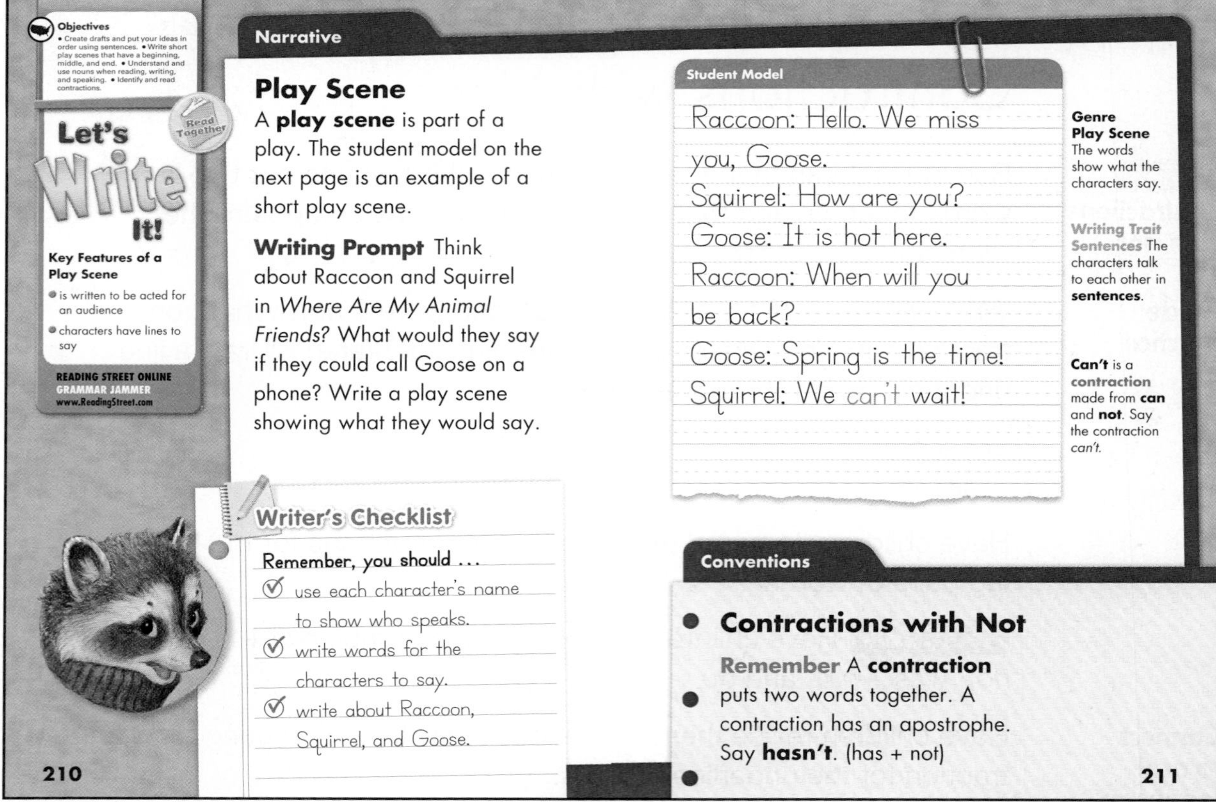

Student Edition pp. 210–211

Let's Write It!

Teach Use pages 210–211 in the Student Edition. Read aloud the Key Features of a Play Scene and the definition of a play scene. Help children better understand the Writing Prompt by reading it aloud and discussing the Writer's Checklist with children.

Review the student model Then read the student model on page 211 to children. Point out the characters in the play scene. Then point out their lines, or the words they say. Read aloud and briefly discuss the side notes about Genre, the Writing Trait, and Contractions with *not* to help children understand how an author writes a play scene.

Scoring rubric

> **Top-Score Response** Help children understand that a top-score response has characters' names followed by the lines they speak. The lines will be sentences with strong verbs. For a complete rubric see Writing Rubric 18 from the Teacher Resource DVD-ROM.

Connect to conventions Read to children the Conventions note about Contractions with Not. Point out the contraction *can't* in the play scene.

Writing—Play Scene
Writer's Craft: Strong Verbs

MINI-LESSON

Strong Verbs

- **Introduce** Use your idea web from yesterday and Writing Transparency 18A to model using strong verbs in a play scene. When I write my play scene, I will use my web. Yesterday I wrote some simple lines my characters might say. I will use those lines in my play scene. I will pick stronger verbs for my play. I will make sure the lines are in the right order, too. Read aloud the draft on the Transparency to show how to use strong verbs in characters' dialogue.

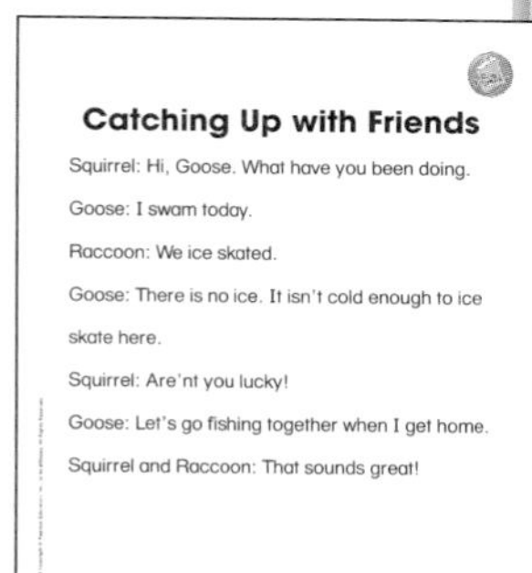

Catching Up with Friends

Squirrel: Hi, Goose. What have you been doing.

Goose: I swam today.

Raccoon: We ice skated.

Goose: There is no ice. It isn't cold enough to ice skate here.

Squirrel: Are'nt you lucky!

Goose: Let's go fishing together when I get home.

Squirrel and Raccoon: That sounds great!

Writing Transparency 18A
TR DVD

- Explain how children can use ideas they recorded yesterday to draft the play scene. They will write their own new ending for the play. Today's goal is to write the play scene but not to rewrite each word perfectly. They can edit later to correct the words.

Guide play scene writing Now it is time to write your play scene. Tell what the characters say to each other. Have children use their webs. Help them finish and arrange ideas. Then guide children as they draft the scenes.

ROUTINE **Quick Write for Fluency** Team Talk

1. **Talk** Have partners take one minute to share their lines.
2. **Write** Each child writes a sentence with a strong verb from the play.
3. **Share** Partners point out verbs in the others' sentences.

Routines Flip Chart

Differentiated Instruction

Advanced

Strong Verbs Children may take the time to think about the strong verbs they want to use. Have them review each of their sentences and make changes to add strong verbs.

Write Guy
Jeff Anderson

Powerful Words, Powerful Verbs

If children have trouble distinguishing complete sentences from fragments, have them ask this question: "Who or what did something? What did they do?" If there is no answer to the question, they know their words may be a fragment. Children can have fun making a complete statement by adding together subjects *(David)* and powerful verbs *(laughed, talked, jumped): David laughed.*

Objectives

- Make an announcement, including all important information.
- Ask questions of a speaker to obtain relevant information.
- Communicate information by making a picture graph.

Listening and Speaking
Give Announcements

Introduce giving announcements

Explain that people give announcements to let people know about something special or important that will happen.

- Good speakers speak slowly and loudly enough to be understood.
- They look at their listeners.
- They tell all the information their listeners need to know.
- Good listeners face the speaker and pay attention.
- If listeners have questions, they politely ask them.

Model

Use the passage below to model giving an announcement.

If I were part of a food drive, I might write an announcement like this. This week our school will collect food to give to needy families. Please remember to bring one or more cans of food from home. Put the cans in the boxes next to the science table. The last day to bring food is Friday. The class that collects the most cans will get their picture in the newspaper, so don't forget!

Guide practice

Tell children that they will make an announcement inviting their classmates to a birthday party. Discuss what they should include in their announcement, and list each type of information on the board.

1. Whose birthday party is it?
2. When will it be?
3. Where will it be?
4. What will happen at the party?

On their own

Have children practice announcing a birthday party to a partner. Then have them give their announcements in small groups. Remind the listeners to pay attention and to ask questions about any important information the speaker forgot to include.

Research and Inquiry
Gather and Record Information

Teach Tell children that today they will gather facts about a topic. They will fill in more of their chart.

Model Think Aloud Display the chart the class created on Day 1. Let's gather some information from your classmates about what they like to do when the seasons change. Also, think about other things that people do when seasons change.

Guide practice Have children ask each other what they like to do when the seasons change. Have them record what they learn in their charts. When they are finished, ask the class to come up with ideas of what people do, in general, when the seasons change.

Spring	Summer	Fall	Winter
Ride my bike	Vacation with my family	Rake leaves	Celebrate the holidays
Walk in the park	Turn on the fan or air conditioning	Wear warmer clothes	Wear very warm clothes
Work in the garden or mow the lawn	Go to the beach	Go back to school	Turn on the heat

On their own Use *Reader's and Writer's Notebook* p. 402.

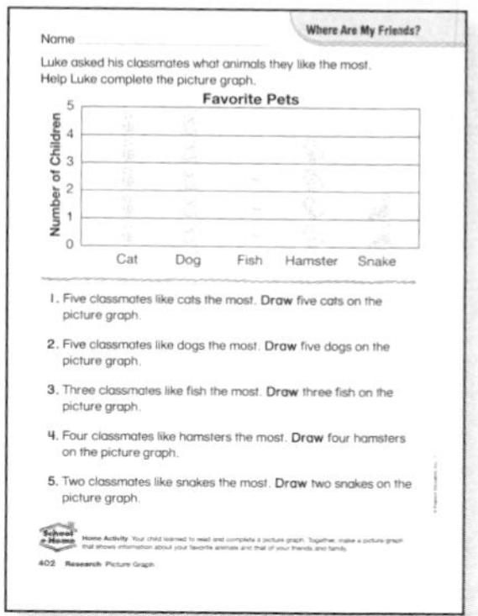
Name

Where Are My Friends?

Luke asked his classmates what animals they like the most. Help Luke complete the picture graph.

1. Five classmates like cats the most. **Draw** five cats on the picture graph.
2. Five classmates like dogs the most. **Draw** five dogs on the picture graph.
3. Three classmates like fish the most. **Draw** three fish on the picture graph.
4. Four classmates like hamsters the most. **Draw** four hamsters on the picture graph.
5. Two classmates like snakes the most. **Draw** two snakes on the picture graph.

402 Research Picture Graph

Reader's and Writer's Notebook p. 402

Wrap Up Your Day

- ✔ **Draw Conclusions** Have children recall *Where Are My Animal Friends?* Describe what will happen to all the characters when spring arrives.
- ✔ **Background Knowledge** Remind children that using everything they already know about a topic, called background knowledge, can help them understand more about a story.

ELL

English Language Learners

Retell Spoken Announcements Remind children that it is important to understand the information in spoken announcements. As children are listening to the announcements spoken by classmates, have them take notes to use as they retell the message.

Tell children that tomorrow they will read a collection of poems about change.

Objectives

- Discuss the concept to develop oral language.
- Build oral vocabulary.
- Identify details in text.

Today at a Glance

Oral Vocabulary
bitterly, weary

Phonemic Awareness
Change Initial Phonemes

Phonics and Spelling
Review *r*-Controlled *er, ir, ur*
Review Contractions *'s, 've, 're*

High-Frequency Words
Review

Comprehension
Poetry

Fluency
Expression and Intonation

Conventions
Contractions with *not*

Writing
Play Scene: Revise

Research and Inquiry
Review and Revise Topic

Concept Talk

Question of the Week

What do animals do when the seasons change?

Build concepts

To reinforce concepts and to focus children's attention, have children sing "Animals All Know" from the *Sing with Me* Big Book. Why can some animals stay in their homes all winter? (Possible response: They gather and store food for the winter, or they eat extra food in summer so they can hibernate, or sleep all winter.)

Sing with Me Big Book Audio

Review Genre: animal fantasy

Have children tell the key features of an animal fantasy: it has animal characters who do things that real animals don't do. Explain that today you will read "Busy Busy Moose" by Nancy Van Laan, a story about another group of forest animals and what they do when the seasons change.

Monitor listening comprehension

Recall that in *Where Are My Animal Friends?*, Raccoon discovers what his animal friends do when winter is coming. Have children listen to "Busy Busy Moose" to find out what keeps Moose busy at different times of the year. Read the selection.

"Busy Busy Moose"

ELL Poster 18

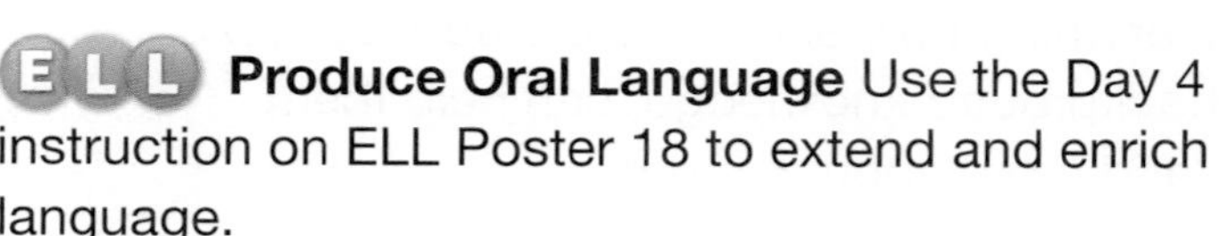
ELL **Produce Oral Language** Use the Day 4 instruction on ELL Poster 18 to extend and enrich language.

Oral Vocabulary
Amazing Words

Teach Amazing Words

Amazing Words Oral Vocabulary Routine

1. **Introduce the Word** Relate the word *weary* to the story. Moose was *weary* from crossing the pond again and again. Supply a child-friendly definition. When you are *weary*, you are very tired. Have children say the word.
2. **Demonstrate** Provide examples to show meaning. The mountain climber was *weary* after a hard day of climbing. The soccer team felt *weary* after practicing all afternoon.
3. **Apply** Have children demonstrate their understanding. What activities do you do that make you feel *weary*?

See p. OV•3 to teach *bitterly*.

Routines Flip Chart

Anchored Talk

Add to the concept map

Discuss what animals do when the seasons change.

- The animals in "Busy Busy Moose" do some things that real animals do. What do they do in the fall? (Beaver makes his winter house; Squirrel hides acorns; Rabbit gathers bark and twigs.) Where should we put each idea in the chart?
- What does Beaver do in winter? (He stays inside his home.) What do Moose and Beaver do in the summer? (Moose grazes; Beaver floats in the pond.) Let's add these to the chart.
- What do birds do in spring? (They nest.) Let's add this to the chart.

Amazing Words

hibernate	freeze
migrate	bitterly
temperature	weary
autumn	

Differentiated Instruction

SI Strategic Intervention

Act Out Have a child act out the meaning of *weary* by walking in a weary manner. Have a child act out the meaning of *bitterly* by showing how uncomfortable people feel when it's bitterly cold (shivering, chattering teeth, rubbing arms, etc.).

English Language Learners

Frontload Listening Before reading, use pictures from the Big Book *What Makes the Seasons?* to help children review what they have learned about the four seasons. Ask questions such as these: What is the weather like in fall? in winter? in spring? in summer? What happens to water outside in winter? What do some animals do in winter?

DAY 4 Get Ready to Read

Objectives

- Form new words by changing the initial phoneme.
- Read words with *r*-controlled vowel sounds and contractions.

Phonemic Awareness
Change Initial Phonemes

Model

This week we read that one animal that flies to warmer weather in the winter, and that is the goose. Listen to the sounds I say in *goose*. Slowly model the sounds: /g/ /ü/ /s/. Now I will change the sound /g/ to the sound /m/: /m/ /ü/ /s/, *moose*. We're going to make new words by changing the beginning sound of a word.

Guide practice

I will say a word. Then you will say a new word by changing the beginning sound to /s/. Say each word below. Guide children in identifying the initial sound and changing it to /s/ to make a new word.

Corrective feedback

If children make an error, model the correct response. Return to the word later in the practice.

more (sore)	**bite** (sight)	**ring** (sing)
pack (sack)	**deal** (seal)	**fame** (same)

On their own

Have children change the initial sound in each word to /p/.

real (peel)	**sink** (pink)	**get** (pet)
door (pour)	**main** (pain)	**toast** (post)

Phonics Review
r-Controlled *er, ir, ur;* Contractions *'s, 've, 're*

Review Sound-spellings

To review last week's first phonics skill, write *her, sir,* and *fur*. You studied words like these last week. What do you know about the vowel sound you hear in these words? (The *sound* is /ėr/. It can be spelled *er, ir,* or *ur*.)

Corrective feedback

If children are unable to answer the questions about the *r*-controlled vowels, refer them to Sound-Spelling Cards 67, 72, and 104.

Review Contractions *'s, 've, 're*

To review last week's second phonics skill, write *it's, we've,* and *we're*. Point to *it's*. You can read this word because you know that it is a contraction. What is the word? (*it's*) What two words make up the contraction? (*it* and *is*) What letter has been replaced by the apostrophe? (*i*) Repeat this procedure for *we've* and *we're*.

Guide practice

Draw a T-chart or use Graphic Organizer Flip Chart 4. When I say a word, hold up one hand if it has the /ėr/ sound or two hands if it is a contraction: *surf, let's, you've, herd, chirp, they're, burn, she's*. Write each word in the appropriate column. Have children read the lists. Ask them to name the two words that make up each contraction.

er, ir, ur	Contractions
surf	let's
herd	you've
chirp	they're
burn	she's

On their own

Use Let's Practice It! on pp. 163–164 on the *Teacher Resource DVD-ROM.*

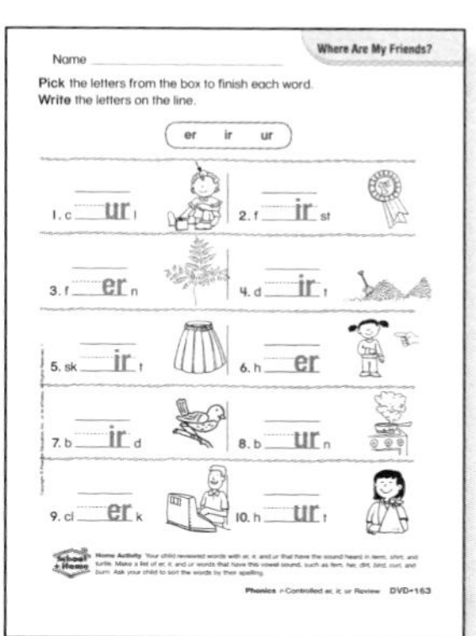
Where Are My Friends?

Name

Pick the letters from the box to finish each word.
Write the letters on the line.

er ir ur

1. c ur l
2. f ir st
3. f er n
4. d ir t
5. sk ir t
6. h er
7. b ir d
8. b ur n
9. cl er k
10. h ur t

Phonics r-Controlled er, ir, ur Review DVD•163

Let's Practice It! TR DVD•163

Where Are My Friends?

Name

Write the contraction for each pair of words.

1. we + have = we've
2. he + is = he's
3. I + have = I've
4. they + have = they've
5. that + is = that's
6. it + is = it's
7. you + are = you're
8. you + have = you've

Here is my balloon.
Here's my balloon.

Find the contraction.
Mark the ⊂⊃ to show your answer.

9. she's / she / sons
10. were / we're / went

DVD•164 Phonics Contractions 's, 've, 're Review

Let's Practice It! TR DVD•164

English Language Learners

Contractions If children have difficulty naming the words that make up a contraction, write the two words on the board and ask children to read them aloud. Then cross out the letter or letters that are replaced by an apostrophe. Write the contraction below the two words and read it aloud. Have children repeat it.

Objectives

- Apply knowledge of sound-spellings to decode unknown words when reading.
- Decode and read words in context and isolation.
- Practice fluency with oral rereading.

Decodable Practice Reader 18C

Comparative Endings *-er, -est;* Consonant Pattern *-dge*

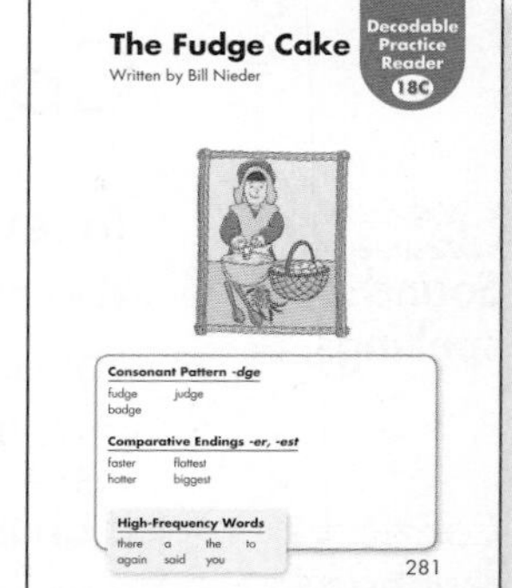

The Fudge Cake
Written by Bill Nieder
Decodable Practice Reader 18C

Consonant Pattern -dge
fudge judge
badge

Comparative Endings -er, -est
faster flattest
hotter biggest

High-Frequency Words
there a the to
again said you

281

Decodable Practice Reader 18C

Decode words in isolation Have children turn to page 281. Have children decode each word.

Review High-frequency words Review the previously taught words *there, to, you, the, again, a* and *said*. Have children read each word as you point to it on the Word Wall.

Preview Have children read the title and preview the story. Tell them they will read words with endings *-er* and *-est* and words with /j/ spelled *dge*.

Decode words in context Pair children for reading and listen carefully as they decode. One child begins. Children read the entire story, switching readers after each page. Partners reread the story. This time the other child begins.

There is a prize
for the best cake.
Penny likes to bake.

282

Penny will bake a cake
to win that prize.
She mixes faster and faster.

283

Decodable Practice Reader 18C

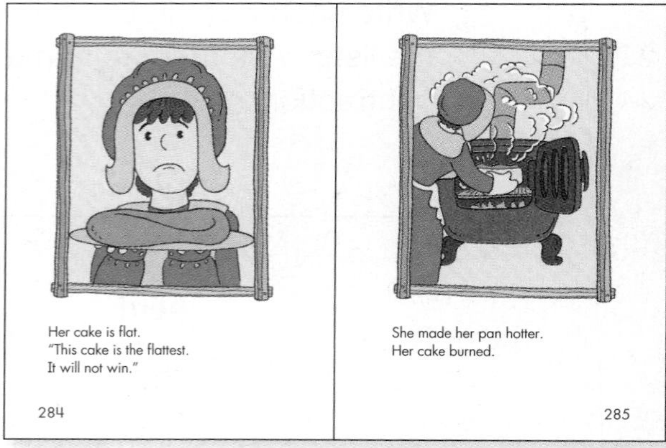

Her cake is flat.
"This cake is the flattest.
It will not win."

284

She made her pan hotter.
Her cake burned.

285

"I will try again," said Penny.
She did not mix as fast.
She added fudge.

286

"Did you make this cake?"
asked the judge with the badge.
"It is the biggest cake."

287

That fudge cake is best.
It wins first prize!

288

Corrective feedback

If... children have difficulty decoding a word,
then... refer them to the Sound-Spelling Cards to identify the sounds in the word. Then prompt them to blend the word.

- What is the new word?
- Is the new word a word you know?
- Does it make sense in the story?

Check decoding and comprehension

Have children retell the story to include characters, setting, and events. Then have children find words with endings *-er* or *-est* and words with /j/ spelled *dge* in the story. Children should supply *faster, flattest, hotter, fudge, judge, badge,* and *biggest*.

Reread for Fluency

Have children reread Decodable Reader 18C to develop automaticity decoding words with endings *-er* or *-est* and words with /j/ spelled *dge*.

ROUTINE Oral Rereading

1. **Read** Have children read the entire book orally.
2. **Reread** To achieve optimal fluency, children should reread the text three or four times.
3. **Corrective Feedback** Listen as children read. Provide corrective feedback regarding their fluency and decoding.

Routines Flip Chart

English Language Learners

Decodable Reader

Beginning Before children read, lead them through *The Fudge Cake*. Tell them that a judge is someone who chooses the winner of a contest. Have children say aloud the words *flattest, hotter, judge, badge,* and *biggest* as they point to the pictures.

Intermediate After children find each *-er, -est,* or *-dge* word in the story, have them use the word in a sentence. For example: *Summer is hotter than winter.*

Advanced/Advanced High After children read, write *faster, flattest, hotter, fudge, judge, badge,* and *biggest* on the board. Have children retell the story using as many of these words as they can.

Objectives

- Read words fluently in context and in isolation.
- Spell words with endings *-er, -est.*
- Spell high-frequency words.

Fluent Word Reading

Spiral Review

Read words in isolation

Display these words. Tell children that they can blend some words on this list and others are Word Wall words.

Have children read the list three or four times until they can read at the rate of two to three seconds per word.

wait	**her**	**know**	**visit**	**turn**
perch	**doesn't**	**I'll**	**swirling**	**clerk**
push	**first**	**we're**	**bird**	**Fern**
we'll	**let's**	**we've**	**done**	**I'm**

Word Reading

Corrective feedback

If... children have difficulty reading whole words,
then... have them use sound-by-sound blending for decodable words, or have them say and spell high-frequency words.

If... children cannot read fluently at a rate of two to three seconds per word,
then... have pairs practice the list until they can read it fluently.

Read words in context

Display these sentences. Call on individuals to read a sentence. Then randomly point to review words and have children read them. To help you monitor word reading, high-frequency words are underlined and decodable words and contractions are italicized.

If <u>the</u> clerk doesn't <u>know</u> <u>what</u> button <u>to</u> <u>push</u>, let's help her.

We've got time <u>to</u> <u>wait</u>, so I'll take <u>a</u> turn.

When we're <u>done</u> with chores, we'll <u>visit</u> Fern first.

I'm swirling like <u>a</u> bird that has left its perch.

Sentence Reading

Corrective feedback

If... children are unable to read an underlined high-frequency word,
then... read the word for them and spell it, having them echo you.

If... children have difficulty reading an italicized decodable word,
then... guide them in using sound-by-sound blending.

Spelling
Words with *-er, -est*

Partner Review Supply pairs of children with index cards on which the spelling words have been written. Have one child read a word while the other writes it. Then have children switch roles. Have them use the cards to check their spelling and correct any misspelled words.

On their own Use *Reader's and Writer's Notebook* p. 407.

Words with -er, -est

Finish the list words.

1. taller 2. shorter
3. tallest 4. shortest
5. sadder 6. biggest
7. bigger 8. saddest

Write the missing words.

Froggy Hopper

9. Hopper is faster than Froggy.
10. Hopper is fastest.

Reader's and Writer's Notebook p. 407

Small Group Time

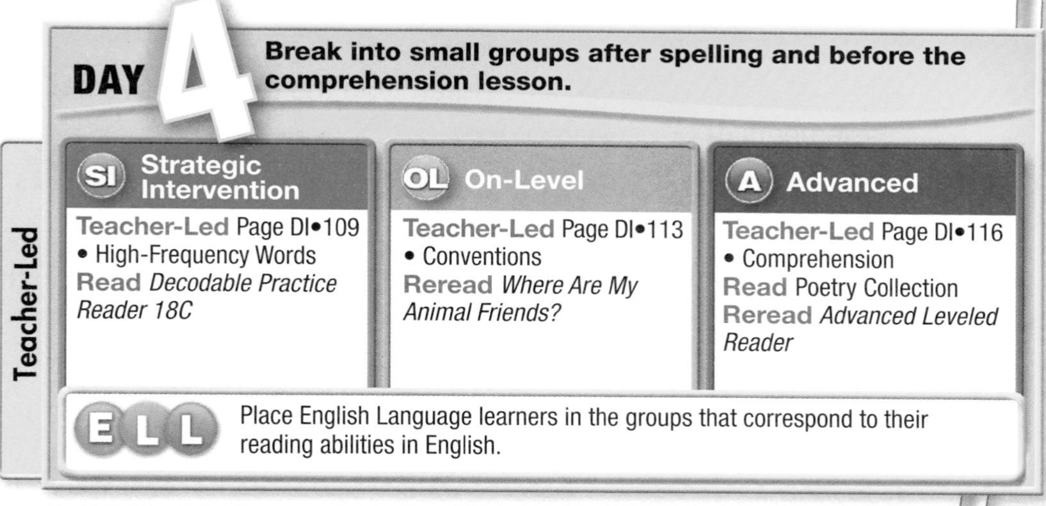

Practice Stations
- Words to Know
- Get Fluent

Independent Activities
- Read independently/Reading Log on *Reader's and Writer's Notebook* p. RR4
- AudioText of Paired Selection

Spiral Review

These activities review

- previously taught high-frequency words *her, done, know, push, visit, wait.*
- /ėr/ spelled *er, ir,* and *ur;* contractions *'s, 've, 're, n't, 'm, 'll.*

English Language Learners

Fluent Word Reading Have children listen to a more fluent reader say the words. Then have them repeat the words.

Objectives

- ◎ Monitor and clarify while reading.
- Recognize structure and elements of poems.
- Relate prior knowledge to new text.
- Set purpose for reading.

Poetry

Preview and predict

Have children read the title of the first poem "This Tooth". Encourage them to look at the pictures. Then ask them to predict what this poem might be about. (Possible response: This poem might be about losing a tooth.)

Let's Think About **Genre**

Poetry Tell children that they will read three **poems.** Review the key elements of a poem: Poems are written in lines and stanzas; stanzas are groups of lines in a poem. Poems often rhyme or have words with the same middle and ending sounds. Poems usually have rhythm, or a regular pattern of beats. Some poems have alliteration.

Activate prior knowledge

Ask children if they've ever had a loose tooth. Have them describe what it felt like.

Set a purpose

Let's Read Together As children read the poems, have them look for elements of poetry.

Let's Think About... Poetry

As you read the selections together, use Let's Think About in the Student Edition to help children focus on the features of poetry.

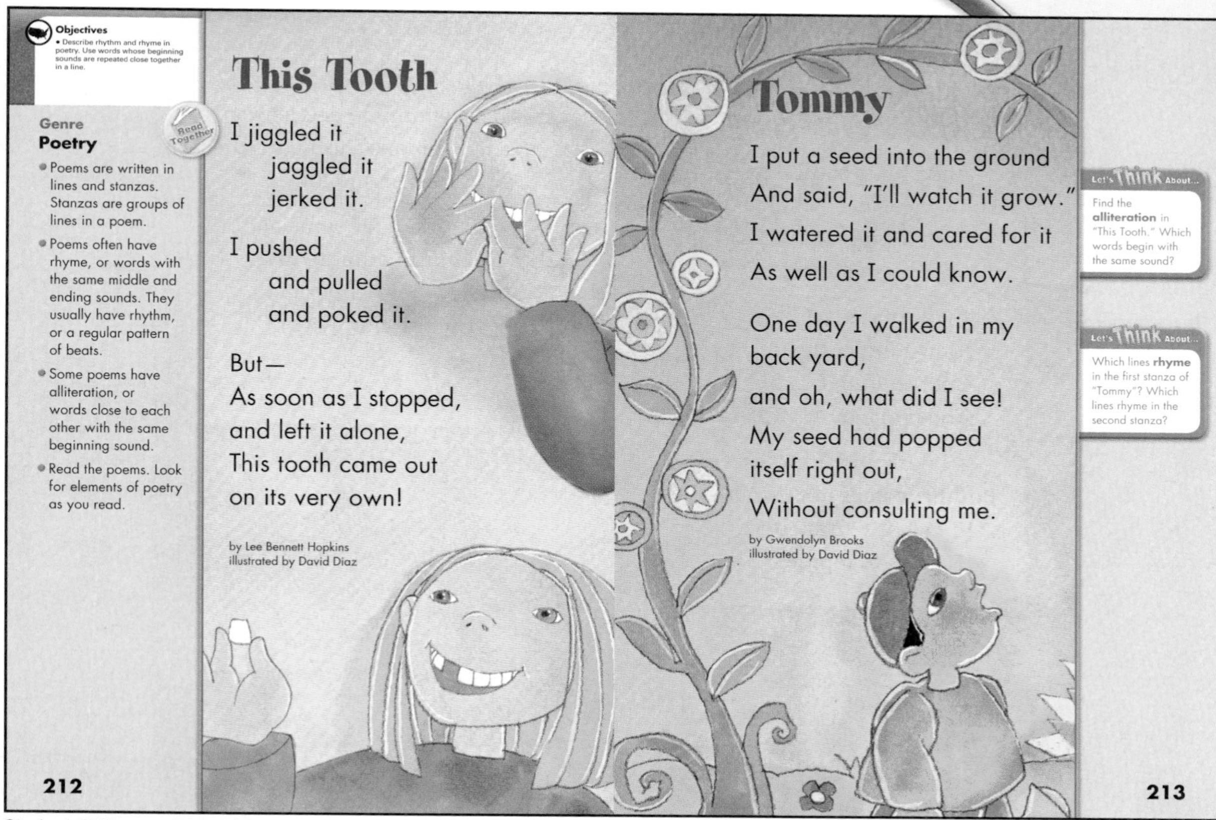

Objectives

• Describe rhythm and rhyme in poetry. Use words whose beginning sounds are repeated close together in a line.

Genre
Poetry

- Poems are written in lines and stanzas. Stanzas are groups of lines in a poem.
- Poems often have rhyme, or words with the same middle and ending sounds. They usually have rhythm, or a regular pattern of beats.
- Some poems have alliteration, or words close to each other with the same beginning sound.
- Read the poems. Look for elements of poetry as you read.

Read Together

This Tooth

I jiggled it
jaggled it
jerked it.

I pushed
and pulled
and poked it.

But—
As soon as I stopped,
and left it alone,
This tooth came out
on its very own!

by Lee Bennett Hopkins
illustrated by David Diaz

212

Tommy

I put a seed into the ground
And said, "I'll watch it grow."
I watered it and cared for it
As well as I could know.

One day I walked in my
back yard,
and oh, what did I see!
My seed had popped
itself right out,
Without consulting me.

by Gwendolyn Brooks
illustrated by David Diaz

Let's Think About...
Find the **alliteration** in "This Tooth." Which words begin with the same sound?

Let's Think About...
Which lines **rhyme** in the first stanza of "Tommy"? Which lines rhyme in the second stanza?

213

Student Edition pp. 212–213

Academic Vocabulary

rhyme words that end with the same sounds: tree, bee; mouse, house

Guide Comprehension

Monitor and Clarify

Think Aloud I can understand a poem better by relating it to my own feelings and experiences. I know what it feels like to have a loose tooth. In "This Tooth," the poet describes how it feels to lose a tooth. My own experience helps me to understand the meaning of the poem.

Alliteration

Think Aloud When I read "This Tooth," I think about alliteration. Alliteration is when words in a selection begin with the same sound. I will look for words that have the same beginning sound in "This Tooth."

Let's Think About... Poetry

The words *grow* and *know* rhyme in the first stanza. The words *see* and *me* rhyme in the second stanza. Possible response: The words *jiggled, jaggled,* and *jerked* all begin with the /j/ sound.

Objectives

- Recognize alliteration in poetry.
- Read aloud fluently with expression and intonation.

Fluency: WCPM
SUCCESS PREDICTOR

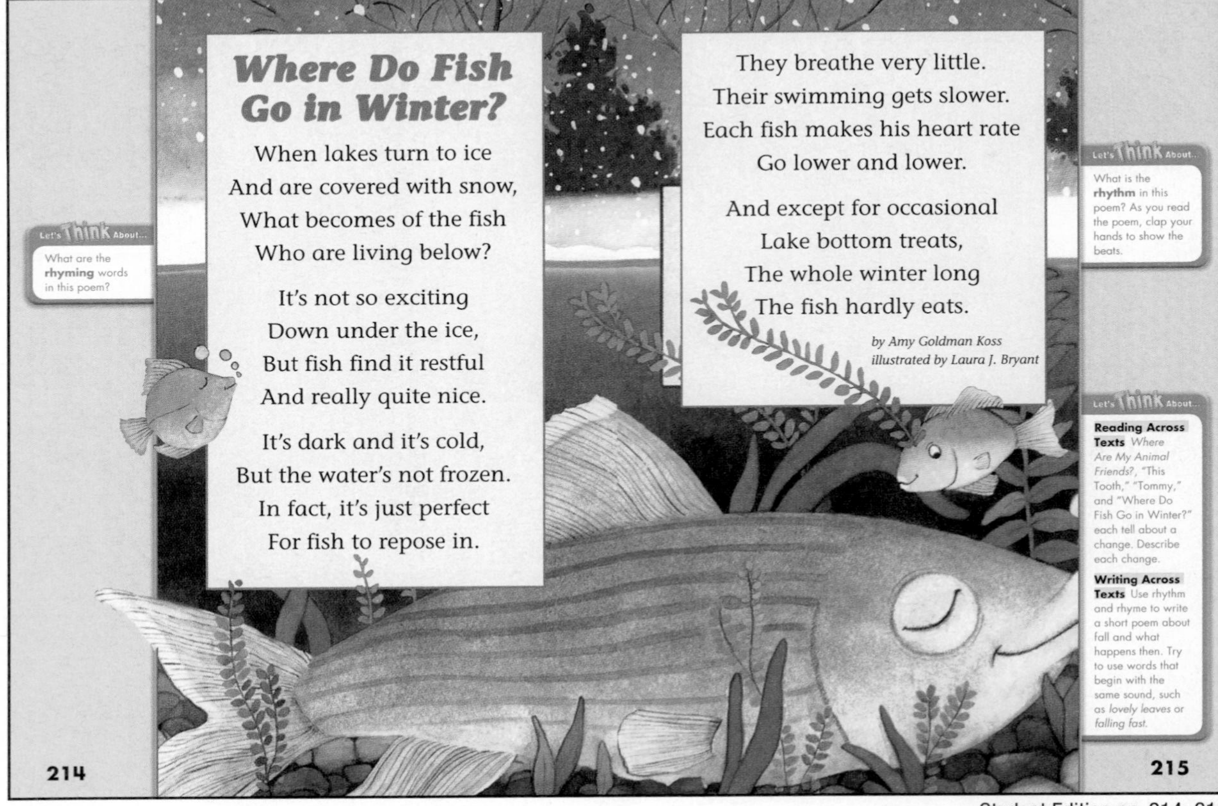

Let's Think About...
What are the **rhyming** words in this poem?

Where Do Fish Go in Winter?

When lakes turn to ice
And are covered with snow,
What becomes of the fish
Who are living below?

It's not so exciting
Down under the ice,
But fish find it restful
And really quite nice.

It's dark and it's cold,
But the water's not frozen.
In fact, it's just perfect
For fish to repose in.

They breathe very little.
Their swimming gets slower.
Each fish makes his heart rate
Go lower and lower.

And except for occasional
Lake bottom treats,
The whole winter long
The fish hardly eats.

by Amy Goldman Koss
illustrated by Laura J. Bryant

Let's Think About...
What is the **rhythm** in this poem? As you read the poem, clap your hands to show the beats.

Let's Think About...
Reading Across Texts *Where Are My Animal Friends?*, "This Tooth," "Tommy," and "Where Do Fish Go in Winter?" each tell about a change. Describe each change.

Writing Across Texts Use rhythm and rhyme to write a short poem about fall and what happens then. Try to use words that begin with the same sound, such as *lovely leaves* or *falling fast*.

214 215

Student Edition pp. 214–215

Guide Comprehension, continued

Let's Think About The rhyming words are *snow, below, ice, nice, slower, lower, treats,* and *eats*.

Use Poetry Have children write a sentence using alliteration. Have them share with a partner.

Reading Across Texts Possible response: The change in *Where Are My Animal Friends?* is the animals preparing for winter. The change in "This Tooth" is the tooth coming out. The change in "Tommy" is a plant growing from a seed. The change in "Where Do Fish Go in Winter?" is how the fish's behavior changes in winter.

Writing Across Texts Answers will vary. You may want to provide examples of alliteration.

Fluency
Expression and Intonation

Guide practice

- Have children turn to pp. 190–191 in *Where Are My Animal Friends?*
- Have children follow along as you read the pages with appropriate expression and intonation.
- Have the class read the pages with you and then reread the pages as a group without you until they read with appropriate expression and intonation. To provide additional fluency practice, pair nonfluent readers with fluent readers.

ROUTINE Paired Reading

1. **Select a Passage** For *Where Are My Animal Friends?,* use pp. 192–193.
2. **Model** First, have children track the print as you read.
3. **Guide Practice** Then have children read along with you.
4. **On Their Own** For optimal fluency, have partners reread three or four times.

Routines Flip Chart

MONITOR PROGRESS Check Fluency WCPM

As children reread, monitor their progress toward their individual fluency goals. Current Goal: 25–35 words correct per minute. End-of-Year Goal: 60 words correct per minute.

If... children cannot read fluently at a rate of 25–35 words correct per minute,
then... have children practice with text at their independent level.

Day 1	Day 2	Day 3	Day 4	Day 5
Check Word Reading	Check Word Reading	Check High-Frequency Words/Retelling	Check Fluency	Check Oral Vocabulary

Success Predictor

Differentiated Instruction

A Advanced

WCPM If children already read at 60 words correct per minute, allow them to read independently.

Fluency Assessment Plan

Do a formal fluency assessment with 8 to 10 children every week. Assess 4 to 5 children on Day 4 and 4 to 5 children on Day 5. Use the reproducible fluency passage, Teacher's Edition, page 217f.

Options for Oral Rereading

Use *Where Are My Animal Friends?* or one of this week's Decodable Practice Readers.

DAY 4 Language Arts

20–25 min.

Objectives

- Recognize correctly spelled contractions with *not.*
- Spelling contractions with *not* correctly.
- Write and act out a scene from a play.

Conventions
Contractions with *Not*

Test practice Use *Reader's and Writer's Notebook* p. 408 to help children understand contractions with *not* in test items. Recall that a contraction is a short way to put two words together. Remind children that in contractions with *not*, an apostrophe takes the place of the *o* in *not*. Model the correct spelling of contractions with *not* by writing these sentences and choosing the one in which *isn't* is spelled correctly. Explain why the others are not correct.

Peppy is'nt a bad cat.

Peppy isnt a bad cat.

Peppy isn't a bad cat.

Then read the *Reader's and Writer's Notebook* p. 408 directions. Guide children as they mark the answer for number 1.

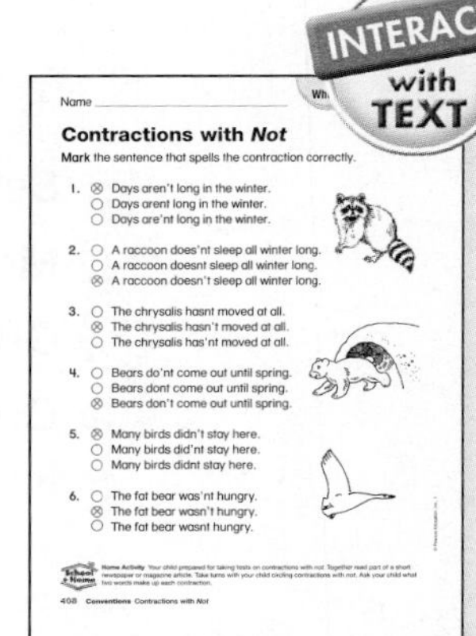

Name ______

Contractions with *Not*

Mark the sentence that spells the contraction correctly.

1. ⊗ Days aren't long in the winter.
   ○ Days arent long in the winter.
   ○ Days are'nt long in the winter.
2. ○ A raccoon does'nt sleep all winter long.
   ○ A raccoon doesnt sleep all winter long.
   ⊗ A raccoon doesn't sleep all winter long.
3. ○ The chrysalis hasnt moved at all.
   ⊗ The chrysalis hasn't moved at all.
   ○ The chrysalis has'nt moved at all.
4. ○ Bears do'nt come out until spring.
   ○ Bears dont come out until spring.
   ⊗ Bears don't come out until spring.
5. ⊗ Many birds didn't stay here.
   ○ Many birds did'nt stay here.
   ○ Many birds didnt stay here.
6. ○ The fat bear was'nt hungry.
   ⊗ The fat bear wasn't hungry.
   ○ The fat bear wasnt hungry.

Home Activity Your child prepared for taking tests on contractions with not. Together read part of a short newspaper or magazine article. Take turns with your child circling contractions with not. Ask your child what two words make up each contraction.

408 **Conventions** Contractions with *Not*

Reader's and Writer's Notebook p. 408

On their own Use *Reader's and Writer's Notebook*, p. 408.

Connect to oral language After children mark the answers to numbers 1–6, review the correct choices. Have children read each correct sentence aloud and say the two words that form the contraction. Then have them say and spell aloud the contraction.

Writing—Play Scene
Revising Strategy

MINI-LESSON

Revising Strategy: Rearranging Sentences

- Yesterday we wrote play scenes of friends talking on the phone. Today we will revise. We can help people who read the play scenes. We can move sentences to make ideas clearer.

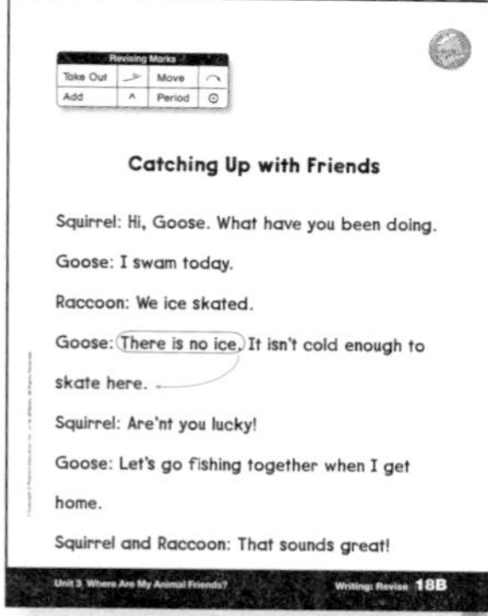

Revising Marks

Take Out		Move	
Add	^	Period	⊙

Catching Up with Friends

Squirrel: Hi, Goose. What have you been doing.
Goose: I swam today.
Raccoon: We ice skated.
Goose: There is no ice. It isn't cold enough to skate here.
Squirrel: Are'nt you lucky!
Goose: Let's go fishing together when I get home.
Squirrel and Raccoon: That sounds great!

Writing Transparency 18B
TR DVD

- Display the Revising Tips. Explain that this is a time for making the play scene clear for anyone who will read it. Tomorrow children will proofread to correct any errors such as misspellings, missing capital letters, or incorrect sentence punctuation.

Revising Tips

- [ ] Make sure your lines sound like people talking.
- [ ] Move sentences to make ideas clear.

- Use Writing Transparency 18B to model rearranging sentences. When Goose says "There is no ice," we don't know where she is talking about. I can fix this by moving the sentence. If it comes after the next sentence, my readers know that she is talking about some place warm. Model transposing the sentences.Tell children that they can move sentences as they revise.

Peer conferencing

Peer Revision Divide children into groups of three. Have children each take a character and read through the scenes. After each one, have children take a few minutes to comment on the play scene. They should tell what is good about the scene and make any suggestions for rearranging sentences to make ideas clearer.

Differentiated Instruction

SI Strategic Intervention

Play Format Explain to children that the play format names the character that speaks the line. When they read the play aloud in their peer groups, they should not say the name of their character before they read the line.

Daily Fix-It

7. today isnt cold.
Today isn't cold.

8. Some birds havent' gon.
Some birds haven't gone.

Discuss the Daily Fix-It corrections with children. Review sentence capitalization, contractions with *not,* and the spelling of *gone.*

English Language Learners

Contractions with Not Be sure children understand that to form a contraction with *not*, they place the apostrophe between the *n* and *t.*

Objectives

- Revise a draft by rearranging sentences.
- Review answers to inquiry questions.

Writing
Play Scene, continued

Guide practice Have children revise their play scenes. For those not sure how to revise, have children refer to the Revising Tips or the Key Features of Play Scenes.

Corrective feedback Circulate to monitor and conference with children as they write. Remind them that they will have time to proofread and edit tomorrow. Today they can move sentences to make their ideas clearer.

ROUTINE Quick Write for Fluency Team Talk

1. **Talk** Read these lines aloud, and have children tell which should come first.

   I am great.
   How are you?
2. **Write** Have children write two lines from a play in the correct order.
3. **Share** Partners can read the lines to one another.

Routines Flip Chart

Research and Inquiry

Review and Revise Topic

Teach Tell children that the next step in the inquiry project is to review our topic to see if we have the information we set out to find. Or, did our answers lead to a different topic?

Model We wanted to answer the question: *What do people do when the seasons change?* We came up with some activities that we like to do. We also thought about some more general things that people do when the seasons change. Display the chart. Now we have a chart of things people do when the seasons change. These ideas answer the original question, *What do people do when the seasons change?* So, we have answered our original topic, and it does not need to change.

Guide practice Have children look at the information they gathered on Day 3. Then instruct them to work with a partner to discuss the entire chart. Do they feel they have enough examples to support the main question? If not, they may wish to ask each other for more ideas, or look for more ideas in magazines and picture books. Finally, tell children that tomorrow they will organize all the information in order to share it with others.

Differentiated Instruction

Advanced

Expand on the Topic Children may wish to investigate what people in other cities, countries, and continents do when the seasons change. For example, what do people do in Canada or Africa? Have students do research in picture books about these places to come up with ideas about what people who live in these places do when the seasons change.

Wrap Up Your Day

- ✔ **Phonics** List several words that end with *-er.* Have children read each word, name the base word, and then build the *-est* form of the word.
- ✔ **Fluency** Write *Oh, no! All my friends are going away!* Have the class reread the sentence until they can do so with appropriate expression and intonation.

Remind children that they heard about a moose that helps others get ready for the changes of the seasons. Tomorrow they will hear about the moose again.

Objectives

- Review the concept: what animals do when the seasons change.
- Build oral vocabulary.
- Identify details in text.

Today at a Glance

Oral Vocabulary
Review

Phonics
◉ Review Comparative Endings *-er, -est*
◉ Review Consonant Pattern *dge*

Comprehension
◉ Draw Conclusions

Story Words
Review

High-Frequency Words
Review

Conventions
Contractions with *not*

Writing
Play Scene

Research and Inquiry
Communicate

Check Oral Vocabulary SUCCESS PREDICTOR

Concept Wrap Up

Question of the Week

What do animals do when the seasons change?

Review Concept

This week we have read and listened to stories about what animals do when the seasons change. Today you will listen to find out what Moose and Beaver do to help each other get ready for winter. Read the story.

- What do Moose and Beaver do to help each other get ready for winter? (Moose builds a rock path across the pond for Beaver's friends. Beaver builds a bigger home so Moose can visit.)

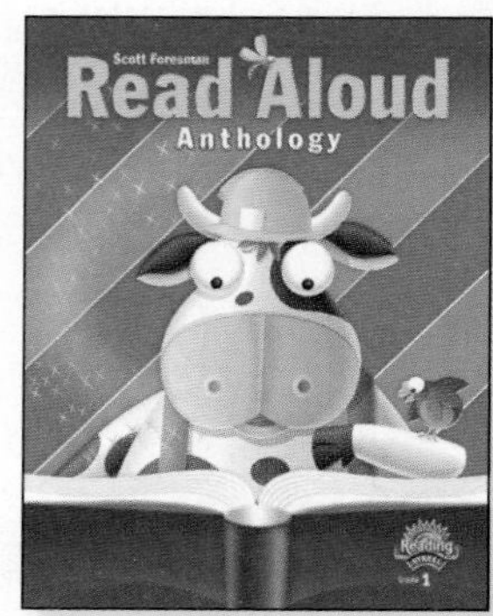

"Busy Busy Moose"

Review Amazing Words

Orally review this week's Amazing Words and concept map. Have children use Amazing Words and the concept map to answer the question "What do animals do when the seasons change?"

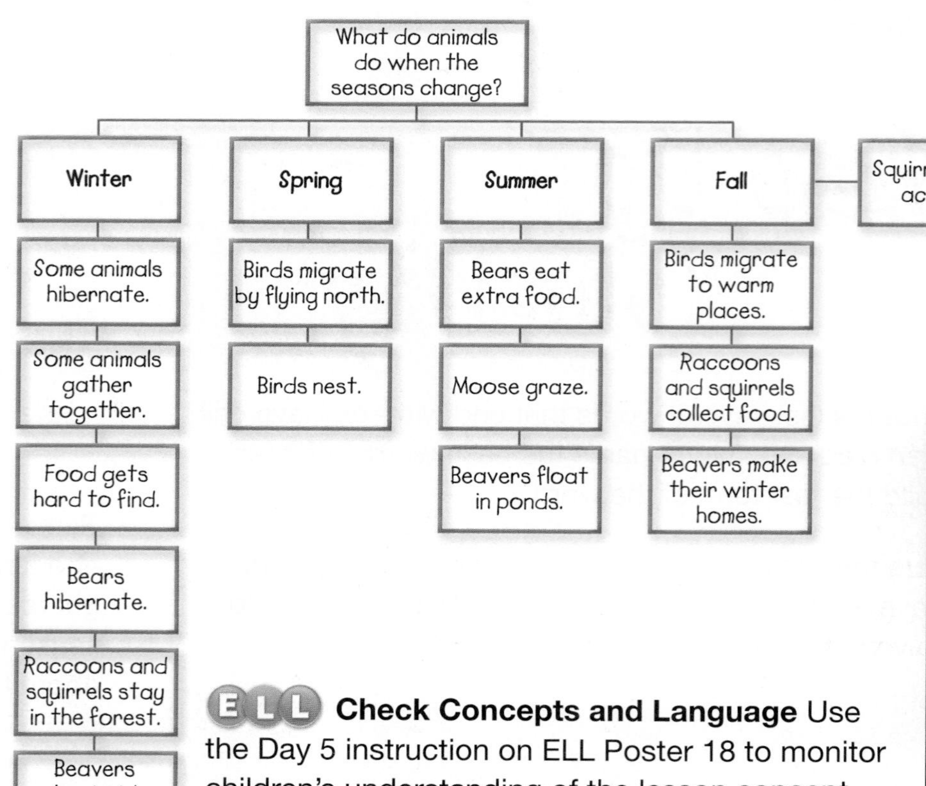

ELL Check Concepts and Language Use the Day 5 instruction on ELL Poster 18 to monitor children's understanding of the lesson concept.

ELL Poster 18

Oral Vocabulary
Amazing Words

Connect to the Big Question

Team Talk Pair children and have them discuss how the Question of the Week connects to this unit's Big Question, "What is changing in our world?" Tell children to use the concept map and what they've learned from this week's Anchored Talks and reading selections to form an Amazing Idea—a realization or "big idea" about **changes**. Then ask each pair to share their Amazing Idea with the class.

Amazing Ideas might include these key concepts:

- In seasons when plants grow, animals eat, store up food, and build homes.
- In winter, animals eat stored food, or they migrate or hibernate.

It's Friday

MONITOR PROGRESS **Check Oral Vocabulary**

Call on individuals to use this week's Amazing Words to discuss what animals do when the seasons change. Prompt discussion with the questions. Monitor children's ability to use the Amazing Words and note which words children are unable to use.

- **If you were a forest animal, would you like to *hibernate* for the winter? Why?**
- **How does the *temperature* tell some animals what to do?**
- **What happens in *autumn* that helps squirrels gather food?**
- **Can a bear catch fish when a lake *freezes*? Why?**
- **What animals can live where it's *bitterly* cold?**
- **Do you think birds get *weary* when they are *migrating*? Why?**

If... children have difficulty using the Amazing Words,
then... reteach the unknown words using the Oral Vocabulary Routines, pp. 183a, 188b, 208b, 212b.

Day 1	Day 2	Day 3	Day 4	Day 5
Check Word Reading	Check Word Reading	Check High-Frequency Words/Retelling	Check Fluency	Check Oral Vocabulary

Success Predictor

Amazing Words

hibernate	freeze
migrate	bitterly
temperature	weary
autumn	

ELL

English Language Learners
Amazing Words Begin by asking questions that review the definitions more directly. For example: What is the *temperature* like in summer? in winter? Use pantomime and gestures to give hints.

Objectives

- ◎ Review comparative endings *-er, -est.*
- ◎ Review consonant pattern *-dge.*
- Review generating rhyming words.
- Review high-frequency words.

Assess

- Spell words with comparative endings *-er, -est.*
- Spell high-frequency words.

Phonological Awareness
Generate Rhyming Words

Review **Rhyming words**

Have children orally generate words starting with consonant blends that rhyme with the following words. If children make an error, model a correct response. Return to the word later in the practice. Sample responses are given.

for (store, floor, score)	**map** (snap, clap, flap, trap)
pass (glass, class, grass)	**if** (sniff, cliff, stiff)
right (fright, flight, bright)	**lone** (blown, stone, grown, flown)

Phonics
◎ Comparative Endings *-er, -est;* Consonant Pattern *-dge*

Review **Target phonics skills**

Write the following sentences on the board. Have children read each one, first quietly to themselves and then aloud as you track the print.

1. **Midge will try to dodge the smallest ball.**
2. **That cat won't budge from the edge of the shorter ledge.**
3. **The biggest dish of hot cereal is the hottest too.**
4. **The greenest wedge of grass is by the park lodge.**

Team Talk Have children discuss with a partner which words have an *-er* or *-est* ending and which words have *dge*. Then call on individuals to share with the class.

Spelling Test
Words with Endings *-er, -est*

Dictate spelling words

Say each word, read the sentence, repeat the word, and allow time for children to write the word.

1. faster	My dog runs **faster** than my cat.
2. bigger	A bus is **bigger** than a car.
3. shorter	This line is **shorter** than that line.
4. saddest	She was **saddest** at the end of the day.
5. fastest	Madge is the **fastest** person in the class.
6. taller	My mom is **taller** than I am.
7. tallest	The **tallest** tree in the park is an oak tree.
8. biggest	That is the **biggest** bird I've ever seen.
9. sadder	Jim looked **sadder** than Jan when we lost.
10. shortest	Let the **shortest** children stand in front.

High-Frequency Words

11. good-bye	We said **good-bye** as we left.
12. before	**Before** you go, stop in to see me.

Small Group Time

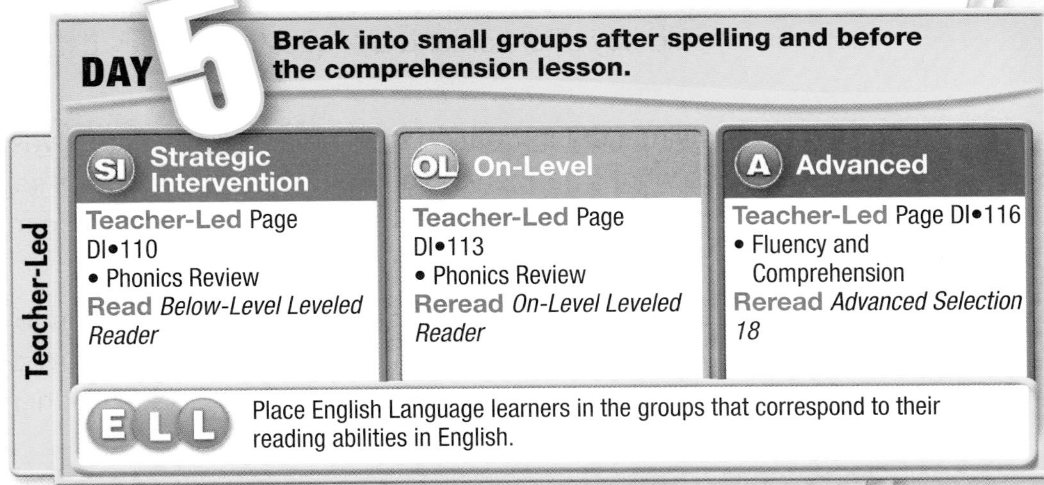
DAY 5 Break into small groups after spelling and before the comprehension lesson.

Teacher-Led

SI Strategic Intervention	OL On-Level	A Advanced
Teacher-Led Page DI•110 • Phonics Review Read *Below-Level Leveled Reader*	Teacher-Led Page DI•113 • Phonics Review Reread *On-Level Leveled Reader*	Teacher-Led Page DI•116 • Fluency and Comprehension Reread *Advanced Selection 18*

ELL Place English Language learners in the groups that correspond to their reading abilities in English.

Practice Stations
- Read for Meaning
- Words to Know

Independent Activities
- Read independently/Reading Log on *Reader's and Writer's Notebook* p. RR4
- Concept Talk Video

Differentiated Instruction

SI Strategic Intervention

Check Spelling Help children spell each word on the test by pronouncing the base word and ending separately. Remind children that when a word with a short vowel sound ends with one consonant, that final consonant is usually doubled before adding *-er* or *-est*.

Advanced

Extend Spelling Have children learn to spell these more difficult words with *-er* and *-est* and write them in original sentences: *colder, stronger, newer, softest.*

ELL

English Language Learners

Spelling Dictation Be sure to clearly enunciate the final /t/ sound in words that end in *–est*, as English learners may have difficulty hearing this sound.

Objectives

- Give an announcement, including all important information.
- Listen attentively.
- Use context clues to determine the correct meaning of multiple-meaning words.
- Read aloud fluently with good expression and intonation.

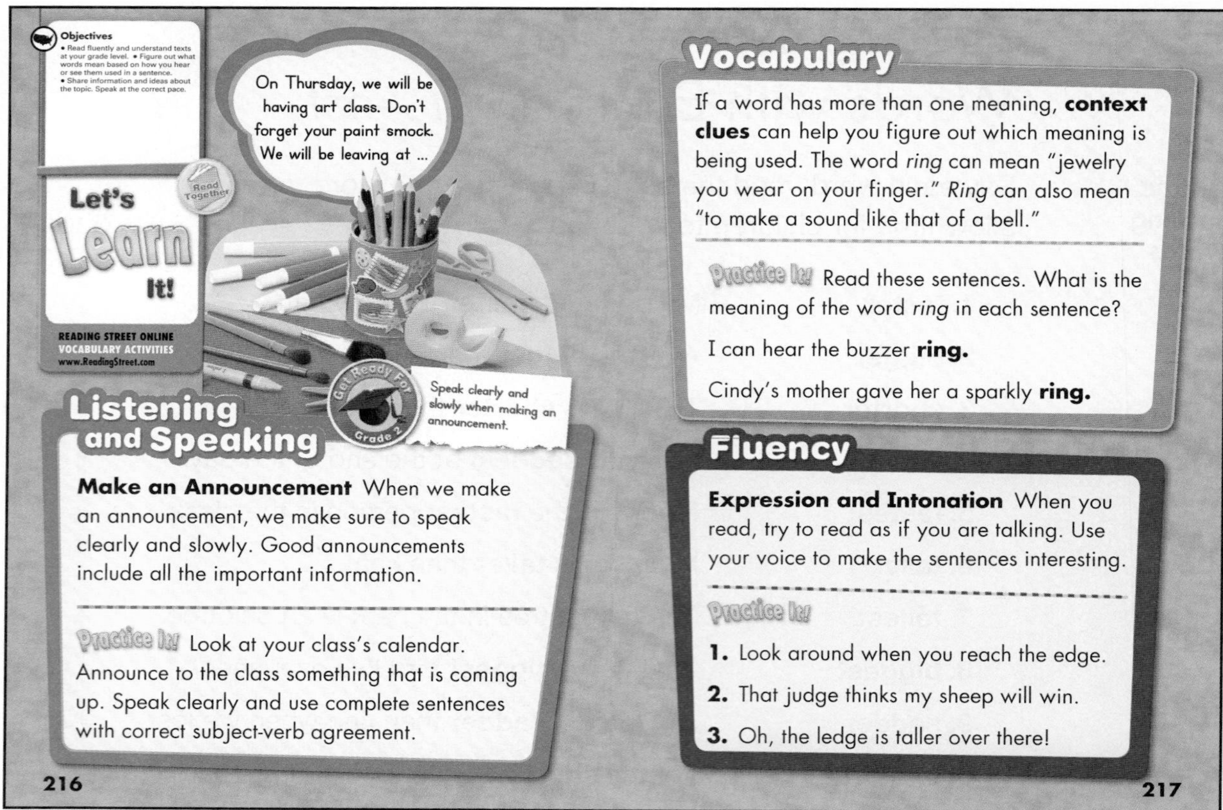

Student Edition pp. 216–217

Listening and Speaking
Give Announcements

Teach Have children turn to pages 216–217 of the Student Edition. Read the announcement aloud. Remind children that an announcement should be given slowly and clearly and should tell all the important information. Listeners should pay attention and ask questions if they didn't hear all the details.

Analyze model Point out the kinds of information that the announcement gives. The first sentence tells what's happening, and on what day. The next sentence tells what to bring. The last sentence tells exactly what time to be ready. Ask children why each kind of information is important.

Introduce prompt Read the Practice It! prompt with the class. Remind children to answer the questions *What's happening?* and *When?*, and to include any other information that their listeners will need to know. Encourage listeners to ask questions if any information was left out.

Team Talk Have pairs plan an announcement together. Tell them to decide first what information is important and then to take turns practicing their announcement, speaking slowly and clearly.

Vocabulary
Context Clues

Teach Read and discuss the Vocabulary lesson on page 217 of the Student Edition. Use the model to explain how to use context clues to understand words that have more than one meaning

Model Point to the first example in the Practice It! section. The words *hear* and *buzzer* are clues that in this sentence *ring* means "the sound of a bell." Point to the second example. The word *sparkly* is a clue that in this sentence *ring* means "jewelry worn on the finger."

Guide practice Write these sentences. Turn *right* at the corner. Josh was *right* about the math test. Read each sentence aloud.

Right can mean "opposite of left" or "correct." What clues tell you which meaning is used in the first sentence? (*Turn* and *corner* are clues that the meaning is "opposite of left.") In the second sentence? (*Math test* is a clue that the meaning is "correct.")

On their own Write and read aloud these sentences: *His bat hit the ball. The bat spread its wings and flew.* Have children discuss the meaning of *bat* in each sentence and the context clues they used.

Corrective feedback Circulate around the room and listen as children discuss context clues for the meanings of *bat*. Provide assistance as needed.

Fluency
Expression and Intonation

Teach Read and discuss the Fluency instructions.

Read words in context Give children a moment to look at the sentences. Then have them read each sentence three or four times until they can read it with good expression and intonation.

Differentiated Instruction

Strategic Intervention
Have a child say the word *ring* twice, each time acting out a different meaning. Ask children what clues in the child's actions showed the meaning of *ring*. Repeat the process for *right* and *bat*.

Give Announcements

To prepare themselves for skills needed at Grade 2, children should be able give announcements, speaking slowly and clearly and including all information that their listeners need to know.

English Language Learners
Context Clues Assign a sound or gesture to stand for each meaning of a multiple-meaning word. For example, children could wave a finger in the air for *ring* as jewelry and say "ding, ding" for *ring* as a sound. Then say sentences using each meaning, and have children make the appropriate gesture or sound to show the correct meaning.

Objectives

- Draw conclusions.
- Read story words.
- Respond to and use rhyme, rhythm, and alliteration.

Comprehension

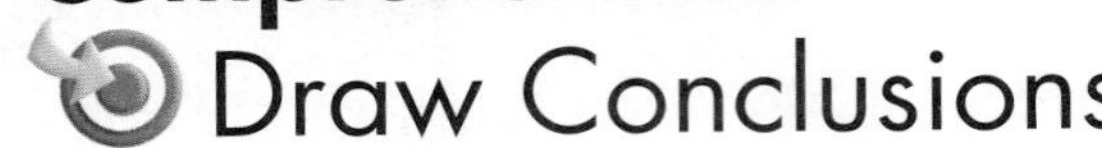

Draw Conclusions

Review
Draw conclusions

Remember good readers think about what they read and what they already know to figure out what the author isn't telling us. What is this called? (drawing conclusions)

To check understanding of drawing conclusions, read aloud the following story and have children answer the questions.

> Two trees stood in Ava's yard. In spring, both trees were covered with green leaves. But one fall, one tree's leaves all turned yellow and the other one's leaves all were red. Ava named one tree *Rosy* and the other *Sunny*. The weather began to get colder and colder, and one day the fall wind blew most of the leaves off the trees. Ava could now see that each tree held a nest in its branches. Ava knew that Rosy and Sunny must be very proud trees.

1. Which tree is Rosy and which tree is Sunny? How do you know? (The tree with red leaves is called Rosy, because roses are usually red. The other one is called Sunny because its leaves were yellow like the sun.)
2. Why does Ava think that both trees are proud? (Possible response: The trees are proud because they had nests in them, which must have been homes to some baby birds. It would make me proud if I could help out a little bird like that.)

Vocabulary

High-Frequency and Story Words

Review
High-frequency words

Review this week's high-frequency words: *does, good-bye, before, won't, oh,* and *right*. Model making up a sentence containing one of the high-frequency words. Example: Oh, you surprised me! Then use gestures or actions to demonstrate the meaning of the word and sentence.

Team Talk Have a child say a sentence using a different high-frequency word. Have another child use gestures or actions to show the meaning of the word and sentence. Repeat for each high-frequency word.

Review
Story words

Write the words *spring, warm, goose, raccoon,* and *butterfly*. Read them aloud together. Then have children tell what each word means.

Corrective feedback

If... children cannot tell what the story words mean,
then... review the definitions on page 184a.

Poetry

Rhyme, Rhythm, and Alliteration

Review Poetry

Review with children that a **poem** is an arrangement of words in lines. A poem sounds like a song but without the music.

Teach

The lines of a poem may have a **rhythm**, or beat. (Clap out the beat of "Mary had a little lamb.") Some of the words may **rhyme**, or end with the same sounds, as in *fish* and *wish*. Some words may begin with the same sound, as in *pretty pink pig*. This is called **alliteration**.

Model

Think Aloud

I enjoy poetry when I can feel its rhythm and hear its special sounds. Read aloud "Where Do Fish Go in Winter?" on pages 214–215, clapping to the rhythm. Point out the rhyming words in each stanza. Then go back to the line "But fish find it restful." In this line, I hear alliteration—words that begin with the same sound. Reread the lines, emphasizing the alliteration. I like the way the /f/ sound repeats in *fish*, *find*, and *restful*.

Guide practice

Have children turn to "This Tooth" on Student Edition page 212. Read the poem aloud with them.

- In the first part, which words begin with the same sound? (jiggled, jaggled, jerked) In the second part? (pushed, pulled, poked)
- Let's read the last part again and clap out the rhythm.
- Which words rhyme in the last part? (alone, own)

On their own

Have children compose silly two-line poems, following this model:

A ________ ________ is in a ________ .
A ________ ________ is in a ________

Explain that the first two missing words in each line must begin with the same consonant sound. The end words must rhyme with each other.

Example:
A fuzzy fly is in a jar.
A merry mouse is in a car.

Differentiated Instruction

Strategic Intervention

Poetry Patterns If children have difficulty following the pattern of the two-line poem, supply the end rhymes and have children provide only the alliterative words. Then do the reverse: supply the alliterative words, and have children provide the end rhymes.

Academic Vocabulary

alliteration the repetition of a sound at the beginning of two or more words

poem an arrangement of words in lines that sometimes rhyme and sometimes have rhythm

rhyme to end with the same sounds

rhythm a regular beat

Assess

- ◎ Comparative Endings *-er, -est*
- ◎ Consonant Pattern *-dge*
- • High-Frequency Words
- • Fluency: WCPM
- ◎ Draw Conclusions

Fluency Goals

Set individual fluency goals for children to enable them to reach the end-of-year goal.

- **Current Goal:** 25–35 WCPM
- **End-of-Year Goal:** 60 WCPM

Assessment
Monitor Progress

For a written assessment of comparative endings *-er*, *-est*, consonant pattern *-dge*, high-frequency words, and drawing conclusions, use Weekly Test 18, pages 139–144.

Assess words in context

Sentence reading Use the following reproducible page to assess children's ability to read words in context. Call on children to read two sentences aloud. Start over with sentence one if necessary.

MONITOR PROGRESS **Sentence Reading**

If... children have trouble reading comparative endings *-er*, *-est* and consonant pattern *-dge*,
then... use the Reteach Lessons on pp. 219–220 in *First Stop*.

If... children cannot read all the high-frequency words,
then... mark the missed words on a high-frequency word list and have the child practice reading the words with a fluent reader.

Assess

Fluency Take a one-minute sample of children's oral reading. Have children read the fluency passage on page 217f.

Comprehension Have the child read the entire passage. If the child has difficulty with the passage, you may read it aloud. Then have the child draw conclusions based on the passage.

MONITOR PROGRESS **Fluency and Comprehension**

If... a child does not achieve the fluency goal on the timed reading,
then... copy the passage and send it home with the child for additional fluency practice, or have the child practice with a fluent reader.

If... a child cannot draw conclusions,
then... use the Reteach Lesson on p. 256 in *First Stop*.

Monitor accuracy

Record scores Have children monitor their accuracy by recording their scores using the Sentence Reading Chart and by recording the number of words read correctly per minute on the Fluency Progress Chart in *First Stop*.

Name ____________________

Read the Sentences

1. Cut this grass before you trim the thickest hedge.

2. That taller judge waved good-bye to us.

3. My shortest horse won't trot to the edge of this cliff.

4. Oh, he just made the smudge on his shirt bigger!

5. Does Tad like my sweetest fudge?

6. Set this darker vase on the right side of that ledge.

MONITOR PROGRESS

- Fluency
- Comparative Endings *-er, -est*
- Consonant Pattern *-dge*
- High-frequency Words

Name ______________________________

Read the Story

Clark had a horse named Star. Star was his fastest 10
horse. Clark wanted Star to jump, but Star didn't jump. 20
If she came to a fence or hedge, she just stopped. She 32
didn't budge. 34

Every day Clark went to the barn. He rode Star all 45
morning. Clark patted Star's neck and spoke to her. 54
"Won't you try jumping?" he asked. 60

One day Clark was humming as he ate figs. "Figs! 70
That is it!" he said. 75

Clark grabbed a bunch of figs. He let Star try one. 86
Then he let Star see him put the figs on the far side of 100
the fence. Star ran faster than ever before. She ran right 111
to the fence and jumped over it! 118

Clark hugged Star. "Oh, what a brave girl!" he said 128
as he fed her a fig. 134

MONITOR PROGRESS

- Check Fluency
- Draw Conclusions

Conventions
Contractions with *Not*

Objectives
- Write contractions with *not* correctly.
- Use contractions with *not* in sentences.

Review Remind children that a contraction is a short way of putting two words together, and that an apostrophe takes the place of a missing letter. Have them give examples of contractions with *not*.

Guide practice Write the following sentences. Have children write the contraction that can take the place of the underlined words.

1. **Steve <u>did</u> <u>not</u> take a cup.**
2. **Kelly <u>has</u> <u>not</u> had her turn.**
3. **Mom <u>does</u> <u>not</u> need the car.**

Connect to oral language Write and read aloud the word pairs below. Have children work with a partner to say the contraction formed by each word pair and use the contraction in a sentence. Then have children share their sentences with the class.

were not **was not** **is not** **are not**

On their own Use Let's Practice It! p. 167 on the *Teacher Resource DVD-ROM.*

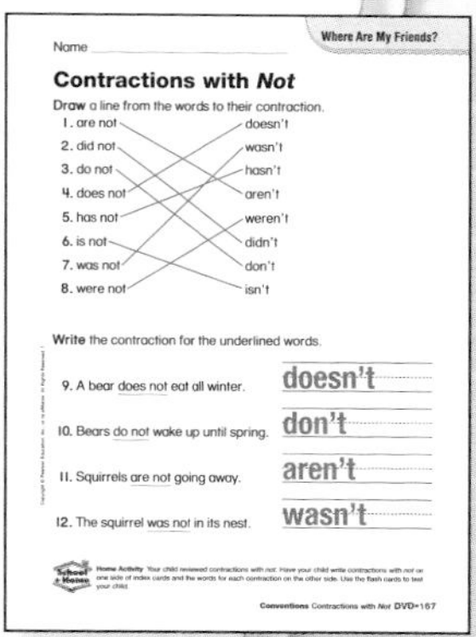
Name ______ Where Are My Friends?

Contractions with *Not*

Draw a line from the words to their contraction.

1. are not — doesn't
2. did not — wasn't
3. do not — hasn't
4. does not — aren't
5. has not — weren't
6. is not — didn't
7. was not — don't
8. were not — isn't

Write the contraction for the underlined words.

9. A bear <u>does not</u> eat all winter. doesn't
10. Bears <u>do not</u> wake up until spring. don't
11. Squirrels <u>are not</u> going away. aren't
12. The squirrel <u>was not</u> in its nest. wasn't

Conventions Contractions with *Not* DVD•167

Let's Practice It! TR DVD•167

Differentiated Instruction

Strategic Intervention

Sentence Production Forming sentences with contractions containing *were, was, is,* and *are* will give children practice with subject-verb agreement for these verbs. Support this skill by giving children corrective feedback on any subject-verb agreement errors in their sentences.

Daily Fix-It

9. this animal is the bigger of all.
   <u>T</u>his animal is the bigg<u>est</u> of all.
10. yesterday some toads hop around.
    <u>Y</u>esterday some toads hop<u>ped</u> around.

Discuss the Daily Fix-It corrections with children. Review capitalization in sentences, comparative endings *-er* and *-est*, and the past tense ending *-ed*.

DAY 5 **Wrap Up your Week** 30–35 min.

Objectives

- Edit a draft for spelling, punctuation, and capitalization.
- Create final draft and present.

Writing—Play Scene
Writer's Craft: Contractions with *Not*

Review Revising

Remind children that yesterday they revised their play scenes. They may have rearranged sentences to make the ideas clearer. Today they will proofread their play scenes.

MINI-LESSON

Proofread for Contractions with *Not*

- **Teach** Mistakes in spelling, punctuation, and capitalization make it hard for readers to understand our writing. We need to correct these kinds of mistakes. We need to check that we have spelled contractions correctly and have used the right punctuation to end our sentences.

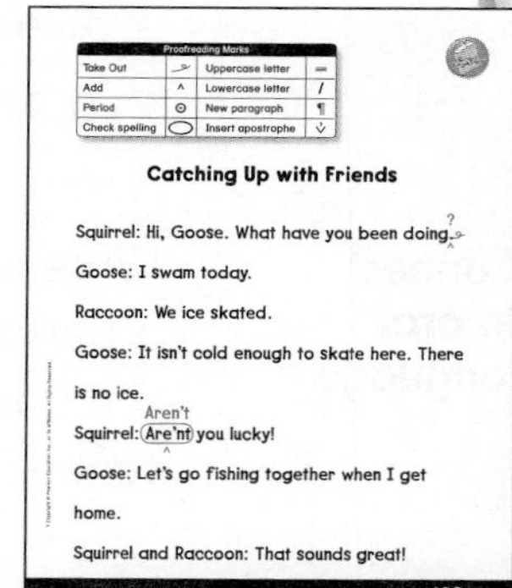

Writing Transparency 18C
TR DVD

- **Model** Let us look at my play scene. Display Writing Transparency 18C. Explain that you will look at the contractions first. Show how you would change any misspellings by correcting the mistake in *aren't*. Then reread for punctuation. Model changing the period to a question mark in the first line of the play.

Proofread

Display the Proofreading Tips. Have children proofread their stories to correct any misspellings, missing capital letters, or errors with periods. Circulate to assist children with contractions.

Proofreading Tips

- ✓ Are my contractions spelled correctly?
- ✓ Are other words spelled correctly? Check a dictionary.
- ✓ Do my sentences begin with a capital letter?
- ✓ Did I punctuate my sentences correctly?

Present

Have children make a final draft of their play scenes with their revisions and proofreading corrections. Help as appropriate.

Choose an option for children to present their play scenes.

Have a play day in which groups of three perform their scenes for the class.	Children can illustrate their play scenes and display them on the class bulletin board.

When they have finished, help them complete a Self-Evaluation form.

ROUTINE **Quick Write for Fluency** Team Talk

1. **Talk** Have partners take one minute to find a contraction in each of their scenes.
2. **Write** Each child writes a new short sentence using one of the contractions.
3. **Share** Partners trade sentences and read them aloud.

Routines Flip Chart

Teacher Note

Self-Evaluation Make copies of the Self-Evaluation form from the Teacher Resource DVD-ROM, and hand them out to children.

English Language Learners

Support Editing Have children work with partners to read aloud their play scenes. Explain that hearing the words often helps them catch errors in spelling, grammar, and punctuation.

Objectives

- Review the concept: what do people do when the seasons change.
- Organize information.
- Create a picture graph.
- Present results of an inquiry project.

Research and Inquiry
Communicate

Teach Tell children that today they will help create a picture graph that tells what their classmates' favorite seasons are.

Model Think Aloud Display the chart. Let's review our chart. We came up with things that people do when the seasons change. We also thought about our favorite things to do when the seasons change. Now I want you to think about all the answers on the chart. I am going to ask you what your favorite season is. Raise your hand when I call out the name of the season that is your favorite.

Guide practice Survey the class for their favorite season. Then make a picture graph on a large posterboard. The left side should name the seasons with a picture (a flower, sun, leaf, and snowflake, for example). The bottom should have numbers listed from left to right. Go as high in numbers as there are children in your class. Look again at Transparency 18 for help. After you have added up the numbers for each favorite season, write the totals on the board.

On their own Have each child come up to the big picture graph and draw a picture in the square for the season they picked as their favorite. When the child is done, have him or her announce, *My favorite season is [name of season]. [Name of fellow classmate], please come up and draw your picture.* Remind children how to be good speakers and listeners:

- Good speakers talk at a pace that everyone can understand. So, be careful not to talk too fast or too slow.
- Good listeners wait until the speaker has finished speaking before raising their hands to ask a question.

Wrap Up Your Week!

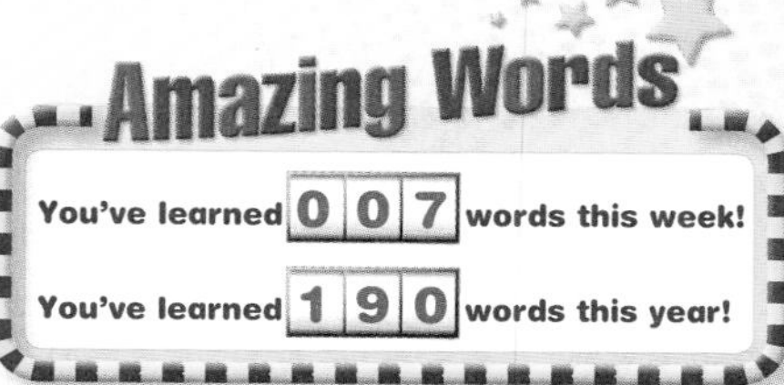

Question of the Week
What do animals do when the seasons change?

Think Aloud

This week we explored the different things that animals do as the seasons change. In the story *Where Are My Animal Friends?*, we read that in fall, as the weather grows colder, some animals get ready for winter by migrating, hibernating, or storing up food. In "Busy Busy Moose," we learned that in spring, as the weather turns warm again, birds that had migrated come back to build new nests and have babies. All of our selections this week have shown us that animals do different things in different seasons, and that their activities fit with the weather and other changes that each season brings to the earth. Have children recall their Amazing Ideas about changes. Then have children use these ideas to help them demonstrate their understanding of the Question of the Week.

English Language Learners

Poster Preview Prepare children for next week by using Unit 4 Week 1, ELL Poster 19. Read the Poster Talk-Through to introduce the concept and vocabulary. Ask children to identify and describe objects and actions in the art.

Selection Summary Send home the summary of *Mama's Birthday Present* in English and the child's home language if available. Children can read the summary with family members.

Preview NEXT WEEK

Tell children that next week they will read about how surprises can be treasures.

Unit Wrap-Up

The Big Question

What is changing in our world?

Understanding By Design

Grant Wiggins, Ed. D.
Reading Street Author

"Good questions elicit interesting and alternative views and suggest the need to focus on the reasoning we use in arriving at and defending an answer . . . They cause us to rethink what we thought we understood and to transfer an idea from one setting to others."

WEEK 1

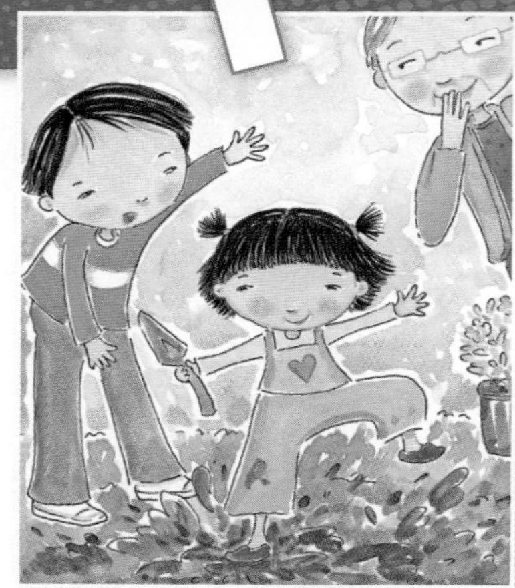

Question of the Week

How do places change?

Concept Knowledge

Children will understand that places:

- grow in size when new people come
- can be made better by people working together
- change to reflect the needs of people

WEEK 2

Question of the Week

What do we learn as we grow and change?

Concept Knowledge

Children will understand that as we grow and change:

- we learn to do new things
- we understand how we are the same as others
- we understand how we are different from others

Discuss the Big Question

Help children relate the concept question for this unit to the selections and their own experiences. Write the question and prompt discussion with questions such as the following:

What changes happen in the stories in this unit?
Possible answers:

- *Ruby in Her Own Time* Ruby grows and changes.
- *The Class Pet* A baby mouse changes in many ways as it grows.
- *Frog and Toad Together* It takes rain, sun, and patience to grow a garden.
- *I'm a Caterpillar* A caterpillar goes through many changes as it becomes a butterfly.

WEEK 3

Question of the Week

What can we learn about animals as they grow and change?

Concept Knowledge

Children will understand that:

- babies go through many changes
- babies learn as they grow
- it is fun to learn something new

WEEK 4

Question of the Week

What changes happen in a garden?

Concept Knowledge

Children will understand that:

- we plant seeds in a garden
- rain and sun help seeds grow
- it takes time for plants to grow

WEEK 5

Question of the Week

What changes can be seen in nature?

Concept Knowledge

Children will understand that:

- some animals undergo amazing changes
- caterpillars change to become butterflies
- the cycle of change repeats itself

WEEK 6

Question of the Week

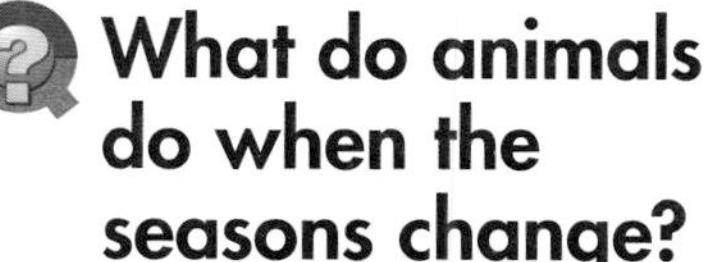

What do animals do when the seasons change?

Concept Knowledge

Children will understand that animals may:

- gather food or feed more in summer and fall
- build new homes in fall and spring
- migrate in fall and spring

What did not change?

Possible answers:

- *A Place to Play* The town is the same.
- *Ruby in Her Own Time* Ruby comes back.
- *The Class Pet* The mouse's home remains the same.
- *I'm a Caterpillar* The cycle of a caterpillar changing is always the same.
- *Where Are My Animal Friends?* Raccoon and Squirrel stay.

Tell about how you changed when you were a baby. Do all babies change in the same way?

Responses will vary.

Assessment Checkpoints for the Week

Weekly Assessment

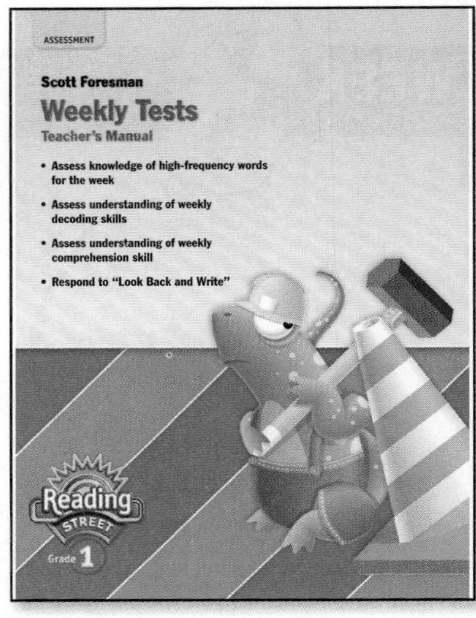

Weekly Tests

Use pp. 139–144 of *Weekly Tests* to check:

- ✔ **Phonics** Comparative Endings *-er, -est*
- ✔ **Phonics** Consonant Pattern *-dge*
- ✔ **Comprehension Skill** Draw Conclusions
- ✔ **High-Frequency Words**

before	oh
does	right
good-bye	won't

Differentiated Assessment

Advanced

OL
On-Level

SI
Strategic Intervention

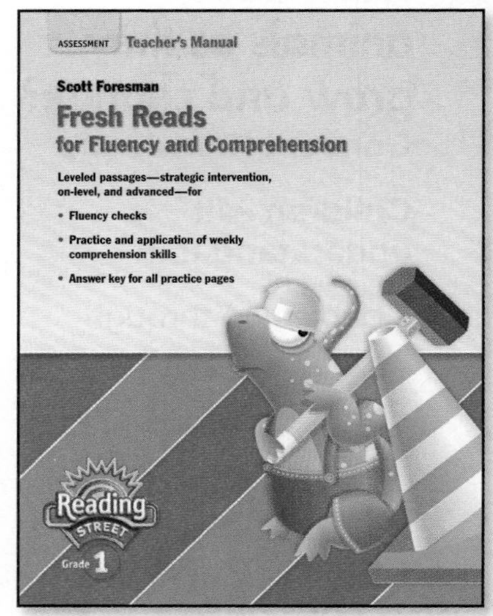

Fresh Reads for Fluency and Comprehension

Use pp. 139–144 of *Fresh Reads for Fluency and Comprehension* to check:

- ✔ **Comprehension Skill** Draw Conclusions
- ✔ Review **Comprehension Skill** Compare and Contrast
- ✔ **Fluency** Words Correct Per Minute

Unit Assessment

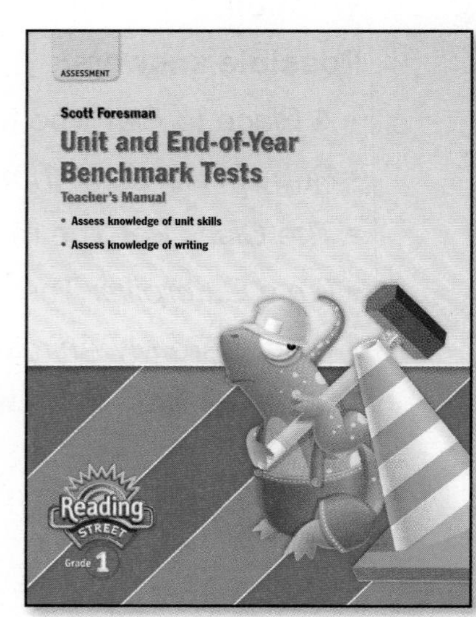

Unit and End-of-Year Benchmark Tests

Use the Unit 3 Benchmark Test to check progress in:

- ✔ **Passage Comprehension**
- ✔ **High-Frequency Words**
- ✔ **Phonics**
- ✔ **Writing Conventions**
- ✔ **Writing**
- ✔ **Fluency**

The Hardest Job

Tim and Jan work outside. They always have jobs to do. They work in spring and summer. They work in fall and winter.

In spring, days are longer and warmer than before. It is the wettest time. Tim and Jan plant gardens. They help the smallest plants grow bigger. They hang flower baskets too. Jan can reach higher than Tim. She can hang the highest baskets.

Summer is the hottest time of the year. It has the longest days. That's good because there is a lot to do! Summer has the greatest number of outside jobs. Summer grass is greener than ever. But it grows the fastest. Tim and Jan cut lots of grass.

Soon cooler days come. It's fall. Tim and Jan are still busy. Who can make the biggest pile of leaves? Some piles are taller than Tim!

Winter is the coldest time of the year. It has the shortest days and longest nights. But winter has the fewest outside jobs. That is, until it snows! Then Tim and Jan have the hardest outside job. They clean streets and paths. They lift heavy snow. Tim is the strongest person Jan knows. And lifting snow is hard, even for him!

Advanced Selection 18 **Vocabulary:** busy, reach

Pacing Small Group Instruction

5 Day Plan

DAY 1	• Phonemic Awareness/ Phonics • Decodable Reader
DAY 2	• Phonemic Awareness/ Phonics • Decodable Reader
DAY 3	• Phonemic Awareness/ Phonics • Leveled Reader
DAY 4	• High-Frequency Words • Decodable Reader
DAY 5	• Phonics Review • Leveled Reader

3 or 4 Day Plan

DAY 1	• Phonemic Awareness/ Phonics • Decodable Reader
DAY 2	• Phonemic Awareness/ Phonics • Decodable Reader
DAY 3	• Phonemic Awareness/ Phonics • Leveled Reader
DAY 4	• High-Frequency Words • Decodable Reader

3 Day Plan: Eliminate the shaded box.

DAY 1

Phonemic Awareness • Phonics

■ **Segment and Blend Phonemes** Reteach pp. 184–185 of the Teacher's Edition. Model segmenting and blending these words. Then have children practice segmenting and blending on their own.

deeper /d/ /ē/ p/ /ə/ /r/	**wettest** /w/ /e/ /t/ /ə/ /s/ /t/
thinner /th/ /i/ n/ /ə/ /r/	**coldest** /c/ /ō/ /l/ /d/ /ə/ /s/ /t/

■ **Comparative Endings *-er, -est*** Reteach p. 185a of the Teacher's Edition. Then write the words below. Have children read the words, identify the endings, and frame the base words. If children have difficulty reading a base word, have them cover the ending and blend the base word. Help them note if the last consonant was doubled before the ending was added.

hardest	**hotter**	**sickest**	**taller**
thicker	**faster**	**slimmest**	**biggest**

Decodable Practice Reader 18A

■ **Review** Review words with comparative endings *-er* or *-est* and the high-frequency words *every, the, day, of, to, ever.* Then have children blend and read these words from the story: *walks, Perky, Lark, Wink, Curly, Sport, King.*

If... children have difficulty with any of these words, **then...** reteach the word by modeling. Have children practice the words, with feedback from you, until they can read them independently.

Have children reread the text orally. To achieve optimal fluency, children should reread the text three or four times.

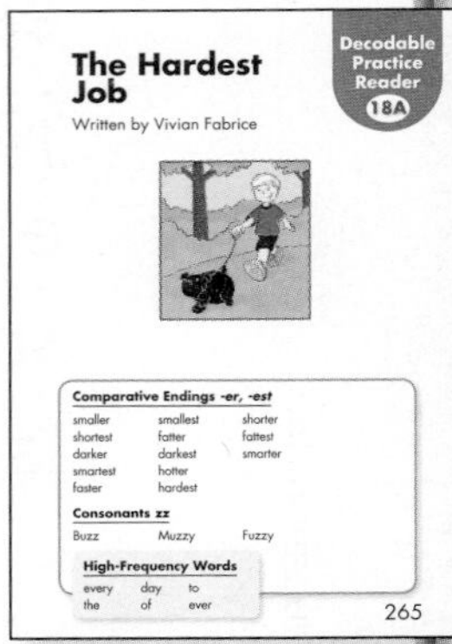

Decodable Practice Reader 18A

Objectives

- Blend spoken phonemes to form two-syllable words, including consonant blends.
- Read base words with inflectional endings.

DAY 2

Phonemic Awareness • Phonics

- **Segment and Blend Phonemes** Reteach p. 188c of the Teacher's Edition. Model segmenting and blending these words. Then have children practice segmenting and blending on their own.

budge /b/ /u/ /j/	**judge** /j/ /u/ /j/	**Madge** /m/ /a/ /j/
bridge /b/ /r/ /i/ /j/	**pledge** /p/ /l/ /e/ /j/	**ridge** /r/ /i/ /j/

- **Consonant Pattern *-dge*** Reteach p. 188d of the Teacher's Edition. Then have children spell *wedge* using letter tiles. Monitor their work.

- Change the *w* in *wedge* to *l*. What is the new word?

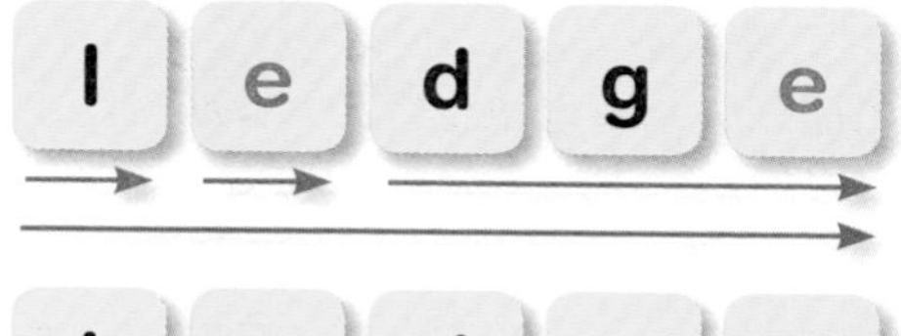

- Change the first *e* in *ledge* to *o*. What is the new word?

- Change the *l* in *lodge* to *d*. What is the new word?

d o d g e

Decodable Practice Reader 18B

- **Review** Review words with the vowel sound in *ball a* and *al* and the high-frequency words *said, where, the, find, to, your, of, a.* Then have children blend and read these words from the story: *let's, first, Bucky, think, asked, seemed, can't, jumped, pink, thanks.*

If... children have difficulty with any of these words, **then...** reteach the word by modeling. Have children practice the words, with feedback from you, until they can read them independently.

Have children reread the text orally. To achieve optimal fluency, children should reread the text three or four times.

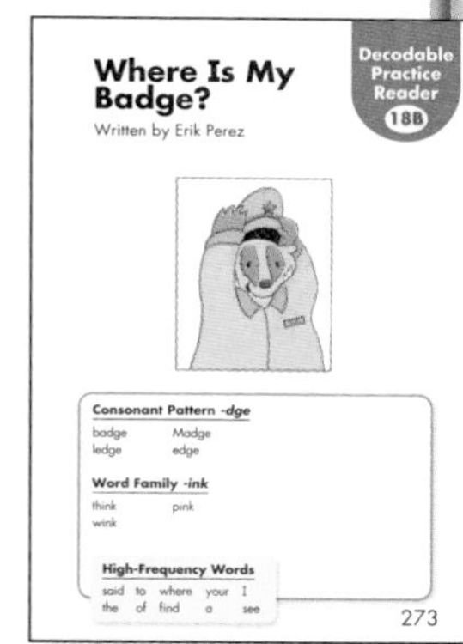

Decodable Practice Reader 18B

More Reading

Use Leveled Readers or other text at children's instructional level to develop fluency.

Objectives

- Decode words in context by applying common letter-sound correspondences, including: consonant digraphs including *-dge*.
- Read base words with inflectional endings.

Phonemic Awareness • Phonics

- **Add Phonemes** Model adding a sound to the beginning of a word to make a new word. Say the word *ridge* and have children repeat it. Now listen as I add the sound /b/ to the beginning of *ridge:* /b/ *ridge*. What is the new word? (bridge).

Have children add the sound shown to the beginning of each word below to make a new word.

/l/ edge **ledge**	/s/ tale **stale**	/k/ lean **clean**	/p/ ride **pride**

- **Comparative Endings *-er, -est* and Consonant Pattern *-dge*** Reteach p. 208e of the Teacher's Edition. Have children blend and read these additional words to help them practice the target phonics skills.

nudge	**fatter**	**pledge**	**reddest**	**sweetest**	**smaller**

For a complete literacy instructional plan and additional practice with this week's target skills and strategies, see the **Leveled Reader Teaching Guide.**

Concept Literacy Leveled Reader

- **Preview and Predict** Read the title and author's name. Have children look at the cover and ask them to describe what they see. Help children activate their prior knowledge by asking them to look through the selection and to use the photos to predict things that they might learn about.
- **Set a Purpose** Remind children that setting a purpose for reading can help them better understand what they read. Guide children to pay attention to the things that different animals do to stay alive in the winter.
- **Read** Provide corrective feedback as children read the selection orally. During reading, ask them if they were able to confirm any of the predictions they made prior to reading.

If... children have difficulty reading the selection individually,
then... read a sentence aloud as children point to each word. Then have the group reread the sentences as they continue pointing. Continue reading in this way until children read individually.

- **Retell** Have children take turns retelling the selection. Help them recall the things different animals do in winter by asking, How do some animal stay warm? How do some animals find food?

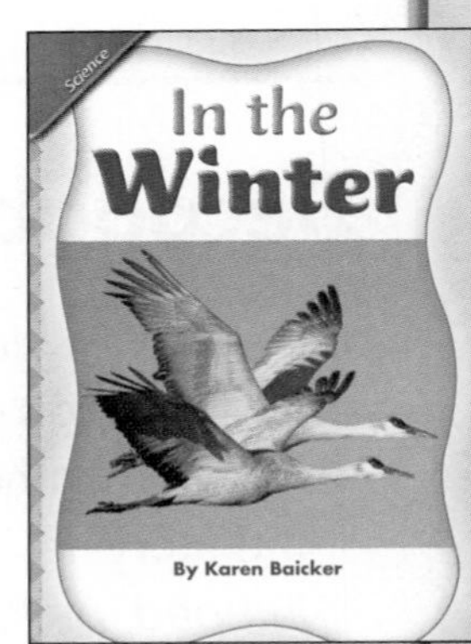

Concept Literacy

Objectives

- Decode words in isolation by applying common letter-sound correspondences, including: consonant digraphs including *-dge*.
- Read base words with inflectional endings.

DAY 4

More Reading

Use Leveled Readers or other text at children's instructional level.

High-Frequency Words

- **Review** Write *does, good-bye, before, won't, oh, right* on the board. Model saying each word. Then have children read each word, spell each word as you point to each letter, and have them say each word again. Allow time for children to practice reading these high-frequency words using the word cards.

Decodable Practice Reader 18C

- **Review** Use the word lists to review comparative endings *-er* and *-est* and consonant pattern *-dge*. Be sure that children understand that *-er* is used to compare two things and *-est* is used to compare three or more things. Point out words in which the final consonant of the base word is doubled before the ending is added. Remind children that *-dge* at the end of a word spells the sound /j/.

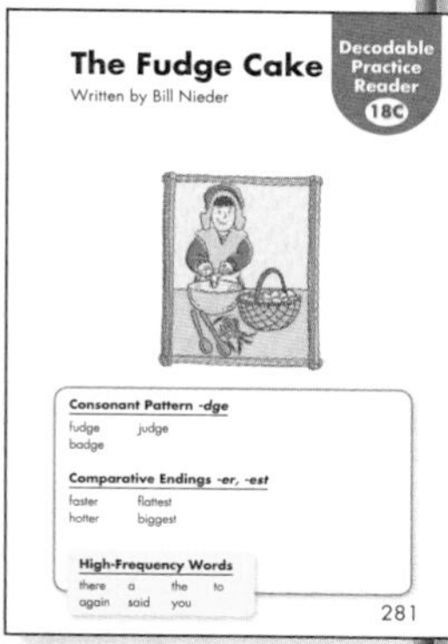
Decodable Practice Reader 18C

If... children have difficulty reading the story individually, **then...** read a sentence aloud as children point to each word. Then have the group reread the sentences as they continue pointing. Continue reading in this way until children read individually.

Check comprehension by having children retell the story including the characters, plot, and setting. Have children locate words in the story that have comparative endings *-er* and *-est* and consonant pattern *-dge*. List the words children identify. Then have children sort the words in a chart with columns labeled *Endings* and *dge*.

Endings	-dge
flattest	fudge
faster	judge
hotter	badge
biggest	

Objectives

- Read base words with inflectional endings.
- Read at least 100 high-frequency words from a commonly used list.

More Reading

Use Leveled Readers or other text at children's instructional level.

Phonics Review

- **Comparative Endings *-er, -est* and Consonant Pattern *-dge*** Write these sentences on the board. Have children read them aloud as you track the print. Then call on individuals to blend and read the underlined words.

Madge ate the biggest wedge of cheese.

This bridge is the fastest way home.

My badge is thinner than a penny.

This pond is deeper at that edge.

For a complete literacy instructional plan and additional practice with this week's target skills and strategies, see the **Leveled Reader Teaching Guide.**

Below-Level Leveled Reader

Preview and Predict Read the title and the author's name. Have children look at the cover and ask them to describe what they see. Help children activate their prior knowledge by asking them to look through the selection and to use the photos to predict things that might take place.

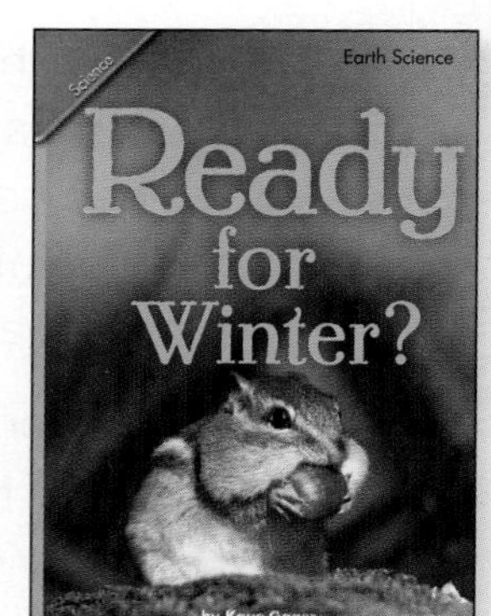

Below-Level Reader

- **Set a Purpose** Remind children that setting a purpose for reading can help them better understand what they read. Have children read this selection to find out how different animals get ready for winter.
- **Read** Provide corrective feedback as children read the selection orally. During reading, ask them if they were able to confirm any of the predictions they made prior to reading.

  If... children have difficulty reading the selection individually,
  then... read each sentence aloud as children point to each word. Then have the group reread the sentences as they continue pointing.

- **Background Knowledge** Ask children what they had already learned about animals and the seasons earlier this week that helped them understand this selection.

Objectives

- Decode words in isolation by applying common letter-sound correspondences, including: consonant digraphs including *-dge*
- Make connections to ideas in other texts.

OL On-Level DAY 1

Phonics • Spelling

- **Comparative Endings *-er, -est*** Write the following words on the board and have children practice reading words with comparative endings *-er, -est.*

  fresher **gladdest** **pinkest** **stiffer**

  Then have children identify the base word and ending in each word.

- **Words with *-er, -est*** Remind children that each spelling word has the *-er* or *-est* ending. Clarify the pronunciation and meaning of each word. For example, say: If I am the *shortest* person, I am the least tall of three or more people. Have children determine whether the final consonant of the base word is doubled in these words: *biggest, fastest, sadder, taller, shortest.*

Objectives

- Read base words with inflectional endings.
- Use phonological knowledge to match sounds to letters to construct words.

Pacing Small Group Instruction 20–30 min.

5 Day Plan

DAY 1	• Phonics • Spelling • Decodable Reader
DAY 2	• Phonics • High-Frequency Words • Decodable Reader
DAY 3	• Leveled Reader
DAY 4	• Conventions • Main Selection
DAY 5	• Phonics Review • Leveled Reader

OL On-Level DAY 2

Phonics • High-Frequency Words

- **Consonant Pattern *-dge*** Write the following words on the board and have children practice reading words with consonant pattern *dge*.

  budge **pledge** **dodge** **trudge**

  Then have children identify the letters that spell the /j/ sound in each word.

- **High-Frequency Words** Hold up this week's High-Frequency Word Cards *(before, does, good-bye, oh, right, won't)* and review proper pronunciation. Continue holding the cards and have children chorally read each word. To help children demonstrate their understanding of the words, provide them with oral sentence frames such as: I hope it _________ rain on our picnic. (won't)

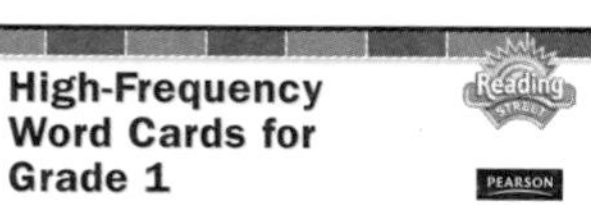

Objectives

- Decode words in isolation by applying common letter-sound correspondences, including: consonant digraphs including *-dge*.
- Identify at least 100 high-frequency words from a commonly used list.

3 or 4 Day Plan

DAY 1	• Phonics • Spelling • Decodable Reader
DAY 2	• Phonics • High-Frequency Words • Decodable Reader
DAY 3	• Leveled Reader
DAY 4	• Conventions • Main Selection

3 Day Plan: Eliminate the shaded box.

Decodable Practice Readers

On-Level

DAY 3

For a complete literacy instructional plan and additional practice with this week's target skills and strategies, see the **Leveled Reader Teaching Guide.**

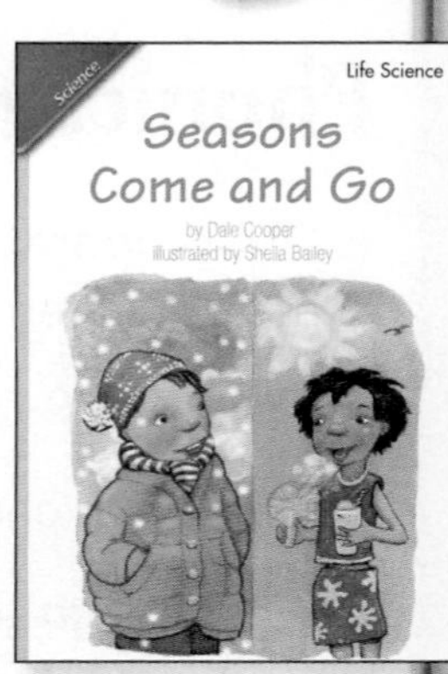

On-Level

On-Level Leveled Reader

- **Preview and Predict** Read the title and the names of the author and illustrator. Have children look at the cover and ask them to describe in detail what they see. Help children preview the selection by asking them to look through the pages and to use the pictures to predict things that they might learn about.
- **Draw Conclusions** Remind children that setting a purpose for reading can help them better understand what they read. Tell children that this selection explains how different animals' bodies change with the seasons, but the author doesn't always say why this happens. Have children read to see if they can figure out why these changes are important to the animals.
- **Read** During reading, monitor children's comprehension by providing higher-order thinking questions. Ask:
  - Why is it important for a bear to get fatter in the fall?
  - How does it help the fox to be one color in summer and another in winter?

To help children gain a better understanding of the text, build upon their responses with a group discussion.

- **Background Knowledge** Have children tell how thinking about what they already knew helped them understand this selection. Ask:
  - What did you learn earlier this week about animals and seasons that helped you understand?
  - What did you know from observing nature yourself that helped you?
- **Text to Self** Help children make personal connections to the selection. Ask:
  - How are winter and summer different for you? What do you do and see outdoors that changes with the seasons?

Objectives

- Make inferences about text.
- Make connections to own experiences.

DAY 4

Conventions

- **Contractions with *Not*** Remind children that a contraction is a short way of writing two words, and that the apostrophe takes the place of the missing letter or letters.
  - Write *has not.* To write *has not* as a contraction, I put the two words together and leave out the *o* in *not*. I replace the *o* with an apostrophe. Write *hasn't*.

    Have children practice writing contractions for these words: *is not, do not, was not.*
  - Write *aren't.* When I read a contraction that ends with *n't,* I know that the apostrophe stands for the *o* in *not.* The words in this contraction are *are not.*
- Write these contractions: *didn't, weren't, haven't, mustn't.* Have children read these contractions and identify the two words that form each.

Objectives

- Use and understand verbs (past) in the context of reading, writing, and speaking.
- Understand and use verbs (present) in the context of reading, writing, and speaking.

DAY 5

Phonics Review

- **Comparative Endings *-er, -est* and Consonant Pattern *-dge*** Have children practice blending and reading words that contain this week's target phonics skills. Write the following words on the board, and say and sound out each word with the children.

grandest	**nudge**	**ledge**	**greener**	**flattest**
ridge	**wetter**	**thickest**	**judge**	**smarter**

Then have children sort the words that have *-er, -est,* and *-dge* into different groups.

Objectives

- Decode words in isolation by applying common letter-sound correspondences, including: consonant digraphs including *-dge.*
- Read base words with inflectional endings.

More Reading

Use Leveled Readers or other text at children's instructional level to develop fluency.

Small Group Time

Pacing Small Group Instruction

20–30 mins.

5 Day Plan

DAY 1	• Phonics • Advanced Selection
DAY 2	• Phonics • Comprehension • Main Selection
DAY 3	• Leveled Reader
DAY 4	• Comprehension • Paired Selection
DAY 5	• Fluency • Comprehension • Advanced Selection

3 or 4 Day Plan

DAY 1	• Phonics • Advanced Selection
DAY 2	• Phonics • Comprehension • Main Selection
DAY 3	• Leveled Reader
DAY 4	• Comprehension • Paired Selection

3 Day Plan: Eliminate the shaded box.

A Advanced — DAY 1

Phonics • Advanced Selection

■ **Comparative Endings *-er, -est*** Have children read these words. Point out that final *y* changes to *i* before *-er* or *-est.*

slower	**brighter**	**cleanest**	**happiest**	**sooner**
fewest	**dimmest**	**funnier**	**louder**	**grayest**

Have children write the words on cards and sort them by ending. Then have them choose several words to use in sentences.

The Hardest Job

Tim and Jan work outside. They always have jobs to do. They work in spring and summer. They work in fall and winter.

In spring, days are longer and warmer than before. It is the wettest time. Tim and Jan plant gardens. They help the smallest plants grow bigger. They hang flower baskets too. Jan can reach higher than Tim. She can hang the highest baskets.

Summer is the hottest time of the year. It has the longest days. That's good because there is a lot to do! Summer has the greatest number of outside jobs. Summer grass is greener than ever. But it grows the fastest. Tim and Jan cut lots of grass.

Soon cooler days come. It's fall. Tim and Jan are still busy. Who can make the biggest pile of leaves? Some piles are taller than Tim!

Winter is the coldest time of the year. It has the shortest days and longest nights. But winter has the fewest outside jobs. That is, until it snows! Then Tim and Jan have the hardest outside job. They clean streets and paths. They lift heavy snow. Tim is the strongest person Jan knows. And lifting snow is hard, even for him!

Advanced Selection 18

■ **Advanced Selection 18** Before reading, have children identify these story words: *busy, reach.* If they do not know these words, provide oral sentences with the words in context to help children determine their meaning. After reading, have children recall two of the most important ideas in the selection.

Objectives

- Read base words with inflectional endings.

A Advanced — DAY 2

Phonics • Comprehension

■ **Consonant Pattern *-dge*** Have children read these words with /j/ spelled *-dge*. Discuss the meanings of unfamiliar words.

gadget	**fidget**	**drudgery**	**partridge**
budget	**misjudge**	**porridge**	**knowledge**

Have children write the words and circle the letters that spell the /j/ sound. Then have them use the words to use in sentences.

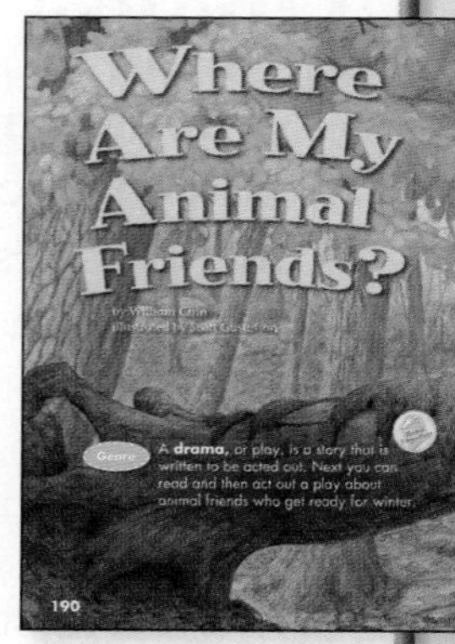

Where Are My Animal Friends?

■ **Comprehension** Have children silently read *Where Are My Animal Friends?* Have them retell the story, identifying characters, setting, and sequence of events. Discuss what makes *Where Are My Animal Friends?* a drama. Point out the features that indicate that the story is meant to be acted out.

Objectives

- Decode words in isolation by applying common letter-sound correspondences, including: consonant digraphs including *-dge*

Advanced

DAY 3

For a complete literacy instructional plan and additional practice with this week's target skills and strategies, see the **Leveled Reader Teaching Guide.**

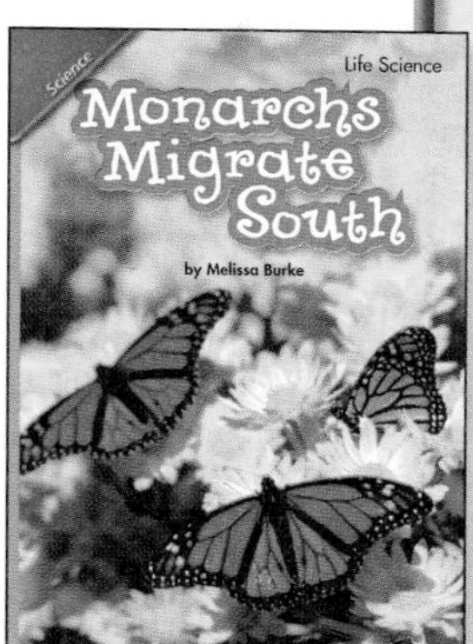

Advanced Reader

Advanced Leveled Reader

- **Activate Prior Knowledge** Read the title and the author's name. Have children look at the cover and describe in detail what they see. Tell them that the word *survive* means "to continue living." Then activate children's prior knowledge by asking them to name things that most animals need in order to survive.
- **Draw Conclusions** Before reading, remind children that setting a purpose for reading can help them better understand what they read. Tell children that in this selection, the author explains some things and lets readers figure out other things for themselves. Have children read to figure out why it's important for monarchs to fit their life cycle to the seasons.
- **Read** During reading, monitor children's comprehension by providing higher-order thinking questions. Ask:
  - Why is it important for monarchs to lay their eggs in spring rather than winter?
  - In what ways are monarch butterflies like birds?

Build on children's answers to help them gain a better understanding of the text.

- **Background Knowledge** Discuss with children how their previous reading and experience helped them understand this selection. Ask:
  - What facts that you learned from *I'm a Caterpillar* helped you understand the pictures on pages 4 and 5?
  - What facts that you already knew about the seasons helped you understand why monarchs migrate in the fall and spring?
- **Text to World** Help children make connections to the selection. Ask:
  - What other insects that you know about have interesting ways of eating, staying safe, and living together? Describe what they do to survive.

Objectives

- Make inferences about text.
- Make connections to the larger community.

More Reading

Use Leveled Readers or other text at children's instructional level.

More Reading

Use Leveled Readers or other text at children's instructional level.

DAY 4

Comprehension

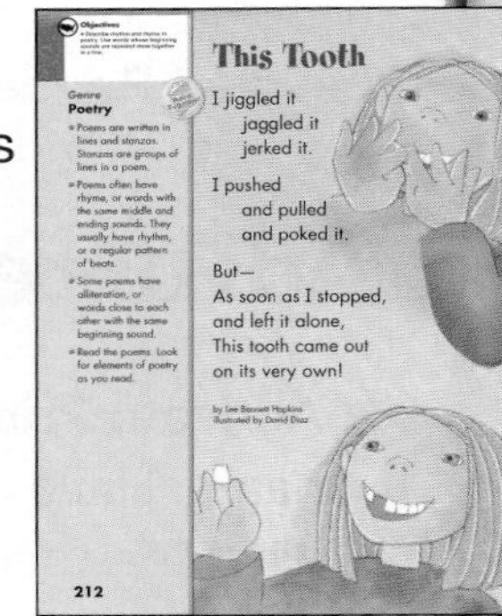
Genre
Poetry
- Poems are written in lines and stanzas. Stanzas are groups of lines in a poem.
- Poems often have rhyme, or words with the same middle and ending sounds. They usually have rhythm, or a regular pattern of beats.
- Some poems have alliteration, or words close to each other with the same beginning sound.
- Read the poems. Look for elements of poetry as you read.

This Tooth

I jiggled it
jaggled it
jerked it.

I pushed
and pulled
and poked it.

But—
As soon as I stopped,
and left it alone,
This tooth came out
on its very own!

by Lee Bennett Hopkins
illustrated by David Diaz

212

Poetry

- **Comprehension** Ask individual children to read aloud the poems from this week's selection. Have children summarize what happens in each poem. Then ask them how each poem fits with the theme of changes in our world.

  Talk about the special features of poetry. Be sure children can identify the use of rhythm, rhyme, alliteration, and stanzas in these poems.

- **Text to Text** Help children make connections to other reading. For example, "Tommy" might remind them of Toad in *Frog and Toad Together*. "Where Do Fish Go in Winter" might remind them of Bear in *Where Are My Animal Friends?*

Objectives

- Respond to rhythm in poetry.
- Make connections to ideas in other texts.

DAY 5

Fluency•Comprehension

The Hardest Job

Tim and Jan work outside. They always have jobs to do. They work in spring and summer. They work in fall and winter.

In spring, days are longer and warmer than before. It is the wettest time. Tim and Jan plant gardens. They help the smallest plants grow bigger. They hang flower baskets too. Jan can reach higher than Tim. She can hang the highest baskets.

Summer is the hottest time of the year. It has the longest days. That's good because there is a lot to do! Summer has the greatest number of outside jobs. Summer grass is greener than ever. But it grows the fastest. Tim and Jan cut lots of grass.

Soon cooler days come. It's fall. Tim and Jan are still busy. Who can make the biggest pile of leaves? Some piles are taller than Tim!

Winter is the coldest time of the year. It has the shortest days and longest nights. But winter has the fewest outside jobs. That is, until it snows! Then Tim and Jan have the hardest outside job. They clean streets and paths. They lift heavy snow. Tim is the strongest person Jan knows. And lifting snow is hard, even for him!

Advanced Selection 18 **Vocabulary** busy, reach

Advanced Selection 18

- **Fluency** Using the first few sentences of Advanced Selection 18, model reading with good expression and intonation. Then have children read the selection to a partner as you listen to their reading. Provide corrective feedback as needed.

- **Comprehension** After they have finished reading the selection, have children summarize the information by stating the main ideas. Then, on the back of the selection page, have them write four sentences telling one job that Jan and Tim do in each season.

Objectives

- Read aloud grade-level appropriate text with fluency (expression).

The ELL lessons are organized by strands. Use them to scaffold the weekly lesson curriculum or during small-group time.

Concept Development

What do animals do when the seasons change?

- **Activate Prior Knowledge** Write the question of the week and read it aloud. Underline the word *seasons* and have children say it with you. A *season* is one of the four natural parts of the year. The four seasons are spring, summer, fall, and winter. Have children name some things that happen when the seasons change.

- **Connect to New Concept** Have children turn to pages 182–183 in the Student Edition. Read the title aloud and have children track the print as you read it. Be sure they understand the implicit ideas in your spoken language by asking them to restate the question in their own words. Guide a discussion about what animals do when the seasons change. For example, point to the birds migrating in the winter. What are these birds doing? (flying) In the winter, birds migrate, or move to warmer places. They stay where it is warm until winter is over. Then they fly back to their homes for the summer.

- **Develop Concepts** Display ELL Poster 18 and have children identify animals they know. (raccoon, duck, bear) What season is it? Have children point to clues about the season on the Poster. (leaves changing color and falling, bear hibernating, raccoon wearing sweater) Use the leveled prompts below to assess understanding and build oral language.

Beginning Ask yes/no questions, such as Is the duck going on vacation? Are the bear and raccoon talking?

Intermediate Ask children questions that can be answered with simple sentences. What season will come after fall? What has the duck packed for his trip south? Which animals are staying where they are?

Advanced/Advanced-High Have children answer the Question of the Week by giving specific examples from the poster and their own experie nces.

- **Review Concepts and Connect to Writing** Review children's understanding of the concept at the end of the week. Ask them to write in response to these questions: What is one thing animals do when the seasons change? What do you do when the seasons change? What English words did you learn this week? Write and display key ideas from the discussion.

Objectives

- Internalize new basic and academic language by using and reusing it in meaningful ways in speaking and writing activities that build concept and language attainment.
- Learn new language structures, expressions, and basic and academic vocabulary heard during classroom instruction and interactions.

Content Objectives

- Describe what animals do when the seasons change.

Language Objectives

- Share information orally.
- Use basic vocabulary for describing what animals do when the seasons change.
- Understand implicit ideas in spoken language.

Daily Planner

DAY 1	• **Frontload Concepts** • **Preteach** Comprehension Skill, Vocabulary, Phonemic Awareness/ Phonics, Conventions/ Writing
DAY 2	• **Review** Concepts, Vocabulary, Comprehension Skill • **Frontload Main Selection** • **Practice** Phonemic Awareness/Phonics, Conventions/Writing
DAY 3	• **Review** Concepts, Comprehension Skill, Vocabulary, Conventions/ Writing • **Reread Main Selection** • **Practice** Phonemic Awareness/Phonics
DAY 4	• **Review Concepts** • **Read ELL/ELD Readers** • **Practice** Phonemic Awareness/Phonics, Conventions/Writing
DAY 5	• **Review** Concepts, Vocabulary, Comprehension Skill, Phonemic Awareness/ Phonics, Conventions/ Writing • **Reread ELL/ELD Readers**

*See the ELL Handbook for ELL Workshops with targeted instruction.

Concept Talk Video

Use this week's Concept Talk Video to help children build background knowledge.

Language Objectives

- Segment phonemes.
- Identify and produce the sounds of comparative endings *-er, -est*.

Transfer Skills

Adjectives that Compare
In Spanish and Hmong, comparisons are expressed with phrases, rather than with adjectives that change form. For example, speakers of these languages may substitute *more red/most red for redder/reddest*. Provide specific practice with these forms.

ELL Teaching Routine

For more practice with comparative endings, use the Whole-Word Blending Routine (*ELL Handbook*, page 493).

ELL English Language Learners

Phonemic Awareness: Blend and Segment Phonemes

■ **Preteach Final Phomemes**

- Have children open to pages 184–185. Explain to children that a word can be segmented into different sounds. Point to the beavers swimming. Model how to segment *swim* into three sounds /sw/ /i/ /m/. Model how to count on your fingers the different sounds heard in *swim*.
- Say the following words aloud: *pan, plan, clan, clap*. Have children repeat the words after you. Tell them to segment and count the sounds in each word.

■ **Practice** Have children segment and count the phonemes in each word. What sound do I add to *pan* to make *plan*? (/l/) What sound do I change in *plan* to make *clan*? (/p/ to /k/) What sound do I change in *clan* to make *clap*? (/n/ to /p/)

Phonics: Words with Comparative Endings

■ **Preteach** Display Sound-Spelling Card 123. This is *taller*. Write the word on the board and underline the base word *tall*. Explain that *tall* is a base word. When we add *-er* to *tall*, we are comparing two things. *Diego is tall, but Philip is taller*. Point out that two people, Diego and Philip, are being compared. Repeat instruction with Sound-Spelling Card 125, using the word *smallest* to compare three or more things.

■ **Listen and Write** Distribute Write and Wipe Boards. Write the following base words. Say each word and have children repeat after you. Then have children write and say each word, adding *-er* to the end of each one: *fast, slow, dark*.

For more practice pronouncing these sounds, use the Modeled Pronunciation Audio CD Routine (*ELL Handbook*, page 501).

Objectives

- Monitor oral and written language production and employ self-corrective techniques or other resources.
- Recognize elements of the English sound system in newly acquired vocabulary such as long and short vowels, silent letters, and consonant clusters.
- Practice producing sounds of newly acquired vocabulary such as long and short vowels, silent letters, and consonant clusters to pronounce English words in a manner that is increasingly comprehensible.

ELL English Language Learners

■ **Reteach and Practice** Remind children we can add /ėr/ and /est/ to the ends of words to make new words. Say the word *happy,* followed by *happier* and *happiest*. Repeat the words, stressing the ending.

Beginning Say the word pairs *hot/hotter; dark/darkest; new/newer;* and *sweet/sweetest.* Tell children to give a thumbs-up if they hear a word with the *-er* or *-est* ending. Repeat until children can distinguish the ending.

Intermediate One by one, say the base words *hot, dark, new,* and *sweet*. Follow each base word with /ėr/ or /est/. Have children say the new word.

Advanced/Advanced-High Have children say the words *hot, dark, new, sweet.* Tell them to make new words by adding /ėr/ and /est/ to the ends of the words.

Phonics: Consonant Pattern *-dge*

■ **Preteach** Have children turn to Envision It! on page 88 of the Student Edition.

- Point to the bridge. What is this? (a bridge) Say the word *bridge* slowly. Show children that in words like *bridge*, the sound /j/ is spelled *-dge*. Write and say the word *bridge*. Underline the letters *-dge* at the end of the word, and tell children that together they are pronounced /j/. Have children repeat the word *bridge* after you. Then reinforce by writing and reading the word *badge*.

■ **Practice** Distribute Letter Tiles *b, a, dge, j, u, e, p, b, l, r,* and *i*.

- Blend the sounds in the word *badge* and have pairs spell *badge* with their tiles: /b/ /a/ /j/, *badge*.
- Replace the *b* and *a*. Spell *judge*.
- Replace the *j* and *u*. Spell *edge*.
- Add a *p* and *l*. Spell *pledge*.
- Replace the *b, r,* and *i*. Spell *bridge*.

Objectives

- Monitor oral and written language production and employ self-corrective techniques or other resources.
- Recognize elements of the English sound system in newly acquired vocabulary such as long and short vowels, silent letters, and consonant clusters.

Language Objectives

- Associate the endings *-er* and *-est* with comparing two or more things.
- Practice /j/ spelled *-dge*.

Catch Up

The letters *a, e, i, o, u*, and sometimes *y* are vowels. Every word in English has at least one of these letters.

Practice Page

ELL Handbook page 274 provides additional practice for this week's skill.

Content Objectives

- Monitor and adjust oral comprehension.

Language Objectives

- Discuss oral passages.
- Learn new language structures.
- Use a graphic organizer to take notes.

ELL Teacher Tip

To help children identify with the concept of migration, lead a discussion about why certain animals migrate to warmer places in the wintertime, such as various types of birds and whales.

ELL English Language Learners

Listening Comprehension

Robin's New Home

Robin lived in the north. She loved her nest. She had plenty of food to eat.

The leaves started falling off the trees. Her friends began flying away. She wanted to know where they were going. She asked Hummingbird. Hummingbird told her that the birds were flying south for the winter.

Robin did not want to leave. She liked her home. Hummingbird told her that she must leave. It would be hard to live in the north when it was winter. He told her that she could build a new home in the south.

Robin and Hummingbird flew south. They found a nice, warm place to build their nests.

Robin loved her new nest. She wanted to live there forever.

Hummingbird told her that she could enjoy her new home for now. But when winter was over, they would go back to the north.

Prepare for the Read Aloud The modified Read Aloud above prepares children for listening to the oral reading "Home Sweet Home" on page 187b.

- **First Listening: Listen to Understand** Write the title of the Read Aloud on the board. This is about a bird who loves her home. Where do the birds go for the winter? Why doesn't Robin want to leave her home? After reading, ask children to discuss why birds migrate.
- **Second Listening: Listen to Check Understanding** Using a Story Predications Chart graphic organizer (*ELL Handbook*, page 505), work with children to predict what will happen in the story and identify if their predictions were correct. Review the completed charts together.

Objectives

- Learn new language structures, expressions, and basic and academic vocabulary heard during classroom instruction and interactions.
- Understand the general meaning, main points, and important details of spoken language ranging from situations in which topics, language, and contexts are familiar to unfamiliar.
- Demonstrate listening comprehension of increasingly complex spoken English by following directions, retelling or summarizing spoken messages, responding to questions and requests, collaborating with peers, and taking notes commensurate with content and grade-level needs.

High-Frequency Words

- **Preteach** Distribute copies of this week's Word Cards (*ELL Handbook*, p. 167). Have children point to or hold up the corresponding card when you say a word in a sentence or make a gesture. When appropriate, use opposites to reinforce meaning.
  - Point to a child in the class. She *does* all her homework.
  - *Good-bye* is what people say when they are leaving. Walk out the door and wave. *Good-bye!*
  - *Before* tells about something that happens earlier than something else. I wash my hands *before* I eat.
  - *Won't* means "will not." Shake your head. I *won't* go home yet.
  - *Oh* is a word used to show surprise, joy, and other feelings. Show a surprised expression. *Oh!*
  - Something that is *right* is the way it should be. Nod your head. Yes, you are *right!*
- **Practice** Briefly repeat each clue. Have children hold up and read the corresponding Word Cards. Then help children memorize the words.
- **Speaking/Writing with High-Frequency Words**
  - **Teach/Model** Write the sentences on the board. Model filling in the missing word from the first sentence. 1. That answer is _______. (right) 2. Put on your hat _______ you go outside. (before) 3. Wave _______ to your grandma. (good-bye) 4. _______ a duck quack? (Does) 5. _______, school was fun today! (Oh) 6. Jeff _______ eat. His tummy hurts. (won't)
  - **Practice** Give each pair of children a set of the Word Cards. Have them work together to find the correct word for each sentence you read.

Leveled Support

Beginning Read the sentences aloud, using a gesture to fill in for each missing word. Have children hold up the correct Word Card for each sentence. Then write each word.

Intermediate Have children write the missing words. Have them use the Word Cards as a spelling resource.

Advanced/Advanced-High Have children write the high-frequency words. Children can make up a sentence with a partner.

Objectives

- Use strategic learning techniques such as concept mapping, drawing, memorizing, comparing, contrasting, and reviewing to acquire basic and grade-level vocabulary.

Language Objectives

- Use accessible language to learn new and essential language.
- Use memorizing to acquire basic vocabulary.
- Use high-frequency English words.
- Understand the general meaning of spoken language.

Mini-Lesson: Speaking and Listening

Use the paired reading as an opportunity to have children listen for general meanings of spoken language. As you read aloud p. 189, have children listen for the general message. If necessary, ask questions to prompt thinking. Then ask children to restate the message to monitor understanding.

Content Objectives

- Draw conclusions by connecting details in the text to real life knowledge and experiences.
- Draw conclusions to aid comprehension.

Language Objectives

- Discuss evidence for drawing conclusions.
- Expand reading skills by using the inferential skill of drawing conclusions from a reading.

ELL English Language Learners

Guide Comprehension
Draw Conclusions

- **Preteach** Sometimes, clues in the pictures or words in a story help you understand something that is not written. Use what you know about real life to tell more about a character or a story.
- **Practice** Have children turn to Envision It! on page EI•6 in the Student Edition. Discuss the picture with children. Have them use the picture and their inferential skills to draw a conclusion about how the boy is feeling. They should use both clues from the text and clues from their own experiences to make their inferences.
- **Reteach/Practice** Distribute copies of the Picture It! (*ELL Handbook*, p. 168). Have children look at the images. Explain that to draw conclusions, you first think about what you know. Then you look for clues in the text. Make a 3 column chart on the board, labeled *What I Know, What the Text Says*, and *Conclusions*. Record what students know about baby birds. Then, read the text to the children. Record what the text tells. Finally, guide the children in drawing conclusions about the passage. (**Answers** 1. She feeds them worms. 2. They are too young to fly away for worms. 3. They are old enough to live alone.)

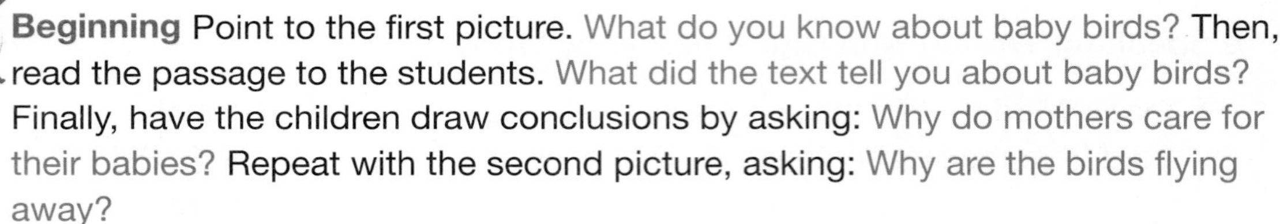

Leveled Support

Beginning Point to the first picture. What do you know about baby birds? Then, read the passage to the students. What did the text tell you about baby birds? Finally, have the children draw conclusions by asking: Why do mothers care for their babies? Repeat with the second picture, asking: Why are the birds flying away?

Intermediate/Advanced/Advanced-High Have the children read the passage with a partner. Write *Why do mother birds care for their babies?* on the board. Ask the children to think about what they know about birds and what the passage tells them to draw a conclusion. Repeat with the second picture, asking: Why are the birds flying away?

Objectives

- Monitor understanding of spoken language during classroom instruction and interactions and seek clarification as needed.
- Understand the general meaning, main points, and important details of spoken language ranging from situations in which topics, language, and contexts are familiar to unfamiliar.

Go Digital!

Envision It! Animations 

eSelections 

Story Sort 

Reading Comprehension

Where Are My Animal Friends?

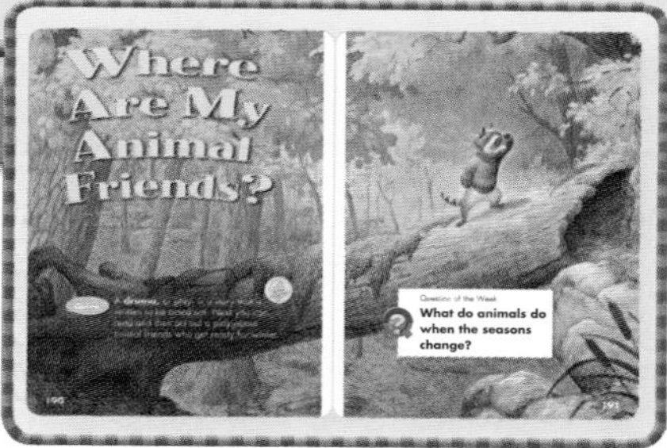

Student Edition pp. 190–191

■ **Frontloading**

- **Background Knowledge** Read the title aloud and discuss it. Who are your friends? Why are friends important?
- **Preview** Guide children on a picture walk through the story, asking them to identify people, places, and actions. Reteach these words using visuals in the Student Edition: *forest* (page 193), *leaves* (page 194), *hummingbird* (page 195), and *sleepy* (page 201)
- **Predict** Who will Raccoon play with in the winter?

Sheltered Reading Ask questions such as the following to guide children's comprehension:

- p. 194: Point to Raccoon and Goose. Who are Raccoon and Goose looking for? (Caterpillar)
- p. 197: Point to the cocoon. Who is inside? (Caterpillar) What happens to Caterpillar in the spring? (turns into a butterfly)
- p. 200: Point to Bear. Why will Bear sleep a long time? (He ate and ate all summer.)
- p. 204: Point to Squirrel. Why will Squirrel stay in the forest all winter? (She has a warm nest and lots of food.)

■ **Fluency: Expression and Intonation** Remind children that reading with expression means to vary their tone of voice. Read page 196, modeling appropriate expression and intonation. Emphasize sentences such as "That's not Caterpillar!" Have pairs read page 198. Have children read with expression and intonation as their partners listen and offer feedback. As children read to each other, they should also strive to understand and demonstrate listening comprehension of the information. Have partners take turns reading aloud and then restating the message of the text.

After Reading Help children summarize the text with the Retelling Cards. Ask questions that prompt children to summarize the important parts of the text.

Objectives

- Use visual and contextual support and support from peers and teachers to read grade-appropriate content area text, enhance and confirm understanding, and develop vocabulary, grasp of language structures, and background knowledge needed to comprehend increasingly challenging language.
- Demonstrate comprehension of increasingly complex English by participating in shared reading, retelling or summarizing material, responding to questions, and taking notes commensurate with content area and grade level needs.

Content Objectives

- Monitor and adjust comprehension.
- Make and adjust predictions.

Language Objectives

- Read grade-level text with appropriate expression and intonation.
- Summarize text using visual support.
- Understand information and demonstrate listening comprehension of spoken language.
- Respond to questions.

Graphic Organizer

Beginning
Middle
End

Audio Support

Prepare children for reading *Where Are My Animal Friends?* by using the eSelection or the AudioText CD.

Mini-Lesson: Answer Questions

Prompt children to demonstrate listening comprehension by answering questions. Have them answer the question in the title: *Where are my animal friends?* Show pp. 196, 199, and 201 of Student Edition and ask children to answer the question as you orally state the question.

For additional leveled instruction, see the **ELL/ELD Reader Teaching Guide.**

ELL Reader

ELD Reader

Comprehension: *As White as Snow*

■ **Before Reading** Distribute copies of the ELL and ELD Readers, *As White as Snow*, to children at their reading level. The ELD Reader has language to linguistically accommodate beginning readers. As children are able, they should move to the ELL Reader.

- **Preview** Read the title aloud with children and allow for them to look through the pages. This story is about how snow can help some animals in the winter. Activate prior knowledge about snow and animals that are white. The story in our book was about what some animals do in the winter. This story is about how snow can help some animals in the winter.
- **Set a Purpose for Reading** Let's read to find out how snow helps some animals.

■ **During Reading** Follow this Reading Routine for both reading groups.

1. Read the entire Reader aloud slowly as children follow along and finger point.
2. Reread the Reader one page at a time, having children echo read after you.

■ **After Reading** Use the exercises on the inside back cover of *As White as Snow* and invite children to share drawings and writings. In a whole-group discussion, ask children to list the animals that can hide in the snow. Encourage children to point to each animal as they list them.

ELD Reader Beginning/Intermediate

■ **pp. 2–3** Point to the snow. What color is snow? Point to the polar bear. What animal is this?

■ **p. 8** What can some animals do in the snow?

Writing Draw a picture of your favorite animal in the story. Find a sentence in the story that tells about the animal. Copy the sentence next to your drawing. Ask children to work in pairs and share their picture and sentence with the whole class.

ELL Reader Advanced/Advanced-High

■ **pp. 2–3** Point to the snow. What does snow do?

■ **p. 6** Point to the weasel. What color is the weasel?

Study Guide Distribute copies of the ELL Reader Study Guide (*ELL Handbook,* page 172). Scaffold comprehension by reviewing how snow can help some animals in the winter. Review their responses together. (**Answers** See *ELL Handbook*, pp. 245–248.)

Objectives

- Understand the general meaning, main points, and important details of spoken language ranging from situations in which topics, language, and contexts are familiar to unfamiliar.

ELL English Language Learners

Conventions
Contractions with *Not*

Preteach Write the words *did* and *not* to start the lesson with the language structure of contractions. Karen did not drink her juice. Explain that when we speak and write, we often combine two words into one word. Karen didn't drink her juice. Repeat the word *didn't*. Tell children that *did not* and *didn't* mean the same thing. Explain that *did* and *not* can be put together to make one word. The one word is a a contraction. Write the word *didn't*. Point out the missing *o* and the apostrophe in its place.

Practice Write the words *can not*. Prompt children to use the two words in a sentence such as, *She can not drive a car.* Tell children to say the contraction for *can not*. (*can't*) Prompt children to say a sentence using the contraction *can't*. Have them identify the letters removed and replaced with an apostrophe. (*n, o*) Demonstrate how to write an apostrophe. Tell children that contractions are part of informal English and that we generally don't use contractions in formal English.

Reteach

- Remind children that contractions are two words that have been combined. Write the words *could not*. Demonstrate how the contraction is formed: combine the two words, erase the letter *o* from *not*, and insert an apostrophe to form the word *couldn't*. Search the Student Edition for examples of contractions, such as those on pp. 199, 201, 203. Have children identify contractions and the words used to form them. Read the contractions aloud and have children spell them correctly.

Practice

Beginning/ Intermediate Have children write the words is not. Have children combine the words into a contraction and use it in a sentence.

Advanced Have children scan books for contractions. Tell them to write three different contractions on a sheet of paper. Then for each contraction, have children write the two words that were combined.

Advanced-High Have children brainstorm a list of contractions using the word *not*. Tell them to use their contractions in simple sentences. Have children edit each other's work, checking for correct subject-verb agreement.

Objectives

- Demonstrate an increasing ability to distinguish between formal and informal English and an increasing knowledge of when to use each one commensurate with grade-level learning expectations.
- Speak using a variety of grammatical structures, sentence lengths, sentence types, and connecting words with increasing accuracy and ease as more English is acquired.

Content Objectives

- Form contractions.

Language Objectives

- Use contractions in sentences.
- Understand when to use informal English.
- Write contractions.
- Comprehend the language structure of contractions and spell contractions correctly.

Transfer Skills

Contractions Some other languages, such as Spanish, include contractions. Provide examples in the home language, such as *a* + *el* = *al* in Spanish. Help children practice pronouncing the final sounds in English contractions. Practice /nt/ until children can blend the phonemes fluently.

Grammar Jammer

For more practice with contractions, use the Grammar Jammer for this target skill. See the Grammar Jammer Routine (*ELL Handbook*, page 501) for suggestions on using this learning tool.

Content Objectives

- Identify and write sentences.
- Identify the characteristics of a friendly letter.

Language Objectives

- Write sentences.
- Share feedback for editing and revising.
- Know when to use formal English.

Mini-Lesson: Formal English

Talk with children about formal English. A friendly letter sounds like it could be written in informal English, but a written message may be more formal than a spoken one. Work with children on using formal English: complete sentences and correct use of conventions.

Mini-Lesson: Subject-Verb Agreement

Remind children that the subject and verb of a sentence must agree. That means they both mean one or more than one. In the sentence *Raccoon, Squirrel, and Goose are friends,* "Raccoon, Squirrel, and Goose" is the subject and is more than one. The verb *are* is used for more than one. Have children edit their friendly letters for subject-verb agreement.

ELL English Language Learners

Write a Friendly Letter

- **Introduce Terms** Write *friendly letter* on the board and explain the terms as you point to them. Something that is friendly is kind and helpful. A letter is a message that you write to someone. Circle the word *friend* inside *friendly*. A friendly letter is a letter that you might write to a friend.

- **Describe Sentences** Letters are messages that are written between two people. Think about Raccoon and Squirrel from *Where Are My Animal Friends?* Their friend, Goose, left to go south for the winter. How did this make Squirrel and Raccoon feel? In a letter, the writer tells the reader how he or she feels about something that has happened to him or her.

- **Model** Draw three large boxes connected with arrows on the board. Label them *First, Next*, and *Last*. Engage children in naming three things that Raccoon and Squirrel might want to tell Goose in their letter. Write sentences for each statement in the boxes.

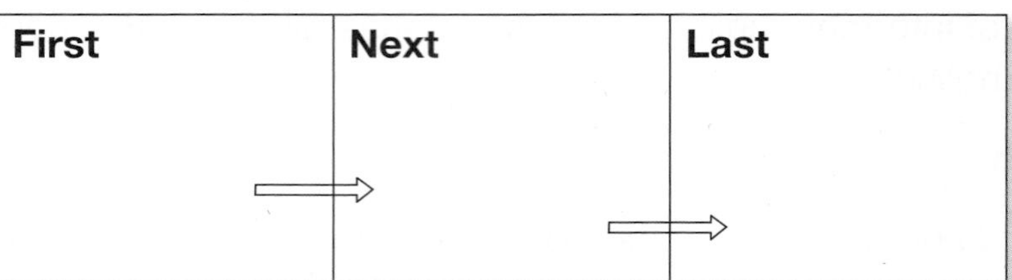

- **Write** Have children draw three boxes on their paper and label them *First, Next*, and *Last*. Have partners work together to think of three things they would want to tell Goose in a letter. What would they tell her first? What would they tell her next? What would they tell her last?

Beginning Supply the graphic organizer. Write the words *First, Next*, and *Last* in your boxes. Pretend you are Raccoon or Squirrel. What three things would you want to tell Goose? Have children tell about their pictures. Supply vocabulary as needed.

Intermediate Guide children's writing. What do you want to tell Goose? Help children with their spelling.

Advanced/Advanced-High Have children use their chart for prewriting. Then have them write their sentences in letter form.

Objectives

- Write using newly acquired basic vocabulary and content-based grade-level vocabulary.

Customize Your Writing

Weekly Writing Focus

Writing Forms and Patterns

- Instruction focuses on a different **product** each week.
- Mini-lessons and models help children learn key features and **organizational patterns**.

Grade 1 Products poetry, personal narrative, realistic story, play scene, letter, and so on

Grade 1 Organization Patterns beginning, middle, and end, main idea and details, sequence, and so on

Daily Writing Focus

Quick Writes for Fluency

- Writing on Demand Use the Quick Write routine for **writing on demand**.
- The Quick Write **prompt and routine** extend skills and strategies from daily writing lessons.

Unit Writing Focus

Writing Process 1 2 3 4 5

- Six **writing process** lessons provide structure to move children through the steps of the writing process.
- One-week and two-week pacing allows lessons to be used in **Writing Workshop**.

Steps of the Writing Process Plan and Prewrite, Draft, Revise, Edit, Publish and Present

Grade 1 Writing Process Products personal narrative, letter, expository article, realistic story, short report

MINI-LESSON

- Daily 10-minute mini-lessons focus instruction on the **traits** and **craft** of good writing.
- Instruction focuses on one writing trait and one writer's craft skill every week.

Traits focus/ideas, organization, voice, word choice, sentences, conventions

Craft drafting strategies, revising strategies, editing strategies

Read Like a Writer

- Use **mentor text** every week as a model to exemplify the traits of good writing.
- **Interact with text** every week to learn the key features of good writing.

Mentor Text Examine literature in the Student Edition.

INTERACT with TEXT Underline, circle, and highlight model text in the *Reader's and Writer's Notebook.*

Write Guy
Jeff Anderson

Need Writing Advice?

Writing instruction is all about creating effective writers. We don't want to crush the inner writer in a child by over-correcting and over-editing. What makes effective writing instruction? Children need to write, write, write! But is that enough? Probably not. All kinds of instruction and guidance go into making an effective writer.

The Write Guy offers advice on teacher and peer conferencing, focusing on writing traits, revising strategies, editing strategies, and much, much more.

Customize Your Writing

Alternate Pacing Plan for Unit Writing Projects

Sometimes you want to spend more time on writing—perhaps you do a **Writing Workshop**. This one- or two-week plan for the unit level writing projects can help.

1 Week Plan	Day 1	Day 2	Day 3	Day 4	Day 5
1 **Plan and Prewrite**					
2 **Draft**					
3 **Revise**					
4 **Edit**					
5 **Publish**					

2 Week Plan	Day 1	Day 2	Day 3	Day 4	Day 5	Day 6	Day 7	Day 8	Day 9	Day 10
1 **Plan and Prewrite**										
2 **Draft**										
3 **Revise**										
4 **Edit**										
5 **Publish**										

Grade 1 Unit Writing Projects

Internet Guy
Don Leu

Unit Writing Project 1–21st Century Project

Unit 1 Trading Card

Unit 2 Pen Pal E-mail

Unit 3 Photo Essay

Unit 4 Story Exchange

Unit 5 E-Newsletter

Unit Writing Project 2–Writing Process

Unit 1 Personal Narrative

Unit 2 Letter

Unit 3 Expository Article

Unit 4 Realistic Story

Unit 5 Short Report

Customize Your Writing

Common Core Standards and the Writing Process

Process Writing and the Common Core Standards for English Language Arts

This unit's Writing Process assignment will provide you with opportunities to instruct children in the steps of process writing: Plan and Prewrite, Draft, Revise, Edit, and Publish. Discuss these tips with children before they begin writing.

Process Writing Steps	Common Core Standards for English Language Arts	Tips for Unit 3 Process Writing
1 **Plan and Prewrite**	**Writing 2.**	As children prepare to prewrite, help them narrow their choices to one topic.
2 **Draft**	**Writing 2.**	Before children begin their drafts, show them how to use a Main Idea and Details Chart to help them organize their ideas.
3 **Revise**	**Writing 5.**	As children revise their drafts, remind them to use the *Revising Checklist* to make their writing clearer and more interesting to read.
4 **Edit**	**Language 1.; Language 2.**	Before children edit their articles, suggest that they read their articles aloud to help them find errors.
5 **Publish**	**Writing 6.**	When children are ready to publish their writing, have them use the Scoring Rubric to evaluate their own writing.

Writing Trait Skills Trace

All of the writing traits taught in Scott Foresman *Reading Street* are dimensions of good writing. In this unit's Writing Process project, children will write Expository Articles. The chart below shows you how the writing traits taught each week of the unit match the elements of the Scoring Rubric for Expository Articles and criteria from the highest score point of the rubric.

	Writing Trait of the Week / Weekly Selection	Scoring Rubric Top Score Point Criteria (The complete Expository Article Scoring Rubric is located on page CW•15.)
Week 1	• Organization *A Place to Play*	Main idea is supported by facts
Week 2	• Voice *Ruby in Her Own Time*	Clearly shows you are interested in the topic
Week 3	• Conventions *The Class Pet*	Uses good spelling and capitalization
Week 4	• Sentences *Frog and Toad Together*	Sentences are complete, clear, and not all alike
Week 5	• Focus/Ideas *I'm a Caterpillar*	Has a strong main idea and interesting details
Week 6	• Sentences *Where Are My Animal Friends?*	Sentences are complete, clear, and not all alike

Writing Resources

Use the resources to the right to build writing skills during and after the teaching of Unit 3.

Writing Resources

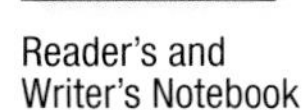
Reader's and Writer's Notebook

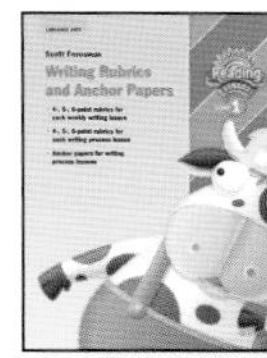
Writing Rubrics and Anchor Papers

Digital Resources
- Online Writing Transparencies

Teacher Resources DVD-ROM
- Reader's and Writer's Notebook
- Let's Practice It!
- Graphic Organizers
- Writing Transparencies

ISBN-13: 978-0-328-64370-7
ISBN-10: 0-328-64370-X

Expository Article

Writing Prompt

Write about a place or thing in nature. Describe the place or thing.

Purpose Inform

Audience Classmates

Introduce genre and prompt

Tell children that in this lesson they will learn about a kind of writing called an expository article. An expository article is a piece of writing about real people, places, or things. When you write an expository article, you use facts to tell about your topic.

Introduce key features

Key Features of an Expository Article

- tells about real people, places, or things
- uses facts to tell about the main idea
- uses specific words to make facts clear

Academic Vocabulary

Expository Article In an expository article, the writer uses facts to tell readers about a main idea.

English Language Learners

Introduce Genre Point out that an expository article tells about real people, places, or things. Explain that the writer uses facts to tell readers about the topic. Discuss with children the key features of an expository article that appear on this page.

Objectives

- Understand and identify the features of an expository article.
- Generate ideas for writing by drawing, sharing ideas, and listing key ideas.
- Select a topic.

Plan and Prewrite

MINI-LESSON

Read Like a Writer

- **Examine Model Text** Let's look at an example of an expository article. Display and read aloud to children "Thunderstorms" on Writing Transparency WP13. Point out the main idea of the article, which is stated at the beginning. Ask children to identify the facts the writer tells about thunderstorms in the middle (rain, lightning, thunder, wind). Ask them to also identify the strong verbs the writer uses (*pours, flashes, booms, blows*). Point out the end and discuss how it ties to the beginning.

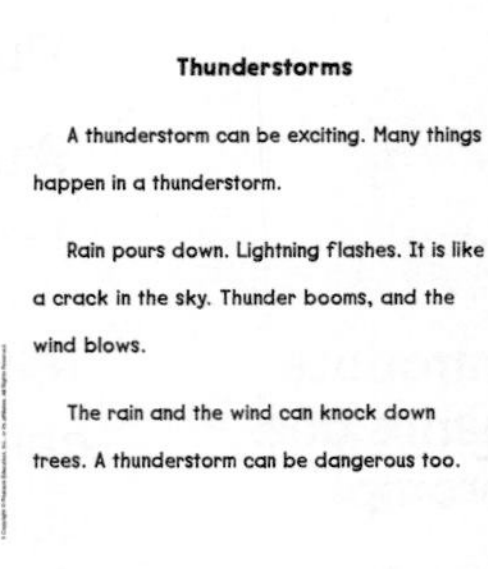

Thunderstorms

A thunderstorm can be exciting. Many things happen in a thunderstorm.

Rain pours down. Lightning flashes. It is like a crack in the sky. Thunder booms, and the wind blows.

The rain and the wind can knock down trees. A thunderstorm can be dangerous too.

Unit 3 Expository Article • PLAN and PREWRITE   Writing Process 13

Writing Transparency WP13
TR DVD

- **Evaluate Model Text** Display "Traits of a Good Expository Article" on Writing Transparency WP14. Discuss each trait with children. First read the name of the trait and remind them what it means. Then read aloud the statement, explaining any unfamiliar words to children. Finally, help children understand how the statement applies to the model expository article.

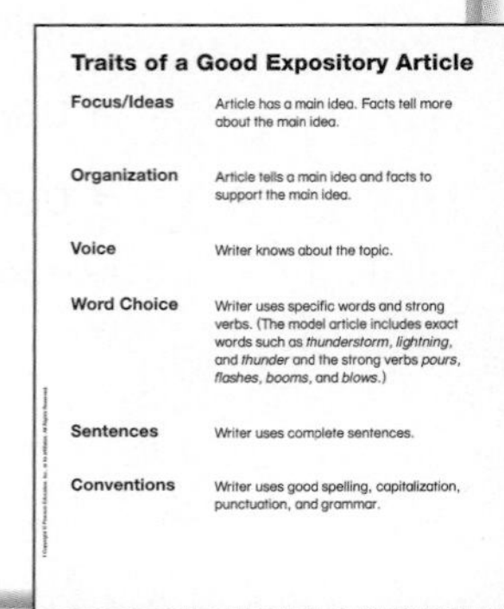

Traits of a Good Expository Article

Focus/Ideas	Article has a main idea. Facts tell more about the main idea.
Organization	Article tells a main idea and facts to support the main idea.
Voice	Writer knows about the topic.
Word Choice	Writer uses specific words and strong verbs. (The model article includes exact words such as *thunderstorm, lightning,* and *thunder* and the strong verbs *pours, flashes, booms,* and *blows.*)
Sentences	Writer uses complete sentences.
Conventions	Writer uses good spelling, capitalization, punctuation, and grammar.

Unit 3 • Expository Article • PLAN and PREWRITE   Writing Process 14

Writing Transparency WP14
TR DVD

Generate ideas for writing

Reread the writing prompt (on page CW11) to children. The writing prompt asks you to write about a place or thing in nature. Encourage children to generate ideas for their expository articles using these strategies:

- ✔ With a partner, share ideas about natural places they have enjoyed.
- ✔ Draw pictures of places and things in nature they think are beautiful.
- ✔ Make a list of as many ideas as possible. Circle their best ideas.

Corrective feedback

If... children have difficulty thinking of a place or thing to write about,
then... display pictures of natural places such as mountains, beaches, and forests and ask children to describe the pictures.

Narrow topic

Have children ask themselves questions about the ideas on their list. They might ask: *Do I know facts about this topic? Is the topic too big? Too small?* Model how to narrow the choices on a list to one topic using the example list shown.

Think Aloud I thought of three ideas. Now I will choose one. I think the ocean is too big a topic for a short article. There would be too many facts to choose from. On the other hand, I don't think I know enough about grass to write an article. Fall is my favorite season. I know facts about it, and I can also describe it. That will be my topic.

Topic Ideas
ocean
grass
fall

Use Mentor Text

Help children recall an article they have read, such as *The Class Pet* in this unit, that tells facts about a topic. Children need to hear and reflect on writing that resembles what they are learning to do. Tell them that they will write an expository article about a place or thing in nature, using facts to tell about it.

Differentiated Instruction

Alternative Writing Prompt
Think about a place you have visited that had interesting plants or animals. Name the things you liked. Tell why you liked them.

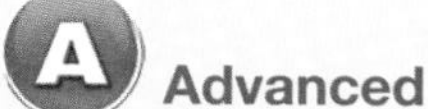

Alternative Writing Prompt
For your expository article, find three facts for your main idea in books. Summarize the facts in your article.

UNIT 3 Writing Process

Objectives

- Understand the criteria for an effective expository article.
- Plan an expository article by organizing ideas.
- Sequence ideas in sentences to prepare to write a first draft.

1 Plan and Prewrite

MINI-LESSON

Planning a First Draft

- **Use a Main Idea and Details Chart** Display Writing Transparency WP15 and read it aloud to children.

  Think Aloud I use this chart to sequence the ideas for my article. First I write my main idea sentence at the top. It tells what my article will be about. Then I write my detail sentences. They tell facts about the main idea. Now I can start writing a first draft of my expository article.

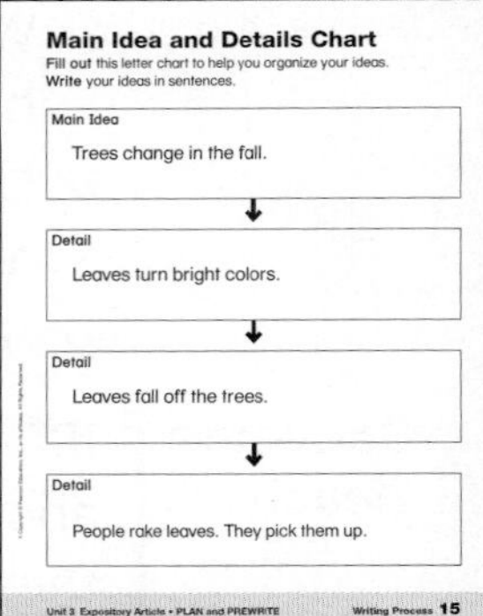

Main Idea and Details Chart

Fill out this letter chart to help you organize your ideas. Write your ideas in sentences.

Main Idea
Trees change in the fall.

Detail
Leaves turn bright colors.

Detail
Leaves fall off the trees.

Detail
People rake leaves. They pick them up.

Unit 3 Expository Article • PLAN and PREWRITE   Writing Process 15

Writing Transparency WP15
TR DVD

- Have children use the Main Idea and Details Chart graphic organizer on *Reader's and Writer's Notebook* page 611 to help them sequence the ideas in their expository article. Before you begin writing, decide what your main idea and details are. The details are facts about the main idea. Then write sentences for the beginning and middle of your article. Then think of a sentence for the end that sums up your main idea.

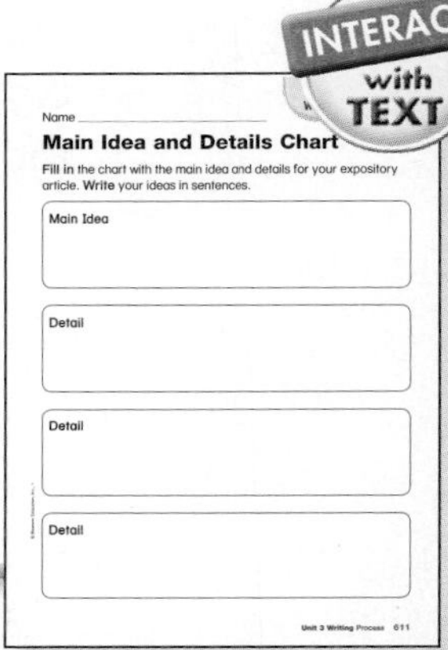

Name ______

Main Idea and Details Chart

Fill in the chart with the main idea and details for your expository article. Write your ideas in sentences.

Main Idea

Detail

Detail

Detail

Unit 3 Writing Process 611

Reader's and Writer's Notebook p. 611

Draft

Display rubric Display Scoring Rubric WP3 from the *Teacher Resource DVD-ROM*. Read aloud and discuss with children the traits and criteria that you choose. Encourage children to think about these criteria as they develop drafts of their expository articles. Tell them that rubrics such as this one are often used to evaluate and score writing.

Scoring Rubric: Expository Article

	4	3	2	1
Focus/Ideas	Has a strong main idea and interesting details	Has a main idea and some details	Has a weak main idea and few details	Has no main idea or supporting details
Organization	Main idea is supported by facts	Has main idea and some facts.	Main idea and facts are not clear.	Does not have facts.
Voice	Clearly shows you are interested in the topic	Shows your interest in the topic a little	Does not show your interest in the topic very well	Does not show you are interested in the topic
Word Choice	Uses specific words to help make ideas clear	Some words help make ideas clear	Words do not help make ideas clear	Words are hard to read
Sentences	Sentences are complete, clear, and not all alike	Sentences are complete and clear	Some sentences are not complete or not clear	Sentences not complete or clear
Conventions	Uses good spelling and capitalization	Uses fair spelling and capitalization	Uses poor spelling and capitalization	Uses very poor spelling and capitalization

Prepare to draft Have children look at the main idea and detail charts they worked on earlier. Ask them to make sure that their main idea and detail charts are complete. If they are not, have children finish them now. Use your main idea and details chart as you write a draft of your expository article. You will have a chance to revise your draft later.

Corrective feedback **If...** children do not understand how the Scoring Rubric can be used to evaluate writing,
then... show them how you can use the Scoring Rubric to evaluate and score one or more traits of the model expository article on Writing Transparency WP13.

Differentiated Instruction

SI Strategic Intervention

Plan a First Draft Some children will need additional guidance as they plan and write their articles. You might give them the option of writing an article with a partner under your supervision or pair them with more able writers who can help them with the process.

English Language Learners

Prepare to Draft Have children name key details they want to include in their articles. Help them restate the key details as complete sentences. Record the sentences and have children copy them.

Objectives

- Use strong verbs to make writing vivid.
- Write a first draft of an expository article.
- Revise a draft of an expository article.

2 Draft

MINI-LESSON

Writing Trait: Word Choice

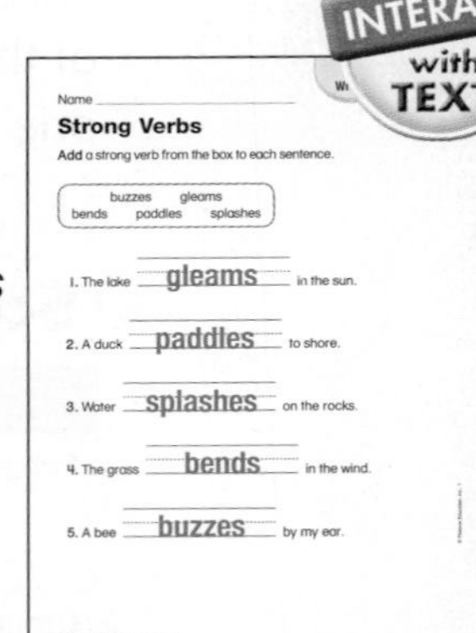

Reader's and Writer's Notebook p. 612

- **Use Strong Verbs** List the strong verbs on the board. Explain that these verbs can be used in place of the weak verb *go* to create a more vivid picture for readers. Say this sentence: *The horses go across the meadow.* Then say the sentence with each strong verb. Ask children what they picture the horses doing when they hear each sentence.

Strong Verbs
walk
trot
gallop
wander

- Have children use *Reader's and Writer's Notebook* page 612 to practice using strong verbs.

Develop draft Remind children that when they write their first drafts, they want to get their ideas down on paper. Suggest that they try these drafting strategies:

✔ Write their details in a different order. Choose the order that makes the most sense.

✔ Write one additional sentence that tells more about each detail.

3 Revise

MINI-LESSON

Writer's Craft: Adding or Deleting a Word, Phrase, or Sentence

- Explain to children that when writers revise, they may add words, phrases, or sentences to give more details. Writers may also delete, or take out, phrases or sentences that aren't needed or aren't about the topic. Help children add a detail phrase to the first example sentence and delete an unnecessary phrase in the second example sentence.

  Red roses grow. (Red roses grow in the garden.)
  The beach sand on the beach is tan. (The beach sand is tan.)

- Have children use *Reader's and Writer's Notebook* page 613 to practice adding or deleting a phrase or sentence.

INTERACT with TEXT

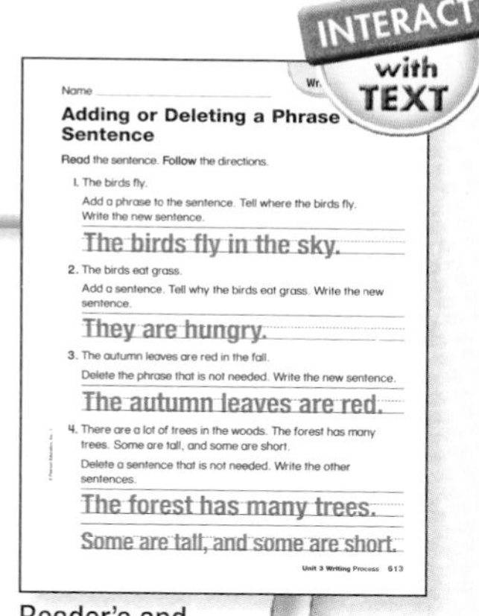

Name

Adding or Deleting a Phrase or Sentence

Read the sentence. Follow the directions.

1. The birds fly.
   Add a phrase to the sentence. Tell where the birds fly. Write the new sentence.
   The birds fly in the sky.
2. The birds eat grass.
   Add a sentence. Tell why the birds eat grass. Write the new sentence.
   They are hungry.
3. The autumn leaves are red in the fall.
   Delete the phrase that is not needed. Write the new sentence.
   The autumn leaves are red.
4. There are a lot of trees in the woods. The forest has many trees. Some are tall, and some are short.
   Delete a sentence that is not needed. Write the other sentences.
   The forest has many trees.
   Some are tall, and some are short.

Reader's and Writer's Notebook p. 613

Revising Tip

Compound Sentences If children wrote only short sentences, suggest that they make some of them into compound sentences. A compound sentence is made up of two simple sentences joined by a comma and the word *and, but,* or *or.* Emphasize that the two simple sentences must be about the same idea.

Revise model Use Writing Transparency WP16 to model how to revise an expository article.

Think Aloud I changed the unclear verb *go* to the stronger, more specific verb *change.* I want my readers to understand exactly what I'm describing about the leaves. I deleted the phrase *with their bright colors* because it is not needed. I already mentioned the colors and used the word *bright.* I added the phrase *on the ground* to create a clearer picture of what the leaves do for my readers.

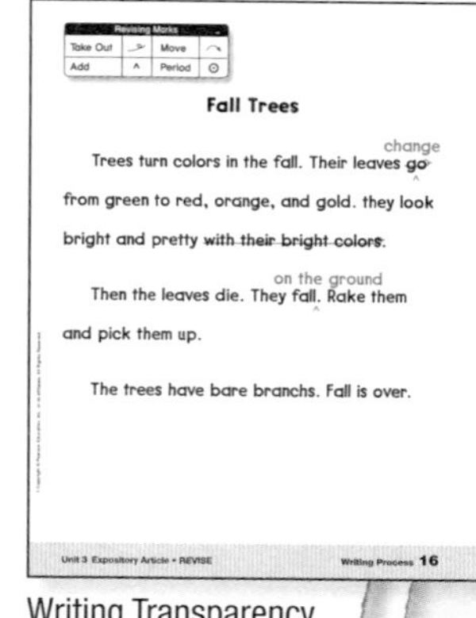

Revising Marks			
Take Out		Move	
Add	^	Period	⊙

Fall Trees

Trees turn colors in the fall. Their leaves ~~go~~ change from green to red, orange, and gold. they look bright and pretty ~~with their bright colors~~.

Then the leaves die. They fall on the ground. Rake them and pick them up.

The trees have bare branchs. Fall is over.

Writing Transparency WP16, TR DVD

ELL

English Language Learners

Revise for Word Choice To help children add strong verbs to their writing, work with them to develop word webs, each with a weak verb in the center and around it strong verbs that can replace it. Encourage children to use children's dictionaries, if available, to find strong verbs. Children can refer to their word webs when they are writing their expository articles.

Writing Process

Objectives

- Revise a draft of an expository article.
- Edit a revised draft of an expository article to correct errors in grammar, punctuation, capitalization, and spelling.

Revise

Revise draft

We have written first drafts of our expository articles. Now we will revise our drafts. When we revise, we try to make our writing clearer and more interesting to read.

Peer conferencing

Peer Revision Write the questions that you choose from the Revising Checklist on the board. If you elect to use peer revision, help pairs of children exchange and read each other's drafts. Read aloud the checklist, one question at a time. Ask children to answer each question about their own draft or their partner's draft. Remind them to think about where a phrase or sentence could be added or deleted to improve the writing.

Have children revise their expository articles using their own ideas or their partner's comments as well as what they have learned about expository articles.

Revising Checklist

- ✔ Does the expository article tell about a real place or thing in nature?
- ✔ Does the article have a main idea and details that support the main idea?
- ✔ Does the article have facts?
- ✔ Does the writer use specific words and strong verbs to make the ideas clear?
- ✔ Will adding or deleting a phrase or sentence help make the article clearer or more interesting?

4 Edit

MINI-LESSON

Editing Strategy: Read Your Work Aloud

- Explain this editing strategy to children: Read your work aloud to help you find errors. Sometimes it is easier to find errors when you hear them. Model this strategy using Writing Transparency W17. If you elect to teach proofreading marks, explain what they mean and how they are used as you discuss the errors on the transparency.

Think Aloud I will listen for errors as I read my article aloud. Something doesn't sound right in the sixth sentence. It does not tell who rakes the leaves. I will add the subject *People* so the sentence will say *People rake them*. Reading aloud helped me find that mistake. I also see two other errors to fix. The first word, *they,* is not capitalized in the fourth sentence. The word *branches* needs a spelling correction.

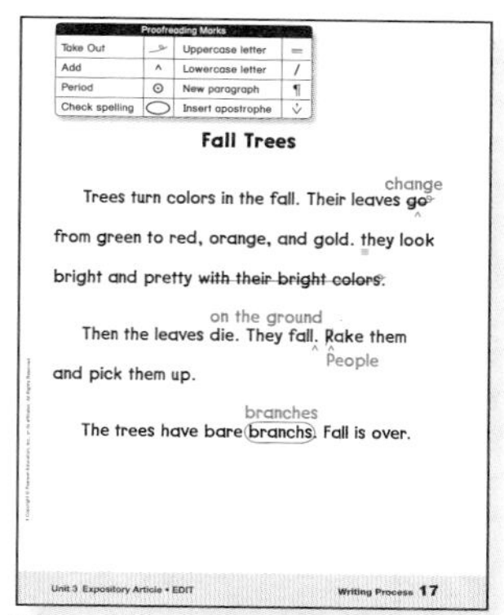

Proofreading Marks			
Take Out		Uppercase letter	≡
Add	^	Lowercase letter	/
Period	⊙	New paragraph	¶
Check spelling	◯	Insert apostrophe	˅

Fall Trees

Trees turn colors in the fall. Their leaves go [change] from green to red, orange, and gold. they look bright and pretty ~~with their bright colors~~.

Then the leaves die. They fall [on the ground]. [People] Rake them and pick them up.

The trees have bare branchs [branches]. Fall is over.

Unit 3 Expository Article • EDIT   Writing Process 17

Writing Transparency WP17
TR DVD

- Have children edit the sentences on *Reader's and Writer's Notebook* page 614. Encourage them to use proofreading marks.

Help children edit their own drafts. Have them check their spelling, grammar, punctuation, and capitalization. Make a simple rubric so children can use it to check the grammar, punctuation, spelling, and capitalization criteria you select for this writing. Make a simple rubric so children can use it to check the grammar, punctuation, spelling, and capitalization criteria you select for this writing.

INTERACT with TEXT

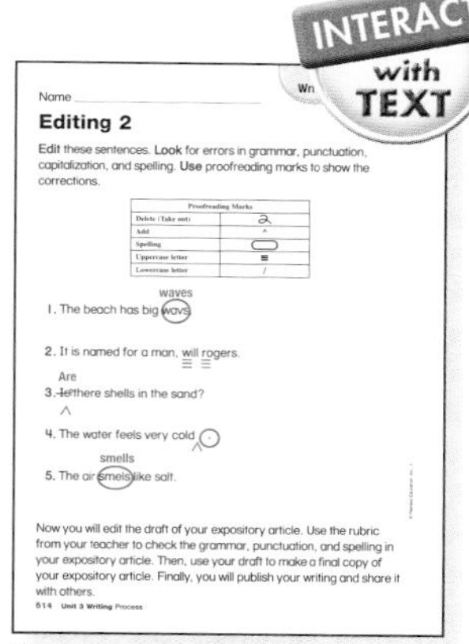

Name ______________________

Editing 2

Edit these sentences. Look for errors in grammar, punctuation, capitalization, and spelling. Use proofreading marks to show the corrections.

Proofreading Marks	
Delete (Take out)	ᘐ
Add	^
Spelling	◯
Uppercase letter	≡
Lowercase letter	/

1. The beach has big wavs [waves].
2. It is named for a man, will rogers.
3. Is [Are] there shells in the sand?
4. The water feels very cold ⊙
5. The air smels [smells] like salt.

Now you will edit the draft of your expository article. Use the rubric from your teacher to check the grammar, punctuation, and spelling in your expository article. Then, use your draft to make a final copy of your expository article. Finally, you will publish your writing and share it with others.

614 Unit 3 Writing Process

Reader's and Writer's Notebook p. 614

Technology Tips

Children who type their expository articles on computers may find this tip useful as they edit:

✔ When they have questions about how to do something on the computer, ask a friend or use the Help menu.

Differentiated Instruction

Advanced

Apply Editing Skills As they edit their work, children can consider these ways to improve it.

- Check that every sentence begins with a capital letter.
- Make sure words are spelled correctly.

Adding Without Leaving Readers Hanging

Children may add worthwhile information but write sentence fragments. Help them recognize "sentences" that "leave the reader hanging." *Picking up leaves* is not a complete sentence. Ask children, "Who is picking up leaves?" *People are picking up leaves.* That doesn't leave readers hanging. Children can understand that.

English Language Learners

Support Editing When reviewing a child's draft, focus on ideas more than errors. Keep in mind that a consistent grammatical error may reflect the writing conventions of the home language. Use the appropriate lessons in the *ELL Handbook* to explicitly teach the English conventions.

Objectives
- Write and present a final draft of an expository article.
- Evaluate one's own writing.

Publish and Present

Present

Remind children of the writing process steps they read about on *Reader's and Writer's Notebook* page 614. After they have revised and edited their expository articles, have children write a final draft. Explain that it is time for them to share their writing with others. Offer children two ways to present their work:

Read aloud their articles in small groups. Group members may ask questions about the articles.	Draw or find pictures to go with their articles. Post both on a bulletin board.

MINI-LESSON

Evaluating Writing

- Prepare children to evaluate their expository article. Display and read aloud Writing Transparency WP18. Model the self-evaluation process.

  Think Aloud In my expository article, I stated my main idea about fall trees in the beginning. In the middle and end, I told facts about the main idea in an order that makes sense. Strong verbs (*change, die, fall, rake*) and specific words (*trees, leaves, branches*) help make my ideas clear. I used short and long sentences. My spelling and capitalization are good.

Fall Trees

Trees turn colors in the fall. Their leaves change from green to red, orange, and gold. They look bright and pretty.

Then the leaves die. They fall on the ground. People rake them and pick them up.

The trees have bare branches. Fall is over.

Unit 3 Expository Article • PUBLISH Writing Process 18

Writing Transparency WP18
TR DVD

- Help children use the Scoring Rubric to evaluate their expository articles. They can save their work in a portfolio to help them monitor their development as writers. Encourage them to build on their skills and to note areas to improve.

Customize Literacy in Your Classroom

Table of Contents
for Customize Literacy

Customize Literacy is organized into different sections, each one designed to help you organize and carry out an effective literacy program. Each section contains strategies and support for teaching comprehension skills and strategies. *Customize Literacy* also shows how to use weekly text sets of readers in your literacy program.

Weekly Text Sets
to Customize Literacy

The following readers can be used to enhance your literacy instruction.

	Decodable Readers	Concept Literacy Reader	Below-Level Reader	On-Level Reader	Advanced Reader	ELD Reader	ELL Reader
Unit 3 WEEK 4	*Hopping Buffy; Day at the Farm; Jogging in the Park*	*Changes in the Gardens*	*The Seasons Change*	*Plans Change*	*All About the Weather*	*Grow Tomatoes*	*Grow Tomatoes*
Unit 3 WEEK 5	*Burt and Gert; She's Flying; We've Made Shirts!*	*Caterpillars Change*	*Animals Change and Grow*	*Let's Visit a Butterfly Greenhouse*	*Learn About Butterflies*	*My Apple Tree*	*My Apple Tree*
Unit 3 WEEK 6	*The Hardest Job; Where Is My Badge?; The Fudge Cake*	*In the Winter*	*Ready for Winter?*	*Seasons Come and Go*	*Monarchs Migrate South*	*As White As Snow*	*As White As Snow*

Customize Literacy in Your Classroom

Customize Instruction
to Improve Reading Behaviors

Instruction in comprehension skills and strategies provides readers with avenues to understanding a text. Through teacher modeling and guided, collaborative, and independent practice, students become independent thinkers who employ a variety of skills and strategies to help them make meaning as they read.

Mini-Lessons for Comprehension Skills and Strategies

Unit R	Character, Setting, Plot, Realism and Fantasy, Questioning, Monitor and Clarify, Background Knowledge
Unit 1	Character, Setting, Plot, Main Idea and Details, Cause and Effect, Summarize, Important Ideas, Story Structure
Unit 2	Sequence, Cause and Effect, Author's Purpose, Compare and Contrast, Predict and Set Purpose, Inferring
Unit 3	Sequence, Compare and Contrast, Fact and Opinion, Author's Purpose, Draw Conclusions, Visualize, Text Structure
Unit 4	Draw Conclusions, Theme, Facts and Details, Cause and Effect, Important Ideas, Questioning
Unit 5	Literary Elements, Draw Conclusions, Compare and Contrast, Main Idea and Details, Sequence, Theme, Monitor and Clarify, Summarize

Envision It! A Comprehension Handbook

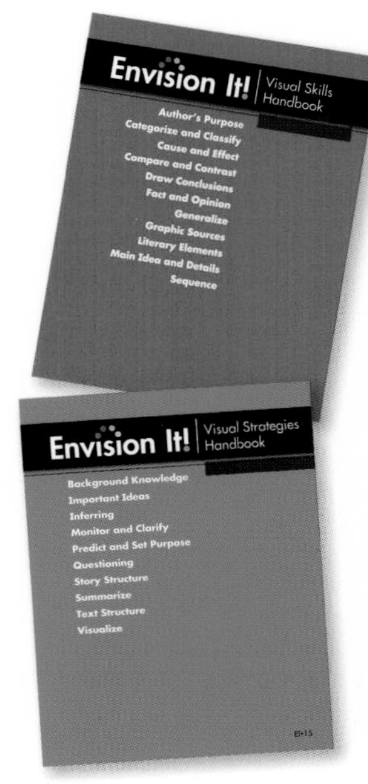

Anchor Chart Anchor charts are provided with each strategy lesson. These charts incorporate the language of strategic thinkers. They help students make their thinking visible and permanent and provide students with a means to clarify their thinking about how and when to use each strategy. As students gain more experience with a strategy, the chart may undergo revision.

See pages 107–128 in the *First Stop on Reading Street* Teacher's Edition for additional support as you customize literacy in your classroom.

Good Readers DRA2 users will find additional resources in the *First Stop on Reading Street* Teacher's Edition on pages 110–111.

Contents

Pacing Guide

This chart shows the instructional sequence from *Scott Foresman Reading Street* for Grade 1. You can use this pacing guide as is to ensure you are following a comprehensive scope and sequence. Or, you can adjust the sequence to match your calendar, curriculum map, or testing schedule.

Grade 1 READING

	UNIT R						UNIT 1	
	Week 1	Week 2	Week 3	Week 4	Week 5	Week 6	Week 1	Week 2
Phonemic Awareness	Match Initial Phonemes	Match Initial Phonemes	Match Final Phonemes	Isolate Final Phonemes	Isolate Phonemes	Isolate Medial Phonemes	Blend and Segment Phonemes	Blend and Segment Phonemes
Phonics	/m/ spelled *m*, /s/ spelled *s, ss* /t/ spelled *t*, /a/ spelled *a*	/k/ spelled *c*, /p/ spelled *p*, /n/ spelled *n*	/f/ spelled *f, ff*, /b/ spelled *b*, /g/ spelled *g*, /i/ spelled *i*	/d/ spelled *d*, /l/ spelled *l, ll* /h/ spelled *h*, /o/ spelled *o*	/r/ spelled *r*, /w/ spelled *w*, /j/ spelled *j*, /k/ spelled *k*, /e/ spelled *e*	/v/ spelled *v*, /y/ spelled *y*, /u/ spelled *u*, /kw/ spelled *qu*, /z/ *z, zz*	Short *a* Final *ck*	Short *i* Final *x*
High-Frequency Words	*I, see, a, green*	*we, like, the, one*	*do, look, you, was, yellow*	*are, have, they, that, two*	*he, is, to, with, three*	*where, here, for, me, go*	*on, way, in, my, come*	*take, up, she, what*
Comprehension Skill	Character	Setting	Plot	Realism/ Fantasy	Plot	Realism/ Fantasy	Character and Setting	Plot
Comprehension Strategy	Questioning	Predict and Set Purpose	Story Structure	Questioning	Monitor and Clarify	Background Knowledge	Monitor and Clarify	Summarize
Fluency	Oral Rereading	Oral Rereading	Oral Rereading, Paired Reading	Oral Rereading, Paired Reading	Oral Rereading, Paired Reading	Oral Rereading, Paired Reading	Accuracy	Accuracy

	UNIT 3						UNIT 4	
	Week 1	Week 2	Week 3	Week 4	Week 5	Week 6	Week 1	Week 2
Phonemic Awareness	Segment Phonemes	Blend and Segment Words	Add Phonemes	Blend and Segment Syllables	Isolate Medial and Final Phonemes	Add Phonemes	Substitute Initial Phonemes	Substitute Final Phonemes
Phonics	Vowel Sounds of *y* Long Vowels (CV)	Final *ng, nk* Compound Words	Ending *-es*, Plural *-es* *r*-Controlled *or, ore*	Inflected *-ed, -ing* *r*-Controlled *ar*	*r*-Controlled *er, ir, ur* Contractions *'s, 've, 're*	Comparative Endings *dge*/j/	Long *a: ai, ay* Possessives	Long *e: ea* Inflected Endings
High-Frequency Words	*always, become, day, everything, nothing, stays, things*	*any, enough, ever, every, own, sure, were*	*away, car, friends, house, our, school, very*	*afraid, again, few, how, read, soon*	*done, know, push, visit, wait*	*before, does, good-bye, oh, right, won't*	*about, give, enjoy, would, worry, surprise*	*colors, drew, over, sign, draw, great, show*
Comprehension Skill	Sequence	Compare and Contrast	Fact and Opinion	Author's Purpose	Fact and Opinion	Draw Conclusions	Draw Conclusions	Theme
Comprehension Strategy	Summarize	Inferring	Monitor and Clarify	Visualize	Text Structure	Background Knowledge	Monitor and Clarify	Visualize
Fluency	Accuracy/ Rate	Phrasing	Phrasing	Expression/ Intonation	Expression/ Intonation	Expression/ Intonation	Expression/ Intonation	Accuracy/ Rate

Are you the adventurous type? Want to use some of your own ideas and materials in your teaching? But you worry you might be leaving out some critical instruction kids need? **Customize Literacy** can help.”

Week 3	Week 4	Week 5	Week 6
Blend and Segment Phonemes	Blend and Segment Phonemes	Blend and Segment Phonemes	Blend and Segment Phonemes
Short *o* -*s* Plurals	Inflected Endings *-s, -ing*	Short *e* Initial Blends	Short *u* Final Blends
blue, little, get, from, help, use	*eat, her, this, too, four, five*	*saw, small, tree, your*	*home, into, many, them*
Character and Setting	Main Idea and Details	Main Idea and Details	Cause and Effect
Visualize	Important Ideas	Story Structure	Text Structure
Rate	Accuracy/ Rate	Phrasing	Phrasing

UNIT 2

Week 1	Week 2	Week 3	Week 4	Week 5	Week 6
Blend and Segment Phonemes	Blend and Segment Phonemes	Distinguish Long/Short Sounds	Distinguish Long/Short Sounds	Distinguish Long/Short Sounds	Distinguish Long/Short Sounds
Digraphs *sh, th* Vowel Sound in *ball*	Long *a* (CVC*e*) *c*/s/ and *g*/j/	Long *i* (CVC*e*) Digraphs *wh, ch, tch, ph*	Long *o* (CVC*e*) Contractions *n't, 'm, 'll*	Long *u*, long *e* (CVC*e*) Inflected Endings *-ed*	Long *e: e, ee* Syllables VCCV
catch, good, no, put, want, said	*be, could, horse, old, paper, of*	*live, out, people, who, work*	*down, inside, now, there, together*	*around, find, food, grow, under, water*	*also, family, new, other, some, their*
Sequence	Cause and Effect	Author's Purpose	Sequence	Author's Purpose	Compare and Contrast
Predict and Set Purpose	Monitor and Clarify	Important Ideas	Inferring	Background Knowledge	Questioning
Accuracy/ Rate	Phrasing	Phrasing	Accuracy/ Rate	Phrasing	Accuracy/ Rate

Week 3	Week 4	Week 5	Week 6
Substitute Phonemes	Substitute Phonemes	Segment Syllables	Blend and Segment
Long *o: oa, ow* Three-letter Blends	Long *i: ie, igh* *kn*/n/ and *wr*/r/	Compound Words Vowels *ew, ue, ui*	Suffixes *-ly, -ful* Vowels in *moon*
found, once, wild, mouth, took	*above, laugh, touch, eight, moon*	*picture, room, thought, remember, stood*	*told, because, across, only, shoes, dance, opened*
Facts and Details	Facts and Details	Theme	Cause and Effect
Important Ideas	Questioning	Story Structure	Predict and Set Purpose
Expression/ Intonation	Accuracy/ Rate/ Expression	Phrasing	Expression/ Intonation

UNIT 5

Week 1	Week 2	Week 3	Week 4	Week 5	Week 6
Delete Initial Phonemes	Blend and Segment Phonemes	Add Final Phonemes	Substitute Final Phonemes	Blend and Segment Phonemes	Delete Phonemes
Diphthongs *ow, ou* Syllables C + *le*	Vowel Patterns *ou, ow* Syllables V/CV, VC/V	Vowels in *foot* Inflected Endings	Diphthongs *oi, oy* Suffixes *-er, -or*	Syllable Patterns	Prefixes *un-, re-* Long Vowels *i, o*
along, behind, eyes, never, pulling, toward	*door, loved, should, wood*	*among, another, instead, none*	*against, goes, heavy, kinds, today*	*built, early, learn, science, through*	*answered, carry, different, poor*
Character, Setting, and Plot	Draw Conclusions	Compare and Contrast	Main Idea and Details	Sequence	Theme
Monitor and Clarify	Background Knowledge	Monitor and Clarify	Summarize	Text Structure	Inferring
Accuracy/ Rate/ Expression	Accuracy/ Rate/ Expression/ Phrasing	Expression/ Intonation	Phrasing	Expression/ Intonation	Phrasing

Pacing Guide

Grade 1

LANGUAGE ARTS	UNIT R Week 1	Week 2	Week 3	Week 4	Week 5	Week 6
Speaking, Listening, and Viewing	Participate in a Discussion	Share Information and Ideas	Follow, Restate, Give Instructions	Give Instructions	Ask Questions	Retell
Research and Study Skills	Parts of a Book	Parts of a Book	Signs	Map	Calendar	Library/ Media Center
Grammar	Nouns: People, Animals, and Things	Nouns: Places	Verbs	Simple Sentences	Adjectives	Sentences
Weekly Writing	Sentences	Sentences	Sentences	Sentences	Sentences	Sentences
Writing						

LANGUAGE ARTS	UNIT 1 Week 1	Week 2
Speaking, Listening, and Viewing	Ask Questions	Share Information and Ideas
Research and Study Skills	Parts of a Book	Media Center/ Library Resources
Grammar	Sentences	Subjects
Weekly Writing	Story/Voice	Fantasy Story/ Conventions
Writing		

	UNIT 3 Week 1	Week 2	Week 3	Week 4	Week 5	Week 6
Speaking, Listening, and Viewing	Relate an Experience	Share Information and Ideas	Give Descriptions	Present a Poem	Share Information and Ideas	Give Announce-ments
Research and Study Skills	Interview	Glossary	Classify and Categorize	Diagram	Technology: My Computer	Picture Graph
Grammar	Action Verbs	Verbs That Add *-s*	Verbs That Do Not Add *-s*	Verbs for Past and for Future	*Am, Is, Are, Was,* and *Were*	Contractions with *Not*
Weekly Writing	Realistic Story/ Organization	Comments About a Story/Voice	Summary/ Conventions	List/ Sentences	Captions and Pictures/ Focus/Ideas	Play Scene/ Sentences
Writing	Photo Writing/Expository Article					

	UNIT 4 Week 1	Week 2
Speaking, Listening, and Viewing	Give Descriptions	Share Information and Ideas
Research and Study Skills	Interview	Chart and Table
Grammar	Adjectives	Adjectives for Colors and Shapes
Weekly Writing	Letter/ Organization	Invitation/ Word Choice
Writing		

Week 3	Week 4	Week 5	Week 6
Give Introductions	Share Information and Ideas	Give Descriptions	Give Directions
Picture Dictionary	Chart	List	Notes
Predicates	Declarative Sentences	Interrogative Sentences	Exclamatory Sentences
Short Poem/ Sentences	Personal Narrative/ Voice	Realistic Story/ Organization	Brief Composition, Focus/Ideas
Keyboarding/Personal Narrative			

UNIT 2

Week 1	Week 2	Week 3	Week 4	Week 5	Week 6
Relate an Experience	Share Information and Ideas	Give Announce-ments	Informal Conversation	Share Information and Ideas	Follow Directions
Parts of a Book	Interview	Map	Periodicals/ Newsletters	Alphabetical Order	Picture Dictionary
Nouns	Proper Nouns	Special Titles	Days, Months, and Holidays	Singular and Plural Nouns	Nouns in Sentences
Friendly Letter/ Organization	Poster; Brief Composition/ Sentences	Explanation/ Conventions	Poem/ Organization	Description/ Voice	Expository Paragraph/ Focus/Ideas
Electronic Pen Pals/Letter					

Week 3	Week 4	Week 5	Week 6
Present a Poem	Purposes of Media	Purposes of Media	Purposes of Media
Bar Graph	Glossary	Technology: Using E-mail	Alphabetical Order
Adjectives for Sizes	Adjectives for What Kind	Adjectives for How Many	Adjectives That Compare
Poem/ Focus/Ideas	Realistic Story/Voice	Thank-You Note/ Conventions	Directions/ Organization
Story Starters/Realistic Story			

UNIT 5

Week 1	Week 2	Week 3	Week 4	Week 5	Week 6
Techniques in Media	Share Information and Ideas	Techniques in Media	Respond to Media	Techniques in Media	Respond to Media
Reference Sources/ Take Notes	Dictionary	Text Features	Picture Graph	Technology: Web Page	Encyclo-pedia
Imperative Sentences	Pronouns	Using *I* and *Me*	Pronouns	Adverbs	Prepositions and Prepositional Phrases
Animal Fantasy/ Voice	Letter/Voice	Questions/ Word Choice	Persuasive Ad/Focus/ Ideas	Autobiography/ Sentences	Poem/ Conventions
E-Newsletter/Short Report					

Teaching Record Chart

This chart shows the critical comprehension skills and strategies you need to cover. Check off each one as you provide instruction.

Reading/Comprehension	DATES OF INSTRUCTION		
Confirm predictions about what will happen next in text by "reading the part that tells."			
Ask relevant questions, seek clarification, and locate facts and details about stories and other texts.			
Establish purpose for reading selected texts and monitor comprehension, making corrections and adjustments when that understanding breaks down (e.g., identifying clues, using background knowledge, generating questions, re-reading a portion aloud).			
Connect the meaning of a well-known story or fable to personal experiences.			
Explain the function of recurring phrases (e.g., "Once upon a time" or "They lived happily ever after") in traditional folk and fairy tales.			
Respond to and use rhythm, rhyme, and alliteration in poetry.			
Describe the plot (problem and solution) and retell a story's beginning, middle, and end with attention to the sequence of events.			
Describe characters in a story and the reasons for their actions and feelings.			
Determine whether a story is true or a fantasy and explain why.			
Recognize sensory details in literary text.			

"Tired of using slips of paper or stickies to make sure you teach everything you need to? Need an easier way to keep track of what you have taught, and what you still need to cover? **Customize Literacy** can help."

Reading/Comprehension	DATES OF INSTRUCTION		
Read independently for a sustained period of time.			
Identify the topic and explain the author's purpose in writing about the text.			
Restate the main idea, heard or read.			
Identify important facts or details in text, heard or read.			
Retell the order of events in a text by referring to the words and/or illustrations.			
Use text features (e.g., title, table of contents, illustrations) to locate specific information in text.			
Follow written multi-step directions with picture cues to assist with understanding.			
Explain the meaning of specific signs and symbols (e.g., map features).			
Establish purposes for reading selected texts based upon desired outcome to enhance comprehension.			
Ask literal questions of text.			
Monitor and adjust comprehension (e.g., using background knowledge, creating sensory images, re-reading a portion aloud).			
Make inferences about text using textual evidence to support understanding.			
Retell or act out important events in stories in logical order.			
Make connections to own experiences, to ideas in other texts, and to the larger community and discuss textual evidence.			

Objectives:

- Children identify the author of a text.
- Children identify whether they think an author wrote something funny, serious, sad, or exciting.

Author's Purpose

Student Edition 1.3, p. EI•2

What is it? An author may write to persuade, to inform, to entertain, or to express a mood or feeling. At Grade 1, children can identify the author as the person who wrote a book. They begin to talk about whether the author wrote something funny, sad, or exciting. They use information from the text, such as pictures, to support their thoughts.

How Good Readers Use the Skill Children know that they read different kinds of selections for different reasons. Teachers can build on these experiences by introducing specific purposes for writing and helping readers classify things they read. At first, children learn that authors write to inform or entertain. More sophisticated readers learn other purposes; they learn that an author may have several purposes. Eventually we want readers to preview a selection for hints to author's purpose, for example, graphics, dialogue, and sample text. They also think critically about whether an author met his or her purpose.

Texts for Teaching

Student Edition

- *Who Works Here?* 1.2, pages 86–95
- *Life in the Forest,* 1.2, pages 146–159
- *Frog and Toad Together,* 1.3, pages 126–141

Leveled Readers

- See pages 24–29 for a list of Leveled Readers.

Mini-Lesson 1

Teach the Skill

Use the Envision It! lesson on 1.3, page EI•2 to visually review author's purpose.

Remind children that:

- an **author** is the person who wrote a story or selection.
- an author usually has a **reason** for writing something.

Practice

Display several familiar books. Explain what an author is and how to find the name of the author. Help children find the author of each book. Explain that authors have a reason for writing. Authors can write something funny, sad, serious, or exciting. Recall each book with children. Discuss what reason the author might have for writing each book.

If... children have difficulty identifying an author's purpose for writing,

then... have them think about how the book made them feel—happy, sad, or excited. Encourage children to connect how they felt about reading to why the author might have written the book.

Apply

As children read the assigned text, have them think about whether it was funny, sad, serious, or exciting.

Writing

Children can write their name on a piece of writing.

Teach the Skill

Use the Envision It! lesson on 1.3, page EI•2 to visually review author's purpose.

Remind children that:
- an **author** is the person who wrote a story or selection.
- an author usually has a **reason** for writing something.
- authors can write something funny, serious, sad, or exciting.

Practice

Show children a familiar nonfiction book. Explain that authors write to tell about something. Review the book. Have children say what the author was trying to tell them. Show familiar fiction and nonfiction books. Review each one. Use a chart like the one below to sort books by author's purpose.

This Book	Title of Book
Is Funny	
Is Exciting	
Is Sad	
Tells Me Something	

If... children have difficulty identifying author's purpose, **then...** model using the pictures and text to talk about what kind of story the author wrote.

Apply

As children read the assigned text, have them think about the author's reason for writing.

Writing

Children can add their favorite book to the tally sheet.

Teach the Skill

Use the Envision It! lesson on 1.3, page EI•2 to visually review author's purpose.

Remind children that:
- an **author** is the person who wrote a story or selection.
- an author usually has a **reason** for writing something.
- authors can write something funny, serious, sad, or exciting.
- an author doesn't tell you why he or she wrote something. You have to figure it out.

Practice

Show a familiar, short fiction story. Preview the pictures and text features. Think aloud: *I can use the pictures to think about why the author wrote this. I see a dog dressed in a hat and high-heels. I think this story will be funny.* Ask children why the author wrote the story. Read the story to confirm predictions. Have children revise their predictions if they would like. You might also do this with a short nonfiction piece to identify what the author wanted the reader to learn.

If... children have difficulty identifying author's purpose, **then...** ask "why" questions to point out the author's purpose.

Apply

As children read the assigned text, have them think about the author's reason for writing.

Writing

Children can write a sentence about why they think an author wrote a familiar book.

Objectives:
- Define *fact* and *opinion.*
- Use clue words to identify statements as fact or opinion.
- Decide whether or not a fact can be checked.

Fact and Opinion

Student Edition 1.3, pp. EI•4–EI•5

What is it? A **statement of fact** tells something that can be proved true or false. A **statement of opinion** tells a person's ideas or feelings and cannot be proved true or false. At Grade 1, children are identifying statements of fact and opinion. They are determining whether or not a statement of fact can be checked.

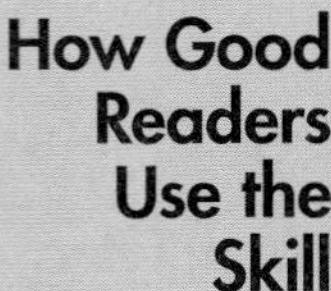

How Good Readers Use the Skill Children meet statements of facts and opinions throughout their day. We want to teach them how to distinguish the two and understand ways to check the veracity of factual statements and be able to judge statements of opinion thoughtfully. Evaluating statements of fact and statements of opinion boosts children' comprehension and helps them avoid being misled.

Texts for Teaching

Student Edition
- *The Class Pet,* 1.3, pages 92–105
- *I'm a Caterpillar,* 1.3, pages 158–173

Leveled Readers
- See pages 24–29 for a list of Leveled Readers.

Mini-Lesson 1

Teach the Skill

Use the Envision It! lesson on 1.3, pages EI•4–EI•5 to visually review fact and opinion with children.

Remind children that:
- a statement of **fact** tells something that can be proved true or false.
- a statement of **opinion** tells a person's ideas or feelings and cannot be proved true or false.

Practice

Write the following on the board and read them with students.
The Story of Ferdinand *was written by Munro Leaf.*
Everybody should read The Story of Ferdinand.
Ask: Which statement is a fact? How can you tell? Which is a statement of an opinion?
Talk with children about how a fact is a statement that can be proved to be true. (They could look at an actual book or they could check the internet or ask a librarian.) Point out the word *should* in the second sentence and explain that opinions often contain judgment words such as *should, I think*, and *best.*
If... children have difficulty distinguishing statements of fact,
then... ask: *Could you check this information out? How?*

Apply

As children read, have them be alert for statements of fact and opinion.

Writing

Children can write an opinion about a favorite book.

Mini-Lesson 2

Teach the Skill

Use the Envision It! lesson on 1.3, pages EI•4–EI•5 to visually review fact and opinion with children.

Remind children that:

- a statement of **fact** tells something that can be proved true or false.
- a statement of **opinion** tells a person's ideas or feelings and cannot be proved true or false.
- clue words and phrases, such as *I think, I believe, cute, best*, and so on, can signal an opinion.

Practice

Give children a familiar nonfiction selection and have partners read it together to identify statements of fact and opinion. Have them complete a chart, listing the statements they identify. Help children suggest how statements of fact can be checked.

Statement	Fact?	Opinion?
The temperature outside is 68°.	Yes. We could look at a thermometer.	No. We can prove it.

If... children have difficulty distinguishing opinions,
then... ask: *Can you prove this is the [cutest] or is that just what someone thinks?*

Apply

As children read, have them look for statements of fact and opinion.

Writing

Children can look at a photograph and write a statement of fact about it.

Mini-Lesson 3

Teach the Skill

Use the Envision It! lesson on 1.3, pages EI•4–EI•5 to visually review fact and opinion with children.

Remind children that:

- a statement of **fact** tells something that can be proved true or false.
- a statement of **opinion** tells a person's ideas or feelings and cannot be proved true or false.
- clue words and phrases, such as *best, in my opinion, I believe, I think*, and so on can signal an opinion.

Practice

Remind children that opinions often have judgment words or phrases: *should, must, best, I think, in my opinion.* Write these sentences on the board and talk about why they are opinions.
I think "Babe" is the best movie ever. Everyone must see it!
Let partners work together to write a paragraph that includes both statements of fact and opinion. Give pairs a topic—such as pets or sports—or let them choose one of their own. Have children complete a chart like the one for Mini-Lesson 2 to show their facts and opinions. Then have children share their paragraphs.
If... children have difficulty writing statements of fact and opinion,
then... give them a topic and sentence starters to complete, such as *The weather today is* ________. *I think this kind of weather* ________.

Apply

As children read, have them look for statements of fact and think about how they would check them out.

Writing

Children can write a few sentences that are facts and then add an opinion, underlining it.

Draw Conclusions

Objectives:

- Use details from a text and put the information together to make a decision.
- Support their conclusions from pictures, text, and their own prior knowledge.

Student Edition 1.3, p. EI•6

What is it? A **conclusion** is a decision a person makes after thinking about some facts and details. Drawing conclusions means figuring out something by thinking about it. Drawing conclusions allows readers to go beyond the literal meaning of a text and put information together in order to make decisions about what they are reading. At Grade 1, children are using information in text to make decisions about what they read.

How Good Readers Use the Skill Drawing conclusions is fundamental in reading and listening comprehension. When readers draw conclusions they synthesize and evaluate information from stories and informational articles as they bring their own life experiences and prior knowledge to the text. The result is a deeper understanding of what they are reading.

Texts for Teaching

Student Edition

- *Where Are My Animal Friends?,* 1.3, pages 190–205
- *Mama's Birthday Present,* 1.4, pages 20–43
- *Mole and the Baby Bird,* 1.5, pages 60–77

Leveled Readers

- See pages 24–29 for a list of Leveled Readers.

Mini-Lesson 1

Teach the Skill

Use the Envision It! lesson on 1.3, page EI•6 to visually review draw conclusions.

Remind children that:

- when they read a story or article or look at a picture, they can figure things out by using what they know about real life

Practice

Show a picture that suggests an emotion, such as a child crying or laughing. Talk about what is going on in the picture asking questions to get children to look closely: What do you see in the picture? What is the [boy, girl] doing? How do you think he or she is feeling? How do you know? Have you ever felt this way? Help children understand that if they have had a similar experience, they have some idea how the person is feeling.

If... students have difficulty drawing conclusions,
then... model your thinking as you draw a conclusion.

Apply

As children read on their own, have them think if they have ever experienced something like what they are reading about.

Writing

Children can write captions for pictures they draw or you provide.

Mini-Lesson 2

Teach the Skill

Use the Envision It! lesson on 1.3, page EI•6 to visually review draw conclusions.

Remind children that:

- when they read a story or article or look at a picture, they can figure things out by using what they know about real life.
- they can practice drawing conclusions by figuring out riddles.

Practice

Have children listen and figure out the answers to the following riddles. Tell them to listen to the words and then use what they already know to figure out the answers. Talk about what they already knew that help them figure out the answers.

I eat carrots and lettuce. I live outdoors. I have long ears. What am I? (a rabbit)

I am a musical instrument. You can play me with your fingers. I have 88 black-and-white keys. What am I? (a piano)

I am a ride at the playground. I can go high. I can go up and down, back and forth. What am I? (a swing)

If... students have difficulty answering the riddles, **then...** supply two answers, one of which is clearly wrong. Ask children to choose the correct answer.

Apply

As children read on their own, have them think about what they already know about the characters, plots, or other information.

Writing

Have children write riddles about familiar objects and have others try to guess the answers.

Mini-Lesson 3

Teach the Skill

Use the Envision It! lesson on 1.3, page EI•6 to visually review draw conclusions.

Remind children that:

- when they read a story or article or look at a picture, they can figure things out by using what they know about real life.

Practice

Read a story to children and have them make decisions about characters, events, or information. Remind children to use what they hear in the text and what they know to figure things out. Ask questions: What happens in the story? What did the characters do that shows you they are nice? mean? strong? smart? What clues helped you decide about the character? Model the process of drawing conclusions about a character by thinking aloud for children. For example, Juanita made cookies for the neighbor. She didn't have to do that. I think that shows she is a nice person.

If... children have difficulty drawing conclusions about a character, **then...** review details about the character and ask: *What kind of person does this?*

Apply

As children read on their own, have them use what they know to figure out more about the characters.

Writing

Children can draw pictures of story characters and label them with details that show what the character is like.

Objectives:

- Understand that text structure is separate from text content.
- Recognize that texts can be organized in sequential order or by description, comparison/contrast, or cause-effect.
- Identify text features of nonfiction.

Text Structure

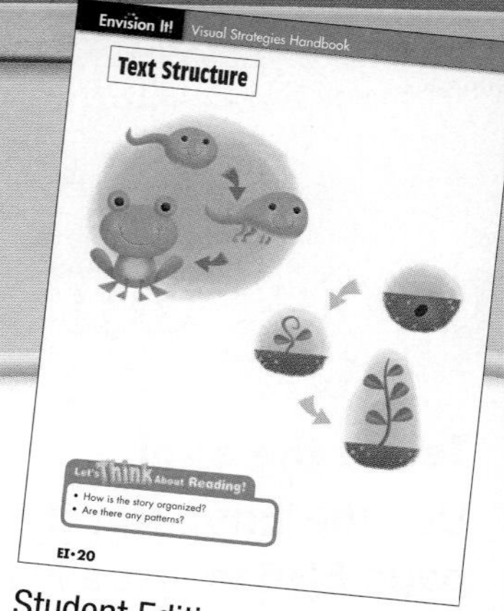

Student Edition 1.3, p. EI•20

Understand the Strategy

Text structure refers to how a nonfiction article is organized. Externally, nonfiction articles include titles, subheads, graphics, and so on. Internally, a nonfiction article is organized in a way that best presents the content. This organization may be sequential, comparative, explanatory (cause-effect), or descriptive. Recognizing text structure helps readers understand and recall ideas.

Teach

Use the Envision It! lesson on 1.3, page EI•20 to visually teach text structure with children.

Tell children that authors organize information in various ways. Provide examples of nonfiction texts and help children begin to identify common text patterns.

Pattern	Text Clues	Examples
Sequence	Words like *first, next, last;* dates, times	Biography, stories about the past, how-to books
Comparison/Contrast	Words like *same, different, both*	Books about animals in different seasons
Cause-Effect	Words like *because, since, as a result;* diagrams	Books that explain how something happens
Description	Lots of pictures of one thing	"all about" books

Practice

Read a short biography with children, pointing out clues to its text structure (sequential). Then have children reread the piece and work in pairs to locate these features on their own. On subsequent occasions, use a science article that explains a process. Over time, have them work with all the patterns listed in the chart.

If... children have difficulty recognizing sequential text structure,
then... talk about how the author shows what happens first, next, and last.

Apply

Ask children to think about how the author arranged the information as they preview and get ready to read.

Anchor Chart

Anchor charts help children make their thinking visible and permanent. With an anchor chart, the group can clarify their thinking about how to use a strategy. Here is a sample chart for text structure.

Texts for Teaching

Student Edition

- *Animal Park,* 1.1, pages 154–163
- *I'm a Caterpillar,* 1.3, pages 158–173
- *Alexander Graham Bell: A Great Inventor,* 1.5, pages 174–193

Leveled Readers

- See pages 24–29 for a list of Leveled Readers.

Text Structure

1. Look over the article before you read. Ask yourself:
What will this be about?
What do the pictures tell me?
Can I figure out a text structure?

2. Look for clues to text structure.
Sequence clues: words like *April, Tuesday, before, after, first, next, last*
Compare/contrast clues: words like *same, different, alike, both*
Cause-effect clues: words like *because, since;* diagrams
Description clues: lots of pictures of one thing or one kind of thing

3. Look for patterns as you read. Ask yourself:
Is this in time order?
Does this tell how to do something?
Does it show how things are alike and different?
Does it tell all about one person, place, or thing?

4. Share your ideas!

Anchor Chart

Using Multiple Strategies

Good readers use multiple strategies as they read. You can encourage children to read strategically through good classroom questioning. Use questions such as these to help children apply strategies during reading.

Questioning

- Who or what is this question about?
- Where can you look to find the answer to this question?
- What do you want to know about ________?
- What questions to do you have about the ________ in this selection? Use the words *who, what, when, where, why,* and *how* to ask your questions.
- Do you have any questions after reading?

Graphic Organizers

- What kind of graphic organizer could you use to help you keep track of the information in this selection?

Monitor and Clarify

- Does the story or article make sense?
- What don't you understand about what you read?
- Do you need to reread, review, read on, or check a reference source?
- Do you need to read more slowly or more quickly?
- What is a ________? Where could you look to find out?

Predict and Set Purpose

- What do you think this story or article will be about? Why do you think as you do?
- What do you think you will learn from this selection?
- Do the text features help you predict what will happen?
- Based on what has happened so far, what do you think will happen next?
- Is this what you thought would happen?
- How does ________ change what you thought would happen?

Preview

- What do the photographs, illustrations, or graphic sources tell about the selection?
- What do you want to find out? What do you want to learn?

Background Knowledge

- What do you already know about ________?
- Have you read stories or articles by this author before?
- How is this selection like others that you have read?
- What does this remind you of?
- How does your background knowledge help you understand ________?
- Did the text match what you already knew? What new information did you learn?

Story Structure

- Who are the characters in this story?
- What is the setting?
- What is the problem in this story? How does the problem get solved?
- What is the point of this story?

Summarize

- What two or three important ideas have you read so far?
- How do the text features relate to the important ideas?
- Is there a graphic organizer that can help you organize the information before you summarize?

Text Structure

- How has the author organized the writing?
- What clues tell you that the text is structured ________?

Visualize

- When you read this, what do you picture in your mind?
- What do you hear, see, or smell?
- What do you think ________ looks like? Why do you think as you do?

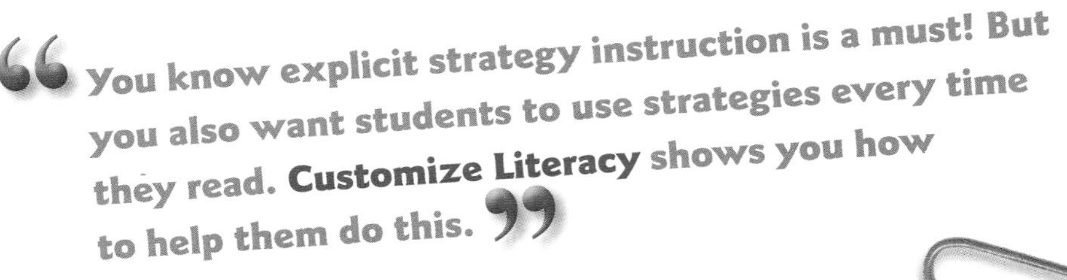

"You know explicit strategy instruction is a must! But you also want students to use strategies every time they read. **Customize Literacy** shows you how to help them do this."

Glossary of Literacy Terms

This glossary lists academic language terms that are related to literacy. They are provided for your information and professional use.

A

alliteration the repetition of a consonant sound in a group of words, especially in poetry

allusion a word or phrase that refers to something else the reader already knows from history, experience, or reading

animal fantasy a story about animals that talk and act like people

answer questions a reading strategy in which readers use the text and prior knowledge to answer questions about what they are reading

antonym a word that means the opposite of another word

ask questions a reading strategy in which readers ask themselves questions about the text to help make sense of what they read

author's point of view the author's opinion on the subject he or she is writing about

author's purpose the reason the author wrote the text

autobiography the story of a real person's life written by that person

B

background knowledge the information and experience that a reader brings to a text

biography the story of a real person's life written by another person

C

cause why something happens

character a person, an animal, or a personified object in a story

chronological order events in a selection, presented in the order in which they occurred

classify and categorize put things, such as pictures or words, into groups

climax the point in a story at which conflict is confronted

compare tell how things are the same

comprehension understanding of text being read—the ultimate goal of reading

comprehension strategy a conscious plan used by a reader to gain understanding of text. Comprehension strategies may be used before, during, or after reading.

conclusion a decision or opinion arrived at after thinking about facts and details and using prior knowledge

conflict the problem or struggle in a story

context clue the words, phrases, or sentences near an unknown word that give the reader clues to the word's meaning

contrast tell how things are different

D

details small pieces of information

dialect form of a language spoken in a certain region or by a certain group of people that differs from the standard form of that language

dialogue written conversation

diary a day-to-day record of one's activities and thoughts

draw conclusions arrive at decisions or opinions after thinking about facts and details and using prior knowledge

E

effect what happens as the result of a cause

etymology an explanation of the origin and history of a word and its meaning

exaggeration a statement that makes something seem larger or greater than it actually is

expository text text that contains facts and information, also called *informational text*

F

fable a story, usually with animal characters, that is written to teach a moral, or lesson

fact piece of information that can be proved to be true

fairy tale a folk story with magical characters and events

fantasy a story that could not really happen

fiction writing that tells about imaginary people, things, and events

figurative language the use of language that gives words a meaning beyond their usual definitions in order to add beauty or force

flashback an interruption in the sequence of events of a narrative to include an event that happened earlier

folk tale a story that has been passed down by word of mouth

foreshadowing the use of hints or clues about what will happen later in a story

G

generalize make a broad statement or rule after examining particular facts

graphic organizer a drawing, chart, or web that illustrates concepts or shows how ideas relate to each other. Readers use graphic organizers to help them keep track of and understand important information and ideas as they read. Story maps, word webs, Venn diagrams, and KWL charts are graphic organizers.

graphic source a chart, diagram, or map within a text that adds to readers' understanding of the text

H

historical fiction realistic fiction that takes place in the past. It is an imaginary story based on historical events and characters.

humor writing or speech that has a funny or amusing quality

hyperbole an exaggerated statement not meant to be taken literally, such as *I'm so hungry I could eat a horse.*

I

idiom a phrase whose meaning differs from the ordinary meaning of the words. *A stone's throw* is an idiom meaning "a short distance."

imagery the use of language to create beautiful or forceful pictures in the reader's mind

inference conclusion reached on the basis of evidence and reasoning

inform give knowledge, facts, or news to someone

informational text writing that contains facts and information, also called *expository text*

interview a face-to-face conversation in which someone responds to questions

irony a way of speaking or writing in which the ordinary meaning of the words is the opposite of what the speaker or writer is thinking; a contrast between what is expected and what actually happens

J

jargon the language of a special group or profession

L

legend a story coming down from the past about the great deeds of a hero. Although a legend may be based on historical people and events, it is not regarded as historically true.

literary elements the characters, setting, plot, and theme of a narrative text

M

main idea the big idea that tells what a paragraph or a selection is mainly about; the most important idea of a text

metacognition an awareness of one's own thinking processes and the ability to monitor and direct them to a desired goal. Good readers use metacognition to monitor their reading and adjust their reading strategies.

metaphor a comparison that does not use *like* or *as,* such as *a heart of stone*

meter the pattern of beats or accents in poetry

M

monitor and clarify a comprehension strategy by which readers actively think about understanding their reading and know when they understand and when they do not. Readers use appropriate strategies to make sense of difficult words, ideas, or passages.

mood the atmosphere or feeling of a written work

moral the lesson or teaching of a fable or story

motive the reason a character in a narrative does or says something

mystery a story about mysterious events that are not explained until the end, so as to keep the reader in suspense

myth a story that attempts to explain something in nature

N

narrative a story, made up or true, that someone tells or narrates

narrator the character in a selection who tells the story

nonfiction writing that tells about real things, real people, and real events

O

onomatopoeia the use of words that sound like their meanings, such as *buzz* and *hum*

opinion someone's judgment, belief, or way of thinking

oral vocabulary the words needed for speaking and listening

outcome the resolution of the conflict in a story

P

paraphrase retell the meaning of a passage in one's own words

personification a figure of speech in which human traits or actions are given to animals or inanimate objects, as in *The sunbeam danced on the waves.*

persuade convince someone to do or to believe something

photo essay a collection of photographs on one theme, accompanied by text

play a story that is written to be acted out for an audience

plot a series of related events at the beginning, middle, and end of a story; the action of a story

poem an expressive, imaginative piece of writing often arranged in lines having rhythm and rhyme. In a poem, the patterns made by the sounds of the words have special importance.

pourquoi tale a type of folk story that explains why things in nature came to be. *Pourquoi* is a French word meaning "why."

P

predict tell what a selection might be about or what might happen in a text. Readers use text features and information to predict. They confirm or revise their predictions as they read.

preview look over a text before reading it

prior knowledge the information and experience that a reader brings to a text. Readers use prior knowledge to help them understand what they read.

prop an item, such as an object, picture, or chart, used in a performance or presentation

R

reading vocabulary the words we recognize or use in print

realistic fiction a story about imaginary people and events that could happen in real life

repetition the repeated use of some aspect of language

resolution the point in a story where the conflict is resolved

rhyme to end in the same sound(s)

rhythm a pattern of strong beats in speech or writing, especially poetry

rising action the buildup of conflicts and complications in a story

S

science fiction a story based on science that often tells what life in the future might be like

semantic map a graphic organizer, often a web, used to display words or concepts that are meaningfully related

sensory language the use of words that help the reader understand how things look, sound, smell, taste, or feel

sequence the order of events in a selection or the order of the steps in which something is completed

sequence words clue words such as *first, next, then,* and *finally* that signal the order of events in a selection

setting where and when a story takes place

simile a comparison that uses *like* or *as,* as in *as busy as a bee*

speech a public talk to a group of people made for a specific purpose

stanza a group of lines in a poem

steps in a process the order of the steps in which something is completed

S

story map a graphic organizer used to record the literary elements and the sequence of events in a narrative text

story structure how the characters, setting, and events of a story are organized into a plot

summarize give the most important ideas of what was read. Readers summarize important information in the selection to keep track of what they are reading.

supporting detail piece of information that tells about the main idea

symbolism the use of one thing to suggest something else; often the use of something concrete to stand for an abstract idea

T

tall tale a humorous story that uses exaggeration to describe impossible happenings

text structure the organization of a piece of nonfiction writing. Text structures of informational text include cause/effect, chronological, compare/contrast, description, problem/solution, proposition/support, and ask/answer questions.

theme the big idea or author's message in a story

think aloud an instructional strategy in which a teacher verbalizes his or her thinking to model the process of comprehension or the application of a skill

tone author's attitude toward the subject or toward the reader

topic the subject of a discussion, conversation, or piece of text

V

visualize picture in one's mind what is happening in the text. Visualizing helps readers imagine the things they read about.

Leveled Readers Skills Chart

Scott Foresman Reading Street provides more than six hundred leveled readers. Each one is designed to:

- Practice critical skills and strategies
- Build fluency
- Build vocabulary and concepts
- Develop a lifelong love of reading

Grade 1

Title	Level*	DRA Level	Genre	Comprehension Strategy
Bix the Dog	A	1	Realistic Fiction	Summarize
Time for Dinner	B	2	Realistic Fiction	Important Ideas
Sam	B	2	Realistic Fiction	Monitor and Clarify
Mack and Zack	B	2	Realistic Fiction	Monitor and Clarify
The Sick Pets	B	2	Realistic Fiction	Summarize
On the Farm	B	2	Realistic Fiction	Visualize
At Your Vet	B	2	Realistic Fiction	Story Structure
Fun in the Sun	B	2	Expository Nonfiction	Text Structure
We Are a Family	B	2	Nonfiction	Predict and Set Purpose
Where They Live	C	3	Realistic Fiction	Visualize
Which Fox?	C	3	Realistic Fiction	Important Ideas
Which Animals Will We See?	C	3	Realistic Fiction	Text Structure
Let's Go to the Zoo	C	3	Nonfiction	Predict and Set Purpose
A Play	C	3	Realistic Fiction	Monitor and Clarify
A Class	C	3	Nonfiction	Monitor and Clarify
Here in My Neighborhood	C	3	Nonfiction	Important Ideas
Look at My Neighborhood	C	3	Realistic Fiction	Important Ideas
Look at Dinosaurs	C	3	Expository Nonfiction	Inferring
Around the Forest	C	3	Nonfiction	Background Knowledge
Learn About Worker Bees	C	3	Expository Nonfiction	Questioning
In My Room	C	3	Nonfiction	Summarize
Hank's Song	C	3	Fantasy	Inferring
Gus the Pup	C	3	Realistic Fiction	Monitor and Clarify
What Animals Can You See?	D	4	Expository Nonfiction	Text Structure
The Dinosaur Herds	D	4	Expository Nonfiction	Inferring
People Help the Forest	D	4	Expository Nonfiction	Background Knowledge
Honey	D	4	Nonfiction	Questioning
Let's Build a Park!	D	4	Fiction	Summarize
Mac Can Do It!	D	4	Fantasy	Inferring
The Seasons Change	D	4	Nonfiction	Visualize

* Suggested Guided Reading Level. Use your knowledge of students' abilities to adjust levels as needed.

The chart here and on the next few pages lists titles of leveled readers appropriate for students in Grade 1. Use the chart to find titles that meet your students' interest and instructional needs. The books in this list were leveled using the criteria suggested in *Matching Books to Readers: Using Leveled Books in Guided Reading, Grades K–3* by Irene C. Fountas and Gay Su Pinnell. For more on leveling, see the *Reading Street Leveled Readers Leveling Guide.*

Target Comprehension Skill	Additional Comprehension Instruction	Vocabulary
Plot	Sequence	High-Frequency Words
Main Idea and Details	Compare and Contrast	High-Frequency Words
Character and Setting	Draw Conclusions	High-Frequency Words
Character and Setting	Main Idea and Details	High-Frequency Words
Plot	Draw Conclusions	High-Frequency Words
Character and Setting	Plot	High-Frequency Words
Main Idea and Details	Theme	High-Frequency Words
Cause and Effect	Author's Purpose	High-Frequency Words
Sequence	Draw Conclusions	High-Frequency Words
Character and Setting	Theme and Plot	High-Frequency Words
Main Idea and Details	Compare and Contrast	High-Frequency Words
Cause and Effect	Setting and Plot	High-Frequency Words
Sequence	Compare and Contrast	High-Frequency Words
Cause and Effect	Main Idea and Details	High-Frequency Words
Cause and Effect	Author's Purpose	High-Frequency Words
Author's Purpose	Draw Conclusions	High-Frequency Words
Author's Purpose	Compare and Contrast	High-Frequency Words
Sequence	Cause and Effect	High-Frequency Words
Author's Purpose	Cause and Effect	High-Frequency Words
Compare and Contrast	Sequence	High-Frequency Words
Sequence	Author's Purpose	High-Frequency Words
Compare and Contrast	Realism and Fantasy	High-Frequency Words
Fact and Opinion	Cause and Effect	High-Frequency Words
Main Idea and Details	Compare and Contrast	High-Frequency Words
Sequence	Draw Conclusions	High-Frequency Words
Author's Purpose	Cause and Effect	High-Frequency Words
Compare and Contrast	Draw Conclusions	High-Frequency Words
Sequence	Author's Purpose	High-Frequency Words
Compare and Contrast	Realism and Fantasy	High-Frequency Words
Author's Purpose	Draw Conclusions	High-Frequency Words

Leveled Readers Skills Chart *Continued*

Grade 1

Title	Level*	DRA Level	Genre	Comprehension Strategy
Animals Change and Grow	D	4	Nonfiction	Text Structure
Ready for Winter?	D	4	Expository Nonfiction	Background Knowledge
A Party for Pedro	D	4	Realistic Fiction	Monitor and Clarify
Space Star	D	4	Realistic Fiction	Visualize
Our Leaders	D	4	Nonfiction	Important Ideas
Grandma's Farm	D	4	Realistic Fiction	Questioning
A New Baby Brother	D	4	Realistic Fiction	Story Structure
My Babysitter	D	4	Narrative Nonfiction	Predict and Set Purpose
What Brown Saw	D	4	Animal Fantasy	Monitor and Clarify
Fly Away Owl!	D	4	Realistic Fiction	Background Knowledge
What A Detective Does	D	4	Realistic Fiction	Monitor and Clarify
The Inclined Plane	D	4	Expository Nonfiction	Summarize
Using the Telephone	D	4	Expository Nonfiction	Text Structure
A Garden for All	D	4	Nonfiction	Inferring
Big Wishes and Her Baby	E	6–8	Realistic Fiction	Monitor and Clarify
Plans Change	E	6–8	Realistic Fiction	Visualize
Let's Visit a Butterfly Greenhouse	E	6–8	Nonfiction	Text Structure
Seasons Come and Go	E	6–8	Expository Nonfiction	Background Knowledge
Special Days, Special Food	E	6–8	Expository Nonfiction	Monitor and Clarify
The Art Show	F	10	Realistic Fiction	Visualize
Treasures of Our Country	F	10	Nonfiction	Important Ideas
A Visit to the Ranch	F	10	Realistic Fiction	Questioning
My Little Brother Drew	F	10	Realistic Fiction	Story Structure
The Story of the Kids Care Club	F	10	Expository Nonfiction	Predict and Set Purpose
Squirrel and Bear	G	12	Animal Fantasy	Monitor and Clarify
Puppy Raiser	G	12	Expository Nonfiction	Background Knowledge
A Mighty Oak Tree	G	12	Expository Nonfiction	Monitor and Clarify
Simple Machines at Work	G	12	Expository Nonfiction	Summarize
Carlos Picks a Pet	H	14	Realistic Fiction	Monitor and Clarify
That Cat Needs Help!	H	14	Realistic Fiction	Summarize

* Suggested Guided Reading Level. Use your knowledge of students' abilities to adjust levels as needed.

You know the theory behind leveled books: they let you match books with the interest and instructional levels of your students. You can find the right reader for every student with this chart.

Target Comprehension Skill	Additional Comprehension Instruction	Vocabulary
Fact and Opinion	Sequence	High-Frequency Words
Draw Conclusions	Sequence	High-Frequency Words
Draw Conclusions	Author's Purpose	High-Frequency Words
Theme	Realism and Fantasy	High-Frequency Words
Facts and Details	Cause and Effect	High-Frequency Words
Facts and Details	Plot	High-Frequency Words
Theme	Realism and Fantasy	High-Frequency Words
Cause and Effect	Main Idea	High-Frequency Words
Character, Setting, and Plot	Realism and Fantasy	High-Frequency Words
Draw Conclusions	Cause and Effect	High-Frequency Words
Compare and Contrast	Cause and Effect	High-Frequency Words
Main Idea and Details	Cause and Effect	High-Frequency Words
Sequence	Author's Purpose	High-Frequency Words
Theme	Sequence	High-Frequency Words
Fact and Opinion	Setting	High-Frequency Words
Author's Purpose	Setting	High-Frequency Words
Fact and Opinion	Author's Purpose	High-Frequency Words
Draw Conclusions	Compare and Contrast	High-Frequency Words
Draw Conclusions	Author's Purpose	High-Frequency Words
Theme	Plot	High-Frequency Words
Facts and Details	Cause and Effect	High-Frequency Words
Facts and Details	Compare and Contrast	High-Frequency Words
Theme	Realism and Fantasy	High-Frequency Words
Cause and Effect	Author's Purpose	High-Frequency Words
Character, Setting and Plot	Realism and Fantasy	High-Frequency Words
Draw Conclusions	Main Idea	High-Frequency Words
Compare and Contrast	Draw Conclusions	High-Frequency Words
Main Idea and Details	Compare and Contrast	High-Frequency Words
Character and Setting	Compare and Contrast	Amazing Words
Plot	Sequence	Amazing Words

Leveled Readers Skills Chart *Continued*

Grade 1

Title	Level*	DRA Level	Genre	Comprehension Strategy
Loni's Town	H	14	Realistic Fiction	Visualize
Baby Animals in the Rain Forest	H	14	Expository Nonfiction	Important Ideas
Cary and the The Wildlife Shelter	H	14	Realistic Fiction	Story Structure
Around the World	H	14	Narrative Nonfiction	Text Structure
The Communication Story	H	14	Expository Nonfiction	Text Structure
Marla's Good Idea	H	14	Realistic Fiction	Inferring
Rules at School	I	16	Animal Fantasy	Predict and Set Purpose
School: Then and Now	I	16	Expository Nonfiction	Monitor and Clarify
Mom the Mayor	I	16	Realistic Fiction	Important Ideas
The Dinosaur Detectives	I	16	Expository Nonfiction	Inferring
All About Food Chains	I	16	Expository Nonfiction	Background Knowledge
Bees and Beekeepers	I	16	Expository Nonfiction	Questioning
A New Library	I	16	Narrative Nonfiction	Summarize
Paul's Bed	J	18	Traditional Tales	Inferring
Britton Finds a Kitten	J	18	Realistic Fiction	Monitor and Clarify
All About the Weather	J	18	Expository Nonfiction	Visualize
Learn About Butterflies	J	18	Expository Nonfiction	Text Structure
Monarchs Migrate South	J	18	Narrative Nonfiction	Background Knowledge
Cascarones Are for Fun	J	18	Expository Nonfiction	Monitor and Clarify
Jamie's Jumble of Junk	J	18	Realistic Fiction	Visualize
America's Home	K	20	Nonfiction	Important Ideas
Go West!	K	20	Legend	Questioning
Double Trouble Twins	K	20	Realistic Fiction	Story Structure
What Makes Buildings Special?	K	20	Expository Nonfiction	Predict and Set Purpose
Grasshopper and Ant	K	20	Fable	Monitor and Clarify
Ways to be a Good Citizen	K	20	Expository Nonfiction	Background Knowledge
Great Scientists: Detectives at Work	L	24	Expository Nonfiction	Monitor and Clarify
Simple Machines in Compound Machines	L	24	Nonfiction	Summarize
Over the Years	L	24	Expository Nonfiction	Text Structure
Cody's Adventure	L	24	Realistic Fiction	Inferring

* Suggested Guided Reading Level. Use your knowledge of students' abilities to adjust levels as needed.

You know the theory behind leveled books: they let you match books with the interest and instructional levels of your students. You can find the right reader for every student with this chart.

Target Comprehension Skill	Additional Comprehension Instruction	Vocabulary
Character and Setting	Theme	Amazing Words
Main Idea and Details	Author's Purpose	Amazing Words
Main Idea and Details	Sequence	Amazing Words
Cause and Effect	Main Idea	Amazing Words
Sequence	Compare and Contrast	High-Frequency Words
Theme	Sequence	High-Frequency Words
Sequence	Character	Amazing Words
Cause and Effect	Draw Conclusions	Amazing Words
Author's Purpose	Cause and Effect	Amazing Words
Sequence	Draw Conclusions	Amazing Words
Author's Purpose	Cause and Effect	Amazing Words
Compare and Contrast	Main Idea	Amazing Words
Sequence	Author's Purpose	Amazing Words
Compare and Contrast	Character	Amazing Words
Fact and Opinion	Setting	Amazing Words
Author's Purpose	Plot	Amazing Words
Fact and Opinion	Cause and Effect	Amazing Words
Draw Conclusions	Author's Purpose	Amazing Words
Draw Conclusions	Sequence	Amazing Words
Theme	Character, Setting, Plot	Amazing Words
Facts and Details	Cause and Effect	Amazing Words
Facts and Details	Theme	Amazing Words
Theme	Realism and Fantasy	Amazing Words
Cause and Effect	Draw Conclusions	Amazing Words
Character, Setting and Plot	Cause and Effect	Amazing Words
Draw Conclusions	Compare and Contrast	Amazing Words
Compare and Contrast	Compare and Contrast	Amazing Words
Main Idea and Details	Cause and Effect	Amazing Words
Sequence	Draw Conclusions	Amazing Words
Theme	Sequence	Amazing Words

What Good Readers Do

You can use the characteristics and behaviors of good readers to help all your children read better. But what are these characteristics and behaviors? And how can you use them to foster good reading behaviors for all your children? Here are some helpful tips.

Good Readers enjoy reading! They have favorite books, authors, and genres. Good readers often have a preference about where and when they read. They talk about books and recommend their favorites.

Develop this behavior by giving children opportunities to respond in different ways to what they read. Get them talking about what they read, and why they like or dislike it.

This behavior is important because book sharing alerts you to children who are somewhat passive about reading or have limited literacy experiences. Book sharing also helps you when you select books for the class.

Good Readers read independently for longer periods of time.

Develop this behavior by taking note of the level of support children need during guided reading. Use this information to gauge independent reading time accordingly.

This behavior is important because children become better readers when they spend time reading many texts at their independent level.

Good Readers select books they can read.

Develop this behavior by providing a range of three or four texts appropriate for the child and then letting the child choose.

This behavior is important because children gain control over reading when they can choose from books they can read. This helps them become more independent in the classroom.

Good Readers use text features to help them preview and set purposes.

Develop this behavior by having children use the title and illustrations in fiction texts or the title, contents, headings, and other graphic features in nonfiction texts to make predictions about what they will be reading.

This behavior is important because previewing actually makes reading easier! Looking at features and sampling the text enables readers to predict and set expectations for reading.

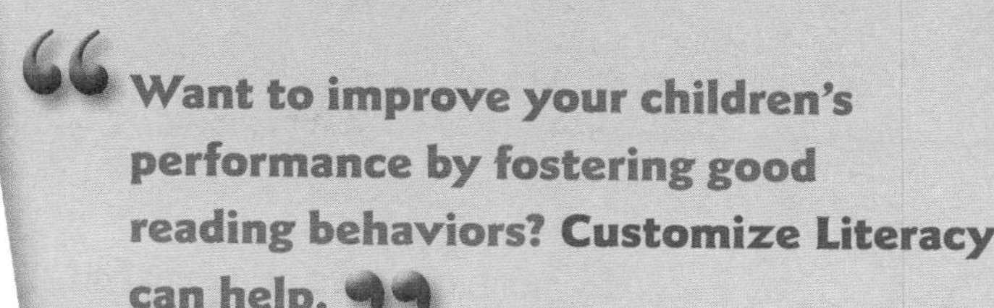

Good Readers predict and ask questions before and while they read.

Develop this behavior by asking questions. After reading a passage, ask children what they think will happen next in a fiction text. Have them ask a question they think will be answered in a nonfiction text and read on to see if it is.

This behavior is important because when children predict and ask questions as they read, they are engaged. They have a purpose for reading and a basis for monitoring their comprehension.

Good Readers read aloud at an appropriate reading rate with a high percent of accuracy.

Develop this behavior by timing children's oral reading to calculate their reading rates. You can also record children's miscues to determine a percent of accuracy. This will help identify problems.

This behavior is important because when children read fluently texts that are "just right," they find reading more enjoyable. A fluent reader is able to focus more on constructing meaning and is more likely to develop a positive attitude toward reading.

Good Readers read meaningful phrases aloud with appropriate expression.

QU-

ST-

Develop this behavior by giving children lots of opportunities to read orally. As they read, note children's phrasing, intonation, and attention to punctuation and give help as needed.

This behavior is important because reading fluently in longer, meaningful phrases supports comprehension and ease in reading longer, more complex texts.

Section 3 Matching Books and Readers

Good Readers use effective strategies and sources of information to figure out unknown words.

CH-
QU-
ST-

Develop this behavior by teaching specific strategies for figuring out unknown words, such as sounding out clusters of letters, using context, reading on, and using references.

This behavior is important because when readers have a variety of strategies to use, they are more able to decode and self-correct quickly. Readers who do these things view themselves as good readers.

Good Readers construct meaning as they read and then share or demonstrate their understanding.

Develop this behavior by having children retell what they read or write a summary of what they read in their own words.

This behavior is important because the ability to retell or write a summary is essential for success in reading. It shows how well a child has constructed meaning.

Good Readers locate and use what is explicitly stated in a text.

Develop this behavior by asking questions that require children to go back into the text to find explicitly stated information.

This behavior is important because the ability to recall, locate, and use specific information stated in a text enables readers to respond to literal questions, as well as to support opinions and justify their responses.

Good Readers make connections.

Develop this behavior by asking questions to help children make connections: *What does this remind you of? Have you ever read or experienced anything like this?*

This behavior is important because making connections helps readers understand and appreciate a text. Making connections to self, the world, and other texts supports higher-level thinking.

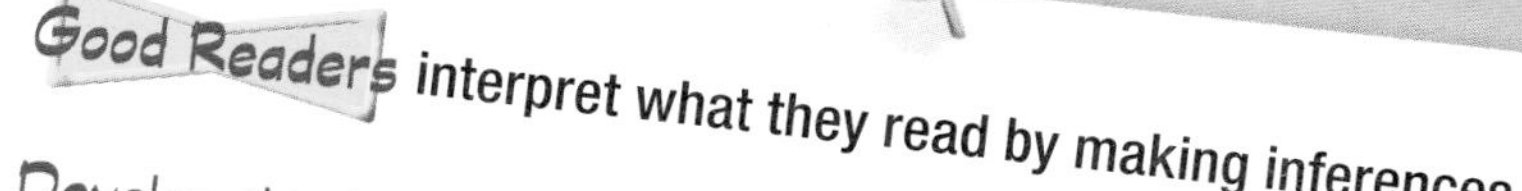

Good Readers interpret what they read by making inferences.

Develop this behavior by asking questions to help children tell or write about what they think was implied in the text: *Why do you think that happened? What helped you come to that conclusion?*

This behavior is important because the ability to go beyond the literal meaning of a text enables readers to gain a deeper understanding. When children make inferences, they use background knowledge, their personal knowledge, and the text to grasp the meaning of what is implied by the author.

Good Readers determine importance and evaluate what they read.

Develop this behavior by always having children identify what they think is the most important message, event, or information in a text.

This behavior is important because readers must be able to sort out important from interesting information. The ability to establish and/or use criteria and provide support when making judgments is an important critical-thinking skill.

Good Readers support their responses using information from a text and/or their own background knowledge.

Develop this behavior by always asking children to give the reason(s) they identified an event, message, or ideas as most important.

This behavior is important because the ability to justify one's response is important for all learners. It enables others to know the basis for a decision and provides an opening for further discussion.

Conversation Starters

Asking Good Questions When children read interesting and thought-provoking books, they want to share! You can encourage children to think critically about what they read. Use questions such as the following to assess comprehension as well as evoke good class/group discussions.

Author's Purpose

- Who wrote this selection?
- Why did the author write this piece?

Cause and Effect

- What is one thing that happens in the story? Why did it happen?
- Is there one thing that causes several other things to happen?

Compare and Contrast

- What shows that the author is comparing people in this story?
- How are the characters and events in this story like and/or different from real people and events you know of?

Draw Conclusions

- Based on what you have read, seen, or experienced, what can you conclude about this event in the selection?
- This story seems to be a fantasy. Why might you conclude this?
- What can you decide about the characters?

Realism and Fantasy

- What parts of this story could be make-believe? Why?

Graphic Sources

- This selection has many pictures. Which one or ones best help you understand the events or ideas in the selection? Why?

Literary Elements: Character, Setting, Plot, Theme

- Who are the main characters in the story? What are they like?
- Where does the story take place?
- What does the main character want at the beginning of the story?
- Retell the story, putting the things that happen in the right order.
- What is the big idea of the story? What lesson did you learn?

Main Idea

- What is this selection mostly about?
- What details tell more about the main idea?
- What might be another good title for this selection?

Sequence

- How is the sequence of events important in the text?
- Is the order of events important in this story? Why or why not?

Section 3 Matching Books and Readers

Connecting Science and Social Studies

Scott Foresman Reading Street Leveled Readers are perfect for covering, supporting, or enriching science and social studies content. Using these books ensures that all children can access important concepts.

Grade 1 Leveled Readers

Science

Earth and Space Science

Nonfiction Books

- *All About the Weather*
- *The Communication Story*
- *Over the Years*
- *Ready for Winter?*
- *Using the Telephone*

Fiction Books

- *Cody's Adventure*
- *Marla's Good Idea*
- *What a Detective Does*

Life Science

Nonfiction Books

- *All About Food Chains*
- *Animals Change and Grow*
- *Around the Forest*
- *Around the World*
- *Baby Animals in the Rain Forest*
- *Bees and Beekeepers*
- *The Dinosaur Detectives*
- *The Dinosaur Herds*
- *Fun in the Sun*
- *Honey*
- *In My Room*
- *Learn About Butterflies*
- *Learn About Worker Bees*
- *Let's Go to the Zoo*
- *Let's Visit a Butterfly Greenhouse*
- *Look at Dinosaurs*
- *A Mighty Oak Tree*
- *Monarchs Migrate South*
- *People Help the Forest*
- *The Seasons Change*
- *Seasons Come and Go*
- *What Animals Can You See?*

Life Science

Fiction Books

- *Bix the Dog*
- *Britton Finds a Kitten*
- *Carlos Picks a Pet*
- *Cary and the Wildlife Shelter*
- *Mac Can Do It!*
- *Mack and Zack*
- *Plans Change*
- *Sam*
- *The Sick Pets*
- *Time for Dinner*
- *What Brown Saw*
- *Which Animals Will We See?*
- *Which Fox?*

Physical Science

Nonfiction Books

- *The Inclined Plane*
- *Simple Machines at Work*
- *Simple Machines in Compound Machines*

Grade 1 Leveled Readers

Social Studies

Citizenship

Nonfiction Books
- *A Class*
- *A Garden for All*
- *Great Scientists: Detectives at Work*
- *Here in My Neighborhood*
- *A New Library*
- *Puppy Raiser*
- *The Story of the Kids Care Club*
- *Ways to Be a Good Citizen*

Fiction Books
- *The Art Show*
- *At Your Vet*
- *Big Wishes and Her Baby*
- *Double Trouble Twins*
- *Fly Away Owl!*
- *Grasshopper and Ant*
- *Hank's Song*
- *Let's Build a Park!*
- *Look at My Neighborhood*
- *My Little Brother Drew*
- *On the Farm*
- *Paul's Bed*
- *A Play*
- *Rules at School*
- *Space Star*
- *Squirrel and Bear*
- *That Cat Needs Help!*

Culture

Nonfiction Books
- *Cascarones Are for Fun*
- *My Babysitter*
- *Special Days, Special Food*
- *We Are a Family*
- *What Makes Buildings Special?*

Fiction Books
- *Go West!*
- *Grandma's Farm*
- *Gus the Pup*
- *Jamie's Jumble of Junk*
- *A New Baby Brother*
- *A Party for Pedro*
- *A Visit to the Ranch*
- *Where They Live*

History

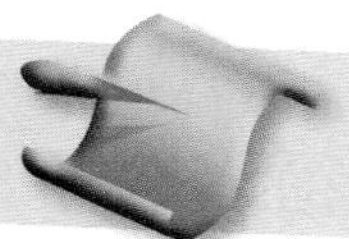

Nonfiction Books
- *School: Then and Now*
- *Treasures of Our Country*

Fiction Books
- *Loni's Town*

Government

Nonfiction Books
- *America's Home*
- *Our Leaders*

Fiction Books
- *Mom the Mayor*

Connecting Science and Social Studies

Need more choices? Look back to Grade K.

Grade K Leveled Readers

Science

Earth and Space Science	Life Science	Physical Science
Fiction Books • *We Can Do It!*	**Nonfiction Books** • *A Winter Home* • *What Can You Do?* • *The Trip* • *Pigs* • *Frog's New Home* • *A Small Trip* • *Safe Places for Animals* **Fiction Books** • *A Walk in the Forest* • *Looking for Animals* • *Skip and Run* • *Big Cats* • *My Pal Fran* • *Fun with Gram* • *They Will Grow* • *Sad and Glad*	**Fiction Books** • *Catch the Ball!* • *The Best Club Hut*

Grade K Leveled Readers

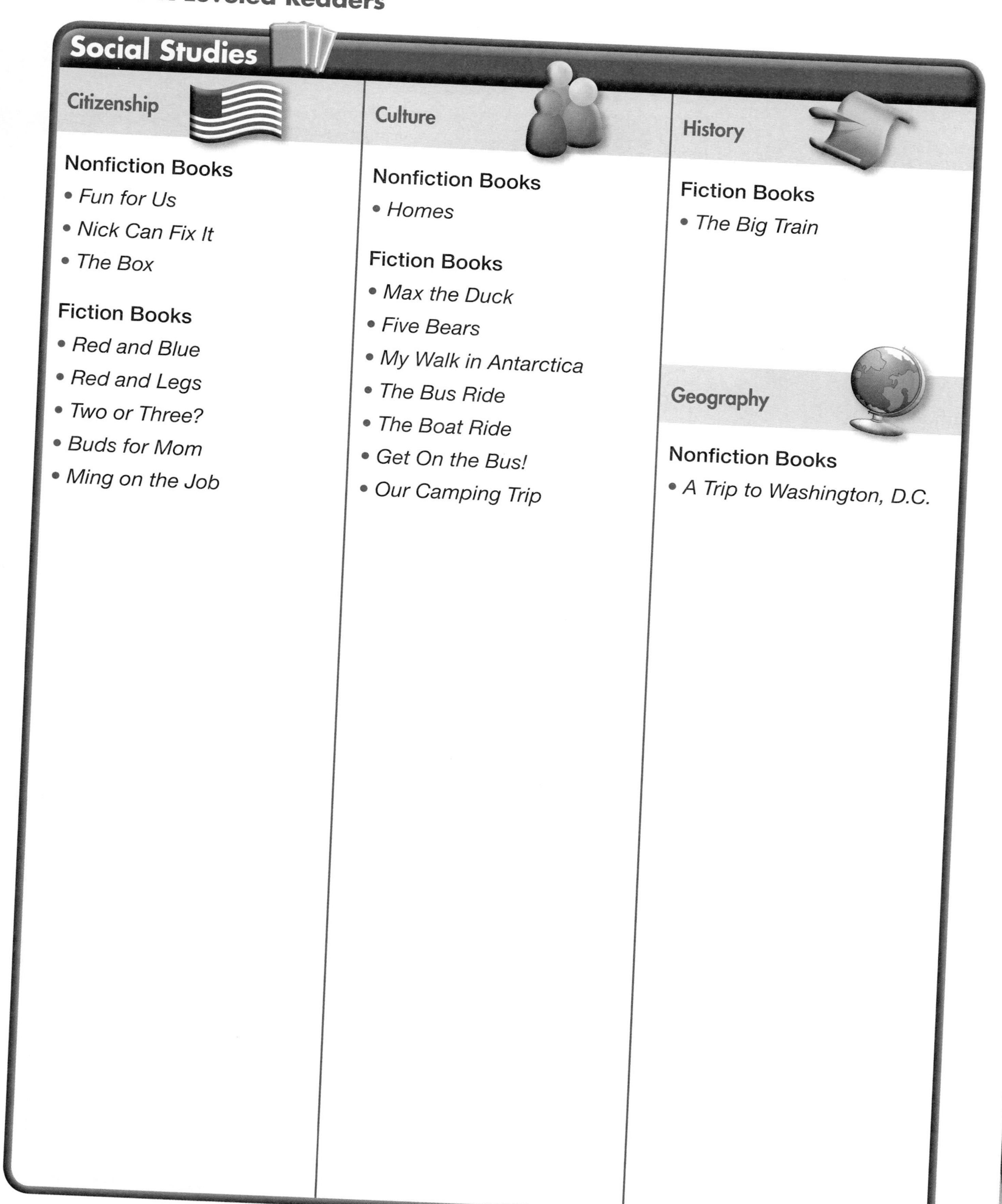

Social Studies

Citizenship

Nonfiction Books
- *Fun for Us*
- *Nick Can Fix It*
- *The Box*

Fiction Books
- *Red and Blue*
- *Red and Legs*
- *Two or Three?*
- *Buds for Mom*
- *Ming on the Job*

Culture

Nonfiction Books
- *Homes*

Fiction Books
- *Max the Duck*
- *Five Bears*
- *My Walk in Antarctica*
- *The Bus Ride*
- *The Boat Ride*
- *Get On the Bus!*
- *Our Camping Trip*

History

Fiction Books
- *The Big Train*

Geography

Nonfiction Books
- *A Trip to Washington, D.C.*

Connecting Science and Social Studies

Need more choices? Look ahead to Grade 2.

Grade 2 Leveled Readers

Science

Earth and Space Science

Nonfiction Books

- *All About Astronauts*
- *An Astronaut Space Walk*
- *Desert Animals*
- *Deserts*
- *Hurricane!*
- *Look at Our Galaxy*

Fiction Books

- *Blizzard!*
- *Maggie's New Sidekick*
- *Rainbow Crow Brings Fire to Earth*
- *A Slice of Mud Pie*

Life Science

Nonfiction Books

- *Arachnid or Insect?*
- *Compost: Recycled Waste*
- *Farming Families*
- *How a Seed Grows*
- *How Can Animals Help?*
- *How Do Plants Grow?*
- *How to Grow Tomatoes*
- *Plants Grow Everywhere*
- *A Vet for All Animals*

Fiction Books

- *Annie Makes a Big Change*
- *Camping at Crescent Lake*
- *Growing Up*
- *Too Many Rabbit Holes*
- *Where Is Fish?*

Physical Science

Nonfiction Books

- *Many Types of Energy*
- *Sink or Float?*

Fiction Books

- *The Hummingbird*
- *Our School Science Fair*

Grade 2 Leveled Readers

Social Studies

Citizenship

Nonfiction Books

- *America's Birthday*
- *The Barn Raising*
- *Be Ready for an Emergency*
- *Everyone Can Make a Difference!*
- *Join an Adventure Club!*
- *Keeping Our Community Safe*
- *Protect the Earth*
- *The Rescue Dogs*
- *Service Workers*
- *Special Animal Helpers*
- *Using a Net*
- *What Can You Do?*
- *Working Dogs*

Fiction Books

- *Andrew's Mistake*
- *Camping with Pup*
- *Freda the Signmaker*
- *Hubert and Frankie*
- *Let's Work Together!*
- *Marty's Summer Job*
- *Sally and the Wild Puppy*
- *Stripes and Silver*
- *Too Many Frogs!*
- *Training Peanut*

Culture

Nonfiction Books

- *Celebrations and Family Traditions*
- *Living in Seoul*
- *Showing Good Manners*
- *Special Chinese Birthdays*
- *A World of Birthdays*

Fiction Books

- *Ana Is Shy*
- *The Camping Trip*
- *Country Friends, City Friends*
- *Dotty's Art*
- *The First People to Fly*
- *Glooskap and the First Summer: An Algonquin Tale*
- *Happy New Year!*
- *The International Food Fair*
- *Just Like Grandpa*
- *Living on a Ranch*
- *The New Kid in Bali*
- *Voting Day*

Economics

Nonfiction Books

- *Services and Goods*

Fiction Books

- *Country Mouse and City Mouse*
- *A Quiet Place*
- *Snakeskin Canyon*

History

Nonfiction Books

- *A Few Nifty Inventions*
- *The Hoover Dam*
- *Living in a Democracy*
- *Making Travel Fun*
- *Saint Bernards and Other Working Dogs*
- *Starting a New Life*
- *Women Play Baseball*

Fiction Books

- *At Home in the Wilderness*
- *A Class Play*
- *A Cowboy's Life*
- *Down on the Ranch*
- *Hank's Tortilla Factory*

Government

Nonfiction Books

- *Communicating Then and Now*
- *Let's Send a Letter!*

More Great Titles

Biography

- *American Revolution Heroes*
- *Baseball Heroes Make History*
- *Thomas Adams: Chewing Gum Inventor*
- *Three Great Ballplayers*

Planning Teacher Study Groups

Adventurous teachers often have good ideas for lessons. A teacher study group is a great way to share ideas and get feedback on the best way to connect content and students. Working with other teachers can provide you with the support and motivation you need to implement new teaching strategies. A teacher study group offers many opportunities to collaborate, support each other's work, share insights, and get feedback.

Think About It

A weekly or monthly teacher study group can help support you in developing your expertise in the classroom. You and a group of like-minded teachers can form your own study group. What can this group accomplish?

- Read and discuss professional articles by researchers in the field of education.
- Meet to share teaching tips, collaborate on multi-grade lessons, and share resources.
- Develop lessons to try out new teaching strategies. Meet to share experiences and discuss how to further improve your teaching approach.

Let's Meet!

Forming a study group is easy. Just follow these four steps:

1. **Decide on the size of the group.** A small group has the advantage of making each member feel accountable, but make sure that all people can make the same commitment!
2. **Choose teachers to invite to join your group.** Think about whom you want to invite. Should they all teach the same grade? Can you invite teachers from other schools? Remember that the more diverse the group, the more it benefits from new perspectives.
3. **Set goals for the group.** In order to succeed, know what you want the group to do. Meet to set goals. Rank goals in order of importance and refer often to the goals to keep the group on track.
4. **Make logistical decisions.** This is often the most difficult. Decide where and when you will meet. Consider an online meeting place where group members can post discussion questions and replies if people are not able to meet.

What Will We Study?

Use the goals you set to help determine what your group will study. Consider what materials are needed to reach your goals, and how long you think you will need to prepare for each meeting.

How Will It Work?

Think about how you structure groups in your classroom. Then use some of the same strategies.

- **Assign a group facilitator.** This person is responsible for guiding the meeting. This person comes prepared with discussion questions and leads the meeting. This could be a rotating responsibility dependent on experience with various topics. This person might be responsible for providing the materials.
- **Assign a recorder.** Have someone take notes during the meeting and record group decisions.
- **Use the jigsaw method.** Not everyone has time to be a facilitator. In this case, divide the text and assign each portion to a different person. Each person is responsible for leading the discussion on that particular part.

Meet Again

Make a commitment to meet for a minimum number of times. After that, the group can reevaluate and decide whether or not to continue.

> **"Have some great teaching tips to share? Want to exchange ideas with your colleagues? Build your own professional community of teachers. Customize Literacy gets you started."**

Trial Lessons

Use your colleagues' experiences to help as you think about new ways to connect content and students. Use the following plan to create a mini-lesson. It should last twenty minutes. Get the support of your colleagues as you try something new and then reflect on what happened.

Be Creative!

As you develop a plan for a mini-lesson, use these four words to guide planning: *purpose, text, resources,* and *routine.*

- **Purpose:** Decide on a skill or strategy to teach. Define your purpose for teaching the lesson.
- **Text:** Develop a list of the materials you could use. Ask your colleagues for suggestions.
- **Resources:** Make a list of the available resources, and consider how to use those resources most effectively. Consider using the leveled readers listed on pages CL24–CL29 and CL36–CL41 of Customize Literacy.
- **Routine:** Choose an instructional routine to structure your mini-lesson. See the mini-lessons in Customize Literacy for suggestions.

Try It!

Try out your lesson! Consider audio- or videotaping the lesson for later review. You may wish to invite a colleague to sit in as you teach. Make notes on how the lesson went.

How Did It Go?

Use the self-evaluation checklist on page CL45 as you reflect on your trial lesson. This provides a framework for later discussion.

Discuss, Reflect, Repeat

Solicit feedback from your teacher study group. Explain the lesson and share your reflections. Ask for suggestions on ways to improve the lesson. Take some time to reflect on the feedback. Modify your lesson to reflect what you have learned. Then try teaching the lesson again.

Checklist for Teacher Self-Evaluation

How Well Did I ...	Very Well	Satisfactory	Not Very Well
Plan the lesson?			
Select the appropriate level of text?			
Introduce the lesson and explain its objectives?			
Review previously taught skills?			
Directly explain the new skills being taught?			
Model the new skills?			
Break the material down into small steps?			
Integrate guided practice into the lesson?			
Monitor guided practice for student understanding?			
Provide feedback on independent practice?			
Maintain an appropriate pace?			
Assess student understanding of the material?			
Stress the importance of applying the skill as they read?			
Maintain students' interest?			
Ask questions?			
Handle student questions and responses?			
Respond to the range of abilities?			

Books for Teachers

Children aren't the only ones who need to read to grow. Here is a brief list of books that you may find useful to fill your reading teacher basket and learn new things.

A Professional Bibliography

Adams, M. J. "Alphabetic Anxiety and Explicit, Systematic Phonics Instruction: A Cognitive Science Perspective." *Handbook of Early Literacy Research.* The Guilford Press, 2001.

Adams, M. J. *Beginning to Read: Thinking and Learning About Print.* The MIT Press, 1990.

Afflerbach, P. "The Influence of Prior Knowledge and Text Genre on Readers' Prediction Strategies." *Journal of Reading Behavior,* vol. XXII, no. 2 (1990).

Armbruster, B. B., F. Lehr, and J. Osborn. *Put Reading First: The Research Building Blocks for Teaching Children to Read.* Partnership for Reading, Washington, D.C., 2001.

Bear, D. R., M. Invernizzi, S. Templeton, and F. Johnston. *Words Their Way.* Merrill Prentice Hall, 2004.

Beck, I., M. G. McKeown, and L. Kucan. *Bringing Words to Life: Robust Vocabulary Instruction.* The Guilford Press, 2002.

Biemiller, A. "Teaching Vocabulary in the Primary Grades: Vocabulary Instruction Needed." *Vocabulary Instruction Research to Practice.* The Guilford Press, 2004.

Blachowicz, C. and P. Fisher. "Vocabulary Instruction." *Handbook of Reading Research,* vol. III. Lawrence Erlbaum Associates, 2000.

Cunningham, P. M. and J. W. Cunningham. "What We Know About How to Teach Phonics." *What Research Says About Reading Instruction,* 3rd ed. International Reading Association, 2002.

Daniels, H. *Literature Circles.* 2nd ed. Stenhouse Publishers, 2002.

Dickson, S. V., D. C. Simmons, and E. J. Kame'enui. "Text Organization: Instructional and Curricular Basics and Implications." *What Reading Research Tells Us About Children with Diverse Learning Needs: Bases and Basics.* Lawrence Erlbaum Associates, 1998.

Diller, D. *Making the Most of Small Groups: Differentiation for All.* Stenhouse Publishers, 2007.

Duke, N. K., V. S. Bennett-Armistead, and E. M. Roberts. "Bridging the Gap Between Learning to Read and Reading to Learn." *Literacy and Young Children: Research-Based Practices.* The Guilford Press, 2003.

Duke, N. K. and C. Tower. "Nonfiction Texts for Young Readers." *The Texts in Elementary Classrooms.* Lawrence Erlbaum Associates, 2004.

Ehri, L. C. and S. R. Nunes. "The Role of Phonemic Awareness in Learning to Read." *What Research Has to Say About Reading Instruction.* 3rd ed. International Reading Association, 2002.

Fountas, I. C. and G. S. Pinnell. *Guided Reading: Good First Teaching for All Children.* Heinemann, 1996.

Fountas, I. C. and G. S. Pinnell. *Matching Books to Readers: Using Leveled Books in Guided Reading,* K-3. Heinemann, 1999.

Harvey, S. and A. Goudvis. *Strategies That Work: Teaching Comprehension to Enhance Understanding.* 2nd ed. Stenhouse Publishers, 2007.

Hiebert, E. H. and L. A. Martin. "The Texts of Beginning Reading Instruction." *Handbook of Early Literacy Research.* The Guilford Press, 2001.

Indrisano, R. and J. R. Paratore. *Learning to Write, Writing to Learn. Theory and Research in Practice.* International Reading Association, 2005.

Juel, C., G. Biancarosa, D. Coker, and R. Deffes. "Walking with Rosie: A Cautionary Tale of Early Reading Instruction." *Educational Leadership* (April 2003).

National Reading Panel. *Teaching Children to Read.* National Institute of Child Health and Human Development, 1999.

Pressley, M. *Reading Instruction That Works: The Case for Balanced Teaching,* 3rd ed. The Guilford Press, 2005.

Smith, S., D. C. Simmons, and E. J. Kame'enui. "Word Recognition: Research Bases." *What Reading Research Tells Us About Children with Diverse Learning Needs: Bases and Basics.* Lawrence Erlbaum Associates, 1998.

Snow, C., S. Burns, and P. Griffin, eds. *Preventing Reading Difficulties in Young Children.* National Academy Press, 1998.

Vaughn, S., P. G. Mathes, S. Linan-Thompson, and D. J. Francis. "Teaching English Language Learners at Risk for Reading Disabilities to Read: Putting Research into Practice." *Learning Disabilities Research & Practice,* vol. 20, issue 1 (February 2006).

WEEK 4 Oral Vocabulary for

Frog and Toad Together

Let's Learn Amazing Words

Definitions, examples, and applications to use with the Oral Vocabulary in each lesson.

Amazing Words Oral Vocabulary Routine

nature

1. *Nature* is a name for things not made by people, such as plants, animals, or the weather.
2. **Examples** You can see *nature* at the park. We took a *nature* walk through the woods. My favorite part of *nature* is a beautiful sunset.
3. **Apply to the Instruction** Name something in nature that you like to watch or do.

sprout

1. *Sprout* means "to grow or spring up."
2. **Examples** Seeds *sprout* and little plants come out of the ground. After I plant my garden, I look every day to see which seeds have *sprouted*. In the spring, trees *sprout* new buds that soon become leaves.
3. **Apply to the Instruction** Name something that *sprouts*.

shade

1. The *shade* of a color is how dark or light the color is.
2. **Examples** The leaves were a beautiful *shade* of green. Her dress was a light *shade* of blue. If you add white to purple paint, you will get a lighter *shade* of purple. If you add black to purple paint, you will get a darker *shade*.
3. **Apply to the Instruction** Show how you can use a pencil to make different *shades* of black. Use the word *shade* when you tell about what you did.

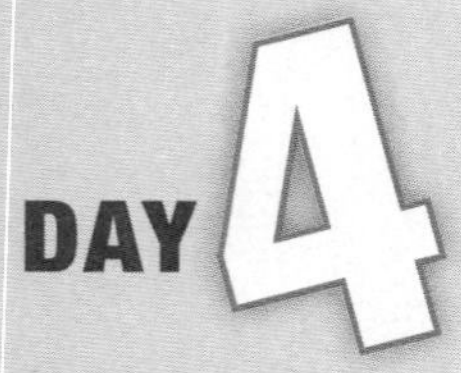

destroy

1. *Destroy* means "to put an end to" or "to ruin."
2. **Examples** A fire can *destroy* a forest. Insects will eat sprouts and *destroy* a garden. A tornado can *destroy* a town.
3. **Apply to the Instruction** Name one thing that could destroy your clothes.

Oral Vocabulary for

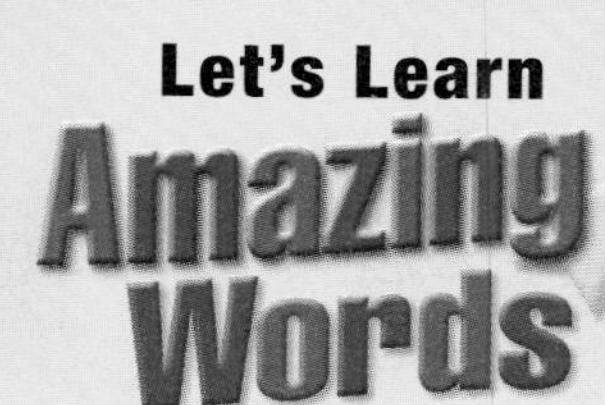

I'm a Caterpillar

Amazing Words Oral Vocabulary Routine

develop

1 *Develop* means "to go through stages of growth."

2 **Examples** A sprout will *develop* into a plant. A child will *develop* into a teenager and then an adult. A caterpillar will *develop* into a butterfly.

3 **Apply to the Instruction** Name the stages something goes through to *develop* into something else. Use the word *develop* to tell about the process.

insect

1 *Insect* is a name for a bug, such as a butterfly or a bee.

2 **Examples** We looked at the *insect* and decided it was a fly. The *insect* buzzed around the flowers looking for food. *Insects* like termites can ruin a house.

3 **Apply to the Instruction** Name your favorite *insect*. Tell something about it.

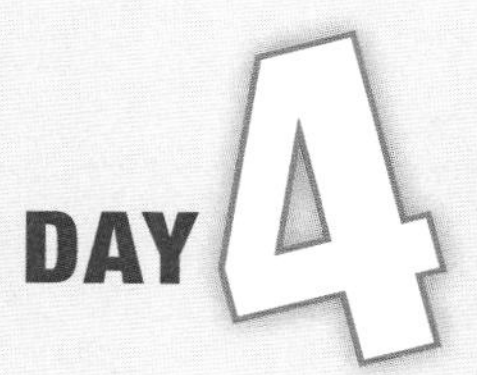

emerge

1 *Emerge* means "to come out from."

2 **Examples** I saw the sun *emerge* from behind a cloud. When the movie is over, people will *emerge* from the theater. The video showed the chick *emerging* from the egg.

3 **Apply to the Instruction** Name a word or words that mean the opposite of *emerge*. Name a word that means almost the same as *emerge*.

vessel

1 A *vessel* is a tube that carries blood inside your body.

2 **Examples** Blood *vessels* carry blood throughout your body. A vein is a type of blood *vessel*.

3 **Apply to the Instruction** Show me a blood *vessel* in your wrist.

Oral Vocabulary for

Let's Learn **Amazing Words**

Definitions, examples, and applications to use with the Oral Vocabulary in each lesson.

Where Are My Animal Friends?

Amazing Words Oral Vocabulary Routine

migrate

1. *Migrate* means "to move from one place to another."
2. **Examples** Some birds *migrate* south in the fall. If a bird doesn't *migrate*, it has to find food where it lives. Animals that *migrate* return when the seasons change.
3. **Apply to the Instruction** If an animal *migrates*, does it live in the same place all year? Explain your answer.

temperature

1. *Temperature* is how hot or cold something is.
2. **Examples** Water freezes at a *temperature* of 32°F. The boy had to stay home from school because he had a *temperature* of 101°F. The weather forecaster warned that the *temperature* would drop.
3. **Apply to the Instruction** When the *temperature* goes up, does it get hotter or colder?

bitterly

1. *Bitterly* means "in a sad or painful way."
2. **Examples** I wore a scarf over my face because of the *bitterly* cold wind. The children were *bitterly* disappointed after their team lost the game.
3. **Apply to the Instruction** Would you like to be outdoors on a *bitterly* cold day? Why or why not?

Acknowledgments

Teacher's Edition

KWL Strategy: The KWL Interactive Reading Strategy was developed and is used by permission of Donna Ogle, National-Louis University, Skokie, Illinois, co-author of *Reading Today and Tomorrow,* Holt, Rinehart & Winston Publishers, 1988. (See also the *Reading Teacher,* February 1986, pp. 564–570.)

Understanding by Design Quotes: Wiggins, G. & McTighe, J. (2005). *Understanding by Design.* Alexandria, VA: Association for Supervision and Curriculum Development.

Illustrations

Cover Daniel Moreton

Running Header Steven Mach

Photographs

Every effort has been made to secure permission and provide appropriate credit for photographic material. The publisher deeply regrets any omission and pledges to correct errors called to its attention in subsequent editions.

Unless otherwise acknowledged, all photographs are the property of Pearson Education, Inc.

Student Edition

Acknowledgments

Text

Grateful acknowledgment is made to the following for copyrighted material:

Page 52: From *Ruby in Her Own Time* by Jonathan Emmett, illustrated by Rebecca Harry. Text copyright © 2003 by Jonathan Emmett, illustrations copyright © 2003 by Rebecca Harry. Reprinted by permission of Scholastic, Inc. Also from *Ruby Flew Too!* written by Jonathan Emmett and illustrated by Rebecca Harry (Copyright © 2004 Macmillan Publishers Ltd., London, UK), reprinted by permission of Macmillan Publishers Ltd.

Page 126: "The Garden" by Arnold Lobel from FROG AND TOAD TOGETHER. Text Copyright © 1971, 1972 by Arnold Lobel. Used by permission of HarperCollins Publishers.

Page 158: From "I'm a Caterpillar" by Jean Marzollo, illustrated by Judith Moffat. A Hello Science Reader! Scholastic Inc./Cartwheel Books. Text copyright © 1997 by Jean Marzollo, illustrations copyright © 1997 by Judith Moffat. Used by permission.

Page 212: "This Tooth" by Lee Bennett Hopkins. Copyright © 1970 by Lee Bennett Hopkins. First appeared in *ME!*, published by Seabury Press. Reprinted by permission of Curtis Brown, Ltd. All rights reserved.

Page 213: "Tommy" by Gwendolyn Brooks. Reprinted by Consent of Brooks Permissions.

Page 214: From "I'm a Caterpillar" by Jean Marzollo, illustrated by Judith Moffat. A Hello Science Reader! Scholastic Inc./Cartwheel Books. Text copyright © 1997 by Jean Marzollo, illustrations copyright © 1997 by Judith Moffat. Used by permission.

Note: Every effort has been made to locate the copyright owner of material reproduced on this component. Omissions brought to our attention will be corrected in subsequent editions.

Illustrations

EI4, EI5 Mary Anne Lloyd

14 Nathan Hale

20-36 Maryann Cocca-Leffler

39-41 Nan Brooks

46 Steve Simpson

78-81 Paul Eric Roca

84 Dani Jones

110-115 Viviana Garofoli

116 Erwin Haya

150 Orlando Ramirez

184 Ron Lieser

190-204 Scott Gustafson

212, 213 David Diaz

Photographs

Every effort has been made to secure permission and provide appropriate credit for photographic material. The publisher deeply regrets any omission and pledges to correct errors called to its attention in subsequent editions.

Unless otherwise acknowledged, all photographs are the property of Pearson Education, Inc.

Photo locators denoted as follows: Top (T), Center (C), Bottom (B), Left (L), Right (R), Background (Bkgd)

12 ©Joseph Sohm/Visions of America/Corbis, ©Rudy Sulgan/Corbis

42 (T) ©Don Mason/Brand X/Corbis

43 (B) ©Larry Williams/Corbis, (C) ©Photomorgana/Corbis

45 (T) ©Janette Beckman/Corbis, (B) ©Rana Faure/Getty Images

82 ©Lynn M. Stone/Nature Picture Library, ©Rolf Nussbaumer/Nature Picture Library

83 ©Rolf Nussbaumer/Nature Picture Library, Radius Images/Jupiter Images

96 (CL) ©De Meester/ARCO/Nature Picture Library, (BL) ©DK Images, (TL) Emilia Stasiak/©iStockphoto

97 (B) Stephen Hayward/©DK Images

99 (B) Jane Burton/©DK Images

100 (B) ©Jane Burton/Nature Picture Library

101 (B) ©Jose B. Ruiz/Nature Picture Library, (C) Kim Taylor/©DK Images

102 (B) ©Barrie Watts/©DK Images

103 (B) ©Jane Burton/Nature Picture Library

118 ©Max Spreewald/Getty Images

119 ©Robert Harding Picture Library Ltd/Alamy Images

146 (B) Dave King/DK Images

147 (CL) ©D. Boone/Corbis, (BL) William Taufic/Corbis

150 Digital Vision

151 ©Eric Baccega/Nature Picture Library, ©Ross Hoddinott/Nature Picture Library

182 (B) ©George McCarthy/Corbis

230

Student Edition p. 230

UNIT 3

Teacher Notes

Teacher Resources

Looking for Teacher Resources and other important information?

- Dear First Grade Teacher
- Research into Practice on Reading Street
- Guide to Reading Street
- Assessment on Reading Street
- Customize Writing on Reading Street
- Differentiated Instruction on Reading Street
- ELL on Reading Street
- Customize Literacy on Reading Street
- Digital Products on Reading Street
- Teacher Resources for Grade 1
- Index

Teacher Resources

Looking for Teacher Resources and other important information?